Critical Perspectives
on Social Control *and* Social Regulation *in* Canada

Critical Perspectives
on Social Control *and*
Social Regulation
in Canada

edited by Mitch D. Daschuk,
Carolyn Brooks, *and* James F. Popham

Fernwood Publishing
Halifax & Winnipeg

Editing: Jenn Harris
Cover design: John van der Woude
Printed and bound in Canada

Published by Fernwood Publishing
32 Oceanvista Lane, Black Point, Nova Scotia, B0J 1B0
and 748 Broadway Avenue, Winnipeg, Manitoba, R3G 0X3
www.fernwoodpublishing.ca

Fernwood Publishing Company Limited gratefully acknowledges the financial support of the Government of Canada, the Canada Council for the Arts, the Manitoba Department of Culture, Heritage and Tourism under the Manitoba Publishers Marketing Assistance Program and the Province of Manitoba, through the Book Publishing Tax Credit, for our publishing program. We are pleased to work in partnership with the Province of Nova Scotia to develop and promote our creative industries for the benefit of all Nova Scotians.

Library and Archives Canada Cataloguing in Publication

Title: Critical perspectives on social control and social
regulation in Canada / edited by Mitch
Daschuk, Carolyn Brooks, and James Popham.
Names: Daschuk, Mitch, 1981- editor. | Brooks, Carolyn,
editor. | Popham, James, 1981- editor.
Description: Includes bibliographical references and index.
Identifiers: Canadiana 20200158694 | ISBN 9781773631196 (softcover)
Subjects: LCSH: Social control—Canada. | LCSH: Deviant
behavior—Canada. | LCSH: Conformity—Canada.
| LCSH: Canada—Social conditions.
Classification: LCC HM661 .C75 2020 | DDC 303.3/30971—dc23

Contents

Section Three: The Culture of Control / 234

Section Four: Surveillance and Resistance
to Social Control / 348

Acknowledgements

Together, we have over thirty years of teaching experience in the sociology of deviance and social control at the undergraduate and graduate levels; we have taught — but more importantly, learned from — thousands of students. It was from conversations with these students and others that we were inspired to write this book. Thank you to all of our students, whose compassion for justice and fairness and whose curiosity about social control pushed us to create a volume that tried to connect real life events and experiences to the rich and diverse theoretical and academic literature. To the extent that we have succeeded, we are extremely thankful for each other and indebted to the inspiring research and scholarship of all of the authors throughout this book and their excellent contributions.

Our sincere appreciation goes to the many people whose work directly shaped this book. We have benefited from the diverse and thought-provoking faculty, sessionals, and colleagues at and affiliated with the University of Saskatchewan and Wilfrid Laurier University. We continue to be inspired by their insights, their thoughtful research, and many conversations. Thank you to Dr. Bernard Schissel for his immensely knowledgeable mentorship, especially toward writing books to enhance teaching and learning. We are also grateful to Gillian Larkin for her excellent editing, as well as Colleen Krushelinski, Cerah Dube, and Kayla Arisman for their creative and organizational assistance and their interest in this work.

Thank you to everyone at Fernwood Publishing for their tireless work, support, and their commitment to publishing books on topics connected to social justice and resistance. In particular, a special thank you to Jenn Harris and Tanya Andrusieczko for their very thoughtful and thorough editing, constructive and insightful comments, and ability to see those details that had become invisible to us. A special thank you also to Wayne Antony for his critical sociological mindfulness and insightful support toward the development of this project, to Beverley Rach for her production work, and to Curran Faris and Nancy Malek for their work with marketing and the catalogue.

Each of us is grateful for the extraordinary support from our family, friends, and furry friends. Mitch expresses his bottomless appreciation to Dr. Karen Sigfrid, Dr. Kristen Sigfrid, and the staff at Northeast Veterinary Services in Tisdale, Saskatchewan for their expertise and compassion; Carolyn sends heartfelt thanks to Sean, Rob, Mel, Ben, Declan, Alice, Delaney, Brendan, and Toby; and James thanks Cara, Riley, and Allister for their patience and is forever grateful to all of the communities he joined in Saskatoon.

About the Authors

Kayla Arisman graduated from the University of Saskatchewan in 2018 with a Bachelor of Arts Honours in sociology (highest honours) and a certificate in criminology and addictions. She is currently an MA candidate in the Department of Sociology at the University of Saskatchewan, where her research focuses on companion animals as a barrier to leaving intimate partner violence. She intends to continue on to law school, where she wants to specialize in family law. In 2018, Kayla published a paper exploring influential prostitution legislation in the *University of Saskatchewan Undergraduate Research Journal* (USURJ).

Celine Beaulieu is an undergraduate student completing a Bachelor of Arts Honours in sociology and a certificate in criminology and addictions at the University of Saskatchewan. She plans on pursuing a Master of Arts following her graduation. Her areas of research interest include criminology, Indigenous Peoples and settler colonialism, surveillance, and religious liberty practices, specifically on First Nations reserves historically.

Danielle Bird (*Nehiyaw*) is a member of the Saddle Lake Cree Nation in Alberta and has familial ties to the Mistawasis Nehiyawak in west central Saskatchewan. She graduated from the University of Saskatchewan in 2016 with a Bachelor of Arts in sociology and a minor in Indigenous studies (with great distinction). Bird is currently an MA student in the Department of Indigenous Studies at the University of Saskatchewan, where her research focuses on concepts of resilience among formerly incarcerated Indigenous women in Saskatchewan.

Kandis Boyko obtained dual bachelor degrees in psychology and sociology from the University of Saskatchewan. She uses an interdisciplinary approach in her employment in both corrections and mental health and addictions. Her research interests stem from her passion to address the stigma attached to vulnerable populations evident within her employment and academic pursuits.

Kirby Brigden graduated from the University of Saskatchewan in 2016 with a Bachelor of Arts in sociology with a minor in political studies (with high honours). She is currently an MA student in the Department of Sociology at the University of Saskatchewan. Her research, for which she received CGSM SSHRC funding, focuses on a critical analysis of sexual violence policies at Canadian universities through contemporary feminist theoretical frameworks. In addition to topics of violence against women, Brigden is also interested in LGBTQ+ issues and advocacy.

Carolyn Brooks is department head and an associate professor of sociology at the University of Saskatchewan. Her research focuses on youth resilience, violence, and theoretical criminology. She is the co-editor, with Bernard Schissel, of three editions of *Marginality and Condemnation: A Critical Introduction to Criminology.*

Mitch D. Daschuk received a PhD in sociology from the University of Saskatchewan in 2016. His graduate research centers around youth culture, counter-hegemonic art, and punk ideology.

Cerah Dubé graduated from the University of Manitoba with a Bachelor of Arts Honours in criminology and a minor in history (with first-class honours) in 2018. She is presently a master's student at the University of Saskatchewan in the Department of Sociology. Her areas of research include violence against women, the MMIWG2S crisis, the over-incarceration of Indigenous women in the Prairie provinces, the prison-industrial complex, neoliberal risk and responsibilization discourses, and decolonial theories and strategies of de-carceration.

Matthew Ferguson is a PhD student in the Department of Criminology at the University of Ottawa and research assistant for the Carceral Cultures Research Initiative funded by the Social Sciences and Humanities Research Council of Canada.

Sean P. Hier is a professor of Sociology at the University of Victoria. He studies moral panics and social problems.

Julie Kaye is an assistant professor in the Department of Sociology at the University of Saskatchewan. Working in the areas of critical criminology, community research and organizing, and feminist, decolonial scholarship, Dr. Kaye's research examines settler colonialism and Indigenous-led responses to colonial gender violence and criminalization as well as harm reduction, consent, self-determination, and body sovereignty. She is the author of *Responding to Human Trafficking: Dispossession, Colonial Violence, and Resistance among Indigenous and Racialized Women*, which examines anti-trafficking responses in the context of settler colonialism in Canada.

Jeffrey Monaghan is an assistant professor at the Institute of Criminology and Criminal Justice, Carleton University. He is the author of *Security Aid: Canada's Development Regime of Security*, co-author with Andrew Crosby of *Policing Indigenous Movements: Dissent and the Security State*, and co-editor with Lucas Melgaço of *Protests in the Information Age: Social Movements, Digital Practices and Surveillance*.

Connor Morrison is a master's student at the University of Saskatchewan in the Department of Sociology, where he also completed a Bachelor of Arts Honours in sociology with a minor in psychology in 2019. His research areas include news media, communication technology, social media, discourse analysis, and online surveillance.

James F. Popham is an assistant professor of criminology at Wilfrid Laurier University, where he researches issues of cyber-criminality, technology, and social empowerment.

Prairie Schappert is employed by the Government of Canada. She convocated from the University of Saskatchewan in 2018 with a Bachelor of Arts with high honours in sociology, a Bachelor of Arts in psychology, achieving great distinction, and a certificate in criminology and addictions. Prairie published a paper on broken windows theory in 2017 in the *University of Saskatchewan Undergraduate Research Journal* (USURJ).

Kristen M.J. Thomasen is an assistant professor of law, robotics and society at the University of Windsor, Faculty of Law. She is also completing her PhD in law on the topic of drones and privacy in public at the University of Ottawa, where she is under the supervision of Dr. Ian Kerr, Canada Research Chair in ethics, law, and technology. Her doctoral work received a SSHRC Joseph-Armand Bombardier Canada Graduate Scholarship. Kristen researches and writes about the legal, social, and ethical implications of robotic and autonomous machines, and she teaches robotics law and policy at the University of Windsor. Prior to starting her PhD, Kristen clerked for the Honourable Madam Justice Rosalie Abella at the Supreme Court of Canada. She also clerked for the Alberta Court of Queen's Bench. Kristen is a member of the Law Society of Alberta.

Scott Thompson is an assistant professor in the Department of Sociology at the University of Saskatchewan and associate editor of the journal *Surveillance & Society*. Having been called "the genuine historian of surveillance studies," Scott primarily uses historical case studies in order to explain and address current and pressing issues in the areas of criminology, sociology, and surveillance studies. His publications include work on surveillance and colonial/First Nations relationships, surveillance and the control of liquor consumption (*Punched Drunk*), national registration and identity cards, and the taking up of "new" surveillance technologies by police services.

Thania Vega is a PhD candidate in the Department of Politics at York University. They use feminist political economy analysis and a critical disability approach to examine the working conditions of migrant nurses at the intersections of Canadian immigration, health care, and labour-market policies. They are also a member of *Upping the Anti*'s editorial collective and an active member of CUPE 3903.

Kevin Walby is the chancellor's research chair and an associate professor of criminal justice at the University of Winnipeg. He is co-author with R. Lippert of *Municipal Corporate Security in International Context* (Routledge, 2015). He has co-edited with R. Lippert *Policing Cities: Urban Securitization and Regulation in the 21st Century* (Routledge, 2013) and *Corporate Security in the 21st Century: Theory and Practice in International Perspective* (Palgrave, 2014). He is co-editor of *Access to Information and Social Justice* with J. Brownlee (ARP Books, 2015) and *The Handbook of Prison Tourism* with J. Wilson, S. Hodgkinson, and J. Piché (Palgrave, 2017). He is co-editor of the *Journal of Prisoners on Prisons* as well as book review editor for *Surveillance & Society* and *Security Journal*.

Edward Hon-Sing Wong is a doctoral candidate in York University's social work PhD program. With a background in mental health practice and community organizing, his work centres on social work abolitionism and draws on anticolonial and anti-racist theory. His published writings include discussions of disablism within Canadian immigration policy, Canadian social work and colonialism, abolitionism in Hong Kong, and discourses of race in Canadian mental hygiene movement literature.

Karen Wood: Drawing from her professional experience as an early childhood educator, social worker, and educator, Dr. Wood's passion is fuelled by a deeply held commitment to eliminating violence that is informed by decades of community practice and academic teaching and research. As academic lead for RESOLVE Saskatchewan at the University of Saskatchewan, Karen's research explores the complexity of preventing, intervening in, and healing from the impacts of violence and abuse.

Introduction

The Study of Social Control and Social Regulation

Mitch D. Daschuk, James F. Popham, and Carolyn Brooks

After reading this chapter, you will be able to do the following:

1. Explain the concepts of social control and social regulation.
2. Identify the four foundational concepts of social control studies.
3. Name the theoretical perspectives associated with understanding social control and regulation.
4. Illustrate how "agents of socialization" shape the way that we understand the world.
5. Demonstrate how sociology helps us to understand social inequality, social conflict, and social change.

How Much Control Do We Really Have over Our Lives?

Many people would say that we have a great deal of control over our own lives. Some of us may reflect on the opportunities for self-direction that we encounter on a daily basis, from details such as choosing our outfit for the day and personal grooming to the bigger things such as our career ambitions and the relationships we form. We also may have a sense of autonomy in our leisurely pursuits, spiritual beliefs, and political opinions. In every case, we are provided with a range of options and in many ways the liberty to determine how we conduct ourselves.

How might a sociological perspective question the "freedom" to act within these examples? To answer, consider the sources of the inspiration underlying many of these decisions — for instance, the necessity of social participation within numerous social systems and institutions — and their influence over the way we think about these options. Western society is organized around the imperative that we, as social actors, must find employment, exchange our time and energy to earn a wage, and do what we need to do to stay alive. The fact that we have choice in determining our careers or educational pursuits does not counter the principle that we have little choice but to participate with these economic practices and institutions. Simply put, as members of a society, we are required to conform to certain expectations should we wish to enjoy the benefits of collective living. We may choose how we present ourselves at work, but we have little choice in deciding whether *to* work. Much of our conduct, put another way, is regulated in accordance with the goal of ensuring the smooth operation of our social institutions, including that of the capitalist economy.

While this observation dispels the notion that we have complete control over our lives, other important questions remain. For instance, you might interject that we still have a great deal of liberty when presenting ourselves. After all, you are free to choose the music you like, the clothes you wear, and whether you style your hair with frosted tips or a combover. Beyond the institutionalized demand that we work, our day-to-day conduct is also regulated and restricted by innumerable cultural norms and expectations. For example, many young people in Canada work part-time in the retail industry. Generally, employers will mandate that employees wear a uniform or wardrobe to promote a sense of "organizational citizenship" (Stamper and Van Dyne 2003). In preparing for the day before a shift begins, can you really say that individuals employed by these companies had much "choice" in what they wore? What about the business person who wears a suit and collared shirt: can it really be said that their wardrobe choices were made out of personal choice rather than social expectation?

If you can agree that much of our daily conduct and self-presentation conform to institutional necessities, economic pressures, and cultural expectations — people *do* need jobs, after all — you might still take solace in the fact that most people nevertheless have great independence in choosing their leisure activities, politics, spirituality, or the types of entertainment that they enjoy. In other words, behind the layers of institutional and cultural expectations (such as the obligation to work and dress appropriately), we nevertheless enjoy liberties centred on our individual beliefs and preferences.

But a sociological lens invites a critical reconsideration of these assumptions. Our economic position greatly influences what forms of leisure we can reasonably afford and how much time we have outside of work hours;

gendered expectations influence our entertainment choices; and our upbringing plays a significant role in shaping our religious credos. Indeed, sociologists frequently contend that many of the personal "tastes" and "beliefs" that define us are, instead, influenced to a great

> The very qualities that we associate with our standing as free-thinking individuals can be traced back to the specific methods through which our significant others compelled us to recognize and interact with "the world"; these are often based on habits or ideas that were posed to us not as choices, but *inevitabilities.*

degree by the specific forms of socialization that our parents, peers, and other authoritative figures impressed upon us as we first began to "make sense" of our material surroundings. The very qualities that we associate with our standing as free-thinking individuals can be traced back to the specific methods through which our significant others compelled us to recognize and interact with "the world"; these are often based on habits or ideas that were posed to us not as choices, but *inevitabilities.*

Broadly speaking, this text provides an analysis and critical reappraisal of the factors — institutional, cultural, ideological, or other — that compel members of a society to conform to a range of social expectations. These sociological initiatives to explain how and why society presses us to conform to dominant expectations are affiliated with concepts such as social control and social regulation. Traditionally, research around **social regulation** focused on how our social institutions ensure that we engage in forms of belief and conduct that protect and reinforce the existing structure of society. These perspectives assess how the construction and enforcement of laws and institutional rules characterize some "ways of being" as normal and valid while delegitimizing or criminalizing others. These forms of analysis aspire to understand how the authority to determine "acceptable" and "unacceptable" conduct is maintained by institutions and over general publics, often promoting practices and beliefs that reinforce the legitimacy of those institutions and caution against drastic forms of change. Research pertaining to **social control**, on the other hand, focuses more so on the role played by our culture (or prevalently recognized belief and value systems that inform our understanding of the world) in impressing expectations of proper conduct and thought upon us. These perspectives consider the role that we all play in reinforcing notions of propriety, be it through compelling others to act in accordance with unwritten but widely recognized conduct expectations, or through the internal processes with which we impress expectations of proper behaviour or thought upon ourselves. The fact that both of these concepts still carry currency within different corners of the sociological discipline demonstrate the shifting focus of social control studies — from early initiatives centred on explaining and preventing unconventional conduct to more recent analyses of how notions of "normal" are reinforced through our daily interactions. This text does not, however, privilege one term over the other. Instead, we feel these contrasting perspectives both make important contributions to our understanding of conformity and ought not be approached as mutually exclusive.

Foundational Concepts in Social Control

Though a variety of sociological traditions extend analyses related to the topics of social regulation and control, these terms rarely explicitly surface within the academic literature. Instead, sociologists have more commonly focused on closely related concepts. As we unpack the connotations that each term implies, we can gather a better sense of how sociology has approached social control research and note how the adoption of these key concepts signal shifting academic perspectives.

Deviance

The study of social control is most prevalently associated with the concept of **deviance**. Defined in a purely scientific manner, deviance refers to actions that are unanticipated or contradictory to expectations. For example, February deviates from the general rule that months have set days, and koalas are deviant bears given that they are marsupials as opposed to actual bears. In popular usage, "deviance" often implies criminality, immorality, and danger, and this is reflected in the systems and social rituals that seek to treat, rehabilitate, and reform those labelled as "deviants." Sociological analysis has sought to explain how we collectively interpret and respond to deviance, and why some forms of conduct lose their status as "deviance" while others persist (see Cohen 1985).

Normativity

Over time, the study of deviance has informed sociological reappraisals of the function of social norms and the processes through which they promote certain ways of acting, thinking, and being as normal, natural, and inevitable. The concept of **normativity** has increasingly been endorsed as a means of assessing exactly how, and why, societies come to impress expectations of "proper" conduct upon their members, and why we consensually participate in a variety of processes through which to regulate and correct those deemed abnormal.

While some perspectives correlate normativity with our innate desire to interact with predictable and safe social contexts, others suggest that expectations surrounding "normative" conduct can be found to restrict or forbid ways of being or thinking associated with underprivileged social populations (Sellin 1938). Normativity, then, is

> Normativity, then, is approached at different turns as a unifying social force or as a process through which to justify the regulation and correction of those groups who cannot, or do not wish to, conform. Many social thinkers have extended these accounts to explain how certain forms of conduct come to constitute "the normal" and why some ways of being become socially authoritative while others are forbidden.

approached at different turns as a unifying social force or as a process through which to justify the regulation and correction of those groups who cannot, or do not wish to, conform. Many social thinkers have extended these accounts to explain how certain forms of conduct come to constitute "the normal" and why some ways of being become socially authoritative while others are forbidden.

Power

Given that expectations surrounding social conduct serve to both label and justify the correction of "deviant" people, some lines of sociological inquiry approach the phenomenon of normativity as an opportunity to critically assess the distribution of **power** in society. Broadly approaching power as the capacity to make people behave or think in ways that they would not otherwise do on their own, these traditions of inquiry assess how different forms of normativity can be described as serving the interests and continued empowerment of some social groups while disadvantaging others (for discussion, see Bourdieu 1979).

Beyond noting the presence of "gender norms" or "sexual norms" and the repercussions associated with acting out of accordance with them, these perspectives allow for a deeper consideration of the interests that social conventions reinforce. Some suggest those who hold positions of power and authority within a society aspire to "shape" morality in a manner that perpetuates various forms of social inequality — most prevalently related to class, race, gender, sex, sexuality, age, ability, and belief. Our cultural and institutional landscapes are designed in ways that benefit those who have the power to create and enforce laws, and they contribute to forms of normativity that reinforce the inequitable distribution of social power.

Other traditions in social thought, however, go so far as to suggest that power imbalances are built into the very linguistic and communicative processes

> Actions that can be read as "deviating from normativity," in this sense, can instead be approached as instances whereby groups develop tactics through which to resist how those with power continue to organize the world to their advantage.

through which we make sense of the material world. The conventions we use to navigate and optimize our interactions with the world serve to empower certain ways of existing and denigrate other forms of conduct as "abnormal" and threatening.

Resistance

Finally, given the emergence of perspectives affiliating deviance and norms with the inequitable distribution of power, sociologists have reappraised conduct that has traditionally been approached as forms of deviance as, instead, expressions of resistance — acts that draw attention to the inequitable distribution of power in society, articulate the negative consequences faced by some social populations, and advocate for movements toward challenging these imbalances. Actions that can be read as "deviating from normativity," in this sense, can instead be approached as instances whereby groups develop tactics through which to resist how those with power continue to organize the world to their advantage.

Sociological Perspectives on Social Control

Various traditions of sociological thought have brought theorists to different conclusions about the presence, and nature, of social control and social regulation. While the discipline offers a plurality of approaches, this section explains how, broadly speaking, certain categories begin to emerge. Each of these sociological perspectives entails central assumptions of the function of social norms and differing analyses of how they coincide with specific cultural and institutional interests.

Symbolic Interactionist Perspectives

Popularized throughout the early 1900s, **symbolic interactionist perspectives** suggest social stability is maintained as human actors develop systems of communication, and collective notions of expected practice, to achieve and reinforce an overarching consensus of how the world works. From this vantage, human beings seek a degree of comfort and security as we interact with others, and we legitimize social norms to reinforce our collective recognition of a **"natural attitude"** (Schütz 1967). Symbolic interactionism argues that the presence of different types of beliefs or conduct expectations draw their force from the fact that a majority of the public believes the world should be ordered in a certain way and approaches deviations from these expectation as threatening practices that require regulation and deterrence. We continue to abide by normative expectations, then, as a means to ensure our own safety and security and to reinforce the authority of social norms with which we have organized our own understanding of "how the world works."

Marxist Perspectives

Inspired by Karl Marx and Friedrich Engels (1970), **Marxist perspectives** suggest societies are structured by the perpetuation of unequal relationships between social groups and that our norms and institutions are designed to benefit those who already possess wealth and social authority. From a Marxist vantage, the power to shape collective norms and social institutions is distributed unequally, and those who have such power use it to ensure the continuation of their privilege and authority. We are, essentially, a society of "haves" and "have-nots" and those who "have" protect their interests by constructing norms to justify their empowerment. As Marxist sociologists explain, one particularly efficient tactic of the powerful involves embedding values and ideologies that promote their interests into our social institutions. This contributes to normative practices that justify inequitable relationships between owners and workers, promotes that we form our identities by purchasing consumer goods, and accredits processes that characterize groups that might threaten these social arrangements as "abnormal," "deviant," "and dangerous."

Critical Perspectives

Critical perspectives, most closely affiliated with the postmodernist theories of Michel Foucault (1980), focus less on the interests of those who hold positions of social power than the forms of "truth" or "knowledge" that grant them such authority. From this perspective, the very systems of communication that we use to orient our understanding of what the world expects of us, including the "truths" around which our norms and institutions are based, are structured in such a way that we grant "knowledge" the authority to determine appropriate and inappropriate forms of conduct. This perspective advocates for a critical interrogation of the forms of truth that inform the operation of our institutions and legitimize the authority of key social actors. Employing a critical perspective involves assessing the power dynamics embedded within the "facts" that inform "the practice of medicine," as opposed to considering the personal

These perspectives advance differing analyses regarding where notions of deviance and normativity draw their authority. Symbolic interactionists argue this authority stems from the collective will of the broader society; Marxist perspectives focus on the interests of those who hold positions of power; and critical perspectives interrogate the very forms of knowledge and truth that serve as the foundations of what we know about the material world.

interests and aims of any given medical professional alone. Critical perspectives contest the prospect that the "objective truths" that orient our world are value-neutral or unbiased, instead approaching these systems of knowledge themselves as possessing the power to assess and optimize the conduct of human populations.

Summary

Collectively, these perspectives advance differing analyses regarding where notions of deviance and normativity draw their authority. Symbolic inter-actionists argue this authority stems from the collective will of the broader society; Marxist perspectives focus on the interests of those who hold positions of power; and critical perspectives interrogate the very forms of knowledge and truth that serve as the foundations of what we know about the material world. Though differentiated by key central assumptions, all three traditions advocate for their perspectives by looking at common variables associated with the process through which we come to understand the world and our position within it. Comparing and contrasting these perspectives can consider the different ways in which they approach the study of commonly identified **agents of socialization**.

Agents of Socialization

Socialization refers to the process through which we are exposed to a range of social groups and institutions that shape our understanding of how the world works, and these cause us to become familiar with the conduct or roles we are expected to endorse in different situations. Often, socialization is approached as a multi-stage process that we continue to experience throughout our lives. The term **primary socialization** refers to situations to which we are exposed throughout our earliest years and how we become familiar with the tools through which we communicate and recognize the presence of social roles and conduct expectations. This pertains to the development of speech (learning how to form words and understanding what they represent) and an awareness of crucial social practices, such as ensuring personal hygiene, respecting the authority of parents, and becoming familiar with the forms of conduct associated with different social roles (Derrida 1969). Once we have the capacity to communicate and a general sense of how the world works, processes of **secondary socialization** inform us of the purpose of our social systems and the specific roles we must take on in the interest of reinforcing social order. Sociologists commonly identify these actors and institutions as agents of socialization and describe their task as ensuring that commonly recognized patterns of social conduct remain orderly and predictable from generation to generation. Four of the most significant agents of socialization are the family, peer groups, educational institutions, and mass media.

The Family

Without doubt, the agent of socialization with which we become most intimately familiar is the institution of the family. Classifying the family as an *institution* may seem curious to some, given that most do not think of the institution of the family in the same way as a correctional institution (though some certainly would). However, it bears keeping in mind that *the family*, as a concept, refers to an institutionalized collection of cultural practices. While *your* family likely consists of at least one parental figure and perhaps some siblings, *the* institution of the family is based around perpetuating normative social practices centred on raising children for the benefits the smooth operation of our social systems.

From the symbolic interactionist perspective, the family is regarded as the institution with the largest influence over our primary socialization and, by extension, the specific ways that we perceive and interact with the world around us (Berger and Luckmann 1984). Beyond imparting us with communication skills, families also implicitly guide the process of how we come to recognize and abide by gender roles as well as the expectations placed upon us within different social environments. Theorists in the Marxist tradition, on the other hand, suggest that the family functions to condition our inevitable participation in the mainstream workforce and they therefore approach the family as an institution through which to manufacture our consent to participate in exploitative economic systems (Willis 1981). Finally, critical perspectives take note of the scientific literature surrounding the "functional family," arguing that this knowledge grants the institutional world the authority to intervene should parents be perceived as engaging in abnormal parenting practices (Agger and Shelton 2007).

Peer Groups

As in the case of the family, our peer groups (the people we interact with throughout the course of our day-to-day lives) also contribute to our socialization. In many cases, peer groups reinforce the socialization to which we are initially exposed in the home, yet they inform how we should conduct ourselves as we interact with the world outside our homes (see Akers 1998). Further, our peer groups inform the processes through which we engage in the construction of our notions of self and individuality, popularize forms of conduct that translate into claims to personal status, and demonstrate the negative repercussions associated with straying from these conventions.

Beyond assessing how our peer groups reinforce our endorsement of the "natural attitude," symbolic interactionist researchers note how some peer groups promote beliefs or practices that would be interpreted as "deviant" by mainstream society, yet these contribute toward survival strategies for those within marginalized populations (Sutherland and Cressey 2006). Marxist traditions suggest a peer group's primary duty, as an agent of socialization, revolves around popularizing forms of leisure or "self-building" that directly perpetuate consumerism. Peer groups, then, take on the task of promoting that we, similarly, build ourselves through the purchasing of consumer products. Critical perspectives analyze the manner in which we impress cultural expectations and forms of regulation upon each other, often based on our uncritical acceptance of the "knowledge" surrounding conduct and the corresponding compulsion to "correct" or "normalize" the conduct of others.

Education

The education system is another significant agent of socialization. Tasked with the explicit goals of imparting students with the "knowledge" required to properly interact with the world as well as ensuring students learn to conform to "proper" expectations of conduct, the institution of formal education serves to reinforce and expand processes related to primary socialization.

Symbolic interactionists argue that the school environment also serves as our initial exposure to forms of secondary socialization, as we are taught how to "properly" conduct ourselves in relation to our peers and the authority figures whom we encounter. From the Marxist perspective, the educational system's primary goal is to condition us to respect authority and develop skills that will (once again) facilitate our transition into the workforce and the social reproduction of class inequalities — with different forms of education being extended to students on the basis of their social class standing (Gramsci 2008). Critical perspectives follow a similar line of logic, suggesting that the institution of education should best be approached as one that places youth under constant surveillance to ensure their conformity with normal expectations; this justifies that they be disciplined should they instead elect to engage in "deviant" or "abnormal" forms of conduct.

Mass Media

The fourth agent of socialization considered here is mass media. Unlike other agents of socialization, mass media does *not* contribute to the socialization process by directly interacting with individuals. While our families, peer groups, and the education system popularize social norms within the context of our lived experiences, mass media distributes information to a broad pool of diverse recipients at the same time. Whereas the socialization agents discussed above educate us on how things work *within our own social settings*, mass media informs us as to the state of the world *outside our personal surroundings*. As such, mass media is a primary resource for forming thoughts and feelings about those regions and social populations with whom we do not interact in our daily lives (see Cohen 1985; Faith and Jiwani 2002). While the news media is tasked with the role of informing us as to "what is happening" so as to ensure our informed participation in the organization of society (via the mainstream political process), entertainment media function to inform our use of leisure time and allow us the opportunity to "relax" and "wind down."

Symbolic interactionists suggest mass media content reflects the values and normative expectations that the wider society values and wishes to see reinforced (Berger 1972). The prevalence of police procedurals and superhero tales demonstrate our desire for justice and security, while situational comedies celebrate and reflect our affinity for humour and relatable content, and romantic comedies reinforce the significance of Western courtship rituals and companionship. From a Marxist perspective, the goals of mass media are far more nefarious and are perceived to further reinforce our support for the perpetuation of inequitable social systems (Horkheimer and Adorno 2002). Marxism posits that news media content aims to create a climate of fear and suspicion, often characterizing social minority groups as sources of risk and danger, to condition our consent for increasingly strict crime control methods. Entertainment media, on the other hand, functions to lead us to "tune in" to this form of media and "tune out" our day-to-day struggles and concerns — as opposed to critically assessing our position in life and whether "the way things are" actually serves to benefit the majority of the population. Critical theorists approach media content as yet another channel through which to orient institutional notions of "proper" and "improper" conduct, as well as an agent that leads us to impress similar expectations of conduct and belief upon others, as well as ourselves.

Current Issues and Social Control

Given this overview of the key concepts and theoretical perspectives with which the social sciences make sense of social control, we now briefly consider some of the themes you will encounter throughout this text.

Understanding Inequality

In some cases, the concepts and perspectives previously presented have been applied in considering the processes through which social norms, institutional regulation, and the contents of "knowledge" have historically contributed to privileging certain groups and justifying the maltreatment of others. Normative social expectations and characterizations of deviance are approached as long-serving means to justify the cultural and structural marginalization of people and populations based on gender, sexuality, ethnicity, body type, class status, ability, "mental health," and age, as well as forming public consensus that such "deviants" *must* be subject to various forms of surveillance, regulation, "treatment," or "correction." While these initiatives often result in the social, economic, and cultural disempowerment of such "nonconformists," these groups can also engage in various forms of collective and individual resistance, be they creative forms of self-performance and self-expression, the formation of subcultural communities that champion values contrasting those of the mainstream society, or other ways to contest the "common sense" of social organization through related rites of rebellion and dissent. The perspectives introduced here do not only attempt to explain historical sources of normativity and power, but they also aim to better assess the symbolism associated with forms of deviance and resistance.

Understanding Conflict

Contemporary events and emerging forms of conflict can also be better understood by "unpacking" the forms of power and expressions of resistance that continue to unfold as a variety of groups strive for equitable treatment and the reorganization of the social landscape. At this current stage in Western society, it could be said that many of the "commonsense" or "taken-for-granted" assumptions that have anchored the "natural attitude" are increasingly being challenged, often by groups that organize and mobilize through the use of technological and communicative capacities. The study of social control allows for a better understanding of the goals of these movements, as well as the emergent tactics — such as the use of social media — that they employ in advocating for change. These areas of study can also help us to understand how mainstream society reacts to these mobilizations – be it through institutions or the mobilization of counter-movements.

Understanding Change

Social control research also aids in the assessment of successful initiatives toward changing aspects of our social and cultural systems and contributes information that informs the social movements of the future. While we will consider a variety of case studies meant to demonstrate the extent to which normativity and power resist challenges, we will also have the opportunity to consider the slow but steady forms of progress that have materialized. These lines of inquiry also demonstrate that significant movements toward change can — and *have* — been instigated by lone individuals and dedicated groups who articulate their grievances in such a manner as to establish common ground among the various "standpoints" that we all inhabit.

A Brief Overview of the Text

This text consists of four sections. The first section provides an overview of influential theories and methods related to "deviance" and social regulation. We discuss examples of historical and present-day social regulation and power, as well as methodological approaches to understand social regulation and control. In part, this section aspires to help students understand the variety of sociological theories in this area. These chapters provide the touchstone perspectives and theorists related to the sociological study of norms, deviance, regulation, normalization, and power. Section two focuses on the construction of deviant and normalized identities, particularly related to addiction, sexuality, disability, and youth. Although we flush out a variety of perspectives on the social control of identity, from consensus to critical and feminist theories, we rely heavily on a social constructionist paradigm that focuses on the standpoints of those defined as deviant and who have experienced social control. Section three explores the culture of control. The chapters in this section raise questions about institutional social control through, for example, media

Each of us is compelled to conform with normative social expectations, respect figures of authority, and support forms of conduct in line with the forms of knowledge and truth that we approach as "common sense" or "beyond reproach."

and moral panics; the control of sex work; and misrepresentations and responses to murdered and missing Indigenous women and girls. The final section aims to familiarize readers with the process through which modern technologies have contributed to new forms of social control and the social movements that emerge to challenge traditional notions of "deviance" and engage in forms of resistance. In reinforcing the prospect that "deviant" labels and social regulatory initiatives depend largely upon the construction of knowledge, the emergence of the internet as a significant communication platform has not only ushered in an age of new surveillance technologies, but it also allows for the development and distribution of "counter-knowledges" through which dominant conceptions of deviance are increasingly being challenged.

Conclusion

At its core, the study of social regulation and social control assists us in understanding why we organize society as we do, how social norms gain authority, and the repercussions that emerge as different people or populations engage in movements toward conformity and nonconformity. Beyond analyzing how notions of deviance, normativity, power, and resistance actively shape our social world, different theoretical perspectives contribute a range of standpoints from which to consider these relationships. Symbolic interactionists suggest that we, as a society, create notions of deviance and normality to suit our collective interests. Marxist perspectives suggest those with social power shape our perceptions of "proper" and "improper" conduct to serve their interests and claims to social privilege. Critical perspectives consider the contents and social effects of the forms of "knowledge" and "truth" that orient our understanding of the material world and the systems we construct based on these truths. Whether being applied to historical case studies or current events, each of these concepts and methods of analyzing social order expands our awareness of the systems and cultural movements that, at different turns, reinforce and challenge long-standing conventions in social organization.

Meanwhile, it is useful to recognize that each of us is compelled to conform with normative social expectations, respect figures of authority, and support forms of conduct in line with the forms of knowledge and truth that we approach as "common sense" or "beyond reproach." By the conclusion of this collection, you may have a different assessment of the amount of control you have over your own life, as well as a newfound familiarity of strategies through which to change this assessment.

Discussion Questions

1. What is one significant difference between the concepts of social regulation and social control?
2. How have you previously understood the concept of "deviance" and what are some forms of conduct that you consider to be deviant?
3. Can you identify some of the "truths" or "forms of knowledge" that have influenced your perspective regarding "the way the world works"? Have you ever had cause to second-guess their credibility?
4. Have you witnessed or participated in any acts of collective resistance? If so, for what purpose?

Glossary

agents of socialization: the social institutions that contribute toward informing us as to how the world works, as well as how we should act.

critical perspectives: sociological theories arguing that systems of communication and forms of knowledge contribute to unequal power dynamics among social groups.

deviance: actions that contrast with cultural expectations or institutional rules.

Marxist perspectives: sociological theories arguing that our social systems are shaped by powerful social groups to protect their privilege.

natural attitude: taken-for-granted assumptions that we uncritically use to inform our beliefs and social conduct.

normativity: the process through which certain behaviours and beliefs take on authority and become standardized expectations.

power: the ability to make an individual or group act in ways that they otherwise would not.

primary socialization: the process through which we become familiar with methods of communication and recognize social roles.

resistance: challenging, or refusing to abide by, normative expectations and the power of those who enforce them.

secondary socialization: the process through which we become familiar with the social roles that we are expected to fill as a means of ensuring social order.

social control: the process through which dominant cultural beliefs compel members of society to conform to conduct expectations as well as pressure others to conform to dominant conduct expectations.

social regulation: the process through which our social institutions are designed to ensure we engage in forms of belief and conduct that protect and reinforce the current structure of society.

socialization: the processes through which we become oriented with the material and social worlds.

symbolic interactionist perspectives: sociological theories arguing that our social systems are actively shaped and reinforced by popular consensus among social actors.

References

Agger, B., and B.A. Shelton. 2007. *Fast Families, Virtual Children: A Critical Sociology of Families and Schooling*. New York: Routledge.

Akers, R. 1998. *Social Learning and Social Structure: A General Theory of Crime and Deviance*. Boston: Northeastern University Press

Berger, J. 1972. *Ways of Seeing*. London: Penguin.

Berger, P., and T. Luckmann. 1984. *The Social Construction of Reality: A Treatise in Sociology of Knowledge*. New York: Penguin.

Bourdieu, P. 1979. "Symbolic Power." *Critique of Anthropology* 4, 13–14.

Cohen, S. 1985. "Introduction." *Visions of Social Control: Crime, Punishment and Classification*. Cambridge: Polity Press.

Derrida, J. 1969. "The Ends of Man." *Philosophy and Phenomenological Research* 30, 1.

Faith, K., and Y. Jiwani. 2002. "The Social Construction of 'Dangerous Girls' and Women." In C. Brooks and B. Schissel (eds.), *Marginality and Condemnation: An Introduction to Critical Criminology*. Black Point: Fernwood Publishing.

Foucault, M. 1980. *Power/Knowledge: Selected Interviews and Other Writings 1972–1977*. New York: Pantheon Books.

Gramsci, A. 2008. *Selections from the Prison Notebooks*. New York: International Publishers.

Horkheimer, M., and T. Adorno. 2002. *Dialectic of Enlightenment: Theoretical Fragments*. Stanford: Stanford University Press.

Marx, K., and F. Engels. 1970. *The German Ideology: Part One*. New York: International.

Schütz, A. 1967. *Phenomenology of the Social World*. Evanston: Northwestern University Press.

Sellin, T. 1938. "Culture Conflict and Crime." *American Journal of Sociology* 44, 1.

Stamper, C.L., and L. Van Dyne. 2003. "Organizational Citizenship: A Comparison Between Part-Time and Full-Time Service Employees." *Cornell Hotel and Restaurant Administration Quarterly* 44, 1.

Sutherland, E.H., and D.R. Cressey. 2006. "A Theory of Differential Association." In T. Cullen and R. Agnew (eds.), *Criminological Theory: Past to Present, 3rd edition*. Los Angeles: Roxbury Company.

Willis, P. 1981. *Learning to Labour: How Working Class Kids Get Working Class Jobs*. New York: Columbia University Press.

A History of Perspectives of Social Deviance, Control, and Governance

Science has played a phenomenal role in framing our perception of the world. We have used scientific analysis to better understand human biology, outline the laws of physics, map out the contents of the human brain, and identify the elements from which all matter is derived. Given the degree to which science continues to shape society, it is surprising to consider that science has only very recently come to frame our understanding of the world (relative, of course, to a timeline beginning at the *very* beginning). Pre-modern European societies derived *their* understanding of the world from myths and religious doctrines. The authority to lead was granted to kings and queens believed to be the direct descendants of the gods and who thus had the "divine right" to govern. Natural disasters such as plagues and drought were attributed to supernatural forces working through morally culpable individuals engaging in forms of thought or conduct that were forbidden by authorities and sacred texts. Those who did not fall in line with the dominant beliefs and conduct expectations of the era were held responsible for the hardships encountered in the material world. This line of reason contributed to the onset of the European witch craze and the execution of untold numbers of women between the fourteenth and seventeenth centuries.

Narratives surrounding the genesis of the human sciences often begin with the "age of Enlightenment" of sixteenth- to seventeenth-century Europe, when scientific understanding became the dominant lens through which the world was observed and explained. The gradual accumulation of scientific perspectives gave way to the belief that science could optimize humankind's use of the natural world, improve the lives of all members of society, and help to determine the best methods of social organization. The enlightenment also contributed to a reconsideration of human nature and popularized the notion that people harboured the capacity to reasonably participate in the role of deciding upon their systems of government. The long-accepted truths that

had guided pre-modern European societies were supplanted by new questions and the analytical tools of the scientific method and rational thought.
This section consists of chapters that demonstrate the range of theoretical
orientations, concepts, and research methodologies that the social sciences
thereafter produced to analyze and explain practices of normativity and
patterns of social control. Individually, these chapters orient students with
concepts and themes that crop up throughout the remainder of this collection and demonstrate the variety of tools and forms of critical inquiry that
the social sciences have developed to date.

This section begins with Sean Hier's chapter, "Beyond Harm: Conditions,
Claims, and Social Problems Frames." Hier considers the value-laden process
through which social phenomena are framed and codified as sources of danger. Focusing on prevalent forms of social discourse surrounding risk, Hier
provides a series of examples to illustrate how practices that entail comparable
levels of risk come to be defined as problems in need of regulation or prohibition in some cases yet are culturally accepted as "the cost of modern living"
in others. Noting a long-standing process whereby the degree of harm posed
by a practice or phenomenon does not coincide with the degree to which
it is problematized, Heir draws attention to the role of the vested interests
and claims-making activities of social authorities and those in positions of
institutional and economic power. The construction of social problems, then,
facilitates and reinforces public consensus that those in positions of power
are deserving of their authority. In addition to providing a chapter that well
complements Hier's subsequent analysis of how panic discourse has evolved
in the wake of internet communication technologies (see Chapter 9), "Beyond
Harm" illustrates how a critical analysis of authoritative social discourse can
help us to unpack the ideologies and intentions that are embedded in the
framing of social problems.

The chapters that follow are concerned with sociological theories surrounding the imperative of normativity, the application and effects of deviant
labelling, how ideologies that naturalize social inequality find popular acceptance, and how different forms of "truth" and "normality" come to be accredited.
In Chapter 2, "Consensus Perspectives: Classical Notes on Norms, Deviance,
and Identity," Mitch D. Daschuk discusses early theories pertaining to the
genesis of social norms and deviant labels. It considers classic sociological
views on social order and the hypothesis that our willingness to conform
with normative social expectations led to our collective construction of the
social world. It also introduces symbolic interactionist concepts that seek

to make sense of how normative expectations take on social authority and become embedded in the institutional and cultural processes that are used to prevent and punish acts of transgression. These perspectives suggest, first, that normativity derives force from our collective human desire for safety and predictability in the navigation of our daily lives and, second, that popular consensus guides the process whereby certain ways of being, thinking, and acting are deemed immoral, deviant, or abnormal. Chapter 2 also elaborates on interactionist perspectives pertaining to the function of "deviant" designations. While deviant labels assist in demonstrating public consensus that certain acts or ways of being should be prohibited, acts of deviance also function to indicate that evolving public perspectives on acceptable or prohibited conduct no longer coincide with the regulations entrenched within our social institutions. By the conclusion of the chapter, students will appreciate that norms play a crucial role in informing our collective recognition of a common world, but that deviance likewise plays a decisive role in informing movements toward social change.

Chapter 3, Carolyn Brooks's "Defining Deviance: Critical, Feminist, and Anti-Oppressive Theories of Social Control," engages with sociological perspectives more closely associated with the conflict pole of the theoretical spectrum. Whereas the thinkers highlighted in Chapter 2 deduce that processes of social control draw their power from public consensus, Brooks highlights concepts to suggest, instead, that those in positions of social power promote beliefs and entrench institutions to protect and legitimize their authority. Brooks discusses the neo-Marxist perspective that categories of deviance come to be constructed and dispersed to allow those with economic and cultural power to marginalize and exploit the underprivileged. The chapter presents early neo-Marxist scholarship based around considerations of class exploitation and highlights how subsequent orientations, including feminist and postcolonial perspectives, sought to problematize the sexism and racism that pervaded our social systems. Moving on to a consideration of the perspectives of Michel Foucault, Brooks discusses the interrelations between forms of truth, institutional authorities, and the mechanisms of power that compel society to validate some ways of being and condemn others. A consideration of Foucault's concept of governmentality demonstrates how the regulatory forces that compel our conformity are both external and internal. Brooks furthermore questions these critical theories for failing to include gender, race, class, and the voices of those experiencing oppression. The last part of her chapter therefore includes feminist and anti-oppressive theories that integrate an understanding of the intersectionality of oppressions as well as the voices of those often labelled deviant.

The final chapter of the section, James Popham's "Research Methods, Statistics, and Listening to Unheard Voices," highlights how research in the study of social control is conducted. Popham provides an overview of quantitative and qualitative research methods while carefully highlighting how each can contribute critical analysis of often taken-for-granted features of the social world. While Popham notes that statistical methods can contribute to the decontextualization of the phenomena that they wish to understand, he demonstrates that they can, nevertheless, inform the creation of progressive social policy. The chapter identifies different forms of data accumulation, expectations related to methodological validity, and the evolving opportunities that contemporary communication platforms extend to social researchers. Popham directs equal attention to the merits and drawbacks associated with the research tactics he identifies and pulls no punches in citing significant instances of methodological error. Foreshadowing themes to be encountered throughout the final section of the text, the chapter considers how recent internet communicative technologies compile "big data" to learn about the online habits of individuals and, in some contexts, predict their future conduct. Popham closes his chapter by advocating for mixed-methods studies that allow for rigorous quantitative analysis while offering further empowerment and emancipation to those populations upon whom research is being conducted.

Looking Forward

The chapters presented in this section touch upon several enduring sociological concepts. Collectively, they testify to the variety of theoretical perspectives and methodologies provided by social science and allow insight on the range of variables that shape, restrict, and regulate our collective practices and personal conduct. These are some of the most revered tools with which to critically consider why we act as we do at this stage in history. That said, every one of these tools has been forged through processes of scientific inquiry and, therefore, is contingent on science's continuing status as the paramount lens through which we understand the world. Indeed, it is difficult to fathom how we might supplant the authority of the scientific method. It is worth keeping in mind, however, that the monarchs and religious authorities of fifteenth-century Europe would have found it difficult to fathom a means of engaging with the world that would supplant the authority of their religious perspectives.

1

Beyond Harm

Conditions, Claims, and Social Problems Frames

Sean P. Hier

After reading this chapter, you will be able to do the following:

1. Describe what is meant by the term *social problem*.
2. Identify the problem with tautological reasoning.
3. Explain variables related to defining social harms.
4. Illustrate how the problem of synchronization relates to the presence of harms that are not recognized as social problems.
5. Contrast constructivist and realist perspectives on social problems.

A social problem is a source of danger or risk that is collectively recognized by the members of society. Once identified, **social problems** often become the target of new laws, policies, or practices that are designed to reduce the risk that they pose. It is often through attracting a great deal of attention from politicians, media figures, and experts that social problems become recognized by the wider population. Imagine asking a class of college or university students in North America to identify the most important social problems right now. They might suggest teen sexting, excessive police violence, climate change, mass shootings, Islamic terrorism, childhood obesity, white nationalism, cyber-bullying, precarious employment, vaccine hesitancy, transgender washrooms rights, sexual violence, and campus rape culture.

Now let's imagine that we asked the same question to students living in the first few years of the 1980s. They would register different issues: nuclear disarmament, IRA terrorism, Colombian drug cartels, South African apartheid, the emergence of HIV, and crack babies. This demonstrates that social

By studying social problems analytically, sociologists explain how social phenomena, sometimes having persisted for decades (like premarital sex, domestic violence, workplace bullying), become understood as social problems only at certain moments in time, in particular places, and among members of specific social groups. They pay attention to social problems to understand how notions of "deviance" and "normativity" assemble, evolve, and decline in relation to shifting public attitudes.

problems change over time and across generations (even within our own lifetime), and explaining what constitutes a social problem is often difficult without examples. When we define social problems as problematic issues, we are using a form of logic called **tautological reasoning**: relying on a self-reinforcing pretense whose conclusion is the same as its premise. An example of tautological reasoning is trying to define what a human being is by pointing to your friend Joanne: you say the same thing twice using different words. Although it is true that Joanne is a human being, drawing attention to her as a human is not sufficient to define "human being." A definition requires explaining exactly why and how Joanne is a definitive characterization of the concept.

Consider racism — an enduring social issue that is also identified as a social problem. What benefit is derived from referring to racism, albeit indirectly, as a social problem? Sociologists are fully capable of investigating racial biases in educational curricula, incarceration rates, immigration policies, hiring practices, and popular culture without mentioning the term social problem. Understanding racism and racial discrimination does not hinge on defining racism as a social problem. If it's necessary to conceptualize racism as a social problem to strengthen explanations of racial prejudice and discrimination, we need specific explanatory criteria that will enhance our understanding of racism in society. Otherwise, referring to racism as a social problem is tautological and offers very little sociological value.

The definition matters to sociologists because they are concerned not only with commenting on and investigating important current-day social issues and events, but also with **analytical frameworks** anchored by criteria that clearly explain what makes a social problem socially problematic in the first place. By studying social problems analytically, sociologists explain how social phenomena, sometimes having persisted for decades (like premarital sex, domestic violence, workplace bullying), become understood as social problems only at certain moments in time, in particular places, and among members of specific social groups. They pay attention to social problems to understand how notions of "deviance" and "normativity" assemble, evolve, and decline in relation to shifting public attitudes. They assess *who* or *what* is being defined as a problem, *why* and *how* the problem is being defined as such, *who* is doing the defining, *what* should be done about the problem, and how a specific strategy will reduce the risk of further harm. They also account for the ways in which social phenomena once considered social problems are sustained over time or decline in importance. Finally, sociologists are becoming increasingly interested in how social issues that appear to be obvious candidates for social problem framing fail to attract sustained public attention and debate.

Social Problems, Harmful Conditions, and Social Definitions

One factor that is common to all social problems is **harm**. As Allessio (2016: 3) explains, "[a] social problem is a condition that involves harm to one or more individuals and/or one or more social entities." Social problems arise when social conditions (e.g., behavioural norms, daily conventions, resource allocations, structural inequities, consumption patterns, leisure activities) pose harm to individuals, organizations, communities, animals, and the natural environment.

Cigarette smoking is an obvious example of how people have problematized harmful social conditions and taken actions to mitigate their undesirable effects. The Canadian Cancer Society (2017) estimates that smoking is responsible for 45,000 deaths per year in Canada — almost one of every five deaths is related to smoking. Media, government, industry representatives, and cancer coalitions have moderated the risks associated with cigarette smoke and de-normalized smoking as a popular social activity by introducing cigarette filters, light cigarettes, age restrictions, advertising regulations, packaging rules, e-cigarettes, vaping, increased costs, specific taxes, new tobacco blends, public information campaigns, nicotine cessation programs, and smoke-free policies that limit the number of social and physical spaces where people can smoke.

The threat of cybercrime is another good example. Statistics Canada (2018) estimates that there were 17,532 reported cases of identity theft and identity fraud in Canada in 2017. Identity theft occurs when cybercriminals steal someone's personal information and identity (RCMP n.d.); for the victim, this can result in monetary losses in the form of counterfeit credit card charges, duplicitous bank withdrawals, and, in some cases, fraudulently refinanced mortgages and home equity credit lines. Victims of identity theft experience emotional distress, physical ailments, and the enormous inconveniences involved in repairing their credit profile (Golladay and Holtfreter 2016).

> We run into a problem when we use the concept of *harm* as the central defining characteristic of social problems: many harmful conditions (some of which have been harmful for decades) are not recognized as social problems. So harm is not a sufficient definition for social problem.

Banks, retail outlets, financial security professionals, and surveillance experts have tried to moderate the risks of consumer financial fraud by incorporating computer chips onto credit and debit cards, as well as advising consumers to protect their passwords and PINs, shred financial documents, and keep their credit cards and passports in radio-frequency identification (RFID) sleeves.

A final example is climate change. Informed by Article 2 of the United Nations Framework on Climate Change, the Intergovernmental Panel on Climate Change (2014) reported not only that climate change is caused by humans, but also that greenhouse gas emissions are the highest in history. They outlined that, in each of the last three decades, the Earth's surface has been warmer than any preceding decade since 1850; changing precipitation patterns and melting snow and ice are affecting marine systems, water resources, and crop yields; and without additional efforts to mitigate the effects of climate change, the end of the twenty-first century may experience severe, possibly irreversible environmental damage. Solutions to the harmful conditions associated with climate change over the past two decades, ranging from disasters like flooding and wildfires to climate-related issues like warming oceans and the rapid decline of plankton, have involved a range of interventions from intergovernmental policy agreements (the Kyoto and Paris Accords) to changes in individual consumption and lifestyle practices (recycling and home energy-use reduction): cap-and-trade programs, carbon taxing, mandatory automobile exhaust tests, green technologies, restrictions on car idling, alternative transportations, and electric or hybrid smart cars have all been floated as ways to mitigate the harms of climate change.

Few people living in North America today deny that the conditions of smoking, identity theft, and climate change pose serious harms to human, animal, and environmental well-being (even if there are people who deny the extent to which climate change is caused by human activity). We run into a problem when we use the concept of *harm* as the central defining characteristic of social problems: many harmful conditions (some of which have been harmful for decades) are not recognized as social problems. So harm is not a sufficient definition for social problem.

For example, numerous studies have documented the relationships between tobacco and lung cancer, emphysema, heart disease, and cardiovascular complications. Over the past fifteen years, these studies have moved public opinion to accept that smoking is harmful to human health. Smokers, especially pregnant ones, are now stigmatized, isolated, and at times ostracized (interestingly, comparable stigmas do not apply to other addictions, such as alcohol or prescription drugs). It makes sense to conclude that the detrimental health effects associated with tobacco use are what makes smoking socially problematic.

But smoking was harmful to human health long before it was widely recognized as a social problem. In fact, the Surgeon General's Advisory Committee on Smoking and Tobacco Report officially linked smoking to lung cancer, laryngeal cancer, and chronic bronchitis in 1964, at which point laws required warnings on cigarette packages and prohibitions on television and radio advertising. Prior to the mid-1960s, smoking was not only socially acceptable but also encouraged; advertising campaigns, positive media images, dubious medical advice, and favourable Hollywood film portrayals made smoking appealing. Activism between 1970 and 2000 to reduce the prevalence of smoking, especially in public places, resulted in a classroom smoking ban in the late 1980s; by the mid-1990s, the majority of US hospitals became smoke-free, by the late 1990s smoking was prohibited on all domestic and international airline flights, and in the 2000s most restaurants across North America restricted indoor smoking.

People were committing identity fraud (using another person's personal information without authorization, to deceive or defraud) long before the term was coined in the 1960s. Tampering with votes, falsifying passports and identification, and running credit card scams caused harm to retailers, security agencies, banking institutions, and consumers even prior to the advent of online banking services, global electronic credit systems, and point-of-purchase credit and debit card "taps." Yet the growing popularity of and mass access to the internet through the 1990s, combined with the influence of popular films such as *The Net* and *Identity Thief*, contributed to transforming identity fraud from a persistent yet marginal and scantly recognized set of criminal activities into a prominent social problem that is familiar to millions of people today.

Likewise, the human dimensions of climate change have been linked to the Industrial Revolution. Global increases in rates of deforestation, population growth, and CO_2 emissions into the atmosphere over the last 200 years are among the contributing factors to global warming, although these existed long before the term *climate change* was coined in the 1970s. Although Swedish scientist Svante Arrhenius (1896) pointed out as early as 1896 that fossil fuel combustion could eventually result in global warming, it was not until the early 1990s that climate change abruptly appeared on the public radar and became a household concern (Stehr and von Storch 1995). Popularized in part by movies such as *The Day After Tomorrow* and the documentary *An Inconvenient Truth*, climate change — a concept that denotes a set of physical changes to global climate patterns and weather systems — is fully understood, in a scientific sense, honouring all of its complexities, by only a small number of scientists. The significant point to take is that the increasing attention that the North American public now devotes to climate change cannot be taken to suggest that climate change is just presently becoming a social problem. Nor can it be expected that members of the general public and climate scientists would use the same points of reference when discussing the most prevalent social problems posed by rising global temperatures. These differing perspectives of understanding could also contribute to differing analyses of the most effective ways to curb the risks — a good reminder that perspectives regarding how to best deter threats posed by social problems may not be consistent or universally accepted.

The Problem of Synchronization

The discrepancy that we see between harmful conditions (such as smoking, identity fraud, and climate change) and the incongruent methods through which the members of a society collectively recognize and validate some harmful conditions as socially problematic (while discounting others) can be understood as the **problem of synchronization**. The problem of synchronization is a routine feature of social interaction characterized by recurring inconsistencies between what people define as harmful social problems at any given time and what evidence suggests that they should (or should not) define as socially problematic. Objectively harmful conditions undoubtedly play an influential role in motivating people to problematize various social activities and arrangements. Yet, as the introductory examples demonstrate, there is *no necessary relationship* between objectively harmful conditions and problematizing activities. This does not mean that there is *necessarily no relationship* between harmful conditions and the problematization of harm; it merely suggests that the relationship between harmful conditions and problematizing activities is not guaranteed (Hall 1986).

The problem of synchronization is commonly expressed in the form of **latent social problems** (Loseke 2003), which include potentially harmful conditions that persist for some time before being recognized and framed as social problems. Smoking, identity fraud, and climate change are good examples of latent social problems whose harmful effects were ongoing long before they were problematized. Other examples of latent social problems whose harms are increasingly being problematized include the refined sugars in commercial foods, factory farming, toxic household cleaning chemicals, long periods of sitting, third-hand smoke, and the carcinogenic properties of latex condoms.

While the problem of synchronization is often explained through a retrospective lens, latent social problems don't only belong to the past. Many other harmful conditions are not likely to ever be explicitly framed in terms of an urgent or life-threatening social problem, regardless of the fact that they pose abiding harms to human health and well-being. Popular hazards in our everyday lives appear benign. But imagine learning that engineers developed a revolutionary new technology that promises to get you places faster, increase the number of chores you can accomplish in a single day, and bring some greater enjoyment to your life. The catch is that this invention will kill upwards of forty thousand people in North America and over a million people around the world each year (to say nothing about the staggering number of injuries that will result). How likely is it that you would eagerly embrace, let alone pay large sums of money to enjoy, this new technology in your everyday life?

Without much embellishment, the new revolutionary technology in question is the automobile! In North America alone, people drive trillions of miles each year. Transport Canada (2014) reports that between 1995 and 2014, there were approximately 2,300 traffic fatalities in Canada each year — about six people a day. It is hard to deny that driving is an objectively harmful, life-threatening condition.

Some of the harmful effects associated with driving are extensively problematized. Government agencies, consumer protection advocates, and the automobile manufacturing industry have introduced design regulations, speed limits, road signs, airbags, seatbelt laws, anti-lock braking mechanisms, and advanced safety warning systems to make driving safer. But mass motorization itself is rarely problematized as a harmful condition. Because the culture of auto-centred transportation is so deeply ingrained in our lifestyles and daily routines, it is hard to imagine viable mass transportation alternatives. Rather than problematizing the harmful condition of driving, safety interventions problematize the age and experience of drivers, or the myriad activities related to driving: distracted driving, careless driving, nighttime driving, texting while

A popular hazard is a harmful activity that millions of people knowingly participate in each day, like driving, drinking alcohol, having unprotected sex, shooting a gun, using a playground, bouncing on a trampoline, or riding a skateboard. These activities are common and usually legal, but they are hazardous in the sense that they cause substantial, though not in most cases immediate, harm to individuals and social groups.

driving, drinking and driving, pollution caused by driving.

The discordance between the objectively harmful condition of driving and the ways in which we selectively problematize the risks associated with auto-centred transportation is an example of what Joel Best (2017) calls a **popular hazard**. A popular hazard is a harmful activity that millions of people knowingly participate in each day, like driving, drinking alcohol, having unprotected sex, shooting a gun, using a playground, bouncing on a trampoline, or riding a skateboard. These activities are common and usually legal, but they are hazardous in the sense that they cause substantial, though not in most cases immediate, harm to individuals and social groups.

To better appreciate the relationship between popular hazards and the problem of synchronization, consider the difference between harm caused by driving and harm associated with international terrorist attacks in the United States. Between September 2001 and December 2014, 2,961 Americans died in terrorist attacks on US soil. Of those, 2,902 resulted from the 2001 9/11 attacks in Washington and New York alone. What this means is that, barring the 9/11 attacks, 59 deaths resulted from terrorist attacks in the United States in the thirteen-year period spanning 2001–14 (National Consortium for the Study of Terrorism and Responses to Terrorism 2015). This number is less than the deaths resulting from only one day of driving in America. Even though the risk of death by driving is higher, international terrorism was far more extensively problematized than driving in this time period. Consider all of the ways — globally, nationally, and individually — that the harms associated with terrorism were problematized in just the first decade of the twenty-first century. Immigration and border controls, intelligence sharing, secret military operations, media speculation about sleeper cells, surveillance of self-radicalized fundamentalists, monitoring ISIS networks, and airport security measures as granular as requiring passengers to remove their shoes prior to boarding commercial aircraft are among the dozens of problematizing activities that continue to sustain the social problem frame of terrorism as an imminent threat.

The problem of synchronization is a helpful way to think about the contradictions that characterize popular social reactions to real and perceived harmful conditions; it also helps us to develop analytical insights into what actually makes a social problem socially problematic. Consider how it can take decades to respond to the objective harms posed by latent social problems (like smoking) and at other times how we

> Halloween trick-or-treating is a very dangerous activity (sugar intake, risk of pedestrian-automobile collision), but there is no evidence that Halloween sadists are anything more than an urban legend. This means that, even though Halloween sadism didn't cause any demonstrable harm to anyone, it was nonetheless treated as a social problem. Harm must not be the factor that defines a social problem.

avoid responding to objectively harmful conditions by deflecting attention away from obvious sources of risk in our daily lives (like driving). A third way to think about the variability of social problem framing is to consider social issues that are extensively problematized even though they are not associated with any objectively harmful condition at all.

The classic example of a non-existing condition that is widely recognized as a social problem is Halloween sadism. Halloween sadism refers to the belief that sadistic strangers contaminate Halloween treats with either poisons or dangerous objects like pins or razors and distribute them to trick-or-treating children. Children are annually instructed to hand over their Halloween treats to their parents for inspection before eating them. For more than twenty years, hospitals have offered to X-ray candy as added assurance. In some places, malls are alternative venues for trick-or-treating. Elsewhere, trick-or-treating is outright banned. In DuPage County, Illinois, the sheriff's office went so far as to open its crime lab for forty-eight hours in 2009, offering to inspect "suspicious sweets using technology that's usually reserved for homicide, sexual assault and burglary" (TIME 2009).

But were people really tampering with candies? Between 1958 and 1984, Best and Horiuchi (1985) examined whether Halloween sadism was a widespread (let alone real) condition. They examined US newspapers to find coverage of the issue, reasoning that, if strangers were annually poisoning and maiming children, the crisis would surely receive extensive public attention. Best (2008) updated the study of print, and subsequently social, media in the years to follow. Each investigation reached the same conclusion: Halloween trick-or-treating is a very dangerous activity (sugar intake, risk of pedestrian-automobile collision), but there is no evidence that Halloween sadists are anything more than an urban legend. This means that, even though Halloween sadism didn't cause any demonstrable harm to anyone, it was nonetheless treated as a social problem. Harm must not be the factor that defines a social problem.

Studying Social Problems

If harm is not a reliable indicator for explaining the socially problematic aspects of a social problem, what are the defining features that differentiate social issues or conditions from social problems? In the 1970s, sociologists started to explicitly study social problems by investigating **claims-making activities**. Claims-making activities are the verbal and non-verbal ways that people define social issues and conditions as social problems. Claims-making activities can be protests, social media posts, YouTube videos, memes, newspaper stories, tweets, congressional hearings, comic strips, Hollywood movies, documentaries, acts of civil disobedience, statistical reports, symbols, and university lectures. Social problems are fundamentally characterized by a wide range of **claims makers** (such as celebrity activists, social movement organizations, politicians, journalists, and professors) who try to convince various audiences (students, conservatives, parents, and members of the LGBTQ+ community) about a real or perceived harm to human, animal, and/ or environmental well-being.

When social problems are studied in terms of claims-making activities, sociologists work with the assumption that the issues or conditions people routinely recognize as social problems cannot be studied apart from human processes of representation, symbolization, and interpretation. Many issues and conditions influence people's lives and life chances, but only a small number of those issues, many of which are indeed harmful to human health and well-being, get defined as and addressed in terms of social problems. This does not mean that those who study claims making deny that harmful conditions exist independently of human consciousness and experience; it simply implies that harm is a poor, or at least imprecise, predictor of what people define as a social problem.

The argument that social problems are the product of claims-making activities rather than objectively harmful, real-world material conditions may seem reductive at first blush. Considering all the suffering and inequity in the world, how can social problems be reduced to a set of claims? Surely, the pervasiveness of sexual violence and torture in Syria, the overrepresentation of Indigenous persons in Canadian prisons, the proliferation of pedophile networks in the deep web, and the thousands of South Sudanese people on the verge of starvation in 2017 indicates there is something more objectively real to social problems than subjective human processes of interpretation and representation.

Sociologists have struggled to come to terms with the counterintuitive argument that claims-making activities are what render social problems socially problematic. For adherents to the claims-making perspective (sometimes referred to as **social constructionists**), social problems are composed of claims about alleged conditions that pose harm to human, animal, and environmental well-being (Spector and Kitsuse 1977). The claims-making approach is based on the argument that we can never understand the harm posed by various social conditions apart from cultural, social, political, and linguistic influences. The reality of harm, in other words, is always symbolically mediated through processes of human communication and interpretation. Because all claims about harm are interpreted through images, texts, metaphors, allegories, and allusions, the best we can do is study claims about what we assume to be an objective social reality. If nothing else, appealing to the objective material reality of social problems does not, as we have seen, get us any closer to understanding the lack of synchronization between alleged harms and social problematization.

On the other side of the debate, adherents to the condition-based perspective reject the argument that social problems are no more than a set of claims (Dello Buono 2015). Condition-based researchers (sometimes referred to as **realists**) believe that objectively measurable harms to human, animal, and environmental well-being are what make social problems socially problematic. Some realists readily concede that we can only know about objective reality through human perception and experience. Still, they hold the view that our interpretations of reality do not fundamentally change the fact that a reality independent of perception can be investigated, measured, and known. For the constructionists, the realists maintain, claims making is the cause, the outcome, and the entirety of reality itself (Thibodeaux 2014).

Although the realist position makes sense intuitively and philosophically, substituting a condition-based perspective with an activities-based one presents a different set of challenges. We have already seen that harm is not always or even regularly a reliable indicator for predicting what people define as, think about, and address in terms of social problems. For example, why do millions of children living in the Global South die from easily preventable diseases every year (like measles and tetanus) if objective harm is what informs social problem framing and the accompanying strategies to eradicate life-threatening conditions? By the same token, why are terrorist attacks in

London and Manchester instantly problematized and addressed in terms of military fortification and securitization while the objectively greater harm that is wreaked by terrorism in Nigeria and Yemen barely attracts attention? There are complicated political answers to these questions, of course, but they are not found in the objectively harmful components that define social problems in an a priori manner.

> In some cases, the framing of social problems leads to collective political actions aimed at mitigating the harms associated with undesirable social conditions.

Most of us are willing to accept the argument that harmful conditions exist, regardless of whether we define them as social problems and attend to their damaging effects. The main point of contention between realists and constructionists, however, is not if harmful conditions exist but rather the value in conceptualizing social problems in terms of harmful conditions. Many constructionists have no problem with researchers who investigate the harms associated with conditions ranging from tooth decay to distracted driving. Constructionists, like most other people, recognize the value of documenting various kinds of harm and developing evidence-based strategies to reduce the risks of human hardship and suffering. But many constructionists are also quick to point out that documenting the harm associated with various conditions gets us no closer to understanding how and why we problematize some harmful conditions and not others.

Beyond the academic conceptual debates about what actually makes a social problem socially problematic (that is, debates that shape how researchers investigate social problems and craft their arguments), social constructionists are also interested in the political and material consequences of **social problem framing** (that is, the actual effects that social problem frames have on real peoples' lives). In some cases, the framing of social problems leads to collective political actions aimed at mitigating the harms associated with undesirable social conditions. The remarkable uptake of the blue box recycling system that began in the 1980s is an example of how social problem framing about pollution and waste management can lead to changes in collective behaviour. Yet in other cases, the framing of social issues that pose seemingly unambiguous harm to human safety and well-being struggles to produce the kinds of political changes that would otherwise be expected.

> Yet in other cases, the framing of social issues that pose seemingly unambiguous harm to human safety and well-being struggles to produce the kinds of political changes that would otherwise be expected.

The social construction of mass

shootings in the United States is a clear example of the differences that social problem framing can make to life itself. Former president Barack Obama candidly addressed the enduring problem of synchronization pertaining to gun access in America when he addressed the White House press gallery (TIME 2015) in response to the forty-fifth mass shooting in 2015, and the 994th since he took office:

> In the coming days, we'll learn about the victims — young men and women who were studying and learning and working hard, their eyes set on the future, their dreams on what they could make of their lives. And America will wrap everyone who's grieving with our prayers and our love. But as I said just a few months ago, and I said a few months before that, and I said each time we see one of these mass shootings, our thoughts and prayers are not enough. It's not enough. It does not capture the heartache and grief and anger that we should feel. And it does nothing to prevent this carnage from being inflicted someplace else in America — next week, or a couple of months from now. We don't yet know why this individual did what he did. And it's fair to say that anybody who does this has a sickness in their minds, regardless of what they think their motivations may be. But we are not the only country on Earth that has people with mental illnesses or want to do harm to other people. We are the only advanced country on Earth that sees these kinds of mass shootings every few months.

Obama argued that, even in the face of the unambiguously monumental harm posed by permissive gun laws in certain US states (the carnage wreaked by routine mass shootings in America), the social problem of gun violence is regularly framed by media, politicians, and lobbyists as one of mental illness, anomaly, aberration, and resolve. Rather than addressing the harm posed by the uniquely recurring phenomenon of mass shootings in America by restricting gun access and adopting stronger laws on the types of guns that can be obtained, the debate has taken the form of a narrow interpretation of the second amendment right to bear arms (Carlson 2016).

For sociologists studying a wide range of social problems, this suggests that it is not enough to only investigate "subjective" claims-making activities (like public statements by victims' families, media frames, NRA lobbying activities). It is also necessary to develop a more complete understanding of why, for example, so many Americans are resistant to stronger guns laws.

In addition to describing specific claims and problematizing frames, claims-making activities should be situated in a broader historical and cultural context to understand the norms, values, conventions, and expectations that condition claims making in the present. The interesting challenge confronting sociologists is to explain how "putatively problematic conditions, once assembled as meaningful objects of discourse and practice, might become dialectically related to the discursive claims made about them" (Weinberg 2009: 62). In other words, rather than juxtaposing "objective" material conditions with "subjective" social definitions, an alternative way of thinking about social problem claims making is to explore how historical packages of claims become objective rhetorical resources that are used to inform how perceived problems are framed in the present. In this way, the social construction of social problems entails the study of claims-making activities in the present, as well as the cultural and historical context in which claims are made, resisted, revised, subverted, and acted upon.

Discussion Questions

1. Why are sociologists interested in studying social problems?
2. What are some harmful conditions that are not recognized as social problems?
3. What is the significance of claims-making activities in relation to social problems?
4. What is the difference between "constructionist" and "realist" perspectives on social problems?
5. Who are the people and groups who frame social problems?

Recommended Resources

1. *Devil Worship: Exposing Satan's Underground* (Geraldo Riviera Specials, 1988)
2. *Marijuana* (Avanti Films, 1968).
3. *The Insider* (Buena Vista Pictures, 1999).

Glossary

analytical frameworks: standardized hypotheses through which to contextualize the study of social phenomena.

claims makers: people with institutional or cultural prominence who have the authority to identify social problems.

claims-making activities: practices through which harmful conditions are redefined as social problems.

harm: an assessment of dangers posed by specific conditions and used to inform collective perceptions of social problems.

latent social problems: harmful conditions that exist but are not popularly characterized as social problems.

popular hazard: harmful conditions or practices with which social actors nevertheless engage.

problem of synchronization: instances in which social problems are identified despite the absence of harmful conditions.

realists: those with the analytical perspective assuming that social problems exist objectively and independent of collective recognition as social problems.

social constructionists: those with the analytical perspective assuming that social problems exist by virtue of their being collectively recognized as social problems.

social problem framing: processes through which the presence of social problems is authoritatively associated with specific practices or populations.

social problems: issues of collective concern among members of society that, though taken as self-evident, are constructed through social interaction.

tautological reasoning: a form of faulty logic based around rephrasing an assertion as evidence in support of itself.

References

Allessio, John. 2016. *Social Problems and Social Inequality: Social Responsibility through Progressive Sociology.* New York: Routledge.

Arrhenius, Svante. 1896, "On the Influence of Carbonic Acid in the Air upon the Temperature of the Ground." *Philosophical Magazine and Journal of Science* 41, 5.

Best, Joel. 2017. "Popular Hazards and Policy Rhetoric. *Sociological Forum* 42, 3.

____. 2008. "Halloween Sadism: The Evidence." <udspace.udel.edu/handle/19716/726#files-area>.

Best, Joel, and Gerald Horiuchi. 1985. "The Razor Blade in the Apple: The Social Construction of Urban Legends." *Social Problems* 32, 5.

Canadian Cancer Society. 2017. "Smoking Causes 1 in 5 of All Deaths, Costs $6.5 Billion in Healthcare in Canada Each Year: Study." October 16. <cancer.ca/en/about-us/for-media/media-releases/national/2017/cost-of-tobacco/?region=on>.

Carlson, Jennifer. 2016. "Moral Panic, Moral Breach: Bernard Goetz, George Zimmerman, and the Racialized News Reporting in Contested Cases of Self-Defense." *Social Problems* 63, 1.

Dello Buono, Ricardo A. 2015. "Presidential Address: Reimagining Social Problems: Moving Beyond Social Constructionism." *Social Problems* 62, 3.

Geraldo Riviera Specials. 1988. "Devil Worship: Exposing Satan's Underground." <youtube.com/watch?v=0mytkRybjNI&feature=youtu.be>

Golladay, Katelyn, and Kristy Holtfreter. 2016. "The Consequences of Identity Theft Victimization: An Examination of Emotional and Physical Health Outcomes." *Victims and Offenders* 12, 5.

Hall, Stuart. 1986. "*The Problem with Ideology: Marxism Without Guarantees.*" *Journal of Communication Inquiry* 10, 2.

Intergovernmental Panel on Climate Change. 2014. *Climate Change 2014: Impacts, Adaptation, and Vulnerability.* <bjs.gov/content/pub/pdf/vit14.pdf>.

Loseke, Donileen. 2003. *Thinking About Social Problems.* New York: Aldine De Gruyter.

Mann, Michael. 1999. *The Insider* [film]. Buena Vista Pictures.

Marijuana [film]. 1968. Avanti Films. <youtube.com/watch?v=sfZqDRul3nw>

National Consortium for the Study of Terrorism and Responses to Terrorism. 2015. "Fact Sheet: American Deaths in Terror Attacks." <start.umd.edu/pubs/START_AmericanTerrorismDeaths_FactSheet_Oct2015.pdf>.

RCMP (Royal Canadian Mounted Police). n.d. "Identity Theft and Identity Fraud." <rcmp-grc.gc.ca/scams-fraudes/id-theft-vol-eng.htm>.

Spector, Malcolm, and John Kitsuse. 1977. *Constructing Social Problems.* New York: Transaction Publishers.

Statistics Canada. 2018. "Police-Reported Crime Statistics in Canada, 2017." <www150.statcan.gc.ca/n1/en/pub/85-002-x/2018001/article/54974-eng.pdf?st=Bg52Fdrz>.

Stehr, Nico, and Hans von Storch. 1995. *Climate and Society: Climate as Resource, Climate as Risk.* Singapore: World Scientific Publishing.

Thibodeaux, Jarrett. 2014. "Three Versions of Constructionism and their Reliance on Social Conditions in Social Problems Research." *Sociology* 48, 4.

TIME. 2015. "Transcript: Read the Full Text of Obama's Statement on the Shooting in Oregon." October 1. <time.com/4058961/oregon-shooting-president-obama-transcript-speech/>.

____. 2009. "Is Trick-Or-Treating Dangerous? October 30. <content.time.com/time/nation/article/0,8599,1933329,00.html>.

Transport Canada. 2014. *Canadian Motor Vehicle Traffic Collision Statistics 2014.* <tc.gc.ca/media/documents/roadsafety/cmvtcs2014_eng.pdf>.

Weinberg, Darin. 2009. "On the Social Construction of Social Problems and Social Problems Theory: A Contribution to the Legacy of John Kitsuse." *American Sociologist* 40.

2

Consensus Perspectives

Classical Notes on Norms, Deviance, and Identity

Mitch D. Daschuk

After reading this chapter, you will be able to do the following:
1. Explain why Durkheim argues that deviance can be "functional" for society.
2. Identify the types of "adaptations" identified by Merton's Strain Theory.
3. Name the variables that Hirschi's social control theory associates with conformity.
4. Describe how our development of our identities is a social process.
5. Differentiate between Goffman's three forms of stigma.

This chapter discusses early sociological perspectives on the genesis of social norms, the function of social deviance, and the influence that being designated a deviant has on the formation of identity. These consensus perspectives, which date back to the inception of sociology in the latter nineteenth century, suggest that dominant interpretations of normality and deviance are actively shaped through the implicit consensus of the social majority. This consensus is reflected, and made routine, through institutions designed to ensure conformity and systems designed to combat deviancy. Social norms and state regulations conform to the will of the public at large, and we all engage in reinforcing their authority in choosing to abide by them. Consensus perspectives are often — and perhaps unfairly — defined by the ways in which they differ from conflict perspectives, which purport that our

> Social norms and state regulations conform to the will of the public at large, and we all engage in reinforcing their authority in choosing to abide by them.

cultural practices and institutions are shaped through conflict and competition between social groups. People in positions of power shape the rules and regulations to which we are subject, and they reinforce and justify the unequal distribution of wealth and social power. As subsequent chapters of this collection will illustrate, the conflict perspective has become the dominant theoretical frame through which deviance and the social control mechanisms that ensure our conformity are examined. From a macro-sociological perspective — that is, when examining how social order is maintained through social institutions that address our collective needs and maintain order — conflict perspectives certainly do provide a great deal of insight. However, this chapter contends that consensus perspectives — and especially those associated with the symbolic interactionist theories of the early 1900s — still provide significant value when considering how normativity and deviance are constructed at a micro-sociological perspective. These conceptual tools are of particular use when considering how all of us reinforce the authority of dominant norms and conduct expectations as we interact with others and intellectually reflect on our own notions of "self." Theorists associated with the consensus perspectives can still contribute toward contextualizing the process through which social norms emerge, the collective imperatives that they aspire to serve, and the consequences for their transgression. This chapter highlights key contributions from consensus perspectives regarding the genesis of social norms, the significance and sources of deviant conduct, and the ways in which attracting condemnation as "deviant" harbours implications in the formation of identity. Following an overview of Emile Durkheim's foundational perspectives on norms, the genesis of social facts, and the significance of deviance in instigating social change, this chapter demonstrates how these concepts informed contrasting movements in strain and social control theories. It then considers interactionist perspectives surrounding the significance of the "natural attitude," the social process through which we derive our perspectives on ourselves, and the repercussions associated with attracting deviant **stigma**. The chapter concludes with an overview of how classical consensus perspectives, collectively, suggest the presence of a vicious cycle in linking the application of deviant labels with the internalization of deviant identities.

Durkheim on Mechanical Solidarity, the Collective Conscience, and Social Facts

Emile Durkheim, often described as one of the founders of sociology, sought to explain the historical emergence of social institutions and cultural norms. Durkheim's 1964 [1893] publication *The Division of Labour in Society* described how the transition from "pre-modern" to "modern" societies ushered in new methods through which to ensure harmonious relationships in diverse populations. Durkheim argued that prior to the Industrial Revolution, social groups in Europe primarily consisted of small, mostly self-sufficient populations. Because they were small and insular, they maintained order because they shared a set of beliefs and conduct — a **collective conscience**. These small groups had a uniform interpretation of the world and a sense of spiritual *connectivity* among members. Durkheim characterized these social groupings with a strong collective conscience as mechanically solidified societies. With the onset of industrialization, the growth of cities, the coalescence of cultural groups, and improvements in manufacturing and distributing goods, social groups organized, and in the cities that emerged around these centres of production, patterns of organization based around insularity became dysfunctional. New ideals of interdependence among different cultural groups created organically solidified societies organized around principles of increased interdependence upon other community members for necessary goods and services. While urban living allowed for more efficient methods of production, the sheer number of cultures and belief structures within the cities deterred the development of uniform beliefs and values. Durkheim explained that **mechanical solidarity** "is possible only insofar as the individual personality is absorbed into the collective personality; [and **organic solidarity**] is possible only if each person has a sphere of action which is peculiar to them; that is, a personality" (1964 [1893]: 131). In the absence of shared beliefs around proper conduct, societies create explicit rules and regulations.

Given the concentration of people in cities, Durkheim explained that modern societies must maintain social order by developing social institutions, such as the judicial and education systems, to promote social norms and ensure that our social systems operate stably. We conform with these normative expectations because these institutions, in turn, serve as our agents of socialization. From this perspective, human societies engage in the process of constructing social norms that align with the requirements of institutional order. Durkheim takes care to argue that members of the general public play an active role in constructing the norms that inform our ways of life. The

> Our judicial system only exists insofar as people engage with and codify the rituals that take place throughout the judicial system. Without motivated individuals to take on the roles of judges, jury members, and lawyers, our courthouses would be empty buildings.

interactive process through which we actively create and reinforce social norms operates through what Durkheim calls social facts: "a category of facts which present very special characteristics: they consist of manners of acting, thinking, and feeling external to the individual, which are invested with a coercive power by virtue of which they exercise control over him" (1938: 52). Social facts are the widely held beliefs that inform the conduct expectations associated with different social roles, and these draw their authority from the widespread social consensus that "this is the way that things should be done." Though social facts gain authority as the members of a society recognize and act in accordance with them, many social facts exist only because people heed them. For example, gender can be considered a social fact, given that we are not biologically hardwired to "act" like boys or girls. While people have different reproductive organs, there is no biological basis for men to develop an affinity for big automobiles or for women to shave their legs. Instead, we take on "masculine" or "feminine" gender practices because we are socialized to recognize gender as a "real thing" even though it does not exist independent of the cultural practices in which we engage. Justice can also be characterized as a social fact. While we have judges and lawyers who conduct criminal trials, the judicial system itself has no basis in material reality beyond the practices that those who assume the social roles of "judges" and "lawyers" actively reinforce. Our judicial system, then, only exists insofar as people engage with and codify the rituals that take place throughout the judicial system. Without motivated individuals to take on the roles of judges, jury members, and lawyers, our courthouses would be empty buildings. Social facts, then, exist by virtue of the patterned forms of interaction between the members of a society.

Durkheim differentiates between two types of social facts. Material social facts are reinforced through the creation of social institutions (e.g., criminal justice, education, and politics) and take on authority due to their embodiment in material structures (such as the courthouse, school, and Houses of Parliament). Non-material social facts, on the other hand, are reinforced through patterns in human conduct (e.g., gender roles, proper etiquette) and acquire authority through the presence of other people (such as parents, peers, and teachers) who impress upon us the importance of abiding by conduct expectations. For Durkheim, social harmony is maintained as people accept and internalize social facts as representations of "the way the world is" and consent to their authority.

Social Bonds and Anomie

Given the onset of industrialization and the transition from rural to urban populations, Durkheim argued that it was crucial that members of a shared society find strong spiritual connection with one another. He identified two problems in collective conscience that urban living introduced. On an individual level, Durkheim argued that feeling spiritually disconnected from, and "out of sync" with, the social majority could propel a person into a state of anomie: a feeling of disconnection with the norms of the dominant society that makes a person less likely to identify with, and therefore conform to, the expectations of the wider community. In his landmark 1897 study, *On Suicide*, Durkheim analyzed suicide trends throughout Europe between 1841 and 1872; he associated different types of suicide with social variables, including one's integration into mainstream society and one's ability to successfully conform with the practices celebrated therein. Egoistic suicide, for example, occurs with people who cannot identify with their fellow community members and experience an absence of meaningful interpersonal relationships. Anomic suicide stems from instances in which individuals experience drastic (and negative) change, such as the dissolution of relationships or sudden changes in their social positioning.

On a group level, Durkheim contends that the loss of collective conscience would pose a problem for groups with cultural practices or belief systems that differ from those of the dominant society. These groups might find it difficult to acclimatize to and nurture the social bonds that promote the recognition and acceptance of common norms. An absence of social bonds at the group level would also mean that some groups might feel little allegiance to dominant norms and values and therefore be prone to engaging in contravening acts and practices.

Deviance, Order, and Change

While Durkheim does not use the term *deviance* specifically, his perspectives on the transgression of social norms are a critical part of understanding contemporary examples of social conflict and change. For Durkheim, the punitive institutional responses by police and judiciaries to the transgression of rules reinforce public consensus on the perpetuation of norms and make clear to members of the society exactly what types of practices are prohibited by social norms. For example, even if a community has some sense of the importance of abiding with normative expectations, specific knowledge of certain rules might not be clearly recognized until someone is caught in the act and subjected to institutional reprimand. Further, rituals surrounding public responses to acts of social transgression — such as through criminal trials or, more recently, the "cancellation" of entertainers who make inappropriate statements — are approached as reinforcing the shared communal bonds of the upstanding members of a society. Collective processes, in which the members of a community react to instances of social deviance, clarify and reinforce norms. Durkheim went so far as to suggest that the reinforcement of social norms can *only* occur through instances whereby individuals transgress those norms; acts of deviance are necessary for the members of a society to know what constitutes prohibited practice.

Durkheim also notes the additional significance of acts of social transgression, as they instigate the process whereby the members of a community, at times collectively, decide to modify what constitutes acceptable behaviour. The evolution of social norms depends upon situations whereby the wider community takes issue with the basis on which certain individuals come to be declared "deviant." Durkheim wrote:

> To make progress, individual originality must be able to express itself. In order that the originality of the idealist whose dreams transcend this century may find expression, it is necessary that the originality of the criminal, who is below the level of his time, shall also be possible. One does not occur without the other.... Aside from this indirect utility, it happens that crime itself plays a useful role in this evolution. Crime implies not only that the way remains open to necessary changes but also that in certain cases it directly prepares these changes. Where crime exists, collective sentiments are sufficiently flexible to take on a new form, and crime sometimes helps to determine the form they will take. How many times, indeed, it is only an anticipation of future morality — a step towards what will be. (1938: 71–72)

Durkheim suggests that the members of a community are not wholly uncritical about transgressive acts: in some cases, the public might take issue with the basis on which actors come to be declared deviant, and they voice dissatisfaction with the normative grounds upon which such declarations are made. For example, when Rosa Parks was arrested for refusing to abide by an Alabama racial segregation law dictating that African-Americans sit at the back of the bus, she inspired a critical mass of protests among African-American communities. The civil rights movement eventually won a repeal of racial segregation laws.

To summarize, Durkheim approaches social norms as a crucial prerequisite to social stability and perceives such norms as representing the general will of the majority public. Deviance occurs when individuals feel that these normative expectations do not coincide with their own beliefs, or they can no longer act in accordance with them. Still, acts of deviance serve different functions within different social contexts. Deviance reinforces social normativity but can also spark re-evaluations of normative expectations.

Durkheim's Influence: Strain and Social Control Theories

Durkheim's sociological concepts captured the attention of sociologists who sought to build the field. Robert K. Merton (1968) incorporated Durkheim's concept of anomie in trying to explain the social influences that led to crime in Western society. Travis Hirschi (1969), meanwhile, incorporated Durkheim's concept of **social bonds** into a social control theory that sought to identify individualized precursors to criminal and otherwise transgressive behaviour.

Strain Theory: Deviance and the Disjunction between Goals and Means

Merton understood prevalent social norms to serve two purposes: familiarizing people with the values and goals they should espouse and also showing how to acceptably achieve them. In the context of North America (and especially the United States), these values and goals revolved around the accumulation of wealth, personal success, and claims to social power and distinction. Pursuing these goals meant having a healthy work ethic and abiding by the conduct expectations of social institutions such as the judicial and education systems. Merton saw a problem, though:

> Contemporary American culture continues to be characterized by a heavy emphasis on wealth as a basic symbol of success, without a corresponding emphasis upon the legitimate avenues on which to march toward this goal. What, in short, are the consequences for the behavior of people variously situated in a social structure of a culture in which the emphasis on dominant success-goals has become

increasingly separated from an equivalent emphasis on institutionalized procedures for seeking these goals? (1968: 193)

Merton developed strain theory, which advances the argument that this
disjuncture between culturally universalized social goals and the inequitable
distribution of opportunities inspired different social populations to endorse
different forms of "adaptations." He outlined five strategies of adaptation that
could manifest in normative or deviant forms of conduct, depending on the
degree to which an individual or group accepts or rejects these cultural goals
and whether they accept or have access to the institutional means to pursue
them.

The first strategy outlined by Merton is **conformity**: accepting both
culturally promoted goals and the institutional means of pursuing them.
For example, conformity could be demonstrated through attempting to get
a good job by earning a university degree. A second strategy for adaptation
is **innovation**: accepting culturally promoted goals but either rejecting or
bypassing the institutionalized means of attaining them. Innovators can
range from people who develop unconventional strategies to achieve wealth
and status (such as becoming social media "influencers," inventing new forms
of crypto-currency, or becoming wealthy through means that do not require
a traditional education) to organized criminal groups that pursue wealth by
profiting from crime. The third strategy is **ritualism**, which involves accepting
and abiding by the institutionalized means for achieving cultural goals even
if the prospect of achieving those goals is gone. This category would include
the types of people often celebrated in the lyrics of mainstream country
music: hard workers who work as a matter of pride, or to make ends meet,
but who don't have any hope of achieving wealth or social status. Merton's
fourth strategy is **retreatism**: effectively rejecting culturally prevalent goals
and turning away from the institutionalized means through which to meet
them. By Merton's account, this category largely consists of people who have
little hope of a prosperous future and instead opt to engage in alcohol and
substance use as a means of dropping out of mainstream society. Finally,
Merton's fifth adaptation strategy is **rebellion**, which consists of persons who
reject popular cultural goals, reject the institutionalized means of achieving
them, and instead opt to formulate their own norms of conduct and patterns
of social organization. Among these five forms of adaptation, all but those
who classify as conformists and, to a lesser extent, ritualists are regarded as
"deviant" by Merton's typology.

Social Control Theory: Social Bonds

Merton's focus on the relationship between deviance and macro-social variables finds a suitable counterpart in Hirschi's (1969) social control theory, which focuses on micro-social variables in explaining an individual's propensity to engage in criminal or deviant conduct. Rather than echoing the perspective that normativity is maintained throughout collective internalization of collective values, Hirshi argues that we instead engage in a continual process of weighing the benefits of deviance against associated risks:

> The idea, then, is that the person invests time, energy, [themselves], in a certain line of activity — say, getting an education, building up a business, acquiring a reputation for virtue. When or whenever [they consider] deviant behavior, [they] must consider the costs of this deviant behavior, the risk [they run] of losing the investment [they have] made in conventional behavior. (1969: 20)

Social control theory correlates one's propensity for deviance with qualities internalized by the individual, including, most significantly, the degree to which they feel attached to others. Hirschi identifies four variables relevant to individuals' integration into their communities that ought to be considered in explaining the cause of deviance: attachment, commitment, involvement, and belief. The variable of **attachment** indicates the extent to which a person feels a level of connection with, or affinity for, their fellow community members and the broader community culture. It refers to an individual's capacity to feel empathy for their fellow human beings and implicitly draws inspiration from psychological approaches correlating deviancy with personality disorders, such as psychopathy, that inhibit an individual's ability to humanize others. Hirschi suggests that people lacking the capacity for empathy will be more likely to challenge and transgress rules and regulations, as they lack the ability to sympathize with those whom they might harm with their deviant conduct. Similarly, the variable of **commitment** attempts to assess the degree to which one values, and opts to pursue, goals promoted by the wider community or culture. Hirschi suggests that individuals who either do not accept mainstream cultural goals as their own or reject the institutionalized methods of achieving them will be more likely to engage in acts of delinquency.

Hirschi's third variable is **involvement**, or the degree to which an individual comes to participate in mainstream cultural activities. While the variable of involvement is significant, in part because persons engaged in

These consensus-based approaches to deviance differ in what they see as the origins of transgressive conduct, from broader social contexts to highly individualized variables. While Merton's analysis affiliates transgressive behaviour with institutionalized inequality, Hirschi's view pathologizes deviant behaviour. He draws a correlation between an individual's inability to abide by social conventions and a cognitive incapacity to empathize with others.

institutionally sanctioned activities or groups would literally have less free time with which to engage in criminal or deviant activities, the act of involving oneself in such group activities also reinforces an individual's attachment to their fellow community members and their commitment toward internalizing prevalent cultural goals. For example, a young person's enrolment in organized sports would reduce their likelihood of engaging in deviant or criminal behaviour, as participants learn to approach the game with a team mentality and pursue cultural goals (winning and achieving success) through culturally sanctioned means like hard work and dedication. Finally, Hirsch associates an individual's propensity to engage in deviance with the variable of **belief**, or the degree to which the actor identifies with prevalent cultural values and perspectives on morality and, moreover, accepts the authority of the socio-legal institutions that guide our collective conduct. This perspective suggests that social actors will be much more likely to accept and abide by the social values and codified laws that shape social conduct if they endorse such values as their own, but less likely if their own beliefs do not conform with those of the wider society.

These consensus-based approaches to deviance differ in what they see as the origins of transgressive conduct, from broader social contexts to highly individualized variables. While Merton's analysis affiliates transgressive behaviour with institutionalized inequality, Hirschi's view pathologizes deviant behaviour. He draws a correlation between an individual's inability to abide by social conventions and a cognitive incapacity to empathize with others. Hirschi's analysis would lend support to initiatives that aim to combat deviance and criminality by focusing on the correction of "the deviant" — best epitomized in the Reagan-era neoliberal discourse that put the onus for correct behaviour on individuals and reduces deviance to the presence of "bad people" and "bad communities." Reagan's popularization of a neoliberal American culture coincided with his administration's initiative to do away with the welfare state by cancelling social assistance programs meant to help those facing poverty to stave off food and housing insecurities (Stoez and Karger 1993).

Interactionist Perspectives: The Social Influence on the Self

While Durkheim described the institutional roots of normativity, symbolic interactionism seeks to explain how social actors internalize and reinforce these expectations. Whereas the theorists we have considered to this point contributed to the study of deviance by primarily considering criminal conduct, symbolic interactionism considers how interactions between people reinforce notions of deviance, how certain demographic groups come to be associated with deviant traits, and what effects this characterization has on people. Popularized in the early 1900s, the symbolic interactionist perspective merged the burgeoning social sciences with aspects of psychology to consider how social interactions contribute to our collective recognition of reality and our individual claims to identity. Symbolic interactionists followed Durkheim in striving to explain how social norms are granted authority through the development of public consensus and collective practice. While theorists such as Mead and Schütz sought to identify how we perceive of the world in uniform ways, Cooley, Goffman, and Lemert considered the processes through which we develop notions of self, as well as how being labelled "deviant" influences this process.

Explaining Normativity: Shared Symbols and the Constitution of the Lifeworld

The founder of the interactionist perspective, George H. Mead sought to demonstrate how social forces inform and influence the ways in which we reflect upon our own identities. Mead wanted to counter the perspective that personality stems exclusively from biological influence (1934); he was among the first to characterize identity formation as a highly social process, arguing that we can only understand the constitution of "the individual" by appreciating the influence of "the social." Mead argued for the importance of understanding how we come to perceive of our surroundings in a uniform way and hypothesized that this was accomplished in part through the development of significant symbols. Simply put, without a shared concept of our material world, social cohesion is impossible. Thus, we consecrate significant symbols — including language, texts, and images — to ensure that we perceive "reality" in a uniform way. For example, the Canadian flag serves as a symbol to reinforce our collective perception that a particular geographic region is a country and, more specifically, is Canada. As these symbols become entrenched in our shared perception of the world and embedded into the systems and

Popularized in the early 1900s, the symbolic interactionist perspective merged the burgeoning social sciences with aspects of psychology to consider how social interactions contribute to our collective recognition of reality and our individual claims to identity. Symbolic interactionists followed Durkheim in striving to explain how social norms are granted authority through the development of public consensus and collective practice.

institutions that structure social relations, their legitimacy is further enforced through the socialization process. Throughout our early life experiences, we are made aware of the Canadian flag and its connection to recognizing ourselves as Canadians. Mead argues that the perpetuation of our shared symbolic world assists our development of the reflexive ability to take the position of "the generalized other" or assume the standpoint of, and empathize with, other persons in society. We feel a sense of connection or kinship with other Canadians due to the prospect that, as Canadians, we ostensibly share uniform beliefs, have similar values, and perceive of the wider world in the same way. Ultimately, Mead links this capacity for empathetic and "moral" conduct with the uniformity of the symbolic world and our engagement with the institutions put in place to maintain it.

Alfred Schütz, a highly influential thinker most closely affiliated with **phenomenology**, also argued that language and systems of communication shape our interactions with others and the material world. However, whereas Mead considers how shared symbols inform our ability to empathize with others, Schütz (1967) focuses on how they allow us to predict the conduct of others by engaging in processes of **intersubjectivity**: drawing from notions of social convention to anticipate what other people are feeling and thinking or are likely to do. These anticipated traditions in conduct and belief come to constitute a **lifeworld** that we actively reinforce but perceive of as objective "realities of the world" that exist independent of human conduct. As Schütz explains,

> Our everyday world is, from the outset, an intersubjective world of culture. It is intersubjective because we live in it as men among other men [sic], bound to them through common influence and work, understanding others and being an object of understanding for other. It is a world of culture because, from the outset, the lifeworld is a universe of significations to us, i.e., a framework of meaning ... which we have to interpret, and of interrelations of meaning which we have to institute only through our action in this life-world. (1967: 133)

Schütz suggests that we approach the lifeworld as an inevitable reality that exists external to us, and we therefore do not critically consider the possibility of ushering in new forms of social organization. Instead, we abide by a "natural attitude" that perceives the status quo as beyond reproach. Schütz also considers the cognitive processes through which we make sense of the world. He suggests that human cognition revolves around the creation of **typifications** that allow us to make assumptions, or predictions, about different groups and social phenomena. Put another way, typifications are categorical assumptions that we make daily to help us better predict how others will conduct themselves in the course of daily interactions. We associate certain characteristics or "ways of being" with expectations of conduct and hypothesize how to best anticipate or manage our interactions in line with these expectations. As we use typifications to categorize those whom we encounter based on demographic factors such as gender, ethnicity, age, and so on, we associate those categorical assessments with anticipated qualities or characteristics. In some cases, these assumptions might be inspired by our own experiences. In other cases, we might instead refer to socially prevalent beliefs regarding persons of a given demographic group.

Deviant Labels and Identity: Stigma, Racialization and Labelling Theory

The interactionist perspective also suggests that being designated as "deviant" by others carries major ramifications with respect to how we perceive ourselves. This position is best reflected in the enduring popularity of Charles H. Cooley's (1922) concept of the **looking-glass self**. Arguing that our individual identities are produced in social interaction, Cooley argues that processes of self-recognition

> seem to have three principle elements: the imagination of our appearance to the other person; the imagination of [their] judgement of that appearance, and some sort of self-feeling, such as pride or mortification ... the thing that moves us to pride or shame is not the mere mechanical reflection of ourselves, but an imputed sentiment, the imagined effect of this reflection upon another's mind. (1922: 152)

For Cooley, identify formation consists of three stages. At the first stage, we try to take the position of others and imagine how we most likely appear to them. There are, of course, a host of factors we might focus on: physical appearance, gender identity, ethnic heritage, or even our attire or general level of cleanliness. Once we have imagined how we are likely to appear to others, the second stage involves trying to ascertain what types of judgments others are likely making about us. If we think of ourselves as less attractive than our peers, we might assume they believe we are ugly. If we believe those around us make negative assumptions about people based on gender or ethnic background, we might imagine they make negative assumptions about us. At this stage, our own internalized awareness of conventional normality affects how we think about others. Finally, Cooley suggests that we ultimately come to form perspectives on ourselves based on the judgments that we believe others have made about us. If we assume that others perceive us as inadequate, we may perceive ourselves as somehow inadequate. Cooley goes so far as to suggest that assuming others think negatively of us contributes to a **self-fulfilling prophecy**: we internalize these negative characterizations of ourselves and act in line with what others expect. For Cooley, then, the process of identity formation is highly influenced by interacting with others and the assumption that they assess us against normative social standards and expectations.

Of course, we do not always have the luxury of making assumptions about what other people believe about us; how others *actually* treat us can speak volumes. Another early interactionist theorist, Erving Goffman, dealt with this issue in his landmark 1963 publication *Stigma: Notes on the Management of Spoiled Identity*. In his own *dramaturgical* analysis of how people form and reinforce their personal identities (1959), Goffman argues that we both reinforce our notions of self and derive our notions of self-value through numerous **interaction rituals**. These rituals, informed largely by what we believe others expect of us, help to ensure that our interactions are governed by common expectations. Goffman's theory of dramaturgy strives to make sense of the divide between the "identities" that we enact (or perform) in a public social context and our internal, individualistic thought processes. Goffman compares interacting with others to putting on a performance, arguing that social harmony is maintained as we recognize and abide by prevalent **social scripts** or expectations of conduct in different contexts. In a sense, social scripts are comparable to Durkheim's notion of social facts: they place certain expectations of behaviour in accordance with people's social roles or demographic features. In our daily interactions, we regulate our own conduct in line with these social scripts, conforming to expectations we believe others have of us in hopes of being looked upon favourably. Goffman describes the process of assessing our own performance against the standards that we assume others hold us to as engaging in **impression management**.

Goffman suggests that individuals or groups who do not conform with social scripts are prone to "being reduced in our minds from a whole and usual person to a tainted, discounted one. Such an attribute is a stigma, especially when its discrediting effect is very extensive" (Goffman 1963: 3). Stigma is the process through which members of the mainstream society symbolically designate as abnormal those who might not abide by social scripts. Goffman identifies three types of stigma. First, stigma surrounding aspects of the body assigns people with physical or biological anomalies as inferior to "normal" members of society and enables discrimination against them. The second form of stigma is against people whose practices or ways of living contradict dominant notions of normality. Goffman provides a brief list of the types of social populations most often stigmatized based on these grounds: those with physical or cognitive conditions, criminalized people, people with substance abuse issues, non-heterosexual people, underemployed workers, and even those who hold radical political ideals. The third form of stigma Goffman identifies is tribal stigma, which is applied to people of an alternative ethnic group, nationality, or religion. This type of stigma is applied to "those who are initially socialized in an alien community … and who then must learn a second way of being that is felt by those around them to be the real and valid one" (1963: 35). Regardless of the type of stigma that a person or population experiences, Goffman suggests that all three contribute to the same process in the context of social interaction:

> An individual who might have been received easily in ordinary social intercourse possesses a trait that can obtrude itself upon attention and turn those of us whom [they] meet away from [them], breaking the claim that [their] other attributes have on us … we [then] construct a stigma-theory, an ideology to explain [their] inferiority and account for the danger they represent … we tend to impute a wide range of imperfections on the basis of the original one. (1963: 5)

For Goffman, it is important to understand how stigma and attendant prejudices and discrimination can have an indelible impact on the self-perceptions of those stigmatized. Goffman identifies commonplace responses on the part of those who come to recognize their own stigmatization and notes that, while some strive to *correct* the "problematic" aspects of their conduct, others accept what Goffman calls their *spoiled identity* and conform with the behaviour implied by the stigma.

Goffman's notes on the influence of social stigmatization coincide with perspectives put forward half a century earlier by W.E.B. Du Bois. A significant contributor to the establishment of critical race theory, Du Bois's (1903) *The Souls of Black Folk* advances the term **racialization** to denote how ethnically or culturally minoritized groups come to be disparaged in mainstream social classification. Du Bois argues that "race" becomes not only the primary frame through which members of a majority society perceive members of minority groups, but it is also the primary frame through which members of those minority groups perceive themselves. African-Americans within Western society thus experience a **double consciousness**, as they are simultaneously expected to embody roles as "Americans" and "persons of colour." Coupled with the material effects of poverty and being subjected to various forms of racism, the process of assessing one's own value through the stigmatic perspective of the majority society creates detrimental effects on one's sense of identity and capacity for hope. The experience of being of non-white heritage in North America at the end of the nineteenth century (a time that was not far removed from the era of slavery) placed additional strain upon those who assessed themselves in line with Eurocentric expectations, leading many to experience anomic sensations. Du Bois (1903: 2) describes double consciousness as

> [A] peculiar sensation [of] always looking at one's self through the eyes of others, of measuring one's soul by the tape of a world that looks on in amused contempt and pity. One ever feels his two-ness, an American, a Negro; two souls, two thoughts, two unreconciled strivings; two warring ideals in one dark body, whose dogged strength alone keeps it from being torn asunder.

The concepts of the looking-glass self and spoiled identity complement Edwin Lemert's (1951) reflections on social deviance and his highly influential labelling theory. Lemert elaborates on how we might internalize stigma in the development of our own identities. Labelling theory proposes that being stigmatized leads a person to eventually accept the "deviant" designation and conform to the negative expectations of the wider society. Labelling theory differentiates between acts of **primary deviance** and **secondary deviance**. Acts of primary deviance occur when an individual does something to attract condemnation from others. Reflecting the values and beliefs of the majority, that action leads the person to be labelled "criminal" or "amoral" or "abnormal." Lemert explains that on the first instance of "criminality," the deviant label does not necessarily become permanent, but it does result in the offender being subjected to increased surveillance. In instances of secondary deviance, the deviant label is reinforced, and in these cases, Lemert argues, the actor might internalize their stigma and, through doing so, come to recognize their **master status** as a "deviant" first and foremost. Ultimately, recognizing and accepting their negative characterization justifies further deviant conduct as they effectively begin to act in accordance with these negative expectations. Lemert suggests those who attract deviant stigmatization internalize this role as a significant facet of identity, acting in line with these expectations.

> Collectively, consensus perspectives regarding the relationship between normativity, deviance, and identity formation show us that there is a vicious cycle that perpetuates social inequality and socially transgressive conduct. Research surrounding stigmatization and deviant labels shows that these processes, in and of themselves, instigate and inspire the very forms of deviant conduct they mean to condemn.

Conclusion: Consensus Perspectives and the Vicious Cycle

Collectively, consensus perspectives regarding the relationship between normativity, deviance, and identity formation show us that there is a vicious cycle that perpetuates social inequality and socially transgressive conduct. Research surrounding stigmatization and deviant labels shows that these processes, in and of themselves, instigate and inspire the very forms of deviant conduct they mean to condemn. Meanwhile, these deviant actions contribute to a public consensus that something is wrong with — and something must be done about — the people who disobey. In the wake of this newly perceived threat, the public at large calls for renewed movements toward ensuring public safety that may lead to the creation of new laws (as enforced by police) or the recognition of new health conditions requiring treatment or therapy (as enforced by medical experts). The way people are categorized as "deviants" occurs not only through, as Durkheim conceptualizes it, constructing social facts surrounding criminality and law, but also in health and medicine, education, mass media, the political system, and the ways in which we treat others on an individual level. Stigmatization and the internalization of deviant labels occur in various institutional and interactive contexts, and each of those contexts carries out different mechanisms to remedy or prohibit the forms of conduct deemed maladaptive or threatening.

Despite the oversights and omissions of consensus theories, notions of normativity come from our common wish to live in a safe, predictable, and welcoming society. The many streams of consensus theory consider, on the one hand, the effects of being structurally excluded from pursuing cultural goals and, on the other, being persistently treated as inferior or dangerous by peers. One of the aforementioned oversights and omissions associated with consensus perspectives is how they consider power: who possesses it, how it is maintained, how it is wielded using cultural and institutional mechanisms, and how its unequal distribution often goes unnoticed. While a great number of social thinkers have since focused on power as manifested in class exploitation, patriarchy, Eurocentrism, and other forms of inequality, early trends in consensus research have helped us remember how these broader social tendencies are experienced at the individual level: they surely contribute to feelings of anomie and processes of negative self-reflection in some cases, but also to feelings of self-affirmative practices of collective resistance and communal bonding.

Discussion Questions

1. What influence did the transition from mechanical solidarity to organic solidarity have on the development of individualism?
2. What is the difference between material and non-material social facts?
3. How are Merton's strain theory and Hirschi's control theory different?
4. According to Schütz, how do social actors maintain intersubjectivity?
5. How can Du Bois's description of experiencing double consciousness be related to Goffman's concept of stigma and Lemert's labelling theory?

Recommended Resources

1. *Social Guidance and Gender Roles: Habit Patterns* (McGraw-Hill 1954). Footage from Charlie Dean Archives.
2. "Subconscious Racial Bias in Children" (CNN 2012).
3. *Pleasantville* (New Line Cinema 1998).

Glossary 2

anomie: the feeling one experiences when they feel disconnected from the wider society. It is the state of social normlessness.

collective conscience: the degree to which members of a society share in uniform beliefs and values.

double consciousness: the concept that members of ethnic or racial minorities perceive of themselves from the perspective of the dominant culture.

generalized other: the capacity for individuals to empathize with or "put themselves in the place" of others.

impression management: the practice of acting in accordance with normative expectations for the sake of being received positively by others.

interaction rituals: collectively recognized expectations of conduct that inform our interactions with others and engagement with society.

intersubjectivity: the ability to empathize with, or put ourselves in the position of others, as based on our sharing uniform beliefs and values.

lifeworld: routinized practices and beliefs that inform our shared perception of social reality.

looking-glass self: the process through which we base our perspectives of ourselves on the impressions that we believe others have of us.

master status: the point at which the actor accepts their criminal or deviant label as their primary identity and acts in accordance with expectations.

material social facts: normative beliefs and conduct expectations that are embedded within material structures.

mechanical solidarity: societies that are organized around the presence of a low division of labour and a strong collective conscience.

non-material social facts: normative beliefs and conduct expectations that are reinforced through collective practices.

organic solidarity: societal organization around the presence of a high division of labour, including the development of institutions to account for a weak collective conscience.

phenomenology: the study of human consciousness and the culturally entrenched ways in which we comprehend a shared reality.

primary deviance: stemming from initial criminal or a deviant act by the actor, potentially leads observers to assign the actor a criminal or deviant label.

racialization: the process through which ethnically or culturally minoritized groups are socially classified with often disparaging racial terms.

secondary deviance: stemming from a subsequent criminal or deviant act; instigated by the application of the criminal or deviant label.

self-fulfilling prophecy: the process whereby we form identities and engage in conduct based on how we assume others expect us to act.

social bonds: the degree to which members of a society feel connected to one another; related to the strength of the collective conscience.

social facts: normative expectations that are promoted by social institutions and cultural practices, but which do not exist independent of human interactions.

social scripts: the widely recognized conduct expectations that we abide by while interacting with others.

stigma: the process whereby persons who are perceived as engaging in "deviant" or "abnormal conduct" have their identities discredited by the majority society.

typifications: the cognitive categorizations that allow us to quickly appraise our surroundings to assess our safety.

References

CNN. 2012. "Subconscious Racial Bias in Children." <youtube.com/watch?v=nFbv BJULVnc>.

Cooley, Charles H. 1922. *Human Nature and the Social Order*. New York: Scribner's Sons.

Du Bois, W.E.B. 1903. *The Souls of Black Folk: Essays and Sketches*. Chicago: A.C. McClurg & Co.

Durkheim, Emile. 1964 [1893]. *The Division of Labor in Society*. New York: Free Press.

____. 1938. *The Rules of Sociological Method*. New York: Free Press.

____. 1897. *On Suicide*. New York: Free Press.

Goffman, Erving. 1963. *Stigma: Notes on the Management of Spoiled Identity*. Englewood Cliffs: Prentice Hall.

____. 1959. *The Presentation of Self in Everyday Life*. Garden City: Doubleday.

Hirschi, Travis. 1969. *Causes of Delinquency*. Berkeley: University of California Press.

Lemert, Edwin. 1951. *Social Pathology: A Systematic Approach to the Theory of Sociopathic Behavior*. New York: McGraw Hill.

McGraw-Hill. 1954. "Social Guidance and Gender Roles: Habit Patterns." <youtube. com/watch?v=km4CR1uGYxA>.

Mead, George H. 1934. *Mind, Self and Society*. Chicago: University of Chicago Press.

Merton, Robert. 1968. *Social Theory and Social Structure*. New York: Free Press.

Pleasantville. 1998. New Line Cinema.

Schütz, Alfred. 1967. *Phenomenology of the Social World*. Evanston: Northwestern University Press.

Stoez, David, and Howard Jacob Karger. 1993. "Deconstructing Welfare: The Reagan Legacy and the Welfare State." *Social Work* 38, 5.

3

Defining Deviance

Critical, Feminist, and Anti-Oppressive
Theories of Social Control

Carolyn Brooks

After reading this chapter, you will be able to do the following:

1. Explain the shift in deviance discourses from analyzing behaviours of so-called nuts, sluts, and perverts to understanding oppression, suffering, and power.

2. Describe how critical theories such as neo-Marxism, governmentality, risk management, and others from Foucault link deviant labels to power and social regulation.

3. Explain the importance of feminist, postcolonialism, and anti-oppressive theory in the understanding of deviance and social regulation.

4. Explain the idea that deviants would not exist except for those who control them.

This chapter focuses on power, social control, and the theoretical models that address the relationships between social inequality and demographic variables such as class, race, gender, age, knowledge, power, and individual resistance. The first section introduces a number of theories based in the critical tradition, including neo-Marxist conflict perspectives and Foucault's notion of **governmentality**. The second section explores theories of gender and race, including critical feminist, anti-oppressive, and postcolonial theories. Rather than focusing on explaining *deviant behaviour*, these theories instead seek to account for the social construction of *deviance* and how those populations

Examples of anti-poverty and anti-homelessness laws in different Canadian cities include fines for sleeping on sidewalks in British Columbia, panhandling prohibition bylaws in Nova Scotia and New Brunswick, the *Safe Streets Act* in Ontario, as well as the new focus on defensive design.

branded "deviant" have experienced oppression.

To demonstrate the social construction and criminalization of entirely different types of deviants, let's look at examples related to policies surrounding homelessness and poverty, focusing specifically on homelessness policies, squeegee kids, and those who discriminate against the poor.

Defining Deviance: Policies toward Homelessness and Squeegee Kids

Much current policy toward homelessness can be summed up as follows: "We don't like that you're homeless, so we'll punish you for being homeless" (Scott 2017). Examples of anti-poverty and anti-homelessness laws in different Canadian cities include fines for sleeping on sidewalks in British Columbia (Aleman 2017), panhandling prohibition bylaws in Nova Scotia and New Brunswick (CTV Atlantic 2018), the *Safe Streets Act* in Ontario (O'Grady and Bright 2002), as well as the new focus on defensive design.

Since late 2016, homeless people in Kelowna, British Columbia, have been criminally culpable for sleeping and sitting on public sidewalks at any point of the day or night. Those who are caught are penalized with a $50 fine (Aleman 2017). In Halifax, Nova Scotia, and Moncton, New Brunswick, the act of panhandling is penalized under local bylaws by issuing tickets (CTV Atlantic 2018). In Halifax, the ticket fine for a first-time offense of approaching a motorist or vehicle in the street is $180; for second and third offenses, the ticket price rises to $237.50 and $354.50, respectively (CTV Atlantic 2018). And in Ontario, the *Safe Streets Act*, enacted by the Harris government in 2000 and still in effect today, criminalized aggressive solicitation and "captive persons" solicitation, meaning it was illegal for people to approach motorists waiting at red lights to wash their windshields for money; it also became illegal to solicit people waiting for public transit, using a pay telephone or public toilet, or departing from an automated teller. A similar version of Ontario's *Safe Streets Act* was passed in British Columbia in 2004. Most Canadian cities have some type of panhandling and squeegeeing bylaw (Graham 2011), and debate persists about the effectiveness of fining people who are begging for money.

The *Safe Streets Act* criminalizes those trapped in poverty and, as Toronto activist and lawyer Joanna Nefs explains, "you can't fine someone out of addiction and poverty" (Scott 2017). News articles also repeat and cement the assumption that poverty is connected with bad behaviour. For example, some report that there is no place on the streets for squeegee kids, the underprivileged persons (usually youth) who make an income by cleaning the windshields of motorists in transit (Scott 2017). Referring to the same incident, a *Toronto Star* headline advised, "Don't challenge squeegee kids, police warn after attack" (Rush 2011), and the *National Post* published a photo under the headline "Squeegee kid beat driver, police say" of a bloodied man on a cellphone holding an ice pack to his head (Switzer 2011). This stigmatizes the young people as dangerous or violent. In the incident, the man asked a squeegee kid to stop squeegeeing his car window, and the interaction escalated. The *National Post* article said this incident was another in a "long battle against aggressive panhandlers" and reported that Ontario Member of Provincial Parliament Mike Colle referred to these young people as a "plague" in 1996.

Some argue these laws infringe upon the rights enshrined in the *Charter of Rights and Freedoms*, including the violation of freedom of expression (Robinson 2017). Although in 2007 the Supreme Court of Canada dismissed an application to strike down the *Safe Streets Act*, activists continue to challenge the legislation and fight for the repeal of such laws (Robinson 2017). Advocacy groups argue the act limits people's freedom of expression, is too hostile toward panhandlers, and fails to address issues of marginalization, while those who question the law contend the implementation of such acts means we are now using policing and the criminal justice system as a way to control or "manage" homelessness (Gaetz, O'Grady, and Buccieri 2010).

Homelessness is one of the most extreme forms of poverty and social exclusion a person can experience (Olsen and Benjaminsen 2017). Deprived of the security of a place to stay or sleep, people experiencing homelessness must actively search for a location to stay, even temporarily. Homelessness is a form of poverty that is visible in everyday society when it occupies public spaces such as sidewalks, parks, and underpasses (Gaetz, Scott, and Gulliver 2013). The regulation of homelessness by the state is increasingly reliant on the regulation of public spaces, including through the alteration of the physical design of public spaces and environments in an effort to forcibly deter and exclude homeless people from them (Antony 2019; Schindler 2015). This tactic is referred to as hostile architecture or defensive design (see Box 3-1).

**Box 3-1: Defensive Design: Social Regulation
of Homelessness through Hostile Architecture**

by Cerah Dubé

Defensive design is a tactic of mitigating the visible signs of poverty in Canadian cities by erasing homeless populations.

At first, defensive design may not be evident or appear overtly hostile (Antony 2019). Some designs may be subtle or visually appealing to conceal their true purpose, which is to push out those who are deemed "vagrants" and "loiterers" from a space. An example is colourfully painted or artistically designed rocks in alcoves outside of restaurants or businesses that intentionally take up space as a means of preventing people from staying or camping overnight (Pelley 2019; Musset 2019). Another, more overt use of hostile design is using tall cage-like structures to gate off spaces under bridges, where people may seek shelter, particularly in harsh weather conditions.

Uncomfortable park bench

One common example of hostile architecture is public park or city benches with a third or middle armrest (Pelley 2019). This design makes it uncomfortable and nearly impossible for someone to rest or sleep on the bench (Antony 2019).

Using defensive design, cities regulate the use of public spaces and control behaviours in these spaces (Schindler 2015). Because homelessness is an unacceptable social behaviour, hostile infrastructure sends the clear message: keep out; you are not allowed in this space. The regulation of homelessness intentionally removes poverty from the sight of those who are not experiencing it.

Discriminating against Homeless People

While homeless and poor communities are heavily policed, criminalized, and stereotyped, those who discriminate against the poor escape the same damning notions of deviance. In one example, the CBC reported the following:

> A Montreal man has been ordered to pay $8,000 to a panhandler after an email he wrote complaining about her presence outside a liquor store was deemed discriminatory by the province's human rights commission.... The letter [email from the man] goes on to talk about the city abolishing its prohibition on begging, and the problems he believed it has created. He then suggests five "solutions," including one labeled the "Chinese solution" that proposes a bullet to the neck and send the bill for the bullet to the deceased bum's family. (CBC News 2013)

The Human Rights Commission criticized the man's actions as "highly reprehensible." He was ordered to pay the victim $8,000.

The aforementioned examples demonstrate the social construction of entirely different types of *deviants*. On the one hand, the panhandler is defined as deviant under the law, which is upheld by public complaints, images in the media, and legal responses. On the other hand, discrimination *against* those who are panhandling is defined as deviant by the Human Rights Commission, and this is reinforced in the media and the law. The following sections of this chapter outline theories for understanding just how *deviance* and *deviants* are socially constructed. Sociologists have not always challenged what we deem to be deviant. Historically, courses in deviance and social control were concerned with "nuts, sluts, and perverts," and many among us actively slotted people into these categories while attempting to explain behaviours. Alexander Liazos (1972: 119) infamously demonstrated how sociologists were guilty of *not* exploring the issue of power:

> As a result of the fascination with "nuts, sluts, and perverts," and their identities and subcultures, little attention has been paid to the unethical, illegal, and destructive actions of powerful individuals, groups and institutions in our society. Because these actions are carried out quietly in the normal course of events, the sociology of deviance does not consider them as part of its subject matter. This bias is rooted in the very conception and definition of the field.

Liazos argued that "we should banish the concept of 'deviance' and speak of oppression, conflict, persecution, and suffering."

Liazos argued that "we should banish the concept of 'deviance' and speak of oppression, conflict, persecution, and suffering" (1972: 119). A focus on power, social control, and theoretical models that address the interrelationship between social inequality and an array of demographic variables illuminates how deviance is applied and how the label changes over time and in different places.

Critical Theory and Neo-Marxism

Investigating how norms and specific deviant acts are socially constructed requires critical perspectives. The present-day understanding of social conflict is derived from the work of Karl Marx, who considers the influence of unequal distribution of resources as the leading cause of social conflict. Marx explains that a major source of conflict comes from our society being shaped by competition between the social classes of the bourgeoisie and proletariat. The bourgeoisie is the wealthy or *ruling* class that owns and controls the means of economic production. They have the power to influence our customs and social institutions to serve their own interests. The proletariat is the *working* class that must work for a wage and is exploited by the bourgeoisie. Marx and Engels suggest the bourgeoisie keep the proletariat oblivious to their own exploitation, chalking up their deprivation to personal capacities or their own failures as opposed to an unjust system (Marx, Engels, Moore, and McLellan, 1992). If the proletariat began to think critically about their conditions, they would gain a class consciousness (the collective awareness of a shared experience of exploitation) and agitate for a revolution that would change the ways in which power is distributed.

Marx and Engels advanced their perspectives on the tense relationship between the bourgeoisie and proletariat over 160 years ago, but subsequent neo-Marxist theorists have largely grouped themselves into distinct variations of the Marxist perspective. We focus here on the instrumentalist and structuralist Marxists.

Instrumentalist and Structuralist Marxists: Power and Ideology

While instrumentalist and structuralist Marxism share many common elements, the two theoretical camps part ways when considering whether current industrialized economic relations are meant to benefit the interests of capitalists or the system of capitalism itself. In our example of the squeegee kids, instrumentalist Marxists would argue that panhandling street youth are criminalized because capitalists (as a social group) benefit when people are blamed for their own poverty and subject to the laws of our criminal justice system. While structuralist Marxists may agree on this point, they would add that this social control of marginalized peoples is done to hide — and thus benefit — the *real* workings of the economic system of capitalism. For example, by creating an ideology in which people are led to believe the criminal justice system is working in everyone's interest and protects law-abiding citizens against dangerous or deviant populations (such as unruly, squeegee-brandishing youth), the underlying causes of homelessness, including structural factors, systems failures, and some individual circumstances (Gaetz, Donaldson, Richter, and Gulliver 2013) remain concealed. More specifically, underlying causes of homelessness left unaddressed are "the interplay between structural factors (poverty, lack of affordable housing), systems failures (people being discharged from mental health facilities, corrections, or child protection services into homelessness) and individual circumstances (family conflict and violence, mental health and addictions)" (Gaetz et al. 2013: 4).

Instrumentalist Marxists, who are often seen as the more radical of the two theorist groups, argue there is a direct link between the dominant elites in society and the institutions or "superstructure" that organizes social life. Marxists such as Ralph Miliband (1969) saw the state as a tool for class rule. For him, elite members of the bourgeoisie dominate the state and act to maintain the status quo. This, in turn, means the elite have *direct control* over our social institutions, including the law, media, and education system.

From an instrumentalist Marxist perspective, the *Safe Streets Act* is legislation that plays a role in wealth making. Rather than questioning the injustice related to the distribution of wealth and focusing on those who are rich, the legislation criminalizes acts associated with poverty and, as a result, rationalizes inequalities by blaming poor people for their own plight in life. John Clarke, a prison abolitionist, takes an instrumentalist approach:

> Social regulation of the poor means less and less income and housing programs and, more and more, takes the form of police patrols, courtrooms and prison cells.... The homeless population in major

cities is mushrooming.... This starts to become highly problematic for those that the law serves. Widespread and visible homelessness starts to interfere with commercial development, tourism, upscale residential redevelopment, etcetera.... Acts of survival like petty drug dealing or prostitution are focused on but the real agenda is the "social cleansing" of the homeless. (2000: 82)

Structuralist Marxists also argue that state institutions work in the interests of the elite in society. However, they contend the state is relatively autonomous from (or does not *directly* engage in) any class control. Rather than serving the interests of the ruling class explicitly, the state instead provides legitimation for the prospect that our current laws and social norms work toward the benefit of all members of a shared society. However, this theory also suggests that, despite appearances, the state behaves in a way that maintains and reproduces capitalist logics and structures. Legitimation means people in society must believe they are living in the best of all possible worlds. The state must appear to be working — at least formally, if not substantially — in the interest of all classes to avoid raising the ire of the lower classes. In fact, examining the legitimation function of the structuralist Marxist position is one way in which we can most effectively see power at work.

Structuralist Marxists argue that those who own the means of material production also own the means of mental production. In other words, the leading *material* force in society is also the leading *intellectual* force. Marx and Engels state that individuals who own the news media, endow the universities, and finance the publication of books are those who have a prevailing say in society, not only regarding economics but also moral and ethical knowledge. Above and beyond linking those who create and disseminate knowledge with an implicit moral entrepreneurial role, Marx and Engels advance the argument that individuals in society are thus "sold an ideology" (Reiman and Leighton 2017) that tells them life will get no better so there is no reason to complain or fight. As such, many structuralist Marxists draw on Antonio Gramsci's (1971) notion of **hegemony**. Hegemony means the elite class manipulates the ideas, knowledge, and morals of the working public to make them believe the system is working in their best interests and does so in a fair and legitimate way. Gramsci argues that hegemony draws on social legitimacy in two ways: first, by allowing representatives of the state to apply force upon those who do not conform to the expectations of the system and, second, the degree to which members of the public themselves consent that these figures and institutions maintain the authority to lead. Gramsci links the maintenance of this public consensus to the presence of intellectuals — politically and culturally significant individuals who embody these ideologies — who "sell" the public on the prospect that the current social order is the best possible arrangement.

> Hegemony means the elite class manipulates the ideas, knowledge, and morals of the working public to make them believe the system is working in their best interests and does so in a fair and legitimate way.

The *Safe Streets Act* reflects hegemonic power (Brooks 2015). It was created under the public safety pretense of making streets safer from the risk of injury or victimization by a criminalized "other" who need regulation and sanction (e.g., panhandlers and young people who squeegee). The legislation does not consider panhandlers and squeegeers as a population in need of care. While the media has painted a picture of a squeegee kid posing a risk to the public and involved in crime, critical researchers ask what would happen if we considered alternative types of employment for squeegee kids, who are quite entrepreneurial. O'Grady, Bright, and Cohen (1998), for example, note that squeegee kids lead quite structured days because they are working and making money. Squeegee kids in Toronto, they argue, are less likely to be involved in other forms of deviance such as crime, selling drugs, or violence than other street-involved youth.

The existence of squeegeers and panhandlers indicates something is not quite right in our social fabric — an observation that could potentially upset the status quo and the privileged position of the dominant class. It demonstrates the continued existence of people who suffer poverty, are homeless, and find themselves in precarious circumstances such that they must squeegee to live. But the way they are characterized by the media and the law arguably leads bystanders to fear for their own personal safety rather than asking *why* homelessness and destitution persist in Canada. The *Safe Streets Act* does not address the underlying issues of youth poverty; it only removes poor people from public view. Janet Mosher (2002: 52) demonstrates the effects:

> Prior to the *Safe Streets Act*, squeegee workers often cleaned the windshield of my car as I was driving my five-year-old daughter to and from school. On many occasions we used those moments to talk about poverty, homelessness and our responsibilities to each other.... For several months now, since the enactment of the *Safe Streets Act*, there have been no squeegee workers at the intersections where we had come to expect — indeed rely — upon them. And while, of course, I can still talk to my daughter about poverty and homelessness,

Social justice concerns from a neo-Marxist perspective would ask why squeegee youth are on the streets in the first place and draw our attention to poverty and growing social inequalities in the context of global capitalism, including the difficulties of getting good jobs and housing.

these issues have clearly become less visible.

Social justice concerns from a neo-Marxist perspective would ask why squeegee youth are on the streets in the first place and draw our attention to poverty and growing social inequalities in the context of global capitalism, including, as Mosher (2002) and O'Grady, Bright, and Cohen (1998) have pointed out, the difficulties of getting good jobs and housing.

The 2017 Report Card on Child and Family Poverty in Canada tells us that one in five children (17.4 percent) lives in poverty, even twenty years after the House of Commons passed a unanimous resolution to end child poverty in Canada (Family Services Toronto 2017). The situation is much worse for Indigenous people and particularly Indigenous youth, 37.9 percent of whom live in poverty (Family Services Toronto 2017). To understand increasing rates of poverty and homelessness, critical authors and researchers often draw attention to increased inequalities amongst social classes. For example, the top 1 percent of the population of Canada now holds 14 percent of the income, up from 8 percent in the 1980s (Broadbent Institute 2012). Oxfam (2017) recently reported that "since 2015, the richest 1% has owned more wealth than the rest of the planet; [and] eight men now own the same amount of wealth as the poorest half of the world."

Critical neo-Marxists understand the rich are not innately more deserving or the poor innately less deserving in this distribution of wealth. As Jeffry Reiman and Paul Leighton point out in *The Rich Get Richer and the Poor Get Prison* (2017), we have been sold an ideology that social problems, including poverty, are the fault of the individual. Talking about the United States, Reiman (2009: 189–90) states:

> We are nowhere near offering all Americans a good education and an equal opportunity to get ahead, we have no right to think that the distribution of income reflects what people have truly earned. The distribution of income in America is so fundamentally shaped by factors such as race, educational opportunity, and the economic class of one's parents that few people who are well-off can honestly claim they deserve all that they have. Those who think that they do should ask themselves where they would be today if they had been

born to migrant labourers in California or to a poor black family in the Harlem ghetto.

From these neo-Marxist perspectives, the *Safe Streets Act* can be approached as legislation that also omits discussions of persistent inequalities in the distribution of income and how this is impacted by inequalities in race, class, gender, educational opportunities, and so on. Growing class inequalities, high levels of poverty, and crimes of the elite are depoliticized while the behaviours of those deemed criminal or deviant are regulated. Hermer and Mosher (2002: 16) state,

> Squeegee kids have come to symbolize a certain form of disorder that has been central to how and why the government is justified in neo-conservative reforms. A central aspect of how the Ontario government has successfully carried out neo-conservative reforms is through its ability to construct "disorderly people." Squeegee kids, welfare cheats, coddled prisoners, violent youth, aggressive beggars are part of a modern rogues gallery in the public character of government.

In this way, the public narrowly views expressions of social and economic inequality as criminal justice and legal problems rather than social issues; "the ever expanding activities of the criminal justice system, persistent cutbacks to social spending, sky rocketing costs of housing in large urban centres and growing gaps of income inequality show us that society is becoming more exclusive" (O'Grady and Bright 2002: 39). This is also evidenced in broken windows theory and policing methods, as outlined in Box 3-2.

Abolitionism, Peacemaking, and Green Criminology

Other theories, including prison abolition and peacemaking, also draw upon this neo-Marxist analysis of the connection between marginality and the criminal justice system. These perspectives understand deviance and crime as social constructions and aim to achieve long-term structural change.

Abolitionists and peacemaking theorists argue that prisons are a form of social control; they are warehouses for victims of structures related to class, race, and gender. It is only by addressing societal inequalities that we may begin to address the root social issues of crime.

Box 3-2: Broken Windows Theory

by Prairie Schappert

Similar to the *Safe Streets Act,* broken windows policing targets those who are poor, racialized, and under scrutiny by the police:

> The "broken windows" policing strategy has become the subject of intense controversies breaking out across US cities. Recent waves of racialized police violence have sparked countrywide mobilizations against broken windows ... the most explosive being in Baltimore, New York City, Philadelphia, and Ferguson, Missouri. In New York City, after the city failed to try an officer who killed an unarmed 43-year-old black male, Eric Garner, mass demonstrations against broken windows policing erupted at several of the city's most iconic sites. (Jefferson 2016: 1)

Broken windows theory is based on two main claims: first, that crime is a result of urban disorder; and second, that levels of minor disorder and subsequent levels of violent crime are linked (Boggess and Maskaly 2014). Broken windows theory asserts that visible disorders, both social and physical, in public spaces beckon deviance and violent crime (Jefferson 2016). Disorder becomes a source of fear and anxiety that leads to community destabilization. The fear-disorder relationship is mediated by intervening social mechanisms such as authority, legislation, policy, and police forces (Gau, Corsaro, and Brunson 2014). Fixing broken windows or cleaning up disorder (i.e., deviance) in neighbourhoods has become the central element of crime-prevention strategies and policies that are implemented by police. Such strategies range from order maintenance and zero-tolerance policing, where police attempt to impose order through strict enforcement, to community and problem-oriented policing, where police attempt to produce order and reduce crime through co-operation with communities (Braga, Welsh, and Schnell 2015).

Critics of broken windows theory and policing say that it "targets the poor, especially the homeless, who are obliged to live in public space" (Berti and Sommers 2010: 63). The approach solidifies a link between structural inequality and crime by targeting neighbourhoods ridden with social and physical disorders. These disorders are targeted as deviant and become criminalized (Jefferson 2016). Berti and Sommers (2010: 63–64) attest that the approach "gives its proponents a way of talking about poverty without dealing with the structural and institutional conditions through which poverty is generated. Poverty is rendered a problem of public order." This theory has influenced the *Safe Streets Act*, which also criminalizes and marginalizes anti-social behaviours associated with poverty and homelessness (O'Grady, Gaetz, and Buccieri 2013). Marginalized groups become scapegoats punished by police and policymakers trying to "clean up" individuals or areas considered problematic.

regarding inequalities in race, class, and gender (Brown and Schept 2016). Abolitionists and peacemaking theorists argue that prisons are a form of social control; they are warehouses for victims of structures related to class, race, and gender. It is only by addressing societal inequalities that we may begin to address the root social issues of crime. For these theorists, crime and other social problems are no different and the solution therefore lies in the community, not the criminal justice system. These theorists also argue the prison system is dangerous and, in the end, increases rather than decreases crime:

> Abolitionists and peacemaking criminologists have exposed the dysfunctional and dangerous features of the criminal (in)justice system ... document[ing] the physical and psychological problems of imprisonment and demonstrat[ing] the abuses in the system: solitary confinement, forced transfer, inadequate health care, overcrowding and excessive sentences. (Brooks 2015: 78)

These theories argue for social rights for all — including housing, employment, nutritious and safe food, safe environments, and clean water — as part of a broader movement toward substantive equality in health, education, employment, and living (Reiman and Leighton 2017). The emphasis on deviance, criminalization, and imprisonment diverts public focus and funding away from these essential health and social justice–building strategies. Similarly, other neo-Marxist theories may suggest that, rather than calling panhandling and squeegeeing deviant, we should define as deviant those actions that allow people to live in poverty in the first place.

In summary, critical neo-Marxist theories assert that public resources that could be directed toward aiding the marginalized and displaced are instead diverted to the criminal justice system. If we invest in healthy communities, we would save costs related to institutions meant to deal with the fallout of unhealthy communities. This type of theory also demonstrates the flexibility and power attributed to what is labelled as deviance.

Foucault: From Torture to Discipline and the Panopticon

Breaking with the neo-Marxist perspective that power originates from privileged social classes and their institutions, French post-structuralist theorist Michel Foucault takes a more decentralized view. Foucault advances the idea that social control

Foucault advances the idea that social control is distributed throughout society — from the state to social institutions, to professions, and to individuals themselves.

is distributed throughout society — from the state to social institutions, to professions, and to individuals themselves.

In the eighteenth century, sovereign power was forceful, concrete, and physical. The sovereign, the person representing the Crown — a monarch, in most cases — maintained power through direct, visible force. Sovereign control was characterized by extreme measures of violence and torture, intended to deter disobedience by instilling fear in their subjects (Foucault 1977: 3). Sovereigns' use of public punishment shifted in the early nineteenth century toward imprisonment, a move that some people considered to be humanitarian. Foucault, however, argued that this was merely a move to a subtler form of power.

Foucault borrows Jeremy Bentham's infamous concept of the **panopticon** to provide a clear example of how power operates through disciplinary technology. The panopticon is an architectural prison design that consists of a tower in the centre of a courtyard, around which stand buildings with cells and windows facing the tower. This design allowed prison guards to continuously watch the behaviour of prisoners from the tower. A prisoner under surveillance was "the object of information, never a subject of communication" (Foucault 1977: 200). Because the prisoner could be seen from within the tower but could not see the guard in the tower, the surveillance was never-ending; in fact, no guard needed to be present because the prisoner was disciplined by the mere possibility of being watched. This power was continuous, anonymous, and disciplinary. In this circumstance, the prisoners ultimately begin to control themselves and become docile.

The control that Foucault describes in the panopticon works both inside as well as outside of the prison. Those who challenge or transgress the law are labelled "criminal" and their imprisonment is assumed to keep both society and the prisoner safe; it also gives the state more knowledge about prisoners to then purportedly reduce criminal behaviour. From a Foucauldian perspective, the problem is that this approach places all responsibility for crime on the individual; this is similar to Marxist perspectives. Combining this critique with the neo-Marxist critique developed previously allows us to see how the state reinforces a certain definition of "crime" (often street crime) and depoliticizes the criminogenic conditions in society: rising inequalities, weakening social programs, and rampant racism. Criminogenic conditions are defined as those conditions that make people more likely to engage in criminal activity (Ewing 2017).

Foucault stresses that panoptic technology can be used wherever individuals

are made observable and productive, such as in factories, schools,
the military, hospitals, and offices.
This form of disciplinary power
means that "prisoners could be
reformed, patients treated, students
instructed, workers supervised, and
so on" (Brock 2012: 22). This idea
of disciplinary power has been used as a model of surveillance and social control in various social institutions, to create conformist, lawful, and so-called
right-minded individuals (Brock 2012).

> Foucault stresses that panoptic technology can be used wherever individuals are made observable and productive, such as in factories, schools, the military, hospitals, and offices. This form of disciplinary power means that "prisoners could be reformed, patients treated, students instructed, workers supervised, and so on."

Psychiatry, medicine, and corrections distinguish between deviant and
normal, criminal and lawful, healthy and sick, and good and evil. Chapter
6 discusses how sexuality has been defined through psychiatry and the
law at different times and places as a mental illness and/or criminal; a
Foucauldian perspective criticizes this for forcing individuals to conform
to a single sexual identity. Over time, what was once considered deviant
can also change. For example, same-sex marriage is now legal and normal
in many countries, and gender and sexual diversity is increasingly also
accepted by the state and social institutions. State acceptance is usually far
behind the social movements that fight against normalized and prevalent
forms of oppression. However, acceptance by the state does not mean an
end to social markers of deviance.

Governing Ourselves: Responsibilization

Foucault later expanded his theory of social control to include concepts of
governmentality and **responsibilization**, arguing that people behave in ways
that align with the needs of the status quo. He wrote that neoliberalism — a
set of ideals that favours free-market capitalism rather than a strong welfare
state (Mosher 2016) and which he defines as a politics of truth — is not
simply an ideological shift but a change in governing relations. Under neoliberalism, governmentality is conduct that emphasizes *individual responsibility*
and de-emphasizes the connection
between economic opportunity
and social structural conditions.
In other words, individual citizens'
failures and successes are correlated
with their own work ethic and

> Under neoliberalism, governmentality is conduct that emphasizes *individual responsibility* and de-emphasizes the connection between economic opportunity and social structural conditions.

Self-control and self-policing are key in a neoliberal society, which extends to the social regulation of those who contribute to disorder. Thus, those who consider themselves active, responsible citizens must pit themselves against those who contribute to disorder (such as squeegee kids).

personal characteristics, and the fact that individuals come from different socioeconomic realities (with inequitable access to the tools needed to succeed) is not perceived as a credible hindrance to success. While neoliberalism emphasizes self-discipline and the responsibility of the individual, governmentality and responsibilization define processes that create a compliant public and minimize resistance (Soneryd and Uggla 2015). Self-control and self-policing are key in a neoliberal society, which extends to the social regulation of those who contribute to disorder. Thus, those who consider themselves active, responsible citizens must pit themselves against those who contribute to disorder (such as squeegee kids). As Sommers (2013: 372) states,

> major cities across North America have experienced a rise in middle class families returning from the suburbs to live in the city.... As more families call the city home, forms of physical disorder, like graffiti or litter, and social disorder, like homelessness, become less tolerated.

Within governmentality, Nikolas Rose (1996, 2000) identifies two major forms of social control: *inclusion* and *exclusion*. Inclusionary control means that citizens are rewarded for so-called proper decisions surrounding consumerism and their lifestyle. In this form of control, citizens are responsibilized to care for their own destiny, security, and health as well as the well-being of their family and community. In other words, unemployment, ill health, homelessness, and poverty are no longer considered socioeconomic problems or collective problems facing society, but rather the responsibility of individuals. In exclusionary control, people are punished and cast out if they fail to be wealthy, secure, healthy, and so on. Under governmentality and neoliberalism, social problems and social risks become the responsibility of individuals and communities.

Foucault argues that individuals have become more docile and self-regulating, having learned to control their behaviour to fit within the status quo. Identities become tied to consumerism and success is externally defined.

Foucault argues that individuals have become more docile and self-regulating, having learned to control their behaviour to fit within the status quo. Identities become tied to consumerism and success is externally defined. In contrast, those defined as "deviant" are rejected because they have not regulated themselves to the "correct" standards and are not successfully responsibilized. All of this depoliticizes structural inequalities and reinforces a mentality of self-conscious alienation.

Risk Management

Lianos and Douglas (2000) build on Foucault's governmentality to theorize that deviance is replaced by risk and probability. Based on the probability of risk, the members of the public seek to increase their own security, which ends up dividing our society into *safe* and *unsafe* spaces. This, in turn, contributes to further dividing people into *us* and *them*. By labelling individuals, communities draw divisions between the areas they deem *acceptable* and *unacceptable*. Increased security thus results in the creation of walled cities and ceaseless surveillance, which deepens our collective fear of people we have learned to view as high risk based on visible social and physical disorder. Safety and fear are therefore cyclical because the more we exclude, use surveillance, and avoid those spaces and people we deem high risk, the more fearful we become and the more we then increase surveillance and social exclusion.

Gated communities are one such product of a fearful society. A number of sociologists (e.g., Bruhn 2005) describe the connections between gated communities, risk management, and social exclusion. In particular, as Blakely and Snyder (1997: 8) note:

> Exclusionary segmentation imposes social costs on those left outside; it reduces the number of public spaces that all can share, and thus the contacts that people from different socioeconomic groups might otherwise have with each other ... the growing divisions between city and suburb and rich and poor are creating new patterns that reinforce the costs that isolation and exclusion impose on some at the same time that they benefit others.

The governmentality and risk perspectives would consider the social exclusion of squeegee kids and panhandlers or other forms of criminalized poverty and marginality as a disguised form of *advanced social control* primarily intended to popularize narrow political and economic agendas. Built on misunderstandings of risk

> Safety and fear are therefore cyclical because the more we exclude, use surveillance, and avoid those spaces and people we deem high risk, the more fearful we become and the more we then increase surveillance and social exclusion.

Built on misunderstandings of risk and justified by sensational media through anecdotal evidence, we exclude and fear those we do not understand.

and justified by sensational media through anecdotal evidence, we exclude and fear those we do not understand. This theme takes on particular significance when considering the emergence of the feminist and anti-oppressive perspectives, to which we now turn.

Feminist and Anti-Oppressive Theories

The 1968 publication of Frances Heidensohn's *The Deviance of Women* openly criticized sociology for its neglect of women's deviance. Over the years, feminist scholars have taken up Heidensohn's challenge and, today, gendered analysis is a crucial part of the sociology of social deviance and control, however marginalized it often remains (Miller 2010). Feminist theories argue for the importance of taking women's voices into account while also recognizing that women's **agency** — the ability to act and make decisions — is not only shaped by, but also shapes, larger relations of power and social control. Feminist-based theories can thus be said to engage deviance on the spectrum between human agency and social structure.

The three traditional varieties of feminist theory — first-, second-, and third-wave feminism — all have their own assumptions concerning the root of gender marginalization as well as the best potential means to strive for the empowerment of girls and women. The first wave started in the United States with the women's suffrage movements in the mid- to late 1800s; the second wave came one hundred years later, in the 1960s and 1970s with women's civil rights and liberation movements (Burgess-Proctor 2006); and the third wave began in the 1990s. The second wave was the first to make inroads into criminology and deviance studies and, as such, we begin our discussion there. The various waves continue to inform different variants of feminist work today but each has also been criticized for focusing on advances made by white feminists.

Feminist theories argue for the importance of taking women's voices into account while also recognizing that women's **agency** — the ability to act and make decisions — is not only shaped by, but also shapes, larger relations of power and social control.

Second-Wave Feminism

Second-wave feminists focus on the inclusion of experiential knowledge (knowledge gained by one's life experiences) and the voices of girls and women in social sciences theory

(Moosa-Mitha 2015). However, second-wave feminists privileged considerations of gender over those of ethnic or racial identity and social class; they also focused on problems related to women of a certain profile — namely white, middle class, and heterosexual. This feminism incorporated liberal, radical, socialist, and Marxist perspectives.

> Second-wave theories draw attention to how violence, poverty, and lower incomes contribute to women's criminality, deviance, and increased positioning as targets of discrimination and stigmatization.

Second-wave theories draw attention to how violence, poverty, and lower incomes contribute to women's criminality, deviance, and increased positioning as targets of discrimination and stigmatization (Barrett, Allenby, and Taylor 2010; Brooks 2015). This perspective, similar to neo-Marxist theories, has a dual focus on social class and gender. The criminalization of poverty in Canada, for example, is one way in which the state perpetuates gender inequality at a socioeconomic level and regulates marginalized women in society. Women make up a majority of the poor across Canada and, subsequently, are more likely to be criminalized for being poor than their male counterparts (Comack 2014a).

Prior to the 1980s, the state took on the social responsibility of providing its citizens with a social safety or security net. This included the provision of welfare and social assistance to those who required it. However, with the rise of neoliberalism — a socioeconomic ideology premised on individualism, free-market economics, and self-reliance — the state withdrew its collective care for those in need of social assistance (Comack 2014b). In coordination with the rise of neo-conservativism — a socio-political ideology built on traditional concepts of hierarchy and authority — governments began to "crack down" on the allotment and availability of their social services, resulting in severe reforms to welfare practices and policies (Comack 2014b; Mosher 2014). The state became increasingly focused on finding welfare "fraudsters" or "cheats" it presumed were taking advantage of the system. This shift in state ideology resulted in a new conceptualization of welfare fraud to "welfare *as* fraud" (Chunn and Gavigan 2014; see also Box 3-3).

Feminist criminologists observe that the majority of imprisoned women are young, unskilled, poor, and Indigenous (Brooks 2015). Many also have drug and/or alcohol addictions and have been victims of sexual or physical abuse (Barrett, Allenby, and Taylor 2010). These women most often commit non-violent property crimes, which indicates the correlation between criminality and women's lower social and economic status (Barrett et al. 2010). Similarly,

Box 3-3: The Feminization of Welfare Fraud: The Case of Kimberly Rogers

by Cerah Dubé

The crackdown on social welfare disproportionately affected women. In Ontario, it happened through the strict welfare reform enacted by the Harris Conservative government in the late 1990s and early 2000s. The government set up welfare fraud "snitch" hotlines, restricted eligibility conditions, set lifetime bans for fraudsters, and heightened the policing of welfare recipients (Chunn and Gavigan 2014). These strict reforms resulted in increased and harsher penalization of poor women on social assistance, such as 40-year-old Kimberly Rogers.

Rogers was a recent graduate of a community college social work program in Sudbury, Ontario, and she had student loans. While she was unemployed and looking for work after graduation, she also applied for welfare assistance. Prior to 1997, Ontario legislation permitted student loans to be held while simultaneously receiving welfare assistance. However, by 2001, legislation had changed as a result of strict welfare policy reform, and Rogers was charged with welfare fraud, or theft over $5,000. She pled guilty and was sentenced to six months of house arrest. Rogers was pregnant and had no financial resources to house or feed herself in light of the new "zero-tolerance" benefits ban placed upon those convicted of welfare fraud. She was permitted to leave her house only on Wednesday mornings for three hours — to grocery shop and for doctor appointments — and her only method of transportation was public transit. Although interim assistance was reinstated by court order until her case was to be heard, the amount Kimberly received was pitiful: $450 of her $468 monthly assistance went to rent, leaving her with $18 for food and other needs for the remainder of the month (Chunn and Gavigan 2014; Mosher 2014). "I ran out of food this weekend. I am unable to sleep and I cry all the time," she stated to the court (as cited in Chunn and Gavigan 2014). While the state intended to punish Rogers for welfare fraud, it was starving her and depriving her of access to mental health resources she needed to deal with her diagnosed depression.

On August 11, 2001, eight months pregnant, Rogers died of a prescription drug overdose in her small apartment in Sudbury during a heatwave. While her death was ruled a suicide, many argued it was no doubt at least in part due to the dire conditions of her house arrest resulting from draconian welfare policies (Mosher 2014). Chunn and Gavigan (2014) point out that, up until 2014, Rogers would still be liable for a conviction of welfare fraud under current welfare legislation.

research on street youth and squeegee kids shows that girls who are living on the street in Canada have experienced physical, sexual, and psychological violence against them, with this directly linked to ending up in conflict with the legal system (Parnaby 2002). The state's continued criminalization of poverty is distinctly gendered in nature and continues to have disproportionately disastrous effects on marginalized women, whose true crime is being poor.

Third-Wave Feminism

In contrast to second-wave feminists, third-wave feminists argue that women's experiences are varied and cannot be lumped together. While appreciating that women may share common experiences, these feminists focus on bringing forth women's voices to show different perspectives. Third-wave feminist theories also contest the first and second waves' critiques of gender, patriarchy, and capitalism, denouncing their universalist tendencies (Hill Collins 2000, 2007); rather, they note that people do not experience inequalities in the same way. Third-wave feminists instead argue there is no ultimate truth, and that truth is always partial, political, constructed, and subject to change. Because third-wave feminism is as diverse as the people about which it attempts to speak, we divide it here into standpoint and anti-oppressive theories.

Standpoint Feminism

Standpoint feminists acknowledge that women's experiences are affected by language and discourse, as well as structural oppressions (as we saw in neo-Marxism and second-wave feminist thought), but also that these play out in the everyday lives of women in diverse ways (introducing agency). Agency is defined as the capacity of a person to act not only by engaging with social structures, but to have the individual capacity and level of reflexivity to think for oneself.

Dorothy Smith (2005) argues that we must begin with the standpoint of people. Standpoint feminism contends that we should study how the dynamics of class, race, and gender impact the everyday lives of women without imposing categories on them (Smith 2005; Comack 1999). This results in what standpoint feminists call "a faithful telling" of the social world. Comack used a standpoint feminist perspective in *Women in*

> Standpoint feminism contends that we should study how the dynamics of class, race, and gender impact the everyday lives of women without imposing categories on them. This results in what standpoint feminists call "a faithful telling" of the social world.

Trouble. In speaking on the use of this framework, she states:

> In taking the women's lives as my starting point, my aim has been
> to develop a way of knowing ... that is capable of shedding light on
> the factors and conditions which brought them into conflict with
> the law. Central to the formulation of this standpoint is the attempt
> to situate their lives within the nexus of the class, race and gender
> relations of our society. (1996: 34)

Comack completed research with twenty-four incarcerated women in
Manitoba and revealed experiential evidence of the connection between
the women's incarceration and the history of violence and abuse against
them. The lived experiential knowledge of the women in conflict with the
law was developed into a unique standpoint, whereby they shared common
or similar backgrounds. However, she is careful to say that their common
background does not mean they have had the same experiences. A standpoint analysis of squeegee kids would place their stories at the centre to
understand the diversity of their experiences while also recognizing their
common backgrounds.

Anti-Oppressive Theories: Intersections
of Race, Gender, Class, and Agency

While adopting the strengths of postmodern deconstruction and standpoint
feminism's focus on experiential knowledge, anti-oppressive theories draw
attention to how colonialism, neocolonial realities, racial identity, and cultural
identity intersect with gender and class. In arguing for an intersectional
analysis of oppressions, these theories contend that we cannot single out, for
example, racial oppression, but rather that forms of oppression are interrelated
(hooks 1989, 1990; Hill Collins 2000, 2007).

Anti-oppressive theories believe it is essential to begin with the standpoint
of the oppressed and hear the voices that have traditionally been silenced. This
means it is important to start with the stories of those who we have defined
as deviant. However, while similarities exist between groups of people or
communities, these theories also recognize the difference between people's
experiences. Patricia Hill Collins
(2000: 347–48), for instance, aims
to bring forward the voices and
experiences of African-American
women while acknowledging both

Anti-oppressive theories believe it is
essential to begin with the standpoint of the
oppressed and hear the voices that have
traditionally been silenced.

the differences in experiences and similarities in the collective background of communities:

The heavy concentration of US Black women in domestic work coupled with racial segregation in housing and schools meant that US Black women had common organizational networks that enabled them to share experiences and construct a collective body of wisdom.

> The combination of critical and anti-oppressive approaches to sociological research provides a lens to understand how gender, racialization, class, and historical positioning (especially colonial and neocolonial realities) shape people's voices and experience.

This means, for example, that African-American women share certain experiences of discrimination in relation to housing and employment as well as being watched or discriminated against in their everyday lives.

Postcolonial Indigenous theory and anticolonial feminism are examples of anti-oppressive theories. These theories contextualize racism within systemic and historical conditions. In Canada, colonizing discourses about Indigenous women are a part of history but also persist today (Browne and Fiske 2001; Browne, Smye, and Varcoe 2008). For example, although women experience domestic violence disproportionately to men, Indigenous women experience it at an even greater disproportionate rate: they report violent victimization at levels nearly three times that of non-Indigenous women and are also more likely to experience severe types of violence (Brennan 2011). These women are thus victim to the violence associated with the discourse as well as the stereotypes of what they represent, placing their entire lives within the margins (Jiwani and Young 2006). Anticolonial Indigenous theorists and postcolonial feminists agree that the perspectives of marginalized peoples must thus be the starting point for developing knowledge and deconstructing race.

The combination of critical and anti-oppressive approaches to sociological research provides a lens to understand how gender, racialization, class, and historical positioning (especially colonial and neocolonial realities) shape people's voices and experience. Together, these theories inform questions about the historical and social determinants of deviance and social control. These anti-oppressive approaches emphasize critical and inclusive analyses that listen and make space for marginalized voices.

Summary

Studies of deviance and social control have not historically questioned what we define as deviant but have instead participated in the ongoing labelling of individuals as "nuts, sluts, and perverts." This chapter focused on the social construction of deviance and its connection to power and social control.

Critical theories contribute to our understanding of social determinants of deviance and the control inherent within social institutions such as law, medicine, and media. As we have seen and will see in coming chapters, there is an abundance of literature on the social determinants and environmental factors related to deviance and crime and on the importance of social class, the production process, racism, economic cycles, and material and social conditions.

Neo-Marxism helps us to discern dominant injustices while also linking knowledge to material, historical, and social contexts. From this perspective, the very ideas of what we define as deviant are rooted in unequal social arrangements. The neo-Marxist approach emphasizes the experiences of people from a human rights perspective and critiques how society is often structured in the interest of high-status groups. This perspective combines the social and economic determinants of deviance and questions why certain groups are labelled deviant or criminal. An important measure of a society, from this lens, would be how we treat the poorest and most disadvantaged among us. The uniqueness of neo-Marxist approaches is their focus on the connections between deviance, crime, and the organization of our political, social, and economic structures. Foucauldian and governmentality perspectives address power, privilege, injustice, collective rights, and the role of government in relation to deviance and social control. We learn from Foucault of panopticon-esque and responsibilized control, which creates citizens (or subjects) who are surveilled and become their own controllers — learning how to behave, how to be good consumer citizens, as well as how to think, look, and belong.

Deviance and social control literature has been questioned for failing to include gender, age, race, and class, and many scholars argue this has still not been fully corrected. The combined social forces of class, race, and gender, as well as the importance of human agency and voice, must be considered. Finally, critical theories are sometimes disparaged for not bringing in the actual standpoints of people affected by social control. Feminist and anti-oppressive theories, on the contrary, include those voices that are not always heard, recognizing that agency is shaped by but also shapes larger relations of power and social control.

In the pages that follow, we draw on current deviance and social control research and engage multiple levels of theories. We introduce research that attempts to bring forward the voices of people who have experienced social control and been labelled as deviant, as well as processes of social regulation in the areas of youth studies, addiction, sexuality, surveillance, imprisonment, violence, body image, sexuality, surveillance, and resistance.

Discussion Questions

1. How have studies in deviance and social control shifted from analyzing behaviours of so-called nuts, sluts, and perverts to understanding social oppression and power?
2. How are deviant labels linked to power and social regulation?
3. How can Foucault's critique of the panopticon be applied to understanding social media as a virtual panopticon?
4. Explain the idea that deviants would not exist except for those who control them.
5. This chapter puts forward the importance of a gendered and anti-oppressive analysis as a crucial part of the sociology of social deviance and control. Do you agree with this assessment? Why or why not?

Recommended Resources

1. Silver, Jim. 2014. *About Canada: Poverty*. Fernwood Publishing.
2. O'Grady, Bill, Stephen Gaetz, and Kristy Buccieri. *Can I See your ID? The Policing of Youth Homelessness in Toronto*. Toronto: JFCY and the Homeless Hub.
3. Reiman, Jeffry, and Paul Leighton. 2017. *The Rich Get Richer and the Poor Get Prison*, 11th edition. Boston: Allyn and Bacon.
4. Burchell, C., C. Gordon, and P. Miller (eds.). *The Foucault Effect: Studies in Governmentality*. University of Chicago Press.
5. The Homeless Hub: "Finding Solutions to End Homelessness." <homelesshub.ca/>.

Glossary 3

agency: the capacity of a person to act not only by engaging with the social structure, but to have the individual capacity and a level of reflexivity to think for oneself.

governmentality: coined by Foucault, this refers to how the state governs the populace.

hegemony: the concept that the elite class manipulates the ideas, knowledge, and morals of the working public to make them believe that the system is working in their best interest and that it does so in a fair and legitimate way.

instrumentalist Marxism: the understanding that those in positions of social power and economic privilege consciously use social institutions to further perpetuate inequitable class relations.

intersectionality: contends that we cannot single out, for example, racial oppression, but rather that forms of oppression are interrelated with one another.

liberal feminism: recognizes women's unequal position in society and aims to increase their status through liberal ideas of equality and inclusion.

Marxist feminism: focuses on capitalism and unequal class positions, demonstrating women's unequal position within labour and the value of their traditional productive labour.

panopticon: architectural design of a tower in the centre of a prison courtyard with cells and windows facing the tower allowing continuous surveillance of the cells from the tower. This power is viewed a continuous, anonymous, and disciplinary.

postcolonial feminism: illuminates connections between gendered positioning, class, and racialization while acknowledging colonial histories, neocolonialism, and the effects of these on current lives, choices, and opportunities.

radical feminism: calls for the end of sex-based discrimination and defines the oppression of women as being based in relations of domination and subordination between the sexes.

responsibilized: to behave in ways that align with the needs of the status quo.

socialist feminism: focuses on class and patriarchal gendered relations, providing attention to both women's exploitation within labour as well as realizing men's control over women.

standpoint feminism: acknowledges that women's experiences are affected by language and discourse (as postmodernists teach) as well as structural oppressions in race, class, and gender, but it also puts forward that these are worked out in the everyday lives of women in diverse ways (introducing agency).

structuralist Marxism: the understanding that capitalist economic relations inherently trend toward perpetuating inequitable class relations independent of the will of those in positions of social power and economic privilege.

References

Aleman, A. 2017. "Why Do Governments Criminalize the Homeless?" Homeless Hub Blog, February 17. <homelesshub.ca/blog/why-do-governments-criminalize-homeless>.

Antony, J. 2019. "Using Defensive Design to Effect Change: From Hostile Architecture to Guerilla Gardening." *EQ3 Stories*, November 8. < stories.eq3.com/en/2019/09/hostile-architecture>.

Barrett, Meridith Robeson, Kim Allenby, and Kelly Taylor. 2010. *Twenty Years Later: Revisiting the Task Force on Federally Sentenced Women*. Correctional Service Canada, July. <csc-scc.gc.ca/005/008/092/005008-0222-01-eng.pdf>.

Berti, Mario, and Jeff Sommers. 2010. "'The Streets Belong to People Who Pay for Them': The Spatial Regulation of Street Poverty in Vancouver." In Diane Crocker and Val Marie Johnson (eds.), *Poverty, Regulation and Social Justice: Readings on the Criminalization of Poverty*. Halifax: Fernwood Publishing.

Blakely, Edward J., and Mary Gail Snyder. 1997. *Fortress America: Gated Communities in the United States*. Washington, DC: Brookings Institution Press.

Boggess, Lyndsay N., and Jon Maskaly. 2014. "The Spatial Context of the Disorder-Crime Relationship in a Study of Reno Neighborhoods." *Social Science Research* 43C.

Braga, Anthony A., Brandon C. Welsh, and Cory Schnell. 2015. "Can Policing Disorder Reduce Crime? A Systematic Review and Meta-analysis." *Journal of Research in Crime and Delinquency* 53, 4.

Brennan, Shannon. 2011. *Violent Victimization of Aboriginal Women in the Canadian Provinces, 2009*. Ottawa: Juristat — Canadian Centre for Justice Statistics.

Broadbent Institute. 2012. "Towards a More Equal Canada: A Report on Canada's Economic and Social Inequality." <d3n8a8pro7vhmx.cloudfront.net/broadbent/pages/4483/attachments/original/1438883643/towards_a_more_equal_canada.pdf?1438883643>.

Brock, Deborah R. 2012. "Thinking about Power: Exploring Theories of Domination and Governance." In Deborah R. Brock, Rebecca Raby and Mark P. Thomas (eds.), *Power and Everyday Practices*. New York: Nelson Education Ltd.

Brooks, Carolyn. 2015. "Critical Criminology." In Carolyn Brooks and Bernard Schissel (eds.), *Marginality and Condemnation: An Introduction to Criminology in Canada*. Halifax: Fernwood Publishing.

Brown, Michelle, and Judah Schept. 2016. "New Abolition, Criminology and a Critical Carceral Studies." *Punishment and Society* 19, 4. <journals.sagepub.com/doi/abs/10.1177/1462474516666281>.

Browne, Annette J., and Jo-Anne Fiske. 2001. "First Nations Women's Encounters with Mainstream Health Care Services." *Western Journal of Nursing Research* 23, 2.

Browne, Annette, V.L. Smye, and Colleen Varcoe. 2008. "Postcolonial-Feminist Theoretical Perspectives and Women's Health." In Marina Morrow, Olena Hankivsky, and Collen Varcoe (eds.), *Women's Health in Canada: Critical Perspectives on Theory and Policy*. Toronto: University of Toronto Press.

Bruhn, John G. 2005. "Communities of Exclusion and Excluded Communities." *The Sociology of Community Connections*: 133–59. <springer.com/gp/book/9780306486166#aboutBook>.

Burgess-Proctor, Amanda. 2006. "Intersections of Race, Class, Gender and Crime: Future Directions for Feminist Criminology." *Feminist Criminology* 1, 27.

CBC News. 2013. "Man Ordered to Pay Panhandler $8,000 for Discrimination." <cbc.ca/news/canada/montreal/man-ordered-to-pay-panhandler-8-000-for-discrimination-1.1380361>.

Chunn, D., and S. Gavigan. 2014. "From Welfare Fraud to Welfare as Fraud: The Criminalization of Poverty." In G. Balfour and E. Comack (eds.), *Criminalizing Women: Gender & (In)justice in Neo-Liberal Times*, 2nd edition. Winnipeg & Halifax: Fernwood Publishing.

Clarke, J. 2000. "Serve the Rich and Punish the Poor: Law as the Enforcer of Inequality." In W. Gordon West and Ruth Morris (eds.), *The Case for Penal Abolition*. Toronto: Canadian Scholars' Press.

Comack, E. 2014a. "The Feminist Engagement with Criminology." In G. Balfour and E. Comack (eds.), *Criminalizing Women: Gender & (In)justice in Neo-Liberal Times*, 2nd edition. Winnipeg & Halifax: Fernwood Publishing.

____. 2014b. "Part II: Introduction." In G. Balfour and E. Comack (eds.), *Criminalizing Women: Gender and (In)justice in Neo-Liberal Times*, 2nd edition. Winnipeg & Halifax: Fernwood Publishing.

____. 1999. "Producing Feminist Knowledge: Lessons from Women in Trouble." *Theoretical Criminology* 3, 3.

____. 1996. *Women in Trouble: Connecting Women's Law Violation to their Histories of Abuse*. Halifax: Fernwood Publishing.

CTV Atlantic. 2018. "Halifax Police Issue Hundreds of Tickets to Panhandlers Who Ask Motorists for Money." May. <atlantic.ctvnews.ca/halifax-police-issue-hundreds-of-tickets-to-panhandlers-who-ask-motorists-for-money-1.3910647>.

Ewing, Benjamin. 2017. "Recent Work on Punishment and Criminogenic Disadvantage." *Law and Philosophy* 37.

Family Services Toronto. 2017. "Report Card on Child and Family Poverty in Canada." <campaign2000.ca/wp-content/uploads/2017/11/EnglishNationalC2000Report Nov212017.pdf>.

Foucault, Michel. 1977. *Discipline and Punish: The Birth of the Prison*. New York: Pantheon Books.

Gaetz, Stephen, Jesse Donaldson, Tim Richter, and Tanya Gulliver. 2013. *The State of Homelessness in Canada 2013*. The Homeless Hub. <homelesshub.ca/sites/default/files/attachments/SOHC2103.pdf>.

Gaetz, Stephen, Bill O'Grady, and Kristy Buccieri. 2010. *Surviving Crime and Violence Street Youth and Victimization in Toronto*. Toronto: JFCY & Homeless Hub.

Gaetz, S., F. Scott, and T. Gulliver (eds.). 2013. *Housing First in Canada: Supporting Communities to End Homelessness*. The Homeless Hub. <homelesshub.ca/sites/default/files/attachments/HousingFirstInCanada_0.pdf>.

Gau, Jacinta M., Nicholas Corsaro, and Rod K. Brunson. 2014. "Revisiting Broken Windows Theory: A Test of the Mediation Impact of Social Mechanisms on the Disorder-Fear Relationship." *Journal of Criminal Justice* 42, 6.

Graham, Stephen. 2011. *Cities Under Siege: The New Military Urbanism*. London: Verso Books.

Gramsci, Antonio. 1971. *Selections from the Prison Notebooks of Antonio Gramsci*. New York, International Publishers.

Heidensohn, F. 2010 [1968]. "The Deviance of Women: A Critique and an Enquiry." *The British Journal of Sociology — The BJS: Shaping Sociology Over 60 Years*. [Originally published in 1968 *British Journal of Sociology* 19, 2.]

Hermer, Joe, and Janet E. Mosher. 2002. *Disorderly People: Law and the Politics of Exclusion in Ontario*. Halifax: Fernwood Publishing.

Hill Collins, Patricia. 2007. "Black Feminist Thought (1990/2000)." In S. Appelrouth and L. Desfor Edles (eds.), *Sociological Theory in the Contemporary Era*. London: Pine Forge Press/Sage Publications.

____. 2000. *Black Feminist Thought: Knowledge, Consciousness, and the Politics of Empowerment*, 2nd edition. New York: Routledge.

hooks, bell. 1990. *Yearning: Race, Gender and Cultural Politics*. Boston: South End Press.

____. 1989. *Boneblack: Memories of Girlhood*. New York: Henry Holt.

Jefferson, Brian Jordan. 2016. "Broken Windows Policing and Constructions of Space and Crime: Flatbush, Brooklyn." *Antipode: A Radical Journal of Geography* 48, 5.

Jiwani, Yasmin, and Mary Lynn Young. 2006. "Missing and Murdered Women: Reproducing Marginality in News Discourse." *Canadian Journal of Communication* 31, 4.

Lianos, Michalis, and Mary Douglas. 2000. "Dangerization and the End of Deviance: The Institutional Environment." *British Journal of Criminology* 40, 2.

Liazos, Alexander. 1972. "The Poverty of the Sociology of Deviance: Nuts, Sluts, and Perverts." *Social Problems* 20, 1.

Marx, K., F. Engels, S. Moore, and D. McLellan. 1992. *The Communist Manifesto*. Oxford: Oxford University Press.

Miliband, Ralph. 1969. *The State in Capitalist Society*. New York: Basic Books.

Miller, Jody. 2010. "Commentary on Heidensohn's 'The Deviance of Women': Continuity and Change over Four Decades of Research on Gender, Crime and Social Control." *British Journal of Sociology* 61, 1.

Moosa-Mitha, Mehmoona. 2015. "Situating Anti-Oppressive Theories within Critical and Difference-Centered Perspectives." In Susan Strega and Leslie Brown (eds.), *Research as Resistance: Critical, Indigenous and Anti-Oppressive Approaches*. Toronto: Canadian Scholars' Press.

Mosher, Janet E. 2016. "Social Class and Invoking Criminality." In C. Brooks and B. Schissel (eds.), *Marginality and Condemnation: A Critical Introduction to Criminology*. Halifax: Fernwood Publishing.

____. 2014. "The Construction of 'Welfare Fraud' and the Wielding of the State's Iron Fist." In E. Comack (ed.), *Locating Law: Race, Class, Gender, Sexuality Connections*, 3rd edition. Halifax and Winnipeg: Fernwood Publishing.

____. 2002. "The Shrinking of the Public and Private Spaces of the Poor." In Janet E. Mosher and Joe Hermer (eds.), *Disorderly People: Law and the Politics of Exclusion in Ontario*. Halifax: Fernwood Publishing.

Musset, B. 2019. "Vancouver's 'Defensive Architecture' Is Hostile to Homeless, Says Critics." *Vancouver Courier*, June 24.

O'Grady, Bill, and Robert Bright. 2002. "Squeezed to the Point of Exclusion: The Case of Toronto Squeegee Cleaners." In Joe Hermer and Janet Mosher (eds.), *Disorderly People: Law and the Politics of Exclusion in Ontario.* Halifax: Fernwood Publishing.

O'Grady, Bill, Robert Bright, and Eric Cohen. 1998. "Sub-Employment and Street Youths: An Analysis of the Impact of Squeegee Cleaning on Homeless Youths." *Security Journal* 11, 2–3.

O'Grady, Bill, Stephen Gaetz, and Kristy Buccieri. 2013. "Tickets … and More Tickets: A Case Study of the Enforcement of the Ontario Safe Streets Act." *Canadian Public Policy* 39, 4.

Olsen, G.M., and L. Benjaminsen. 2017. "Homelessness and Social Policy." In B. Greve (ed.), *Routledge Handbook of the Welfare State.* London: Routledge.

Oxfam. 2017. "Oxfam Briefing Paper — Summary." January. <d1tn3vj7xz9fdh.cloudfront. net/s3fs-public/file_attachments/bp-economy-for-99-percent-160117-summ-en. pdf>.

Parnaby, Patrick. 2002. "Disaster Through Dirty Windshields Law, Order and Toronto's Squeegee Kids." *Canadian Journal of Sociology* 28, 3.

Pelley, L. 2019. "How 'Defensive Design' Leads to Rigid Benches, Metal Spikes, and 'Visual Violence' in Modern Cities." cbc *News*, July 2.

Reiman, Jeffery. 2009. *The Rich Get Richer and the Poor Get Prison: Ideology, Class and Criminal Justice*, 9th edition. New York and London: Routledge.

Reiman, Jeffery, and Paul Leighton. 2017. *The Rich Get Richer and the Poor Get Prison: Ideology, Class and Criminal Justice*, 11th edition. New York and London: Routledge.

Robinson, Alex. 2017. "Legal Clinic to Challenge Safe Streets Act." *Law Times*, April 10. <lawtimesnews.com/author/alex-robinson/legal-clinic-to-challenge-safe-streets-act-13290/>.

Rose, Nikolas. 2000. "Government and Control." *British Journal of Criminology* 40, 2.

_____. 1996. "The Death of the Social? Re-Figuring the Territory of Government." *Economy and Society* 25, 3.

Rush, C. 2011. "Don't Challenge Squeegee Kids, Police Warn After Attack." *Toronto Star*, June 8. <thestar.com/news/crime/2011/06/08/dont_challenge_squeegee_kids_ police_warn_after_attack.html>

Schindler, S.B. 2015. "Architectural Exclusion: Discrimination and Segregation Through Physical Design of the Built Environment." *Yale Law Journal* 124, 6.

Scott, Lauren. 2017. "Repeal the Ontario Safe Streets Act." *The Leveller*, January 25. <leveller.ca/2017/01/safe-streets-act/>.

Smith, Dorothy. 2005. *Institutional Ethnography: A Sociology for People.* Lanham: Rowman Altamira.

Sommers, Rory. 2013. "Governing the Streets: The Legal, Social and Moral Regulation of Homeless Youth." In Stephen Gaetz, Bill O'Grady, Kristy Buccieri, Jeff Karabanow, and Allyson Marsolais (eds.), *Youth Homelessness in Canada: Implications for Policy and Practice.* Toronto: Canadian Homelessness Research Network Press.

Soneryd, Linda, and Ylva Uggla. 2015. "Green Governmentality and Responsibilization: New Forms of Governance and Responses to 'Consumer Responsibility.'" *Environmental Politics* 24, 6.

Switzer, Jane. 2011. "Squeegee Kid Beat Driver, Police Say." *National Post*, June 7. <nationalpost.com/posted-toronto/squeegee-kid-beat-driver-police-say>.

4

Research Methods, Statistics, and Listening to Unheard Voices

James F. Popham

After reading this chapter, you will be able to do the following:
1. Explain methodological validity.
2. Explain construct and content validity.
3. Critically assess research strategies.
4. Identify sampling issues.
5. Identify inherent biases to big data analytics.
6. Explain the value of mixed methods and qualitative research approaches.

In 1999, the "House Hippo" public service announcement first aired on Canadian television (Concerned Children's Advertisers 1999). The documentary-style footage shows hippopotami in a middle-class home, inferring that a seemingly impossible mouse-sized sub-species of *H. amphibious* commonly dwells in kitchens and mouse holes throughout North America. The imagery is surprisingly well done and even includes a voiceover reminiscent of nature documentaries such as the *Mutual of Omaha's Wild Kingdom* or *David Attenborough's Planet Earth*. This reality is shattered after about forty-five seconds, when a placard with the logo of the *Concerned Children's Advertisers* appears and a narrator asks: "That looked really real, but you knew it couldn't be true, didn't you?" (Concerned Children's Advertisers 1999).

The PSA encouraged young people to question the information they encountered daily through different media sources (Muto 2004). Produced at a time when computer-augmented imagery was beginning to infiltrate popular

> A great deal of the power that comes from the use of statistical knowledge to prove a point comes from the fact that much of the public is under-educated about what these figures and ratios mean.

media, the non-profit *Concerned Children's Advertisers* (now called *Companies Committed to Kids*) was employing demonstrative tactics to raise awareness about the influence of tempting imagery on our perceptions of "truth." This approach reflected the work of Marshall McLuhan (1964), who, in the 1960s, warned that the way people use or employ information, rather than the information itself, is what should be of concern. Thus, the "reality" of house hippos is a measure of a person's interpretation of the information presented to them, rather than the veracity of the sixty-second vignette in which it appears.

McLuhan's focus on how information is conveyed and how we make use of it, rather than the nature of the information itself, rings true in many fields beyond media studies. This is a particularly important critique for the popular use of quantitatively derived statistical data — or "stats" for short. A great deal of the power that comes from the use of statistical knowledge to prove a point comes from the fact that much of the public is under-educated about what these figures and ratios mean (O'Neil 2016; Field 2016). Popular depictions of statistics, such as in the 2011 film *Moneyball* (De Luca, Horovitz, Pitt, and Miller 2011), tend to frame them as a black box of mystery and use convoluted or downright obtuse formulae to draw stunning conclusions. These projections of statistics tend to dissuade people from critically thinking about the numbers presented to them, and instead encourage them to invest a great deal of credence in what they have been told — after all, it's in the math (Field 2016). However, all statistical calculations are built upon a foundation of decisions, many of which are subject to the opinions and interpretations of researchers. While the calculations behind these conclusions might be mathematically correct, statistics can nonetheless act as a subjective mechanism of social control when these decisions are made in error, intentionally or not.

On January 16, 2018, US president Donald Trump used social media to share the results of a government report that he connected with anti-immigration rhetoric that had been central to his 2016 election campaign. He cited figures collected by the US Department of Justice (DOJ)'s National Security Division estimating that people born outside of the United States accounted for approximately 73 percent of international terrorism-related convictions between September 11, 2001, and December 31, 2016. In a tweet, Trump told his 51.5 million followers at the time that "nearly 3 in 4 individuals convicted of terrorism-related charges are foreign-born."

The issue with President Trump's tweet lies in the way the information was presented rather than its accuracy. The DOJ report that he was citing lists 549 terror-related convictions against unique individuals that had occurred in the United States over a fifteen-year period and explains that 254 of the individuals were not US citizens while an additional 148 were foreign-born naturalized US citizens. Mathematically speaking, the DOJ's assertion that 73 percent of international terrorism-related convictions were foreign-born is correct, as was President Trump's phrasing of "nearly 3 in 4." What was missing from this dialogue was context: the terror-related convictions make up a miniscule fraction of the total number of criminal offences that occur within the United States in any given year. Specifically, approximately 18.5 million violent offences were recorded during this time period, and in the five years between 2012 and 2016, 74,900 people were charged with murder in the United States. The vastness of these numbers makes it difficult to comprehend the risks or dangers that they pose, so statisticians will often standardize crime rates to give a sense of how many people in a population (generally 100,000) will be affected. For 2016, the violent crime rate in the United States stood at 384 incidents per 100,000, and the murder rate 5.4 per 100,000 (Federal Bureau of Investigations, 2020). Assuming that all 549 convictions occurred in a single year, the rate of terror-related crimes would have been 0.17 per 100,000. Further, if the rate was reduced to only foreign-born residents of the United States (the segment of the population that President Trump was decrying, accounting for approximately forty-three million Americans), terror-related incidents would have occurred at approximately 1.25 per 100,000 in 2016 (Federal Bureau of Investigations 2020).

The standardization of data described above is an important point when discussing statistics. **Standardizing** data entails presenting it in a way that allows comparison of different measures; you do this when you convert your exam scores into percentages, which helps you to determine how well you are doing in your class (Tukey 1977). The standardization process is particularly helpful when looking at large groups of people, such as the population of a city or country. Consider a town of 10,000 people that has 1,000 internationally born residents versus a city of 200,000 with 2,000 internationally born residents. While the gross number of immigrants in the city is larger than the town, the town's rate of immigrants is 10,000 per 100,000 residents versus the city's rate of 1,000 immigrants per 100,000 residents. The statistics cited by President Trump were used to advance a stereotype of the unsafe immigrant by suggesting that this group of people are responsible for most acts of terror occurring within the United States. The president and his administration used this information as a platform to implement the "immigration ban" — Executive Order 13780 (2018) — that drastically limited the number of refugees allowed to enter the United States. The executive order was later amended to impose travel bans for people travelling from Chad, Iran, Libya, North Korea, Somalia, Syria, Venezuela, and Yemen (Fullerton 2017).

Statistics are a powerful tool that, when used appropriately, can provide valuable insights into social trends and help to inform policy. For instance, we know that the crime rate in Canada has followed a downward trend since the mid-1990s and stabilized at levels similar to those experienced in the 1970s. Similarly, we know that the level of crime severity has also declined over that period, indicating that Canada as a whole has grown safer (Allen 2016). These statistics have informed shifts in Canadian policing strategies, such as growing investment in community safety (Webster and Doob 2015). On the other hand, misuse of data can have dire consequences that empower new mechanisms of social control, as demonstrated above. The purpose of this chapter therefore echoes the "house hippo" PSA: Its goal is to develop a critical discussion about quantitative research methodologies — stats — without undermining their impact. The hope is that you will pause when encountering stats in the wild and challenge the ways in which "definitive" statements about social issues are framed.

The first section of this chapter introduces questions about methodological validity in quantitative method, which is a "test" of how well the questions asked align with what needs to be determined. The second section then explores who is being asked in this research, demonstrating how shortcomings in locating research participants can alter the results of quantitative research and its applications. Third, the chapter considers "big data" and offers critiques about the latent biases present in digitized approaches to research. The chapter concludes with a discussion of mixed-methods research, emphasizing the importance of multidimensional research when exploring and responding to social questions. The chapter uses a case-study approach to identify examples where systemic exclusion might occur and to develop critical thinking skills.

What's In a Question?

The odds are that you have, at some point or another, completed a survey. Surveys generally consist of a series of closed-ended questions designed to focus the respondents' answers in some sort of comparable manner. In *Survey*

Methodology, Groves et al. (2004: 2) define surveys as "a systematic method for gathering information from (a sample of) entities for the purpose of constructing quantita-

> Every time you complete a survey, you contribute toward datasets used by various stakeholders to produce knowledge about the public, or demography.

tive descriptors of the attributes of the larger population of which the entities are members." This approach to research has become a ubiquitous feature of society (Loosveldt and Joye 2016), accelerated by the social media–driven internet (Hays, Liu, and Kapteyn 2015). You have no doubt encountered quizzes posted by friends (trying to determine the colour of your aura or the celebrity you most resemble) or been asked to provide feedback to online companies to improve their services or rate your transactions with them.

You have also completed surveys when participating in social situations, such as getting your driver's licence or applying for a passport. In fact, you need not look any further than your initial registration with the post-secondary institution that you are currently attending. The administration likely asked you to provide basic information, such as your personal address and phone number, as well as demographic data about your age, immigration status, or gender. You might also have been asked to describe your personal sleep habits or respond to a series of hypothetical situations to assist with locating an appropriate roommate for your residence placement. Similarly, if you were a resident of Canada in 2016, you or someone in your household would have completed the Canadian census. Using Groves et al.'s (2004) definition, these systematic research tools are frequently used to collect demographic information about the population and its subsets. Every time you complete a survey, you contribute toward datasets used by various stakeholders to produce knowledge about the public, or demography (see Groves et al. 2004; O'Neil 2016; Prewitt 2018).

But is the **survey methodology** and the data that it produces as straightforward as it seems? Thinking again about your experience with surveys, what do you do when a question does not exactly apply to you, or does not provide answers that resonate with you? Perhaps you were asked to provide an opinion on something that did not matter to you. In that circumstance, would you choose the midpoint on the scale (for example, choosing 3 on a scale of 1 to 5)? What about instances where you were asked to choose between categories that overlap (for example, choosing between chocolate or cheese as your favourite dip). In circumstances where you are provided with only exclusive options, what do you do when you like both or neither? These concerns become ever more prescient when we begin to consider the infinitesimal variation of the human condition across broad populations — such as ranking one's level of mental health or defining one's sexuality.

Consider the ubiquitous **Likert-style scaling** often employed in surveys. First proposed by social psychologist Rensis Likert in 1932, this question design entails reading a proposition or series of statements paired with a ranking system that generally uses a scale of some sort (e.g., ranking your happiness on a scale of 1 to 5). This approach allows a degree of flexibility in responding to a question by providing participants with a range of options that reflect their feelings or interpretations. Likert-style questions also tend to be provided in a series rather than as standalone questions, and they are designed to provide a cumulative measure of the trait being tested (Norman 2010). Despite the flexibility, though, Likert-style surveys are still prone to underrepresenting the breadth of possible responses. Alwin and Krosnick (1991) point out that attitudinal measures such as this tend to be paired with ambiguous language and generalizations in order to account for as broad a range of responses as possible. Thus, a question might ask people to state how satisfied they are with a given product but not really clarify what the researchers mean by "somewhat satisfied" or "not satisfied at all."

Challenges such as this are often framed as issues of "validity," or the ability of research tools to effectively represent the attitudes and ideas that they are meant to measure. Jennifer L. Schulenberg (2016) identifies eight separate tests of validity: face validity, content validity, criterion validity, concurrent validity, predictive validity, construct validity, convergent validity, and discriminant validity. A brief synopsis of each concept is covered in Box 4-1. Each dimension of validity plays an important role in determining what interpretations, called "inferences," can be made from the resulting answers. An inherent limitation of the survey methodology therefore lies in the relative simplicity of its questions: the controlled scope of possible responses to a set of questions directly affects the depth of information collected. For example, a poll of fifty students about their final grades in a semester will give a great indication of their grade-point average (GPA), but it cannot easily quantify how the personal experiences of each individual affected their academic performance. Groves et al. (2004: 40) frame these as **inferential limitations**, relating to the "formal logic that permits description about unobserved phenomena based on observed phenomena." You could infer that students of a certain group (year of study, program of study, and so on) are doing well in their classes based on their grades, but little else.

Box 4-1: Dimensions of Validity

Face validity: a validity test in which a person's judgment validates a measure based on its appearance and appropriateness.

Content validity: a validity test in which a knowledgeable person's judgment validates a measure by concluding that it covers the range of the concept.

Criterion validity: a validity test that compares a measurement's scores to an external, established instrument or criterion.

Concurrent validity: a validity test that determines the extent to which the scores from one measure correspond to those of an existing measure.

Predictive validity: a validity test that examines the degree to which a measurement instrument can predict a future behaviour or event.

Construct validity: a validity test that finds the extent to which scores from multiple indicators are related to one another as predicted by theory.

Convergent validity: a validity test that assesses whether two measures associate in a manner consistent with theoretical predictions.

Discriminant validity: a validity test that determines whether two concepts differ from one another as predicted by theory.

Source: Schulenberg, J. L. 2016. The Dynamic of Criminological Research. Toronto: Oxford University Press, page 82.

Questionnaires that ignore the implications of inferential limitations run the risk of producing misleading or even harmful data that recreates mechanisms of social control for subject communities, rather than empowering these communities with evidentiary knowledge. This might stem from simple omissions, such as employing a binary gender question (e.g., male/female), or might venture into extreme and intentionally leading designs, such as push polls that employ affective wording intended to shape the opinion of the person taking the survey and to manipulate the data (for an example of a push poll, which is usually intended to demonize political opponents, see Box 4-2). Hodge and Gillespie (2003) point out that the unidirectional formatting of surveys, which often use a Likert-style design and ambiguous definitions, leads to confusing and often exclusive categories that fail to measure the continuum of social characteristics. This is of particular significance when considering two of the more important tests of validity — construct and content — and

> Questionnaires that ignore the implications of inferential limitations run the risk of producing misleading or even harmful data that recreates mechanisms of social control for subject communities, rather than empowering these communities with evidentiary knowledge.

Box 4-2: Affective Wording and Push Polls

What do you think?

☐ **I agree with my MP Lawrence Toet!**
We must take additional action to
protect Canada from terrorism.
☐ **I disagree!** Terrorists are victims too.

In March of 2015, the Honorable Lawrence Toet, legislative representative for the
Elmwood-Transcona riding near Winnipeg, Manitoba, came under public
scrutiny for a controversial mail-out. The flyer, which had been distributed to
addresses within his constituency by his office, took on the appearance of a
newsletter and provided highlights of the Conservative Party of Canada's
controversial Bill C-51. The flyer concluded with a brief poll that asked recipients
what they thought of the government's work, but the question was worded so
as to suggest people who disagreed with the content of C-51 would be
sympathetic to terrorists. This mail-out is an example of a "push poll," a
controversial political tactic that uses misleading language to pose questions
with only one reasonable answer, generally in line with the campaign promises
of the politician who circulated it (Saul 2012). This use of loaded questions —
ones that seem to have a pre-determined answer — is referred to as "affective
wording" in research circles and can also be called the *argumentum ad logicam*
philosophical fallacy.

---

their relationship to inferential limitation (Maxfield and Babbie 2014). The
omission of survey options, or the use of misleading and unclear language,
can lead to the exclusion of certain groups from representation in "official"
statistics presented by public bodies. Since these stats often inform policy
development, the omission of groups can translate into inadequate or even
detrimental laws and rules that control bodies and identities (Campbell 1984).
In 2010, Canadian researchers Akwasi Owusu-Bempah and Paul Millar
(2010: 99) explained how Correctional Service Canada's long-standing policy
of not collecting race-based data from incarcerated individuals was harming
justice policy, as the "paucity of official justice statistics" made it impossible to
identify and redress racial discrimination within the administration of justice.

Construct Validity

The first test of validity defines potential flaws in the apparatus, or "constructs,"
used to test the presence of an underlying, or latent, trait. A construct is a
series of questions that, when considered together, help to identify an individual's attitude, opinion, or traits. Imagine you wanted to identify students

with good study habits. You could ask them if they had good habits, but you would likely have a high proportion of students who claim they do regardless of their actual habits. A better approach would be to ask them a series of overlapping questions that are related to study habits, such as their use of mnemonic devices, the number of hours spent in a library, and their use of rewards. When considered together, these indicators form a construct that can help researchers quantify latent traits (in this case, study habits). **Construct validity** indicates how well the interrelated components actually reflect the desired outcome, and it can be jeopardized when researchers either use ineffective measures for the identified trait or develop constructs that identify poorly defined traits (Schriesheim et al. 1993). In some cases, the constructs employed by researchers are reflections of their personal predispositions toward a given subject, or they are a recreation of previous researchers' predispositions.

In what he called "value judgements," Max Weber (1949) studied opinion and emotion in empirical research. The presence of value judgments in constructs plays an important role for critical discussions of "race" in empirical studies. The "race question," a tool for categorizing an individual's physical characteristics based on arbitrarily defined features, is at best an ambiguous attempt to pin down socially constructed concepts (see Chapters 2 and 14). Brunsma and Rockquemore (2002) challenge the validity of race as a discursive or analytical unit, explaining that they have not been able to locate or define a universal nomenclature for races and their related characteristics; rather, they find that racial constructs are often employed in confounding ways. They observe:

> As sociologists, we consider concepts to be valid to the extent that the descriptions of empirical reality they express are correct. Applying this assumption to racial categorization begs the question: are the ways that we understand "black" reflective of empirical reality? The answer to that question often depends on one's politics, theoretical orientation, discipline, profession, position in the class structure, and/or one's race. Though various interest groups may justify the existence of particular self-serving definitions of what black means, membership in a collective body should not alter consensus on the validity of a concept. Furthermore, the continued use of invalid constructs in research, policy debates, and public discourse results in their reification, affecting the very experiences of the individuals and groups that the original construct has misrepresented. (103)

Durand et al. (2016) raised similar concerns in their review of the language and options for Indigenous self-identification in Canadian census questionnaires. Upon reviewing a number of comparable studies of Indigenous demographics, the authors conclude that identification boundaries are fuzzy and that individuals might fluidly choose between Indigenous or non-Indigenous labels based on a number of social, cultural, and methodological contexts. These points illustrate the challenges that questions raise regarding the validity of social concepts like race, demonstrating how "absolute" concepts and categories actually carry a great deal of variability.

Content Validity

Content validity refers to a question's ability to encapsulate existing academic knowledge about relevant concepts (Maxfield and Babbie 2014). Many sociological studies of human behaviour employ a range of measures designed to inquire about a given subject that are grounded in past research, representing the legacy of academic research that informed the approach. For instance, the social learning theory championed by Ronald Akers (1998) accounts for four domains of influence that may lead a person into deviant behaviours, which he calls differential association, differential reinforcement, definitions, and modelling. Each of these domains has specific questions or statements designed to assess its presence (or absence) in an individual's outlook. In many cases, these questions ask people to indicate, using a Likert-style scale, how much they agree with certain statements (e.g., "my friends encourage me to drink alcohol"). In the case provided previously, a question about friends encouraging alcohol consumption effectively measures peer pressure (an indicator of differential reinforcement) but doesn't really measure definitions (the idea that drinking alcohol is acceptable behaviour). Content validity is therefore a measure of the cumulative expert research on a subject, with the expectation that a question, or group of questions, aligns with successful methods established in previous study (Ayre and Scally 2014). Lawshe (1975) developed a measure of content validity that compares the total number of research experts or publications on a given concept with the total number of times that a specified research method occurs within them (see Formula 4-1). Therefore, the underlying theory of content validity is that good research replicates the successes of the past and discards the failures, creating an environment of continual improvement.

This assumption becomes increasingly difficult to ascertain with deeper consideration of the meaning of expertise. For instance, sociologist Pierre Bourdieu (1975: 22) examined academic knowledge production and found

Formula 4-1: Lawshe's (1975) *Content Validity Ratio (CVR)*

$$CVR = \frac{n_e - {}^{N}/_{2}}{{}^{N}/_{2}}$$

Where n_e is the number of experts who consider an item to be essential and N is the total number of experts.

that fields of study are subject to the "play of opposing forces in a struggle for scientific stakes," suggesting that "valid" concepts often achieve this status due to a researcher's prestige. He argues that "scientific authority" is a form of social capital rather than an objective measure of ability, and that it is accumulated when other researchers in a de facto state of competition with one another recognize each other's abilities. Bourdieu (1975) suggests that new and contradictory approaches will face enormous resistance through criticism and symbolic violence from those who stand to lose social capital when their work is discredited, and that leading ways of thinking in a given academic field rarely earn their position through purely objective means. By the same measure, his writing questions the logic of content validity, which relies on the assumption that conceptual measures are constructed through an iterative, objective process.

These limitations can be illustrated by examining a pair of case studies. The first deals with Charles A. Murray and Richard Herrnstein's 1994 book that connected measures of intelligence with socioeconomic status in the United States. Murray and Herrnstein argue that criminality relates to intelligence and demonstrate this point by connecting the depth of justice system experiences with the reported IQ level of young white men. Their textbook defines a "demography of intelligence" (341), but their discussion of crime is a case of inferential overreach based on false assumptions of content validity. The authors fail to control for the numerous external factors that affect one's contact with the justice system (e.g., the impact of neighbourhood on the frequency that one encounters the police) and disregard debates about socio-legal approaches to crime (e.g., assuming that encountering the justice system equates with criminality) (see Cullen et al. 1997; Gendreau, Little, and Goggin 1996; Rosoff, Pontell, and Tillman 2002). In this case, content validity was undermined by the false assumption that empirical measures of one's experiences with the justice system can be extrapolated to infer levels of criminality, contrary to the majority of criminological knowledge (Cullen et al. 1997) (see Box 4-3).

Box 4-3: The Bell Curve: Intelligence and Class Structure in American Life

An example of statistics being used beyond their inferential limitations extends from the controversial text *The Bell Curve: Intelligence and Class Structure in American Life*, written by Charles Murray and Richard Herrnstein in 1994. The book proposed that intelligence is a predictor for crime and social disorder, among other social ills, and the authors connected intelligence with ethnicity and particularly what they termed the "black-white divide" (Murray and Herrnstein 1994: 271). Their conclusions called for a radical transformation of society, including a suggestion that affirmative action policies — designed to ensure fair opportunities for job applicants regardless of racial or ethnic characteristics — should be abandoned as a fruitless and economically harmful practice. Notably, the IQ test has been long contested by social scientists as an accurate measure of intelligence, as it often tests concepts that require memorization rather than any sort of innate intellectual capacity (see Jeffery and Schakleford 2018). Moreover, arbitrary distinctions like "racial" characteristics are themselves fraught with controversy and often defined by controlling interests (explored in this chapter; see also Chapter 13 of this text). Murray and Herrnstein's work tested the boundaries of statistical inference, using controversial evidence as the foundations for arguments that could have had enormous social consequence. Indeed, Murray's earlier work on an arbitrarily defined group of individuals he called "the underclass" has often been employed as leveraging point in popular calls for welfare reform (Reese 2005).

The second example is a paper authored by a team of university researchers and health practitioners that challenges the meaning of "disability." Thomas-MacLean et al. (2009) interviewed forty breast cancer survivors who had undergone some form of mastectomy. Many of the survivors explained that they had experienced arm morbidity following their operations. To the authors' surprise, many of the participants recounted that their disability was overlooked by their doctors, who had assumed that being cancer-free meant being healthy. Thomas-MacLean et al. (2009) concluded that clinical definitions of disability need to be expanded to include the symptoms of cancer treatment — something that had not been considered in past research. In this case, Thomas-MacLean et al.'s (2009) work demonstrates how the cumulative knowledge in a given field is not necessarily exhaustive; rather, they point out that commonly accepted, narrow definitions inhibited deeper exploration of meaning. Content validity must account for the ways in which foundational knowledge is subject to the intentions, goals, or whims of those who first created it, as well as their ambitions to remain a leading scholar in their field.

Upon reading this section of the chapter, you should feel empowered to

question the breadth of information provided by statistical analysis
of issues, as the mode of data collection employed in quantitative
approaches does not allow for
detailed responses or background

> Content validity must account for the ways
> in which foundational knowledge is subject
> to the intentions, goals, or whims of those
> who first created it, as well as their ambitions
> to remain a leading scholar in their field.

considerations of a question. Moreover, you should also now feel more aware
of some of the basic limitations of connecting language to emotion and therefore be able to identify where constructs could go wrong. Finally, you should
also have a sense of the tenuous nature of expertise in scholarship and how
it relates to the content validity of a questionnaire.

Who's Being Asked?

Think about the last day of your first semester at a post-secondary institution.
After writing your final exam, you probably packed up a few essentials and
made your way home, where you waited for your final grades, an indication of
your achievements as a student. A higher average might affect your eligibility
for scholarships and bursaries, whereas a lower average can jeopardize your
status as a student and might even land you in dreaded academic probation.
It hardly seems fair that such major, life-changing decisions are based on just
a handful of grades. Even if you were to score an A (85 percent) in four out
of five classes, a single D- (50 percent) would drop your average down to 78
percent and boot you off of the dean's list!

In a second scenario, imagine that the university's administration decided
that they wanted to identify the priority areas for improving student life on
campus. The university administers a survey to fifty randomly selected students to accomplish this. The data tells the university that students would
prefer an expanded library collection over other options such as an on-campus
café or increased funding for social events. Regardless of your own thoughts
on expanded library collections, would you be happy with this process?
Considering that the average Canadian institution has nine thousand full-
time undergraduate students, do fifty students represent the interests of the
entire student body?

The examples provided previously are not intended to give you anxiety,
but rather to demonstrate another consideration about quantitative research:
important decisions about social issues are often made based on the answers
provided by relatively small groups of individuals. This process is known in
statistics as "sampling" and is founded on the rationalization that it would be

virtually impossible to poll everyone in a large group of people (a "population"). To address this problem, researchers will often administer their questionnaires to a random selection of individuals and use the resulting data from that **sample** to make inferences about the general population. This approach of selecting a "probability sample" means that all members of a population have at least some chance of being selected to participate in the research project. Additionally, more than three centuries of statistical exploration have established that, as sample size reaches an adequately large threshold, the responses coming from the sample of people have a high likelihood of closely resembling the responses of the population (Field 2016).

Systemic Failures in Sampling

Probabilistic applications of statistics therefore rely on an assumption of universal opportunity — that is, that everyone will have a chance to answer the same questions. However, in many cases, the methods to locate and contact would-be survey respondents are flawed based on the manner in which the survey is administered. This is known as **sampling bias**. One way that sampling bias might emerge is by taking inadequate measures to locate participants. Groves et al. (2004: 94) call this "systemic failure," explaining that "if some persons in the sampling frame have a zero chance of selection and they have different characteristics on the survey variable, then all samples selected with that design can produce estimates that are too high or too low." To illustrate, imagine that the university administration described previously decided to poll their sample of participants by randomly calling dormitory rooms. We know that many university students do not actually live on campus, so the off-campus students would have zero chance of providing feedback about improving campus life. In this case, any policy decisions resulting from this survey will be likely to misrepresent the opinions of non-residential students at the university as their opinions would not be included in the data.

One of the most infamous cases of systematic failure occurred during the 1936 US election. The election pitted the incumbent, Democrat Franklin D. Roosevelt, against Republican Alfred M. Landon. Held in the midst of the Great Depression, the thirty-eighth election occurred during a time of enormous social upheaval and a central point of debate was social security (Fadely 1989). To predict the outcome of the election, the editors at the influential magazine the *Literary Digest* mailed out ten million ballots to potential respondents drawn from automobile registration lists and telephone books; more than two million people sent in their responses (Freedman, Pisani, and

Purves 1998). After analysis, the results were clear-cut: the *Literary Digest* predicted that Landon would receive 55 percent of the popular vote compared to 41 percent for Roosevelt, declaring a landslide victory for the Republicans. In reality, President Roosevelt was re-elected with 61 percent of the popular vote. George Gallup also ran a poll with a sample of fifty thousand people, and he more accurately predicted 66 percent of the vote in favour of the incumbent (Freedman, Pisani, and Purves 1998). Peverill Squire's (1988) analysis of the *Digest's* poll suggests, first, that the initial sample was biased because many people in the 1930s did not have a car, telephone, or subscribe to an expensive magazine and second, the overall response rate was poor, leading to a phenomenon called "nonresponse bias," in which assumptions were made about the opinions of those who chose not to return their surveys.

Haphazard Sampling

A second, more common concern about sampling is that researchers in many cases employ "haphazard sampling" techniques that intentionally employ non-random sampling strategies. This is cause for significant debate in many academic circles as the representativeness of so-called non-probability sampling can be questionable (Sousa, Zauszniewski, and Musil 2004; Popham 2011; Griffin et al. 2015). Researchers, often pressed for time and finances, may employ targeted recruitment techniques to quickly locate a large sample of participants. Two commonly encountered non-probability tactics are the use of "convenience" and "purposive" samples. The first process entails collecting responses from a group of people who are readily available to the researcher, such as an undergraduate class or patrons at a shopping centre (Groves et al. 2004). The second approach entails a more rigorous method of recruitment that specifically seeks out individuals who represent a specific group within the population, such as religious faiths or age groups. These methods provide reliable data (Griffin et al. 2015), but remaining inconsistencies adversely affect conclusions (Young 2011; Widaman, Early, and Conger 2013). These methods are also prone to inferential limitations as they tend to seek out motivated respondents. As Sousa, Zauszniewski, and Musil (2004: 130) suggest, "because convenience samples use voluntary participation, this fact increases the probability of researchers to recruit those individuals who feel strongly about the issue in question and may favor certain outcomes."

Thirty years ago, David O. Sears (1986), concerned with psychological research relying on responses from undergraduate students tested in academic labs, wrote a lasting critique of the use of non-probability samples. He was concerned that psychological research conducted in academic settings from the 1960s onward had become increasingly dependent on responses provided by a "narrow methodological base" (516), namely undergraduate students tested in academic labs. Sears (1986: 520) felt that academic research designed to infer behavioural traits upon the general population using observations of undergraduate psychology students failed: "the absence of research on the general population in natural situations can leave the experimental social psychologist ignorant of the actuarial mainstream, unaware of what the critical sources of variation are, or are not, in 'natural' social processes."

Sears's (1986) work developed an important and rarely considered intro-spective critique of research methods. Widaman, Early, and Conger (2013: 59) revisited this work to develop "special populations" research, referring to empirically distinct subgroups of a heterogeneous population. They point out that the most common reference groups (the sample that forms academic knowledge about a given subject) are limited to those who volunteer answers and are inordinately made up of young, white, male, educated participants. Widaman, Early, and Conger (2013) demonstrate that presumptive meth-odological approaches to quantitative research tend to obfuscate the nuances of alternative viewpoints coming from already marginalized populations:

> If we disregarded the presence of special populations, then we might develop a corpus of scientific findings that applies to "the" population — whatever that is — but in actuality applies to very few individuals or, at least, fails to apply to members of important special popula-tions. (76–77)

In *The Criminological Imagination*, criminologist Jock Young (2011) recounts a critique by Harvard professor of zoology John Lewontin, who was responding to a pair of textbooks that claimed to be "definitive surveys" (Young 2011: 25) on sexuality in the United States. These texts, authored by a team of sociologists from leading US institutions, used a sample of 3,432 individuals to make a series of observations about sexual practices in the United States. Citing Lewontin (1995), Young (2011) points out that this survey was rife with systemic and sampling failures. For example, this relatively small sample did not include non-English speakers, people who were outside of ages 15–59, or those who were homeless/institutionalized. The researchers had a response rate of approximately 79 percent, meaning that almost a quarter of all of the people who received the survey chose not to respond. Young (2011) explains that an unexplored causal factor may have influenced this specific group of individuals to not respond, making these missing respondents more than likely a non-probability sample of the sample. Young (2011) calls into question the representativeness of the survey based on these shortcomings, pointing out that those who are most likely to be affected by harms related to sexuality were the most likely to be omitted from this survey (for more information, see Poteat, Malik, and Beyrer 2018).

This raises an important point about the role of empirical research in social control, particularly when addressing sensitive issues like sexuality. The report was set against the looming HIV/AIDS crisis of the 1980s and was initially designed to inspire sexual health–related policies. Given the lack of response, what conclusions might have been erroneously drawn about safe sex in the United States? Perhaps, as Young (2011) infers, those who are most affected by unsafe sexual practices were among those who chose not to respond to a government-funded survey requesting highly personal information. Mechanical functions behind the production of objective-seeming knowledge might themselves be subject to the whims of the researcher and respondents. Researchers often use a sample of people to make determinations about a larger population. The probability assumption relies on the difficult-to-attain principle of non-zero chance; in many cases academic research with practical barriers will omit probability, and these approaches can further omit important perspectives. Armed with this knowledge, you should be able to critically assess everyday presentations of statistical "knowledge" and consider how these limitations might have affected it.

"Big Data" Analytics and Their Challenges

Big data refers to the collection and analysis of personal information produced during our interactions with modern technologies, ranging from social media likes to credit card purchases to health records. This technologically driven approach to interpreting human behaviour uses algorithms to identify patterns in our interactions and link seemingly disparate actions together. Big data is often touted as the answer to many of the methodological challenges described in this chapter. Specifically, big data analytics operate under the assumption that personal traits, behaviours, and opinions can be estimated through observation of everyday interactions without direct intervention by researchers. The big data response to construct validity, for instance, is that constructs no longer exist; rather, machine-learning processes identify dynamic constructs and can include or exclude variables based on an infinite set of possible individual characteristics that are reflective of temporal, spatial, and environmental conditions (O'Neil 2016). Similarly, the issues of sampling are eliminated because the reach of data collection tools simplifies exhaustive access to entire populations (Mayer-Schönberger and Cukier 2013); in fact, big data analysts must often work to pare down their sample size in order to simplify statistical computations (Wu et al. 2014). In essence, big data allegedly takes the researcher out of the research equation.

This new approach to research is dependent on modern technologies and people's dependence on devices and programs (see Chapter 15). As we go through our day-to-day interactions online and in person, we leave a trail of breadcrumbs (and the occasional cookie) that are collected and stored in digital repositories. These might include your search history, online shopping wish lists, or even the speed you were travelling while using a mapping application. These big datasets are able to pair a number of our personal details with our consumer characteristics by connecting various pieces of information collected through different services. Consider your social media use. On any given day you might share your location, your meals, and even your feelings with your social network. You might also click on articles or news items that appear in your various social media feeds, and even on the occasional advertisement. Embedded functions within these services record every action that you take while on their websites and will often extend to your actions beyond the website, such as the next website you visit or the type of browser you use (Elish and Boyd 2018). When paired with high-powered computing technologies, this information can inform profiles about you as well as people with similar characteristics.

Data collected from users, such as you, have been routinely aggregated and used under many circumstances since the dawn of social media and the rise of the interactive "internet of things." One of the most burgeoning facets to big data analytics has been the move to the "smart city" (alternatively called the real-time city) (Kitchin 2014), in which municipalities analyze service-use statistics to improve the delivery of services on demand. For example, the City of Chicago launched an online service called "Plow Tracker" (Townsend 2013: 149), which allowed citizens to look up the location of snowplows to gauge the state of the city's roads during snowstorms. In addition to appeasing concerns about the progress of these services, the website also included a tool that sent volunteer snow clearers — the "snow corps" (Townsend 2013: 149) — to the homes of snowbound senior citizens who might not otherwise be able to clear the snow from their walkways.

Latent Biases

Despite beneficial appearances, researchers like Cathy O'Neil (2016) have raised concerns about the way big data is collected and, more importantly, how it might exclude marginalized populations. In *Weapons of Math Destruction* (2016), O'Neil warned that big data analytics could accelerate inequality rather than ameliorate it. Specifically, she writes that analytic tools are often protected as the intellectual property of their creators and therefore the underlying processes that inform decisions remain opaque or hidden from review. The underlying computational models are prone to reflecting the inherent biases of their creators, intentionally held or not (O'Neil 2016). For instance, a programmer leading the development of an analytical framework might only think about gender as a binary, excluding nonbinary people from analysis (Puschmann and Burgess 2014). O'Neil (2016) also points to the risk of creating pernicious feedback loops in analytic processes, whereby the data created by analytical procedures are recycled as an input, or indicator, of the social problem being addressed.

O'Neil uses the example of a predictive policing software suite called PredPol, used by police services to identify "hot spots" for certain crimes (Mohler et al. 2015). She suggests that relatively minor infractions (vagrancy or panhandling) included in PredPol can overrepresent the crime rate in an area. She observes that:

> These nuisance crimes are endemic to many impoverished neighbourhoods. In some places police call them antisocial behavior, or ASB. Unfortunately, including them in the model threatens to skew the analysis. Once the nuisance data flows into a predictive model, more police are drawn into those neighbourhoods, where they're more likely to arrest more people.... These types of low-level crimes populate their models with more and more dots, and the models send the cops back to the same neighbourhood. (O'Neil 2016: 86–87)

As O'Neil explains, these overrepresentations tend to disproportionately affect already marginalized populations through tautological measures of criminality. She argues that the people designing big data analytic processes tend to recreate biased frames of judgment within their models. Designers are not intentionally targeting certain individuals or

> The underlying computational models are prone to reflecting the inherent biases of their creators, intentionally held or not.

groups, but the processes themselves reflect long-standing systemic barriers against marginalized populations (see Sherman, Gartin, and Buerger 1989). Targeting certain communities and people predates digital innovations, and the justifications for targeted policing have therefore carried over into new technologies. O'Neil's (2016) concern here is that blind faith in the power of machine learning will dissuade critical discussion and encourage the legitimization of biases, jeopardizing construct and content validity.

Representativeness

Despite collecting aggregate and universal data, big data remains subject to sampling limitations. Access to the internet comes at significant financial cost through service provider contracts. Similarly, mobile internet via cell networks requires expensive devices (as well as the ability to charge them). These costs put access to technology out of reach for many people in North America (Gonzales 2016), which excludes them from data collection processes. Longo et al. (2017) call this form of dual marginalization "**digital invisibility**," arguing that it can affect the accuracy of big data and subsequent policy decisions. To demonstrate this impact, the researchers recorded the temperatures experienced by homeless individuals in Phoenix, Arizona, during a hot summer day and juxtaposed them with a comparison group of university students. Longo et al. (2017) found that the homeless participants encountered greater fluctuation in temperatures and also had a higher likelihood of experiencing heat stress. The researchers explain that the digital divide experienced by homeless individuals means that, despite being a high-risk population for heat-related illness and death, their locations and experiences with dangerous ambient temperatures are far less likely to be recorded in health-related datasets. This omission has a cascading effect on policy development, raising the spectre of systemic failure in sample development (Kitchin 2014).

Big data analytics are a modern variation of largely unchanged institutional processes and therefore subject to many of the same methodological limitations (Wall 1999). Longo et al. (2017) explain that these limits are often masked by the presumptive objectivity espoused by positivistic approaches to problem solving and writing:

> This new enthusiasm for ubiquitous data and policy analytics rests on the widespread belief that large data sets offer a higher form of intelligence, revealing objective and accurate truth. However, if this movement fails to acknowledge some of the limitations of new forms

of data collection and analytics, the core critiques of post-positivism will go unanswered. (83)

As outlined in O'Neil's explanation, failure to critique big data analytic methods runs the risk of empowering nefarious applications of the technology, whether by intention or not. This point is of particular relevance, as at the time of writing this chapter, the data analytic firm Cambridge Analytica is under extreme scrutiny for its access to and mishandling of data collected through the Facebook social media platform (see Cadwalladr and Graham-Harrison 2018; Confessore 2018; Elish and Boyd 2018). While this section has only provided a cursory overview of the panacea of analytics, you should once again have formulated some important questions about how these data are collected and from whom.

Reconciling Statistics with Unheard Voices

Despite the pitfalls, statistical knowledge paired with opportunities to share the experiences of marginalized communities can be a powerful tool for overcoming systemic mechanisms of exclusion. Well-designed statistical methods can develop a top-down perspective on populations and trends (van de Sande and Byvelds 2015) and can present compelling demography (such as differences in income among population groups), provide context on social questions through longitudinal analysis (such as year-over-year changes to the crime rate), and reveal public opinions (van de Sande and Byvelds 2015; Field 2016). More complex quantitative methodologies can also produce insightful knowledge about correlations between two or multiple variables, such as the relationship between gender and annual income or level of education and affinity for cats (Field 2016).

That said, statistical research is less effective at providing contextual knowledge about individual-level decisions or opinions. This is an inherent facet of survey research; at its core, this methodology is designed to elicit comparable responses (Schulenberg 2016) and so requires that absolute limits be placed on the types of answers people give. As discussed previously, quantitative researchers will often develop constructs to help identify latent traits in individuals, but these approaches are nonetheless vested in producing knowledge through volume. Other approaches to research can help to fill in these epistemological gaps by providing greater context at the cost of sample size. Consider Figure 4-1. Each of these images provides you with some level of knowledge about Yellowknife, Northwest Territories. The map of Canada situates Yellowknife within the enormous expanse of the North. You can use it to determine Yellowknife's location relative to other provincial and territorial capitals, as well as the US border, and other features of Canada. The second image provides a street map of the city, from which you might infer how closely people live together in Yellowknife, the number of city parks, and other municipal details. This increased level of detail comes at the cost of the contextual information gleaned from the first image. Finally, the third image is a street-level photograph of Yellowknife. You can infer much more knowledge about this specific location, such as the prevalence of certain foliage or the preferred colour for houses on the street, but in doing so you sacrifice the detail at the two other levels discussed.

Mixed-Methods Research

The three images of Figure 4-1 encapsulate the value of mixed-methods research for questions of exclusion and resistance. **Mixed-methods research**

Figure 4-1: Three Images about Yellowknife, NWT

Source: E Pluribus Anthony, transferred to Wikimedia Commons by Kaveh (log), optimized by Andrew pmk. <commons.wikimedia.org/wiki/File:Political_map_of_Canada.png>, Political map of Canada, marked as public domain.

Source: Trevor MacInnis <commons.wikimedia.org/wiki/File:Downtown_Yellowknife_2.jpg>,
"Downtown Yellowknife 2", marked as public domain.

entails combining the deeply personal information collected through qualitative research (e.g., interviews, focus groups, document analysis) with the
inferential capacities of quantitative research. As Schulenberg (2016) points
out, the level of integration between these two methods ranges from study to
study, making a concrete definition hard to pin down. Still, a significant body of

literature has demonstrated the benefit of incorporating multiple methods of inquiry into research projects (Johnson, Onwuegbuzie, and Turner 2007), and these advances have affected the way that policy is designed and administered:

> The subsequent post-positivist movement led to calls for a balancing of softer skills along with technical mastery, and approaches such as participatory design, stakeholder involvement, citizens' input, qualitative methods, and mixed methodology, among others, were advanced.… Based on this revised appreciation of the actual work of the policy analyst, policy analysis skills came to include case study methods, interviewing and qualitative data analysis, organizational culture analysis, political feasibility analysis, stakeholder engagement, and small-group facilitation. (Longo et al. 2017: 81)

You might think about mixed-methods research as a sort of wiki (a user-built website) for a TV series. On the main page, you will find a listing of all of the episodes, air dates, viewership, participating actors, and other pertinent information. Wikis also provide links to greater depth about many of the concepts on the main page, so if you click on one of the episodes you might be directed to a synopsis of the plot of that specific episode. Figure 4-2 provides an illustrative example using a table of the first season of the hit series *Game of Thrones*. The table provides a summary of key information points about the program, such as average viewership, and if you were to click on any one episode title, you would find additional background information and detail about it. Recalling Longo et al.'s (2017) quote above, the basic information about the series would be primarily positivistic knowledge, while the episode details would be the product of the so-called softer skills.

The illustrative power of qualitative research used in conjunction with quantitative methods cannot be overemphasized. A study by Findlay, Popham, and Ince (2013) was designed to understand training programs for women incarcerated at a federal prison in Saskatchewan. At the outset, the researchers' demographics statistics about the women indicated that the population was primarily Indigenous single mothers. The researchers were able to find information about skills training programs in the institution, including the number and type of programs delivered, their schedules, and the total number of service hours provided, as well as the number of participants who enrolled. In program evaluation research, these facets are often referred to as the "inputs" and "outputs" used to inform the "outcomes" of a project (Vito and Higgins 2015). Had they used a strictly quantitative approach, Findlay, Popham, and

Figure 4-2: Table of *Game of Thrones* Episodes

No. overall	No. in season	Title	Original air date	US viewers (millions)
1	1	"Winter Is Coming"	April 17, 2011	2.22
2	2	"The Kingsroad"	April 24, 2011	2.20
3	3	"Lord Snow"	May 1, 2011	2.44
4	4	"Cripples, Bastards, and Broken Things"	May 8, 2011	2.45
5	5	"The Wolf and the Lion"	May 15, 2011	2.58
6	6	"A Golden Crown"	May 22, 2011	2.44[
7	7	"You Win or You Die"	May 29, 2011	2.40
8	8	"The Pointy End"	June 5, 2011	2.72
9	9	"Baelor"	June 12, 2011	2.66
10	10	"Fire and Blood"	June 19, 2011	3.04

Ince (2013) could have concluded that Correctional Service Canada's "works programs" were attaining their objectives because the inputs, outputs, and outcomes had all been statistically fulfilled. However, the study also incorporated a semi-structured interview component that invited incarcerated women to share their experiences with in-house programming, ranging from general complaints about mistreatment and cultural accommodation to more introspective concerns about their own capacity to return to their families based on the programs that they had received. See Box 4-4 for an example of the statements from one of the participants of this study.

A second important facet of mixed-methods research is the opportunity for discovery. As Schulenberg (2016) notes, mixed-methods research will occasionally employ a "top-down" (inductive) approach to research, meaning that researchers will first engage with and interview participants before determining their research questions. This approach is particularly effective in participatory action research activities, as it allows participating communities to incorporate their concerns into the study before investigations begin (Lingard, Albert, and Levinson 2008). The researchers can "discover" key areas of inquiry that might not have otherwise been acknowledged following more traditional "bottom-up" (deductive) approaches to research (van de Sande and Schwartz 2011). Westhues et al. (2008) provide an interesting case study for this approach. Their research team was tasked with improving mental health service delivery to various diasporas in southern Ontario, accounting for cultural sensitivities. The researchers opted to avoid addressing

> **Box 4-4: Statement of an Unnamed Woman Incarcerated at a Federal Institution**
>
> I was just getting up; I was feeling good about myself. I was having a good day because that morning they asked me if I could wash the kitchen walls because we had all of the tables moved because of that smell. We moved into the day room to eat and stuff, but that morning, the staff Sherry asked me nicely to pay me five bucks just to wash the walls and sweep, so I did that and I felt good about it because I went to the boss there and I said, "Oh, how is this now? I washed the walls, I did it all that you guys asked," and she says, "Oh, that's good enough. Yeah, you did lots, thank you," and I felt good. I was feeling good about what I did, and then the shift change is going on and another staff came on shift and now she says to me, and that wasn't a joke because she would have laughed and giggled about it if it was a joke, but she didn't. She just said, "Oh, you're always stinking up this place," or like that. And honestly, she just put my self-esteem right down. Like I was feeling really, really good that day and then the way I went after, the way I felt, my anger in me built up and built up and I just had to go walk it off. I was just saying prayers in my head to help me cope, to help me take the anger out of me because I just wanted to just lash out at this woman, but I stayed calm and I just went for a walk and talked to one of my friends.

this question with preloaded theories by first interviewing key informants from various cultural communities. Through these conversations, the team learned that the respondents saw the mental health system as replete with Eurocentric, neocolonial perspectives on healing that often conflicted with the cultural beliefs of non-English service users. This revelation then informed additional layers of data collection, including a service provider survey that incorporated questions relating to institutional cultures and their potential impact on service recipients (Westhues et al. 2008). The case study previously outlined confers the importance of reflexivity in one's approach to research: we must always be prepared to acknowledge how our own biases can form barriers to the emancipatory power of empirical knowledge (Saldaña 2015).

The spectrum of research design beyond purely quantitative surveys is virtually endless. You should understand the ways in which human experiences might be introduced through empirical methods, including but not limited to quantitative methodologies. The wiki example showed that each bit of information collected about an individual or group carries a significant amount of underlying meaning.

Conclusion

Let's return to our earlier discussion of the house hippo. No matter how hard you wish, you will never see a miniature hippopotamus fending off your pet in real life; however, with enough effort and Hollywood glitz you might be persuaded of the possibility. This same holds for the misuse of quantitative methodology: compelling presentations of statistics, without critical assessment, can and have been used to mislead the public.

Throughout this chapter, we explored some of the important critical questions in statistical knowledge. We started off with a discussion about validity and focused on the concepts of content and construct validity, both of which underscore the importance of asking good questions to produce good data. While multiple other forms could be considered (for example, Schulenburg [2016] identifies eight dimensions of validity), the two that we focused on are particularly important tests for the accuracy, or veracity, of the questions that researchers might ask. In other words, if a researcher fails to ensure that their questions agree with existing knowledge about a subject, or fails to actually test what they are intended to test, then the resulting data could provide misleading answers about their research question.

We also considered who is being asked. While it is virtually impossible to ask a question to every single person in a population, we know that statisticians using mathematical proofs have established that a random sampling of individuals within a frame can provide an accurate sample of answers. However, the sampling approach can be prone to systemic failure if it does not locate the sample appropriately. Non-probability samples can also have detrimental effects on the applications of statistics. You will recall the critique of Donald Trump's tweet about international terrorism charges at the beginning of the chapter. Statistics should be held to rigorous standards when they are used to represent the interests or actions of any group of people.

Third, we examined some of the barriers that might affect the reliability of statistics drawn from big data and algorithmic computing. Computers remain fickle machines that are unable to critically examine their instructions, and they are therefore subject to the inherent flaws of their programmers. As was demonstrated in this chapter, many critics have pointed out where gaps exist between what ought to be included versus what actually is. While this exciting new approach holds promise, its validity and representativeness must be critically assessed in much the same framework as more traditional approaches to quantitative research.

Finally, the last section introduced the value of incorporating qualitative research into emancipatory research as a mechanism to empower the marginalized voices that are otherwise omitted in traditional quantitative methods. Specifically, it demonstrated how taken-for-granted knowledge might be turned upside down when additional interpretive layers are added. While qualitative research is also subject to its own limitations (see Brinkmann 2013; Saldaña 2015; van de Sande and Schwartz 2011), it introduces multidimensional ways of framing observation. In so doing, it empowers empirical tools for resisting exclusion.

Discussion Questions

1. Find an example of statistics in the media. How might your example mislead the public?
2. What considerations should you make about validity when creating a questionnaire about race and crime?
3. How could the *Literary Digest* have improved its polling for the thirty-eighth presidential election?
4. Create a scenario where haphazard sampling is used. What considerations should be made in sampling? How can this knowledge affect public narratives?
5. Should big data analytics and machine learning be used to shape public policy? Why or why not?

Recommended Resources

Vigen, T. 2015. *Spurious Correlations*. New York: Hachette Books.
Huff, D. 1993. *How to Lie with Statistics*. New York: W.W. Norton & Company.
O'Neil, C. 2016. *Weapons of Math Destruction*. New York: Crown.

Glossary

big data: catch-all phrase that describes the enormity of personal information collected through automated, digital processes.
construct validity: a measure of how well a series of questions can be used to make inferences about a given topic.
content validity: a measure of how well a series of questions represents the concept they are designed to test.
digital invisibility: certain segments of the population, generally dictated along socioeconomic stratum, may be omitted from big data analytics due

to their diminished level of access to the technologies that collect said data.

inferential limitation: the extent to which numerically derived statistics can be used to make inferences on a broader population. Generally limited by the size and nature of the sample.

Likert-style scaling: a style of question that asks respondents to provide feedback using a ranking system, such as 1 to 5 or 1 to 10.

mixed-methods research: an approach to research that dovetails the strengths of qualitative and quantitative information gathering. There is no fixed procedure to mixed methods; some studies are more quantitative while others are more qualitative.

sample: a smaller segment of the population whose answers to a survey can be used to represent larger groups of people.

sampling bias: a critique of statistical research based on how well a sample actually depicts the population that it's meant to represent.

standardizing: using mathematic and statistic principles to make two disparate concepts comparable, such as the rate of crime per 100,000 residents in a city.

survey (survey methodology): collecting information about human behaviours using a series of closed-ended questions.

References

Akers, R. 1998. *Social Learning and Social Structure: A General Theory of Crime and Deviance*. Boston: Northeastern University Press.

Allen, M. 2016. "Police-Reported Crime Statistics in Canada, 2015." *Juristat: Canadian Centre for Justice Statistics* 1.

Alwin, D.F., and J.A. Krosnick. 1991. "The Reliability of Survey Attitude Measurement: The Influence of Question and Respondent Attributes." *Sociological Methods and Research* 20, 1.

Ayre, C., and A.J. Scally. 2014. "Critical Values for Lawshe's Content Validity Ratio: Revisiting the Original Methods of Calculation." *Measurement and Evaluation in Counseling and Development* 47, 1.

Bourdieu, P. 1975. "The Specificity of the Scientific Field and the Social Conditions of the Progress of Reason." *Information (International Social Science Council)* 14, 6.

Brinkmann, S. 2013. *Qualitative Interviewing*. London: Oxford University Press.

Brunsma, D.L., and K.A. Rockquemore. 2002. "What Does 'Black' Mean? Exploring the Epistemological Stranglehold of Racial Categorization." *Critical Sociology* 28, 1–2.

Cadwalladr, C., and E. Graham-Harrison. 2018. "Revealed: 50 Million Facebook Profile Harvested for Cambridge Analytica in Major Data Breach." *Guardian*, March 17. <theguardian.com/news/2018/mar/17/cambridge-analytica-facebook-influence-us-election>.

Campbell, T.J. 1984. "Regression Analysis in Title VII Cases: Minimum Standards, Comparable Worth, and Other Issues Where Law and Statistics Meet." *Stanford*

Law Review.

Concerned Children's Advertisers. 1999. "The Hidden World of the House Hippo" [Television commercial]. <youtube.com/watch?v=TijcoS8qHIE>.

Confessore, N. 2018. "Cambridge Analytica and Facebook: The Scandal and the Fallout So Far." *New York Times*, April 4. <nytimes.com/2018/04/04/us/politics/cambridge-analytica-scandal-fallout.html>.

Cullen, F.T., P. Gendreau, G.R. Jarjoura, and J.P. Wright. 1997. "Crime and the Bell Curve: Lessons from Intelligent Criminology." *Crime and Delinquency* 43, 4.

De Luca, M., R. Horovitz, B. Pitt (Producers), and B. Miller (Director). 2011. *Moneyball* [motion picture]. Culver City: Columbia Pictures.

Durand, C., Y.E. Massé-François, M. Smith, and L.P.P. Ibarra. 2016. "Who Is Aboriginal? Variability in Aboriginal Identification between the Census and the APS in 2006 and 2012." *Aboriginal Policy Studies* 6, 1.

Elish, M.C., and D. Boyd. 2018. "Situating Methods in the Magic of Big Data and AI." *Communication Monographs* 85, 1.

Executive Order No. 13780, 3 C.F.R. 1-11 (2018). Washington, DC: Department of Homeland Security.

Fadely, J.P. 1989. "Editors, Whistle Stops, and Elephants: The Presidential Campaign of 1936 in Indiana." *Indiana Magazine of History.*

Federal Bureau of Investigation (US). 2020. "Crime Data Explorer" <crime-data-explorer.fr.cloud.gov/>.

Field, A. 2016. *An Adventure in Statistics: The Reality Enigma.* Thousand Oaks: Sage Publications.

Findlay, I., J. Popham, and P. Ince. 2013. *Through the Eyes of Women: What a Co-Operative Can Mean in Supporting Women During Confinement and Integration.* Saskatoon: Centre for the Study of Co-operatives, University of Saskatchewan.

Freedman, D., R. Pisani, and R. Purves. 1998. *Statistics.* New York: Norton and Company.

Fullerton, M. 2017. "Trump, Turmoil, and Terrorism: The US Immigration and refugee Ban." *International Journal of Refugee Law* 29, 2.

Gendreau, P., T. Little, and C. Goggin. 1996. "A Meta☒Analysis of the Predictors of Adult Offender Recidivism: What Works!" *Criminology* 34, 4.

Gonzales, A. 2016. "The Contemporary US Digital Divide: From Initial Access to Technology Maintenance." *Information, Communication and Society* 19, 2.

Griffin, J., T. Abdel-Monem, A. Tomkins, A. Richardson, and S. Jorgensen. 2015. "Understanding Participant Representativeness in Deliberative Events: A Case Study Comparing Probability and Non-Probability Recruitment Strategies." *Journal of Public Deliberation* 11, 1.

Groves, R., F. Fowler Jr., M. Couper, J. Lekowski et al. 2004. *Survey Methodology.* New York: John Wiley and Sons.

Hays, R.D., H. Liu, and A. Kapteyn. 2015. "Use of Internet Panels to Conduct Surveys." *Behavior Research Methods* 47, 3.

Hodge, D.R. and D. Gillespie. 2003. "Phrase completions: An alternative to Likert scales." *Social Work Research* 27, 1.

Huff, D. 1993. *How to Lie with Statistics.* New York: W.W. Norton & Company.

Jeffery, A.J., and T.K. Shackelford. 2018. "Moral Positions on Publishing Race Differences in Intelligence." *Journal of Criminal Justice*, 59.

Johnson, R.B., A.J. Onwuegbuzie, and L.A. Turner. 2007. "Toward a Definition of Mixed Methods Research." *Journal of Mixed Methods Research* 1, 2.

Kitchin, R. 2014. "Big Data, New Epistemologies and Paradigm Shifts." *Big Data and Society*, 1, 1.

Lawshe, C.H. 1975. "A Quantitative Approach to Content Validity." *Personnel Psychology* 28, 4.

Lewontin, R.C. 1995. "Sex, Lies, and Social Science." *New York Review of Books* 42, 7.

Likert, R. 1932. "A Technique for the Measurement of Attitudes." *Archives of Psychology* 22.

Lingard, L., M. Albert, and W. Levinson. 2008. "Grounded Theory, Mixed Methods, and Action Research." *BMJ* 337.

Longo, J., E. Kuras, H. Smith, D.M. Hondula, and E. Johnston. 2017. "Technology Use, Exposure to Natural Hazards, and Being Digitally Invisible: Implications for Policy Analytics." *Policy and Internet* 9, 1.

Loosveldt, G., and D. Joye. 2016. "Defining and Assessing Survey Climate." In C. Wolf, D. Joye, T. Smith, and Y. Fu (eds.), *The SAGE Handbook of Survey Methodology*. Thousand Oaks: Sage Publishing.

Maxfield, M.G., and E.R. Babbie. 2014. *Research Methods for Criminal Justice and Criminology*. Toronto: Nelson Education.

Mayer-Schonberger, V., and K. Cukier. 2013. *Big Data: A Revolution That Will Transform How We Live, Work, and Think — A Review*. New York: Houghton Mifflin Harcourt.

McLuhan, M. 1964. *Understanding Media: The Extensions of Man, 2nd edition*. New York: New American Library.

Mohler, G.O., M.B. Short, S. Malinowski, M. Johnson et al. 2015. "Randomized Controlled Field Trials of Predictive Policing." *Journal of the American Statistical Association* 110, 512.

Murray, C., and R. Herrnstein. 1994. *The Bell Curve: Intelligence and Class Structure in American Life*. New York: Free Press.

Muto, S. 2004. "Children and Media." *Young Consumers* 6, 1.

Norman, G. 2010. "Likert Scales, Levels of Measurement and the 'Laws' of Statistics." *Advances in Health Sciences Education*, 15, 5.

O'Neil, C. 2016. *Weapons of Math Destruction: How Big Data Increases Inequality and Threatens Democracy*. New York: Broadway Books.

Owusu-Bempah, A., and P. Millar. 2010. "Research Note: Revisiting the Collection of 'Justice Statistics by Race' in Canada." *Canadian Journal of Law & Society/La Revue Canadienne Droit et Société* 25, 1.

Popham, J. 2011. "Factors Influencing Music Piracy." *Criminal Justice Studies* 24, 2.

Poteat, T.C., M. Malik, and C. Beyrer. 2018. "Epidemiology of HIV, Sexually Transmitted Infections, Viral Hepatitis, and Tuberculosis Among Incarcerated Transgender People: A Case of Limited Data." *Epidemiologic Reviews* 40, 1.

Prewitt, K. 2018. "The Census Race Classification: Is It Doing Its Job?" *The Annals of the American Academy* 677.

Puschmann, C., and J. Burgess. 2014. "Big Data, Big Questions — Metaphors of Big Data." *International Journal of Communication* 8, 20.

Reese, E. 2005. *Backlash against Welfare Mothers: Past and Present*. Los Angeles: UC Press.

Rosoff, S.M., H.N. Pontell, and R. Tillman. 2002. *Profit Without Honor: White-Collar Crime and the Looting of America*. Upper Saddle River: Prentice Hall.

Saldaña, J. 2015. *Thinking Qualitatively: Methods of Mind*. Thousand Oaks: Sage.

Saul, J.M. 2012. *Lying, Misleading, and What is Said: An Exploration in Philosophy of Language and in Ethics*. Oxford: Oxford University Press.

Schriesheim, C.A., K.J. Powers, T.A. Scandura, C.C. Gardiner et al. 1993. "Improving Construct Measurement in Management Research: Comments and a Quantitative Approach for Assessing the Theoretical Content Adequacy of Paper-and-Pencil Survey-Type Instruments." *Journal of Management* 19, 2.

Schulenberg, J. 2016. *The Dynamics of Criminological Research*. Oxford: Oxford University Press.

Sears, D.O. 1986. "College Sophomores in the Laboratory: Influences of a Narrow Data Base on Social Psychology's View of Human Nature." *Journal of Personality and Social Psychology* 51, 3.

Sherman, L.W., P.R. Gartin, and M.E. Buerger. 1989. "Hot Spots of Predatory Crime: Routine Activities and the Criminology of Place." *Criminology* 27, 1.

Sousa, V.D., J.A. Zauszniewski, and C.M. Musil. 2004. "How to Determine Whether a Convenience Sample Represents the Population 1." *Applied Nursing Research* 17, 2.

Squire, P. 1988. "Why the 1936 Literary Digest Poll Failed." *Public Opinion Quarterly* 52, 1.

Thomas–MacLean, R., A. Towers, E. Quinlan, T.F. Hack et al. 2009. "'This Is a Kind of Betrayal': A Qualitative Study of Disability after Breast Cancer." *Current Oncology* 16, 3.

Townsend, A.M. 2013. *Smart Cities: Big Data, Civic Hackers, and the Quest for a New Utopia*. New York: Norton and Company.

Trump, D.J. [realDonaldTrump]. 2018. [Tweet] January 16. <twitter.com/realDonaldTrump/status/953406423177859073>.

Tukey, J. 1977. *Exploratory Data Analysis*. London, UK: Addison-Wesley Publishing.

van de Sande, A., and C. Byvelds. 2015. *Statistics for Social Justice: A Structural Perspective*. Winnipeg: Fernwood Publishing.

van de Sande, A. and K. Schwartz. 2011. *Research for Social Justice: A Community-Based Approach*. Winnipeg: Fernwood Publishing.

Vigen, T. 2015. *Spurious Correlations*. New York: Hachette Books.

Vito, G., and G. Higgins. 2015. *Practical Program Evaluation for Criminal Justice*. London: Anderson Publishing.

Wall, D. 1999. "Cybercrimes: New Wine, No Bottles?" In P. Davies, P. Francis and V. Jupp (eds.), *Invisible Crimes*. London: Palgrave Macmillan.

Weber, M. 1949. *The Methodology of the Social Sciences* (E.A. Shils and H.A. Finch, trans. and eds.). New York: Free Press.

Webster, C.M., and A.N. Doob. 2015. "US Punitiveness 'Canadian style'? Cultural Values and Canadian Punishment Policy." *Punishment and Society* 17, 3.

Westhues, A., J. Ochocka, N. Jacobson, L. Simich et al. 2008. "Developing Theory from Complexity: Reflections on a Collaborative Mixed Method Participatory Action Research Study." *Qualitative Health Research* 18, 5.

Widaman, K., D. Early, and R. Conger. 2013. "Special Populations." In Tod Little (ed.), *The Oxford Handbook of Quantitative Methods, Volume 1: Foundations*. London: Oxford University Press.

Wu, X., X. Zhu, G.Q. Wu, and W. Ding. 2014. "Data Mining with Big Data." *IEEE Transactions on Knowledge and Data Engineering* 26, 1.

Young, J. 2011. *The Criminological Imagination*. New York: Polity Press.

The Regulation of Identities

Identities — such as those attributed to race, gender, age, sexuality, beauty, ability, addiction, and personalities — are often taken for granted. While we certainly have some influence over how others identify us, in some situations, we have less control and our identity seems to be unchangeable and defined by others. Section 2 focuses on the construction of deviant and normalized identities, particularly related to addiction, sexuality, disability, and youth. Here, we see the relations between institutional regulations, self-policing, discipline, and constructions of identity. Throughout the chapters in this section, we identify various means of social control — some subtle, some not — that define certain groups as deviant, sick, pathological, addicted, or criminal. These very definitions are socially constructed through time and place, and they often deflect attention from problems of oppression, inequality, and the ways in which social disadvantages become normalized. We will explore a variety of perspectives on the social control of identity but will also rely heavily on a social constructionist paradigm that prioritizes the standpoints of those defined as deviant and who have experienced social control.

In Chapter 5, Mitch Daschuk maps out the social control of substance use and users. Drawing on an understanding of how addiction is represented, he demonstrates how social control of certain substances is often more informed by political than health goals. Although some jurisdictions in Canada endorse harm-reduction policies and client-centred programming, regulations continue to be highly influenced by ideologies of a dangerous "other" better served through the criminal justice system than health care initiatives. He demonstrates the complexity and the many ways that substance control is constructed by also acknowledging the Liberal government's recent decriminalization of marijuana.

While acknowledging the inherent health risks of many illicit drugs, Daschuk's work recognizes how political rhetoric and media have shaped public perceptions of people who supposedly pose a danger to society or themselves. As an example, he outlines Canadian legal policy surrounding the possession, sale, and manufacturing of prescribed substances as well as arguments that suggest criminalization has less to do with the potential for social harm from the prescribed substances themselves and more to do with the people associated with their use. Using this lens, he shows a link between Canada's history of drug control and the social control of immigrant populations, beginning with anxieties surrounding Asiatic immigration in the mid-nineteenth century. He extends this to more recent media narratives on rave culture and the overestimation of ecstasy-related deaths. Using these examples and more, Daschuk demonstrates how ideologies about specific populations — such as racialized "others," youth subcultures, or socially underprivileged populations — become linked to moral decline and establish a rhetoric whereby certain groups become viewed as social and/or political threats and thus in need of more regulation. This moralistic framework then becomes reified in medicine, mental health, law, and the media.

Daschuk's chapter also shows how institutional misrepresentations of addiction contribute to the stigmatization of substance users and continued criminalization, and he links this to different levels of perspectives on social control. By detailing individual, community, and culture-based conditions that contribute to addiction as well as different approaches to dealing with it, he captures the importance of understanding colonization, intergenerational trauma, systemic discrimination, socioeconomic marginalization, sexual orientation, gender identity, ability, and more as important contextual factors for understanding substance use and its control. In the end, this chapter demonstrates the social construction behind which drugs are accepted and which drugs are forbidden, as well as our approach to the populations and individuals that use them.

The social construction of deviant identities and social control through media, medicine, law, and identity is taken up again by Brooks and Brigden in Chapter 6, "The Creation of Sexual Deviance: Social Control of Lesbian, Gay, Bisexual, Transgender, and Queer Plus (LGBTQ+) People in Canada." This chapter provides an overview of the methods of social control used against LGBTQ+ persons by individual, social, legal, and institutional practices. The authors canvas Canadian history for examples of laws and policies used to repress LGBTQ+ persons through the denial of jobs, housing, and the ability to marry and raise children. Other examples of social control are also covered, such as hegemonic discourse in institutions of psychiatry, military, medicine, police, and media, whereby LGBTQ+ individuals have been treated as sick, pathological, deviant, or criminal and requiring treatment or punishment.

The voices of LGBTQ+ individuals are brought in to demonstrate more about the workings of power and to uncover truths from the standpoints of those who have been oppressed. The social construction of so-called normative sexualities has often labelled those who fall outside of defined scripts as deviant/sick/pathological/criminal, resulting in devastating individual and social consequences. Presented with personal stories throughout, LGBTQ+ people are shown to be at increased risk of hate crimes, intimate partner violence, becoming street involved, and suicide.

Brooks and Brigden address intersecting places of oppression such as racism, homophobia, sexism, and socioeconomic disparity, all of which affect the ability of LGBTQ+ individuals to create positive identities and communities. This chapter, however, also notes positive stories of individuals thriving and feeling supported and loved. This is made clear in the introduction of this chapter and the description of Prime Minister Trudeau's November 28, 2017, apology to the LGBTQ+ community for the cruel and unjust methods used to identify and persecute LGBTQ+ persons working in public service, actions referred to as "the purge." Thus, this chapter addresses the diverse and complex history of public opinion, homophobia, heterosexual hegemony, homonormativity, transgender representations, anti-LGBT history, as well as LGBTQ+ rights, transgender rights, and resistance to sexual scripts in Canada and around the world.

Chapter 7, by Edward Hon-Sing Wong and Thania Vega, uses a similar social construction approach to show that disability has had different meanings and uses throughout history, and it has been used as a means of social control based on social constructions of who is productive or unproductive, desirable or undesirable. The authors show a link between disability and race, and the ways in which both categories have worked to exclude bodies by upholding particular socially constructed norms about citizenship and who deserves to belong. The authors describe how Canadian immigration policies, although shifting through time, were and are still used to bar those considered undesirable using justifications that link race, disability, and perceptions of citizenship. They clearly demonstrate how race- and disability-based fears are interrelated.

The authors detail and critique four key approaches to understanding disability: charity, eugenics, medical, and social movement. The traditional charity approach is discussed and critiqued for most often stripping those defined as disabled of agency by putting them forward as objects of pity and failing to make visible the underlying discrimination they experience. In outlining the eugenics approach, Wong and Vega show the deeply disturbing histories of social control through forced sterilization, gender-segregated institution-alization, the targeting of racialized people, and more. Next, they show how the medical approach shifts social control to a medically informed standard whereby the disabled body is deemed dependent as opposed to independent and ideal. The medicalization approach thus shows that what is considered deviant or abnormal is connected to expanding diagnostic categories. The rights and social movements approach focuses on addressing environmental issues, such as education, culture, and transportation. This approach aims to conceptualize disabled individuals much differently and ensure their access to the broader society. Although rights-based approaches have opened up opportunities, the authors argue that this approach nonetheless fails to alter disablist and oppressive logic within the Canadian immigration system.

Wong and Vega conclude by proposing an alternate and radical approach that places the construction of disability in the context of power. Similar to the other chapters, their model of understanding "disability" views its very construction as a means to further stigmatize marginalized individuals. Thus, their aim is to resist the broader dynamics of power that are linked to the social construction of disability, realize interlocking oppressions, and envision a more inclusive society.

A key aspect of the social construction and control of deviant identities is how they are used to exclude large categories of people — especially more socially marginalized and racialized people — from society; this also shifts over time and place. Despite social exclusion and oppressive categories of deviance, however, individuals are shown to thrive in the face of adversity and stigmatization. This is the topic of Chapter 8, the final chapter in this section by Kandis Boyko and Mitch Daschuk, whose work focuses on the resiliency of youth who thrive despite marginalization and deviant identity construction.

Boyko and Daschuk trace the history and definitions of youth/adolescence/ teenagerdom. They show how youth have been the target of consumerism, which reinforces a marketing of self-building strategies. Interestingly, they demonstrate how this also includes a marketing strategy focused on teen-age rebellion. While targeted for consumption, youth are also shown to be an easily exploitable labour pool. Alas, Boyko and Daschuk then introduce the construction of prolonged parental dependence and the complexity of a market that exploits yet depends on youth. Concepts such as surveillance and medicalization are drawn on here to demonstrate how adolescence is controlled through constructed diagnoses such as oppositional defiance dis-order. Rebellious youth might then be targeted both through consumerism as well as by being pressured to meet societal demands as an obedient worker, feeding a thriving drug industry.

Similar to the social control of addictions, sexuality, and disability, ideologies of adolescence are also shown to be influenced by media and popular culture, often leading to the stigmatization of youth and labelling of marginalized youth as those to fear. Boyko and Daschuk detail the rich literature on moral panics, showing how marginalized youth might be blamed for their own misfortunes by labelling them through media as "folk devils" and subjecting them to correction through punishment and treatment. Media has been shown to focus on sensationalistic acts done by only a few youths while also highlighting unorthodox youth cultures, furthering public fear, surveillance, and regulation of youth conduct.

This final chapter also addresses the intersection of race, sexuality, gender, and age, showing the impact of these variables on homelessness, street involvement, criminalization, teen pregnancy, single parenting, and more. Overlap occurs between the chapters on disability, sexuality, and addiction, as we recognize, for example, that queer and transgender youth have unique challenges through their encounters with homophobia and transphobia and thus are at increased risk of discrimination, addiction, mental illness, and self-harm. Boyko and Daschuk also draw attention to the circumstances of Indigenous youth, the repercussions of residential schools and colonialism, and the foster care system and overrepresentation of Indigenous youth in the child protection and the criminal justice systems. Finally, Boyko and Daschuk put forward the complex nature of youth resilience, realizing that some actions defined as deviance might be better understood as resilience strategies and that reinterpretation of many resilience strategies demonstrates adaptive mechanisms with both positive and sometimes dangerous repercussions.

The final note in Boyko and Daschuk's chapter resonates with the theme of listening to the perspectives of those who are the target of social control, specifically shifting perspectives on power to the margins. Carefully refining concepts of deviance, resilience, social justice, and control might be best met by understanding the lives of those who have experienced social control.

Looking Forward

The chapters all point to the importance of listening to those whose identities have been shaped and constructed by systems of power, rather than by understanding real struggles and resilience. While LGBTQ+ individuals are shown to be controlled through law, psychiatry, media, military, and social norms, they also resist. These chapters also address stigmatization, rejection, multiple oppressions experienced among LGBTQ+ people but also celebrate thriving and embracing diversity. Research on addictions is now also focusing on the real experiences of those people who may be prone to higher rates of substance abuse. This work leads researchers to address social marginalization and stigmatization, as well as personal and collective trauma and mental illness. Disability studies are similarly learning from those who experience disability. This experiential approach leads to deeper understandings of interlocking oppressions, including hardships caused by colonial violence and other social processes of disablement. The last chapter in this section points to the important work of listening to and respecting street-involved youths.

Definitions of addiction, sexuality, disability, and youth are socially constructed and often deflect attention from oppression, inequality, and the normalization of social disadvantages. Drawing attention to the standpoints of those defined as deviant and who have experienced social control allows a new understanding of oppression and the social construction of identity.

5

Representations of Addiction

The History and Continuing Repercussions of Canadian Drug Rhetoric

Mitch D. Daschuk

After reading this chapter, you will be able to do the following:

1. Explain the significance of political rhetoric surrounding illicit substances and substance users.
2. Describe rates of substance use and drug-related arrests in Canada.
3. Indicate how media representations have historically influenced Canadian narcotics policies.
4. Differentiate between sociological perspectives on pathways toward substance use.
5. Demonstrate how political rhetoric influenced changes to Canada's national drug treatment strategy.

Since the 1980s, Vancouver's Downtown Eastside (DTES) has had the reputation of being one of Canada's most impoverished neighbourhoods. Though known for incredible rates of homelessness[1] and substance use, the area has also been a hotbed for progressive social programs. In 2003, Insite, Canada's first needle exchange and safe-injection drug site, opened on East Hastings Street. Above and beyond offering needle sterilization to reduce the risk of transmitting communicable diseases, Insite also prevented overdose deaths by providing intravenous substance users access to medical staff. The federal government granted Insite a three-year exemption from aspects of Canada's *Controlled Drugs and Substances Act* (CDSA), but Insite needed to

Sociologists have sought to understand how prevalent forms of drug rhetoric, often steeped in ideological biases, inform legislative responses against the threat of "drug epidemics" and stigma surrounding those who use illicit drugs. Given the slim margin of characteristics separating "illegal drugs" and "acceptable substances" (such as alcohol and, to a dwindling extent, nicotine), drug rhetoric's influence is powerful.

show evidence that the program had a positive impact on clients and the surrounding community.

Over the course of rigorous evaluations, reports suggested that Insite did have a positive impact: infectious disease transmission and overdose mortality rates declined notably, and Insite improved community relations and social program awareness throughout the DTES (Wood, Kerr, Lloyd-Smith et al. 2004; Wood, Tyndall, Montaner, and Kerr 2006; British Columbia Centre for Excellence in HIV/AIDS 2009). Despite these findings, and although Insite's CDSA exemption was extended to 2008, the federal health minister, Tony Clement, announced that the federal government would not grant Insite any further exemptions from federal drug legislation. He said, "allowing and or encouraging people to inject heroin into their veins is not harm reduction, it is the opposite…. We believe it is a form of harm addition" (*Globe and Mail* 2008). Regardless of the demonstrably positive benefits of the Insite program, Clement and others in the government objected to Insite's ideological position on illicit substances and sought its closure. In response, Vancouver's Portland Hotel Society (PHS) Community Services Society and harm reduction activists (and former Insite clients) Dean Wilson and Shelly Tomic launched a Supreme Court case to determine whether preventing Insite from operating contradicted liberties guaranteed by the *Charter of Rights and Freedoms* (Pivot Legal Society n.d.). Specifically, the plaintiffs wished to know if disallowing Insite an exemption from the CDSA effectively put the health and safety of Insite's clients at undue risk. In a landmark 2011 decision, the Supreme Court unanimously decided that preventing Insite from operating did indeed violate the charter rights of Insite clients.

This chapter critically considers the history — and continued prevalence — of Canadian rhetoric surrounding substance use and users. Sociologists have sought to understand how prevalent forms of drug rhetoric, often steeped in ideological biases, inform legislative responses against the threat of "drug epidemics" and stigma surrounding those who use illicit drugs. Given the slim margin of characteristics separating "illegal drugs" and "acceptable substances" (such as alcohol and, to a dwindling extent, nicotine), drug rhetoric's influence is powerful. Further, an analysis of changes made to Canada's national drug policy under the Harper government highlights the ideological undertones that deny substance users the best possible treatment. Above all else, this chapter demonstrates the ways in which popular rhetoric surrounding substance use informs policies and how mainstream perspectives reinforce the stigmatization and marginalization of substance-using populations.

Classifying Substances and Assessing their Use in Canada

The possession, sale, and manufacture of illicit substances falls under the 1996 *Controlled Drugs and Substances Act*. Passed into Canadian law by the Liberal government in 1996, the CDSA prohibits substances when there are "reasonable grounds to believe that the controlled substance constitutes a potential security, public health or safety hazard" (Government of Canada 1996: 28). Further, the CDSA identifies a range of prohibited substances (including derivatives of opium, cannabis, and barbiturates) and outlines the corresponding punishments for their sale or possession. As noted in Table 5.1, different schedules of prohibited substances carry different penalties in terms of both possession and trafficking.

The most recent data on substance use rates provided by the Canadian Centre for Substance Abuse (2018, 2019a, 2019b) suggest that, excluding nicotine, the most common drugs used by Canadians are alcohol, cannabis, hallucinogens, cocaine or crack cocaine, and ecstasy. As Table 5.2 notes, the two substances most often reportedly used by the general population of Canadians, independent of age, are alcohol (78 percent of respondents) and cannabis (9.1 percent), with cocaine and crack (0.9 percent), ecstasy (0.7 percent), and hallucinogens (0.6 percent) rounding out the top five. When factoring in the age of respondents, slight variations in rates of use emerge. While rates of youth alcohol consumption (70.8 percent) are lower than adult alcohol consumption (79.3 percent), a larger proportion of youth (21.6 percent) than adults (6.7 percent) report using cannabis. Finally, and though extrapolated from small sample sizes, these results suggest that youth are more likely to use ecstasy (2.6 percent) and hallucinogens (2.0 percent) while adult populations are more prone to use cocaine and crack (0.7 percent).

Recent data from Statistics Canada (2017) demonstrates police-reported rates of drug-related arrests. As Table 5.3 demonstrates, police-reported figures indicate 95,417 people were arrested for drug offences in Canada in 2016, with the highest proportion related to the possession (44,301 persons) and trafficking, production, or distribution (10,639 persons) of cannabis. Rates of drug-related arrests in 2012 (Statistics Canada 2013) suggests that there was an overall decrease in drug-related arrests (especially regarding cannabis and

Table 5-1: The Controlled Drugs and Substances Act

CDSA Schedule	Schedule I Substances	Schedule II Substances	Schedule III Substances	Schedule IV Substances
Substances included	Opium, cocaine, methamphetamine, amphetamine	Cannabis, marijuana, marijuana resin	Psylocybin, mescaline	Barbituates, benzodiazepines, anabolic steroids
Punishments (Possession)				
First offence	Guilty of offence punishable on summary conviction, fine not exceeding $1,000 and/or prison term not exceeding six months			
Second offence	Guilty of offence punishable on summary conviction, fine not exceeding $2,000 and/or prison term not exceeding one year			
Third offence	Guilty of indictable offence, prison term not exceeding seven years	Guilty of indictable offence, prison term not exceeding five years less a day	Guilty of indictable offence, prison term not exceeding three years	Guilty of indictable offence, prison term not exceeding eighteen months
Punishments (Trafficking)				
First offence	Guilty of an indictable offence, liable to imprisonment for life		Guilty of summary conviction, prison term not exceeding eighteen months	Guilty of summary conviction, prison term not exceeding three years
Second (or subsequent) offence			Guilty of indictable offence, prison term not exceeding ten years	Guilty of summary conviction, prison term not exceeding one year
Third offence				Guilty of indictable offence, prison term not exceeding three years

cocaine offences), but arrests related to substances once in the general category of "other drugs" — including methamphetamine and heroin — have increased sharply. Whether these trends best correlate with patterns in substance use, changes in federal and law enforcement policy, or unforeseen variables, they nevertheless constitute the types of "official" statistics that influence new directions in policy and enforcement.

Table 5-2: Top Five Substances Used by Canadians, 2011
(Self-Report Survey)*

	#1	#2	#3	#4	#5
General Population (15+)	Alcohol (78.0%)	Cannabis (9.1%)	Cocaine/crack (0.9%)*	Ecstasy (0.7%)*	Hallucino-gens (0.6%)*
Youth (15–24)	Alcohol (70.8%)	Cannabis (21.6%)	Ecstasy (2.6%)	Hallucino-gens (2.0%)*	N/A (suppressed)
Adults (25+)	Alcohol (79.3%)	Cannabis (6.7%)	Cocaine/crack (0.7%)*	N/A (suppressed)	N/A (suppressed)

Note: Asterisks (*) denote results pulled from small sample sizes.

The Cultural History of Canadian Drug Policy

Canada was the first Western country to institute laws to criminalize the use and possession of certain substances. Research about early Canadian drug legislation, including the 1908 *Opium Act* and the 1929 *Opium and Narcotic Drug Act*, contradicts the assumption that drugs are determined to be illegal based on the severity of harm they cause. Instead, and as Sniderman (1999: 86) contends, "the drugs of choice of the so-called 'moral center' — the so-called solid citizens, the professionals and business classes, the police, politicians, etc. — don't get criminalized." He argues, "what determines whether a particular drug is criminalized is not its inherent properties and/or potential for social harm but rather the kinds of people associated with its use." This position implies that substances such as alcohol and tobacco have largely been spared illegal designation due to both their popularity with privileged people and their use as sources of legitimate industry.

The introduction of Canada's initial *Opium Act* coincided with anxieties surrounding Asian immigration (Giffen, Endicott, and Lambert 1991; Green 1979). In the mid-nineteenth century, many Chinese immigrants came to Canada in large part to construct the trans-Canadian railroad. During this time, opium importation was legal (though subject to federal taxation) and the drug was widely used medicinally. Nevertheless, as Green (1979: 44) notes, "employment opportunities had severely contracted [by the early 1880s] and the Chinese, who were willing to work for far less money than white labourers, increasingly became objects of public — and particularly labour movement — resentment." Legislation drastically reduced rates of Chinese immigration, and the 1908 *Opium Act* was advanced, in part, as a means of

Table 5-3: Comparison of Police Reported Rates of Drug Offences, 2012–2016

Type of Drug Offence	2012 — persons (rate)	2016 — persons (rate)	2012–2016 rate change
Total Drug Offences	109,455 (314)	95,417 (263)	-51
Possession			
Cannabis	57,429 (165)	44,301 (122)	-43
Cocaine	7,847 (22)	7,056 (19)	-3
Methamphetamine	n/a	7,673 (21)	
Heroin	n/a	2,143 (6)	
Methylenedioxyamphetamine	n/a	255 (1)	
Other drugs	10,661 (31)	7,695 (21)	18*
Trafficking, production, or distribution			
Cannabis	15,674 (45)	10,639 (29)	-16
Cocaine	10,553 (30)	7,161 (20)	-10
Methamphetamines	n/a	2,153 (6)	
Heroin	n/a	912 (3)	
Methylenedioxyamphetamine	n/a	196 (1)	
Other drugs	7,291 (21)	5,233 (14)	3*

Note: Asterisks (*) indicate rate change based on total of all substances not explicitly identified in 2012 statistics.

deterring immigration through rendering opium (and its importers) criminal. According to Green (1979: 58),

> the conclusion that the increasingly severe nature of Canada's narcotic laws was politically facilitated by the assumption that their impact would fall mainly upon the Asiatic population appears impossible to avoid. And, in fact, enforcement records support this assumption as Dominion Bureau of Statistics data for 1923 reveal that the racial origin of over 1,100 of the 1,858 persons convicted of narcotics-related offences that year was Chinese.

Although the *Opium Act* increased regulation and surveillance of Asian immigrants, Prime Minister Mackenzie King tried gaining support for this legislation by advancing a narrative of the moral character of Canadian society, and this would be taken up over the next two decades by a range of moral entrepreneurial forces. Among these was Canadian magistrate Emily Murphy, who advocated for the criminalization of further substances, including marijuana and cocaine. Murphy was a prominent public figure due to her early advocacy for women's rights. Her argument that recreational substance use posed a distinct moral threat to conventional Canadian society carried weight with the general Canadian public. While Murphy's moral crusade began with the publication of a series of particularly sensationalistic *Maclean's* magazine articles, "whose stated purpose was to pressure the government to enact stricter drug laws" (Sniderman 1999: 87), she became a self-appointed expert in the dangers of substances with the publication of *The Black Candle* (1922). Though Green (1979: 53) notes that Murphy had "marshaled significant social, medical, statistical and pharmacological data from Canada, the United States and the United Kingdom," it is nevertheless notable that

> her style tended more to sensationalist rhetoric than impartial reportage ... the effects of the various drugs were not clearly distinguished, but it hardly mattered as Murphy was convinced that they all produced the same general [effects]: moral degeneration, crime, physical and mental deterioration and disease, intellectual and spiritual wastage and material loss through drug-induced negligence.

Murphy's writings would use a risk discourse that connected recreational substance use with trends in moral decline and the assumed dangers posed by immigrant populations: "the role of the villain in her anecdotal accounts was almost always played by conspicuous 'foreign' persons, and she cautiously suggested that narcotics were part of an international conspiracy to injure the bright-browed races of the world'" (Green 1979: 53). Ultimately, Murphy was not only successful in influencing Canadian narcotic policy but also in crafting a moralistic rhetoric that continues to permeate Canadian attitudes about substance users.

Drug Panics, Political Rhetoric, and Mass Media Representations

Just as early Canadian attitudes toward recreational substance use were highly influenced by the inception of drug legislation, sociologists continue to assess public perspectives on illicit drug use and the influence of moral entrepreneurial drug rhetoric. While social anxieties regarding dangerous drugs are not purely "socially constructed" in the sense that the use of many illicit drugs can lead to overdose and death, popular discourse surrounding the dangers of drugs often overstates the risks inherent to using problematic substances and overestimates the prevalence of their use (Goode 2007). Akin to our account of the genesis of Canadian drug legislation, many researchers point to the significant influence of political rhetoric and mass media representations in shaping North American attitudes regarding substances. We will consider examples of each in turn.

Political Rhetoric: Reagan and the War on Drugs

Political **rhetoric** — or the way in which politicians, authorities, and social elites talk about certain social issues — influences how mass media and the public perceive the harms posed by substance use (Beckett 1995; Jernigan and Dorfman 1996; Sharp 1992). One of the most pertinent examples of how political rhetoric appears to have greatly influenced public attitudes toward drugs stems from US president Ronald Reagan's declaration of a "War on Drugs" in the early 1980s. While Reagan was not the first president to correlate recreational substance use with a decline in proper American morals (that distinction goes to Richard Nixon), research suggests that Reagan's decidedly sensationalistic brand of political rhetoric had a profound effect in shaping public anxieties surrounding trends in American drug abuse and, particularly, the pronounced dangers posed by the relatively recent invention of crack cocaine. As Goode (2007) notes, Reagan's anti-drug discourse is likely responsible for the 1985 Gallup public opinion poll findings that Americans identified illegal drug use as the country's most pressing social problem, even though actual rates of illicit drug use had decreased dramatically since the 1970s. Reagan characterized illegal drugs as an affront to mainstream American morals and, specifically, a threat targeting youth and young adult populations.

Why did Reagan's administration focus on the dangers of recreational drug use despite decreasing rates? As Sniderman (1999) contends, aspects of the War on Drugs were an affront against the youth-directed social movements of the 1960s — and the "hippie" culture specifically. Elwood (1995) suggests that the Reagan administration might have tried to instigate a drug panic to shore up the political endorsement of the American "moral majority" while correlating dangerous drug use with America's underprivileged and racial minority populations. As

> Reagan's decidedly sensationalistic brand of political rhetoric had a profound effect in shaping public anxieties surrounding trends in American drug abuse.

the neoliberal fiscal policies of the Reagan administration (also known as "Reaganomics") had contributed to the decline of the American welfare state, Elwood implies that Reagan's War on Drugs discourse might have functioned to characterize those populations negatively, affected by Reaganomics as a public danger as opposed to targets of unsavoury government policy. In

Reagan's anti-drug discourse is likely responsible for the 1985 Gallup public opinion poll findings that Americans identified illegal drug use as the country's most pressing social problem, even though actual rates of illicit drug use had decreased dramatically since the 1970s. Reagan characterized illegal drugs as an affront to mainstream American morals and, specifically, a threat targeting youth and young adult populations.

any event, and as Hawdon (2001: 429–30) notes, "President Reagan skillfully used communitarian arguments to define drug use as a problem. He frequently defined drug use as a choice and identified the folk devil responsible for the problem. By 1987, the media had popularized this punitive position … and, once accomplished, public opinion and political rhetoric reinforced each other."

Mass Media Representations

The content and influence of mass media representations of the "dangers" posed by drugs have also attracted critical attention. Although contemporary media might not possess the same creative licence as Murphy took in *Black Candle*, they still contribute to comparable trends in media sensationalism. According to Orcutt and Turner (1993), the "crack panic" that preceded Reagan's "War on Drugs" was not merely instigated by political rhetoric; mainstream media reinforced and accredited its existence by broadcasting incorrect information pertaining to substance use rates throughout the United States. Jernigan and Dorfman (1996), who conducted a content analysis of broadcast news during the peak of the War on Drugs, found that media largely parroted the moralistic rhetoric of the Reagan administration as opposed to using credible data on the use and effects of drugs. Neo-Marxist analysis of Reagan's War on Drugs explains these collusive relations between the media and the state as maintaining public consent toward ineffective (and predatory) policies. Similarly, Agar and Reisinger (2000) critically analyze Baltimore's media-facilitated heroin drug panic in the late 1990s. Though the sheer number of media reports relating to the dangers of heroin held steady throughout the decade, the information became framed differently: Media discourse around the panic increasingly revolved around a common narrative (that suburban heroin use was becoming a problem), and there was a gradual increase of sensationalistic language and imagery alongside heightened coverage correlating heroin with America's moral decline.

Sociologists have investigated the highly moralistic content of media representations of substance users, which fall into two general categories based upon the demographic qualities of the groups under analysis: those that extend a discourse revolving around "populations in danger" and those that revolve around "populations that pose danger." Whereas those social groups who are seen as susceptible to negative cultural influences (such as youth and young adults) are often grouped in with the former, those framed as posing a danger are more often racialized, poor, or culturally sanctified (like mothers).

"Populations in Danger" versus "Dangerous Populations "

Analysis of early Canadian media claims surrounding drug use (including Murphy's series of *Maclean's* articles) indicates an abundance of narratives linking the legality of opium with risk to the moral integrity of Canada — specifically, in making Canadians susceptible to the "villainous" intentions of Asian immigrants. More recent analyses of Canadian media reports regarding ecstasy-related deaths suggest that little has changed in this respect. Analysis of media narratives relating to cases of ecstasy-related death have, comparatively, noted tendencies toward causally linking the dangers of ecstasy with the emergence of rave subculture (Baldwin, Miller, Stogner, and Hach 2012; Hier 2002). Beyond highlighting media narratives centred on the emergence of a new and dangerous manifestation of youth culture, these researchers suggest the ensuing public panic functioned to reinforce many common Canadian ideologies revolving around youth, namely that youth conduct must be regulated through legislative means. In this manner, media representations pertaining to youth substance use reinforce two common ideologies at once: one characterizing illicit substance use as a pronounced social threat and another characterizing youth as being incapable of individual responsibility and in dire need of legislative regulation.

> In this manner, media representations pertaining to youth substance use reinforce two common ideologies at once: one characterizing illicit substance use as a pronounced social threat and another characterizing youth as being incapable of individual responsibility and in dire need of legislative regulation.

While media discourse of substance use among "vulnerable" social populations, such as young people, uses a protectionist rhetoric, media discourse takes a decidedly different tone when it comes to minority populations represented as a dangerous "other." Whiteacre

(2005: 10) suggests that media representations affiliating substance use with minority populations reinforce discourse that characterizes substance users as "symbolically associated with disease, the subterranean, and low self-control." This observation complements the critical position that prevalent social discourses surrounding the dangers of drugs might carry the latent function of reinforcing the stigmatization of racialized peoples.

Sociological Perspectives on Addiction and Patterns in Substance Use

Historically, and beyond influencing public perspectives on the nature of illicit substances, discourse extending from the fields of medicine, mental health, law, and mainstream media also contributed to prevalent social understandings regarding "drug addicts." Chances are quite good, in fact, that mere mention of the term "drug addict" may evoke common cultural stereotypes: that they are inherently criminal, with deficiencies in impulse control and a propensity for violent conduct. These stereotypes of substance users as risks has largely remained stable, dating back to the early twentieth century, and they continue to inform how mainstream Canadian society perceives of, and responds to, substance-using populations.

Somewhat ironically, while public perspectives surrounding the dangers posed by drug addiction have remained relatively unchanged, the concept of addiction has recently undergone changes. Throughout the twentieth century, addiction referred to people who had a physical dependency upon a substance, explicitly defined as "an adaptive state of the body that is manifested by physical disturbances when drug use stops" (Milby 1981: 3). Today, the Centre for Addiction and Mental Health (CAMH) affiliates addiction with the presence of the "four C's": cravings; an individual's inability to control the frequency of their engagement with the practice; the presence of a compulsion to engage in the behaviour; and, finally, an inability to cease engaging in the behaviour despite detrimental consequences.

While mass media and moral entrepreneurial representations of the perils of drug addiction (and the dangerousness of drug-addicted populations) undoubtedly contribute to the reinforcement of prevalent Western drug ideologies and the stigmatization of substance users, sociological theories can explain trends in drug use that are not predicated upon the assumed "immorality" of substance users. These explanations come from two traditions: those that strive to account for substance-using practices by incorporating community and cultural considerations (macro-level perspectives) and others

While mass media and moral entrepreneurial representations of the perils of drug addiction (and the dangerousness of drug-addicted populations) undoubtedly contribute to the reinforcement of prevalent Western drug ideologies and the stigmatization of substance users, sociological theories can explain trends in drug use that are not predicated upon the assumed "immorality" of substance users.

that strive to deduce individualistic correlates with substance use (micro-level perspectives).

Community and Culture-Based Perspectives

Community and culture-based perspectives suggest that features in collective social organization, as opposed to individual traits, can best be correlated with heightened rates of substance use and abuse. Many of these perspectives stem from the tradition of social disorganization theories. Some theorists (Haynie, Silver, and Teasdale 2006; Stewart, Simons, and Conger 2002; Zimmerman and Vasquez 2011) have posited that neighbourhoods defined by rampant poverty, poor living and school conditions, and limited access to social supports can be expected to demonstrate higher rates of nonconformist practices. Other theorists (Kornhauser 1978; Sampson and Groves 1989) have entertained the prospect that corresponding sensations of anomie and community disconnectedness also play a prevalent role. While social disorganization perspectives speak to a "commonsensical" relationship between social marginalization and substance use, recent research has tried to investigate this correlation — but with mixed results. While some quantitative researchers have reported findings to support social disorganization perspectives on substance use and addiction (Hayes-Smith and Whaley 2009; Scheier, Botvin, and Miller 2000), others have found little grounds on which to correlate trends in drug use with community characteristics (Fagan, Wright, and Pinchevsky 2013; Steen 2010).

More recently, and due in part to focusing distinctly upon the presence of heightened trends of alcoholism and substance abuse among ethnically minoritized communities, sociologists have considered the relationship between trends in substance use and the concepts of historical and intergenerational trauma. This research was conducted with Holocaust survivors, which correlated their collective experience of attempted genocide with "symptoms of denial, depersonalization, isolation, somatization, memory loss, agitation, anxiety, guilt, depression, intrusive thoughts, nightmares, psychic numbing and survivor guilt" (Whitbeck, Adams, Hoyt, and Chen 2004: 130). The researchers argued that survivors of culturally shared trauma not only gravitate toward substance use as a means of coping with their experiences but that their symptoms of trauma (and, by extension, the use of substances as a coping mechanism) are passed down over generations. To date, **historical trauma** is commonly defined as "a collective complex trauma inflicted on a group of people who share a specific group identity or affiliation — ethnicity, nationality and religious affiliation" and as "the legacy of numerous traumatic events a community experiences over generations" (Evans-Campbell 2008: 320). Collective historical trauma includes the loss of traditional language, the loss of traditional cultural practices, the loss of lands, the loss of rights of self-governance, and, for many, the resultant inability to connect with their traditions, culture, and communities. The concept of **intergenerational trauma**, on the other hand, "conceptualizes the trauma inflicted on entire communities of people who have been subject to abuses based on their ethnicity and group identity, and explores the ways in which the children of those people also carry the traumatic effects, even though those children did not directly experience the traumatic events themselves" (Haskell and Randall 2009: 67). As Menzies (2007) cautions, however, many communities and cultures have suffered historical trauma and systemic discrimination to such an extent that these experiences "[become] normalized to the point that the group does not realize how social conditions continue to oppress them" (373). Given a state of perpetual trauma and a lack of options for recourse and remedy, they may turn to alcohol and substances for temporary escape.

While research with Canada's Indigenous populations strongly correlates contemporary trends in alcohol and substance use with historical experiences of colonization and assimilation as well as the residential school system, Haskell and Randall (2009) also suggest the continued relevance of those positions stemming from the social disorganization theory tradition:

> The injustices and colonialism in the lives of Canada's First Nations peoples are not merely relics of a distant or even a recent past. Instead, these injustices continue to be found and are even entrenched in the contemporary social conditions of inequality in which a great many of Canada's First Nations peoples live. Many aspects of the lives of Aboriginal peoples, therefore, are *continuously traumatic*. This is a fundamental insight which cannot be over emphasized, and which must be fore-grounded in any discussion of the impact of trauma on Aboriginal peoples of Canada. (50)

In sum, community- and culture-based perspectives suggest that heightened trends of alcohol and substance use among marginalized and underprivileged populations can be better contextualized against the recognition of unsavoury historical experiences and their continuing contemporary effects. Nonetheless, and in being considered separately, disorganization and trauma-based perspectives do well in correlating heightened trends in problematic substance use with cultural experiences of discrimination and disempowerment.

Individual-Based Approaches

Sociologists recognize that individual persons often develop substance-use issues by virtue of unique circumstances, social pressures, and their own personal experiences and biographies. As such, the concept of **pathways** is often used to refer to "the unique circumstances through which a person comes to problematically use alcohol and other substances" (Daschuk, Dell, and Duncan 2012: 36) and argues that any individualized case of problematic substance use is likely influenced and inspired by a range of unique factors. Nevertheless, just as the concept of community or cultural trauma has come to be recognized as a significant precursor to problematic substance use, research now suggests that persons with pre-existing mental health issues — including those instigated by traumatic experiences — are more likely to develop issues with problematic substance use (Kirst, Frederick, and Erickson 2011; Sellman 2009). A wealth of studies undertaken throughout North America have correlated depression and traumatic experiences with trends in substance use among adult and homeless youth populations (Drake et al. 2001; Foster et al. 2010; Tsemberis, Gulcur, and Nakae 2004; Kirst, Frederick, and Erickson 2011; Slesnick and Prestopnik 2005), high school students (Clark, Ringwalt, and Shamblen 2011), heavy drinkers (Lukassen and Beaudet 2005), and socioeconomically marginalized single and expecting parents (Linden, Torchalla, and Krauz 2013).

For some researchers, studies linking problematic substance use with pre-existing mental health issues suggest the applicability of Khantzian's (1985) **self-medication hypothesis.** The general principle that persons with pre-existing mental health conditions might gravitate toward problematic substance use as a means of coping with strain, or altering and improving their emotional state, is attracting increasing popularity within the fields of sociology and public health alike (Clark, Ringwalt, and Shamblen 2011). Indeed, many health care professionals in the field of substance abuse treatment argue that increased public awareness regarding the strong relationship between pre-existing mental health conditions and subsequent trends in substance abuse might challenge and contradict those prevalent social stereotypes that equate addiction with personal weakness and moral failings.

Subcultural Perspectives

An additional pathway through which people might gravitate toward the increased use of illicit substances is their introduction into "deviant" or "outsider" groups that use substances because of social discontent. Subcultural groups often endorse nonconformist practices as a means of engaging in social critique, and research pertaining to **drug cultures** suggests these collectives celebrate the use of illicit substances as a sign of "legitimate" group membership and belonging (Johnson, Bardhi et al. 2006; Becker 1965). Sidran's (1981) early research on the bebop musical subculture suggests that the term "cool" may have originated based upon the collective experiences with prevalent heroin use among bebop musicians and their audience, as "[heroin] spoke kindly to the 'cool' style of the hipster for three reasons: it suppresses emotional excess; it establishes an in-group of users and dealers; and it eases anxieties not directly concerned with procuring it" (113). The "hippie" subculture of the 1960s (Davis and Munoz 1968), the New York art scene and punk rock subculture of the 1960s (McNeil and McCain 2006; Bockris 1989), the aforementioned "rave" culture of the 1990s (Wilson 2002; Measham, Parker, and Aldridge 1998; Thornton 1996), and a range of music-based subcultures (Pederson 2009) are other examples of subcultural groups that have used recreational alcohol and drugs as an indication of "insider" belonging — or as a sign of social contempt and resistance. Ironically, and in considering how youth or socially nonconformist subcultural groups often come to attract (or wish to attract) designation as Western cultural "folk-devil" populations, it follows that their endorsement of illicit substance use further reinforces perspectives equating substance use with unruly, nonconformist, and dangerous behaviour.

To date, the sociological literature largely suggests that substance users in Canada come from populations that have been made vulnerable due to long-standing experiences with marginalization, lower socioeconomic status, and

> To date, the sociological literature largely suggests that substance users in Canada come from populations that have been made vulnerable due to long-standing experiences with marginalization, lower socioeconomic status, and cultural disempowerment. While this characterization undoubtedly contrasts with prevalent social representations of the "drug addict," it is very much in keeping with the perspectives of persons employed within the fields of addiction treatment and outreach services.

cultural disempowerment. While this characterization undoubtedly contrasts with prevalent social representations of the "drug addict," it is very much in keeping with the perspectives of persons employed within the fields of addiction treatment and outreach services. As the following section will demonstrate, this awareness surrounding the realities of substance use has, throughout Canada and beyond, popularized initiatives and programs that employ a harm-reduction philosophy.

Drug Treatment Strategies in Canada: A Tale of Duelling Drug Ideologies

Mainstream Canadian views surrounding illicit drugs and substance users are still informed by the same ideologies underpinning the 1908 *Opium Act*. But on the "ground level" of treatment and outreach, rather than approaching problematic substance users as inherently criminal, morally bankrupt, or damningly impulsive, most treatment services in Canada have adopted a "client-centred" approach that instead sees problematic substance users as vulnerable populations whose use may stem from any number of distinct pathways, including experiences of emotional or cultural trauma, concurrent mental health issues, socioeconomic marginalization, and social disempowerment.

Whereas the Canadian federal government is responsible for creating drug laws and legislation, the responsibility for administering substance abuse treatment programs and outreach falls under the jurisdiction of provincial, territorial, and municipal governments. Beyond providing services to assist clients in combating their substance-use issues, many provide services such as counselling, spiritual guidance, and the development of self-esteem and pro-social skills (including communicative skills and courses attuned toward helping clients find employment). Canadian substance abuse and treatment programs also typically offer a wide array of services tailored toward the distinct needs of certain populations. For example, programs based around principles of **gender sensitivity** take note of the fact that men and women often come to develop problematic substance use issues due to unique factors and experiences: whereas men are more likely to resort to substance use due to such factors as job loss, financial instability, or an inability to measure up to Western standards of masculinity, the well-travelled pathways toward substance abuse for women involve experiences with domestic violence, the unique burden of single-parenthood, and a self-perceived inability to conform with cultural expectations surrounding femininity. Further, an increasing number of programs tailored toward Indigenous Peoples take care to ensure that their programs are culturally sensitive, which entails not only recognizing the influence of historical and intergenerational trauma but also basing service components around Indigenous traditions. Client-centred programs can also be tailored on the basis of age, sexual orientation, gender identity, and ability.

Substance abuse programs and services that abide by a client-centred approach toward substance abuse treatment are often described as endorsing a treatment philosophy of harm reduction. According to Boyd (2004), the harm reduction treatment philosophy, which first took on prominence in Britain and the Netherlands, strives to "[offer] practical programs that focus on minimizing drug-related harms to both the individual and society" (175). While a harm reduction philosophy doesn't expect that clients will eventually abstain from substances, it understands that abstention may lead prospective clients to disengage with treatment services and thus puts them at the risk of further preventable harms. Notably, the harm reduction philosophy's endorsement of a "value-neutral view" of substance use does not merely strive to ensure that program clients are not approached as overly criminalistic, immoral, or impulsive, but it aims to guarantee that treatment centres function as "safe spaces" where clients are treated with respect and compassion. Finally, harm reduction advocates that treatment "success" or "recovery" be defined in different ways for each client on a case-by-case basis and depending upon considerations such as development of pro-social skills and improvements in personal health as opposed to merely whether a client has ceased to use substances in a problematic manner.

While substance use treatment programs fall under provincial, territorial, or municipal jurisdiction, the federal government of Canada has nevertheless developed and endorsed strategies aimed at curbing national rates of substance use. Canada's first federal drug strategy, developed in 1987 with the participation of various levels of government, initially abided by a philosophy based on four pillars: treatment, prevention, enforcement, and harm reduction. The fourth pillar demonstrated that the government endorsed the perspective that substance addiction ought to be approached as a public health issue as opposed to a crime issue and, by extension, that substance users ought be approached as persons in need of suitable health care assistance. Indeed, this pillar led to the foundation of Vancouver's Insite clinic. However, following the 2004 election of a minority Conservative government, Canada's national drug strategy underwent ideological revisions. Notably, the 2007 passage of Canada's *National Anti-Drug Strategy* drew criticism on two significant fronts: it increased mandatory minimum incarceration sentences relating to

The national drug strategy amendments suggest that, in many respects, recent trends in Canadian drug legislation discourse parallel and popularize the drug rhetoric once promoted by the likes of Emily Murphy and Ronald Reagan: that illicit substances constitute a pronounced social danger best combated through criminal judicial recourse as opposed to health care initiatives.

the distribution and possession of illicit substances, and it eliminated the pillar of harm reduction. In response, the Centre for Addiction and Mental Health (2014) noted:

> The exclusion of harm reduction from the federal anti-drug strategy is a result of a deliberate shift in federal drug policy. Canada's drug strategy prior to the current administration included harm reduction programs and policies. This shift in policy has included an emphasis on abstinence and deterrence through the criminal justice system. Evidence from the USA has shown using the criminal justice system to solve substance use problems has resulted in increased numbers of individuals incarcerated and increased health related harm.... This shift in policy does not reflect the lessons learned in the United States, nor is it in step with drug strategies across Canada. (3–4)

The national drug strategy amendments suggest that, in many respects, recent trends in Canadian drug legislation discourse parallel and popularize the drug rhetoric once promoted by the likes of Emily Murphy and Ronald Reagan: that illicit substances constitute a pronounced social danger best combated through criminal judicial recourse as opposed to health care initiatives. Nevertheless, it is perhaps too early to suggest that Canadian society has *wholeheartedly* embraced moral entrepreneurial positions surrounding substance use. The fact that Justin Trudeau's election as prime minister in 2015 coincided with his promise to decriminalize recreational marijuana use in Canada suggests conservative drug ideologies do not attract the same degree of public consent they once did.

Conclusion

Canadian drug rhetoric speaks to the socially constructed nature of our collective approach to the subject of illicit narcotics and the people who use them. Rather than declaring substances either legal and culturally sanctioned or illegal and culturally prohibited based on the negative health effects and public danger which they pose, research instead suggests that a variety of alternative factors inform the illegality of some narcotics (and the legality of others). These alternative factors include the type of social populations who are associated with the use of a given substance and the types of social populations that advocate for their criminal status.

Describing Canadian drug ideology as being socially constructed points to the ambiguous process whereby some drugs are deemed forbidden while others — in spite of demonstrable dangers they pose — are accepted. Harkening back on the genesis of Canadian drug legislation, however, Canada's moral consensus on drugs was actually instigated through the production of moral entrepreneurial discourse and Canadian anxieties surrounding the moral risks posed by immigrants. In some cases, the evidence that guided amendments to Canada's earliest drug legislation appears to be based on little more than sensational and fictitious accounts of the effects of substances such as marijuana. The case study of the Reagan administration's War on Drugs can even be taken to suggest that drug policies, at times, stem from aspirations of sheer political gains and ideological hegemony. Drugs and their users have long served as adequate targets of moral panic that might only be "defeated" by way of publicly sanctioned judiciary responses.

Research conducted with people who seem prone to higher rates of substance use does little to confirm the popular assumption that drug addicts are morally flawed and inherently criminalistic. Instead, experiences of social marginalization, personal and collective trauma, and general experiences of disempowerment are better correlatives with substance addiction. An improved understanding of the connection between substance abuse and pre-existing mental health issues suggests that substance-addicted people ought to be approached as in need of better health care provisions as opposed to incarceration or other forms of punishment. Drug consumption has also been used to signify social discontentment and rebellion among some subcultural groups — and often in a manner that serves to reinforce popular public associations between drug use and "abnormal" or "deviant" social populations.

As Canada's current movement toward decriminalizing the use of marijuana suggests, neither prevalent drug ideologies nor legislative drug policies remain static over time. Given that Canadian society continues to critically question the illegality of some substances (while critically questioning the legality of others), Canadian drug rhetoric and corresponding policies stand a great chance of evolving drastically over the course of our lives. As few fields of inquiry speak to the often ambiguous and contradictory process through which we construct our perspectives on social reality, the realm of drug policy will doubtless remain a popular target of critical sociological research.

Discussion Questions

1. Why are safe-injection sites controversial despite their documented benefits?
2. What influence did Emily Murphy's *The Black Candle* have on Canadian narcotics policy?
3. What are the "four Cs" that the Centre for Addictions and Mental Health use to identify the presence of addiction?
4. What is the harm reduction treatment philosophy?
5. What significant changes in narcotics policy occurred with the 2007 passage of Canada's *National Anti-Drug Strategy*?

Recommended Resources

1. Canadian Centre on Substance Use and Addiction Website. <ccsa.ca/>.
2. The Fifth Estate: "Staying Alive" (CBC 2008).
3. *Reefer Madness* (Motion Picture Ventures 1936).

Glossary 5

addiction: the presence of a dependence on substances or practices as indicated in the presence of cravings, loss of control, the presence of compulsions and use despite negative consequences.

cultural sensitivity: the process of ensuring that substance-use treatments and services are respectful of issues and concerns specific to the cultural affiliations of clients.

drug cultures: groups that celebrate the use of narcotics as a collective practice and indicator of legitimate insider status.

gender sensitivity: the process of ensuring that substance-use treatments and services respect the issues and concerns related to clients' gender identity.

harm reduction: a treatment philosophy that involves reducing negative consequences as opposed to promoting complete abstinence.

historical trauma: acknowledgement that the negative repercussions of traumatic historical events (like colonialism) reverberate through generations.

intergenerational trauma: the process through which persons with experiences of victimization pass on the associated trauma in subjecting their children to similar forms of victimization.

pathways: the unique contexts and pre-existing variables that can be associated with a person's gravitating toward substance use.

rhetoric: forms of authoritative discourse that are distributed by persons in positions of power to popularize their point of view on an issue or topic.

self-medication hypothesis: the perspective that people with mental wellness issues gravitate toward substance use as a form of treatment.

Note

1. While there is no document identifying specific rates of homelessness within the East Hastings region, a homeless count conducted by the City of Vancouver (2019) indicated that the city of Vancouver recorded 614 "unsheltered" homeless persons; 62 percent of whom are located in the Downtown Eastside. The population of homeless persons with access to shelter, meanwhile, was recorded as 1,609 individuals (geographic distribution unknown).

References

Agar, Michael H., and Heather Schact Reisinger. 2000. "Read All About It: Media Construction of a Heroin Epidemic." *Substance Use & Misuse* 35, 11.

Baldwin, Julie M., Bryan Lee Miller, John Stogner, and Steve Hach. 2012. "The Night the Raving Died: The Social Construction of a Local Drug Panic." *Deviant Behavior* 33, 9.

Becker, Howard S. 1965. *Outsiders: Studies in the Sociology of Deviance*. London: Free Press of Glencoe.

Beckett, Katherine. 1995. "Media Depictions of Drug Abuse: The Impact of Official Sources." *Research in Political Sociology* 7.

Bockris, Victor 1989. *The Life and Death of Andy Warhol*. New York: Bantam Books.

Boyd, Susan. 2004. *From Witches to Crack Moms: Women, Drug Law, and Policy*. North Carolina: Academic Press.

British Columbia Centre for Excellence in HIV/AIDS. 2009. "Findings from the Evaluation of Vancouver's Pilot Medically Supervised Safer Injection Facility — Insite." <bccsu. ca/wp-content/uploads/2016/10/insite_report-eng.pdf>

Canadian Centre on Substance Use and Addiction Website. n.d.

Canadian Centre on Substance Abuse. 2014. "Canadian Drug Summary: Cannabis." <ccsa.ca/sites/default/files/2019-04/CCSA-Canadian-Drug-Summary-Cannabis-2018-en.pdf>.

____. 2019a. "Canadian Drug Summary: Alcohol." < ccsa.ca/sites/default/files/2019-09/ CCSA-Canadian-Drug-Summary-Alcohol-2019-en.pdf>.

____. 2019b. "Canadian Drug Summary: Cocaine." < ccsa.ca/sites/default/files/2019-04/ CCSA-Canadian-Drug-Summary-Cocaine-2019-en.pdf>.

CBC *Fifth Estate*. 2008. "Staying Alive." <cbc.ca/player/play/1367469592>.

Centre for Addiction and Mental Health. 2014. "Addiction." <camh.ca/en/hospital/ health_information/a_z_mental_health_and_addiction_information/drug-use-addiction/Pages/addiction.aspx>.

City of Vancouver. 2019. "Homeless Count." <vancouver.ca/people-programs/homeless-count.aspx>.

Clark, Heddy K., Chris Ringwalt, and Stephen Shamblen. 2011. "Predicting Adolescent

Substance Use: The Effects of Depressed Mood and Positive Expectancies." *Addictive Behaviors* 36.

Daschuk, Mitch, Coleen Dell, and C. Randy Duncan. 2012. *First Steps First: A Community-Based Workbook for Evaluating Substance Abuse and Mental Health Programs in Canada*. Saskatoon: University of Saskatchewan Department of Sociology and School of Public Health.

Davis, F., and L. Munoz. 1968. "Heads and Freaks: Patterns and Meanings of Drug Use Among Hippies." *Journal of Health and Social Behavior* 9, 2.

Drake, R., S. Essock, A. Shaner, K. Carey, K. Minkoff, L. Kola et al. 2001. "Implementing Dual Diagnosis Services for Clients With Severe Mental Illness." *Psychiatric Services* 52, 4.

Elwood, William. 1995. "Declaring War on the Home Front: Metaphor, Presidents and the War on Drugs." *Metaphor and Symbolic Activity* 10, 2.

Evans-Campbell, Teresa. 2008. "Historical Trauma in American Indian/Native Alaska Communities: A Multi-Level Framework for Exploring Impacts on Individuals, Families and Communities." *Journal of Interpersonal Violence* 23, 3.

Fagan, Abigail, Emily Wright, and Gillian Pinchevsky. 2013. "Racial/Ethnic Difference in the Relationship Between Neighborhood Disadvantage and Adolescent Substance Use." *Journal of Drug Issues* 43, 1.

Foster, S., C. LeFauve, M. Kresky-Wolff, and L. Rickards. 2010. "Services and Supports for Individuals with Co-Occurring Disorders and Long-Term Homelessness." *Journal of Behavioral Health Services & Research* 37, 2.

Giffen, P.J., Shirley Endicott, and Sylvia Lambert. 1991. *Panic and Indifference: The Politics of Canada's Drug Laws*. Ottawa: Canadian Centre on Substance Abuse.

Globe and Mail. 2008. "Clement's Insite Attack Leaves WHO Red-Faced." August 6. <theglobeandmail.com/life/clements-insite-attack-leaves-who-red-faced/article1058485/>.

Goode, Erich. 2007. *Drugs in American Society*. New York: McGraw-Hill.

Government of Canada. 1996. "Controlled Drugs and Substances Act." <laws-lois.justice.gc.ca/PDF/C-38.8.pdf>.

Green, M. 1979. "A History of Canadian Narcotics Control: The Formative Years." *University of Toronto Faculty Law Review* 37.

Haskell, Lori, and Melanie Randall. 2009. "Disrupted Attachments: A Social Context Complex Trauma Framework and the Lives of Aboriginal Peoples in Canada." *Journal of Aboriginal Health* November.

Hawdon, James. 2001. "The Role of Presidential Rhetoric in the Creation of a Moral Panic: Reagan, Bush and the War on Drugs." *Deviant Behavior* 22, 5.

Hayes-Smith, Justin, and Rachel Whaley. 2009. "Community Characteristics and Methamphetamine Use: A Social Disorganization Perspective." *Journal of Drug Issues* 39, 3.

Haynie, Dana, Eric Silver, and Brent Teasdale. 2006. "Neighborhood Characteristics, Peer Networks, and Adolescent Violence." *Journal of Quantitative Criminology* 22, 2.

Hier, Sean. 2002. "Raves, Risks and the Ecstasy Panic: A Case Study in the Subversive Nature of Moral Regulation." *Canadian Journal of Sociology* 27, 1.

Jernigan, David, and Lori Dorfman. 1996. "Visualizing America's Drug Problems: An Ethnographic Content Analysis of Illegal Drug Stories on the Nightly News."

Contemporary Drug Problems 23.

Johnson, Bruce, Flutura Bardhi, Stephen Sifaneck, and Eloise Dunlap. 2006. "Marijuana Argot as Subculture Threads: Social Constructions by Users in New York City." *British Journal of Criminology* 46.

Khantzian, E.J. 1985. "The Self-Medication Hypothesis of Addictive Disorders: Focus on Heroin and Cocaine Dependence." *American Journal of Psychiatry* 142, 11.

Kirst, Maritt, Tyler Frederick, and Patricia Erickson. 2011. "Concurrent Mental Health and Substance Use Problems among Street-Involved Youth." *International Journal of Mental Health and Addiction* 9.

Kornhauser, Ruth. 1978. *Social Sources of Delinquency*. Chicago: University of Chicago Press.

Linden, Isabelle, Iris Torchalla, and Michael Krauz. 2013. "Addiction in Maternity: Prevalence of Mental Illness, Substance Use, and Trauma." *Journal of Aggression, Maltreatment & Trauma* 22.

Lukassen, Jennifer, and Marie Beaudet. 2005. "Alcohol Dependence and Depression Among Heavy Drinkers in Canada." *Social Science & Medicine* 61, 8.

McNeil, Legs, and Gillian McCain. 2006. *Please Kill Me: The Uncensored History of Punk*. New York: Grove Press.

Measham, Fiona, Howard Parker, and Judith Aldridge. 1998. "The Teenage Transition: From Adolescent Recreational Drug Use to the Young Adult Dance Culture in Britain in the Mid-1990s." *Journal of Drug Issues* 28, 1.

Menzies, Peter. 2007. "Understanding Aboriginal Intergeneration Trauma from a Social Work Perspective." *Canadian Journal of Native Studies* 27, 2.

Milby, Jesse. 1981. *Addictive Behavior and Its Treatment*. New York: Springer.

Murphy, Emily. 1922. *The Black Candle*. Toronto: Thomas Allison.

National Anti-Drug Strategy. n.d. "Canadian Drugs and Substances Strategy." <nationalantidrugstrategy.gc.ca/prevention/youth-jeunes/index.html>.

Orcutt, James, and J. Blake Turner. 1993. "Shocking Numbers and Graphic Accounts: Quantified Images of Drug Problems in the Print Media." *Social Problems* 40, 2.

Pedersen, Willy. 2009. "Cannabis Use: Subcultural Opposition or Social Marginality? A Population-Based Longitudinal Study." *Acta Sociologica* 52, 2.

Pivot Legal Society. n.d. "The Historic Insite Decision in a Nutshell." <pivotlegal.org/pivot-points/blog/the-historic-insite-decision-in-a-nutshell>.

Reefer Madness [film]. 1936. Motion Picture Ventures. <youtube.com/watch?v=zhQlcMHhF3w>.

Sampson, Robert, and W. Byron Groves. 1989. "Community Structure and Crime: Testing Social-Disorganization Theory." *American Journal of Sociology* 94, 4.

Scheier, Lawrence, Gilbert Botvin, and Nicole Miller. 2000. "Life Events, Neighborhood Stress, Psychosocial Functioning, and Alcohol Use Among Urban Minority Youth." *Journal of Child & Adolescent Substance Abuse* 9, 1.

Sellman, D. 2009. "The 10 Most Important Things Known About Addiction." *Addiction* 105, 1.

Sharp, Elaine. 1992. "Agenda-Setting and Policy Results: Lessons from Three Drug Policy Episodes." *Policy Studies Journal* 20, 4.

Sidran, Ben. 1981. *Black Talk*. New York: DaCapo Press.

Slesnick, N., and J. Prestopnik. 2005. "Dual and Multiple Diagnoses Among Substance

Using Runaway Youth." *American Journal of Drug and Alcohol Abuse* 31, 1.

Sniderman, Barney. 1999. "Just Say No to the War on Drugs." In Nick Larsen and Brian Burtch (eds.), *Law in Society: Canadian Readings*. Toronto: Harcourt Canada.

Statistics Canada. 2017. "Police Reported Crime Statistics in Canada, 2016." <statcan. gc.ca/pub/85-002-x/2017001/article/54842-eng.htm>.

___. 2013. "Police Reported Crime Statistics in Canada, 2012." <statcan.gc.ca/pub/85-002-x/2013001/article/11854-eng.pdf>.

Steen, Julie. 2010. "A Multilevel Study of the Role of Environment in Adolescent Substance Use." *Journal of Child & Adolescent Substance Abuse* 19, 5.

Stewart, Erica, Ronald Simons, and Rand Conger. 2002. "Assessing Neighborhood and Social Psychological Influences on Childhood Violence in an African-American Sample." *Criminology* 40, 4.

Thornton, Sarah. 1996. *Club Cultures: Music, Media and Subcultural Capital*. Middletown: Wesleyan University Press.

Tsemberis, Sam, Leyla Gulcur, and Maria Nakae. 2004. "Housing First, Consumer Choice, and Harm Reduction for Homeless Individuals With a Dual Diagnosis." *American Journal of Public Health* 94, 4.

Whitbeck, L., G. Adams, D. Hoyt, and X. Chen. 2004. "Conceptualizing and Measuring Historical Trauma Among American Indian People." *American Journal of Community Psychology* 33, 3–4.

Whiteacre, Kevin. 2005. "Criminal Construction of Drug Users." In Wilson R. Palacios (ed.), *Cocktails and Dreams: Perspectives on Drug and Alcohol Use*. Toronto: Pearson.

Wilson, Brian. 2002. "The Canadian Rave Scene and Five Theses on Youth Resistance." *Canadian Journal of Sociology* 27, 3.

Wood, Evan, Thomas Kerr, Elis Lloyd-Smith, Chris Buchner, David Marsh, Julio Montaner, and Mark Tyndall. 2004. "Methodology for Evaluating Insite: Canada's First Medically Supervised Safer Injection Facility for Injection Drug Users." *Harm Reduction Journal* 1, 9.

Wood, Evan, Mark Tyndall, Julio Montaner, and Thomas Kerr. 2006. "Summary of Findings from the Evaluation of a Pilot Medically Supervised Safer Injecting Facility." *Canadian Medical Association Journal* 175, 11.

Zimmerman, Gregory, and Bob Edward Vasquez. 2011. "Decomposing the Peer Effects on Adolescent Substance Use: Mediation, Nonlinearity, and Differential Nonlinearity." *Criminology* 49, 4.

6

The Creation of Sexual Deviance

Social Control of Lesbian, Gay, Bisexual, Transgender, and Queer Plus (LGBTQ+) People in Canada

Carolyn Brooks and Kirby Brigden

After reading this chapter, you will be able to do the following:

1. Understand the social construction of sexuality, heterosexual hegemony, heteronormativity, and homonormativity.
2. Describe the institutional social control of sexuality, including current LGBTQ+ rights in Canada and global LGBTQ+ rights.
3. Discuss different theories about sexuality and how these contribute to the debate on regulation.
4. Explain the importance of resistance to sexual social control and listening to the voices of those who have been controlled.

On November 28, 2017, Prime Minister Justin Trudeau officially apologized to Canada's **lesbian, gay, bisexual, transgender,** and **queer plus (LGBTQ+)** community for the injustices they faced at the hands of the government. In his speech (Trudeau 2017), he discussed the legal and social discrimination of LGBTQ+ persons, from the impact that settlers had on the destruction of Indigenous Two-Spirit and LGBTQ+ identities to ongoing increased rates of discrimination, suicide, and homelessness among LGBTQ+ youth. In particular, Trudeau apologized for the government's actions between the 1950s and early 1990s. During this time, often referred to as "the purge," the Canadian government used a variety of cruel and unjust methods to identify and persecute LGBTQ+ persons working in the country's public service (Trudeau 2017). The purge resulted in people's loss of friends, families, careers,

In this speech, he famously declared, "There's no place for the state in the bedrooms of the nation," acknowledging that government has played a significant role in the social control of the LGBTQ+ community.

health, and dignity while simultaneously normalizing discriminatory behaviour against LGBTQ+ people. He concluded by recognizing that LGBTQ+ persons continue to face various forms of discrimination and inequality, vowing that the government of Canada would make every effort to correct this damaging treatment moving forward. Fifty years prior, during Pierre Elliot Trudeau's time as justice minister, Justin Trudeau's father made a landmark speech proposing radical amendments to the Criminal Code. In this speech, he famously declared, "There's no place for the state in the bedrooms of the nation," acknowledging that government has played a significant role in the social control of the LGBTQ+ community.

Canada's history has been marked by many discriminatory acts towards LGBTQ+ populations. In Montreal in 1989, Joe Rose was kicked, struck, and stabbed to death by a group of teens for being gay. While this attack initiated activism against such violence at the time, in 2012, a journalist found that Rose had been all but forgotten by students at the school he had attended. It was not until the following year that a plaque was hung to honour him (Burnett 2015). In 2010, Shannon Barry, a lesbian woman living in Edmonton, was attacked by a man yelling sexual epithets; she suffered a broken jaw, crushed eye socket, and facial nerve damage (Rusnell 2010). Then, in 2013, Scott Jones was stabbed in the back and left paralyzed in New Glasgow, Nova Scotia (CBC News 2013). This attack spurred the "Don't Be Afraid" campaign. Jones said of homophobia, "everyone thinks its 2013 and it shouldn't be happening … but it's happening. It's like racism. It's always going to be there unless you talk about it and there's education" (CBC News 2013). In 2012, 185 hate crimes motivated by sexual orientation were reported to police in Canada (Allen 2014). The stories of hate crime are tragic and all too common.

Sociologists have studied the social construction of sexual scripts and normative sexualities, as well as how individuals falling outside of defined cultural sexual scripts have often been labelled as deviant/sick/pathological/mentally ill and/or criminal. Today, sexuality that is defined as deviant and criminal ranges from acts that involve non-consenting adults or children to various forms of paraphilia, which are marked by behaviour involving objects, humiliation, and/or suffering, such as exhibitionism, pedophilia, voyeurism, or zoophilia. The focus of this chapter is on acts that involve consenting individuals, but they have regardless been defined throughout time and place as

deviant or pathological. In particular, the focus is on members of the
LGBTQ+ community. In addition
to the aforementioned identities,
the "plus" refers to other identities

According to the Gay & Lesbian Alliance
Against Defamation, 20 percent of
millennials currently identify with some label
under the LGBTQ+ umbrella.

that are not **heterosexual** or **cisgender**, such as **Two-Spirit** (a term used by
Indigenous people to describe a variety of nonbinary gender and/or sexual
identities), **genderqueer** or **gender nonbinary** (refers to someone whose gender exists outside of or beyond the binary concept of gender), **polyamorous**
(those who have romantic and/or sexual relationships involving more than
two people), **asexual/aromantic, demisexual/demiromantic**, or **grey-sexual/
grey-romantic** (terms referring to varying degrees of sexual and/or romantic
attraction), or **pansexual** (refers to someone attracted to any gender).

The specific focus of this chapter is to develop an understanding of: (1)
current mental health and justice issues facing LGBTQ+ people; (2) public
attitudes, including homophobia, hate crimes, and resistance and advocacy;
and (3) institutional social control of sexuality, with a special focus on (a)
historical and comparative legal policy and (b) shifts in mental health policy
and psychiatry. We conclude with a discussion on resistance to sexual social
control, hate crimes, and homophobia, and we challenge readers to listen to
the voices of those who have experienced oppression and have been silenced
simply because of their sexual orientation.

LGBTQ+ Mental Health, Violence, and Resilience

> I tried to explain the conflict to her between religion, my personal
> values, [and my same-sex attractions] ... and she just kind of said,
> "Well, I don't see what your problem is. Just pick one." She didn't seem
> much help. She just didn't quite get it. —Lee Beckstead 2001: 97

Research on experiences of LGBTQ+ individuals has often demonstrated
pervasive anti-gay and homophobic attitudes that persist in Canada (Taylor
and Peter 2011) and elsewhere (Norton and Herek 2013). People who
identify as LGBTQ+ frequently become targets for social stigma, rejection, and
violence. Such stigmatization affects everyone no matter what their sexual
identity, especially young people whose sexual identities might not yet have
fully formed. According to the Gay & Lesbian Alliance Against Defamation
(GLAAD 2017), 20 percent of millennials currently identify with some label
under the LGBTQ+ umbrella. Young people and adults who identity as

> Hottes, Ferlatte, and Gesink reveal that Canadian bisexual and gay men are likewise four times more likely to have attempted suicide.

lesbian, gay, bisexual, transgender, Two-Spirit, and/or queer have consistently shown to be at a higher risk of suicide, addictions, anxiety and depression, and other mental health issues (Lea, de Wit, and Reynolds 2014). Specifically, several Canadian studies have explicitly shown an increased risk among LGBTQ+ individuals. Egale Canada Human Rights Trust (Dyck and ECHRT 2012) asserts that LGBTQ+ youth are at significantly greater risk of suicide than their heterosexual and cisgender peers. About half of LGBTQ+ youth have considered suicide, and they are over four times more likely to attempt suicide than their non-LGBTQ+ peers. Hottes, Ferlatte, and Gesink (2014) reveal that Canadian bisexual and gay men are likewise four times more likely to have attempted suicide. They further argue that this continues to be a very pressing social and political issue: suicide surpassed HIV as the leading cause of premature mortality for gay and bisexual men in 2007.

Sexual minorities continue to experience high rates of violence against them as well as day-to-day oppressions (D'Augelli, Pilkington, and Hershberger 2002; Hatzenbuelher 2011). Youth talk about experiencing difficulties within their family (D'Augelli et al. 2006), school (D'Augelli, Pilkington, and Hershberger 2002; Kosciw, Greytak, and Diaz 2009), and religion (Rostosky, Danner, and Riggle 2007), as well as other social environments that are not supportive of LGBTQ+ individuals (Hatzenbuehler 2011). The words of youth and adults, when made visible, point to experiences of fear, stigma, and rejection. Higa et al. (2014) bring forward the words of youth who talk about why they continue to be fearful in their neighbourhood and community:

> A pretty bad thing that happened to me was I was on the bus and I was spit on because I was commenting on someone's purse and I was wearing purple nail polish. I got spit on six times before I got off the bus. (646)

Another youth from the same study shared the following:

> My ex-girlfriend's little brother, he's gay and he lived in [city name], and now he's laying in a coma that he's been in for the past six months because some kids started beating the shit out of him because they knew he was gay. (646)

Hate crimes in Canada motivated by sexual orientation more than doubled from 2007 to 2008 (Dauvergne 2010). As of 2015, rates of sexual orientation–based hate crimes have decreased, but hate crimes perpetrated against sexual minority individuals are still more likely to be violent than other hate crimes. Nearly six in ten attraction-motivated crimes are violent, and four in ten result in reported injury. The rate of reported attraction-motivated hate crimes is likely lower than the actual rate of occurrence, as many victims do not understand what constitutes hate crime, some feel as though their experiences may not be severe enough to warrant police attention, and others believe that certain negative experiences are not worth reporting due to their frequency (Magic 2014). Many LGBTQ+ victims of hate crime worry that reporting victimization will reflect poorly on the community as a whole (Magic 2014).

> An American survey conducted in 2010 showed that 44 percent of lesbians and 60 percent of bisexual women had experienced rape, physical violence, or stalking by an intimate partner in their lifetime compared to 35 percent of heterosexual women; corresponding rates were 26 percent for gay men, 37 percent for bisexual men, and 29 percent for heterosexual men.

LGBTQ+ people are also at heightened risk for intimate partner violence (IPV) and sexual violence. An American survey conducted in 2010 showed that 44 percent of lesbians and 60 percent of bisexual women had experienced rape, physical violence, or stalking by an intimate partner in their lifetime compared to 35 percent of heterosexual women; corresponding rates were 26 percent for gay men, 37 percent for bisexual men, and 29 percent for heterosexual men (NISVS 2010). In Canada, 74,000 sexual assaults reported to Statistics Canada in 2014 were perpetrated against **homosexual** or bisexual persons. Bisexual people alone made up 57,000 of these assaults (Statistics Canada 2014).[1]

Lesbian and bisexual women are three to four times more likely than heterosexual women to have experienced spousal violence (Statistics Canada 2016; see also Box 6-1). Rates of IPV occur at similar rates among same-sex couples (Finneran and Stephenson 2013; Guadalupe-Diaz and Barredo 2013; Halpern et al. 2004; Kelley, Lewis, and Mason 2015; Luo, Stone, and Tharp 2014; Martin-Storey and Fromme 2016; Messinger 2011); however, despite public perceptions that men are generally at lower risk of experiencing IPV overall, men who have sex with men (MSM) experience IPV at the same rate as heterosexual women (Finneran and Stephenson 2013).

Much of the literature on the continued discrimination and experiences of LGBTQ+ individuals also draws attention to those who experience multiple oppressions — based on sexual orientation as well as race, gender, and class. In

Box 6-1: Sexual Violence against Lesbian and Bisexual Women: Focus

Several studies have found that lesbian and bisexual women experience increased rates of sexualized violence compared to their male counterparts (Alexander et al. 2016; Gilmore et al. 2014; Hequembourg, Livingston, and Parks 2013; Hughes et al. 2010; Molina et al. 2015; Rothman, Exner, and Baughman 2011). Victimization often occurs following a woman's disclosure of her sexual identity, often referred to as "coming out" (Hequembourg, Livingston, and Parks 2013). Additionally, bisexual women are more often subject to harsher incidents of sexual violence than lesbian women (Hequembourg, Livingston, and Parks 2013). As a result, women who have sex with women have higher rates or depression, post-traumatic stress disorder, and suicidal ideation than other sexual minorities and heterosexual women (Alexander et al. 2016).

The reasons bisexual women appear to be at greater risk for sexual violence have not been sufficiently studied. However, one hypothesis suggests that it could be due to a perception of bisexual women as hyper-sexual. Due to their attraction to multiple genders, bisexual women have often been stereotyped as simultaneously involved with multiple partners (Molina et al. 2015), depicted as using their attraction to women as a ploy to garner the attention of men (Angelides 2001; Baumeister 2000; Fahs 2012; Hequembourg, Livingston, and Parks 2013), or solicited by male partners to engage in bisexual behaviours (Fahs 2012). Consequently, this hyper-sexualization reinforces the notion that bisexual women are an object created to fulfill men's desires.

addition, mental health problems are often viewed as a direct effect of ongoing discrimination and social determinants related to multiple intersecting factors. The Canadian Mental Health Association of Ontario (2014) states that "LGBTQ individuals may experience multiple forms of marginalization or disadvantage at the same time. For example, an individual's experience may be shaped at the same time by their sexual orientation, racialization, gender, disability and income (e.g., a bisexual South Asian woman may have an anxiety disorder and be living in poverty)" (para. 8). A recent Ontario study found that 50 percent of transgender people have an income of less than $15,000 per year (Tjepkema 2008; Bauer et al. 2010). Transgender people in Canada and the United States have repeatedly faced discrimination in seeking employment, housing, and other services related to health and violence against them (Bauer et al. 2010), showing the influence of sexuality on socioeconomic status. In addition, others argue that LGBTQ+ youth are at greater risk of becoming street involved (Renna 2012).

The importance of understanding multiple and intersecting oppressions and considering the impact of race, class, gender, and sexuality on experience (remember Chapter 3 and the anti-oppressive feminist work!) is also demonstrated through studies with, for example, young Black gay men. LaSala and Frierson's (2012) work draws on an awareness of the intersection of sexism, (gender), racism (race), homophobia (sexuality), and classism. Issues related to cultural prescriptions of masculinities and their intersection with race is evident in the following interview with one study participant: "Oh, my God! As a black man you have everything going against you — and now this! This will just make your life so much harder" (LaSala and Frierson 2012: 434).

Multiple and intersecting places of oppression, such as racism, homophobia, and sexism, are also faced by Two-Spirit persons and other Indigenous LGBTQ+ individuals. Understanding intersecting multiple oppressions has been key in recent literature on social work and health practices. For example, in addressing critical social work practice with Indigenous LGBTQ+ people, Alaers (2010: 72) states: "with various intersecting oppressions such as racism, homophobia, sexism, socioeconomic disparities and the potential for intergenerational difficulties, creating a positive identity that unites sexuality and culture must be nourished." Similarly, in discussing risks facing Black men who have sex with men in Canada and the United States, Nelson et al. (2014) point to the importance of interventions that address racism, religious oppression, religious assets, cultural assets, and other aspects of multiple oppressions that may impact vulnerability for HIV; they recommend "the development and integration of social justice tools for nursing practice that aid in addressing the impacts of racism and other oppression on HIV vulnerability of black men who have sex with men (MSM)" (270).

While we address much of this in the final section, it is important to also bring forward some of the words of individuals who have faced adversity but thrived, as well as wonderful stories of support and love. We draw on the words of two youth:

> I have strong internal principles. I have faced enough adversity over the years in various forms and I know I am, and I'm sticking to that because I figure I've paid my dues with what I've been through — and I owe it to myself to make something out of it, or else like what's the point of going through all this? I'm going to do what I want to do. (Cited in Higa et al. 2014: 673)

> Like the best experience you could have asked for coming out, I had with my parents. And they were a hundred percent accepting, and I was really happy. (Cited in Higa et al. 2014: 673)

LGBTQ+ People and Public Opinion

Homophobia refers to the dislike of or prejudice against LGBTQ+ people. Numerous studies have tried to understand the persistence of homophobia. In this section, we briefly examine some of the literature that has linked the construction of homophobic attitudes to gender, class, religion, scripture, as well as physical attraction and social media.

Hooghe, Claes, Harell, Quintelier, and Dejaeghere (2010) examine anti-gay and homophobic attitudes in Canada and Belgium, with results showing that youth commonly hold negative feelings toward gay activism. The strongest opposition was found among teenage boys (in comparison to teenage girls) and those in more religious groups, especially Muslim youth in Western societies. This study draws attention to differences across religious groups and interpretations of religious texts. They note that "despite the fact that Jewish and Christian denominations refer to the same biblical references with regard to homosexuality, their vision with regard to LGTB rights seem to diverge ... apparently, the interpretation of these texts or the more specific cultural traditions of religious communities are more important than the texts themselves" (395–96).

The persistence of negative feelings and homophobia towards LGBTQ+ individuals and activists is concerning. Taylor and Peter's 2011 survey of 3,700 Canadian high school students between 2007 and 2009 agreed that homophobia exists to a high degree in schools. This study also found, however, that girls and young women are more likely than boys and young men to suffer physical and verbal harassment based on sexual orientation.

Numerous studies have documented public approval and disapproval over time for LGBTQ+ individuals and advocates. In both the United States and Canada, the majority of people support same-sex marriage, although this differs with age: "79% of Canadians aged 18 to 29 are in favor, as compared to 55% of those aged 60 and older. In the US, 70% of those born after 1980 support same-sex marriage as compared to 31% of those born between 1928 and 1945" (Adams 2013: para. 5).

In Canada, findings from polls show that opinions on same-sex marriage are linked to province of origin, knowing someone who identifies as LGBTQ+, low income, and differences along political lines. Opinions on same-sex marriage are notably different between

> People from Saskatchewan, Manitoba, and Alberta were the least supportive of same-sex marriage; in fact, the majority of people in Alberta have said they do not support marriage of same-sex couples.

Canadian provinces. People from Saskatchewan, Manitoba, and Alberta were the least supportive of same-sex marriage; in fact, the majority of people in Alberta have said they do not support marriage

> Active social media users are more likely to support same-sex marriages than inactive or more passive social media users (56 percent versus 50 percent and 47 percent, respectively; see also Box 6-2).

of same-sex couples (Carlson 2012). The more complicated demographic in Canada is socioeconomics. Carlson (2012) suggests that lower-income Canadians are said to be less likely to know someone who is gay or in a same-sex marriage and least likely to support it; however, they are more likely to identify as LGBTQ+. Finally, Conservative voters are least likely to support same-sex marriage, showing only a 45.8 percent approval versus New Democratic Party voters at 79.8 percent (Carlson 2012).

An Ipsos Global poll was conducted in an online panel system from April 1 to 15, 2014, in fifteen developed countries and it had 12,001 participants. Some of the findings linked religion, knowing someone who is LGBTQ+, and demographics to opinions on same-sex marriage and relationships. Two additional influential factors were access to social media and culture, suggesting that active social media users are more likely to support same-sex marriages than inactive or more passive social media users (56 percent versus 50 percent and 47 percent, respectively; see also Box 6-2). Inactive and passive users are also more likely to not be certain about their views (Ipsos 2014). Overall, this

---

Box 6-2: Transgender Representation in the Media: Focus

Media, both on- and offline, have shaped depictions of transgender characters (McInroy and Craig 2015). While some visibility of transgender individuals may be seen as better than none, the majority of trans people have found transgender depictions in the media to be negative and inaccurate (Trans Media Watch n.d.). A study conducted by GLAAD found that 54 percent of a catalogued 102 episodes of scripted television collected over a ten-year period contained negative representations of transgender characters. Additionally, 35 percent were categorized as problematic, and only 12 percent were considered groundbreaking, fair, and accurate (GLAAD 2012).

As has been explored in this chapter, LGBTQ+ youth are at particular risk of harassment, discrimination, and victimization. However, positive media representations may be useful in mitigating negative experiences and help to foster self-esteem (Craig et al. 2014). Positive representations of transgender individuals can not only provide a place of escape for trans individuals, but can also promote resilience (Craig et al. 2014).

poll found that 51 percent believe same-sex couples should be able to marry and 76 percent believe gay and lesbian individuals should have the choice to live as they please.

Stigmatization as a function of homophobia and upheld in public attitudes has occurred within institutions and ideologies/discourse. We now shift the focus to understanding social theory and the extent to which law, psychiatry, and other practices have and continue to uphold sexual norms and stigmatization of LGBTQ+ individuals as well as contribute to their definition as deviant, criminal, and/or pathological.

Social Creation of Deviance: Heterosexual Hegemony, Heteronormativity, and Homonormativity

Related to literature on homophobia, public attitudes, and social control of sexuality are the concepts of **heterosexual hegemony, heteronormativity,** and **homonormativity.** Heterosexual hegemony is a key term in the social constructionist literature and refers to those practices that define heterosexuality as "normal" and LGBTQ+ as "deviance." Heteronormativity is the assumption that heterosexual relationships are normal (i.e., assumes everyone is straight) and only between **cisgender** people. Authors in the sociology of deviance and social control have drawn on the ideas of heterosexual hegemony and/or heteronormativity. Popular theories that will be explored in this chapter include neo-Marxism, Foucauldian theories, and feminist and queer theories.

Neo-Marxism and Heterosexual Hegemony

> Coercive laws, police practices, "queer-bashing," and limited social options all attempt to make heterosexuality compulsory (or compulsive). — Gary Kinsman 2006: 103

Gary Kinsman (2006: 87) uses a neo-Marxist and feminist framework to shatter "the ahistorical character of heterosexual hegemony [disclosing] the oppressions lying beneath the 'natural' appearance of this hegemony." Kinsman (2006) points to how sexualities are created, problematizing the idea that sexuality is natural. This neo-Marxist position asks about the relationship between state formation, class, and sexual rule and maintains that sexual relations are

> Heteronormativity is the assumption that heterosexual relationships are normal (i.e., assumes everyone is straight) and only between **cisgender** people.

important in the formation of class relations and vice versa.

Hegemony occurs by normalizing some practices, sexual and otherwise, granting legitimacy to the status quo and the larger need related to capitalist economies. The dominant culture represents itself as the most all-embracing culture, dominating understanding of what is considered acceptable. In Kinsman's (2006: 103) discussion of heterosexual hegemony, he provides an understanding of how discourse is constructed through different institutions:

> The entry of heterosexual hegemony into public "common sense" involves many variants of heterosexist discourse.... These include homosexuality as a sin (in religious discourse); as unnatural (in both religious and secular discourse); as an illness (in medicine and psychiatry) ... as deviance (in some Sociology theory); ... as national security risk (...in military organization); ... and as a criminal offence or a social menace (in police campaigns, "moral panics," and the media).

Considering power relations is key to understanding how heterosexual hegemony and heterosexism have been created and upheld within societal institutions.

Heterosexual hegemony has meant subordinating LGBTQ+ individuals, who have become defined as "deviant," "patient," and "criminal." Kinsman's adaptation of standpoint feminism brings back the voices of LGBTQ+ individuals to learn even more about the workings of power: "There is no pure unmediated "telling of experience, as this is always affected by social discourse, but starting with the experiences of the oppressed and marginalized and then making them problematic locates our investigation in a very different place ... this allows us to see the workings of ruling relations from the standpoint of the oppressed" (2006: 99).

Foucault and the History of Sexuality

There is no escaping from power, that it is always-already present constituting that very thing which one attempts to counter it with.
—Michel Foucault 1978

Foucauldian scholars (and Foucault himself) provide an analysis of sexuality that develops links between professional discourse and language (such as psychiatry or medicine). Rather than attempt to define any sexuality as "truth," Foucault aims to understand how it has come into being. He likewise provided a critique of psychoanalysts (as we will see in this section) who encourage an exploration of sexual secrets to uncover sexual and emotional health, and Foucault asks instead how discourses such as psychoanalysis produce sexual representation.

Foucault argues that the idea of homosexuality did not develop until the 1870s; it is not a discovered identity but a constructed category. He acknowledges the existence of sexual practices between men and men as well as women and women, but viewing oneself as a "homosexual" became an identity to be studied and understood only at a particular point. In other words, although diverse sexualities have long been practised, they weren't viewed as part of an individual's identity and did not have labels or categories such as homosexuality. It was only through confession to a professional psychiatrist or other doctor that the term "homosexuality" was established.

In the sixteenth century, sodomy was considered a sinful act. By the nineteenth century, homosexuality was instead a scientifically determined condition inherent in the individual to be studied as a "species," with the pathologized deviant subject to control. If an individual confessed to being homosexual, for example, they were studied, interpreted, categorized, and "cured." Foucault (1978: 43) explained:

> Homosexuality appeared as one of the forms of sexuality when it was transposed from the practice of sodomy onto a kind of interior androgyny, a hermaphrodism of the soul. The sodomite had been a temporary aberration; the homosexual was now a species.

Foucault paved the way to understanding the relationship between sexuality and power differently. Social control of sexuality was not about controlling behaviours but about policing and constructing identity. Foucault offers an understanding on "technologies of the self" and "technologies of power," whereby the self is studied (recall the panopticon in Chapter 4) and objectified through science (Foucault 1978) but it also constitutes itself as a subject (see Foucault 1985). Technologies of power are techniques that aim to shape the

By the nineteenth century, homosexuality was instead a scientifically determined condition inherent in the individual to be studied as a "species," with the pathologized deviant subject to control.

conduct of individuals in ways desired by the market. Psychiatry, for example, could define proper behaviour, and under the guise of helping, provide people cures with desired effects. Technologies of the self are the techniques that individuals use to transform themselves in ways defined by powerful others to pursue happiness and higher qualities of life. "[Foucault investigated] those practices whereby individuals, by their own means or with the help of others, acted on their own bodies, souls, thoughts, conduct, and way of being in order to transform themselves and attain a certain state of perfection or happiness, or to become a sage or immortal, and so on" (Martin, Gutman, and Hutton 1988: 4).

Queer Theory

> A queer identity implies not everyone is queer in the same way. — April S. Callis 2009

Drawing from Foucault, feminism, and the ideas of formation of identity (i.e., one is not born, but *becomes* a woman or man), queer theory rejects defined categories of heterosexual/homosexual/ male/female and deconstructs hegemonic heteronormative discourse (Sullivan 2003). In fact, in queer theory, the ideas of heterosexuality, homosexuality, and bisexuality are all called into question; put forward instead are diverse and fluid ideas of sexualities, identities, and relationships. Categories and identities are problematized:

> To the queer theorist, heterosexuality and homosexuality are binary social constructs that hold saliency only in certain historical moments, rather than [as] descriptors of innate sexual types.... Rather than studying the homosexual or heterosexual individual, the queer theorist studies the webs of power and discourse that create and uphold the idea that such individuals exist, and that defining individuals by sexual object choice is somehow natural. (Callis 2009: 215)

Drawing from a Foucauldian perspective, then, queer theory analyzes categories for sexuality to expose how a society functions. Gender and sexuality are viewed as fluid. In this literature, we are also introduced to the idea of homonormativity, which is the idea that queer people inherently want to be like heterosexual people — and this is not necessarily the case. In other words, contesting homonormativity in turn critiques the idea that we have to pin things down or define identities at all.

Heterosexual hegemony, heteronormativity, and homonormativity have

Heterosexual hegemony, heteronormativity, and homonormativity have involved the subordination of gay, lesbian, and bisexual individuals as well as all other forms of sexuality and gender identity. With reference to much of the legal and **medical control** of LGBTQ+ individuals, we begin to understand that the creation of deviance does not mean that one is absent from discourse, but it does mean that individuals are given a subordinate status from which to speak — as "criminal," "pervert," or "deviant" — thus shaping identities and changing lives.

Historical Social Controls of Sexuality: Mental Health Policy and Psychiatry

> I wouldn't wish this on anybody. I would rather have cancer. That's how I look at it honestly. I have said this many times because cancer doesn't affect my eternal progression ... theoretically, I can be cut off from my wife and be cut off from God ... so this is much worse than any kind of disease that I could ever have. — A. Lee Beckstead 2001: 95

It was not until the nineteenth century that the term *homosexuality* was created — coined by Havelock Ellis (1859–1939) — and the public became fascinated with the scientific study of sexuality. Through psychiatry, homosexuality came to be viewed as a mental disorder and classified along a scale of normalization and pathologization. If a diagnosis of perversion was scientifically established, then corrective technologies could be applied as a form of "cure." As noted, though, Foucault argues that this is a form of power and coercion.

Until 1973, homosexuality was viewed as a mental disorder in need of fixing. This is an example of psychiatry defining what is normal or deviant, leading to the suppression of sexuality from the seventeenth to the twentieth century. Not until the third revised version of the *Diagnostic and Statistical Manual of Mental Disorders* (DSM) — and, importantly, through efforts from gay rights activists and dissenting academics — was homosexuality officially declassified as a form of mental illness. However, the category "ego-dystonic homosexuality" replaced it and continued to allow psychiatrists to engage in reorientation therapies with individuals who experience distress about their sexuality. Ego-dystonic sexuality meant lesbian women and gay men could be diagnosed with a mental disorder if they appeared distressed or dissatisfied with their own sexual orientation. In 1987, ego-dystonic homosexuality was removed and a new diagnosis of "sexual disorder not otherwise specified" was applied where a marked or persistent distress over sexual orientation is shown. An example by Silverstein (1972) helps make sense of why marked distress may persist based on social factors rather than simply mental pathologies:

> To grow up in a family where the word "homosexual" was whispered, to play in a playground and hear the words "faggot" and "queer," to go to church and hear of "sin" and then to college and hear of "illness," and finally to the counselling center that promises to "cure," is hardly to create an environment of freedom and voluntary choice. (cited in Beckstead 2001: 90)

Reorientation therapies, also called conversion therapy, are a type of sexual orientation therapy to change a person from homosexual or distressed to heterosexual. This form of therapy has been subject to intense moral debate, with the most high-profile advocates being conservative Christian and other religious groups. This therapy and efforts by mental health and pastoral care support providers aim to convert individuals to heterosexuality using aversion treatments. Treatments range from the use of electric shock to genitals or hands to drugs that induce nausea while the individual watches homoerotic content. Other techniques are reconditioning masturbatory responses, psychoanalytic therapies, as well as spiritual interventions, visualizations, and more. Some have undergone surgical interventions such as spinal cord cauterizations, castration, ovary removal, lobotomies, and clitoridectomies to rid themselves of an unwanted sex drive. Others hoped convulsive methods, such as electric shocks, seizures, or drugs, might disrupt brain traces created by their sexual ideas that were non-traditional for their gender — and the list goes on (Beckstead 2012).

There are many criticisms of reorientation therapy. Some argue that one cannot change their sexual orientation and that attempts might cause further harm. In fact, some authors define reorientation therapy as "consumer fraud" because it is a practice that "simply does not work" (Hadleman 1991: 150, 160, cited in Beckstead 2001: 91). And for Foucault, this process of classification and "fixing" is symbolic of a power to force individuals to conform to a single sexuality and identity, which, he argues (as do many others), does not exist.

The problematization of homosexuality or its diagnosis as a mental illness has also been criticized by theorists, such as in the infamous 1948 work of Alfred Kinsey and colleagues, who argue that society has come to see sexuality as Black and white, gay or straight, male or female. The spectrum of sexuality and of gender is explained to be much more complicated than this assumes.

Kinsey's groundbreaking research, done more than fifty years ago, argued that sexuality lies on a continuum and that terms such as gay, lesbian, bisexual, and straight are misleading for many people. Kinsey's study challenged the very idea that sexual orientation can be fit neatly into categories at all. Kinsey and his colleagues completed over 21,000 face-to-face interviews and reported that 50 percent of men were exclusively heterosexual (category 1) throughout their lifetimes while 4 percent were exclusively homosexual throughout their lifetimes. The others were somewhere between, and the term **bisexual** is appropriate for these. Key to his findings was the considerable change in the proportions over time and within subgroups. He used the following categories in his study:

0 = Exclusively heterosexual with no homosexual
1 = Predominately heterosexual, only incidentally homosexual
2 = Predominately heterosexual, but more than incidentally homosexual
3 = Equally heterosexual and homosexual
4 = Predominately homosexual, but more than incidentally heterosexual
5 = Predominately homosexual, but incidentally heterosexual
6 = Exclusively homosexual

Kinsey defined these points in his study in terms of both behaviour and orientation or preference. He was also interested in the self-definition or self-conception of the individual (how they defined themselves) (Kinsey, Pomeroy, and Martin 2003). Kinsey's concept of sexual continuums was retested in a 2012 study conducted over the internet, with 17,785 subjects in forty-eight countries, including the United States (Epstein et al. 2012). The results of this study suggest that sexual orientation should not be forced into a small number of pre-given categories:

> The entire debate about sexual orientation choice is based on a fundamental misconception, after all. The assertion that everyone is naturally straight becomes impossible when we recognize that sexual orientation lies on a continuum. The pain that some individuals suffer around sexual orientation may be based less on societal pressure to be straight than on the nearly impossible task of assigning a single label to tendencies that cannot accurately be categorized in that way. (Epstein et al. 2012: 1377)

The findings provided additional support to Kinsey, Wardell, and Martin's (1948) research that sexual orientation supports a fluid-continuum model. The 2012 authors also argue that their study provides a foundation to question the assumption that as many as 90 percent of individuals are heterosexual and a small number gay or bisexual, instead suggesting that researchers might have an obligation to use a continuum perspective in their view of sexual orientation:

> In the present sample, only 6.2% of the respondents had a perfect straight score, and only 1.2% of the respondents had a perfect gay score, leaving 92.6 percent of the sample with past or present attractions to both genders ... suggesting the inadequacy of these labels. (Epstein et al. 2012: 1377)

Other recent research has found that women have a more flexible sexual orientation than men (Mosher, Chandra, and Jones 2005). Additionally, internet quizzes and explanations about the Kinsey scale have become a popular way for internet users to understand and categorize their sexual identities anonymously, as well as providing an instrument for individuals to understand their sexuality on their own terms and allow them to feel less alone (Drucker 2010). Others reject the idea that a scale can accurately measure and define something as complex as identity, and that the Kinsey scale is too limited to express all possibilities of sexual identity (Galupo et al. 2014). Kinsey's scale has also been challenged due to its entrenchment in Western ideals, failing to account for different cultural values of sexuality and sexual behaviour (Burleson 2008).

The idea of the continuum of sexual orientation engages the "choice debate." Tests such as those proposed by Kinsey et al. (1948) or Epstein et al. (2012) do not demonstrate if an individual has flexibility in determining how to express their sexual orientation. This is also the subject of heated debate, as many individuals argue that individuals have no choice and others suggest sexual orientation or its expression is a choice. Even Kinsey et al. (1948) note that societal pressure to be heterosexual would certainly influence expression of this type. This engages the social constructionist discussion once again about sexual scripts in certain cultures and the social control over sexual expression. This literature also suggests that sexual cultures may also shift when individuals challenge sexual scripts (Epstein et al. 2012; see also Box 6-3).

The institutions of law, psychiatry, and medicine have identified "normal" and "legal" sexual orientations while problematizing and making others deviant and illegal. Disciplinary practices have created divisions of healthy/ill, sane/

> **Box 6-3: Canada's Anti-LGBT History: The "Fruit Machine"**
>
> Canada has had a tumultuous history with LGBTQ+ rights. Numerous LGBTQ+ persons have been denied jobs, housing, and the ability to adopt and raise children (Fisher 2004). It was not until 1995 that same-sex couples were allowed to file a joint application for adoption in Canada (CBC News 2012).
>
> One particular strain on Canada's relations with LGBTQ+ persons occurred during the 1960s. In the Cold War era, a prevailing fear was that homosexuals were at greater risk of exposing national secrets to Russian spies (Knegt 2018). In collaboration with a Carleton University researcher, the federal government developed a tool that came to be known as the "fruit machine" (Fisher 2004; Hauen 2017). This "machine," which consisted of a series of questions, was devised to identify gay and lesbian Canadians. During this time, more than eight thousand LGBTQ+ persons were investigated by the RCMP, and an estimated 150 lesbian and gay civil servants lost their jobs.

mad, legal/delinquent, normal/deviant as effective means of normalization. These practices, even though they have shifted, continue at the micro and personal level, internalized as ideological frameworks and identities.

Institutional Social Control of Sexuality

Any sociological understanding of sexuality begins, then, with an awareness of the sexual norms and sanctions imposed by society for violating those norms, as well as the impact of these on individuals, groups, and societies. We turn to a discussion of how heterosexual hegemony, heteronormativity, and homonormativity (although not talked about as such) have been embodied in Canada and other countries (and through time) in the criminal code, denial of rights, media, family, psychiatry, medicine, and more.

LGBTQ+ Rights in Canada

Homosexuality was defined in the Canadian Criminal Code until 1969 (CBC News 2012). In 1982, the crime of "gross indecency" was only applied to sexual acts between men, leading to arrest and criminalization. In the 1950s, the label "criminal sexual psychopath" was used to refer to men committing acts of a homosexual nature. The Criminal Code still contains an anti-sodomy law (Section 159) (*Criminal Code* 1985), originally used to criminalize homosexual men; however, it is in the process of being repealed.

Stigma against homosexuality increased in Canada following World War II, as belief grew that LGBTQ+ people were not only deviants but were also prone to "communist subversion" (Historica Canada 2017). Many other countries, however, were increasingly tolerant toward LGBTQ+ communities at this time; based on a 1957 report, British parliament legalized private, consensual homosexual acts between adults. However, Prime Minister Diefenbaker was toughening Canadian law, recommending that homosexual acts be met with a life sentence in prison, as these acts would cause injury, pain, or evil and were likely to be committed multiple times (Historica Canada 2017).

Everett George Klippert was the only Canadian to be declared a dangerous sexual offender and sentenced to life in prison simply for being homosexual. Born in Kindersley, Saskatchewan, before moving to the Northwest Territories to become a mechanic, Klippert acknowledged to police that he was gay and had had sex with men for more than twenty-four years and, alas, was quite unlikely to change. The decision to define him as a sexual offender in 1965 was backed up by the Supreme Court of Canada in 1967. The justice minister, Gérald Fauteux, stated that the majority decision was informed by the likelihood that Klippert would commit the same kind of offences (Historica Canada 2017).

In response to the Supreme Court ruling, Klippert's Member of Parliament told CBC that it was "ridiculous that any man ... would be put in jail because they are affected by [a] social disease" (Historica Canada 2017: para. 11). It was also at this time that Pierre Trudeau, then justice minister, introduced an omnibus bill to legalize consensual homosexual acts. In 1969, a different version of this bill became law, but Klippert was not released from prison until July 20, 1971. He died in 1996 due to kidney failure (Historica Canada 2017). In 2016, Prime Minister Justin Trudeau recommended that Klippert be granted a pardon posthumously and that the government consider pardoning all gay men convicted under gross indecency laws (Historica Canada 2017; Trudeau 2017).

In 1977, Quebec amended its *Charter of Rights and Freedoms* to prohibit discrimination based on sexual orientation. By 2001, a number of other Canadian provinces and territories, excluding Prince Edward Island, the Northwest Territories, and Alberta, had enacted the same amendment. That same year, homosexuals were no longer deemed an inadmissible class under the newest *Immigration Act*. Previous legislation gave Canadian immigration officials the power to exclude people from entering Canada under the label of "immoral purpose." In addition to denying entry to Canada, this legislation allowed for immediate deportation if they "practiced homosexuality" (*Immigration Act* 1976, 1977, 1978). Changes made in 1977 did not include amendments to the definition of family or spouse, which remained defined as one of the opposite sex.

Despite the decriminalization of homosexual acts, Canadian history remains marked by several injustices against LGBTQ+ individuals and groups. For example, a raid of gay bathhouses in Toronto in 1981 sparked a protest of more than three thousand people, the largest LGBTQ+ rights protest in the country's history. An instructor at King's College in Edmonton, Alberta, was fired for being homosexual — but because the province's *Individual Rights Protection Act* did not cover sexual orientation at the time, the case was not investigated until it was amended in 1997.

In the past two decades, LGBTQ+ rights have grown significantly. In 1992, individuals who defined themselves as gay or lesbian were permitted to enter the Canadian Armed Forces, lifting a long-time ban on homosexuals in the military. The adoption of children by same-sex couples was legalized in Ontario in 1995, and this was followed by similar legislation in British Columbia, Nova Scotia, and Alberta. In 1996, the Supreme Court of Canada ruled that the definition of spouse violated the *Charter of Rights and Freedoms*, and it changed the definition from "a man and a woman" to "two persons." This ruling ensured that same-sex couples would receive many of the same benefits and be subject to the same obligations as opposite-sex couples. Following a statement by Prime Minister Jean Chretien, same-sex marriage was legalized in Ontario and British Columbia in 2003, then by Saskatchewan, Manitoba, Nova Scotia, and Newfoundland and Labrador in 2004. Bill C-38, the *Civil Marriage Act*, was passed in the House of Commons in 2005, formally legalizing same-sex marriage in all of Canada. Globally, Canada was the fourth country to legalize same-sex marriage at the federal level, following the Netherlands, Belgium, and Spain, respectively (Gray 2017).

Global LGBTQ+ Rights

Globally, much remains to be done to repair the effects of the social control of LGBTQ+ populations. As of 2017, seventy-three countries still consider homosexual activity to be illegal (Gray 2017). In some of these countries, such as Turkmenistan, Sierra Leone, and Zimbabwe, same-sex conduct is illegal between men but not between women (Gray 2017). In Iran, Afghanistan, Mauritania, and Saudi Arabia, homosexual activity can be punishable by death (Gray 2017). Only five countries — Bolivia, Ecuador, Fiji, Malta, and the United Kingdom — explicitly guarantee equality for citizens on the basis of gender and sexual orientation (as cited in Gray 2017). Same-sex marriage is legal in only forty countries worldwide, though 123 countries are working toward such legislation. While some countries — such as Australia, Germany, and Malta — have legalized same-sex marriage in the past few years, other countries, such as Botswana, have made it illegal (Gray 2017).

There are even fewer rights guaranteed for transgender people. In 2016, Bill C-16 was passed in the Canadian House of Commons and lists gender identity and expression as a prohibited ground for discrimination in the *Canadian Human Rights Act* (Trans Equality Canada 2017). Various countries have created a legal recognition of sex reassignment and allow for the change of gender on birth certificates. However, many countries, such as Russia, France, China, and South Africa, require surgical transition before citizens can adjust documents (Gray 2017). The requirement of surgery is an obstacle, as transgender individuals wishing to **transition** are typically required to undergo hormone therapy for a certain amount of time before being considered for surgery. The surgery itself can be prohibitively expensive, and many transgender individuals have no desire to surgically transition at all (Weinberg 2009). In Europe, twenty countries require sterilization before gender recognition is legal, but in 2017 the European Court of Human Rights ruled that requiring sterilization for legal gender change was a violation of human rights. Those twenty countries are now in the process of adjusting their legislation (Transgender Europe 2017).

Transgender rights have been frequently discussed in American media over the past few years. Perhaps most notable is the ongoing battle over bathroom rights. As of 2017, sixteen states have considered legislation that would restrict access to bathrooms and other sex-segregated facilities based on a definition of sex or gender that refers to an individual's assigned sex at birth. Weinberg (2009: 147) notes the discomfort over transgender bathroom usage is "the result of a legal and social landscape that has adopted a 'separate spheres' ideology, in which the construction of sex segregated bathrooms and preoccupation with anatomical difference remain unchallenged." Overall, transgender rights have been under-discussed and under-implemented worldwide.

Resistance to Sexual Social Control: Voices through the Silence

Resistance takes the form of human rights networks; lobbying and activism; scholarship and research; art, symbols, novels, and creative writing; global and local pride events; educational and media reforms; and much more. International LGBTQ+ human rights activism has formed networks and professional organizations focused on political, social lobbying, and human rights claims. In some cases, human rights organizations have merged with international groups for human rights, such as Amnesty International and Human Rights Watch, and released very strong international rights statements. Browne and Nash (2014: 324) offer a few powerful examples, including "the signing of the Declaration of Montreal (2006) on the application of international human rights law in relation to 'sexual orientation' and 'gender identity' ... [and] international LGBT human rights approaches [which] have sought to use global and supranational organizations to influence domestic policy and national citizenship debates around LGBTQ+ rights."

WorldPride events promote LGBTQ+ pride at international and local levels. Involving festivals, parades, and cultural activities, these events have received support as well as opposition. The fourth celebration of WorldPride was held in Canada and was the first-ever such event in North America. Over 120,000 marchers took part in the final parade in downtown Toronto. Prior WorldPride events have been held in Rome, Jerusalem, and London (CTV News 2014).

Literary, artistic, and photographic pieces also aim to increase support for and knowledge of LGBTQ+ individuals. For example, a recent academic research project entitled "Using Theatre to Disseminate LGBTQ+ Peoples' Experiences" used "forum theatre," in which audiences watch a mini-play and then respond and react (Tarasoff et al. 2014). Other studies have used photovoice, a participatory action research method, as a method for suicide prevention with LGBTQ+ youth and as a means to understand LGBTQ+ older adults. In photovoice, participants take pictures to document their realities and engage in critical reflection individually and in a group process, using images and stories to advocate for community and policy-level changes. Individuals have likewise used social media and visual methods to share their experiences. *Out in the Silence* is one of a series of GBTQ2S+ videos that demonstrates the controversy and events following Joe Wilson's marriage to another man in Pennsylvania (British Columbia Teachers' Federation 2020).

A number of local and global programs target classrooms, religious organizations, media, and government with public awareness campaigns that aim to challenge gender role beliefs and create respectful, inclusive, and accepting schools and communities. A few efforts at Canadian schools include the following: in the Yukon Territory, all high schools are required to enact proactive strategies that are welcoming for LGBTQ+ youth and families, including having a safe contact staff member as well as visual images and positive statements;

Edmonton public schools introduced a policy in 2011 that comprehensively supported LGBTQ+ youth, families, and staff, gay-straight alliances, and policies that ensure staff address homophobic, transphobic, and sexist comments; and, in 2014, the Vancouver School Board emphasized a curriculum reflecting rights and positive messages with respect to LGBTQ+ students and their families as well as more explicitly addressing rights for trans students.

Advocacy and scholarship also address the problem of homonormativity to ensure some are not demonized for the liberation of others. The six-colour rainbow stripes of the LGBTQ+ flag are understood globally to represent sexual freedom, togetherness, and diversity. Michael Stipe, ex-member of the rock band REM, said of the colors and of queer and fluid sexual identities:

> It is the final, completely obvious contemporary acceptance and understanding that this enormous world of beauty, sexuality, identity, lust, feeling, excitement, and love isn't just black and white, or simple, at all — it is literally every shade and gradation of the rainbow. It doesn't just lie in one of two camps. It includes accepting and supporting positions that you may not even completely understand; and to arrive at that conviction is so, so beautiful, and to quote my great friend Casey Legler: "Fierce!" (Stipe 2014: para. 6)

Awareness is increasing of diverse genders and sexualities as well as multiple and intersecting oppressions. Efforts are being made to understand heterosexism, heteronormativity, homonormativity, and the ways in which sexual oppression is interconnected with race, gender, class, and age.

Conclusion

Hate crimes and other forms of discrimination against LGBTQ+ persons still make media headlines in Canada, as noted in the following examples:

- Hate crimes against gays doubled in Canada (Cohen, CanWest News Service, 2014).
- A gay couple was banned from PEI home (Logan, *Daily Extra*, November 23, 2010).
- A man accused of murdering gay activist Raymond Taavel should never have been released (Cross, *National Post*, April 18, 2012).
- Scott Jones says he was attacked for being gay (CBC News 2013).
- A man was found guilty in a Vancouver gay-bashing case (Mickelburgh, *Globe and Mail*, August 11, 2010).

We have also witnessed the decriminalization of consensual sexual orientation, further protections through human rights codes, legalized same-sex marriages, celebrated activism, and changed school curriculums.

Governing strategies of consensual sex have been shown to involve legal, medical, psychiatric, religious, and other forms of heterosexist discourse. This means that, over time, LGBTQ+ individuals have been labelled as criminal (through law), sick (through psychiatry), deviant (in media), security risks (through the military), glorified (through celebrities), and socially problematic. Heterosexual hegemony, heteronormativity, and homonormativity have prevailed in public attitudes, showing up in continued pain and discrimination. Yet, despite all of this, there is much resistance and resilience, including support, advocacy, and persistent calls for addressing stigmatization, rejection, violence, and multiple oppressions experienced by LGBTQ+ youth and adults.

Inquiry into historical processes and developed identities means we give voice to pain and suffering as well as resilience, thriving, and the celebration of diversity. As Stephanie Mott (2016) said in "The Truth About Anti-Trans* Slurs,""if it harms even one person, if it gives rise to someone's pain, it becomes personal. Expect me to say so."

Discussion Questions

1. How have heterosexual hegemony, heteronormativity, and homonormativity been embodied in the Canadian state? Draw on examples in the Criminal Code, media, family, psychiatry, and medicine.
2. In what ways have LGBTQ+ individuals been subject to multiple and intersecting oppressions?
3. What is reorientation therapy? Why is Foucault critical of psychoanalysis and these forms of curative techniques?
4. What is the difference between heteronormativity and homonormativity? Why is the concept of homonormativity useful in understanding queer theory?

Recommended Resources

1. Dyck, D.R., and ECHRT (EGALE Canada Human Rights Trust). 2012. *Report on Outcomes and Recommendations.* LGBTQ Youth Suicide Prevention Summit 2012. <egale.ca/wp-content/uploads/2013/02/YSPS-Report-online.pdf>.
2. GLAAD (Gay & Lesbian Alliance Against Defamation). 2017. "Ac-

celerating Acceptance." <glaad.org/publications/accelerating-accep-tance-2017>.

3. Kinsman, Gary. 2010. "Against National Security: From the Canadian War on Queers to the 'War on Terror.'" In Bruno Charbonneau and Wayne S. Cox (eds.), *Locating Global Order: American Power and Canadian Security after 9/11*. Vancouver: UBC Press.

4. Trans Equality Canada. 2017. "Trans Equality Rights in Canada." <transequalitycanada.com/>.

5. Trans Media Watch. n.d. "Why It Matters." <transmediawatch.org/why.html>.

Glossary

asexual/aromantic: describes a person who experiences little or no sexual/romantic attraction.

bisexual/biromantic: describes a person who is attracted to two or more genders.

cisgender: describes a person whose gender identity matches their sex/gender assigned at birth.

demisexual/demiromantic: describes a person who experiences attraction only after a strong emotional bond has been formed.

gay: typically refers to men who are attracted to men; sometimes used as an umbrella term for anyone who is not heterosexual.

genderqueer/gender nonbinary: terms to describe persons who identify and/or express themselves in ways that differ from society's binary norms of sex/gender.

grey-sexual/grey-romantic: terms used to describe persons who experience low amounts of attraction, or only under certain conditions.

heterosexual: describes a person who is attracted to the other binary gender.

heterosexual hegemony/heteronormativity: ideas and practices that view heterosexuality as the norm and LGBTQ+ identities as deviant.

homonormativity: the idea that queer people inherently want to be like heterosexual people — and this is not necessarily the case. Contesting homonormativity in turn critiques the idea that we have to pin things down or define identities at all.

homophobia: dislike or fear of, or prejudice against, homosexual people.

homosexual: describes a person who is attracted to people of their own gender.

lesbian: describes women who are attracted to other women.

LGBTQ+: acronym for lesbian, gay, bisexual, transgender, queer (plus), which refers to people belonging to sexual or gender minority identities.

polyamorous: the practice or desire to be involved in relationships involving more than two people.

queer: an umbrella term to describe LGBTQ+ identities and people to describe sexual and/or gender identities that fall outside of societal norms.

transgender: an umbrella term used to describe persons whose gender identity does not match their sex/gender assigned at birth.

transition: the process of pursuing changes (social, medical, surgical, etc.) to affirm one's gender.

Two-Spirit: an umbrella term used by various Indigenous groups to describe persons of various gender and/or sexual minority identities.

Note

1. Due to the population size, Statistics Canada requests that these numbers be used with caution.

References

Adams, M. 2013. "Why Do We Support Gay Rights? Because We Know Each Other." *Globe and Mail*, July 2. <theglobeandmail.com/opinion/why-do-we-support-gay-rights-because-we-know-each-other/article12894193/>.

Alaers, J. 2010. "Two-Spirited People and Social Work Practice: Exploring the History of Aboriginal Gender and Sexual Diversity." *Critical Social Work* 11, 1.

Allen, M. 2014. "Police-Reported Hate Crime in Canada, 2012." *Juristat* 3, 85-002.

Angelides, S. 2001. *A History of Bisexuality*. Chicago: University of Chicago Press.

Bauer, G., M. Boyce, T. Coleman, M. Kaay et al. 2010. "Who Are Trans People in Ontario." *Toronto: Trans PULSE E-Bulletin*.

Baumeister, J. 2000. "Gender Differences in Erotic Plasticity." *Psychological Bulletin* 126.

Beckstead, A.L. 2012. "Can We Change Sexual Orientation?" *Archives of Sexual Behavior* 41, 1.

____. 2001. "Cures versus Choices: Agendas in Sexual Reorientation Therapy." In Ariel Shidlo, Michael Schroeder and Jack Drescher (eds.), Sexual Conversion Therapy: Ethical, Clinical and Research Perspectives. New York: Haworth Medical Press.

British Columbia Teachers' Federation. 2020. "LGBTQ2S+ Video Resources." <bctf.ca/SocialJustice.aspx?id=47512>.

Browne, K., and C.J. Nash. 2014. "Resisting LGBT Rights Where 'We Have Won': Canada and Great Britain." *Journal of Human Rights* 13, 3.

Burleson, W.E. 2008. "The Kinsey Scale and the Pashtun: The Role of Culture in Measuring Sexual Orientation." *Journal of Bisexuality* 8, 3–4.

Burnett, R. 2015. "Prejudice to Pride: The Forgotten Murder of Joe Rose." *Montreal Gazette*, March 3. <montrealgazette.com/health/Prejudice+pride+forgotten+mur

der+Rose/9619291/story.html>.

Callis, A.S. 2009. "Playing with Butler and Foucault: Bisexuality and Queer Theory." *Journal of Bisexuality* 9, 3–4.

Canadian Mental Health Association of Ontario. 2014. *Lesbian, Gay, Bisexual, Trans & Queer Identified People and Mental Health.* Toronto: Canadian Mental Health Association. <ontario.cmha.ca/documents/ lesbian-gay-bisexual-trans-queer-identified-people-and-mental-health/>.

Carlson, K.B. 2012. "The True North LGBT: New Poll Reveals Landscape of Gay Canada." *National Post*, July 6. <nationalpost.com/news/canada/ the-true-north-lgbt-new-poll-reveals-landscape-of-gay-canada>.

CBC News. 2013. "Scott Jones Says He Was Attacked for Being Gay." December 11. <cbc.ca/news/canada/nova-scotia/scott-jones-says-he-was-attacked-for-being-gay-1.2459289>.

____. 2012. "Timeline: Same-Sex Rights in Canada." January 12. <cbc.ca/news/canada/ timeline-same-sex-rights-in-canada-1.1147516>.

Cohen, Tobi. 2014. "Hate Crimes Against Gays Doubled in Canada." CanWest News Service. <canada.com/LIFE/HATE+CRIMES+AGAINST+GAYS+DOUBLE D+CANADA/3155968/STORY.HTML>.

Craig, S.L., L. McInroy, L.T. McCready, and R. Alaggia. 2014. "Media: A Catalyst for Resilience in Lesbian, Gay, Bisexual, Transgender, and Queer Youth." *Journal of LGBT Youth* 12, 3.

Criminal Code, RSC. 1985. C-46.

Cross, Allison. 2012. "Man Accused of Murdering Gay Activist Raymond Taavel Should Never Have Been Released: Lawyer." *National Post*, April 18. <nationalpost.com/ news/canada/man-accused-of-murdering-gay-activist-raymond-taavel-should-never-have-been-released-lawyer>.

CTV News. 2014. "Rainbow of Revellers in Toronto WorldPride Parade." June 29. <ctvnews. ca/canada/rainbow-of-revellers-in-toronto-worldpride-parade-1.1891489>.

D'Augelli, A.R., A.H. Grossman, N.P. Salter, J.J. Vasey et al. 2006. "Predicting the Suicide Attempts of Lesbian, Gay, and Bisexual Youth." *Suicide and Life-Threatening Behavior* 35, 6.

D'Augelli, A.R., N.W. Pilkington, and S.L. Hershberger. 2002. "Incidence and Mental Health Impact of Sexual Orientation Victimization of Lesbian, Gay, and Bisexual Youths in High School." *School Psychology Quarterly* 17, 2.

Dauvergne, M. 2010. "Police Reported Hate Crime in Canada, 2008." *Juristat: Canadian Centre for Justice Statistics* 30, 2.

Drucker, D.J. 2010. "Male Sexuality and Alfred Kinsey's 0-6 Scale: Toward 'A Sound Understanding of the Realities of Sex.'" *Journal of Homosexuality* 57, 9.

Dyck, D.R., and ECHRT (EGALE Canada Human Rights Trust). 2012. *Report on Outcomes and Recommendations.* LGBTQ Youth Suicide Prevention Summit 2012. <egale.ca/ wp-content/uploads/2013/02/YSPS-Report-online.pdf>.

Epstein, R., P. McKinney, S. Fox, and C. Garcia. 2012. "Support for a Fluid-Continuum Model of Sexual Orientation: A Large-Scale Internet Study." *Journal of Homosexuality* 59, 10.

Fahs, B. 2012. "Compulsory Bisexuality? The Challenges of Modern Sexual Fluidity." In J. Alexander and S. Anderlini-D'Onofrio (eds.), *Bisexuality and Queer Theory:*

Intersections, Connection and Challenges. New York: Routledge.

Finneran, C., and R. Stephenson. 2013. "Gay and Bisexual Men's Perceptions of Police Helpfulness in Response to Male-Male Intimate Partner Violence." *Western Journal of Emergency Medicine* 14, 4.

Fisher, J. 2004. "Outlaws or In-Laws: Successes and Challenges in the Struggle for LGBT Equality." *McGill Law Journal* 49.

Foucault, M. 1985. *The Use of Pleasure: The History of Sexuality, vol. 2* (R. Hurley, trans.). New York: Pantheon.

____. 1978. *The History of Sexuality: An Introduction. vol. 1.* New York: Vintage.

Galupo, M.P., K.S. Davis, A.L. Grynkiewicz, and R.C. Mitchell. 2014. "Conceptualization of Sexual Orientation Identity Among Sexual Minorities: Patterns Across Sexual and Gender Identity." *Journal of Bisexuality* 14, 3–4.

Gilmore, A.K., K.H. Koo, H.V. Nguyen, H.F. Granato et al. 2014. "Sexual Assault, Drinking Norms, and Drinking Behaviour Among a National Sample of Lesbian and Bisexual Women." *Addictive Behaviors* 39, 1.

GLAAD (Gay & Lesbian Alliance Against Defamation). 2017. "Accelerating Acceptance." <glaad.org/publications/accelerating-acceptance-2017>.

____. 2012. "Victims or Villains: Examining Ten Years of Transgender Images on Television." <glaad.org/publications/victims-or-villains-examining-ten-years-transgender-images-television>.

Gray, A. 2017. "What You Need to Know About LGBT Rights in 11 Maps." World Economic Forum. <weforum.org/agenda/2017/03/what-you-need-to-know-about-lgbt-rights-in-11-maps/>.

Guadalupe-Diaz, X.L., and J. Barredo. 2013. "An Exploration of Predictors for Perpetration of Same-Sex Intimate Partner Violence in a Community Sample of Lesbians, Gays and Bisexuals." *Sociation Today* 11, 2.

Halpern, C.T., M.L. Young, M.W. Waller et al. 2004. "Prevalence of Partner Violence in Same-Sex Romantic and Sexual Relationships in a National Sample of Adolescents." *Journal of Adolescent Health* 35, 2.

Hatzenbuehler, M.L. 2011. "The Social Environment and Suicide Attempts in Lesbian, Gay, and Bisexual Youth." *Pediatrics,* 127, 5: 896–903.

Hauen, J. 2017. "Canada 'Poured Thousands and Thousands' into 'Fruit Machine' — A Wildly Unsuccesful Attempt at Gaydar." *National Post,* May 24. <nationalpost.com/news/canada/the-fruit-machine>.

Hequembourg, A.L., J.A. Livingston, and K.A. Parks. 2013. "Sexual Victimization And Associated Risks Among Lesbian and Bisexual Women." *Violence Against Women* 19, 5.

Higa, D., M.J. Hoppe, T. Lindhorst, S. Mincer et al. 2014. "Negative and Positive Factors Associated with the Well-Being of Lesbian, Gay, Bisexual, Transgender, Queer, and Questioning (LGBTQ) Youth." *Youth and Society* 46, 5.

Historica Canada. 2017. "Everett Klippert Case." <thecanadianencyclopedia.ca/en/article/everett-klippert-case/>.

Hooghe, M., E. Claes, A. Harell, E. Quintelier, and Y. Dejaeghere. 2010. "Anti-Gay Sentiment Among Adolescents in Belgium and Canada: A Comparative Investigation into the Role of Gender and Religion." *Journal of Homosexuality* 57, 3.

Hottes, T.S., O. Ferlatte, and D. Gesink. 2014. "Suicide and HIV as Leading Causes of Death Among Gay and Bisexual Men: A Comparison of Estimate Morality and

Published Research." *Critical Public Health* 25, 5.

Hughes, T.L., L.A. Szalacha, T.P. Johnson, K.E. Kinnison et al. 2010. "Sexual Victimization and Hazardous Drinking among Heterosexual and Sexual Minority Women." *Addictive Behaviors* 35, 1.

Ipsos Global Trends Survey. 2014. "Global Trends 2014." <ipsos.com/sites/default/files/publication/1970-01/ipsos-mori-global-trends-2014.pdf>.

Kelley, M., R. Lewis, and T. Mason. 2015. "Discrepant Alcohol Use, Intimate Partner Violence, and Relationship Adjustment among Lesbian Women and Their Same-Sex Intimate Partners." *Journal of Family Violence* 30, 8.

Kinsey, A.C., W.R. Pomeroy, and C.E. Martin. 2003. "Sexual Behavior in the Human Male." *American Journal of Public Health* 93, 6.

Kinsey, A., P. Wardell, and C. Martin. 1948. *Sexual Behavior in the Human Male*. Indiana University Press.

Kinsman, Gary. 2006. "The Creation of Homosexuality as a 'Social Problem.'" In A. Glasbeek (ed.), *Moral Regulation and Governance in Canada: History, Context and Critical Issues*. Toronto: Canadian Scholars' Press.

____. 2010. "Against National Security: From the Canadian War on Queers to the 'War on Terror.'" In Bruno Charbonneau and Wayne S. Cox (eds.), *Locating Global Order: American Power and Canadian Security after 9/11*. Vancouver: UBC Press.

Knegt, P. 2018. "The Fruit Machine: Why Every Canadian Should Learn About This Country's 'Gay Purge.'" *CBC News*, May 30. <cbc.ca/arts/the-fruit-machine-why-every-canadian-should-learn-about-this-country-s-gay-purge-1.4678718>.

Kosciw, J.G., E.A. Greytak, and E.M. Diaz. 2009. "Who, What, Where, When, and Why: Demographic and Ecological Factors Contributing to Hostile School Climate for Lesbian, Gay, Bisexual, and Transgender Youth." *Journal of Youth and Adolescence* 38, 7.

LaSala, M.C., and D.T. Frierson. 2012. "African-American Gay Youth and Their Families: Redefining Masculinity, Coping with Racism and Homophobia." *Journal of GLBT Family Studies* 8, 5.

Lea, T., J. de Wit, and R. Reynolds. 2014. "Minority Stress in Lesbian, Gay, and Bisexual Young Adults in Australia: Associations with Psychological Distress, Suicidality, and Substance Use." *Archives of Sexual Behavior* 8.

Luo, F., D.M. Stone, and A.T. Tharp. 2014. "Physical Dating Violence Victimization Among Sexual Minority Youth." *American Journal of Public Health* 104, 10.

Magic, J. 2014. "Social and Psychological Factors Influencing Reporting of Homophobic Hate Crime." *Socialno Delo* 53, 6.

Martin, Luther H., Beck Gutman, and Patrick H. Hutton. 1988. *Technologies of the Self: A Seminar with Michel Foucault*. Massachusetts: University of Massachusetts Press.

Martin-Storey, A., and K. Fromme. 2016. "Trajectories of Dating Violence: Differences by Sexual Minority Status and Gender." *Journal of Adolescence* 49.

McInroy, L., and S.L. Craig. 2015. "Transgender Representation in Offline and Online Media: LGBTQ Youth Perspectives." *Journal of Human Behaviour in the Social Environment* 25.

Messinger, A.M. 2011. "Invisible Victims: Same-Sex IPV in the National Violence Against Women Survey." *Journal of Interpersonal Violence* 26, 11.

Mickelburgh, Rod. 2010. "Man Found Guilty in a Vancouver Gay-Bashing Case." *Globe and Mail*, August 11. <theglobeandmail.com/news/british-columbia/

man-found-guilty-in-vancouver-gay-bashing-case/article1381035/>.

Molina, Y., J.H. Marquez, D.E. Logan, C.J. Leeson, K.F. Balsam, and D.L. Kaysen. 2015. "Current Intimate Relationship Status, Depression, and Alcohol Use among Bisexual Women: The Mediating Roles of Bisexual-Specific Minority Stressors." *Sex Roles* 73, 1.

Mosher, William D., Anjani Chandra, and Jo Jones. 2005. *Sexual Behavior and Selected Health Measures: Men and Women 15–44 Years of Age, United States, 2002.* Atlanta: US Department of Health and Human Services, Centers for Disease Control and Prevention, National Center for Health Statistics.

Mott, S. 2016. "The Truth About Anti-Trans* Slurs." *HuffPost*, February 2. <huffingtonpost. com/stephanie-mott/the-truth-about-anti-trans-slurs_b_5393083.html>.

Nelson, L.E., J.J. Walker, S.N. DuBois, and S. Giwa. 2014. "Your Blues Ain't Like Mine: Considering Integrative Antiracism in HIV Prevention Research with Black Men Who Have Sex with Men in Canada and the United States." *Nursing Inquiry* 21, 4.

NISVS (National Centre for Injury Prevention and Control). 2010. *NISVS: An Overview of 2010 Findings of Victimization by Sexual Orientation.* Atlanta: Centers for Disease Control and Prevention.

Norton, A.T., and G.M. Herek. 2013. "Heterosexuals' Attitudes Toward Transgender People: Findings from a National Probability Sample of US Adults." *Sex Roles* 68, 11–12. doi:10.1007/s11199-011-0110-6.

Renna, C. 2012. "Street-Involved Youth in Canada." CATIE. < catie.ca/en/pif/spring-2012/ street-involved-youth-canada>.

Rostosky, S.S., F. Danner, and E.D. Riggle. 2007. "Is Religiosity a Protective Factor Against Substance Use in Young Adulthood? Only if You're Straight!" *Journal of Adolescent Health* 40, 5.

Rothman, E.F., D. Exner, and A.L. Baughman. 2011. "The Prevalence of Sexual Assault Agianst People Who Identify as Gay, Lesbian, or Bisexual in the United States: A Systematic Review." *Trauma, Violence, & Abuse* 12, 2.

Rusnell, C. 2010. "Lesbian Victim of Assault Says It Was a Hate Crime." CBC *News*, April 21. <cbc.ca/news/canada/edmonton/lesbian-victim-of-assault-says-it-was-hate-crime-1.917267>.

Statistics Canada. 2016. "Family Violence in Canada: A Statistical Profile, 2014." *Juristat: Canadian Centre for Justice Statistics.* <www150.statcan.gc.ca/n1/pub/85-002-x/2016001/article/14303-eng.pdf>.

____. 2014. "Personal victimization incidents reported by Canadians, by type of offence and selected demographic and socioeconomic characteristics." <www150.statcan. gc.ca/n1/pub/85-002-x/2015001/article/14241/tbl/tbl04-eng.htm>.

Stipe, M. 2014. "Michael Stipe: Queerness Is a State of Mind Brought About by Understanding." *Guardian*, October 26. <theguardian.com/world/shortcuts/2014/oct/26/ michael-stipe-queerness-is-a-state-of-mind-brought-about-by-understanding>.

Sullivan, N. 2003. *A Critical Introduction to Queer Theory.* New York: New York University Press.

Tarasoff, L.A., R. Epstein, D.C. Green, S. Anderson, and L.E. Ross. 2014. "Using Interactive Theatre to Help Fertility Providers Better Understand Sexual and Gender Minority Patients." *Medical Humanities* 40.

Taylor, C.G., and T. Peter. 2011. *Every Class in Every School: Final Report on the First National Climate Survey on Homophobia, Biphobia, and Transphobia in Canadian*

Schools. Toronto: EGALE Canada Human Rights Trust.

Tjepkema, M. 2008. "Health Care Use Among Gay, Lesbian and Bisexual Canadians." *Health Reports* 19, 1.

Trans Equality Canada. 2017. "Trans Equality Rights in Canada." <transequalitycanada. com/>.

Trans Media Watch. n.d. "Why It Matters." <transmediawatch.org/why.html>.

Transgender Europe. 2017. "Trans Rights Europe Map & Index 2017." < tgeu.org/ trans-rights-map-2017/>.

Trudeau, J. 2017. "Remarks by Prime Minister Justin Trudeau to apologize to LGBTQ2 Canadians." November 28. <pm.gc.ca/eng/news/2017/11/28/ remarks-prime-minister-justin-trudeau-apologize-lgbtq2-canadians>.

Weinberg, J.D. 2009. "Transgender Bathroom Usage: A Privileging of Biology and Physical Difference in the Law." *Buffalo Journal of Gender, Law and Social Policy* 18.

7

"Is That Man Going to Be of Use to Canada?"

Disability as Social Control in Immigration

Edward Hon-Sing Wong and Thania Vega

After reading this chapter, you will be able to do the following:

1. Differentiate historical approaches to understanding disability as a category of social control: the charity approach, the eugenics approach, the medical approach, and the rights and social models.
2. Explain the intersection of disability and race as a means to uphold norms of belonging and deservingness.
3. Understand the evolution of the regulation of disability as a category of social control through Canadian immigration policy.
4. Draw on disability activism for lessons in developing a meaningfully inclusive society.

Disability as a social category has meant different things in different historical contexts. People's understanding of and identification with what constitutes disability, as well as the state's regulation of disability, have changed over time. Acclaimed disability scholar and activist A.J. Withers (2012) identifies four approaches to understanding disability: (1) the charity approach; (2) the eugenics approach; (3) the medical approach; and (4) the rights and social models. As we will see, how people come to understand disability plays a significant role in shaping policies and perceptions of disabled peoples. Although these approaches emerged and competed with each other at different points in history, all are still in effect today. Canadian immigration policy is particularly helpful in mapping historical shifts in how disability as a social category has been both constructed and used as a means of social control. Immigration policies construct particular bodies as disabled (broadly understood as bodies deemed contagious, deficient, inferior, or as public threats) and, in turn, disability is intertwined with other forms of social identity, especially race, as a means to uphold white, masculinist, disablist norms of citizenship. We conclude by considering an alternative approach to understanding disability: the radical disability justice approach. This approach is integral to resisting the broader dynamics that produce disability and developing a more meaningfully intersectional and inclusive society.

Approaches to Disability

What is disability? And, by extension, who gets identified as disabled? Markers identifying disability are all around us: parking spots and bus seats marked by the stick figure wheelchair icon indicate to us those spaces are reserved for the disabled; the Paralympics is held for athletes who are perceived as disadvantaged or limited relative to Olympic athletes; advertisements of law firms propose to offer legal assistance to people who have been injured or disabled in the workplace or in public; cashiers at the grocery store request donations for organizations that provide seeing-eye dogs to the visually impaired; the list goes on. Yet there seems to be little consensus, not only in terms of what constitutes disability and who the disabled are, but also in terms of what to do about disability — starting with whether it should be screened for prior to birth and how to deal with it in our educational institutions, at work, and in our neighbourhoods. The following framework, adopted from A.J. Withers's (2012) survey of disability history *Disability Politics and Theory*, which draws on existing literature and the work of disability activists, is meant to help distinguish different approaches to understanding disability, the origins and limitations of the different approaches, and how they have manifested in policy.

Charity Approach

The **charity approach** is most prominent in the contemporary understanding of disability; it is evident in advertisements pleading for donations to support war amputees or cancer research. Every year, people run marathons to promote various programs ostensibly to support disabled people, and initiatives such as the Ice Bucket Challenge have gone viral, raising over $100 million for amyotrophic lateral sclerosis (ALS) research (Diamond 2014). While these charitable initiatives are largely secular in basis, they are rooted in Christian formulations of

The **"deserving poor"** were differentiated from the **"undeserving poor"**: able-bodied indigents who were seen as lazy or personally deficient.

disability that understood disabled people as existing for the purpose of bestowing charity. Charity was seen as a quick and easy way for wealthy Christians to gain access to heaven (Stiker 1999). Indeed, such donations funded early iterations of social services in Canada provided by various Christian orders (Finkel 2006).

But charity was provided selectively and only to those defined as disabled. When the charity approach first emerged during the Middle Ages, classifications of disability were not concrete, especially relative to contemporary understandings. The definition was loosely based on a man's inability to engage in productive labour "due to a perceived physical, intellectual or psychiatric abnormality" (Withers 2012: 57). Women were not a part of this calculus until well past the nineteenth century, as they were presumed to be reliant on a husband's labour and income (Thane 1978). Some people "deserved" charity because their capacity to contribute to society was considered to be limited (hence the term "deserving poor"). The **"deserving poor"** were differentiated from the **"undeserving poor"**: able-bodied indigents who were seen as lazy or personally deficient. For example, this distinction was at the heart of a 1677 Quebec policy that banned begging, imposing stiff fines for those deemed able to work and granting licences to beg to people deemed unable to work. By 1688, seigneurs — wealthy landlords who administered much of rural French Canada — were granted the right to differentiate the "undeserving poor," who were forced to take up jobs at low wages and in poor conditions, from the "deserving poor," who were given alms. In urban areas, the distinctions were drawn by the *bureaux des pauvres* (offices of the poor) (Finkel 2006: 35).

Today, charities continue to produce specific notions of what it means to be disabled. The notion of the deserving poor has persisted: disabled people are portrayed as burdensome and pitiable. These representations have been used to channel money to the Canadian non-profit sector, which contributed over $169 billion of economic activity (e.g., in the areas of service provision, advocacy, fundraising, and research) in 2017 alone (Statistics Canada 2019). Yet most disability-focused charities are not run or led by disabled people themselves, reinforcing notions that disabled people are incapable of making their own decisions (Oliver 2009). In other words, while disabled people are represented as burdensome, they are also exploited. And while disabled people are portrayed as objects of pity, they are also stripped of their agency.

More importantly, though, the charity approach also neglects to represent institutional challenges faced by disabled people in securing housing, employment, education, or access to medical services beyond those dealing with their disability. The failure to consider institutional challenges can stall or even work against substantive social change. In her critique of what she calls the "non-profit industrial complex," Andrea Smith (2007) argues the non-profit sector tends to focus on superficially addressing individual needs rather than addressing the root causes of oppression. Just as the almsgiving of the Middle Ages was never meant to "solve 'social problems'" (Greer 1997: 25), contemporary charitable provisions "serv[e] to mask the inadequate distribution of jobs, food, housing, and other valuable resources" (Kivel 2007: 2) as well as relevant underlying causes. The charity approach serves as a means of social control, deflecting attention from problems of oppression and inequity and naturalizing social disadvantage.

Bell Media's *Let's Talk* campaign is a prominent initiative that has raised more than $100 million from its inception in 2011 to 2019 for mental health services and research (CTV 2019), allowing Bell to present itself as a major supporter of disabled people. Portrayed as a "win-win" situation for disabled people and corporations (who benefit through brand promotion leading to increased sales), the campaign obfuscates the ways in which corporations, particularly Bell Media, exacerbate the institutional challenges faced by disabled people. For instance, an employee filed a human rights complaint alleging that Bell failed to accommodate her disability (Johnson 2017). Their corporate practice, which involves pushing for greater productivity from a downsized workforce, has also been reported to produce serious mental health issues for employees, as seen in Box 7-1 (Ho 2016). A CBC investigation reported that "current and former employees describe[d] panic attacks in the workplace, stress-induced vomiting and diarrhea. Some also reported crying before starting call-centre shifts and said taking stress leave is 'common'" (Johnson 2017).

In sum, the charity approach to disability has been problematic because it mainly produces benefits for the *givers* while providing marginal benefits at best and counterproductive results at worst, for the *receivers*. The *givers* get to experience gratification or, in the case of corporate donations, a net financial benefit from an improved public image and tax credits. In contrast, those upon whom charity is bestowed often have little say in terms of how the funds are distributed and may actually see little of the funds. Even more problematically, the appearance that something is being done helps to blind or distract us from tackling the conditions of oppression that are producing or exacerbating the challenges disabled people face.

Box 7-1: Excerpt from Karen K. Ho, "Let's Talk About How My Job at Bell Gave Me Mental Health Issues and No Benefits," Canadaland website, January 31, 2016

I worked at Bell, in their media division. I needed help after working there. The terms of my job meant I was lucky I was able to access it at all.

In 2014, I was hired as a broadcast associate at the specialty television channel Business News Network, also known as BNN. I was officially a freelance employee, paid $15.25 an hour, with no sick days, vacation days, or benefits. As a permalancer, I worked 40 hours per week. Duties included grabbing coffee and water for guests, putting them on set, cutting tape, screening calls, and memorizing hundreds of stock tickers for on-screen charts and graphs. It was an extremely fast-paced, entry-level job and it meant I earned just over $30,000 a year. I thought it would be the start of a great career in multimedia. I was wrong.

The stress level of that position rose to the point where I broke fillings after day-grinding my teeth, a regular twitch started in my right eye and I developed hives for the first time. (I thought they were bed bug bites.) I rarely went through days without a clenching feeling in my chest, or the sentiment I was a complete failure at my job. The margin for error seemed enormously high. I was told I laughed too much, to stop trying to chase produce and if I wanted to write anything for the channel's website it would have to be on my own time and unpaid.

My contract did not grant me access to Bell Media's Employee Assistance Plan, meaning I had no access to mental health care through Bell. Luckily, my executive producer was able to grant me special permission. I'm grateful to her, but critical of Bell. What if I didn't feel comfortable telling my boss I was suffering? Mentioning her name was the only way I could access both counselling services by phone and then in-person as a contract staffer.

What frustrated me most about being inside the company was knowing that my work situation wasn't unique. I knew other BNN contractors who were deeply involved in producing Bell Let's Talk programming, but who also did not have health benefits, including mental health care, because they were contract workers.

This seems to be a trend both at Bell and in the media industry. Bell hasn't confirmed the health care terms for its contractors, but those we reached out to said they couldn't access the Employee Assistance Plan because they weren't permanent staff.

Eugenics Approach

The **eugenics** approach, first popularized in the late nineteenth century, was "the first [set of] cohesive ideas about a class of disabled people" (Withers 2012: 13). Eugenics was defined by Sir Francis Galton in 1865 as

> the science of improving inherited stock, not only by judicious mating, but by all the influences which give more suitable strains a better chance [and as a way] to give the more suitable races a better chance of prevailing speedily over the less suitable. (Galton and Galton 1998: 99)

Eugenics was the science of "improving" the genetic quality of a population by encouraging the procreation of "more desirable" (i.e., white non-disabled people) while preventing the procreation of others understood as defective and inferior (i.e., racialized and disabled people).

The deep entanglements between disability and race in the eugenics approach are not surprising. Eugenics was influenced by and helped justify colonialism by presenting the people of the colonized world as less able, child-like, and sub-human; consequently, their subjugation was not considered a moral transgression — rather, it was simply a natural phase within human evolution (Levine 2010). In fact, in Galton's ranking of people's "fitness" for procreation, Black people were "automatically ranked two grades lower than what he considered to be the least-fit white person" (Withers 2012: 17).

Eugenicist literature promoted the concern that "feeblemindedness is highly hereditary" (Fernald 1919: 104), resulting in people being "poorly" born and "poorly" transitioned to adulthood. In a review of the American *Manual of the Mental Examination of Aliens* published in the *Canadian Journal of Mental Hygiene* (cjmh), a major proponent of eugenics claimed that "in the case of the insane or mentally defective there is imposed a burden which tends to perpetuate itself. Each mental defective may become the progenitor of a line of paupers, vagrants, criminals or insane persons" (Notes and News 1919: 285). Adolf Meyer (1919: 152), the director of the Henry Phipps Psychiatric Clinic, also expressed concerns in the cjmh about "letting them out-marry the marriageable and out-multiply the fit." Drawing from prominent anthropological criminologists such as Cesare Lombroso — who argued that criminality was biological, caused by a reversion to a primitive form of human beings, and identifiable by physical features — the concern by proponents of eugenics was that criminality and pauperism, as forms of "mental defects," would pass from one generation to another. In addition, there was a great fear that the "mentally deficient" would quickly outnumber "normal" citizens.

In Canada, organizations such as the Canadian National Committee of Mental Hygiene (CNCMH) — a founder of the Canadian mental health field and now known as the Canadian Mental Health Association — were responsible for promoting these perspectives, influencing public discourse, and advocating for eugenics policies. These organizations were most active in the late nineteenth to mid-twentieth centuries (Dowbiggin 2003; Joseph 2012, 2015; MacLennan 1987; McLaren 1990; Menzies 1998; Wong 2016). Founded in 1918, the CNCMH promoted American Psychiatric Association president Isaac Ray's (1863: 15) definition of mental hygiene: that mental health was determined by one's lifestyle, including exercise, rest, food, and clothing, but also on a societal level through "laws of breeding." Mental hygienists tied the "laws of breeding" with the perfection of "both the body and mind of man as well as his society" (Richardson 1989: 9).

This fixation with the "laws of breeding" promoted a continued fear that undesirable groups, disabled and non-white, would outnumber the desirable. This fear led eugenicists to reject the charity approach, believing that charity would encourage and "breed poverty and misery" (Withers 2012: 50), preventing the "natural dying out" of undesirable groups. Instead, the CNCMH and other eugenicist organizations advocated for two approaches: *positive eugenics* for "normal" and "supernormals," and *negative eugenics* for "abnormals" (Withers 2012). Positive eugenics refers to policies that encourage reproduction for those deemed desirable and negative eugenics refers to policies that discourage reproduction or eliminate those deemed undesirable.

Examples of negative eugenics include **sterilization** (a procedure that leaves a person unable to reproduce), segregation, and immigration policies that restricted non-white and disabled people (Wong 2012, 2016). Perhaps most infamously, Nazi eugenics policies in Germany, which resulted in the mass murder of Jewish people, also targeted Romani people, queer people, people with mental and physical disabilities, and others. Although these policies were enacted by the Nazis, they were heavily influenced by the North American eugenicist movement (Mitchell and Snyder 2003; Withers 2012). Forced sterilization policies and gender-segregated institutionalization emerged across Canada. These policies disproportionately targeted racialized people, demonstrating how definitions of race and disability are linked. In Alberta, Indigenous women were disproportionately diagnosed as "mentally defective"; doctors used these diagnoses to override requirements for consent. Consequently, a quarter of all sterilizations were conducted on First Nations and Métis people despite this group making up less than 3 percent of the entire population (Stote 2012). While an overt eugenics approach fell out of favour given its association with the horrors of Nazi policies (Barnes 2012; Gallagher 1995), many practices based on eugenic principles remain. Immigration restrictions is one example and will be examined more closely in the following section.

Medical Approach

As the overt advocacy of eugenics became less common, the **medical approach** emerged in its place. While the eugenics approach is largely focused on the elimination of disabled people, the medical approach has a broader interest in investigating the source of disability (Withers 2012). Once the health problem is understood and diagnosed, medical practitioners attempt to "fix" the disabled person, "regulat[ing] and control[ing] sickness by curing and returning 'sick' people back to health" (Barnes 2012: 17).

Steven Smith (2005: 561) defines the medical approach as "associat[ing] being disabled with fixed essential characteristics, seen via the perspective of non-disabled people and experts, that necessarily prelude a life of personal loss or 'tragedy.'" In the case of the medical approach, disability is rooted in the body. The "normal" body is marked by its independence and understood as the ideal, while the disabled body is dependent on the support of others. In 1951, sociologist Talcott Parsons argued that disabled people are obligated to seek assistance. While to be disabled means to be excused from social obligations and personal responsibility (as recovery from their condition cannot be achieved by an act of will), the disabled person must acknowledge their condition is undesirable, seek help, and co-operate in the recovery process as prescribed by medical professionals (Norris and Faircloth 2014).

The major aspect of social control within the medical approach is the power to define behaviour or individuals as deviant (Norris and Faircloth 2014). Definitions of disability are not universal and shift even within this approach. For example, a person whose height occupies the shortest 3 percent for a particular age group and gender is now diagnosed as having "idiopathic short stature"; however, the pathologization of this physical attribute was not possible without the emergence of human growth hormone treatment and without changes in height averages (Withers 2012: 37).

The diagnosis of "extreme shortness" is an example of medicalization, the process of framing certain behaviours or conditions in medical terms and

A medical diagnosis is determined by comparing the body or mind to population averages or norms. When people have been "cured" of their deviant or disabled condition, the norm simply shifts and a new group of people is considered disabled. The central objective of the medical approach, to cure disability, is a paradoxical goal because deviance is never completely eliminated.

using medical practices to eliminate or control those conditions understood as deviant (Norris and Faircloth 2014). Indeed, just as with "extreme shortness," a medical diagnosis is determined by comparing the body or mind to population averages or norms. When people have been "cured" of their deviant or disabled condition, the norm simply shifts and a new group of people is considered disabled. The central objective of the medical approach, to cure disability, is a paradoxical goal because deviance is never completely eliminated (Withers 2012). What is considered abnormal has also broadened in scope. The 1918 *Statistical Manual for the Use of Institutions for the Insane*, a formal catalog of mental health diagnostic labels and a predecessor to the modern *Diagnostic and Statistical Manual of Mental Disorders* (DSM), featured only twenty-two diagnostic categories but, by 2000, the number of diagnoses had grown to a staggering 297 in the DSM, fourth edition, text revision (McCarron 2013).

The primary proponents of the medical approach to disability are in the medical industry (e.g., doctors, social workers, nurses, medical researchers) and the pharmaceutical industry, but also crucial are actors outside of the formal medical industry, including charities (Norris and Faircloth 2014). With these professionals taking centre stage in defining disability, experiences and perspectives held by disabled people themselves are devalued and unacknowledged. The dominant role the medical field plays in defining disability is apparent in many aspects of social policies and practices (Withers 2012). In Ontario, as in other jurisdictions, application for accommodations or social assistance requires documentation from a doctor and supplemental assessments from other professions operating under the medical approach (MCSS 2018).

The perspective held by the medical field and the process of medicalization has often served as justification for other methods of social control. An example of this is drapetomania (Mama 1995), a mental health diagnosis first developed in 1851 by Samuel A. Cartwright. The diagnosis was used to describe Black enslaved people who resisted their predicament by running away. To treat the disorder, doctors suggested using physical violence to return Black enslaved people to their "normal" state of obedience and subservience (Mama 1995). Not only was this diagnosis used to justify physical violence, it naturalized the enslavement of Black people. Similarly, Metzl (2009) argues that the diagnosis of schizophrenia was used to pathologize and detain thousands of Black people who participated in the American civil rights movement of the 1960s and 1970s. Psychiatrists interpreted the violence and behaviours associated with resistance against racism as pathological (Metzl 2009). Other groups targeted with psychiatric pathologization and labelled deviant include "women, homosexuals, vegetarians, masturbators, people on social assistance, and ... others ... because of their identities or actions, all of which are considered medically normal today" (Withers 2012: 41).

While medicalization often targets specific marginalized groups, another of its features is totalization. Totalization refers to the notion that everyone can and should be treated as a patient. Foote and Frank (1999) illustrates this with the example of grief: because everyone has the potential for grief through loss or death, everyone potentially requires medical treatment for grief. The legitimate targets of grief have also expanded to the loss of things such as prized possessions or pets and, thus, so have the target populations for therapy, with the presumption that disabled people have an obligation to get better through medical treatment. Getting better means becoming healthy once again and returning to normal social responsibilities, such as employment. As Foote and Frank (1999: 167) state, "individuals have work that they need to do, that therapy is work, and that in doing this work, bereaved people display themselves as doing what society expects of its members." Being excused from work not only increases the potential for a prompt return to being fully efficient at work, it also ensures that the emotionally distressed person does not interfere with the work of others (Foote and Frank 1999). This illustrates the connections between capitalism and the medical approach. Cushman (1995) adds that medical professionals have provided capitalists with greater control over the workplace through psychological research that erased workers' concerns about the workplace and class relations by "psychologizing" their concerns (Cushman 1995: 72). Workers have long been directed by industrial psychologists to manage concerns such as stress and fatigue through individualistic therapeutic techniques that understand these concerns as problems of "maladjustment." Rather than recognizing the roots of workers' concerns, including monotonous, demanding, and dangerous working conditions in combination with poor compensation, psychology has "served the therapeutic function of containing unrest and deflecting it onto the psyche of the worker" (Cloud 1997: 41).

As we will see in our discussion of immigration policy, medical inspection is a way to control who enters the country; it is intended to deem inadmissible applicants who are considered a danger to public health or whose care costs will potentially exceed what is considered reasonable. In this sense, applicants' disabilities are taken to be fixed, burdensome attributes, rather than possibly rooted in social causes such as Canadian corporations' practices of exploitation and extraction abroad, imperialist foreign policy, or climate change.

Rights and Social Models

In contrast to the preceding approaches, which are rooted in institutions that reinforce existing social arrangement, the rights and **social model** emerged out of the disability social movements of the 1960s (Barnes 2012). These movements challenged the modes of social control directed at disabled people and their underlying discourses. The **rights approach** had particular influence in the United States; informed by the civil rights movement and organization of the LGBTQ+ community, it focused on disabled people's access to the broader society (Roulstone, Thomas, and Watson 2012). This approach conceptualized disabled people as deserving access to broader society and to the rights held by non-disabled people. To achieve this, the movement aimed to change the built and social environments.

Rights can be divided into two categories: positive rights, referring to equality that requires special accommodations, and negative rights, referring to equality based on receiving the same kind of treatment as everyone else. Rights-based advocacy organizations argue that positive rights are necessary to achieve the full participation of disabled people in society. But while these organizations might be credited for bringing about material improvements in the lives of disabled people, they are also critiqued for "focus[ing only] on getting disabled people access to society and changing it only as much as is necessary to establish their desired rights" (Withers 2012: 82). Reformist in nature, this form of advocacy fails to address the central logics that drive discrimination on the basis of disability in society, including capitalism and colonialism. These organizations also inadequately address the unique problems faced by racialized disabled people and other issues relating to the intersections of multiple forms of oppression (Withers 2012).

Examples of organizations that fought for these demands include Rolling Quads, which advocated for physical accessibility, and the Coalition of Provincial Organizations of the Handicapped (CPOH), which successfully advocated for the inclusion of disability as a category within the *Canadian Charter of Rights and Freedoms*. The CPOH, similar to so many organizations that operate through the rights approach, explicitly focused on legal reform: a prohibition of government discrimination of disabled people. This meant that people confined to institutions (e.g., psychiatric hospitals) were now allowed to vote and that public transit had to be accessible. However, adherence to these legal stipulations (especially in relation to public transit) was not always consistent (Withers 2012).

Also emerging out of opposition to discrimination on the basis of disability, the UK social model approach is distinct from the American rights approach. Oliver (2009), an early proponent of the social model, attributes the model's development to *The Fundamental Principles of Disability*, a statement published by the Union of the Physically Impaired Against Segregation (UPIAS) in 1976. This document articulates disability as the socially constructed discrimination of people with impairments: "In our view, it is society which disables physically impaired people. Disability is something imposed on top of our impairments by the way we are unnecessarily isolated and excluded from full participation in society" (Oliver 2009: 42). In other words, *impairment* is understood as the physical component relevant to a disability, which might involve "lacking all or part of a limb, or having a defective limb, organism or mechanism of the body" (UPIAS 1976: 20), but is not understood as the direct cause for the social exclusion of disabled people. Instead, disability, defined as the discriminatory practices and discourses relevant to people with impairments, is the culprit. For instance, UPIAS (1976) considers how visual impairments result in a whole spectrum of experiences in relation to discrimination — from the notably less severe, arguably non-existent, discrimination experienced by those who wear glasses to the major challenges experienced by those with significant visual impairments in terms of navigating built spaces that were designed without consideration of their needs, such as spaces with inadequate lighting or the lack of braille signage (Oliver 2009).

The social model attempts to move away from the notion of exclusion and marginalization as rooted in biological differences and toward recognition that these problems are caused by "disabling environments, barriers and cultures" (Oliver 2009: 45). This emphasis on the environment is apparent in Oliver's (2009: 45) assertion that the "totality of disabling environments" must be examined to understand the impact of disability on daily life. Totality suggests that not just one aspect of the environment contributes to disability, but a culmination of issues — ranging from the labour market to transportation, education, and culture — is what curtails life opportunities.

Although the acknowledgement of the social challenges faced by people with disabilities has been key to the success of rights and social model

> Labelling people as threatening due to their construction as unproductive, defective, and deficient is a process of social control. This process establishes the boundaries between those who should and should not belong to the nation.

approaches, this approach does not fully conceive of impairment as separate from social processes and as fixed attributes identifiable only by medical authorities. We will elaborate more on these limitations in our concluding analysis of the radical disability justice approach.

In the preceding sections, we have established that a number of approaches to disability hold prominence in how people understand disability. Importantly, these approaches are not abstract concepts but rather have practical implications, shaping both how people interact with each other as well as government policies. A notable example of this is the Canadian immigration system's exclusion of disabled people, which will be explored in the following section.

Canadian Immigration Policy: The Social Control of Race and Disability

Labelling people as threatening due to their construction as unproductive, defective, and deficient is a process of social control. This process establishes the boundaries between those who should and should not belong to the nation. One way this operates is through the immigration system, differentiating the "desirable" (those who are permitted entry and permanent stay) from the "undesirable" (those who are barred, deported, or permitted only conditional entry and/or temporary stay). As our overview of immigration policies will show, the justifications behind the regulation of these threatening bodies as well as the means by which these bodies are identified have shifted over time, yet they reflect an ongoing desire to uphold particular citizenship norms. Our aim is therefore to show how the Canadian state's approach with respect to disability has evolved over time, as well as the deep entanglements between disease, disability, and racism as means of social control. The point is not to say that disability and race as social categories are the same, but rather that dis-

> Disability and race have often worked together to exclude or contain bodies considered undesirable or downright dangerous to the nation while simultaneously upholding particular norms around citizenship (i.e., deservingness and belonging).

ability and race have often worked together to exclude or contain bodies considered undesirable or downright dangerous to the nation while simultaneously upholding particular norms around citizenship (i.e., deservingness and belonging).

Disablist Immigration Policy from the Nineteenth to Early Twentieth Century

Throughout the nineteenth and early twentieth centuries, Canada's early immigration policies contained few restrictions but reflected a growing concern with regulating particular kinds of bodies. Many aspects of the initial legislation were justified by claims of need for quarantine and supposed fears of spreading diseases such as cholera and tuberculosis (Hanes 2011). For instance, the 1803 *Passenger Vessels Act* (Weindling 2014) passed by British Parliament and the 1832 *Quarantine Act* (Bilson 1977) passed by the government of Lower Canada (present day Quebec) aimed to improve the sanitary conditions of transport ships and prevent the spread of diseases such as typhus from reaching Canadian shores. For the most part, however, exclusions or "prohibited classes" went far beyond concerns regarding contagions and instead were grounded in a eugenic fear of racial and intergenerational contagion as well as understandings rooted in the charity approach of disabled people as drains on society.

Post-confederation Canada's very first piece of immigration legislation, the *Immigration Act* of 1869, provided border agents and medical superintendents the authority to identify passengers as "lunatic, idiotic, deaf and dumb, blind or infirm" (Canadian Museum of Immigration at Pier 21, 2018). Those identified were prohibited from entry or required to pay a bond to compensate the state and charitable institutions for the additional expense required for their support (Hanes 2011). While this policy did not explicitly bar all disabled migrants, exempting people who could prove they would be cared for by family members or had a job, this provision nonetheless relied on and reinforced the assumption that people with disabilities are unable to contribute to society. Consistent with the eugenic, charity, and medical approaches previously discussed, this inability is understood as inherent to the individual, without questioning the fact that Canadian society creates barriers for people with disabilities aiming to contribute in ways that are traditionally recognized as legitimate, such as through paid employment.

While this framing of disabled people is problematic, these restrictions were thankfully not widely implemented. On the one hand, border inspectors had weak measuring techniques and a poor understanding of how disease spread. On the other hand, the goal of expanding settlement to prevent American annexation of territories to the west of the newly founded Canadian nation-state also meant that inspections were relatively lenient and primarily concerned with assessing the usefulness of immigrants (Whitaker 1991). In the words of the chief medical officer of Canada's provincial Board of Health, the idea was to ask "is that man going to be of use to Canada?" (Fairchild 2003: 146). It was not until the turn of the century that the government shifted toward more selective and restrictive policies, largely due to growing concerns that a more open immigration policy was negatively affecting "national efficiency [and causing] societal degeneration" (Fairchild 2003: 146). By 1906, the classification was expanded and elaborated: "No immigrant shall be permitted to land in Canada, who is feebleminded, an idiot, or an epileptic, or who is insane, or has had an attack of insanity within five years" (Dawson 1906). The act also formalized the deportation of immigrants who had become "public charges" within two years. While these restrictions only resulted in the rejection of 0.46 percent of immigrants arriving from 1902 to 1911, 40 percent of those rejected were excluded for reasons of medical inadmissibility (Fairchild 2003: 146).

As eugenic theories and the fear of intergenerational contagion became increasingly popular in academic and legislative circles as well as in spaces of inspection, the taxonomy of "prohibited" or "inadmissible" classes in immigration policy was expanded. For instance, the 1910 Act included mental conditions, barring those deemed "mentally disabled" from entry into Canada except on the condition of family support (Capurri 2010). Entire families were sometimes rendered inadmissible if their accompanying dependents were labelled as "mentally disabled" (Chadha 2008). The 1927 Act further increased scrutiny and expanded the list of mental disabilities.

Throughout the twentieth century until the 1990s, border officials retained discretionary power in the assessment of disease and disability. Although their means of assessment were crude, they showed a steadfast commitment to approving immigrants who were white and able-bodied, rejecting immigrants who were not. Those admissible were permitted passage to a better life, while those rejected faced the pain of family separation and an arduous trip back to the port of departure (Kelley and Trebilcock 1998).

The Broader Context of Interlocking Disablism and Racism

The regulation of disease and disability has long had deep entanglements with **racialization**. In fact, disease, disability, and race were often indistinguishable, especially during the period when eugenics gained popularity. For instance, Langdon Down, known for his study of Down syndrome, originally described people deemed mentally deficient as "Mongoloids," based on the idea that non-white groups were stuck in earlier stages of species development (Goodey

2011). These perspectives, which suspect racialized people in particular of being diseased, inferior, or defective, inform Canadian state policies. Fear of racial and intergenerational contagion has been quelled either through outright killing or sterilization, or, when it became less normatively acceptable for Indigenous people and other racialized groups to be subjected to explicit violence, through confinement or exclusion (Chapman 2014).

For example, race- and disability-based fears were mobilized by eugenicist organizations to advocate for immigration restrictions and also intertwined with nationalistic goals of strengthening Canada (Wong 2016). In an article published in the CNCMH's official journal, founder Clarence Hincks (1919: 20) states that

> the brains of a nation constitute its most important asset. No country can be truly great, and remain so, with a population possessed of mediocre mentality. Natural resources may be necessary for the success of a country, but alone they are not sufficient, and perforce must take second place to human resources.

Indeed, a nationalist desire for Canada to be "truly great" was a major component of CNCMH's raison d'être, with a particular focus on improving mental aspects of the Canadian people. Lamenting the emphasis on purely material considerations, Hincks (1919) advocated for social policy that could foster the human capacity of the nation. While this language appears innocuous on the surface, the desirable human resources were understood as white and non-disabled, and these were fostered through eugenics policies, including immigration restriction.

The "Mental Hygiene Survey — Province of British Columbia" (1920: 39), published by the CNCMH, includes the following comment:

> Mrs. Harris [a member of the Vancouver Police] stated that she and three other police women pay particular attention to the problem of immorality. It was her opinion that the Chinese contributed to immoral practices through the sale of drugs and the enticing of white women.

Other references to the inherent otherness of the Chinese and deviant behaviours as linked to a mental deficit can be seen throughout the published works of the CNCMH (Clarke 1921; Smith 1919a, 1919b). These ideas are consistent with popular associations of Chinese people with disease and inferiority. In British Columbia, popular culture emphasized that "widespread

poverty, loathsome disease, cruel vanities, and low regard for life were all characteristic of Chinese society" (Ward 2002: 5). In particular, white Canadians
considered Chinese people inferior, unsuited for Canadian life, and inherently prone to leprosy and syphilis. Although the rates of infectious diseases
and opium addiction were indeed relatively high in racialized communities,
this was, of course, not a product of their biological propensity but, rather, a
product of their segregation into condensed urban environments with little
or no access to infrastructure and sanitation (Anderson 1991). Such ideas
reinforced and further propelled nativist campaigns that led to the *Chinese
Immigration Act* of 1885, which imposed a hefty head tax on immigrants from
China and the subsequent ban of Chinese immigrants in 1923.

   Another example of intertwined race and disability in Canadian immigration policy is the government's response to the migration of thousands of
Black families from Oklahoma to the Canadian Prairies in the late nineteenth
century. They arrived after a Canadian government advertisement campaign
in Oklahoma promised land for American farmers to settle in the Prairies.
But the Canadian government issued an order in council that constructed
Black people as inherently disabled, as they were deemed unable to survive
in Canadian territory and climate:

> For a period of one year from and after the date hereof the landing
> in Canada shall be and the same is prohibited of any immigrants
> belonging to the Negro race, which race is deemed unsuitable to the
> climate and requirements of Canada. (Vernon 2011: 37)

While the order in council was retracted two months later to prevent damaging trade relations with the United States, the government continued to
discourage Black immigration by sending immigration agents to Oklahoma
to warn potential immigrants to Canada of "the difficulties of climate and the
general prejudice that was sweeping over Canada against the negro" (Vernon
2011: 37). Likewise, the medical establishment was recruited into playing a
major role in the pathologization of racialized people and others. For example,
the commissioner of Immigration for Western Canada offered money to the
medical inspector at Emerson, Manitoba, for every Black person he rejected
(Vernon 2011).

   The idea that people of colour are inherently diseased, defective, or inferior
no longer explicitly informs immigration policy. However, the intertwining
of race and disability continues to have reverberations that yield similar
results. Medical inspections, concerned with filtering out perceived health

and economic threats, construct migrants as valuable insofar as they can be productive. In this assessment, no attention is paid to how discrimination of disabled people plays a role in disadvantaging them in the workplace, or to the possible

> From the early twentieth century until the late 1960s, immigration policy retained the eugenicist logic of earlier policies, expanding its list and identification methods of diseases and disabilities that shifted decision-making power from border officials to medical doctors.

causes of disability such as how Canadian corporations and foreign policy produce disability abroad. Meanwhile, skill assessments (wherein foreign credentials and manual or feminized labour skills are attributed less value) also serve to stratify access to the Canadian labour market in racialized ways. We explore this in more detail in the following section.

Contemporary Immigration Policies

From the early twentieth century until the late 1960s, immigration policy retained the eugenicist logic of earlier policies, expanding its list and identification methods of diseases and disabilities that shifted decision-making power from border officials to medical doctors. The *Immigration Act* of 1952, introduced when migration increased after the war, distinguished between "preferred" (British, French, and American) immigrants and "undesirable" ones (people with diseases and disabilities, homosexuals, sex workers, single Asian applicants, or people considered unsuitable for Canadian climate and culture).

Despite the lasting impact of eugenics on immigration policies, immigration policy discourse, particularly in relation to "mental disabilities," shifted in the early 1960s in response to a series of societal and political changes and social movements, including a growing distaste for eugenics, the rise of veterans' and disability rights movements that stressed public consultation in the legislative process, and the societal duty to care for and recognize the contributory potential of disabled people (Capurri 2010; Kelley and Treblicock 1998). These changes were reflected in the 1966 *White Paper on Immigration* and subsequent acts. The 1966 White Paper (Marchand 1966), commissioned by Lester B. Pearson's Liberal government, recommended flexibility, informed by scientific and medical changes, for some disabled individuals to be removed from the prohibited classes and granted permission to immigrate. Earlier policies had denied access solely on the basis of physical and mental defect, but the White Paper recommended that people should be admitted if their health showed signs of improving (Hanes 2011).

These recommendations were adopted in the *Immigration Act* of 1976 (c.

52, s. 1), which removed mentions of specific diagnoses and further limited the discretion of immigration officials to identify disease and disability (Kelley and Trebilcock 1998). The act also reflected "more politically acceptable" criteria of inadmissibility, such as the likelihood to place an "excessive demand on health and social services" (Mosoff 1999: 155). The concern with "becoming a public drain" was not new, but in the context of emergent publicly funded health and social services, the "excessive demand" criterion became a seemingly non-discriminatory mechanism that regulated the associated "costs" of disease and disability through a series of scientific calculations. While these changes did not alter the exclusionary logic of immigration policy, they gave the "appearance of social rationality" (Mosoff 1999: 4).

In the 1980s, the equality clause in the *Canadian Charter of Rights and Freedoms* (1982, s. 6(2)(b)) solidified the impression of fairness and neutrality because legislation could no longer formally discriminate against enumerated groups, such as people with disabilities. The 1992 amendment to the 1976 *Immigration Act* removed all references to disease, disorders, impairments, and disability. However, with a prevailing anxiety that disabled immigrants would drain the Canadian health and social system, the process of discrimination simply shifted from the use of diagnostic categories to a measuring of "costs" associated with the disability (Capurri 2010). The legislation's 1992 amendment clarified the meaning of "excessive demand" to mean "demands that the immigrant may reasonably be expected to make on health services and social services ... in the five years following the medical examination of the immigrant, [which] exceed five times the average annual per capita costs in Canada" (Mosoff 1999: 12). The *Medical Officer's Handbook* standardized the costs associated with particular diagnoses (Mosoff 1999).

The 1967 amendment and subsequent changes to immigration policy also removed explicit mentions of race, ethnicity, and national origin as criteria for exclusion. Thus, during this time period, as the connections between race and biology came under challenge, less explicit connections were also made between disease, disability, and race in policy discourse. In reality, however, race and disability still intersect in policy and practice albeit in more latent ways. Though the removal of explicit racial discrimination significantly increased the entry of people from Asia, the Caribbean, Latin America, and Africa (Whitaker 1991), it also established new ways to subject racialized bodies to forms of social control that undermine their worth and belonging to the nation.

The points system, which assigns points to migrants based on the likelihood of their integration into the Canadian workforce and society, is an example of a new mechanism to exclude racialized and disabled people (Knowles 2000). By relying on seemingly non-discriminatory criteria such as education levels and language proficiency (rather than national or ethnic origin), the points system appears to be neutral about race and rather focuses on migrants' qualifications and merits. However, the immigrants who are favoured are those who espouse Western and masculinist understandings of skills (i.e., who have received formal education and training in institutions recognized by Canadian authorities and in traditionally male-dominated fields such as engineering) and with the economic resources to have previously studied or worked in Canada. In contrast, immigrants who are not considered "valuable" are undesirable, leaving behind a vast array of marginalized people of colour unable to escape social and economic hardships (Anderson 2010; Valiani 2012; Walia 2010). Still, even people who have Canadian citizenship cannot completely escape social and economic hardships, given the barriers to nutritious food, housing, health care, secure and well-paid jobs, difficulties translating education and skills into social mobility, and high levels of poverty and criminalization, all of which increase risk of disease and disability (Block and Galabuzi 2011; da Silva Gorman 2016).

In the same way that the points system excludes racialized people, especially women, it also places applicants with disabilities at a disadvantage. Specifically, El-Lahib and Wehbi (2011: 4) find that the emphasis on employment and educational attainment by the points system is exclusionary for people with disabilities because

> if people with disabilities lack the education and employment experience in their countries of origin due to marginalization and exclusion, they are less likely to have the necessary qualifications to meet the selection criteria in the current Canadian immigration point system.

While the points system places all disabled people at a disadvantage given constructions of disabled people as unproductive, it especially targets racialized disabled people who face multiple forms of marginalization and are often made disabled in the first place by colonial violence, including war and occupation (da Silva Gorman 2010, 2016).

Temporary forms of migration have also excluded racialized people under the guise of neutrality. Touted as a quick way for Canadian businesses to fill perceived labour shortages with minimal investment and risk while providing migrants temporary access to better paying jobs and, in some cases, the opportunity to apply for permanent residence, temporary migration is in reality another form of regulation aimed at exploiting the labour of racialized people. Between 1953 and 1963, Canada admitted over 900 nurses from the Caribbean on the basis that their qualifications exceeded those of white nurses and that they would return to their home countries after a short period of time (Calliste 1993). Similar to the exclusion of Black Oklahoman farmers in the early 1900s, Caribbean nurses were assumed to be "biologically incapable of adjusting to the Canadian climate and culturally incapable of assimilating into Canadian society" (Calliste 1993: 89) but also "*inherently* suited to service jobs or those which required heavy physical labour, rather than to positions of authority" (Calliste 1993: 90). In contrast, nurses immigrating from Europe were evaluated and integrated into the workforce as swiftly as possible (McPherson 1996).

From the 1990s onward, temporary migration proliferated. According to the 2006 Canadian census, Canada had more temporary migrants in Canada than permanent migrants, an increase of nearly 60 percent since 1996 (Thomas 2014). Canada boasts a variety of temporary migrant programs including the Caregiver Program (formerly the Live-in Caregiver Program), the Temporary Foreign Worker Program, and the Seasonal Agricultural Worker Program — each with varying degrees of ability to change employers and access permanent residency (Rajkumar Berkowitz et al. 2012).

Temporary migration is a form of social control that puts disability outside the scope of responsibility of the hosting nation-state (Anderson 2010; Walia 2010; Yeates 2009; Valiani 2012). By preventing access to citizenship and its attendant benefits and protections, Canada extracts value from migrant workers without having to care for them if they become injured, ill, or disabled. For instance, in the case of temporary farm workers, injured workers have been sent home despite their right to access the Canadian health care system (Orkin et al. 2014; da Silva Gorman 2016). Live-in caregivers who have been promised permanent residency after three years have been denied immigration status on medical grounds (Keung 2010).

Resisting Disablist Immigration Controls

Resistance from the disability rights movement has been one of the factors behind immigration reforms. In 1984, the Council of Canadians with Disabilities (ccd) demanded federal candidates support accepting fifty or more refugees with disabilities per year. In 1991, the ccd collaborated with the Canadian Disability Rights Council to eliminate the medical examination requirement for permanent resident status applicants. This campaign had broader success in removing specific references to disability in immigration law, though the excessive demand clause remained a fixture (CCD 2013).

Others have tried to reform immigration policies through the courts. In 2003, Angela Chesters, a migrant to Canada who was denied permanent residency, contested the constitutionality of medical inadmissibility in the Canadian immigration system on equality grounds (*Chesters v. Canada* 2002). The government argued that immigrants are "assessed on a personalized basis" and concluded the visa officer's rejection could contain no stereotypical reasoning. The Supreme Court agreed with the government's arguments and judged that inadmissibility was not determined on the presence of disability per se, but rather on the *probability* that admission might amount to an undue burden on society.

More recently, the Juana Tejada Law was established, named after a live-in caregiver and labour activist who faced deportation after she was diagnosed with cancer and deemed medically inadmissible in 2006 (see Box 7-2). Tejada had applied for permanent residency through a program that granted live-in caregivers permanent residency after completing three-year employment assignments (Keung 2009). At the time, ill live-in caregivers would be removed from Canada, even if all other requirements were met. But activists, including Tejada, advocated to eliminate the requirement for a second medical examination after completing the three-year assignment. The law came into effect in 2010, a year after her death (Keung 2010). Limitations to the Juana Tejada Law quickly became apparent, however, as immigration officers still have the discretion to request medical examinations. This was the case for Marcia Piamonte Bandales, who was also diagnosed with cancer and found medically inadmissible as her diagnosis was deemed to "cause extensive demand on social services" (Keung 2010).

Given the limitations of these reforms, one of the last avenues to contest exclusion on the basis of excessive demand has been to file claims based upon humanitarian and compassionate grounds. However, the humanitarian and compassionate (H&C) application reproduces the problems with the charity approach to disability insofar as it relies on the judge's discretion to assess the extent to which the applicants deserve the status, in particular their "ability" and "willingness" to pay for treatment (*Lawyer's Daily* 2018). Furthermore, the 5 percent success rate of all H&C claims suggests this avenue is far from adequate (Agnew 2009).

Despite the discernable changes brought about by rights-based approaches and the opportunities (however slight) of H&C applications, these modes of

Box 7-2: Excerpt from: Nicholas Keung, "Juana Tejada, 39: Nanny Inspired Reforms for Caregivers," *Toronto Star*, **March 11, 2009**

Tiny and soft-spoken, Juana Tejada was a giant till her last breath as the voice for migrant nannies toiling in Canada for a better future for their families in the Philippines.

Tejada, who inspired a grassroots campaign to lobby for reforms to the federal live-in caregiver program, died of cancer Sunday at Toronto General Hospital. She was 39.

"Even though she was bedridden, when we asked her if she was ready to go, she said, 'No.'" said friend Connie Sorio. "Juana was reserved and had very few words, but she would be most remembered for her fighting spirit."

Tejada, a founding member of the United Steelworkers' Independent Workers Association, was also inspirational to a group of Philippine live-in caregivers, all struggling with cancer and immigration.

"When Juana got her (permanent residence) status, she took upon herself as the spokesperson of the campaign to change the (caregiver) program," Sorio recounted. "She never wanted any limelight. You had to prod her to speak. But she was so courageous when speaking for others."

Tejada came here in 2003 through the program, which grants permanent resident status to foreign domestic workers after they complete three-year assignments and obtain medical and criminal record clearances.

She was diagnosed with colon cancer when she applied for permanent residence in 2006 and faced removal because she was deemed a health burden.

She later won an appeal, got her status and lobbied to change the two-step medical exam required for caregivers. Under the program, a caregiver has to pass a medical test to come to Canada and another when applying for immigration. Her supporters are asking the immigration minister to exempt caregivers from the second test.

resistance still don't change the fundamental disablist and oppressive logics of the Canadian immigration system. Although racialized and disabled people are no longer explicitly excluded in immigration policy, both the exclusion of racialized disabled people and the disablement of racialized people remain key components and effects of the policy in practice. To substantively improve conditions faced by disabled people, social movements may need to take a radical approach to disability that acknowledges the complexities of how disablism

> Despite the discernable changes brought about by rights-based approaches and the opportunities (however slight) of H&C applications, these modes of resistance still don't change the fundamental disablist and oppressive logics of the Canadian immigration system.

operates, interlocked with other forms of oppression, and adopt a broader definition of accessibility that moves beyond consideration of physical barriers.

A Radical Approach for the Future

While the social model has been instrumental in challenging problematic ideas around disability and social control, critical thinkers and activists have continued to discuss its pitfalls and limitations. Similar to the social model, the **radical approach** to disability defines disability not in terms of biological categories but as socially constructed (Withers 2012) in the context of power relations. Disability is understood as a means to marginalize and stigmatize people who deviate from the norm; this marginalization not only penalizes disabled people but helps others obtain and maintain power. In the case of immigration policy, for instance, the exclusion of disabled people has enabled Canada to offload the responsibility for their care to countries already facing shortages in care professionals. Withers (2012: 98) explains that "the classification of disabled is a political determination."

The radical approach also differs from the social model because it rejects the impairment/disability distinction, recognizing that the notion of impairment is also socially constructed. As mentioned in the discussion of the medical approach, labelling impairments is largely a process of categorizing perceived deviances along a constructed norm. This is perhaps most apparent in the field of psychiatry, with its ever-expanding classifications of illnesses and disorders. Despite the radical approach's emphasis on disability and impairment as social constructions, it also seeks to acknowledge the range of difficulties people face in relation to their bodies and minds. Withers (2012: 36) explains that these people sometimes struggle to talk about the pain they feel or limitations they face, as they fear it reinforces notions that "disabled people do not have full and rewarding lives." Ultimately, the radical approach intends to challenge these pressures to conceal or erase experiences of hardship faced by disabled people by emphasizing that these difficulties are not solely the product of being disabled; rather, "we experience them because we are human" (Withers 2012: 115). Frustrations with the mind or body are normal, not a so-called pathology or membership in the disability category.

The radical approach also recognizes that these hardships can be directly caused by colonial violence and other social processes in a process called **disablement**. This process is alluded to in our discussion of the role of poverty and criminal justice involvement in increasing the chance of disability for racialized people. Da Silva Gorman (2010) warns that overemphasizing disability as

Indigenous people are recognized as disproportionately disabled, but without consideration of who and what might be responsible for this situation. Canada's role in the disablement of people internationally, many of whom are denied entry into the country because of Canadian immigration policy, is also ignored.

a social category without consideration of disablement can obfuscate colonial processes in producing the conditions faced by disabled and colonized peoples. Thus, instead of recognizing the role of residential schools in the "high rates of trauma, injury, malnourishment, and illness" (Chapman 2014: 35) after discharge, disability associated with Indigenous people is naturalized or individualized. In other words, Indigenous people are recognized as disproportionately disabled, but without consideration of who and what might be responsible for this situation. Canada's role in the disablement of people internationally, many of whom are denied entry into the country because of Canadian immigration policy, is also ignored. Examples include disablement caused by Canadian corporate practices (e.g., mining operations that lead to environmental pollution and armed conflict with locals opposed to business practices) and Canadian participation in war and occupation (Gordon 2010).

Disability studies have traditionally paid little attention to disablement, especially as experienced by racialized people (da Silva Gorman 2010). The radical approach recognizes that experiences of disability do not occur in a vacuum and are, instead, shaped by the interlocking systems of disablism, racism, sexism, capitalism, and other oppressive systems. As Bannerji (1995) argues, understandings of social realities cannot be fragmented or emphasize one part (e.g., disability or class) over another, as our experiences of society result from many forms of oppression coming together at once. Definitions of disability likewise often rely on racist stereotypes that are frequently linked to medical definitions of disability. Failure to recognize interlocking oppression leads to an analysis that defaults to the experiences of white disabled men as representative of all disabled peoples. Some proponents of the social model have called for access to formal paid labour as a means to address social inequalities faced by disabled people, without acknowledging the unpaid labour performed largely by disabled women, such as reproductive labour and housework, and without considering the supports that may benefit those engaged in unpaid work (Withers 2012).

Finally, the radical approach is critical of how proponents of rights and social models tend to contain ideas of accessibility to physical access (e.g., ramps and door sizes), despite the many other barriers to accessing a space.

For example, a building with ramps and large doorways might still be inaccessible if transit is unavailable or unaffordable, if racism prevents a Black man from hailing a taxi, or

> Failure to recognize interlocking oppression leads to an analysis that defaults to the experiences of white disabled men as representative of all disabled peoples.

if fears of deportation prevent a person with precarious immigration status from leaving home. The radical approach is also skeptical of approaches to accessibility based on universality. Epitomized by "universal design," which argues for the creation of products and spaces that are accessible to all (Story, Mueller, and Mace 1998), universalist approaches fail to recognize that "people and their needs change" (Withers 2012: 118). Considering the complexities of access, the radical approach suggests that access needs to involve constant dialogue, whereby "we treat people as people and look at each of our needs and how to collectively meet them" (Withers 2012: 118). These conversations must acknowledge barriers to both the body and mind, and consider not only presence but "comfort, participation and leadership" (Withers 2012: 118).

Conclusion

The different historical approaches to understanding disability as a category of social control — the charity approach, the eugenics approach, the medical approach, and the rights and social models — are not purely intellectual endeavours. They inform policies and practices that have material implications on people's lives. As is apparent through their influence on Canadian immigration policy, these approaches to race and disability intertwine to uphold norms of belonging and deservingness. Nevertheless, resistance and opposition to these practices is also driving a new radical approach to disability that aims to bring about substantive change by challenging the underlying logics and structures that inform the social control of all people, regardless of whether the medical system recognizes them as disabled or not.

Discussion Questions

1. What are some current examples in which you see one of the four approaches (charity, eugenics, medical, rights and social models) being used in social control?
2. What are some of the ways in which contemporary social and labour policies (such as social and employment assistance programs) differentiate between "deserving" and "undeserving" poor?
3. Reflect on experiences with disability and/or illness in your own life.

What limitations and obligations did you face?

4. Is disability burdensome? If so, why and how can we work to mitigate this? If not, how can we better recognize the value that disabled people bring to our societies?

Recommended Resources

1. A.J. Withers's website <stillmyrevolution.org>.
2. Mia Mingus on disability justice, interview with Greg Macdougall for the Icarus Project (video and transcript available at <equitableeducation.ca/2013/mia-mingus-disability-justice>).
3. *The Disability Rights Movement: From Charity to Confrontation* by Doris Zames Fleischer and Frieda Zames.
4. *Why I Burned My Book and Other Essays on Disability* by Paul K. Longmore.

Glossary

charity approach: understands disabled people as "deserving" of charity insofar as their capacity to contribute to society is considered limited. The charity approach serves as a means of social control, deflecting attention away from problems of oppression and inequity.

deserving and undeserving poor: the term "deserving poor" describes disabled people who were "deserving" of charity insofar as their capacity to contribute to society was limited. Conversely, the "undeserving poor" were able-bodied indigents struggling under the social changes of the time, but were seen as having chosen their struggle because of their laziness or personal deficiencies.

disablement: the process of colonial violence and other historical/material conditions causing impairments and physical or emotional hardships.

eugenics: the science of improving the genetic quality of a population by encouraging the procreation of "more desirable" (i.e., white non-disabled people) while preventing the procreation of others understood as defective and inferior (i.e., racialized and disabled people).

medical approach: considers disability as rooted in the body. The "normal" body is marked by its independence and understood as the ideal, while the disabled body is dependent on the support of others.

pathologization: seeing a symptom or behaviour as an indication of disease or abnormality. This process removes the symptom or behaviour from its larger social causes, such as poverty and exploitation, and it also opens up the opportunity for medical or other forms of institutional intervention.

racialization: historically specific processes in which social relations become structured by categorization on the basis of supposed biological or cultural characteristics.

radical approach: more explicitly frames disability as a social construction in the context of power relations. The construction of disability is understood as a means to marginalize and stigmatize people who deviate from the norm. This marginalization not only penalizes disabled people but helps others obtain and maintain power.

rights approach: considers disabled people as deserving access to the broader society and to the rights held by non-disabled people.

social model: considers disability as the socially constructed discrimination of people with impairments. Based on this understanding, disability is rooted in discriminatory practices and perspectives, not in biological difference.

sterilization: a procedure that renders someone unable to reproduce children.

References

Agnew, Vijay. 2009. *Racialized Migrant Women in Canada*. Toronto: University of Toronto Press.

Anderson, Brigit. 2010. "Migration, Immigration Controls and the Fashioning of Precarious Workers." *Work, Employment & Society* 24.

Anderson, Kay. 1991. *Vancouver's Chinatown: Racial Discourse in Canada, 1875–1980*. Montreal: McGill-Queen's University Press.

Bannerji, Himani. 1995. "But Who Speaks for us?" In *Thinking Through: Essays on Feminism*. Toronto: Women's Press.

Barnes, Colin. 2012. "Understanding the Social Model of Disability." In Nick Watson, Alan Roulstone, and Carol Thomas (eds.), *Routledge Handbook of Disability Studies*. New York: Taylor & Francis Group.

Bilson, Geoffrey. 1977. "The First Epidemic of Asiatic Cholera in Lower Canada, 1832." *Medical History* 21.

Block, Sheila, and Grace-Edward Galabuzi. 2011. "Canada's Colour Coded Labour Market." Canadian Centre for Policy Alternatives, March 21. <policyalternatives.ca/publications/reports/canadas-colour-coded-labour-market>.

Calliste, Agnes. 1993. "Women of Exceptional Merit: Immigration of Caribbean Nurses to Canada." *Canadian Journal of Women and the Law* 6, l.

Canadian Charter of Rights and Freedoms. 1982, s 6(2)(b). Ottawa: Government of Canada. <laws-lois.justice.gc.ca/eng/Const/page-15.html>.

Canadian Museum of Immigration at Pier 21. 2018. "Immigration Act, 1869." <pier21.ca/research/immigration-history/immigration-act-1869>.

Capurri, Valentina. 2010. "Canadian Public Discourse around Issues of Inadmissibility for Potential Immigrants with Diseases and/or Disabilities 1902–2002." PhD diss., York University.

CCD (Council of Canadians with Disabilities). 2013. "Immigration and People with Disabilities." <ccdonline.ca/en/socialpolicy/immigration>.

Chadha, Ena. 2008. "'Mentally Defectives' Not Welcome: Mental Disability in Canadian Immigration Law, 1859–1927." *Disability Studies Quarterly* 28, 1.

Chapman, Chris. 2014. "Five Centuries' Material Reforms and Ethical Reformulations of Social Elimination." In Liat Ben-Moshe, Chris Chapman, and Allison C. Carey (eds.), *Disability Incarcerated: Imprisonment and Disability in the United States and Canada*. London: Palgrave Macmillan.

Chesters v. Canada. 2002. *Angela Chesters v. Her Majesty the Queen in Right of Canada as represented by the Minister of Citizenship and Immigration*, IMM-1316-97; 221 FTR 1 — 96 CRR (2d) 337. <canlii.org/en/ca/fct/doc/2002/2002fct727/2002fct727.html>.

Clarke, Charles Kirk. 1921. "A Study of 5,000 Cases Passing Through the Psychiatric Clinic." *Canadian Journal of Mental Hygiene* 3, 2.

Cloud, Dana, L. 1997. *Control and Consolation in American Culture and Politics: Rhetoric of Therapy*. Thousand Oaks: Sage Publications.

CTV. 2019. "Bell Let's Talk Day Raises More than $7.2M, Breaks Previous Record." <ctvnews.ca/mobile/canada/bell-let-s-talk-day-raises-more-than-7-2m-breaks-previous-record-1.4274778>.

Cushman, Phillip. 1995. *Constructing the Self, Constructing America: A Cultural History of Psychotherapy*. New York: Doubleday.

da Silva Gorman, Rachel. 2016. "Disability In and For Itself: Towards a 'Global Idea of Disability." *Somatechnics* 6, 2.

____. 2010. "Empire of Rights: The Convergence of Neoliberal Governance, 'States of Exception,' and the Disability Rights Movement." Paper presented at Cripping Neoliberalism: Interdisciplinary Perspectives on Governing and Imagining Dis/Ability and Bodily Difference, October 8, 2010, Charles University, Prague.

Dawson, S.E. 1906. *An Act Respecting Immigration and Immigrants*. Ottawa.

Diamond, Dan. 2014. "The ALS Ice Bucket Challenge Has Raised $100 Million — And Counting." *Forbes*, August 29. <forbes.com/sites/dandiamond/2014/08/29/the-als-ice-bucket-challenge-has-raised-100m-but-its-finally-cooling-off>.

Dowbiggin, Ian R. 2003. *Keeping America Sane: Psychiatry and Eugenics in the United States and Canada, 1880–1940*. Ithaca: Cornell University Press.

El-Lahib, Yahya, and Samantha Wehbi. 2011. "Immigration and Disability: Ableism in the Policies of the Canadian State." *International Social Work*, 55, 1.

Fairchild, Amy. 2003. *Science at Borders: Immigrant Medical Inspection and the Shaping of the Modern Industrial Labor Force*. Baltimore: Johns Hopkins University Press.

Fernald, Walter E. 1919. "State Programmes for the Care of the Mentally Defective." *Canadian Journal of Mental Hygiene* 1, 2.

Finkel, Alvin. 2006. *Social Policy and Practice: A History*. Waterloo: Wilfred Laurier University Press.

Foote, Catherine E., and Arthur W. Frank. 1999. "Foucault and Therapy: The Disciplining of Grief." In Adrienne S. Chambon, Allan Irving, and Laura Epstein (eds.), *Reading

Foucault for Social Work. New York: Columbia University Press.

Gallagher, Hugh. 1995. *By Trust Betrayed: Patients, Physicians and the License to Kill in the Third Reich*. Arlington: Vandamere Press.

Galton, David J., and Clare J. Galton. 1998. "Francis Galton: and Eugenics Today." *Journal of Medical Ethics* 24, 2.

Goodey, C.F. 2011. *A History of Intelligence and "Intellectual Disability": The Shaping of Psychology in Early Modern Europe*. Ashgate Publishing Ltd.

Gordon, Todd. 2010. *Imperialist Canada*. Winnipeg: Arbeiter Ring.

Greer, Allan. 1997. *The People of New France*. Toronto: University of Toronto Press.

Hanes, Roy. 2011. "None Is Still Too Many: An Historical Exploration of Canadian Immigration Legislation as It Pertains to People with Disabilities." Winnipeg: Council of Canadians with Disabilities. <ccdonline.ca/en/socialpolicy/access-inclusion/none-still-too-many>.

Hincks, Clarence M. 1919. "The Scope and Aims of the Mental Hygiene Movement in Canada." *Canadian Journal of Mental Hygiene* 1, 1.

Ho, Karen K. 2016. "Let's Talk About How My Job at Bell Gave Me Mental Health Issues and No Benefits." Canadaland, January 31. <canadalandshow.com/lets-talk-about-how-my-job-bell-gave-me-mental-health-issues-and-no-benefits>.

Immigration Act. 1976, c. 52, s. 1. <refworld.org/docid/3ae6b5c60.html>.

Johnson, Erica. 2017. "Bell's 'Let's Talk' Campaign Rings Hollow for Employees Suffering Panic Attacks, Vomiting and Anxiety." November 25. <canadalandshow.com/lets-talk-about-how-my-job-bell-gave-me-mental-health-issues-and-no-benefits/>.

Joseph, Ameil J. 2015. *Deportation and the Confluence of Violence Within Forensic Mental Health and Immigration Systems*. Basingstoke: Palgrave-Macmillan.

____. 2012. "Ancestries of Racial and Eugenic Systems of Violence in the Mental Health Sector." In Ian Needham, Kevin McKenna, Mireille Kingma, and Nico Oud (eds.), *Third International Conference on Violence in the Health Sector*. The Netherlands: Kavanah.

Kelley, Ninette, and Michael J. Trebilcock. 1998. *The Making of the Mosaic: A History of Canadian Immigration Policy*. Toronto: University of Toronto Press.

Keung, Nicholas. 2010. "Loophole in New Law Leaves Sick Nannies at Risk." *Toronto Star*, June 6. <thestar.com/news/gta/2010/06/06/loophole_in_new_law_leaves_sick_nannies_at_risk.html>.

____. 2009. "Juana Tejada, 39: Nanny Inspired Reforms for Caregivers." *Toronto Star*, March 11. <thestar.com/news/gta/2009/03/11/juana_tejada_39_nanny_inspired_reforms_for_caregivers.html>.

Kivel, Paul. 2007. "Social Service or Social Change?" In Incite! Women of Color Against Violence (eds.), *The Revolution Will Not Be Funded: Beyond the Non-Profit Industrial Complex*. Cambridge: South End Press.

Knowles, Valerie. 2000. *Forging Our Legacy: Canadian Citizenship and Immigration, 1900–1977*. Ottawa: Public Works and Government Services.

Lawyer's Daily. 2018. "Empathy Needed in Dealing with Health-Care Related Immigration Cases, Say Lawyers." January 18. <thelawyersdaily.ca/articles/5690>

Levine, Philippa. 2010. "Anthropology, Colonialism, and Eugenics." In Alison Bashford and Philippa Levine (eds.), *The Oxford Handbook of the History of Eugenics*. Oxford: Oxford University Press.

Longmore, Paul K. 2003. *Why I Burned My Book and Other Essays on Disability.* Philadelphia: Temple University Press.

MacLennan, David. 1987. "Beyond the Asylum: Professionalization and the Mental Hygiene Movement in Canada, 1914–1928." *Canadian Bulletin of Medical History* 4, 1.

Mama, Amina. 1995. *Beyond the Mask: Race, Gender and Subjectivity.* London: Routledge.

Marchand, Jean. 1966. *White Paper on Immigration.* Ottawa: Queen's Printer.

McCarron, Robert M. 2013. "The DSM-5 and the Art of Medicine: Certainly Uncertain." *Annals of Internal Medicine* 159, 5.

McLaren, Angus. 1990. *Our Own Master Race: Eugenics in Canada, 1885–1945.* Toronto: Oxford University Press.

McPherson, Kathryn M. 1996. *Bedside Matters: The Transformation of Canadian Nursing, 1900–1990.* University of Toronto Press.

MCSS (Ministry of Children, Community and Social Services, Ontario). 2018. "Applying for ODSP Income Support." March 8. <mcss.gov.on.ca/en/mcss/programs/social/odsp/income_support/IS_Application.aspx>.

"Mental Hygiene Survey — Province of British Columbia." 1920. *Canadian Journal of Mental Hygiene* 2, 1.

Menzies, Robert. 1998. "Governing Mentalities: The Deportation of 'Insane' and 'Feebleminded' Immigrants Out of British Columbia from Confederation to World War II." *Canadian Journal of Law and Society* 13, 2.

Metzl, Johnathan Michel. 2009. *The Protest Psychosis: How Schizophrenia Became a Black Disease.* Boston: Beacon Press.

Meyer, Adolf. 1919. "The Right to Marry." *Canadian Journal of Mental Hygiene* 1, 2.

Mitchell, David, and Sharon Snyder. 2003. "The Eugenic Atlantic: Race, Disability, and the Making of an International Eugenic Science, 1800–1945." *Disability & Society* 18, 7.

Mosoff, Judith. 1999. "Excessive Demand on the Canadian Conscience: Disability, Family, and Immigration." *Manitoba Law Journal* 26.

Norris, Claire, and Christopher A. Faircloth. 2014. "Medicalization of Deviance." In Craig J. Forsyth and Heith Copes (eds.), *Encyclopedia of Social Deviance.* Thousand Oaks: Sage Publications.

Notes and News. 1919. *Canadian Journal of Mental Hygiene* 1, 3.

Oliver, Michael. 2009. *Understanding Disability: From Theory to Practice.* London: Palgrave Macmillan.

Orkin, Aaron M., Morgan Lay, Janet McLaughlin, Michael Schwandt, and Donald Cole. 2014. "Medical Repatriation of Migrant Farm Workers in Ontario: A Descriptive Analysis." *CMAJ Open* 2, 3.

Parsons, Talcott. 1951. *The Social System.* Glencoe: Free Press.

Rajkumar, Deepa, Laurel Berkowitz, Leah F. Vosko, Valerie Preston, and Robert Latham. 2012. "At the Temporary-Permanent Divide: How Canada Produces Temporariness and Makes Citizens through its Security, Work, and Settlement Policies." *Citizenship Studies* 16, 3/4.

Ray, Isaac. 1863. *Mental Hygiene.* Boston: Ticknor and Fields.

Richardson, Theresa R. 1989. *The Century of the Child: The Mental Hygiene Movement & Social Policy in the United States and Canada.* Albany: State University of New York Press.

Roulstone, Alan, Carol Thomas, and Nick Watson. 2012. "The Changing Terrain of

Disability Studies." In Nick Watson, Alan Roulstone, and Carol Thomas (eds.), *Routledge Handbook of Disability Studies*. New York: Taylor & Francis Group.

Smith, Andrea. 2007. "Introduction: The Revolution Will Not Be Funded." In Incite! Women of Color Against Violence (eds.), *The Revolution Will Not Be Funded: Beyond the Non-Profit Industrial Complex*. Brooklyn: South End Press.

Smith, Steven R. 2005. "Equality, Identity and the Disability Rights Movement: From Policy to Practice and from Kant to Nietzsche in More than One Uneasy Move." *Critical Social Policy* 25, 4.

Smith, William George. 1919a. "Immigration Past and Present." *Canadian Journal of Mental Hygiene* 1, 1.

___. 1919b. "Oriental Immigration." *Canadian Journal of Mental Hygiene* 1, 3.

Statistics Canada. 2019. "Non-Profit Institutions and Volunteering: Economic Contribution, 2007 to 2017." <www150.statcan.gc.ca/n1/daily-quotidien/190305/dq190305a-eng.htm>.

Stiker, Henri Jacques. 1999. *A History of Disability*. Ann Arbor: University of Michigan Press.

Story, Molly Follette, James L. Mueller, and Ronald L. Mace. 1998. "The Universal Design File: Designing for People of All Ages and Abilities." <ncsu.edu/ncsu/design/cud/pubs_p/pudfiletoc.htm>.

Stote, Karen. 2012. "The Coercive Sterilization of Aboriginal Women in Canada." *American Indian Culture and Research Journal* 36, 3.

Thane, Pat. 1978. "Women and the Poor Law in Victorian and Edwardian England." *History Workshop* 6.

Thomas, Derrick. 2014. "Foreign Nationals Working Temporarily in Canada." <statcan.gc.ca/pub/11-008-x/2010002/article/11166-eng.htm>.

UPIAS (Union of the Physically Impaired Against Segregation). 1976. "Fundamental Principles of Disability." <disability-studies.leeds.ac.uk/wp-content/uploads/sites/40/library/UPIAS-fundamental-principles.pdf>

Valiani, Salimah. 2012. *Rethinking Unequal Exchange: The Global Integration of Nursing Labour Markets*. Toronto: University of Toronto Press.

Vernon, Karina. 2011. "The First Black Prairie Novel: Chief Buffalo Child Long Lance's Autobiography and the Repression of Prairie Blackness." *Journal of Canadian Studies* 45, 2.

Walia, Harsha. 2010. "Transient Servitude: Migrant Labour in Canada and the Apartheid of Citizenship." *Race and Class* 52, 1.

Ward, Peter. 2002. *White Canada Forever: Popular Attitudes and Public Policy Toward Orientals in British Columbia*. Montreal: McGill-Queen's University Press.

Weindling, Paul. 2014. *Healthcare in Private and Public from the Early Modern Period to 2000*. London: Routledge.

Whitaker, Reginald. 1991. *Canadian Immigration Policy Since Confederation*. Ottawa; Canadian Historical Association.

Withers, A.J. n.d. Home page. <stillmyrevolution.org>.

Withers, A.J. 2012. *Disability Politics and Theory*. Winnipeg: Fernwood Publishing.

Wong, Edward Hon-Sing. 2016. "'The Brains of a Nation': The Eugenicist Roots of Canada's Mental Health Field and the Building of a White Non-Disabled Nation." *Canadian Review of Social Policy* 75.

____. 2012. "Not Welcome: A Critical Analysis of Ableism in Canadian Immigration Policy from 1869 to 2011." *Critical Disability Discourses* 4.

Yeates, Nicola. 2009. *Globalizing Care Economies and Migrant Workers: Explorations in Global Care Chains*. Basingstoke: Palgrave MacMillan.

Zames Fleischer, Doris Zames, and Frieda Zames. 2012. *The Disability Rights Movement: From Charity to Confrontation*. Philadelphia: Temple University Press.

8

Living on the Margins

Contextualizing Resiliency Through the Lens of Marginalized Youth

Kandis Boyko and Mitch D. Daschuk

After reading this chapter, you will be able to do the following:

1. Identify variables associated with the social construction of adolescence.

2. Explain how the Western economy exploits adolescents.

3. Demonstrate how the concepts of **"folk devils"** and "moral panics" are relevant for public attitudes on youth populations.

4. Elaborate on factors contributing to youth becoming street involved or out of doors.

5. Critically appraise how practices of resilience among marginalized youth can be interpreted as deviant acts by outsiders.

Adolescence is the social and cultural transitional period between childhood and adulthood, encompassing ages 15 to 24 (Statistics Canada 2016). Youth have long been subject to specific rights and restrictions within Canada, based on the premise that they lack cognitive maturity and require policies designed to prevent their moral corruption and economic exploitation (Barmacki 2007; Schissel 2006; Côté and Allahar 2004). Despite this, adolescents nevertheless hold a precarious position in Western society. Popularly characterized by media, moral entrepreneurs (whom Sean Hier discusses at further length in Chapter 9), and medical experts as a demographic at pronounced risk of disorder and criminal conduct, "teenagerdom" is largely synonymous with anxieties relating to public safety and the moral sanctity of future generations.

Critical sociologists have considered the prevalent forms of discourse associated with "the adolescent," drawing specific attention to how these perspectives normalize the political disempowerment and economic exploitation of young adult populations. The field of critical youth studies has been particularly keen to demonstrate the role that this discourse plays in characterizing marginalized youths' survival strategies as acts of criminality and deviance. Here, we provide an overview of macro-sociological perspectives of adolescence. We then link these themes with micro-sociological perspectives that contextualize "deviant" youth conduct as self-preservation and resilience. We draw particular attention to the evolution of adolescence and, with it, Western ideologies legitimizing the social values of the nuclear family, parental dependence, and mandatory education. We demonstrate how these idealized notions of adolescence contradict the experiences of marginalized youth and, in some cases, contribute to their social marginality.

The Social Construction of Adolescence

Sociologists based in critical youth studies argue that the concepts of "adolescence" and the "teenaged years" gained traction during the transition to industrialized urban societies throughout the 1800s (Coleman 1961; Lapsley, Enright, and Serlin 1985; Fasick 1994). Prior to industrialized methods of production and distribution of goods, families were often responsible for producing their own goods to ensure their self-sustenance. Given these demands on the family, children were expected to take on the role of providers as early as age 10 or 11. As health care and medicine were far less advanced than they are today, high rates of infantile death contributed to bigger family sizes to ensure collective survival. Simply put, pre-industrial families did not well resemble what we know today as the nuclear family (two parents and 2.5 biological children). Trends in familial organization began to change with industrialization, though, and as new economic systems emerged and people migrated to cities from their rural homes, industrialized society gradually revised common assumptions regarding the unique status of pre-adult populations. Fasick (1994) identifies five "demographic transitions" related to the social construction of adolescence: (1) population increase and urbanization; (2) the emergence of the small family system; (3) the development of mandatory education laws; (4) cultural practices based around "parental dependence"; and (5) the onset of "youth culture."

Just as technological and scientific innovations revolutionized the production and distribution of goods, medical advancements lengthened the average life expectancy. As adults now found their odds of living longer to be drastically improved, this meant that youth labour was not only no longer required, but might even impede adult workers with family responsibilities from being employed. Couples were no longer under pressure to produce large families, and within the Canadian context, a sole breadwinner could support a familial unit (with disposable income to spare). Under these conditions, labour legislation throughout much of the industrialized world began to prevent young people from participating in the paid workforce. In Canada, youth age 12 and younger are now entirely prohibited from working, and youth under the age of 17 require parental consent (Ministry of Justice 2019). However, many provincial governments have legislation extending alternate determinations of the age at which adolescents can take on employment with parental consent; whereas Manitoba sets the minimum age at 16, New Brunswick permits youth as young as 14 to work within certain sectors of the economy (LawNow 2014). Though Fasick (1994) concedes that the majority of Western youth sought a public education long before persons under 16 years of age were legally required to stay enrolled in school, the onset of **mandatory education** legislation in the nineteenth century also ensured that youth would be prohibited from entering the Western workforce. Mandatory education also ensured that youth under 16 were unable to survive beyond the confines of the family unit. This concern led to the popularization of a new Western cultural practice — **parental dependence** — whereby parents came to be expected to house and provide for their offspring until they had completed their mandated education. Finally, as the concept of "adolescence" began to take on cultural legitimacy, burgeoning mainstream **culture industries** (see Box 8-1) involved in the production, marketing, and distribution of consumer goods began to market distinct forms of entertainment, fashion, and leisure-time activities to adolescents who — with the support of parents — constituted a new population of consumers. This further contributed to the reification of adolescence and popularized a range of consumer goods through which youth themselves could engage with and broadcast markers of distinct

---

Box 8-1: What Is the Culture Industry?

Marxist theorists Horkheimer and Adorno (1947) focus on the emergence of **culture industries**: the dominant industries and institutions that manufacture and distribute cultural products, such as art, entertainment, and fashion. Adorno and Horkheimer argued that the culture industries promote hegemony by reshaping the ways in which we think about the world and consume homogenized mass entertainment. By their view, the onset of new technologies for cultural reception (radio, photography, film, television) empowered the corporate world to dictate the contents of popular entertainment and consumption items to reinforce our commonsensical perspective that our current systems of social and cultural order are the only possible forms of social organization.

In the culture industries, we have come to approach art and information as sources of amusement, something we engage with to deter intellectual stimulation. As entertainment consumption became a prevalent means of "winding down" following a hard day's work, Horkheimer and Adorno argue that the proletariat became conditioned to amuse themselves instead of analytically reflecting on their position in life and thereby mobilizing toward change.

When we approach entertainment as "nothing to be taken seriously" and uncritically absorb media representations of the world, it is all the easier for cultural products to shape the subconscious ways that we perceive of the world. Consider prime-time network television programs such as sitcoms that depict traditional social roles associated with family life, heteronormativity, and characters who derive much of their self-worth from their claims to a strong work ethic. Adorno and Horkheimer would suggest that these representations are meant to direct audiences toward affinities for these characters based on their similar social contexts while signalling that the hardships associated with working-class life are universal, inevitable, and unchangeable. At the same time, these representations of normativity also inform and reinforce the viewer's commonsensical perspectives on how the world works and what conduct is permissible. In lieu of striving for self-affirmation through creative expression, we substitute this need with the emotional connections we develop through these cultural products. Further, the culture industry conditions us to reinforce our notions of "self" through the act of purchasing consumer goods.

"teenage" cultures based around emergent trends in fashion and a rejection of their parents' culture.

Fasick (1994) asserts that the youth-centred consumer market reinforced the perspective among members of their parents' culture that youth ought to be perceived as a social group with distinct cultural practices. Medovoi (2005) further suggests these narratives would also have an indelible effect on how youth perceived *themselves*. As the mainstream culture industries began to promote jazz, blues, soul, and rock'n'roll to distinctly defined Western youth markets, youth themselves were given the impression that self-actualization and identity formation could be best achieved through the consumption of distinct cultural goods. Noting that the marketing strategies of the mid-twentieth century culture industries framed the concept of identity "as the product of self-defining and self-affirming acts that confront a punitive authoritarian 'other,'" Medovoi suggests that youth cultural goods did not merely serve to naturalize the life stage of adolescence, but they correlated this life stage with "[an individual's] triumphant self-transformation as it detaches itself agonistically from the coerced expectations of 'society,' America, one's elders [and so forth]" (2005: 5). Industries began targeting adolescents with both consumer goods and a corresponding cultural discourse to promote the prospect that forming a distinctly adolescent identity was predicated upon engaging in some measure of nonconformity.

Critical Perspectives on Adolescence: Exploitation and Medicalization

Two Western youth cultural processes are codified by prompting adolescent populations to critique and resist the values of their parents' society through purchasing cultural goods — one whereby youth are urged to engage in practices of "self-building" through the consumption of consumer goods and another whereby the very consumer goods marketed toward youth extend the impression that "teenagers" constitute a unique — and often oppositional — "culture" unto themselves. This suggests that Western notions surrounding the prospect that "teenage rebellion" is a normal, natural, and "commonsense" byproduct of one's voyage through the life cycle might indeed themselves be byproducts of corporate-cultural initiatives centred on manufacturing a new consumer base who might then signify their "social refusal" by consuming the goods — leather jackets, teen magazines, or records — of the very "dominant culture" that they are ostensibly rallying against.

The reaffirmation of conformity through teenage rebellion dovetails well with conflict perspectives on the economic exploitation of adolescent populations. Political

> Western notions surrounding the prospect that "teenage rebellion" is a normal, natural, and "commonsense" byproduct of one's voyage through the life cycle might indeed themselves be byproducts of corporate-cultural initiatives centred on manufacturing a new consumer base who might then signify their "social refusal" by consuming the goods — leather jackets, teen magazines, or records — of the very "dominant culture" that they are ostensibly rallying against.

economy perspectives approach adolescence as a life stage of pronounced social disempowerment, where youth are pressured to find employment and engage in adolescent rites of hyper-consumption, focused on the constitution of identity (Côté and Allahar 2006; Tannock 2001). But adolescents are also subject to Canadian child labour laws that bar those age 14 and under from working for a wage and restrict the types and amount of employment that youth over 14 can access (Schissel 2006). Though characterized as *preventative* measures for exploitation, these restrictions direct adolescents toward minimum-wage positions, often in fast food and retail, while being excluded from accessing employee benefits (Tanner 2010; Schissel 2006).

Adolescents are subjected to a second form of exploitation around their social function as "super-consumers" (Schor 2004; Quart 2003; Frank 1997). Aspects of Western economic stability are dependent on youth consumers having a disposable income. The Western cultural practice of prolonged parental dependence allows industries targeting youth to promote the notion that "identity" can only be established and reinforced through product consumption. In sum, youth resign themselves to exploitative employment for the ability to engage in consumption-centred forms of self-affirmation. This effectively funnels the disposable income of precariously employed youth directly back into the profit margins of the very industries that thrive on their continued economic disempowerment.

Many critical theorists study the evolution of prevalent forms of adolescent discourse, often drawing heavily from Michel Foucault's *History of Sexuality* (1978). Foucault argued that science popularizes forms of clinical "speech" that characterize non-normative forms of conduct as "mental illness." Critical youth research seeks to understand how clinical "expert" discourse informs prevalent assumptions surrounding adolescence, advocating for the heightened surveillance and control of youth (Barmacki 2007; Maurutto 2003; Hill and Fortenberry 1992). Adolescence has been closely associated in the field of cognitive human science with the development of morality, dating back to the foundational perspectives of Piaget (1932) and Kohlberg and Kramer (1969). Drawing upon Foucault's method of critically assessing the validity of scientific "truth-claims," Harwood and Rasmussen (2007) analyzed adolescent-specific disorders identified in the fourth edition of the *Diagnostic and Statistical Manual* (DSM-IV). Critically approaching the conditions of adolescent psychopathology and sexuality-centred "disorders," the authors draw attention to the ambiguous grounds on which these diagnoses are based, suggesting that their endurance derives from moral concerns as opposed to scientific grounds. Similar traditions in critical research integrate political economy perspectives by linking the discovery of youth and young adult conduct disorders — including attention deficit-hyperactivity disorder and oppositional defiance disorder — with aims of rendering youth susceptible to evolving forms of correction (Mather 2012; Harwood 2006). From this perspective, youth who resist authority or exhibit a lack of engagement with educational curricula run the risk of being designated "ill." A medical diagnosis then emphasizes the treatment of these disorders, which serves to both meet the economic demands of an obedient workforce and achieve financial benefits for the prescription drug industry at the same time.

> Cohen's framework has been applied in numerous instances to show how the mass media and other authoritative figures use sensationalistic forms of discourse to convince wider publics of the danger and moral decline that youth represent. The media pundits and moral entrepreneurs of the mid- to late 1980s looked to the burgeoning heavy metal and rap subcultures as a means of denoting pronounced patterns of moral decline among young populations.

Popular ideologies surrounding the Westernized notion of adolescence are heavily influenced by the content produced through mass media and popular culture. Influential theorist Stan Cohen (2002) suggests that societal perceptions of youth are reflected within media representations as being inherently deviant, prone to substance abuse and criminal behaviour.

In a case study of an incident between two groups at a Clacton beach resort over the Easter weekend of 1964, Cohen notes how sensational (if not fabricated) reports characterized a brief melee between members of the "mods" and "rockers" subcultures as a highly destructive — almost riotous — event. The story contributed to a general climate of public apprehension toward adolescents, justifying an increase in police presence in common youth leisure spaces and, ultimately, bylaws prohibiting young people from accessing beach resorts. The media's representations of the mods and rockers functioned to restrict the liberties of British adolescents while saturating the public sphere with alarmist, audience-capturing narratives.

Stereotypes of youth subpopulations provided by the media then become internalized by society, thus furthering the stigmatization and oppression of youth. Media representations of youth deviance (and youth *deviants*) further increase ambivalence toward youth cohorts by adults (Bottrell 2009), serving to naturalize their political disempowerment.

Cohen's framework has been applied in numerous instances to show how the mass media and other authoritative figures use sensationalistic forms of discourse to convince wider publics of the danger and moral decline that youth represent. The media pundits and moral entrepreneurs of the mid- to late 1980s looked to the burgeoning heavy metal and rap subcultures as a means of denoting pronounced patterns of moral decline among young populations (Goodlad and Bibby 2007; Binder 1993). Further, media narratives highlighting the *symbolic* dangers posed by unorthodox youth cultures complement and accredit reportage pertaining to the *concrete* dangers posed by adolescent populations. For example, the initial media reports attempting to deduce why Eric Harris and Dylan Klebold orchestrated the 1999 Columbine High School massacre specifically implicated goth culture and, more generally, the "moral failings" of contemporary youth culture (Frymer 2009). These tendencies in media and moral entrepreneurial discourse legitimize associations between adolescence and danger, further ensuring public support for increasingly punitive forms of judicial correction of youth (Faucher 2009; Minaker and Hogeveen 2009; Schissel 2006; Hogeveen 2005) and the expanding surveillance and regulation of youth conduct (Harwood and Rasmussen 2007; Côté and Allahar 2004).

These previously outlined macro perspectives explain the genesis and continuing implications of "adolescence." As a population demographic, adolescence was gradually codified with the onset of the industrial society and corresponding evolutions within the private and economic spheres. As a cultural construct, adolescence draws sanctification from an array of expert and authoritative discourses that characterize "teenagers" as a population in need of corrective surveillance and socio-political disempowerment. Next, we consider how youth "deviance," when investigated at a micro-sociological level, can be contextualized as responses by marginalized youth in positions of vulnerability and danger.

From Idealism to Intersectional Marginality

Prevalent Western discourse surrounding youth intersects with idealized notions of family stability, the universality of education, and clearly demarcated adolescent-parental relationships. Research conducted with youth in vulnerable positions permits a deeper understanding of how the institutions responsible for producing normative youth pose the danger of further exacerbating their marginality. As neoliberalism emphasizes the family sphere and educational institutions to develop youth into "ideal subjects" easily absorbed into the mainstream work force, any deviation from the societal ideal is then attributed to individual failure and moral deficit. Youth from marginalized backgrounds are particularly affected by the cumulative impact of variables compounding their social oppression.

Marginalized youth often come from families typified by fragmentation, poverty, low educational attainment, and interactions with the criminal justice or social welfare systems. However, it is crucial to recall that the concept of parental dependency is predicated on expectations of economic security and the nuclear family structure. Economic crisis and the negative impact of the conditions of poverty potentially hinder youth from thriving in their environments. Estimates conducted in 2015 suggest that one in six youth are impoverished in Canada, and that this figure rises to four in ten among Indigenous youth (Citizens for Public Justice 2015).

Research conducted with youth in vulnerable positions permits a deeper understanding of how the institutions responsible for producing normative youth pose the danger of further exacerbating their marginality. As neoliberalism emphasizes the family sphere and educational institutions to develop youth into "ideal subjects" easily absorbed into the mainstream work force, any deviation from the societal ideal is then attributed to individual failure and moral deficit.

The emergence of the small-family system and the practice of parental dependency intensified the pressure on families to nurture youth in line with dominant cultural expectations and ascriptions throughout their adolescence. Alvi, Scott, and Stanyon (2010) suggest that frequent familial conflict is a significant precursor for youth becoming homeless or engaging in criminal activity, and youth from economically deprived families often receive severe punishments from parental figures for minor transgressions. Youth dealing with parental "**intolerance of transgressions**" and corresponding forms of punishment might become emotionally withdrawn or begin to seek peer validation by engaging in further forms of rebellious or anti-authoritarian conduct. Moreover, youth might become accustomed to harsh punishments for their minor transgressions, desensitizing them to the consequences associated with more severe infractions. Tendencies toward introversion and rebellion might result in further punitive actions and can contribute toward extreme cases when parents "sever ties" out of frustration, often forcing youth into homelessness or the child welfare system. Such punitive responses have become socially justifiable responses to non-normative behaviours.

Parents who were themselves subjected to physical, emotional, or sexual abuse throughout adolescence are at an increased risk of developing mental health issues and addiction, which may contribute to further forms of family dysfunction (Center for Addiction and Mental Health n.d.). Those who have been subjected to abuse in their own upbringing can perpetuate similar conditions once they assume the role of a parent. Experiences of abuse within the family sphere undermine a youth's ability to develop an emotional attachment to a parent or guardian, influencing them to perceive the world as a volatile and unsympathetic environment. Subsequently, youth may consider aggression and physical abuse as normal and acceptable responses to stressors. Contending that experiencing physical abuse diminishes the development of pro-social coping mechanisms in adolescents, Baron (2013) suggests a higher likelihood that they will endorse violence as a means of demonstrating their authority. Pro-violent attitudes increase the likelihood that youth will engage in violent behaviour, throughout their own adolescence and into adulthood.

For marginalized youth, a propensity for violence can also be approached as a way of accruing status and establishing personal reputations based around displays of strength and aggression. Following the adoption of mandatory education, achievement within the classroom became a significant avenue to characterize and govern the capacities and responsibilities of young individuals. However, critics suggest that the educational environment reinforces inequalities among adolescents by ensuring a division between academic achievers and failures, and this coincides with hegemonic white, middle-class ideologies of society (Bottrell 2007). As the educational system cultivates the social and cultural capital of youth, it often disperses resources based on their socioeconomic status within the academic hierarchy (Bottrell 2009). As labels of deficit or "otherness" are applied, these forms of stigma coalesce into their own claims to identity and self-actualization. Learning difficulties, educational resistance, or lack of participation due to external issues can negatively affect youth within the academic setting, potentially leading them to drop out of school as a means of retaining positive claims to identity (Robinson 2016). Societally marginalized youth are likewise at an increased risk for dropping out of school. In Canada, the cultural and colonial biases of educators as well as the Eurocentric nature of educational curricula subject Indigenous youth to a heightened risk for falling out of the mainstream educational system, with only approximately 50 percent of Indigenous youth obtaining a high school diploma (Preston, Carr-Stewart and Bruno 2012).

Variables relating to sex, gender, sexuality, and ethnicity subject youth subpopulations to a higher likelihood of encountering institutional intervention, homelessness, and other challenges (Alvi, Scott and Stanyon 2010). Teenage pregnancy is one of the leading antecedents to female youth being cast out of the family home. In 2011, approximately thirty thousand Canadian girls aged

15 to 19 became pregnant (Sedgh et al. 2015), with Indigenous girls twice as likely as white girls to become single parents (Baskin 2013). Moreover, adolescent mothers are at an increased risk of lower levels of educational attainment due to their economic responsibilities, hindering their ability to secure higher-wage positions within the mainstream job market (Dryburgh 2000).

Queer and transgender youth are also confronted with unique challenges based on their subversion of dominant Western values surrounding heteronormativity and cis-normativity, as they occupy spaces between socially accepted labels in a constant battle for acceptance and equality (Harvey 2012). The greater likelihood of queer and transgender youth encountering homophobia and transphobia within the domestic sphere and educational system, puts them at further risk of being forced out of doors (Coolhart and Brown 2017; Choi, Wilson, Shelton, and Gates 2015). As these discriminatory ideologies are also embedded within the very systems and institutions meant to cater to at-risk youth, queer and transgender adolescents are often deterred from seeking help when in need for fear of further discrimination (Abramovich 2017; Maccio and Ferguson 2016). Queer and transgender youth also experience significantly higher rates of mental illness, suicidal ideation, and self-harming behaviours compared to other youth populations (Abramovich 2013).

Marginalized youth are likewise at an elevated risk of developing substance dependence and addictions, with experiences of dislocation and economic vulnerability contributing to heightened rates of substance use among disenfranchised youth (Saewyc et al. 2013). The progression of substance dependencies also constitutes a significant pathway toward involvement with the drug trade, both as a means of procuring substances and establishing claims to status in alignment with the "code of the street" (Anderson 2000).

Substance use is often attributed to the presence of mental health issues or experiences with trauma, as displaced youth might self-medicate to cope with the pain of these experiences (Buccieri 2013). Moreover, youth suffering from concurrent disorders (dual diagnoses of both a substance abuse disorder and a mental health disorder) have a further increased risk of contracting infectious diseases, being sexually exploited, and getting involved in the criminal justice system (Kirst and Erikson 2013). In sum, the hardships experienced by marginalized youth, coupled with the individualized strategies to alleviate or cope with the experiences of street life, further reinforce cultural stereotypes regarding the "immorality" of youth culture and street youth culture alike.

Implications and Intersections: Youth on the Margins

While the services and programs extended to at-risk adolescents attempt to support youth in times of pronounced crises, child welfare intervention and foster home/group home placements operate as a form of social control that emphasize the same forms of conduct regulation as the educational system. The most common reason for state intervention is neglect and maltreatment, often correlated to parental substance abuse and poverty (Sinha and Kozlowski 2013; Tait, Henry, and Walker 2013). The effects of the welfare systems can vary. Marginalized girls with a history of involvement in child protective services are also subject to additional forms of state intervention should they become pregnant; however, these same girls are likewise often deterred from reporting abuse and victimization for fear of such intervention.

Parent-child estrangement due to state involvement significantly increases a youth's future engagement in criminal activity. More than half of all home-less and gang-involved youth have past interactions with child protective services, often through multiple out-of-home placements, and Indigenous youth experience higher instances of multiple external placements compared to non-Indigenous youth (Baskin 2013; Tait, Henry, and Walker 2013). In the prairie provinces, Indigenous youth are overrepresented within child protective services; for example, in Saskatchewan, they comprise approximately 80 percent of youth in foster care and group homes (Tait, Henry, and Walker 2013). Youth are typically discharged from group homes and foster care between the ages of 16 and 18. At age 16, when education is no longer mandatory, the responsibility of obtaining employment and housing is on the youth themselves. Youth discharged from this continuously structured environment face impending financial instability and lack educational oppor-tunities and affordable housing, along with depleted support systems (Tait, Henry, and Walker 2013).

In Canada, the cultural genocide of the residential school system continues to marginalize Indigenous Peoples, as Eurocentric ideas about the "best inter-est" of the child discriminate against Indigenous traditions of parenting and culture. Amnesty International (2007) reported that Indigenous children are four to six times more likely to be removed from their residence and placed under state supervision, and Indigenous children with status are fifteen times more likely to be removed by child protective services. The report also concluded that Indigenous reserves receive 22 percent less funding for child welfare services, with child removal being the only strategy available due to the absence of alternative options.

Legally, the term "homeless youth" pertains to persons aged 12 to 24 years who experience chronic instability stemming from a lack of adequate housing, legitimate employment, and access to basic needs. Studies assessing the number of homeless youth in Canada — including the National Homelessness Initiative's 2006 estimation that roughly 150,000 youth classify as out of doors (Gaetz, Dej, Richler, and Redman 2016) — often draw primarily from social service institutions and can neglect data from youth who do not seek assistance. In 2006, the Public Health Agency of Canada (2006) reported that, among youth, there are twice as many street-involved boys compared to girls. The document also deduced that Canada's homeless youth population is comprised of 60 percent Caucasian youth and 33 percent Indigenous youth (a considerable overrepresentation, given the size of the Indigenous youth population throughout Canada), with 40 percent of all youth identifying as a sexual minority.

Despite the research into why young people become homeless, neoliberal ideology shapes prevalent cultural representation of homeless persons as lazy, deviant, potentially dangerous, and without responsibility; commonly, these ideas advance a notion that they should simply "get a job." As Kidd (2013) notes, many prevalent cultural narratives suggest that homelessness is the fault of the homeless alone and, therefore, they are undeserving of compassion and sympathy — blame is deflected from an institutional failing onto an individual deficit. Street-involved youth often suffer from poor nutrition and chronic health problems, which can be exacerbated given their poverty, as well as limited access to health services (e.g., prescriptions), lack of contact information, and limited ability to obtain valid identification. All of these factors serve to entrench their oppression and compound the traumatization inherent to homelessness, as youth are forced into high-risk and stressful environments with continuous exposure to violence and victimization, which in turn have detrimental effects on the physical and mental health of homeless youth (Kidd 2013).

Once youth become street involved, Canadian legislation, cultural attitudes, and the strain of economic marginality intersect with and reinforce one another. When youth become homeless, they leave behind their family networks during a life stage when most are economically and socially dependent (Winland 2013) and face greater obstacles to work; this in turn squeezes them into criminalized economic options like panhandling (Sommers 2013). But critical social research understands criminal activity as an avenue through which youth can regain confidence and social approval in alternative cultural contexts. Being denied access to socially appropriate means of making a living may cause youth to gravitate to street subcultures that encompass a completely different set of norms, rules, and expectations than mainstream society (Baron 2013), including attitudes of "anti-social" conduct, as a means of reaffirming one's status, reputation, and identity.

Resilience and Its Repercussions

In recent years, the field of sociology has reappraised many of the practices associated with marginalized populations as expressions of resilience. According to Bottrell (2009: 600), **resilience** is "positive adaptation despite adversity [in which youth] primarily focus on protective factors that mitigate the risks of adverse conditions and circumstances, allowing for healthy development." Resilience refers to the practices that vulnerable populations develop in hopes of securing what they need to survive (food and shelter), and strategies to develop positive identities and maintain mental wellness (Kolar, Erickson, and Stewart 2012). Resilience is not a trait or an inherent capability, but a coping mechanism anyone can develop in precarious situations, using resources from the environment around them. In the case of street-involved youth, the behaviours and practices that might otherwise be described as "deviant" or "abnormal" must be judged based on how these behaviours positively function for the youth within their situated social contexts. Otherwise, professional supports might perceive their behaviours as maladaptive as opposed to resilient, resulting in street-involved youth being denied assistance and support (Harvey 2012).

Resilience is not a trait or an inherent capability, but a coping mechanism anyone can develop in precarious situations, using resources from the environment around them. In the case of street-involved youth, the behaviours and practices that might otherwise be described as "deviant" or "abnormal" must be judged based on how these behaviours positively function for the youth within their situated social contexts. Otherwise, professional supports might perceive their behaviours as maladaptive as opposed to resilient, resulting in street-involved youth being denied assistance and support.

Kolar, Erickson, and Stewart (2012: 749) identify coping mechanisms associated with resilience in youth, including practices of self-defensive **social distancing**, which they define as "the active attempts of [street-involved youth] to remove themselves from certain social groups or persons, and their development of anti-social coping mechanisms in the form of attitudes and outlooks on life, such as a non-discriminating and intense distrust of others due to hurtful experiences." The authors note that many street-involved youth have histories of negative experiences with professional supports, such as child protective services, causing them to become more suspicious of individuals offering support in the future and leading to survival strategies based around keeping distance from such individuals or service providers for fear of victimization or perceived vulnerability. Social distancing is a "purposive survival strategy" focusing on emotional regulation and self-reliance. While social distancing, in part, leads out-of-doors youth to develop habits of self-reliance as a coping mechanism, engaging in this practice increases a youth's vulnerability to future obstacles by eliminating professional supports.

Kolar, Erickson, and Stewart (2012) highlight street-involved youths' heightened risk of being subject to violence and other forms of predation, as well as the peace of mind that youth derive from proving that they can defend themselves. They caution that, within the street environment, "engaging in violent behavior should not be oversimplified as maladaptive. Rather, violence can serve to defend oneself or to develop a reputation of being able to do so … where violence is prevalent and recourse to police is avoided" (2012: 753–54). By engaging in self-defence behaviours, youth gain a reputation and status on the street, alongside thwarting their own victimization. While using violent and aggressive behaviours is imperative for self-defence, it also produces the opportunity for retributive attacks, the possibility of criminal charges, and potential for being denied access to important services and programs. Moreover, some street-involved youth engage in self-harming/suicidal behaviours that function "as a risk rather than a failure to adapt" (Kolar, Erickson, and Stewart 2012: 755).

Although these practices help to ensure one's personal security on the street, they also potentially alienate service providers, increase involvement in the criminal justice system, and play into some of the public stereotypes surrounding the inherent danger of street-involved youth. The example of the panic around Ontario's "squeegee kids," as discussed in Chapter 3 of this collection, well demonstrates how stigmatic representations of impoverished youth can facilitate public demand for legislative responses such as the *Safe Streets and Communities Act*. This means that the significant resilience strategies that youth develop to cope with their experiences of marginality in fact serve to reinforce the legislative and cultural factors that maintain and "normalize" these unsavory conditions.

Conclusion

While adolescence is a relatively recent cultural construct, the social practices that emerged to better accommodate those transitioning from "teenagerdom" to adulthood have become so engrained within Western ways of life that they are taken for granted as self-evident. Few of us have encountered opportunities to question the notion that it is (and has always been) natural that youth attend school and depend on parents for shelter and finances. A historical interrogation of the emergence of adolescence illustrates that practices around the "best interests" of the young — such as mandatory education and extended periods of parental dependency — can be better associated with the economic repercussions of industrialization and the insights of the burgeoning human sciences. The gradual emergence of "the adolescent" justified the subjection of young adults to increasing periods of institutional exclusion and regulation predicated on notions of irresponsibility and cognitive immaturity. These perspectives would find a measure of reinforcement in the forms of "teenage culture" that emerged throughout the twentieth century, as film, music, and youth-targeted consumer markets associated adolescence with rebellion and the rejection of authority. Representations of adolescents suggested that youth were prone to refusing and resisting the very institutions and practices that had been put in place to ensure their immediate safety and future security, justifying their treatment as the source of public anxiety and targets of new social control measures. Given the simmering climate of moral panic that has long surrounded the subject of adolescents and youth culture, it is not surprising that instances of delinquency or anti-social conduct are correlated, almost instinctually, with problems inherent to the adolescent as opposed to the broader social contexts in which they exist.

The cultural norms surrounding adolescence and the cultural anxieties surrounding "the adolescent" marginalize vulnerable youth, especially street-involved youth, who are commonly characterized by their families, welfare services, and academics as delinquent, criminal, and individually responsible for their positions in life. These forms of stigma are reinforced by their involvement in illicit economies that ensure their survival, as well as the resilience-based self-preservation strategies in which they engage. Ironically, this results in abandoning youth in need of

> The cultural norms surrounding adolescence and the cultural anxieties surrounding "the adolescent" marginalize vulnerable youth, especially street-involved youth, who are commonly characterized by their families, welfare services, and academics as delinquent, criminal, and individually responsible for their positions in life.

social support, even while youth protection is celebrated as a cultural value. Any substantive movement toward rectifying the tendency to associate youth with danger requires listening to street-involved youth and respecting their perspectives and interests.

Discussion Questions

1. How is adolescence a social construction?
2. What are the five demographic transitions that Fasick associates with the social construction of adolescence?
3. Why is it important to consider how youth perceive advantages when they engage with behaviours of resilience?
4. How does dysfunction within the family sphere create a pathway for youth homelessness?
5. What factors influence the identity development of youth?

Recommended Resources

1. Covenant House Toronto website <covenanthousetoronto.ca/>.
2. *Paradise Lost* documentary series (Berlinger and Sinofsky 1996)
3. *Teenage* (Cinereach 2015)

Glossary

culture industries: the dominant industries and institutions that manufacture and distribute cultural products including art, entertainment, and fashion.

folk devils: social groups that are prevalently represented, by media and other authority figures, as deviant and dangerous populations about which something must be done.

intolerance of transgression: the practice whereby youth are ejected from the family home because they act in defiance of their parents' expectations.

mandatory education: the legal requirement that youth attend school until age 16; contributes to labour laws limiting the legal ability for youth to secure employment.

parental dependence: a relatively recent cultural practice whereby youth remain dependent on their parents until they have competed their education.

resilience: the ability to survive and experience self-empowerment despite the presence of hardships and traumatic experiences.

social distancing: a resilience strategy, employed by street-involved youth, of refusing assistance from others as a means of reducing the risk of victimization.

References

Abramovich, Alex. 2017. "Understanding How Policy and Culture Create Oppressive Conditions for LGBTQ2S Youth in the Shelter System." *Journal of Homosexuality* 64, 11.
___. 2013. "No Fixed Address: Young, Queer, and Restless." <homelesshub.ca/sites/default/files/23ABRAMOVICHweb.pdf>.

Alvi, Shahid, Hannah Scott, and Wendy Stanyon. 2010. "'We're Locking the Door': Family Histories in a Sample of Homeless Youth." *Qualitative Report* 15, 5.

Amnesty International. 2007. "*Human Rights for All: NO Exceptions.*" <amnesty.org/download/Documents/60000/amr200012007eng.pdf >.

Anderson, Elijah. 2000. *Code of the Street: Decency Violence and the Moral Life of the Inner City.* New York: W.W. Norton.

Barmaki, Reza. 2007. "The Bourgeois Order and the 'Normal' Child: The Case of Ontario, 1867–1900." *International Journal of Mental Health and Addiction* 5, 3.

Baron, S. 2013. "Why Street Youth Become Involved in Crime." In S. Gaetz, B. O'Grady, K. Buccieri et al. (eds.), *Youth Homelessness in Canada: Implications for Policy and Practice.* Toronto: Canadian Homelessness Research Network Press.

Baskin, C. 2013. "Shaking off the Colonial Inheritance: Indigenous Youth Resist, Reclaim and Reconnect." In S. Gaetz, B. O'Grady, K. Buccieri et al. (eds.), *Youth Homelessness in Canada: Implications for Policy and Practice.* Toronto: Canadian Homelessness Research Network Press.

Berlinger, Joe, and Bruce Sinofsky. 1996. *Paradise Lost* [film]. HBO Films.

Binder, A. 1993. "Constructing Racial Rhetoric: Media Depictions of Harm in Heavy Metal and Rap Music." *American Sociological Review* 58.

Bottrell, Dorothy. 2009. "Dealing with Disadvantage: Resilience and the Social Capital of Young People's Networks." *Youth & Society* 40, 4.
___. 2007. "Resistance, Resilience and Social Identities: Reframing 'Problem Youth' and the Problem of Schooling." *Journal of Youth Studies* 10, 5.

Buccieri, K. 2013. "Back to the Future for Canada's National Anti-Drug Strategy: Homeless Youth and the Need for Harm Reduction." In S. Gaetz, B. O'Grady, K. Buccieri et al. (eds.), *Youth Homelessness in Canada: Implications for Policy and Practice.* Toronto: Canadian Homelessness Research Network Press.

Centre for Addiction and Mental Health. n.d. "Trauma." <camh.ca/en/health-info/mental-illness-and-addiction-index/trauma>.

Choi, Soon Kyu, Bianca Wilson, Jama Shelton, and Gary Gates. 2015. *Serving Our Youth 2015: The Needs and Experiences of Lesbian, Gay, Bisexual, Transgender, and Questioning Youth Experiencing Homelessness.* Los Angeles: Williams Institute with True Colors Fund.

Citizens for Public Justice. 2015. "On the Margins: A Glimpse of Poverty in Canada." <cpj.ca/wp-content/uploads/On-The-Margins.pdf>.

Cohen, Stanley. 2002. *Folk Devils and Moral Panics: The Creation of the Mods and Rockers.*

New York: Routledge.

Coleman, J.S. 1961. *The Adolescent Society: The Social Life of the Teenager and its Impact on Education.* Oxford: Free Press of Glencoe.

Coolhart, Deborah, and Maria Brown. 2017. "The Need for Safe Spaces: Exploring the Experiences of Homeless LGBTQ Youth in Shelters." *Children and Youth Services Review* 82.

Côté, James, and Anton Allahar. 2006. *Critical Youth Studies: A Canadian Focus.* Toronto: Pearson.

____. 2004. *Generation on Hold: Coming of Age in the Late Twentieth Century.* Toronto: Stoddart.

Covenant House Toronto. n.d. Home page. <covenanthousetoronto.ca/>.

Dryburgh, Heather. 2000. "Teenage Pregnancy." *Statistics Canada Health Reports* 12, 1.

Fasick, Frank. 1994. "On the 'Invention' of Adolescence." *Journal of Early Adolescence* 14.

Faucher, Chantal. 2009. "Fear and Loathing in the News: A Qualitative Analysis of Canadian Print News Coverage of Youthful Offending in the Twentieth Century." *Journal of Youth Studies* 12, 4.

Foucault, Michel. 1978. *The History of Sexuality Volume I: An Introduction.* New York: Vintage.

Frank, Thomas. 1997. *The Conquest of Cool: Business Culture, Counterculture, and the Rise of Hip Consumerism.* Chicago: University of Chicago Press.

Frymer, Benjamin. 2009. "The Media Spectacle of Columbine: Alienated Youth as an Object of Fear." *American Behavioral Scientist* 52, 10.

Gaetz, Stephen, Erin Dej, Tim Richter, and Melanie Redman. 2016. *The State of Homelessness in Canada 2016.* Toronto: Canadian Observatory on Homelessness Press.

Goodlad, Lauren, and Michael Bibby. 2007. "Introduction." In L. Goodlad and M. Bibby (eds.), *Goth: Undead Subculture.* London: Duke University Press.

Government of Ontario. 1999. *Safe Streets Act, 1999, S.O. 1999, c. 8.* <ontario.ca/laws/statute/99s08>.

Harvey, Rebecca. 2012. "Young People, Sexual Orientation, and Resilience." In M. Ungar (ed.), *The Social Ecology of Resilience.* New York: Springer.

Harwood, Valerie. 2006. *Diagnosing "Disorderly" Children: A Critique of Behaviour Disorder Discourses.* New York: Routledge.

Harwood, Valerie, and Marie Louise Rasmussen. 2007. "Scrutinizing Sexuality and Psychopathology: A Foucauldian Inspired Strategy for Qualitative Data Analysis." *International Journal of Qualitative Studies in Education* 20, 1.

Hill, Robert, and J. Dennis Fortenberry. 1992. "Adolescence as a Culture-Bound Syndrome." *Social Science & Medicine* 35.

Hogeveen, Bryan. 2005. "'If We Are Tough on Crime, if We Punish Crime, Then People Get the Message': Constructing and Governing the Punishable Young Offender in Canada During the Late 1990s." *Punishment & Society* 7, 1.

Horkheimer, Max, and Theodor Adorno. 1947. *Dialectic of Enlightenment: Theoretical Fragments.* Stanford: Stanford University Press.

Kidd, S. 2013. "Mental Health and Youth Homelessness: A Critical Review." In S. Gaetz, B. O'Grady, K. Buccieri et al. (eds.), *Youth Homelessness in Canada: Implications for Policy and Practice.* Toronto: Canadian Homelessness Research Network Press.

Kirst, M., and P. Erikson. 2013. "Substance Use and Mental Health Problems among

Street-Involved Youth: The Need for a Harm Reduction Approach." In S. Gaetz, B. O'Grady, K. Buccieri et al. (eds.), *Youth Homelessness in Canada: Implications for Policy and Practice.* Toronto: Canadian Homelessness Research Network Press.

Kohlberg, L., and R. Kramer. 1969. "Continuities and Discontinuities in Child and Adult Moral Development." *Human Development* 12.

Kolar, Kat, Patricia Gail Erickson, and Donna Stewart. 2012. "Coping Strategies of Street-Involved Youth: Exploring Contexts of Resilience." *Journal of Youth Studies* 15, 6.

Lapsley, Daniel K., Robert D. Enright, and Ronald C. Serlin. 1985. "Toward a Theoretical Perspective on the Legislation of Adolescence." *Journal of Early Adolescence* 5.

LawNow. 2014. "The Protection of Young Workers in Canadian Employment Law." <lawnow.org/protection-of-young-workers-in-canadian-employment-law/>.

Maccio, Elaine, and Kristen Ferguson. 2016. "Services to LGBTQ Runaway and Homeless Youth: Gaps and Recommendations." *Children and Youth Services Review* 63.

Mather, Barbara. 2012. "The Social Construction and Reframing of Attention-Deficit/Hyperactivity Disorder." *Ethical Human Psychology and Psychiatry* 14, 1.

Maurutto, Paula. 2003. "Moral Reform, Discipline and Normalization: Juvenile Delinquency and Rehabilitation in Ontario." In D. Brock (ed.), *Making Normal: Social Regulation in Canada.* Toronto: Tomson Nelson.

Medovoi, Leerom. 2005. *Rebels: Youth and the Cold War Origins of Identity.* Durham: Duke University Press.

Minaker, Joanne, and Bryan Hogeveen. 2009. *Youth, Crime and Society: Issues of Power and Justice.* Toronto: Pearson.

Ministry of Justice. 2019. "Canada Labour Code." <laws-lois.justice.gc.ca/PDF/L-2.pdf>.

Piaget, Jean. 1932. *The Moral Judgement of the Child.* New York: Free Press.

Preston, Jane, Shelia Carr-Stewart, and Charlene Bruno. 2012. "The Growth of Aboriginal Youth Gangs in Canada." *Canadian Journal of Native Studies* 32, 2.

Public Health Agency of Canada. 2006. "Street Youth in Canada: Findings from Enhanced Surveillance of Canadian Street Youth 1999–2003." <phac-aspc.gc.ca/std-mts/reports_06/pdf/street_youth_e.pdf>.

Quart, Alissa. 2003. *Branded: The Buying and Selling of Teenagers.* New York: Perseus.

Robinson, Anne. 2016. "The Resilience Motif: Implications for Youth Justice." *Youth Justice* 16, 1.

Saewyc, E., C. Drozda, R. Rivers, L. MacKay, and M. Peled. 2013. "Which Comes First: Sexual Exploitation or Other Risk Exposures Among Street-Involved Youth." In S. Gaetz, B. O'Grady, K. Buccieri et al. (eds.), *Youth Homelessness in Canada: Implications for Policy and Practice.* Toronto: Canadian Homelessness Research Network Press.

Schissel, Bernard. 2006. *Still Blaming Children: Youth Conduct and the Politics of Child Hating.* Halifax: Fernwood Publishing.

Schor, Juliet B. 2004. *Born to Buy: The Commercialized Child and the New Consumer Culture.* New York: Scribner.

Sedgh, Gilda, Lawrence Finer, Akinrinola Bankole, Michelle Eilers, and Susheela Singh. 2015. "Adolescent Pregnancy, Birth, and Abortion Rates Across Countries: Levels and Recent Trends." *Journal of Adolescent Health* 56, 2.

Sinha, Vandha, and Anna Kozlowski. 2013. "The Structure of Aboriginal Child Welfare in Canada." *International Indigenous Policy Journal* 4, 2.

Sommers, R. 2013. "Governing the Streets: The Legal, Social and Moral Regulation of

Homeless Youth." In S. Gaetz, B. O'Grady, K. Buccieri, Jet al. (eds.), *Youth Homelessness in Canada: Implications for Policy and Practice.* Toronto: Canadian Homelessness Research Network Press.

Statistics Canada. 2016. "Perspectives on the Youth Labour Market in Canada, 1976 to 2015." <www150.statcan.gc.ca/n1/en/daily-quotidien/161205/dq161205a-eng.pdf?st=cc9kyNRp>.

Tait, Caroline, Robert Henry, and Rachel Loewen Walker. 2013. "Child Welfare: A Social Determinant of Health for Canadian First Nations and Métis Children." *Pimatisiwin: A Journal for Aboriginal and Indigenous Community Health* 11, 1.

Tanner, Julian. 2010. *Teenage Troubles: Youth and Deviance in Canada.* New York: Oxford University Press.

Tannock, Stuart. 2001. *Youth at Work: The Unionized Fast-Food and Grocery Workplace.* Philadelphia: Temple University Press.

Teenage [film]. 2015. Cinereach. <kanopy.com/product/teenage>.

Winland, D. 2013. "Reconnecting with Family and Community: Pathways Out of Youth Homelessness." In S. Gaetz, B. O'Grady, K. Buccieri et al. (eds.), *Youth Homelessness in Canada: Implications for Policy and Practice.* Toronto: Canadian Homelessness Research Network Press.

SECTION THREE

The Culture of Control

The social contract, an assumed unwritten agreement between the public and the state, holds that the public subscribes to certain limitations on its freedoms in exchange for the protections afforded by the state. According to this philosophy, with this protection, we can freely work toward pursuing our goals and securing our happiness, so long as we "play by the rules." For example, as a university professor, I can focus my energies on developing my career based on the assumption that I am protected from other risks. In Canada, we have a form of universal health care, which means I have to spend less time worrying about paying for health care–related costs; we have a criminal justice system that prohibits certain behaviours, so I need not spend excessive time securing myself and my belongings; and we have a series of political institutions devoted to maintaining and improving our infrastructure, which frees me from having to build my own roads or generate my own electricity. At the same time, I have to accept that certain limitations have been placed upon the way I act by various authorities. I cannot, for example, take the latest smartphone model from a store without paying for it. Similarly, I can't make up data about my latest research project and then profess it as the truth. In both cases I would face repercussions for my actions, which generally outweigh the benefits of doing them. Our adherence to the social contract assumes that all of those involved are acting in *good faith*: the state in all of its forms is working toward protecting the interests of the individuals who constitute the public, and the public is equally invested in the state and its regulations.

Our social realities are, however, somewhat different than what might be promised by the ideals of the social contract. There are serious questions about the definitions of freedom and protection: what does it mean to be free, or to act freely, in Canadian society? The answer to this question is wholly dependent on the person who answers it, as different individuals will have different understandings of and experiences with their own personal freedoms. Similarly, what should protection entail in our society? The mechanisms that we rely upon for protection in Canada are inherently subject to the whims of those who define, design, and control them, which alters the meaning of protection. Critical questions like these lead to important observations about the social contract theory. The first observation is that all societies host a range of opinions, ideas, and goals. The structures emerging from the social contract are expected to simultaneously represent multiple interests, which are often in competition with one another. The second observation is that the social contract creates mechanisms that maintain and enforce the security it promises. Thus, there is an inherent need for authorities to adjudicate transgressions and prescribe remedies. The third observation, based on the two prior conditions, is that there will be greater power afforded to those who are in the position to codify certain social ideals — often referred to as "moralities" — over others. Thus, the social contract contributes to a culture of control, with vested interests in maintaining power structures and undermining those who oppose or resist them.

These concepts of control are explored in depth throughout in this next section. Using a range of examples, you will learn about public perceptions of right and wrong, as well as the various social forces that inform them. The first chapter presented in this section raises important questions about the media's role in defining and maintaining social controls: how might media in the twenty-first century affect public dialogue about and interpretations of social issues. Sean Hier calls you to critically consider moral panic theory, which classically held that the public could be motivated to respond on a given social issue by targeted reporting through mass media outlets. The inference of the moral panic theory was that a relatively concentrated group of controlling bodies closely aligned with the social contract dictate their interests to the public through control of the media while excluding alternative perspectives. However, as Hier explains, this idea presupposes that an asymmetrical form of media can unilaterally define popular opinion; this leads him to ask: do the same principles hold true in an era of participatory media? This question helps us consider how (or whether) the internet might achieve its promised utopia of unbiased, immediate informational exchange. In answering this question, Hier explores the Twitter-led response to the police shooting of Michael Brown in Ferguson, Missouri, in 2014 and demonstrates that digitally mediated moral panics reinforce traditional claims-making activities, but they also empower counter-hegemonic claims making.

The second chapter in this section returns to the question of asymmetrical forms of media. In this case, Matthew Ferguson explores how curated museum exhibits about criminal justice contribute to socially engineered narratives of "good" and "bad." Ferguson argues that the language and presentations made by these exhibits provide telling evidence of the social mechanisms that impact public "knowledge" about crime. He analyzes traditional role formation in how patrons are presented with a predisposition toward murder and violence, as well as sympathetic depictions of police surveillance. His chapter deconstructs representations of police, victims of crime, and people who are criminalized. Ferguson also delves into the role of museums as storytelling institutions, relating their inflexible informational presentation to mechanisms of indoctrination for "traditional" interpretations of crime and criminality. One of Ferguson's most compelling observations comes from his discussion of the omitted aspects to criminal justice among the considered exhibitions. For instance, he points out how the crimes of the powerful, such as harmful business practices, are representative of organized forgetting that seeks to undermine counter-power narratives of justice. In relation to this text's focus on social control, Ferguson's chapter provides critical insights into the power of narrative maintenance even within institutions whose mandate focuses on education.

Carolyn Brooks and Karen Wood's chapter on the social control of sex work brings attention to the social construction of harm and its relevance to notions of morality. They consider the competing interests represented under the social contract, starting with a critical examination of legislation regulating the sex trade in Canada and the sociological perspectives that have contextualized the sex industry and sex workers. Differing feminist perspectives are often at odds with one other: some frame the sex trade and the driving forces behind it as a recreation of hyper-masculine norms, while others argue that it is a deviantized yet liberating occupation. In order to reframe this discussion, the authors then point to various forms of sociological inquiry that can be used to empower the voices of those involved with the sex trade and to provide new perspectives that bracket traditional social moralities in order to develop deeper, and more popular, empathy.

Danielle Bird and Julie Kaye conclude this section with a critical deconstruction of the Canadian government's historic responses to the crisis of murdered and missing Indigenous women and girls (MMIWG). This chapter can also be contextualized within the social contract theory as exemplary of the negotiation and pursuit of power at the cost of marginalized communities. Bird and Kaye's chapter examines the othering effect of official responses to MMIWG typical of the government's settler colonial approach to relations. For instance, the authors demonstrate how the dominant tough-on-crime approach present in Canada through the thirty-ninth to forty-first parliaments (2006–2015) emphasized an offender-oriented response to the crisis that entirely omitted the systemic marginalization of Indigenous women and silenced them. They deconstruct the persistent reliance of a singular "truth" within government approaches to MMIWG investigations, identifying its role in reifying public dialogues that portray Indigenous Peoples as uncivilized and infantilized populations. These arguments contribute to Bird and Kaye's cumulative argument that, despite media-friendly politically correct conversations on "truth and reconciliation," the Canadian government's series of MMIWG and related inquiries operate as technologies of control that ultimately maintain mechanisms of social control by concentrating responsive powers into the hands of the governments. Despite these observations Bird and Kaye conclude with a message of hope, focusing on recent efforts to recentre dialogue onto the experiences — and voices — of Indigenous women, in direct contrast to colonial narratives of control.

In summation, this section of chapters provides an insightful consideration of the juxtaposition between marginalized communities (digital social movements; the incarcerated; sex workers; and Indigenous Peoples) and multiple forms of media, identifying the dialogues and discourses that position various deviantized social groups within the social contract. The presumptive safety of this contract does not always extend to everyone in society, and their denial is often legitimized through the framing of omitted groups as "wrong" or "bad." Fortunately, each chapter also identifies pathways to empower the voices of each group and ultimately recentre the dialogue to include their interests.

9

Digitally Mediated Moral Panics

On the Changing Nature of Claims Making, Audience Engagement, and Social Regulation

Sean P. Hier

After reading this chapter, you will be able to do the following:

1. Elaborate on the concept of media claims making.
2. Explain how perspectives on moral panic changed following the development of internet technologies.
3. Define the concept of media logic.
4. Describe the role of moral entrepreneurs in instigating moral panic.
5. Illustrate how social media users have developed tactics to challenge news media narratives.

Chapter 6 introduced Stan Cohen's (2003) concept of **moral panic**, or the process through which news media frame current issues to incite public anxieties and mobilize demands for legislative changes to counter the threats that they depict. Cohen's research suggests that news media engage in processes of **claims making**, or depicting menacing events and populations in a manner that aligns with and promotes the interests of media owners, politicians, police, and other social elites. Reports that depict the onset of crises and issues of collective anxiety compel the general public to demand that authority figures do something about the threat at hand. This process serves to reinforce the stigma and negative stereotypes associated with those groups being characterized as sources of danger while reinforcing the consensus that those with the power to neutralize such threats deserve their authority. Through the 1980s, moral panic was associated with the HIV/AIDS epidemic, Satanic teenagers and daycares, and other issues.

In 1995, Angela McRobbie and Sarah Thornton introduced their influential deconstruction of moral panic studies. They explained how the proliferation of grassroots and non-corporate media outlets, along with the many voices that were contesting meanings of deviance and moral transgression, signalled that relations between media and social regulation have undergone some degree of shift, if not transformation (McRobbie and Thornton 1995). Their deconstruction of the cycles and stages underscoring original moral panic models affected how criminologists explain the relationships among media, crime, and public anxieties. Their arguments about fragmented media sources, the diversity of participants involved in public claims making, and shifting points of social regulation and control also inspired new and innovative advances in moral panic research (e.g., Ungar 2001; Hier 2008).

But in the twenty years following McRobbie and Thornton's critique, as digital communication networks and social media platforms reshape the dynamics of moral panics, criminological moral panic research has not kept up with changes in public claims making, modes of audience engagement, and techniques of social regulation and control. McRobbie and Thornton's critique can no longer fully explain how moral panics are cultivated in digitally (rather than only multi-)mediated social worlds. Further, despite important theoretical and conceptual gains, criminological moral panic research remains curiously silent on the ways in which newer digital media formats are reshaping the dynamics of interactions involved in public claims making, modes of audience engagement, and techniques of social regulation and control. This chapter revisits McRobbie and Thornton's work on the original models of moral panic to show how moral panic remains tied to a tacit set of assumptions that pivot on the logic of mass mediation and to demonstrate what has changed in the digital age.

The argument is presented over three sections. The first section revisits McRobbie and Thornton's assessment of the criminology of moral panic to show how their deconstruction is based on tacit assumptions about the ways in which commercial media representations contribute to the cultivation of deviant identities.

The second section explains how McRobbie and Thornton's insights are bound by the parameters of what Altheide and Snow (1979) originally conceptualized as **media logic**, which explains how mass media influence other institutions, such as criminal justice. McRobbie and Thornton's critique of the relations among media, society, claims making, and social control introduced a significant degree of complexity into the notion of mass media logic as it pertains to processes of **deviance amplification** and social regulation. Still, their framework is based on implicit assumptions surrounding mass media production and reception that have been all but ignored by contemporary criminologists.

The third section uses the example of social reactions to racist police violence on the hashtag #Ferguson to illustrate how changing relations of digital mediation are impacting public claims making, modes of audience engagement, and techniques of social regulation and control. The example of #Ferguson is instructive because it illustrates the differences that digital media make to the mediation of a moral panic about crime and policing and because it contributes to recent arguments that moral panics are not only socially regressive or "bad" but also politically progressive or "good" (Hier 2016).

Moral Panics for Multi-Mediated Social Worlds

McRobbie and Thornton's (1995) deconstruction of classical moral panic theory argues for revisions to the stages of moral panic and the social relations that support it. Writing in late twentieth-century Britain, McRobbie and Thornton surmise that, if moral panics were once conceptualized as the unintended outcome of journalistic practices, they seem to have become a goal of such practices. The authors contrast the changing dynamics of moral panics given the emergence of web-based communicative technologies with the kinds of social relations envisioned in the original studies. On the one hand, they explain that the early moral panic theories formulated by Cohen (2003), Young (1971), and Pearson (1983) approached such instances as cultural control mechanisms that reinforce a single (dominant, conservative) social order. On the other hand, they observe that Hall et al.'s (2009) neo-Marxian framework develops deeper insights into the political dimensions of moral panics by explaining how they function to link the interests of the state and civil society through the ideological components of common sense.

McRobbie and Thornton argued that each of the original models relies on a singularly reductive understanding of "society" and "social reactions." Whether characterized by Cohen's "society," Pearson's "collective memory," or Hall et al.'s "hegemony," classical formulations, according to McRobbie and Thornton, characterize public responses to the onset of moral panic as being highly uniform, predictable, and uncritical of their role in reinforcing the continued empowerment of social elites and authorities. The problem with assuming homogenized public reactions to moral panic is that doing so undermines the complexity of societal relations by advancing "a metaphor which depicts a complex society as a single person who experiences sudden fear about its virtue" (McRobbie and Thornton 1995: 567) as opposed to accounting for the different ways in which different groups are involved in and respond to the onset of panic.

> The styles of youth dress and conduct that moral entrepreneurs tout as trappings of the folk devil resurface as youth repurpose these markers to demonstrate their displeasure with the dominant culture. The culture industries, in turn, appropriate these markers from youth and repackage them as consumption items.

McRobbie and Thornton's perspective on the complexity of responses to moral panic draws heavily from Thornton's (1995) ethnographic investigation of British club cultures. Thornton argues that youth groups, as a segment of British society, do not uniformly lament a safe and stable past, as many theories of society and social control suggest. Conversely, McRobbie and Thornton argue that youth tend to be nostalgic for past transgression (e.g., mods, rockers, punks, New Romantics) that resonates with their often radical bent. Instead of excluding and/or controlling youth groups, disapproving mass media coverage tends to legitimize and authenticate youth cultural movements. McRobbie and Thornton conclude that what classical moral panic theorists identify as deviance amplification can, for youth, entail a process of transforming a scene into a movement. Negative reports centred on the early English punk subculture, for example, served to inform new practices and ideologies based around sensationalistic media representation (Daschuk 2016; Savage 1991). Reports that took creative liberties in cautioning against the onset of a new, violent form of youth culture effectively inspired the popularization of practices that mirrored these (formerly) highly fictionalized accounts.

In addition, McRobbie and Thornton observe that publishing and recording industries are keenly aware of the marketing potential to youth groups looking to cultivate transgression. This means that the instigation of moral panic may lead to the unintended consequence of informing new trends in youth fashion and culture. Sleeve notes on record albums, representations in the style/music press, and articles in niche music magazines routinely capitalize on and exploit "privileged" knowledge of youth hairstyles, dance trends, music genres, fads, and fashions. The styles of youth dress and conduct that moral entrepreneurs tout as trappings of the folk devil resurface as youth repurpose these markers to demonstrate their displeasure with the dominant culture. The culture industries, in turn, appropriate these markers from youth and repackage them as consumption items. Cultural industries are just as adept at deploying panic narratives in the interest of profit as the mainstream mass media is at doing so in the interest of social control.

McRobbie and Thornton suggested that processes related to youth deviance take place partially — if not entirely — externally to youth groups themselves. They claimed that the youth cultures of the 1990s were steeped in the legacy of previous panics about transgressive activities, but that the subcultural formation of a youth movement or lifestyle depended on the commercial interests of the marketing and mainstream media industries. McRobbie and Thornton showed that (deviant) youth movements were galvanized by disapproving mass media coverage, front-page tabloid newspaper stories, and sleeve notes on record albums. In effect, if not intentionally, they theorized that youth culture exists in an asymmetrical relationship with the interests of commercially driven media outlets, whereby transgressive youth cultural identities require disapproving social reactions for cultural (trans) formation and legitimacy.

Further, the argument advanced by McRobbie and Thornton encounters problems based on how they explain the plurality of voices involved in public claims-making activities. McRobbie and Thornton argue that interest groups, pressure groups, lobbies, and campaign experts routinely *intervene* in (rather than incite) panic episodes to contest mainstream media claims. As McRobbie and Thornton (1995: 568) note:

> Moral panic is a favourite topic of the youth press. When the mass media of tabloids and TV [became] active in the "inevitable" moral panic about [the "Acid House" music genre], the subcultural press were ready. They tracked the tabloids every move, re-printed whole front pages, analysed their copy and decried the misrepresentation of Acid House. Some 30 magazines now target and speak up for youth.

Made possible by the proliferation of grassroots and alternative media, they explain that folk devils and their supporters fight back by providing information to established mass media outlets with the intention of reacting to and contesting demonizing narratives. From the vantage point of the mid-1990s, they asserted that resistance to tacitly conservative claims-making activities involves providing information in the form of sound bites for journalists working on tight schedules and budgets in a highly structured media production system (McRobbie and Thornton 1995). McRobbie and Thornton offer intriguing commentary about how specialty magazines, community tabloids, and **niche media** outlets cultivate and reproduce cultural meanings. Yet patterns of subcultural formation and resistance to hegemonic norms are not ultimately explained in terms of folk devils and their supporters *producing* their own constitutive and counter-hegemonic narratives — either in the midst of or beyond volatile and sensational claims-making episodes.[1] McRobbie and Thornton theorize the social construction of deviance in relation to inequitable mass-mediated relations, whereby various interests compete for a dominant voice in a cohesive, if contested and more volatile, public media sphere.

Moral Panics and Media Logic

McRobbie and Thornton's (1995) deconstruction of the core assumptions of classical moral panic theory represents a pragmatic attempt to correct some of the functional simplicity characterizing the original models. They resist conventional tendencies to theorize media, society, claims-making activities, and processes of social regulation and control in a singularly reductive, possibly deterministic manner. Instead, McRobbie and Thornton draw analytical attention to fragmented media sources, diverse social reactions, and the many voices that engender narratives designed to resist the demonization of targeted groups. The critical intervention offered by McRobbie and Thornton continues to influence how panics are theorized and explained. Their critique, however, bears an uncanny, and yet unacknowledged, resemblance to what Altheide and Snow (1979) originally conceptualized as media logic. Altheide and Snow developed this concept to explain the institutionalized assemblage of organizational tactics, formatting codes, and framing techniques that influence how mass media construct representations of social reality (e.g., through issue filtering, narrative structure, aesthetic presentation, source selection, styles of rhetoric). Motivated by the growing influence of television formats on routine social interaction and the politics of everyday life, Altheide and Snow not only formulated the concept of media logic to explain the ways that commercial mass media produce representations of social reality, but also how the framing and presentation of media content that exist among mass media institutions increasingly influence behavioural expectations and routine interactions in social institutions beyond media.

The logic of mass mediation is premised on the notion that information flows in an asymmetrical or one-way direction from mainstream commercial media institutions to the masses. Cultivated through a set of interconnected and highly structured relationships involving professional actors (the production of news according to journalistic norms), commercial interests

Whether the medium is radio, television, or print news, media logic assumes a hierarchical structure to information selection, dissemination, and reception: vast amounts of potentially newsworthy information are filtered through a class of professional journalists and packaged in a familiar, even predictable, format for widespread consumption.

(profit-driven motives), and technological innovations (media of mass communication in their different forms), the operating logic of the mass media is to continually produce authoritative representations of social reality that are received, normalized, internalized, and reproduced by mass audiences.

Whether the medium is radio, television, or print news, media logic assumes a hierarchical structure to information selection, dissemination, and reception: vast amounts of potentially newsworthy information are filtered through a class of professional journalists and packaged in a familiar, even predictable, format for widespread consumption.

McRobbie and Thornton's critique was so influential in moral panic studies because it explained that the journalistic filter process involved in media logic entails a more intricate set of conditioning relations than the original models suggested. They argued that material changes taking place in how information is transmitted across various media require reassessment of the "complex realm of reception" (McRobbie and Thornton 1995: 572). This complex realm of reception is composed of readers, listeners, and viewers, so as to avoid the temptation to homogenize public opinion based on hegemonic representations of social issues appearing in mainstream commercial media discourse. In the early 1990s, McRobbie and Thornton were starting to recognize the impacts of desktop publishing, computer mailing, niche-oriented consumer magazines, and lobby and special interest groups on the direction of public claims making, media discourse, and the social construction of deviance. Rather than conceptualizing news discourse and mass-mediated narratives that demonize marginalized groups in terms of a linear, a priori normative logic tied to (or conditioned by) the political economy of news production, they demonstrated that the creation of media discourses and counter discourses is more nuanced and malleable.

Despite the complexity of conditioning relations that McRobbie and Thornton identify, the overall logic of mass mediation that guides their assessment of moral panic for multi-mediated social worlds is nevertheless based on tacit assumptions about an institutionalized media production system external to or at a distance from the consumers of media content (i.e., audiences). McRobbie and Thornton convincingly demonstrate how cultivating mass-mediated moral panics is considerably more difficult than the original models suggest. Still, from their perspective, the ultimate fate of claims-making activities and framing strategies remains dependent on a systematized logic of asymmetrical *mass mediation*, replete with its own firmly embedded rules, hierarchies, rituals, and routines.

Moral Panics and Digital Media Logic

McRobbie and Thornton's (1995) assessment of moral panic for multi-mediated social worlds appeared on the cusp of profound changes to the cultural, institutional, technological, and communicative relations on which the notion of media logic rests. Their critique focused on emerging alternative media cultures and was buttressed by passing references to the expansion of tabloid television, the rise of infotainment formats, and the entrenchment of specialized, issue-driven audiences. The ultimate aim of McRobbie and Thornton's deconstruction was to complicate overly simplistic explanations for the construction of commercial media discourses that tacitly assume a firm, if not impenetrable, separation between the professional journalists who produce and transmit panic narratives and the audience members who consume them.

Though McRobbie and Thornton provided insights into the nuances of audience engagement and public (counter-)claims making, their work preceded advances in digital computing technologies that were also unfolding through-out the 1980s and early 1990s. For example, McRobbie and Thornton do not consider the file- and message-sharing capabilities of early web-communicative platforms like Internet Relay Chat, Usenet, and bulletin board systems; the URL and search functions associated with Web 1.0; or the growing popularity of modems that connected home and personal computers through telephone (land) lines to an increasingly available and quickly expanding internet. The emerging forms of digitally mediated computer interaction (e.g., blogs, chat rooms, text-based email clients) that quickly morphed into web-based inter-faces, mobile handheld devices, and social media and networking sites at the beginning of the twenty-first century were changing the ecology of everyday communications in ways that McRobbie and Thornton could not have antici-pated when they launched their critique in the early 1990s.

The changing dynamics of social interaction associated with the prolif-eration of interactive digital communication technologies call attention to the importance of revisiting the logic of mass mediation with insights into the structuring principles that ground the logic of digital mediation. Digital media is a broad concept that includes technological developments spanning

Accordingly, the **crisis narratives** that underscore moral panics commonly assume the form of socially regressive claims-making activities that are deployed with the intention of drawing attention to threatening others.

the advent of machine-readable computers and satellite television in the last quarter of the twentieth century to the proliferation of social media and networking sites in the first decade of the twenty-first century. In some ways, contemporary innovations in digital communication media reinforce and exacerbate the ongoing fragmentation of mass audiences into smaller niche publics — a process that was set in motion with earlier innovations in commercial media, including cable television, direct broadcast satellites, VCRs, DVDs, and PVRs. Recent popular debates about digital gatekeepers, echo chambers, and the filter bubble are cases in point (Pariser 2011). In other ways, innovations in digital communication infrastructures are undermining the very notion of the audience and, necessarily, related sociological assumptions about (a) what constitutes "media" and the social agents who produce and receive their contents, (b) the style of claims they engender and the arenas they appear in, and (c) the impacts they have on techniques of social regulation and control.

Media, Audiences, and Users

In keeping with the logic of mass-mediated moral panics, audience members represent distant observers of commercial media content who bear witness to images, stories, and primary and secondary testimony (Frosh and Pinchevski 2009). Eyewitness narratives are cultivated by journalists and media corporations that control the means of cultural production and routinely profit from tales of suffering, injustice, exploitation, and transgression. Rather than passively viewing mass media events, the audience members who are subject to mass-mediated moral panics actively and imaginatively engage with a range of narrated crises that emphasize the urgency of reacting to moral transgressions (Hay 1995). As generations of moral panic researchers have demonstrated, however, the crisis narratives that accentuate mass-mediated moral panics cannot be explained by merely emphasizing the variance between perceived threats and actual harms (i.e., disproportionate representations). Rather, the explanatory power of moral panics is found in the ways that crisis narratives provide a simplified account of moral transgression that is "sufficiently flexible to 'narrate' a great variety of morbid symptoms while unambiguously attributing causality and responsibility" to culpable social agents (Hay 1995: 335).

Accordingly, the **crisis narratives** that underscore moral panics commonly

assume the form of socially regressive claims-making activities that
are deployed with the intention
of drawing attention to threatening others (consider mass media

Framed in this conventional manner, audiences identify with and act in response to narrated crises on the basis of their prejudices, anxieties, bigotries, and fears.

frames about the health and security threats posed by asylum seekers and refugees). Framed in this conventional manner, audiences identify with and act in response to narrated crises on the basis of their prejudices, anxieties, bigotries, and fears. Yet, as Cohen (1999, 2003, 2011) has argued, crisis narratives can also assume the form of socially progressive claims-making activities (i.e., good moral panics) that are deployed to defend the rights and entitlements of vulnerable people (e.g., reporting on human suffering in the context of war and persecution). Framed in this unconventional manner, audience members identify with and act in response to narrated crises on the basis of their emotional identification with the victims of injustices and their cultural connections to a set of shared social responsibilities to care for and demonstrate compassion toward precarious populations (Hier 2016).

As traditional media logic continues to influence modes of audience engagement and social reactivity, the logic of digital mediation is, at the same time, continually reshaping how crises — be they conservatively regressive or socially progressive — are witnessed in, by, and through new and traditional media (e.g., Frosh and Pinchevski 2009). The most obvious differences that digital mediation makes regarding how users witness crises pertain to the scale of participation, the amount of testimonial evidence that can be circulated directly from networked users, and the speed and ease of transmission. Tracing back to the rise of interactive digital communications in the 1990s (e.g., bul-letin board systems, blogs, personal homepages), the web-based collaborative projects (e.g., wikis), content communities (e.g., YouTube), microblogs (e.g., Twitter), and social-networking sites (e.g., Facebook) that proliferated in the early 2000s are publicly available to, created by, and maintained through the routine activities of end users (Kaplan and Haenlein 2010). To be sure, organizations and website owners, often motivated by commercial interests, are able to manipulate interfaces and algorithms to channel users' experiences and shape online content (van Dijck and Powell 2013); however, at the same time, changing forms of digital mediation enable (if not require) networked users to intentionally or inadvertently steer information streams by creating, sharing, liking, filtering, mentioning, recommending, favouriting, tagging, forwarding, commenting on, and linking content.

The moral indignation expressed on the Twitter hashtag #Ferguson in response to the 2014 lethal police shooting of 18-year-old Michael Brown is a case in point. In the hours that followed Michael Brown's death in Ferguson, Missouri, neighbours and community members began posting images and text on Twitter, Instagram, YouTube, and Vine to express their anger and outrage at the killing of an unarmed Black man. In the first week of reaction alone, more than three million posts appeared on Twitter, and by the end of August 2014, #Ferguson had appeared on Twitter more than eight million times (Bonilla and Rosa 2015). The user-generated footage documenting the immediate aftermath of Michael Brown's death, combined with real-time crowd-sourced coverage of the protests and police force that followed, was conveyed across hashtag linkages (e.g., #HandsUpDontShoot, #MichaelBrown) that caused Twitter algorithms to make #Ferguson a trending topic (Bonilla and Rosa 2015).

Reminiscent of social reactions to witnessing similar incidents of racially motivated lethal violence (e.g., #trayvonmartin, #justiceforericgarner/#ICant Breathe, #FreddieGray), #Ferguson highlights the changing ways that moral panics are mediated across digital networks. In their hashtag ethnography of #Ferguson, for example, Bonilla and Rosa (2015) argue that hashtags, which mark conversations on social media platforms, serve as clerical and semiotic indexing systems. As clerical indexing systems, hashtags order information about specific topics and enable the quick retrieval of archived information. Hashtags function more broadly to signify existing social concerns in flexible and dynamic ways. By marking posts with hashtags, digital media users imaginatively and interactively shape what conversations are actually about by linking analogous conversations about prevailing and emerging narratives across hashtags, thereby expanding and strengthening the claims-making domain (e.g., the inter-discursive linkage between hashtags including #Ferguson, #michaelbrown, #TamirRice, #EricGarner, and #BlackLivesMatter).

Although the social media reactions to Michael Brown's death show that participatory digital media provide distant users with an unprecedented set of communication resources to witness and participate in the narration of crises, they also point to other ways that **digital media logic** influences the mediation of moral panics. In sharp contrast to the critical orientation to protest activities and civil disobedience that often characterizes elites' agenda setting and mass media framing, #Ferguson amplified the urgency of reacting to the threat posed by racially motivated police violence by continually managing the contents of the community-based grievance. Before mass media were able to report on the shooting or document the unfolding of events, multiple social media users were already enacting crisis narratives

> Marginalized groups have historically developed networks and alliances beyond mainstream media channels to communicate their goals and have their voices heard.

that amplified racism and police brutality in Ferguson (Bonilla and Rosa 2015).

The initial tweet that drew attention to the shooting (sent within minutes of Michael Brown's death) came from a local resident (@AyoMissDarkSkin) who described witnessing the unarmed innocent boy being executed by Ferguson police. The tone of the initial post contrasted sharply with the only mass media depiction posted on Twitter that day by the St. Louis Post Dispatch (@stltoday): "Fatal shooting by police prompts mob reaction" (Jackson and Foucault Welles 2016: 405). The @stltoday post not only lacked the emotionally charged language that Papacharissi and de Fatima Oliveira (2012) attribute to the narration of crowd-sourced social media crises, it also failed to attract the same level of attention that the #Ferguson hashtag did. In contrast to @stltoday, the claims-making activities of several influential social media users and their followers on #Ferguson amplified the crisis by posting, retweeting, and mentioning influential posts. They also challenged subsequent mass media frames that characterized Michael Brown and his supporters as a threat to social order. This media framing was largely undertaken through the release of security video footage of Brown shoplifting cigars (the crime for which police were initially called) and the broadcast of witness testimonies suggesting that Brown was the aggressor in his confrontation with Wilson (Jackson and Foucault Welles 2016).

In addition to the ways that hashtags enable distant social media users to participate in the narration of crises without relying exclusively on mainstream mass media logic, the digital mediation of the crisis in Ferguson also facilitated the emergence of a hashtag "ad hoc public." Marginalized groups have historically developed networks and alliances beyond mainstream media channels to communicate their goals and have their voices heard. This is the essence of McRobbie and Thornton's (1995) argument about multi-mediated moral panics. But Twitter's user-generated system of hashtags affords platform users the ability to spontaneously react to transgression or injustice by bringing people together around common themes and topics.

As Bruns and Burgess (2011) explain, the use of hashtags to coordinate

But Twitter's user-generated system of hashtags affords platform users the ability to spontaneously react to transgression or injustice by bringing people together around common themes and topics.

political discussions or crisis communication contributes to the formation of ad hoc publics through dynamic networks of communication and connectivity. Such publics, they explain, are organized around issues or events rather than pre-existing social affiliations. In the social media reaction to the crisis in Ferguson, #Ferguson and related hashtags were generative of ad hoc publics that did not represent bounded groups but rather emergent networks that overlapped with pre-existing, broader social justice concerns (such as the Black Lives Matter movement that began to take root in 2013). The significance of the crisis hashtags used to articulate the grievance against racially motivated police violence in Ferguson and elsewhere is not, therefore, only about the way that digital networks link people together around common themes; hashtags function to amplify an assemblage of messages posted by otherwise disconnected people who come together spontaneously to express their anger and outrage at normative transgressions.

The changing ways that people witness transgression in digital environments, combined with the ad hoc publics that form in reaction to the mediation of crisis events over social media platforms, is impinging on the structure of moral entrepreneurship. **Moral entrepreneurs** are conventionally understood as structurally advantaged activists who influence mass media narratives and shape public opinion by forming organizations, giving talks, lobbying governments, and staging protests (Goode and Ben-Yehuda 2013). Be they members of interest groups, social elites, or grassroots campaign networks, moral entrepreneurs represent socially established activists who work in close relation with mass media institutions to establish a preferred position in, and gain control over, media narratives and public claims making.

Because traditional moral entrepreneurs enjoy an intimate relationship with mass media institutions, they have conventionally been explained as having a conservative bent that aligns with media logic and bolsters the agenda-setting priorities of commercial media outlets. The logic of digital mediation has created opportunities for a new kind of unwitting moral entrepreneur to engage in claims making that can take the form of resisting, complying with, and/or inventing new forms of social regulation and control. Indeed, the moral entrepreneurship that developed in response to Michael Brown's death challenged mainstream media narratives that depicted Brown as a threat and protesters as violent and disobedient, that allocated blame to racialized policing practices and state-sanctioned violence, and that galvanized a broad network of (Bl)activists under a common online identity. Emerging from ad hoc publics, the opinion leaders and crowd-sourced elites whose messages were amplified across hashtag linkages represented a small number of overall social media users, yet their messages were mentioned and retweeted to the extent that they became inadvertent leaders in the narration of the crisis (LeFebvre and Armstrong 2016).

In this way, the logic of digital mediation underscoring #Ferguson provided a set of opportunities for members of marginalized populations to bypass gatekeepers, evade censorship, challenge elite claims, and directly document police violence without having to rely on traditional news cycles and logics of mediation. Contrary to McRobbie and Thornton's (1995) influential declaration that alternative niche media play a central role in both instigating and responding to moral panics in multi-mediated social worlds, niche media outlets were almost entirely absent from the initial claims-making package (Jackson and Foucault Welles 2016). Alternatively, community members in Ferguson — many of them young, Black working-class Americans — became primary definers of the crisis in Ferguson between August 9 and 15, 2014, by articulating a grievance that pitted the collective responsibility to protect vulnerable young Black Americans against the specific harm posed by racist police in America (e.g., LeFebvre and Armstrong 2016). When a second "Twitter storm" emerged in the three-week period that led up to and immediately followed the grand jury's verdict not to indict white police officer Darren Wilson (who killed Michael Brown), more than six million tweets were sent using #Ferguson. The contents were carefully controlled by social media users who selectively enlisted the support of elites (e.g., President Obama), retweeted and mentioned posts by influential opinion leaders and celebrity sports stars, and promoted supportive local and national mainstream media outlets by mentioning, linking, forwarding, and retweeting their posts (see Jackson and Foucault Welles 2016).

Claims-Making Arenas and Styles of Claims

The myriad digitally mediated social reactions to racially motivated police violence that have developed under the broad identity of Black Lives Matter clearly demonstrate how participatory digital media provide distant users with an unprecedented set of communication resources to witness crises and challenge traditional ideological biases in the mass media. As the audience becomes increasingly accustomed to the participatory architecture of digital media, it is simultaneously getting used to new ways of making, disseminating, receiving, and acting on claims. Conceptualized through the lens of traditional media logic, claims making entails ongoing cycles of competition among a diverse set of "claims makers" who aspire for status within the broader field of information resources (Hilgartner and Bosk 1988). Sometimes the focus of analysis is trained on the ways in which activists directly intervene in established arenas to influence mass media frames. At other times, the focus of analysis is concentrated on how various coalitions use their own niche media to develop oppositional narratives that are presented alongside hegemonic representations in mainstream media. In either case, **alternative framing strategies** and **oppositional narratives** are understood to offer secondary sites of engagement, always indexed to dominant narratives appearing in the mass media (Meyers 2012).

In contrast to Altheide and Snow's (1979) logic of mediation, millions of images and video files in the past decade have been uploaded/posted to various sites by traditional journalists, online commentators, social movement activists, police agencies, human rights workers, and ordinary citizens. Online images and video files undeniably reflect the ideological orientations and interests of witnesses, who range from humanitarians to bigots. But once content is posted to social media and networking sites, video files and digital images are subjected to an ongoing sequence of editing, sharing, tagging, categorizing, reposting, repositioning, commenting, remixing, and deleting that continually influences the original meaning of uploaded content, the dynamics of witnessing, and the future memory of events.

One of the increasingly common ways that digital images and video files are subjected to reappropriation is through processes of **journalistic verification**. As digital archives (like YouTube) became increasingly popular locations to post a wide variety of eyewitness testimonial visual evidence (sometimes involving hundreds of images and video files capturing different angles of the same event), journalists increasingly relinquished their conventional commitment to breaking news stories. In place of taking the lead on breaking stories, journalists now are more regularly cast in the secondary position of verifying, interpreting, and remediating crowd-sourced content. As Smit, Heinrich, and Broersma (2017) explain, when journalists remix citizen-generated footage, they tend to adopt a detached style of questioning that interrogates the authenticity of events depicted in images and video files (or if they happened in the ways that video evidence suggests). By adopting a skeptical orientation to crowd-sourced content, reassembled files that are uploaded to digital archives reshape the meaning and intention of original footage by introducing voiceovers, installing news tickers, altering interpretations, compiling multiple images into one file, and ultimately questioning the legitimacy of digital witness testimony (Smit, Heinrich, and Broersma 2017).

Journalists are not, however, the sole actors who reappropriate digital files and images. Accompanying the ways that journalists remix online video feeds, photographs, sketches, and symbols is a second powerful form of digital witnessing: internet memes. **Internet memes** are a type of textual genre that is often composed of an image with captioned text. Representing "multimodel artifacts remixed by countless participants" (Milner 2013: 2357), memes play a daily role in online interactions about social, political, and cultural issues and events.

As an important way of conveying information and continuing a conversation in participatory digital media cultures, internet memes are expressed in a variety of forms. For example, memes can be satirical, such as appropriating imagery from corporate advertising to rhetorically comment on everyday conventions and moral transgressions. In this way, memes can function as a style of moral regulation in everyday life that encourages, challenges, and interrogates certain ways of thinking and acting (Hunt 1999). Memes can also serve the interests of political activists, such as the ones that contributed toward popularizing and advancing the grievances launched by the Occupy Wall Street (ows) protests in 2011, during which iconic images — such as the iconic bull statue on Wall Street — were appropriated to amplify corporate deviance and mobilize support (*Huffington Post* 2017).

Returning to the example of #Ferguson, one of the most powerful claims-making styles adopted by ordinary digital media users pertained to #HandsUpDontShoot. Users posted thousands of photos of individuals and groups on various social media sites with their hands in the air (often wearing a hoodie). These images gained considerable traction when students at Howard University created an internet meme depicting hundreds of Black students with their hands in the air (Bonilla and Rosa 2015). The influence of #HandsUpDontShoot was bolstered by several other hashtags, such as #IfTheyGunnedMeDown, that articulated the imperative to collectively manage the risks posed by lethal police harm. Online reaction to Brown's death included a meme, designed by 18-year-old Tyler Atkins and reproduced by the *New York Times*, juxtaposing an endearing childhood photo of Atkins with a photo of him wearing a black T-shirt and bandana. The meme functioned as a rhetorical claim to challenge the stereotyping of Black youth by police (would they shoot me down?) and media tendencies in the representation of Black victims (which photo would they use?).

Changing patterns of journalistic verification and online memetic practices represent two important ways that users witness media crises in newer digital claims-making arenas. Although both forms of witnessing profoundly affect claims-making activities and user reactivity, they are underscored by and partially shaped through the technological affordances of platforms — a third, non-human influence on the remediation of online content. For example, when journalists remix crowd-sourced content (like mobile phone coverage of the shooting of a Black boy), they do not merely alter the original interpretation of uploaded files but also make decisions about anticipated search activity and the ways that platforms sort information, filter content, rank files, and influence user behaviour and experiences (Bucher 2012). By categorizing, describing, and tagging images and frames (including tagging themselves), journalistic verification can subvert the democratic storage functions provided by online archives that enable anyone to post material by manipulating display functions that are susceptible to commercial influences, advertising, platform censorship, and user popularity (Gehl 2009). By the same token, meme generation has hitherto mostly relied on user-generated input of images and text, but algorithm curation models (computations that promote popular links and trending topics) and emerging computations that automatically generate memes (Costa, Olivera, and Pinto 2015) are also capable of animating controversial topics online. Hence, across platforms such as Tumblr, Twitter, Reddit, 4chan, YouTube, and Facebook, practices of remediation play instrumental roles in making claims, amplifying deviance, mobilizing support, influencing mainstream media discourse, shaping political debate, and changing the structure of activism and how people witness dissent (Huntington 2015).

Social Regulation and Control

The rapid reconfiguration of the audience, combined with the changing ways that "produsers" (Bruns 2008) create, experience, receive, and amend claims, reveals the limitations of both conventional and many contemporary theories of social regulation and control. In several important ways, the logic of digital media supplements how traditional media logic connects newsworthy information to issue-publics, commercial advertisers to consumer-publics, and elite national agendas to citizen-publics: It does so by increasing the size of receiving audiences and refining how mass media institutions create and transmit information across digital platforms. Yet in other substantial ways, some of which have been highlighted above, the networked participation that interactive digital media infrastructures require also provides new opportunities for ordinary people to circumvent the agenda-setting activities of elites, subvert the traditional gate-keeping

> The networked participation that interactive digital media infrastructures require also provides new opportunities for ordinary people to circumvent the agenda-setting activities of elites, subvert the traditional gate-keeping role of mass media, and articulate a wide range of grievances against insult and injustice.

role of mass media, and articulate a wide range of grievances against insult and injustice.

In the ongoing mediation of the crisis in Ferguson, the changing dynamics of social regulation and control were clearly demonstrated by social reactions to the *New York Times*' depiction of Michael Brown on the day of his funeral (Eligon 2014). The newspaper described Brown as "no angel," and noted that he used drugs and alcohol, lived in a rough neighbourhood, shoplifted, used vulgar lyrics in his rap songs, and was "a handful" as a boy. Responding to the depiction of Brown as "no angel," the hashtag #NoAngel proliferated on Twitter. Along with #IfTheyGunnedMeDown and #HandsUpDontShoot, #NoAngel was used to challenge victim-blaming in the mainstream press.

Since the 1970s, explanations for the social construction and amplification of deviance that underscore the bulk of studies of moral panic have more or less hinged on tacit assumptions about an interdependent relationship among traditional mass media, established politics, cohesive audiences, and levers of social control sustained by a familiar cast of moral entrepreneurs, including police, politicians, and activists. As the impact of digital media logic continues to transform the dynamics of everyday social interaction, however, deviance amplification is increasingly susceptible to the claims-making activities of an extended range of definers, including bloggers, vloggers, Tweeters, memers, hashtag activists/slacktivists/Blacktivists, citizen journalists, trolls, YouTubers, Viners, gamers, and the millions of ordinary people who have incorporated social media platforms and networking sites into their everyday lives.

Conclusion

In their deconstruction of the classical models of moral panic, McRobbie and Thornton (1995) demonstrated that the relationship between (British) society and mass media at the twilight of the twentieth century was considerably different than it had been imagined when moral panic studies first emerged in the 1960s. Repudiating the main assumptions of the original studies, they drew attention to the diversity of media outlets, to the multifaceted character of claims-making processes, and especially to the patterns of folk-devil resistance that are often involved in constructing modern moral panics. An updated model of moral panic capable of capturing the greater complexity of media communications, social differentiation, and audience fragmentation in the age of multi-mediated social relations was, they convincingly argued, critically important for maintaining and (re)affirming the relevance of moral panic as an explanatory sociological concept.

Notwithstanding the importance of McRobbie and Thornton's empirical insights, their deconstruction of moral panic in the mostly analog world of newspaper stories and niche publishing outlets predates the transformations that have since taken place in digital communication infrastructures and collaborative social media networks. The combination of social, technological, and economic forces that contributed to the proliferation of digital (rather than merely mass) media has altered some of the ways in which claims are created, contested, disseminated, and received. Like never before, digital media users (as opposed to mass "audience" members) are able to share stories, articulate controversies, launch grievances, document transgressions, and witness crises instantaneously, interactively, and globally. In some ways, digital mediation is affecting the traditional power dynamics associated with elite agenda setting and hegemony by providing new and more accessible opportunities to supplement journalistic claims making with alternative points of view. In other ways, digital communication networks are creating opportunities to subvert the traditional gatekeeping role of journalists and elites by providing spatially and temporally distant users with an unprecedented set of opportunities to participate in interactions that range from exposing racially motivated police violence in real time to shaming ordinary people for minor indiscretions.

Despite the obvious influences that the newest digital (particularly social) media platforms are having on claims-making activities and deviance amplification, moral panic scholarship carries on as though we are still living in a world where putative problems play out primarily across the pages of broadsheet newspapers and through asymmetrical channels of mass-mediated communication. Moral panic scholars are in essence caught in the midst of something resembling a paradigm shift in the structure of media and crime communications — a historical transformation that some stubbornly persist in ignoring. It is important to continue investigating how the changing logic of mass mediation affects social interactions in domains within and beyond commercial media outlets. At the same time, however, the proliferation of digital infrastructures calls attention to the importance of understanding how digitally mediated interactions are enabling diverse users to participate in a range of claims-making activities, moralizing campaigns, and righteous crusades that have been met by a curious silence in the burgeoning criminological literature on contemporary moral panics.

Discussion Questions

1. What is moral panic?
2. What are the important distinctions between media logic and digital media logic?
3. How have practices associated with claims making changed with the emergence of digital media?
4. What media practices are involved in journalistic verification?
5. How do hashtags allow social media users to engage in the narration of crises?

Recommended Resources

1. Black Lives Matter. <blacklivesmatter.com>
2. State of Emergency: Ferguson, Missouri (VICE News series)
3. "Citizen Journalism Is Reshaping the World" (TED Talk presented by Brian Conley)

Glossary

claims making: the process whereby media and moral entrepreneurs strive to authoritatively shape public discourse and perspectives surrounding prominent issues and events.

crisis narratives: media communications centred on the onset of crises that can be critically assessed to discern subtextual commentaries regrading responsibility and potential remedies.

deviance amplification: a mainstream media practice whereby numerous reports simultaneously focus on a social issue or perceived threat, thus inflating the prominence and gravity of the threat for audiences.

digital media logic: emergent practices of information distribution whereby a range of actors use social media platforms to contribute information; challenges media authority to determine how current events are framed.

internet memes: images developed and distributed by social media users,

often uniting culturally prevalent imagery with user-determined text, to
critique or humorously comment on current events and social issues.

journalistic verification: emerging practices whereby journalists assert
authority not in "breaking" news, but by critically assessing the ways in
which breaking stories are framed by social media users.

media logic: traditional practices of information distribution whereby a
restricted population of media resources hold the authority to frame
and unidirectionally distribute information to audiences.

moral entrepreneurs: figures of social authority or high social status
whom members of the public trust as valid information resources.

moral panic: the process whereby media representations of perceived dangers manipulate audience emotions to reinforce social consensus validat-
ing the empowerment of authority figures.

niche media: information media that are designed to target restricted
audiences on the basis of select beliefs, ideological positions, or cultural
tastes.

oppositional narratives: alternative accounts surrounding an event or
social issue that are disseminated to counter and challenge the claims of
mass media and other authorities.

Notes

This chapter coincides with a paper that was published in the journal *Crime, Media,
Culture* in 2019.

1. Toward the end of their article, McRobbie and Thornton (1995) make passing
   references to gay/lesbian papers, street papers aimed at homeless readers, and socialist
   and fascist niche papers. They suggest that so-called folk devils can produce their
   own media and, intriguingly, that moral panics are not always hegemonic. Despite the
   significance of the latter suggestion for renewed debate about the prospect that moral
   panics can be "good" (see Cohen 2011), the point is merely asserted descriptively and
   not developed analytically.

References

Altheide, David, and Robert Snow. 1979. *Media Logic*. Beverly Hills: Sage.
Black Lives Matter. n.d. Home page. <blacklivesmatter.com>.
Bonilla, Yarimar, and Jonathan Rosa. 2015. "#Ferguson: Digital Protest, Hashtag
    Ethnography, and the Racial Politics of Social Media in the United States." *American
    Ethnologist* 42, 1.
Bruns, Axel. 2008. *Blogs, Wikipedia, Second Life and Beyond: From Production to Produsage*.
    New York: Peter Lang.
Bruns, Axel, and Jean Burgess. 2011. "The Use of Twitter Hashtags in the Formation
    of Ad Hoc Publics." *Proceedings of the 6th European Consortium for Political Research*

(ECPR) *General Conference 201.* <eprints.qut.edu.au/46515/>.

Bucher, Tania. 2012. "Programmed Sociality: A Software Studies Perspective on Social Networking Sites." PhD thesis, University of Copenhagen.

Cohen, Stanley. 2011. "Whose Side Were We On? The Undeclared Politics of Moral Panic Theory." *Crime, Media, Culture* 7, 3.

_____. 2003 *Folk Devils and Moral Panics: The Creation of the Mods and Rockers,* 3rd ed. London: Routledge.

_____. 1999. "Moral Panics and Folk Concepts." *Paedagogica Historica* 35, 3.

Costa, Diogo, Hugo Olivera and Alexandre Pinto. 2015. "'In Reality There Are as Many Religions as There Are Papers': First Steps Towards the Generation of Internet Memes." *Proceedings of the Sixth International Conference on Computational Creativity.*<researchgate.net/publication/298041856_In_reality_there_are_as_many_religions_as_there_are_papers_-_First_Steps_Towards_ the_Generation_ of_Internet _Memes>.

Daschuk, M.D. 2016. "'What Was Once Rebellion Is Now Clearly Just a Social Sect': Identity, Ideological Conflict and the Field of Punk Rock Artistic Production." University of Saskatchewan Online Thesis Directory. <harvest.usask.ca/ handle/10388/7488>.

Eligon, John. 2014. "Michael Brown Spent Last Week Grappling with Problems and Promise." *New York Times,* August 24. <nytimes.com/2014/08/25/us/michael-brown-spent-last-weeks-grappling-with-lifes-mysteries.html>.

Frosh, Paul, and Amit Pinchevski. 2009. "Crisis-Readiness and Media-Witnessing." *Communication Review* 12, 3.

Gehl, Robert W. 2009. "YouTube as Archive: Who Will Curate This Digital Wunderkammer?" *International Journal of Cultural Studies* 12, 1.

Goode, Erich, and Nachman Ben-Yehuda. 2013. *Moral Panics: The Social Construction of Deviance,* 2nd edition. Malden: Wiley-Blackwell.

Hall, Stuart, Chas Chritcher, Tony Jefferson, John Clarke, and Brian Roberts. 2009. *Policing the Crisis: Mugging, the State, and Law and Order.* London: Macmillan Press.

Hay, Colin. 1995. "Mobilization through Interpellation: James Bulger, Juvenile Crime and the Construction of Moral Panic." *Social Legal Studies* 4, 2.

Hier, Sean P. 2016. "Good Moral Panics? Normative Ambivalence, Social Reaction, and Coexisting Responsibilities in Everyday Life." *Current Sociology* 65, 6.

_____. 2008. "Thinking Beyond Moral Panic: Risk, Responsibility, and the Politics of Moralization." *Theoretical Criminology* 12, 2.

Hilgartner, Stephen, and Charles Bosk. 1988. "The Rise and Fall of Social Problems: A Public Arenas Model." *American Journal of Sociology* 94, 1.

Huffington Post. 2017. "Occupy Wall Street Memes Sprout Up on the Internet." December 6. <huffingtonpost.com/2011/11/24/occupy-wall-street-memes_n_1111848.html>.

Hunt, Alan. 1999. *Governing Morals.* Cambridge: Cambridge University Press.

Huntington, Heidi. 2015. "Pepper Spray Cop and the American Dream: Using Synecdoche and Metaphor to Unlock Internet Memes' Visual Political Rhetoric." *Communication Studies* 27, 1.

Jackson, Sarah, and Brooke Foucault Welles. 2016. "#Ferguson Is Everywhere: Initiators in Emerging Counterpublic Networks." *Information, Communication, and Society* 19, 3.

Kaplan, Andreas, and Michael Haenlein. 2010. "Users of the World, Unite! The Challenges and Opportunities of Social Media." *Business Horizons* 53.

LeFebvre, Rebecca, and Crystal Armstrong. 2016. "Grievance-Based Social Movement Mobilization in the #Ferguson Twitter Storm." *New Media and Society* 20, 1.

McRobbie, Angela, and Sarah Thornton. 1995. "Rethinking 'Moral Panic' for MultiMediated Social Worlds." *British Journal of Sociology* 46, 4.

Meyers, Erin. 2012 "'Blogs Give Regular People the Chance to Talk Back': Rethinking 'Professional' Media Hierarchies in New Media." *New Media and Society* 14, 6.

Milner, Ryan. 2013. "Pop Polyvocality: Internet Memes, Public Participation, and the Occupy Wall Street Movement." *International Journal of Communication* 7.

Papacharsissi, Zizi, and Maria de Fatima Oliveira. 2012. "Affective News and Networked Publics: The Rhythms of Story Telling on #Egypt." *Journal of Communication* 4, 1.

Pariser, Eli. 2011. *The Filter Bubble: How the New Personalized Web Is Changing What We Read and How We Think*. New York: Penguin.

Pearson, Geoffrey 1983. *Hooligan: A History of Respectable Fear*. London: MacMillan.

Savage, Jon. 1991. *England's Dreaming: Sex Pistols and Punk Rock*. London: Faber and Faber.

Smit, Rik, Ansgard Heinrich, and Marcel Broersma. 2017. "Witnessing in the New Memory Ecology: Memory Construction of the Syrian Conflict on YouTube." *New Media and Society* 19, 2.

TEDx Talks. 2012. "Citizen Journalism Is Reshaping the World: Brian Conley at TEDxMidAtlantic." <youtube.com/watch?v=kY-l9UQpf0Y>.

Thornton, Sarah. 1995. *Club Cultures*. Middleton: Wesleyan University Press.

Ungar, Sheldon. 2001. "Moral Panic Versus the Risk Society: The Implications of the Changing Sites of Social Anxiety." *British Journal of Sociology* 52, 2.

van Dijck, Jose, and Thomas Powell. 2013. "Understanding Social Media Logic." *Media and Communication* 1, 1.

VICE. 2014. "State of Emergency: Ferguson, Missouri." <vice.com/en_us/article/pa45dz/state-of-emergency-ferguson-missouri-dispatch-1>.

Young, Jock. 1971. *The Drug Takers: The Social Meaning of Drug Use*. London: McGibbon and Paladin.

10

"The Kids Find It Fascinating"

Museums, Policing, and the Fairy Tale of "Crime"

Matthew Ferguson

After reading this chapter, you will be able to do the following:

1. Explain what "crime" is and how it is socially constructed.
2. Discuss how critical criminology differs from mainstream criminology.
3. Discuss the relevance and significance of museums to criminology.
4. Identify some common myths about "crime" and policing.
5. Understand the concept of penal spectatorship.

On May 4, 2017, a new exhibit opened at the Chimczuk Museum (pronounced CHIM-chuck), a community museum located in downtown Windsor, Ontario. Called "150 Years of Policing Memorabilia," the three-month exhibit traced the history of the Windsor Police Service. It was spearheaded by the newly designated official historian for the police service — a staff sergeant with nearly thirty years of policing experience — along with the help of a few high school students as part of the celebrations for the 150th anniversary of Windsor's Police Service (which was launched April 1, 1867, with the appointment of a single chief and three constables). A local journalist described the collection as "artifacts chronicling the heroes and villains of Windsor's history," while the chief of police, who arrived at the opening of the exhibit in a 1958 Chevrolet Biscayne police car, touted it as "the story of our community" (Wilhelm 2017: 1).

Spread throughout the exhibit space was an assortment of objects, photographs, and video footage related to public policing in the Windsor area.

Among the more popular displays was one near the entrance dedicated to a notorious figure from the 1940s known as the "Slasher," whose real name was Ronald Sears. Several vintage newspaper clippings pasted on a wall recounted the story, with headlines such as "Slasher Charged as Slayer" and "Sears Confession Is Read" ("150 Years of Policing Memorabilia" 2017). Nearby, beside a worn-out firearms registry and a book of mug shots from the 1950s, visitors could peer into a glass display case at a letter sent by the mysterious "Slasher" to police headquarters before his identification and capture ("150 Years of Policing Memorabilia" 2017). Scrawled in red pencil was written:

> Dear Sirs, This is a challenge to you. "I" will strike in the near future. I can not disclose this to you of course. My avenge of these people are great. Nothing shall stand in my way. I will use only the knife on my supposed enemies. I am not a returned soldier. This is no prank. THE SLASHER. Please forgive me but these people have destroyed my whole life.

Below the writing was an unsettling sketch of a knife dripping blood. A few feet to the right, a display was set up in remembrance of a recently slain police officer who had made "The Ultimate Sacrifice," according to a framed newspaper headline, in a shootout with two teenagers ("150 Years of Policing Memorabilia" 2017). Other material in the exhibit included an area dedicated to a highly decorated, hard-nosed detective. According to a story shared in a binder, he was a "crime-fighting legend" who had the remarkable ability to "smell crime" and a "dogged determination to nab criminals" ("150 Years of Policing Memorabilia" 2017). Above this display was a photograph of a police officer clutching an infant found in a bed next to her deceased mother, the victim of a homicide. It was titled, "The Face of Compassion in the Depth of Tragedy" (wall text, "150 Years of Policing Memorabilia" 2017).

On the other side of the room were relics of forensic science. There were old plaster casts of tire tracks and footwear impressions, an antique Korona View camera once used in investigations, and fingerprints obtained by a police officer in 1922. Also present were early textbooks on the study of fingerprint technology, with writing nearby explaining the current process for visitors: "Today a computer system is used to match crime scene fingerprints to known offenders' fingerprints on a National level. Matches generated by the computer are then examined by an accredited fingerprint expert to validate and confirm the match" (display text, "150 Years of Policing Memorabilia" 2017). After three months on display, the exhibit was dismantled and transported back to police headquarters for storage.

The exhibit's curator noted that it received positive feedback and attracted 600–700 Grade 6 students on field trips, numerous members of the policing community, as well as other interested citizens and tourists (personal communication, July 4, 2017). In many ways, these visitors resembled the black-and-white figures on the poster introducing the exhibit: a photograph of police officers, adults, and children gathered around the scene of a bank robbery on August 23, 1947 (poster, "150 Years of Policing Memorabilia" 2017). Along with being a story of community, as the chief framed it, the policing exhibit was also a "story of crime" (Hayward 2010: 4) that captured the attention of police and citizens during the summer months, much in the same way it did seventy years earlier.

This chapter examines how criminalized conflict and harm — or what most people simply refer to as "crime" — is represented in a few of Ontario's police museums and exhibits. The recent "150 Years of Policing Memorabilia" exhibit at the Chimczuk Museum is one example, along with the Ontario Provincial Police (OPP) Museum in Orillia and the Hamilton Police Service Museum in Ancaster. As Hayward (2010: 4) observes, in our media-driven society "the 'story' of crime and crime control is now promulgated as much through the image as through the word." Meanings about criminalized acts are produced through visually striking displays and stories set in particular times and places. Museums are storytellers too, relying on the power of stories to make connections between visitors and content (Bedford 2001). They are authoritative narrators that should be truthful and not attempt to deceive (Crane 1997). The museum is the opposite of the police interrogation room; it is an open, welcoming space to which the public is invited and trusts in the truth of the stories. The objective of this chapter is to turn the tables, so to speak, and critically interrogate the "story of crime" told in two police museums and a policing exhibit. Drawing from criminological literature, it examines how cultural representations communicate messages and shape popular understandings about criminalized harm, victimization, and (in)justice (see Brown 2009; Piché and Walby 2016; Hirschfield and Simon 2010; Christie 1986).

The following section examines the concept of "crime" in greater detail and emphasizes its socially constructed nature. Literature on its representation in mass media and other sites of popular culture highlights how police museums are often overlooked as places where meaning making occurs. The chapter demonstrates how police museums and exhibits foster social distance

The chapter demonstrates how police museums and exhibits foster social distance between penal spectators (i.e., tourists) and those in conflict with the law by representing criminalized individuals as dangerous and cunning authors of "crime," while celebrating police officers as heroic and sacrificial in their "fight" against it.

between penal spectators (i.e., tourists) and those in conflict with the law by representing criminalized individuals as dangerous and cunning authors of "crime," while celebrating police officers as heroic and sacrificial in their "fight" against it. We will also discuss how the

 museums emphasize relatively rare acts of extreme violence committed against innocent victims and ignore illegal conduct committed by corporate and state actors, as well as police officers themselves. The chapter concludes with reflections on the "stories of crime" shared in the museums, which resemble a fairy tale. Marketed for everyone — but especially children, as an educational and recruitment tool — police museums and exhibits are places where what constitutes "crime" and acceptable responses to it are socially constructed by those in power, helping to perpetuate and build pride in a profoundly ineffective, costly, and unjust penal system.

What, if Anything, Is "Crime"?

In his 2004 book *A Suitable Amount of Crime*, Norwegian criminologist Nils Christie (2004: 1) confidently titled his opening chapter, "Crime does not exist." He explains that "only acts exist, acts often given different meanings within various social frameworks" (Christie 2004: 3). For Christie and many other critical criminologists, the word "crime" is a problematic and slippery one. He does not deny the existence of "unwanted acts" (Christie 2004: 7) that have been socially defined as undesirable and criminalized. However, he explains that what we know as "crime" is a fluid and shallow artifact of human creation that changes over time, across societies, and within them daily. This label, he argues, can be applied to an endless number of acts and is dependent on social, cultural, and political conditions. It is also not consistent in its enforcement; for example, an act of theft committed by a teenager against a family member might be considered a family issue, while outside the home it would be criminalized (Christie 2004).

Problematizing the concept of "crime" as an imprecise, socially defined creation differs from the more common, less critical position embraced by mainstream criminologists. Adopting the perspective of the state, these scholars accept the concept of crime and typically consider it to be a violation of the law. As Agnew (2011: 13) notes, "mainstream criminologists spend surprisingly little time discussing the actual definition of crime," because it is considered by them to be self-evident and not require much explanation. As researchers, they focus most of their attention on individual acts of violence, theft, and drug use, or what some refer to as "street crimes" (Agnew 2011: 14). This dominant perspective has been critiqued for numerous reasons, but arguably the biggest risk of remaining uncritical about the concept of "crime" is overlooking what Christie (2004) reminds his readers right from the beginning — that crime is a social construction with no ontological reality (see also Hulsman 1986). According to Bittle and colleagues (2018: 5), the discipline of criminology still fails to take this important point seriously, evidenced by its persistent focus on acts that are mainly committed by the powerless, which receive significantly more criminological attention than the violence committed by powerful people and corporations.

> Crime is a social construction with no ontological reality.

Ontology is the study of being, and to say that something has no ontological reality is to say that it has no reality or essential nature that exists independently in the world. As Hulsman (1986) explains, this accurately describes "crime" because unwanted acts in a society must first be constructed as "criminal" through a social process of criminalization before they exist as such. In other words, without the many laws and institutions in society that criminalize certain behaviour, this category would cease to exist. This means that "crime" is the product of law, not the object of it (Hulsman 1986), and it is a constantly evolving construct that is imbued with meaning, negotiated, reformed, organized, and applied by humans. As Presdee (2004: 44) puts it, "crime can only be created through social relations made within a dominant culture and determined by a dominant morality." Thus, it shifts over time and corresponds to a dominant way of constructing social reality, a powerful "criminal way" (Hulsman 1986: 72) of perceiving and acting in the world. More specifically, it reflects a way of organizing society where certain people are criminalized for transgressing boundaries specified by those with social and political power.

Hulsman (1986) argues that understanding and demystifying the social reality that constructs, shapes, and gives meaning to "crime" requires criminologists to problematize and ultimately reject this concept. That is, they must reject the very concept that forms the organizing foundation of their discipline. If they fail to do so, then they are operating from within the "criminal way" of constructing reality (the subject of their study) and "can never take *an external view* [on this reality] *and ... therefore* [are] *unable to demystify it"* (Hulsman 1986: 71, emphasis in original). Thus, Hulsman and many others have sought to "decriminalize criminology" (Shearing 1989: 169) by expanding its subject matter to include a broad range of harms, such as sexism, racism, and economic exploitation, as well as shifting its focus away from "crime" and toward social order, such as how the dominant order and the harms associated with it are maintained. The next section explains how criminalized conflicts and harms — usually referred to as "crime" or what Nils Christie once called a "big, fat, imprecise word" (*Wired News* 2009: 1) — are depicted in mass media and museums, shaping the meanings people attach to this term and, consequently, the social reality it represents.

Mass Media and Museums: Putting "Crime" on Display

Museums and mass media, which includes video games, movies, and television shows, are filled with representations of criminalized acts and the assemblage of institutions involved in criminalizing them, such as police, courts, and prisons. Though some people have direct experience with these matters, most of what the public knows is acquired from a social distance through cultural representation. According to Hall (1997b: 15), "representation is an essential part of the process by which meaning is produced and exchanged between members of a culture." Acts of representation containing signs and symbols communicate meanings, which are interpreted by people in different ways depending on factors such as cultural and social backgrounds (see Watney 1989; Lidchi 1997). Hall (1980) explains how mass media and other forms of popular culture are contested sites where struggles are waged over representation and the power to produce meaning. Some knowledge systems or "ways of knowing" become elevated through these mediums and legitimized at the expense of others (Howarth 2006). Similar to Hall, Coyle (2013) emphasizes the pivotal role that language plays in this process. He explains how everyday words and phrases used to talk about "justice-related matters" carry powerful yet subtle meanings that encourage social control and punishment. For example, commonly used terms such as "criminal" and "inmate" define others as deviant, stripping away their identity and justifying their social control through exclusionary practices. As Coyle (2013) notes, our language choices have important implications for how we think about and design justice policy.

A significant amount of research has demonstrated the inaccuracies of cultural representations of policing and criminalized harms. As Hirschfield and Simon (2010: 155) explain, "representations in the news media depict crime as an individual moral failing, criminals as irredeemably dangerous, victims as innocent, and police as honest and heroic public servants" (see also Reiner 1985, 2010; Colbran 2014; Greer 2007). Such portrayals have consequences for public perceptions and contribute to what Hulsman (1986: 70) calls "mystification," because they focus on atypical "newsworthy" events and present them in a stereotyped fashion that influences how people understand the world. As a result, news and entertainment media regularly produce and shape meanings about "crime" in ways that distort the reality of it. Research in this area has expanded considerably and is often conducted under a relatively new perspective known as cultural criminology (Ferrell, Hayward, and Young 2008). Situated under the broader umbrella of **critical criminology**, cultural criminology "views crime and the agencies and institutions of crime control as cultural products — as creative constructs" (Aspden and Hayward 2015: 237). It draws on a wide range of perspectives and ideas in an effort to understand and "confront systems of control and relations of power as they operate today" (Ferrell, Hayward, and Young 2008: 7). Along with mass media, museums are another powerful institution in society that produce and communicate cultural meanings.

A large body of research has recently emerged on what Welch (2015) calls penal history museums, defined more precisely by Piché and Walby (2016: 1) as "venues where representations of those in conflict with the law and those employed to uphold it inform public understandings of 'criminal justice.'" Brown (2009: 8) argues that prison museums, along with mass media, are an important domain of "penal spectatorship" that permit citizens to engage with punishment, but from a distance. She notes that "in contexts where individuals only know incarceration at a distance, the dynamics of penal participation are slippery and can quickly devolve into complex, voyeuristic frameworks which privilege various kinds of punitive, individualistic judgment" (Brown 2009: 5). While the criminalized endure the brutal realities of incarceration, everyday onlookers or "**penal spectators**" (Brown 2009: 1) take part in and judge such practices from a remote position. Brown (2009: 37–38) explains that **penal spectatorship** is a "distinctly dangerous way of seeing" but can be contested in ways that provoke deeper reflection about imprisonment and create empathy with prisoners. However, most research has found that prison museums emphasize sensational stories that depict prisoners as dangerous and violent people, expanding the social distance between penal spectators and prisoners and, in the process, building deeper support for needlessly punitive and expensive approaches to addressing socially unwanted acts (see Chen et al. 2016).

While research on prison museums is significant, police museums have received only a small amount of research attention despite existing across Canada and in nearly every country in the world. A number of scholars (e.g., Buffington 2012; Caimari 2012) demonstrate how police museums operating in Latin America legitimize and sensationalize police work. For example, Buffington (2012) discovered that three recently constructed police museums in Mexico are less concerned with providing an accurate history of local policing than with convincing the population that police have transformed into a legitimate and dependable public service. Similarly, McNair (2011) argues that two police museums in Los Angeles, California, disseminate a pro-police narrative of police work as heroic, rightful, and absolutely necessary. She notes how they attempt to erase and remake history by not mentioning prominent scandals and injustices, such as the infamous 1991 assault of Black taxi driver Rodney King by four white police officers (see also Nettelbeck and Foster 2013; Ferguson, Piché, and Walby 2017). The next sections examine how two police museums and a policing exhibit in Ontario construct a distorted reality of criminalized behaviour and, similar to mass media and prison tourism, perpetuate harmful stereotypes and expand the social distance between penal spectators (i.e., tourists) and criminalized individuals.

Representations of "Crime" in Police Museums and Exhibits

This chapter examines the "150 Years of Policing Memorabilia" exhibit at the Chimczuk Museum in Windsor, the Hamilton Police Service Museum in Ancaster, and the OPP Museum in Orillia. Four types of arrangements revealed how "crime" was represented: spatial (i.e., how the material space is organized), visual (i.e., what people see when they look around), narrative (i.e., the ideas conveyed through interactions with guides and text), and performative (i.e., the roles and functions of museum staff and volunteers, as well as how these were performed).

The three museums are a good sample of the different heritage institutions where policing is memorialized in Ontario. They are located in different cities, represent municipal and provincial police services, vary in size, and have different levels of funding and staff resources. The exhibit at the Chimczuk Museum described at the beginning of this chapter was a temporary collection of policing memorabilia. In contrast, the OPP Museum is a permanent police museum located in the publicly accessible front portion of the OPP

General Headquarters, an extremely large, military-style complex in Orillia. The museum employs two staff members and is part of a special communications bureau of the opp. It specializes in the history of policing in Ontario since 1791, with a specific focus on the development of the opp since 1909. The current exhibit is called "Behind the Badge: The Story of the Ontario Provincial Police." Upon arrival, visitors must check in at the security desk and they receive a gallery guide booklet to learn more about everything on display. Some of the topics discussed include the evolution of police uniforms, undercover and surveillance operations, seized material, women in policing, recruiting services, and forensic science. For younger audiences, there is a "Kidzone" at the back of the museum where children can dress up in police uniforms, play with puppets (e.g., police officer, firefighter, construction worker), and learn about topics such as how forensic investigations take place and when to call 9-1-1. The museum receives a wide range of visitors, including retired police officers, families, groups of children, tourists from out of town, and opp recruits, the latter of which are brought into the museum to learn a bit about opp history before they graduate.

In contrast to the opp Museum, the Hamilton Police Service Museum is located in a small historic building called Tisdale House in Ancaster, built circa 1825. A few dedicated volunteers with backgrounds in policing manage the site, which receives no funding from the police service outside of the police service paying the $2/year rent. The area around Tisdale House is picturesque and the Township Hall beside it is a popular location for weddings. The museum occasionally participates by bringing out a ball and chain that was once used to restrain Louis Riel and offering it to the bride or groom to take photos with (volunteer, personal communication, July 7, 2017). Inside Tisdale House, the museum operates in a small room on the north side of the building and includes a table of antique communications equipment, a display about the trial of Louis Riel, and another about the infamous "Torso Murder" trial of Evelyn Dick in Hamilton's "trial of the century" (Hamilton Police Service Museum 2017). The museum receives many families, schoolchildren, and other special groups, including boy scouts and cub scouts (volunteer, personal communication, July 7, 2017).

The amount and types of "crimes" represented in the museums corresponded with their size. In the smallest of these museums, the Hamilton Police Service Museum, only five criminalized acts are represented; at the "150 Years of Policing Memorabilia" exhibit, there are fourteen; and thirty-five at the opp Museum. Additionally, each museum's objectives inform how they emphasize criminalized acts: the two biggest museums devoted a large amount of exhibit space to "crime." This supports the common myth that police are "crime fighters" who are at war with certain members of the community (see Reiner 1985). Waddington (1998: 118) contends that this policing myth has numerous consequences, including legitimizing the use of force against an imaginary group of citizens who appear to "deserve it", and upholding the fictitious notion that the police have a significant impact on preventing criminalized acts. Trophies earned in this "fight" are prominently displayed at the OPP Museum in the form of objects and photographs of seized hauls of drugs, weapons, money, and animal pelts ("Behind the Badge: The Story of the Ontario Provincial Police" 2017). Linnemann (2017: 66) argues that police trophy shots help to perpetuate the myth that "police mark the boundaries between order and chaos." He also notes that "more subtly, police trophy shots remind state subjects of the legal brutality and thievery" (Linnemann 2017: 66) that is a part of police power.

Museum representations are also heavily skewed toward "crimes," with a visibly violent outcome. One prominent act represented at all three sites is murder. These depictions tend to arise from stories shared about notable past police investigations. They are often featured in main displays, while acts such as speeding, sex work, or drunk driving are mentioned in smaller areas. They also feature acts of killing that involve more than one individual, occurring between strangers, and using some form of weapon. For example, the OPP Museum shares a story about an incident in 1981 where two men killed a gas station employee in an apparent robbery and fled by vehicle. Early witnesses who saw the vehicle stated that a simple hit and run had occurred, which led to an underprepared police officer who pulled the vehicle over being shot and killed by the two men as well (gallery guide, "Behind the Badge: The Story of the Ontario Provincial Police" 2017). Both the OPP Museum and the "150 Years of Policing Memorabilia" exhibit also commonly represent theft. Played on repeat at the latter exhibit was a Crime Stoppers advertisement video from 1990 that re-enacted an armed robbery at a bank. The perpetrator and the getaway driver were arrested following anonymous tips to Crime Stoppers. At the end, a tipster is shown discreetly receiving his monetary reward and the words, "ONLY YOU CAN CRACK THE CRIME" flash across the screen (film, "150 Years of Policing Memorabilia" 2017). Other prominently featured acts in main displays include illicit gambling, treason, and bootlegging.

In the "Kidzone" at the OPP Museum, depictions of criminalized harms include a lottery ticket theft, a stolen vehicle, and an unlawful entry into a house

Image 10-1: "Kidzone" area at the opp Museum

(see Image 10-1). Children are invited to help find the individuals responsible for committing these harms. One story begins as follows: "In this crime scene, the green entrance door to a home has been pried open and damaged with a tool. Someone has broken into the house.… See if you can figure out how to use trace evidence to learn more about what happened." This process ends with children looking through a magnifying glass at a piece of fabric caught on the door and comparing it to various fabric samples, one of which was taken from the shirt of a person caught fleeing the scene. Once they identify a match, the activity is over and children can leave satisfied knowing that the "right" person has been caught. Yet they have not learned anything about the individual who committed the act or the wider social, cultural, and political processes in which criminalized harm is rooted.

Notably absent in the museums are critical stories about police wrongdoing (see McNair 2011). Police, especially those working today, are portrayed as "crime-fighters" and community protectors, not public servants who occasionally commit criminalized acts. A small display at the Chimczuk Museum mentions a scandal that hit the Windsor Police Service in the 1950s in which some members of the police service were complicit in illegal gambling and sex work. Few other details are provided outside of the fact that an OPP officer had to be brought in as police

> Notably absent in the museums are critical stories about police wrongdoing.

chief to straighten things out. Similarly, the opp Museum does not mention the 1995 Ipperwash Crisis, during which an opp officer shot and killed an unarmed Indigenous protestor (see Hedican 2008), resulting in an inquiry that led to changes in policing. The Ipperwash Inquiry (2007: 61, 77) concluded that "the opp's lack of communication in this operation was a serious failing," and "the opp, as an institution, also needs to be accountable and take some responsibility for the tragedy." In the museum, a staff member noted that the Ipperwash Crisis and the inquiry that ensued afterwards "doesn't really belong" and visitors who bring it up are connected "with the people whose job it is to have those conversations" (staff member, personal communication, July 13, 2015). The Hamilton Police Service Museum also excludes such depictions, including information on the landmark case *Hill v. Hamilton-Wentworth Police Services Board*, in which a legal principle was established that police are liable for conducting negligent investigations.

These examples are but one aspect of a broader category of "crime" that is missing in the museums, sometimes referred to as "crimes of the powerful" (see Bittle et al. 2018: 1). The museums downplay the harms committed by companies, corporations, and penal system agencies. The decision to not depict them, as if they simply do not happen or are not worth talking about, is a kind of "organized forgetting" (Giroux 2014: 1) that can be conceived of as a form of violence in itself, one that obscures state oppression and injustice (McNair 2011). It is also an example of a type of forgetting that Connerton (2008: 60) calls "repressive erasure," whereby states seek to eliminate traces of an event in an effort to remove it from people's memory. While sometimes applied forcefully, Connerton (2008: 60–61) notes that it can also "be encrypted covertly and without apparent violence" through cultural forms such as museums by discreetly editing out events that do not fit the master narrative. For the police, deliberate acts of forgetting are as important for maintaining the preferred institutional image as that which is celebrated and remembered. Through the interplay of forgetting and remembering, the museums perpetuate the same "mystification about the world" (Hulsman 1986: 70) as mass media and many mainstream criminologists. This helps to maintain the social distance of penal spectators, who receive a one-sided, sanitized version of police history congruent with the interests of those in power.

Representations of the Criminalized

Criminalized individuals are represented in the museums through a mixture of images, text, film, and tour guide narratives. They are labelled criminal, bad guy, crook, offender, thief, murderer, convict, inmate, and killer (see Coyle 2013). The criminalized individuals are represented in the display of empty handcuffs, leg shackles connected to thin air,

> This practice maintains the social distance of penal spectators, who step behind bars for a brief moment while remaining safely distanced from the harsh and inhumane realities of confinement.

and cell bars with vacant space behind them — but the people themselves are rarely seen. Visitors occasionally played the role of criminalized persons. The Hamilton Police Service Museum encourages children to dress up in costumes and have their picture taken standing behind a jail cell door (tour guide, personal communication, July 7, 2017). However, when confinement is reduced to a photograph, it trivializes rather than illuminates the experiences of prisoners. This practice maintains the social distance of penal spectators, who step behind bars for a brief moment while remaining safely distanced from the harsh and inhumane realities of confinement (see Wilson et al. 2017). In contrast to prison museums, police museums rarely feature mannequins of prisoners; instead, mannequins of police officers are prevalent (see Wilson et al. 2017). Police museums are a sanctuary for the police and shrine for fallen service members (see Buffington 2012), even though some visitors to the museums — including criminalized people, who are usually not wanted as visitors — subversively confront and challenge the displays.

Vicious and Threatening

Those who commit "crimes" are generally represented as vicious and threatening people. In many stories, they are stereotypical morally corrupt dangerous "others" who blend in with the community, only distinguishing themselves through acts of violence. Each of the three museums considered here featured in a main display at least one story about an infamous person who brutally killed people. The Chimczuk Museum featured a display dedicated to "Slasher" Ronald Sears, who terrorized the city in the 1940s (newspaper, "150 Years of Policing Memorabilia" 2017). Similarly, the Hamilton Police Service Museum remembers Evelyn Dick — or "The Notorious Mrs. Dick" as the poster board called her (see Image 10-2). According to the text, Evelyn was a "beautiful and proudly promiscuous lady" who was the focus of a high-profile trial when the dismembered corpse of her husband surfaced (wall text, Hamilton Police Service Museum 2017). She was acquitted but served time in prison after the body of her 2-year-old child was found encased in cement in her attic. A perpetrator walk image of her leaving the courthouse is displayed, along with

Image 10-2: Display about Evelyn Dick at the Hamilton Police Service Museum

photographs of her husband's bloody torso, her baby son's body in cement, and one of the possible sites of dismemberment. Her gun is also showcased, as is an Evelyn Dick T-shirt. A volunteer noted that this display is not shown to children and is a bit out of place. However, they were "more or less forced" to include it because of visitor demand — a sign of the challenges and potential benefits that well-known "stories of crime" can bring for museums (personal communication, July 7, 2017) (see Wilson et al. 2017).

Numerous stories shared at the opp Museum also present criminalized individuals as vicious and threatening people. For example, prominently displayed near the entrance is a story about a killing that occurred in 1944 dubbed the "Hot Stove Murder," where a woman was tortured on her kitchen stove (gallery guide, "Behind the Badge: The Story of the Ontario Provincial Police" 2017). She succumbed to burn injuries in the hospital, and three men were hanged for the act; a fourth served life in prison. Their mug shots are on display along with a wanted poster, a piece of the hangman's rope, and a gallows hood used during one of the executions. At the three museums, the emphasis placed on notorious people who

> At the three museums, the emphasis placed on notorious people who committed rare, shocking acts of violence strengthens the prevailing stereotype that all criminalized individuals are evil or dangerous figures who are "different" from so-called ordinary, law-abiding citizens.

committed rare, shocking acts of violence strengthens the prevailing stereotype that all criminalized individuals are evil or dangerous figures who are "different" from so-called ordinary, law-abiding citizens (see Wilson 2008). The message is that, once caught, severe punishment, not compassion or forgiveness, must follow.

Intelligent and Well-Organized

The second way criminalized people are represented is as intelligent and well-organized, adept at committing illicit behaviour and often working in pairs or teams to do so. For example, the OPP Museum features a display dedicated to police surveillance, where numerous depictions are shared of times when police used special investigative tactics to penetrate criminalized operations (gallery guide, "Behind the Badge: The Story of the Ontario Provincial Police" 2017). This is also a theme at the "150 Years of Policing Memorabilia" exhibit, which features a display about an underground casino operating in the 1930s known as the Michigan Club (display text, "150 Years of Policing Memorabilia" 2017). The casino was intricately hidden and designed with only one way in and out in order to avoid detection. However, the police eventually caught wind of it. A large amount of money and other casino-related objects (e.g., chips) were seized, and many people were arrested. Displayed in the exhibit was $600 worth of chips and a set of dice that had survived. These captured objects and similar but more deadly ones displayed at the OPP Museum are what Chen and colleagues (2016: 30) call "artefacts of danger and cunningness." They argue that such objects are prevalent in many penal history museums across Canada and serve to mark criminalized individuals with these attributes, legitimizing the need to monitor, apprehend, and imprison them.

Representations of Police Officers and Victims

Representations of people victimized by criminalized acts fall into two main categories. The first is police officers. The OPP Museum and the "150 Years of Policing Memorabilia" exhibit showcase displays dedicated to police officers killed on duty. These individuals are depicted as heroic and memorialized inside the museum for the sacrifice they made. The second category is vulnerable, innocent, and defenceless citizens. The text below expands on these two categories in greater depth and notes the similarity of these representations to those conveyed in mass media and other forms of popular culture.

Heroic and Sacrificial

Memorial displays honouring deceased police officers are common in police museums (Buffington 2012). The OPP Museum features several displays dedicated to remembering officers and members who lost their lives on duty — including police dogs. One display titled, "Cloud II — A Hero's Life" is about a German shepherd who was the first police dog killed in Ontario (gallery guide, "Behind the Badge: The Story of the Ontario Provincial Police" 2017). Cloud II was a well-known member of the OPP's canine team in the 1970s and assisted in "capturing 123 fugitives" during his time with the service. The gallery guide ("Behind the Badge: The Story of the Ontario Provincial Police" 2017) explains that, in 1974, he was elected into the Purina Animal Hall of Fame for helping to capture "three juvenile offenders" who were armed with a rifle and a knife. Less than a year later, a "suspected murderer who had escaped while awaiting trial" shot and killed the canine. An urn containing his remains is displayed in the museum, along with several pictures of the dog and his handler.

As mentioned in the introduction, the "150 Years of Policing Memorabilia" exhibit also memorializes deceased officers. Near the entrance is a display dedicated to the career of a police officer who worked during the early days of the force. In 1887, he undertook a "heroic Detroit River rescue" that earned him a bravery medal. Display text explains that he was "shot and left for dead" in 1905 and died a few years later of pneumonia, which was attributed to the old wound ("150 Years of Policing Memorabilia" 2017). Across the room is a larger display case dedicated to another police officer killed while on duty (see Image 10-3). Displayed inside are several photographs of the officer and his family, his badge, and newspapers with headlines such as "Farewell to a Hero" and "The Ultimate Sacrifice: 'Good Cop' Killed in Shootout with Teens" ("150 Years of Policing Memorabilia" 2017). Beside the display case is a framed photograph of the funeral service depicting hundreds of uniformed officers and other mourners in attendance. Below this, a chair is positioned with a plaque that, in bold lettering, reads "THIS SEAT IS TAKEN" in memory of the officer.

Representations of police officers killed on duty support the popular though misguided belief that the police profession consists of heroic "crime-fighting" individuals (see Reiner 1985). Rather than engaging with issues such as racial profiling, police brutality, or citizen killings, which "challenge dominant cultural images of crime and the police" (Hirschfield and Simon 2010: 156), the museums depict police as the epitome of honour and duty. The fact that

Display at the Chimczuk Museum dedicated to a police officer killed on duty

they were killed while on duty elevates their status, while those killed by state authorities are often ignored or considered to be "deserving" of death. As Brown (2009) and others (e.g., Chen et al. 2016) note, these depictions foster solidarity between citizens and penal system workers while expanding the social distance between citizens and the criminalized, the latter of which become stereotyped through these displays as ruthless persons determined to upset the status quo.

Innocent and Defenceless

Victimized individuals who are not police officers tend to be portrayed as innocent and defenceless citizens. At the Chimczuk Museum exhibit beside the "Slasher" display — where the victimized individuals were unsuspecting men — was the previously mentioned photograph on the wall titled "The Face of Compassion in the Depth of Tragedy" (wall text, "150 Years of Policing Memorabilia" 2017), which depicted a solemn-faced officer holding a victimized infant wrapped in a blanket. Similarly, a baby was one of those killed in the Evelyn Dick story told at the Hamilton Police Service Museum. At the opp Museum in the "Hot Stove Murder" display, the victim was a woman named Viola Jamieson who was attacked in her home (gallery guide, "Behind the Badge: The Story of the Ontario Provincial Police" 2017). In another area, a story is told about the time when a "convict evaded day parole from Kingston Penitentiary" and kidnapped a 16-year-old girl. The booklet ("Behind the Badge: The Story of the Ontario Provincial Police" 2017) explains that the "armed criminal" was eventually captured in a dramatic rescue and the girl freed.

The museum representations of victims uphold many of the same stereotypes that researchers have identified in mass media (see Hirschfield and Simon 2010; Greer 2007). Discussing media representations of victims, Christie (1986: 18) describes the "ideal victim" as "a person or a category of individual who — when hit by crime — most readily are given the complete and legitimate status of being a victim." He points out two common attributes: the victim is weak and vulnerable, and the victim is completely innocent and blameless for their fate. Christie (1986) explains that people who have these attributes are more readily given the legitimate victim status than others. Also relevant are factors such as class, race, age, and sexuality. The museums reinforce this pervasive stereotype and what Greer (2007: 22) calls a "hierarchy of victimization," which can be thought of as a triangle with ideal victims at the top and "non-deserving" victims at the bottom. Some of those in the latter group include sex workers and Indigenous people, both of whom experience a great deal of victimization, yet this is ignored in the museums (see, for example, Shannon et al. 2009; Boyce 2016).

Conclusion: The Fairy Tale of "Crime"

This chapter examined how criminalized acts are represented in two police museums and a temporary policing exhibit in Ontario. The museums emphasize relatively rare, visible acts of violence and ignore harms committed by powerful actors such as corporate entities and state authorities themselves, which might produce unwanted knowledge and critique of police practices. Criminalized individuals tend to be demonized and depicted as vicious, threatening, intelligent, and well-organized people. In contrast, police officers are portrayed as heroic and selfless "crime-fighting" figures, especially those who have been killed on duty. Victimized individuals are frequently police officers and everyday citizens who fit the ideal victim stereotype as innocent and defenceless actors. Despite their institutional differences, each museum brings a similar "story of crime" to life for visitors that strengthens common myths and stereotypes rather than challenging them. As sites of penal spectatorship, the museums encourage visitors to witness and take part in the work of the penal system from a distance, inviting them into an artificial world "where guilt is punished, innocence avenged and order restored"

> Despite their institutional differences, each museum brings a similar "story of crime" to life for visitors that strengthens common myths and stereotypes rather than challenging them.

(Linnemann 2015: 130). There is no desire to initiate reasoned debate about the limits of police authority and punishment, nor is there an attempt to educate visitors about what "crime" is or what it means to be criminalized. While more research is needed on visitor interpretation, the museums help to perpetuate and build pride in an ineffective, expensive, and unjust penal system (Brown 2009; Ferguson, Piché, and Walby 2015).

As storytelling sites, the museums construct meaning about criminalized harm in ways that resemble works of popular criminology, such as "true crime" literature, as well as fairy tales more generally. The latter is apparent when considering the presence of stereotypical representations and the emphasis each museum places on attracting children. A significant portion of the budget allocated by the Windsor Police Service for their 150th anniversary exhibit went to paying the Chimczuk Museum admission fees for hundreds of local school students (exhibit curator, personal communication, July 4, 2017). Likewise, the "Kidzone" is a popular area at the OPP Museum (exhibit curator, personal communication, July 13, 2015). A staff member noted that several students in the museum program at Georgian College who visited assumed one of the displays "would scar children ... or traumatize visitors," but the staff member remarked that this has not happened; in fact, "the kids find it fascinating" (personal communication, July 13, 2015). In Hamilton, a tour guide explained how the museum, though not an official part of the police service, is a "good recruiting tool for kids" (personal communication, July 7, 2017). Thus, police museums are designed not only to perpetuate myths and stereotypes, but to recruit young people into the policing profession and worldview, thereby maintaining a culture of policing, criminalization, and oppression. As mentioned, these are also sites in which new recruits are brought to learn about the history of the police. However, the omission of the Ipperwash Crisis is evidence that the purpose is not to provide future officers with a complete and accurate history of the organization. As one staff member noted, "it is really a kind of salesmanship and some PR ... to build pride in the organization they just joined" (personal communication, July 13, 2015). More broadly, police museums are a "kind of salesmanship" for the police institution and the status quo, which is aided by "stories of crime" communicated to visitors.

At the three museums, the stories resemble a fairy tale, with an emphasis on violent harms, innocent victims, evil villains, noble heroes, and usually a "happy" ending of imprisonment or death for those responsible. This narrative helps to reproduce myths, such as the myth that "crime" is primarily predatory "street crime" committed by dangerous people, the myth that penal system workers are the "thin line" between social order and social chaos, and the myth that police always "get their man" or woman. The commonalities between law and fairy tales have been noted before — as Roberts (2001: 15) explains, "the goals of the criminal justice system and of the fairy tale are quite in accordance: find the truth, convict the guilty, and acquit the innocent. The tales simply rely more on magic than due process to get the job done." Though they do not depict wicked witches or faraway kingdoms, the museums do have a magical quality to them, in the sense of making the cultural appear natural. In other words, the museums help to transform "crime" from something that is socially and culturally constructed by those with power into something with an existence that can be detected through police work and technologies (Christie 2004). This is accomplished through a combination of stereotypes, myths, erasure, built space, language, and selectively chosen non-fictional elements that fit tightly within a concealed master script that decides what belongs and what does not.

Along with expanding the social distance between penal spectators and those in conflict with the law, the museums present "crime" as something that must be addressed by police and other state institutions through the deprivation of liberty. Moreover, they divide complex human beings into wholly good or evil characters (heroes and villains, to borrow the words of the *Windsor Star* journalist), making retributive justice appear deserved and compassion the oddity (Roberts 2001). The museums also conceal the complex structural inequalities in society that lie beneath criminalized acts, instead emphasizing violent "street crimes" as serious threats facing society. It is not explained that these harms are small in comparison to issues such as poverty, state violence, corporate corruption, environmental degradation, discrimination, and so on — many of which are invisibly wrapped up within the stories shared or erased altogether. The museums draw attention away from more important social issues and hide certain realities of police work that visitors implicitly or explicitly sanction (see Ferguson, Piché, and Walby 2017).

The three museums examined in this chapter, similar to mass media and other forms of popular culture, construct meanings about criminalized harm through a profusion of signs, symbols, and objects that visitors interpret. Hall (1997a: 4) notes that things derive meaning through cultural practices, including when we "weave narratives, stories — and fantasies — around them." Whether gathering around the scene of a bank robbery or gazing at its photograph years later in a museum exhibit, these acts are constantly being interpreted and given meaning. The three museums weaved stories that resembled fairy tales, with each perpetuating harmful stereotypes and reinforcing punitive ways of thinking about criminalized harms rather than encouraging critical reflection about them and the work of the penal system more generally (see Brown 2009; Piché and Walby 2016; Roberts 2001).

Discussion Questions

1. How does critical criminology differ from **mainstream criminology**?
2. What is penal spectatorship? How do museums and other cultural practices contribute to promoting penal spectatorship and how can it be challenged?

Recommended Resources

Brown, Michelle. 2009. *The Culture of Punishment: Prison, Society, and Spectacle*. New York: New York University Press.
Buffington, Robert M. 2012. "Institutional Memories: The Curious Genesis of the Mexican Police Museum." *Radical History Review* 113.
Christie, Nils. 2004. *A Suitable Amount of Crime*. New York: Routledge.
Hulsman, Louk. 1986. "Critical Criminology and the Concept of Crime." *Contemporary Crises* 10.
Wilson, Jaqueline, Sarah Hodgkinson, Justin Piché, and Kevin Walby. 2017. *The Palgrave Handbook of Prison Tourism*. New York: Palgrave.

Glossary

critical criminology: a diverse theoretical field that challenges core assumptions of mainstream criminology and considers the major sources of "crime" to be inequalities in class, race/ethnicity, and gender and sexual relations. There are many versions of critical criminology (e.g., feminist, critical race, Marxist, cultural, postmodernist), but all endeavour to understand and explain social harms by situating them within structural and institutional contexts.

mainstream criminology: criminological theories based on state-defined conceptualizations of crime. This perspective focuses on violations of the law (usually theft, violence, and drug use), emphasizing questions of causation and privilege objectivity, and it tends to support criminal justice responses.

penal spectators: people who witness and take part in punishment (and its correlates of accusation, judgment, detention, and pain) from a distance. Penal spectators play an important, if unwitting, role in reproducing the ideologies and practices of the penal system.

penal spectatorship: the widespread and common practice of looking at the pain of others from a distance and, in the process, reproducing the ideologies and practices of the penal system. Penal spectatorship implies that people largely experience punishment through cultural practices (e.g., movies, television, museums), which are characterized by a problematic social distance from punishment that can deny meaningful reflection about it and diminish the capacity to develop empathy with prisoners.

Note

I am grateful to the editors for their encouraging remarks and useful suggestions. I also wish to thank Justin Piché and Kevin Walby for their helpful comments on earlier versions of the chapter.

References

Agnew, Robert. 2011. *Toward A Unified Criminology: Integrating Assumptions About Crime, People and Society.* New York: New York University Press.

Aspden, Kester, and Keith J. Hayward. 2015. "Narrative Criminology and Cultural Criminology." In Lois Presser and Sveinung Sandberg (eds.), *Narrative Criminology: Understanding Stories of Crime.* New York: New York University Press.

Bedford, Leslie. 2001. "Storytelling: The Real Work of Museums." *Curator: The Museum Journal* 44, 1.

Bittle, Steven, Laureen Snider, Steve Tombs, and Dave Whyte. 2018. "Revisiting Crimes of the Powerful: An Introduction." In Steven Bittle, Laureen Snider, Steve Tombs, and David Whyte (eds.), *Revisiting Crimes of the Powerful: Marxism, Crime, and Deviance.* London: Routledge.

Boyce, Jillian. 2016. *Victimization of Aboriginal People in Canada, 2014.* Ottawa: Statistics Canada.

Brown, Michelle. 2009. *The Culture of Punishment: Prison, Society, and Spectacle.* New York: New York University Press.

Buffington, Robert M. 2012. "Institutional Memories: The Curious Genesis of the Mexican Police Museum." *Radical History Review* 113.

Caimari, Lila. 2012. "Vestiges of a Hidden life: A Visit to the Buenos Aires Police Museum." *Radical History Review* 113.

Chen, Ashley, Sarah Fiander, Justin Piché, and Kevin Walby. 2016. "Captive and Captor Representations at Canadian Penal History Museums." *Qualitative Sociology Review* 12, 4.

Christie, Nils. 2004. *A Suitable Amount of Crime*. New York: Routledge.

____. 1986. "The Ideal Victim." In Ezza Fattah (ed.),

Colbran, Marianne. 2014. *Media Representations of Police and Crime: Shaping the Police Television Drama*. New York: Palgrave.

Connerton, Paul. 2008. "Seven Types of Forgetting." *Memory Studies* 1, 1.

Coyle, Michael J. 2013. *Talking Criminal Justice: Language and the Just Society*. New York: Routledge.

Crane, Susan. 1997. "Memory, Distortion, and History in the Museum." *History and Theory* 36, 4.

Ferguson, Matthew, Justin Piché, and Kevin Walby. 2017. "Representations of Detention and Other Pains of Law Enforcement in Police Museums in Ontario, Canada." *Policing and Society*, Advance Online Edition.

____. 2015. "Bridging of Fostering Social Distance? An Analysis of Penal Spectator Comments on Canadian Penal History Museums." *Crime, Media, Culture: An International Journal* 11, 3.

Ferrell, Jeff, Keith Hayward, and Jock Young. 2008. *Cultural Criminology: An Invitation*. London: Sage.

Giroux, Henry. 2014. *The Violence of Organized Forgetting: Thinking beyond America's Disimagination Machine*. San Francisco: City Lights Publishers.

Greer, Chris. 2007. "News Media, Victims and Crime." In Pamela Davies, Peter Francis, and Chris Greer (eds.), *Victims, Crime, and Society*. New York: Sage.

Hall, Stuart. 1997a. "Introduction." In Stuart Hall (ed.), *Representation: Cultural Representations and Signifying Practices*. London: Sage.

____. 1997b. "The Work of Representations." In Stuart Hall (ed.), *Representation: Cultural Representations and Signifying Practices*. London: Sage.

____. 1980. "Encoding/Decoding." In Stuart Hall, Dorothy Hobson, Andrew Lowe, and Paul Willis (eds.), *Culture, Media, Language*. London: Hutchinson.

Hayward, Keith. 2010. "Opening the Lens: Cultural Criminology and the Image." In Keith Hayward and Mike Presdee (eds.), *Framing Crime: Cultural Criminology and the Image*. New York: Routledge.

Hedican, Edward. 2008. "The Ipperwash Inquiry and the Tragic Death of Dudley George." *Canadian Journal of Native Studies* 28, 1.

Hirschfield, Paul J., and Daniella Simon. 2010. "Legitimating Police Violence." *Theoretical Criminology* 14, 2.

Howarth, Caroline. 2006. "A Social Representation Is Not a Quiet Thing: Exploring the Critical Potential of Social Representations Theory." *British Journal of Social Psychology* 45, 1.

Hulsman, Louk. 1986. "Critical Criminology and the Concept of Crime." *Contemporary Crises*, 10.

Ipperwash Inquiry. 2007. "Report of the Ipperwash Inquiry, The Honorable Sidney B. Linden, Commissioner." Toronto: Publications Ontario.

Lidchi, Henrietta. 1997. "The Poetics and Politics of Exhibiting Other Cultures." In Stuart Hall (ed.), *Representation: Cultural Representations and Signifying Practices*. London: Sage.

Linnemann, Travis. 2017. "Proof of Death: Police Power and the Visual Economies of Seizure, Accumulation and Trophy." *Theoretical Criminology* 21, 1.

___. 2015. "Capote's Ghosts: Violence, Media and the Spectre of Suspicion." *British Journal of Criminology* 55, 3.

McNair, Ayana. 2011. "The Captive Public: Media Representations of the Police and the (Il)legitimacy of Police Power." PhD diss., Department of Critical Studies, University of Southern California, Los Angeles.

Nettelbeck, Amanda, and Robert Foster. 2013. "On the Trail of the March West: The NWMP in Western Canadian Historical Memory." In Adele Perry, Esyllt W. Jones, and Leah Morton (eds.), *Place and Replace: Essays on Western Canada*. Winnipeg: University of Manitoba Press.

Piché, Justin, and Kevin Walby. 2016. "Dark Tourism, Penal Landscapes and Criminological Inquiry." In Michelle Brown (ed.), *Oxford Research Encyclopedia of Criminology and Criminal Justice*. Oxford: Oxford University Press.

Presdee, Mike. 2004. "The Story of Crime: Biography and the Excavation of Transgression." In Jeff Ferrell, Keith Hayward, Wayne Morrison, and Mike Presdee (eds.), *Cultural Criminology Unleashed*. London: Glass House Press.

Reiner, Robert. 2010. "Media Made Criminality: The Representation of Crime in the Mass Media." In Mike Maguire, Rod Morgan, and Robert Reiner (eds.), *The Oxford Handbook of Criminology*. Oxford: Oxford University Press.

___. 1985. *The Politics of the Police*. New York: St. Martins Press.

Roberts, Katherine J. 2001. "Once Upon the Bench: Rule Under the Fairy Tale." *Yale Journal of Law & the Humanities* 13, 2.

Shannon, Kate, Thomas Kerr, Steffanie A. Strathdee, Julio Montaner, and Mark Tyndall. 2009. "Prevalence and Structural Correlates of Gender Based Violence Among a Prospective Cohort of Female Sex Workers." *British Medical Journal* 339.

Shearing, Clifford. 1989. "Decriminalising Criminology." *Canadian Journal of Criminology* 31, 2.

Waddington, Peter. 1998. *Policing Citizens: Authority and Rights*, London: UCL Press.

Watney, Simon. 1989. *Policing Desire: Pornography, AIDS, and the Media*. Minneapolis: University of Minnesota Press.

Welch, Michael. 2015. *Escape to Prison: Penal Tourism and the Pull of Punishment*. Oakland: University of California Press.

Wilhelm, Trevor. 2017. "New Museum Exhibit Chronicles 150-Year History of Windsor Police Service." *Windsor Star*, May 4. <windsorstar.com/news/local-news/new-museum-exhibit-chronicles-150-year-history-of-windsor-police-service>.

Wilson, Jaqueline. 2008. *Cultural Memory and Dark Tourism*. New York: Peter Lang.

Wilson, Jaqueline, Sarah Hodgkinson, Justin Piché, and Kevin Walby. 2017. *The Palgrave Handbook of Prison Tourism*. New York: Palgrave.

Wired News. 2009. "Nils Christie: Empty the Prisons." September 21. <wired.com/2009/09/ff-smartlist-christie/>.

11

The Social Control of Sex Work

Carolyn Brooks and Karen Wood

After reading this chapter, you will be able to do the following:

1. Describe the current regulation of the sex trade in Canada and identify current challenges and debates.

2. Highlight the link between involvement in the sex trade and social conditions related to class, race, gender, and sexuality.

3. Discuss how Indigenous sex workers are racialized and silenced, and why this is best understood in the context of colonization.

4. Understand some of the current realities of the sex trade, including age of entry, social conditions leading to sex work, international dimensions, sexual exploitation of children and youth, and male involvement.

5. Discuss different theories about prostitution and how these contribute to the debate on regulation.

In Canada, the legalities of sex work are complex. Although providing and purchasing sexual services are legal, until recently it was illegal to recruit people into prostitution, to communicate in a public arena pertaining to or for the purposes of prostitution, and to use a certain place (**bawdy house**) for the purposes of prostitution activities (O'Doherty 2011a, 2011b; Perrin 2014; Landsberg et al. 2017). Any act involving the solicitation of sex with a person under the age of 18 is illegal under any terms (Perrin 2014).

Canadian law has recently undergone some major changes regarding sex work. Three women who had been sex workers brought sections 210, 212(1)(j), and 213(1)(c) of the Criminal Code to the Supreme Court of Canada, claiming these prostitution laws violated section 7 of the *Canadian Charter of*

Rights and Freedoms (Perrin 2014). In December 2013, the Supreme Court of Canada ruled that these laws were unconstitutional and in violation of the rights of sex workers to protect themselves. As noted, "the three laws struck down included prohibitions on communicating in public for the purpose of prostitution (sex workers or clients) [section 213(1)(c)], operating a bawdy house [section 210] and living off the avails of prostitution [section 212(1) (j)]" (Krusi et al. 2014: 2). These reforms are based on the idea that the criminalization of sex work is not a human rights-based response.

In a unanimous decision (*Canada v. Bedford* 2013), the Supreme Court of Canada struck down the laws and moved toward what is referred to as the "end demand," "Nordic model," or "third-way" approach, focusing on criminalizing clients and third-party managers. Justice Minister Peter McKay brought forward **Bill C-36**, the *Protection of Communities and Exploited Persons Act*, which decriminalized the sex trade and criminalized **johns** and pimps or anyone exploiting sex workers. The intention behind the legislation is to work towards an end to prostitution.

This chapter introduces: (1) the social control and regulation of the sex trade; (2) the pathways and commonalities among sex trade workers; (3) sex work and colonization; (4) sociological and feminist perspectives that attempt to understand sex trade involvement.

Criminalization of the Sex Trade

At different historical times and places throughout the world, sex work has been, and continues to be, identified as both deviant and normal, morally acceptable/good and morally unacceptable/evil, and healthy and risky. In turn, sex workers have been recognized as celebrated professionals and/or shunned and penalized with imprisonment, public punishments, stoning, and even death. Philosophical and theoretical literature attempts to understand the existence and regulation of sex work as well as the contempt, fear, stereotypes, and ongoing moralizing of sex.

Criminalization continues to be the prominent sex work policy around the world (Armstrong 2016; Vanwesenbeeck 2017), meaning that any aspect of sex work — whether selling sex, buying sex, or organizing sex for pay — might result in punitive measures. These practices vary in enforcement but sex work is actively prosecuted and policed in many countries.

Countries that criminalize prostitution include Afghanistan, Barbados, Bahamas, Egypt, Dominica, Jamaica, Haiti, China, and the Philippines. For a more thorough list, see ProCon.org (2018) or Barnett and Casavant

(2014). An example of the interplay of culture within criminalization policies can be seen through a discussion about prostitution in the Philippines and China. In China, Xiaobing Li and Qiang Fang (2013) state that, "officially, prostitution is illegal in China. Prostitution is banned because — in official language — it 'seriously corrupts people's minds, poisons the social atmosphere, and endangers social stability'" (cited in ProCon.org 2018: 1). In the Philippines, the revised penal code of 2012 provides an example of the definition of prostitution and its punishment. Article 202 reads as follows: "Prostitutes ... women who, for money or profit, habitually indulge in sexual intercourse or lascivious conduct, are deemed to be prostitutes." The punishment put forward is that prostitutes "shall be punished by *arresto menor* or a fine not exceeding 200 pesos, and in case of recidivism, by *arresto mayor* in its medium period to prison correctional, in its minimum period or a fine ranging from 200 to 2,000 pesos or both, in the discretion of the court" (Lawphil Project 2012). In other regions, the sex trade is seen as limitedly legal and limitedly criminalized. In Scotland, England, and Wales, for example, selling and purchasing sexual services for money is legal but other activities — such as brothel keeping, kerb-crawling, and soliciting — are criminalized. Other examples of countries with limited criminalization include the United States, Iceland, Ireland, and Japan.

Criminalization has been criticized for human rights and public health concerns, including increasing stigma, violence, unsafe sex practices, social exclusion, and discrimination (Vanwesenbeeck 2017). Studies point to the connections between the violence against women who engage in sex work and the stipulations, laws, police interactions, and policing strategies they face (Krusi et al. 2012; Vanwesenbeeck 2017). When sex work is criminalized, the women engaging in these activities are displaced from urban areas to more industrialized areas, where they are less likely to have access to protections like policing and community services. Not only does this contribute to building barriers and ideologies around their value as human beings (Shannon and Csete 2010; Krusi et al. 2012), but this displacement also reduces the likelihood of being able to interact safely and successfully negotiate safe sex with a client (i.e., with the use of a condom) (Shannon and Csete 2010; Krusi et al. 2012). The inability to negotiate safe sex puts sex workers at higher risk for interpersonal violence and STDs, including HIV/AIDS (Shannon and Csete 2010; Krusi et al. 2014).

The **decriminalization** and **legalization** of sex work are legal and cultural processes that are distinct from criminalization. In a legalized system, some

---

Box 11-1: Key Legislation on Nevada's Legalized Prostitution

by Kayla Arisman

At the federal level in the United States, prostitution remains criminalized. However, because individual states have control over their own state criminal codes, Nevada created the only system of legalized prostitution in the country. Nevada's Revised State Statute Title 15-subsection 201.380 (NRS) includes an awkward combination of old, new, official, and unofficial local legislation that sets the standards for the state-wide brothel industry (Brents and Hausbeck 2001).

The NRS allows for brothels to be zoned and owned. Brothels must be in a city/county with a population under 400,000 and no brothel may be "situated within 400 yards of any schoolhouse or schoolroom used by any public or common school in the State of Nevada" (State of Nevada 1995a&b). The NRS also mandates that a brothel may not come "within 400 yards of any church, edifice, building or structure erected for and used for devotional services or religious worship in this state" (State of Nevada 1995a&b). The statute makes clear that the only legal form of soliciting a prostitute is within "a licensed house of prostitution." Failure to comply with this law could result in a misdemeanor offence or, in the case of soliciting individuals under the age of 18, in a felony charge and imprisonment of one to four years — including a maximum fine of $5,000 for a first offence (NRS 201.354).

While prostitution is legal at the state level, local county governments have the power to outlaw these acts — even within a county of under 400,000 people, prostitution still may not be legal (Brents and Hausbeck 2005).

---

types of sex work are legally permitted. For example, in the US state of Nevada, sex work in sanctioned brothels is legal, but other forms are illegal (see Box 11-1). Lutnick and Cohan (2009: 38–39) note that sex workers must register with police departments as brothel workers: "Under a legalized framework those businesses and individuals in sex work face regulations and licensing procedures that other business do not." This includes regular testing for STDs as well as stipulated location and working conditions. Decriminalization, on the other hand, means that regulatory practices, including occupational health and safety standards that define other business codes, also regulate sex work (Lutnick and Cohan 2009).

In other words, the focus is not on sex trade activities being legal or illegal; rather, regulations apply just as for any other workplace activity, thereby implicitly condoning the activities as acceptable practices. Decriminalization is found in the Netherlands, New Zealand, and parts of the United States and Australia (Lutnick and Cohan 2009). In the New Zealand Prostitution and Reform Act of 2003, the sex industry was decriminalized; purchasing sex, pimping, and brothels were made legal (Raymond 2018). The framework of the act instilled health, employment, and safety regulations that are strictly enforced within licensed brothels. The act designated employment guidelines such that the rights of those in sex work were safeguarded, public health was protected, and individuals under 18 years of age were prohibited from working (Ministry of Justice 2003).

International comparative research has considered historical examples to determine what decriminalization, legalization, and regulation or strict criminal sanctions might look like. Decriminalization and legalization have been introduced in other countries and often involve conditions that regulate the sex work industry in terms of "age and immigrant status, recruitment strategies, mandatory registration, health checks, geographical locations, building regulations, etc." (Vanwesenbeeck 2017: 1631). In Germany, where clients can window-shop for sex, more than 400,000 women work in brothels. In some places, such as the spa town of Aachen, men can have unlimited sex with many women for only €99 (or approximately C$150) in a brothel that boasts a flat rate: "There are dozens of women in the corridors, sitting on stools where men can walk around checking the women out … there are floors and floors of women; some wear nothing, others very little" (New York Post 2014). Germany's sex work-related legislation has been subject to criticism from reports on the sex trade funded by internal government organizations that the majority of these women were forced into prostitution or were trafficked (New York Post 2014).

In the Netherlands, the sex trade was legalized in 2000, brothels became regulated and taxed with regular inspection, and sex trade workers were unionized. Initial reports on the effectiveness of this system were optimistic yet cautious. For example, Vanwesenbeeck (2017) reports considerable autonomy among sex workers but also considerable control through stigma from brothel owners and managers. Managers continue to control workers' dress and hours of work, and they gain a substantial percentage of the workers' income. This indicates an employee/employer relationship, which undermines the independence of the women.

Researchers have recently questioned and reconsidered legalization, red-light districts, and progressive permissive liberality (see, for example, Vanwesenbeeck 2017; Deinema and Aalbers 2015). Part of this critique is related to the recognition of the global connection between sexual slavery and **human trafficking** with the legalized sex trade, meaning that the individuals

This position is marketed as the "third way," "end demand," and/or the "Nordic model" and involves modifying laws so that johns cannot freely purchase sex while those in the sex trade are not criminalized.

involved are increasingly vulnerable to exploitation and are often forced to participate. This critique is related to the global economy and political discourse on regulating harm. For example, Wonders and Michalowski (2001: 545) found "patterns of sex tourism in [Havana and Amsterdam] are increasingly over-determined by global economic forces, connecting the practice of sex work in both cities with the broader phenomenon of globalized sex tourism." Deinema and Aalbers (2015: 273) assert that problems of trafficking of humans as well as related forms of crime and violence call for the regulation of the sex trade and

> fuel calls for the drastic curtailment of window prostitution in the district, despite the fact that formal legalization was designed to combat such excesses and that window prostitution can be more successfully regulated than alternative, less visible forms of sex work.

Some countries are also criminalizing the purchasing of sex (Vanwesenbeeck 2017). Countries such as Sweden, Norway, Iceland, and, recently, Canada are focusing on ending the demand for sex work. This position is marketed as the "third way," "end demand," and/or the "Nordic model" and involves modifying laws so that johns cannot freely purchase sex while those in the sex trade are not criminalized. In Sweden, for example, individuals who purchase sex can be sentenced to up to one year of imprisonment or be fined, and those who exploit an individual in sex work can be sentenced to up to four years in prison.

This brings us back to our original emphasis on Canada where the landmark case (*Canada v. Bedford* 2013) decriminalized sex work and moved toward this "third way" approach. In response, the federal government of Canada proposed Bill C-36, the *Protection of Communities and Exploited Persons Act*, which names johns and pimps as the exploiters and criminalizes the purchase of sex while decriminalizing sex work. This bill passed the House of Commons on October 6, 2014 by a vote of 156–124 and received Royal Assent on November 6, 2014, coming into effect in December of 2014. The introduction of Bill C-36 in Canada means that sex workers may continue to work in the sex trade but criminalizes those who purchase their services as well as other third parties involved, such as managers (Landsberg et al. 2017).

The Nordic model has garnered mixed responses. While some see it as a well-intentioned form of protection for sex trade workers, others criticize it for treating all clients as perpetrators and all sex workers as victims, thus taking away their livelihood (Landsberg et al. 2017; Scott 2018) and possibly creating a more dangerous environment. The same critics argue that it neglects the diversity within the industry, which includes street-based workers as well as independent, home-based services and escorts across the gender spectrum. In addition, this position neglects to account for the diversity in clientele and the movements to destigmatize johns and advocate for their decriminalization (Murphy 2014). Advocates argue that the "bad" johns do not represent the majority (Murphy 2014) and that the criminalization of johns might mean street-based workers resort to more isolated transactions that are less safe (Kelly and Pacey 2011).

Pathways and Commonalities among Sex Trade Workers

Much of the public debate surrounding prostitution focuses on whether individuals choose to enter the sex trade as well as the resultant social issues. This includes research on the statistics and characteristics of those involved, victimization, homicide, the engagement of men and LGBTQ+ persons in the sex trade, the industry's relationship to transphobia and homophobia, the overrepresentation of Indigenous Peoples and relationships to colonization, and theories that attempt to explain involvement in the sex trade and its regulation.

Statistics about the number and characteristics of people involved in the sex trade are highly debated, especially considering the diversity of those involved and the bias that sometimes exists in analyzing this particular trade (Weitzer 2005a, 2005b). Perrin (2014) suggests that street-level prostitution involves anywhere from 5 to 20 percent of sex workers in Canada. Other researchers agree, noting that street sex work is the most visible form of sex work but the smallest sector (Strega et al. 2014). The age of entry has been debated, but common arguments suggest the majority of people who engage in the sex trade enter between ages fourteen and twenty (Perrin 2014). The overrepresentation of Indigenous women in street sex work is also well documented; Indigenous girls and women likewise enter sex work or become sexually abused by perpetrators and pimps at a younger age (Strega et al. 2014).

Violence experienced by girls and women in the sex trade has been quite thoughtfully documented and is painfully prevalent throughout the industry, with an extremely high rate of sex workers being victims of homicide (Cool 2004; Matthews 2014). Street-based sex workers

> Krusi et al. estimate that between 40 and 70 percent of Canadian sex workers have experienced physical and sexual violence.

Farley, Lynne, and Cotton argue that prostitution is lethal, citing the Special Committee on Pornography and Prostitution's claim that the death rate of women in the sex trade is more than forty times higher than those not in the sex trade.

are disproportionately the victims of violence and rape, more than any other group of women Krusi et al. (2012) estimate that between 40 and 70 percent of Canadian sex workers have experienced physical and sexual violence. A study conducted in Victoria, British Columbia, found that 67 percent of a sample of 200 sex workers had been treated for injuries obtained during work, and 37 percent had been hospitalized due to the abuses they endured within the sex trade (Cool 2004). Cool (2004) adds that both rape and prostitution frequently involve brutality and occur in an atmosphere of humiliation. Farley, Lynne, and Cotton (2005) argue that prostitution is lethal, citing the Special Committee on Pornography and Prostitution's claim that the death rate of women in the sex trade is more than forty times higher than those not in the sex trade. Matthews (2014: 86) estimates that "those involved in prostitution are 15 to 20 times more likely to be killed than other women in the same age group."

Some of the most common reasons cited for entry into the sex trade also involve violence and/or previous abuse, as well as financial need, homelessness, addictions, anti-social personality disorders, and recruitment (Cobbina and Oselin 2011; Farley, Lynne, and Cotton 2005). Marginalized individuals, especially Indigenous persons, are also notably overrepresented among those engaged in street-based sex work (Bittle 2002; Strega et al. 2014).

A Vancouver study of one hundred women working in the sex trade found that 52 percent (a significant overrepresentation) were First Nations, 82 percent reported childhood sexual abuse, and 72 percent reported childhood physical abuse (Farley, Lynne, and Cotton 2005). Moreover, 90 percent reported physical abuse and 78 percent sexual abuse (specifically rape) while in the sex trade. They also found that 95 percent of participants wanted to exit the sex trade and that over 80 percent were experiencing addictions and/or issues related to homelessness.

Cobbina and Oselin's (2011) study found that women have different motivations for entering into street-level sex work depending on their age. Although age groups overlapped, those under nineteen were more likely to engage in sex work to "reclaim control of [their] sexuality" (Cobbina and Oselin 2011: 316) after suffering abuse and to continue sexual experiences that to them were normal or familiar. The older group — those over age nineteen — was more likely to enter the sex trade to "sustain drug addiction[s]" (Cobbina and Oselin 2011: 316) and to earn money to pay for necessities (prostitution as survival). Cobbina and Oselin (2011) also found that members of the younger group had, on average, been involved with sex work for a longer period of time than those in the older group.

In a discussion of repeated violence in the lives of young woman who end up in the sex trade (i.e., before they entered the sex trade), Tutty and Nixon (2003: 71) share the words of a young woman who had been raped prior to her involvement in sexual exploitation through prostitution:

> I got raped when I was about eleven by one of my really good guy friends and after that, I felt like crap about myself. It just went down-hill from there. I made choices based on how I was feeling.

Tutty and Nixon (2003) document that some young women overcome feelings of powerlessness from childhood abuse through sex trade involvement. They share a story of a woman who was abused repeatedly by an uncle who asked her to perform sexual acts. As this young woman explained, "no customer after that really seemed to matter. It never really made a difference. I just made sure I got paid" (70). The link between childhood sexual abuse and later involvement in the sex trade and being sexually exploited by perpetrators and pimps becomes very clear in stories such as these, of which there are far too many.

Victimization of individuals in the sex trade raises issues related to consent and coercion — and, therefore, power and social control (Matthews 2014). Literature citing the words of those working in the sex trade as children shows that those working in the sex trade are often coerced by partners, pimps, parents, and others to reluctantly "consent." Many young women have spoken about different forms of coercion. For example, 18-year-old Jenny talked about tactics of coercion by pimps:

> He introduced himself and he was real cool, or he thought he was. He gave me, "are you live shit?" ... Man, he could read me like a book. He knew I was desperate. (Cited in Hodgson 1997: 45)

Tutty and Nixon (2003: 70) share the words of a young woman who were coerced into the sex trade:

> I was thirteen. I had a gun held to my head. I wasn't sure if it was loaded or not, but at the time I was pretty scared. And they told me that if I went to cops or told my group home staff that they, when

Many transgender sex workers who enjoy the sex trade industry aim to challenge the ideology that sex work is survival.

they got out, or they'll get someone to kill me. So I was pretty scared.... I fell into his game and he addicted me to crack cocaine and put me out on the street to pay for my habit later on.

Men and boys are often omitted from discussions of pathways into the sex trade or are assumed to share experiences and characteristics similar to those of women (Dennis 2008); indeed, much of the literature compares the characteristics and backgrounds of men involved in the sex trade to those of women. Similar to women involved in the sex trade, men are said to enter the sex trade at a young age, having come from difficult home lives that lead them to street involvement, homelessness, and sexual exploitation (Allman and Myers 1998; Ellison and Weitzer 2016). Commonly, young men working in the sex trade have run away from physically and sexually abusive homes (Ellison and Weitzer 2016). Bittle (2002: 3) attests that "male prostitutes had experienced more physical and sexual abuse while growing up, and had witnessed more violence between parents, more drug and alcohol use among family members, and were more likely to identify male partners as their first sexual experience."

LGBTQ+ individuals in the sex trade are also under-researched (Logie et al. 2012). Existing studies about transgender people's backgrounds suggest that their experiences related to trauma and childhood victimization are similar to those of female and male sex workers (Baumann et al. 2018). Many individuals enter prostitution when their choices are limited and/or when they are coerced (Shdaimah and Wiechelt 2012), and those same individuals in the sex trade are highly victimized (Matthews 2014). Other research identifies how transphobia and homophobia shape the lives of transgender sex workers (Fletcher 2013).

Much of this work has the goal of putting forward the voice of transgender sex workers, especially their efforts to challenge assumptions about gender, sexual orientation, and sex work as always being oppressive. Many transgender sex workers who enjoy the sex trade industry aim to challenge the ideology that sex work is survival. Fletcher (2013: 72) believes

we are witnessing a sea of change in Canada; trans people are standing up and fighting back, and queer communities are reexamining their own assumptions about sexual orientation and gender ... people are suffering because of archaic and repressive government policies, not because there is anything inherently unhealthy about being trans or doing sex work.

Discussions of men and LGBTQ+ people in the sex trade might serve to disrupt the potentially destructive moral framing of their engagement in the industry and to expand definitions of gender and sexuality as more fluid. As Fletcher (2013: 72) notes,

> the existence of transgender and transsexual individuals, whose sex, gender, and sexuality exist on a continuum, and who are being forced to address the historical erasure of their embodied experiences as legitimate, presents society with opportunities to expand its understanding of the complexities of sex and gender.

Not all young people who become sexually exploited by perpetrators and pimps and enter the sex trade have experienced sexual and physical abuse, and not every young person who is abused finds themselves in the sex trade, but research has consistently found strong evidence of running away, poverty, abuse, and subsequent sex trade involvement (Bittle 2002). Many youths in these situations are said to have been "thrown away" — they have experienced neglect and all forms of abuse, discrimination, intra-familial violence, and then situational street-involved poverty. Any discussion of youth and subsequent adult involvement in the sex trade must then be understood within broader structural factors, including oppression of youth more widely, unemployment rates, gendered sexual socialization, and violence, as well as poverty and class issues. This ultimately means that the social conditions that make the sex trade a viable option for youth and adults also need to be addressed. This includes the importance of gender, sexual identity, race, and the continued marginalization of Indigenous people.

Sex Work and Colonization

The overrepresentation of Indigenous youth and adults involved in the sex trade (Farley, Lynne, and Cotton 2005; Strega et al. 2014) is linked to violence, ongoing cultural alienation, and the devastating impacts of colonization (Farley, Lynne, and Cotton 2005) that created economic, social, and political barriers. Overrepresentation of both African-American women (Valandra 2007) and Indigenous women in the sex trade is linked to the history of colonialism and vulnerability of racialized women: "The intersection of race, class and gender

> "The intersection of race, class and gender combine to heighten the vulnerability of women of color, particularly poor, urban women of color, to substance use (and HIV/AIDS) and subsequently increase their probability of entry into sex work."

combine to heighten the vulnerability of women of color, particularly poor, urban women of color, to substance use (and HIV/AIDS) and subsequently increase their probability of entry into sex work" (Golder and Logan 2007: 629).

Indigenous youth often find themselves street involved and in the sex trade after they leave troubled family and/or community situations (Bittle 2002). This ill-fated scenario is deeply embedded in colonial legacies. Save the Children Canada (2000: 13) notes that all of the Indigenous youth who participated in a national consultation process "spoke of the physical, sexual and/or emotional abuse they experienced in their home lives, as parents, relatives, care givers, and neighbours continued to suffer from the legacy of cultural fragmentation." The Save the Children Canada report also outlines how prostitution became a choice for many Aboriginal youth who had left troubled home and community situations and ended up on the streets with few educational and job skills/opportunities.

Indigenous individuals' involvement in the sex trade in Canada often reproduces more violence toward those with histories already marked by racial, economic, and sexual victimization (Farley, Lynne, and Cotton 2005; Strega et al. 2014), and their victimization in the sex trade must be understood in the context of colonialism. In Canada, Indigenous women and girls are at high risk for being "trafficked" for **sexual exploitation**, although this is not often viewed as such. Indigenous women and girls have been subject to exploitation and recruitment into the sex trade under very exploitative circumstances and in ways that match the Canadian Criminal Code definitions of trafficking in persons (Sikka 2009). In fact, many authors argue that the continued displacement of poor, rural, and Indigenous women should be viewed as trafficking, where women are moved from the reserve to the city for the purpose of prostitution (Farley, Lynne, and Cotton 2005).

Canada amended its criminal code in 2005 to include trafficking in persons; the definition includes the recruitment, transportation, and harbouring of a person to control them for purpose of exploitation and threatening them if they fail to provide the service — which describes the coercion experienced by the majority of Indigenous youth. Sikka (2009) argues that many Indigenous youth are recruited by people who prey on their vulnerabilities and provides an example of trafficking in prairie cities:

Two youths who were living in a care facility were invited to attend a party in another city with two young male adults. During the trip the men changed license plates on the vehicle and began restricting the girls' phone usage. They picked up another man, who stopped and purchased a large quantity of lingerie, and the girls were subsequently taken to a hotel room in a third city. The care facility was able to reach police in that city in time to prevent any sexual acts from occurring, but it was clear that the intention of the trip was for the purpose of sexually exploiting the girls. (Sikka 2009: 16)

A number of authors draw attention to the problem of race and racism in any discussion of the sex trade. Sherene Razack, for example, examines how racialized bodies and racialized spaces are both marked for prostitution: "this specialized view of justice helps us to see how race shapes the law by informing notions of what is just and who is entitled to justice" (Razack 2002: 155). Similar to Razack, other authors argue that whiteness is protected and reproduced through the negligible judicial response to and media portrayals of racialized individuals (Hugill 2010; Strega et al. 2014). What this means, for example, is that Indigenous sex workers portrayed in the media are often racialized and silenced through a portrayal that they are somehow different and removed from the "respectable" rest (Hugill 2010). This framing of Indigenous sex workers implies they are marked and even deserving of their misfortune and experiences of violence:

These strategic silences contribute to representations of Aboriginal women who are sex workers as deserving of violence … representations of Aboriginal women in Vancouver's Downtown Eastside oscillate between invisibility and hypervisibility: invisible as victims of violence and hypervisible as deviant bodies. (Jiwani and Young 2006: 3)

This is part of the problem leading to the over-policing of Indigenous women's "deviance" and the lack of judicial attention to their victimization.

The media discourse around Robert Pickton and his victims is an example of a negative portrayal of the sex work industry, with an emphasis on Indigenous women. In 2006, Robert Pickton, a multi-millionaire pig farmer and resident of Port Coquitlam, British Columbia, was found guilty of the murder of six sex workers and accused of murdering dozens more. Pickton allegedly picked up his victims in the downtown area of Vancouver between

Box 11-2: Halfbreed

Maria Campbell, a Métis author and playwright, wrote a groundbreaking autobiography in 1973 titled *Halfbreed*. The book powerfully describes the impact of colonization and marginalization on the life of a disenfranchised young woman and how this pushed her and other marginalized Indigenous women into the sex trade (Ferris 2008). Specifically, her work demonstrates how social exclusion, poverty, and isolation from her culture led her into survival sex work that was a symptom of colonization and systemic racism. Ferris (2008: 128–29) suggests that "Campbell's narrative calls for the end not of prostitution itself, but of the state-sponsored and culturally endorsed racial/sexual violence that populates the survival sex industry with Aboriginal women." Maria Campbell creates an intimacy for her readers, leading to a depth of understanding of the culture at that period of time. What her readers did not know was that a section of the original text had been removed by the publisher.

In the spring of 2018, four decades after *Halfbreed* was published, Simon Fraser University's Deanna Reder and Alix Shield discovered the word passage that had been removed; it describes a sexual assault on Maria, who was 14 years old at the time, by RCMP police officers in her own home. The passage contained statements by Campbell describing this incident:

> (Suddenly he [the RCMP officer] put his arm around me and said that I was too pretty to go to jail. When I tried to get away, he grabbed my hair and pulled me to him … all I can recall is being dragged to Grannies bed where the man tore my shirt and jeans. When I came to, Granny was crying and washing me off.

Campbell would like to see this passage put back into the book but would not change anything else in the book, suggesting that her writing spoke to where she was at during that period of time (Deibert 2018).

1978 and 2001, took them to his farm, and killed them. Their remains were found throughout the pig farm (*National Post* 2010).

The high-profile media portrayal of the Pickton case, and the subsequent portrayal of the female victims involved, did little to acknowledge the value of their lives as human beings. The prominence of this case served to magnify the negative framing of sex workers (hyper-visible as deviant bodies) rather than mourning them as murdered women, and reinforcing the stereotype of Indigenous women involved in the sex trade as "a drugged, dazed, deviant, dissolute, and corrupted 'other' whose affiliation with a notorious underworld places [them] in a constant threat of danger and predation" (Hugill 2010: 55). Undermining the value of their lives also undermines the perceived severity of the acts done against them (see Box 11-2).

Sociological and Feminist Perspectives that Attempt to Understand Sex Trade Involvement

How do social theorists make sense of all of the information related to the sex trade? Depending on one's theoretical perspective, the debate and information can be viewed quite differently. With an eye to better understanding the litera-ture on the social deviance and regulation of sex trade, we turn now to theories and research that aim to understand and explain sex trade involvement.

We begin with a few theories that have been deemed "contaminated knowledges" based on historically specific and "ideological blinders," as well as authors who adopt quite extreme versions and arguments about the sex trade (Weitzer 2005a: 974). First, we look at a few extreme examples of pathological theorizing, radical feminist, and pro-sex feminist thought. Although deemed extreme, we acknowledge they have put forward at least a part of the picture toward understanding sex trade involvement and, in the case of radical versus pro-sex arguments, sometimes quite opposite explanations.

Pathological Theorizing: Biological and Psychological Factors

Despite efforts by some scholars in the sociology of deviance to remove moral judgment from enquiry, theory has continued to pathologize over time. Authors such as Lombroso and Ferraro (1895) and Shutt et al. (2011) ques-tion the extent to which people who engage in the sex trade are predestined to be participants through some type of biological or organic constitution. The pathological model attributes the cause of prostitution to individual afflic-tion or abnormalities. Lombroso and Ferraro defined what they deemed to be organic and hereditary features of the prostitute, such as idleness, misery, and alcoholism. Within this paradigm, other characteristics were similarly attributed to women, such as feeblemindedness, having parents with low mentality or unintelligent disciplinary practices, coming from a broken home (Glueck and Glueck 1934), and having compulsive and deep psychoneurotic needs (Benjamin and Masters 1964). The immediate criticism of this paradigm is the focus on women's identity as "prostitutes," which is still quite common both in casual language and in academic literature. To define someone as a prostitute (let alone feebleminded or idle) defines a "type" of "deviant" person.

Although this model is mostly no longer in academic favour (Reeve 2013), a number of authors have continued to understand the sex trade from this pathological perspective. Benjamin and Masters (1964) talk about women in the sex trade as being of two types: compulsive prostitutes who possess

> Early positivist criminologists argued for regulation and discipline but in the form of police lists and not imprisonment, especially because prostitution was necessary to "make sexual intercourse accessible to all dissolute-minded young men" and was therefore a "sexual safety valve."

a psychological abnormality and predisposition towards prostitution, and voluntary prostitutes who engage as a result of poverty and other social or environmental conditions. Other authors have linked post-traumatic stress disorder to women in the sex trade. Shutt et al. (2011), for example, developed a biosocial explanation for the behaviour of johns. Using self-reports of the purchasing of sex, drawing from survey data (N = 14,544), they argue their findings are

> consistent with a growing body of empirical research suggesting that biosocial factors are part of a complete explanation of human and criminal behaviors ... moreover, the existence of such a sexual-resource instinct is consistent with a large and growing body of sex-based disparities in human and non-human sex-partner preferences. (Shutt et al. 2011: 167)

However, these authors also note they do not intend to support a pathological model for prostitution itself but aim to show that males in comparison to females have an instinctive value and that biology and instinct might underlie demand. Other theories, such as functionalism, argue that prostitutes are deviant and mentally unstable but that sex work is universal and provides a safety function for society by protecting the family and providing an outlet for men's sexual needs:

> Enabling a small number of women to take care of the needs of a large number of men, [prostitution] is the most convenient sexual outlet for an army, and for the legions of strangers, perverts and physically repulsive in our midst. It performs a function, apparently, which no other institution fully performs. (Davis 1937: 124)

Early positivist criminologists argued for regulation and discipline but in the form of police lists and not imprisonment, especially because prostitution was necessary to "make sexual intercourse accessible to all dissolute-minded young men" and was therefore a "sexual safety valve" (Gibson 1999: 124). Another criticism of pathological theorizing fails to consider the underlying experiences of the women and the structural factors of sex workers' lives, such as poverty, violence, and racism, that might contribute to their sex trade involvement.

Radical Feminist Theorizing: Gender and Violence

In contrast to understanding individuals in the sex trade as deviant and pathological, early radical feminist theorizing still defined the sex trade as a "deviant
activity" and also as "sexual slavery" (Sanders, O'Neill, and Pitcher 2009: 3).
This model, while also quite extreme, worked hard to raise awareness about
the violence and oppression of women in the sex trade and the importance
of gender violence and inequalities. However, women in the sex trade were
viewed as "deviant" (Barry 1988; Dworkin 1981). This position suggested
women who sold sex were degrading themselves, reproducing societal images
of female inferiority.

Catherine MacKinnon and Andrea Dworkin (1981) define prostitution
(and pornography) as masculine expressions of power that idealize the female
and demonize the male. Dworkin (1981 argues that the male penis signifies
the power of men over women, and male domination allows men to "get laid"
(48–49). Phyllis Chesler (1973: 138) likewise states that

> female prostitution and harems have existed among all races, in nearly
> every recorded culture, on every continent, and in all centuries.... It
> always signifies the relatively powerless position of women and their
> widespread sexual repression. It usually also signifies their exclusion
> from or subordination within the economic, political, religious, and
> military systems.

Millett (1969) examined the trading of women, which she argues is proof
that women are currency in all societies, even those without monetary systems. She asserts that women's sexuality is not for their own pleasure; rather,
through rape, abuse, and incest, women are forced to accept prostitution as a
way of life. Millett argues that patriarchal society kills women's self-respect,
their hope, and their ego.

The gender and violence model has continued to make sense of prostitution
by identifying the social control over female sexuality, women's victimization,
and poverty. For example, Hoigaard and Finstad's (1992) text *Backstreets:
Prostitution, Money and Love* demonstrates the effect of violence in women's
lives, the prevalence of working-class and irregular home lives, and the impact
of oppressive institutions. These authors argue that women's experiences lead
to a breakdown of healthy self-perception and self-esteem.

Schrage (1989, 1994) clearly outlines the dilemma facing radical feminist
theories on prostitution. On the one hand, feminism supports abolishing

The problem with the gender, male violence, and radical feminist models is that they link prostitution to sexual commodification and social control over women's subordinate sexuality.

practices that are discriminatory and punish or harass prostitutes. On the other hand, feminists cannot support prostitution because the work is found morally and politically objectionable (Schrage 1989). The sex industry is, for radical feminists, ultimately organized around values that oppress women, "for prostitution depends upon the naturalization of certain principles that marginalize women socially and politically" (Shrage 1989: 349). For Schrage (1989, 1994), prostitution is part of a patriarchal hegemony embedded in all social institutions, and the answer lies in challenging cultural presuppositions and not necessarily in directly addressing prostitution: "[prostitution] will be remedied as feminists make progress in altering patterns of belief and practice that oppress women in all aspects of their lives" (1989: 360).

The problem with the gender, male violence, and radical feminist models is that they link prostitution to sexual commodification and social control over women's subordinate sexuality. This essentializes prostitution as well as female sexuality, leaving little space for a discussion of women in the sex trade who do not define themselves as victims or as deviants (Gerassi 2015). This work is criticized for being paternalistic (Meyers 2013).

Pro-Sex Feminists: Sex Trade is a Choice and Not Deviance

Challenging the radical feminist views about sex as danger and prostitution as a form of deviance and slavery are the pro-sex and sex-positive feminists, who aim to reclaim sexuality as a normal and healthy form of pleasure for people, including sex trade workers (Snowden 2011; Gerassi 2015). In this line of thought, sex trade workers resist prescriptive notions about their work, challenging the radical feminist view of sex as danger and offering the alternative view of sexuality as a form of pleasure (Gerassi 2015). These feminists conceptualize their profession as erotic labour and argue that sex trade workers are entitled to liberties and human rights. In fact, they view the feminist position cited previously as self-righteous and traitorous:

> I will say that, in my experience, feminists opposed to prostitution, pornography and s/m [sadomasochism] fight with a passion reserved for the truly self-righteous. It is not only that they know they are right, but they know that the safety of women elsewhere depends

on the triumph of their position. Women who disagree are not only enemies but traitors…. My own experience as a designated enemy has not only intensified my hatred of war in any context, it has also raised the stakes for me in wishing to see this conflict resolved. (Chapkis 1997: 5)

This "sex-positive" perspective, advanced by authors such as Gayle Rubin (1984), revealed that, although sex can be dangerous for women, it can also be a source of pleasure. This perspective calls for a recognition of sexual pluralism and an acknowledgement that women can be empowered through sexual pleasure. Rubin (1984) further outlined how hegemonic masculine sexualities are themselves socially constructed and can therefore be uprooted. Rubin argues that prostitutes face hierarchies of sexualities, akin to systems of racism, religious chauvinism, and ethnocentrism. These hierarchies rationalize well-being for those who are sexually privileged, but discrimination and adversity for those who are sexually deviant (Rubin 1984). Brock (2000) points out, however, that Rubin fails to examine women's economic relations that might lead them into prostitution and conflates sexual behaviour with sexual identity. Her error might be in the reduction of all sex workers to an erotic group.

The sex-positive libertarian critique of radical feminism was influenced by sex trade workers/activists. These women emphasize the "pleasure" derived from their work.

Pro-sex feminists likewise continue to highlight the sex trade as a form of erotic labor (Chapkis 1997; Nagle 1997). This position argues that women and men in the sex industry are entitled to human rights and liberties in the same way as any other worker. Jill Nagle (1997) writes as a consumer and sex worker, drawing attention to the work of sex trade activists around the globe. She criticizes traditional feminists' analysis of the sex trade for arguing that sexual oppression is the "only story," and she gives voice to a variety of women in the sex industry who are also feminists. Dudash (1997) writes that sex industry work can empower women, put women in charge of their own sexuality and bodies, help men become more educated about women and sexual needs, and help them to be more effective in dealing with sexual and other harassment. In this way, some authors suggest sex trade work gives women more power and helps to challenge sexual inequalities.

Recent pro-sex feminists also assert that women in the sex trade deserve equal rights and labour laws. Van der Meulen (2012: 63) argues that "it is especially urgent for the labour movement to rise to the challenge of supporting

---

Box 11-3: Critical Community and Legal Groups

A number of community-based and legal groups point to the importance of increasing the safety and rights of sex workers and their access to health care and human rights. For example, Pivot Legal Society is committed to challenging social conditions that are oppressive for sex workers, such as poverty, colonization, homelessness, and addiction. They also aim to address discrimination in the criminal justice system. In Toronto, Ontario, Big Susie's, Sex Professionals of Canada, Sex Workers Action Group Kingston, Maggie's: The Toronto Sex Workers Action Group, Stepping Stone, Stop the Arrests!, and Stella have aligned with other organizations for sex workers to condemn police activities that deceive and intimidate sex workers and lead to their arrest. Police use tactics such as posing as clients, booking appointments, or demanding entry to check for coercion and trafficking. Sex workers say over three hundred of them have been subject to these intimidation tactics, which "pushes us further into the shadows and sets up the same kind of circumstances that the Supreme Court just ruled are unacceptable" (Maggie's Toronto Sex Workers Action Project, 2014). In Vancouver, British Columbia, the Eastside Sex Workers United Against Violence Society (SWUAV) and Pivot Legal Society put forward an initiative to educate sex workers about the Vancouver Police Department's Sex Work Enforcement Guidelines. A new "Know Your Rights Card" was provided to sex workers to explain that the police should not "harass, target, arrest or intimidate you for doing sex work" (Pivot 2014).

---

sex workers' rights to safe and equitable work places." She calls on the labour movement to work with individuals in the sex trade toward these rights. Additionally, she shares research that has asked sex trade workers what an ideal workplace might look like. She notes the absence of frivolous suggestions and that every suggestion she received included some of the most basic rights, including: "establishment of employment contacts, gaining access to workers compensation ... development of discrimination policies ... payment for services provided" (154). Van der Meulen (2012) likewise highlights the historical development of sex workers' rights in Canada, including referring to an organization called Maggie's Toronto and their Sex Workers Action Project — said to be the oldest sex worker–run organization that endorses decriminalization in Canada (see Box 11-3). It has been very creative in promoting sex workers' rights, as evidenced in their twenty-fifth anniversary poster: "It's a business doing pleasure with you" (2012: 154).

A shortcoming of sex-positive ethnographic work is that it fails to connect women's narratives to the larger oppression of women that upholds prostitution. The sex trade (even sexuality itself) seems reified within this work.

Many authors writing about the sex trade divide feminism into two distinct perspectives: (1) prostitution as a form of exploitation that reinforces hegemonic sexuality, underpins patriarchal institutions, and impacts all women negatively versus (2) prostitution as a freely chosen occupation that is deserving of rights and liberties (including freedom from violence). This debate has been labelled the "feminist sex wars" (Kissil and Davey 2010). While some argue that individuals might make a "rational" choice to enter prostitution, others argue that free choice into the industry is often not possible. The added paradox lies in the fact that, for many women, prostitution is a means to independence, alleviation of poverty, and better lives — yet it is also argued that prostitution is unlikely to save individuals from poverty or victimization, as it tends to create more destitution, violence, and poverty (Phoenix 2000, 1999a, 1999b).

These very diverse views of radical and pro-sex feminists, although not drawn upon as heavily in current academic and feminist circles, introduce important aspects of the current debate:

> The arguments are [often] reduced to a small number of basic asser-
> tions which avoid the complexities of prostitution. First, women
> working as prostitutes are exploited by those who manage and
> organize the sex industry (mostly men). Moreover, prostitution and
> the wider sex industry serve to underpin and reinforce prostitution
> as a patriarchal institution that affects all women and gendered
> relations. Second, in contemporary society, prostitution for many
> women is freely chosen as a form of work, and women working in the
> sex industry deserve the same rights and liberties as other workers,
> including freedom from fear, exploitation and violence in the course
> of their work. Additionally, sex work or erotic labor can actually be
> a liberatory terrain. (Sanders, O'Neill, and Pitcher 2009: 5)

Despite the richness of feminist literature, positions about the sex trade are often polarized.

The Intersectionality of Social Structure and Voice

In the following theoretical analysis, we introduce critical feminism and anti-oppressive theories that speak from a number of critical, anti-oppressive and feminist perspectives, including anti-racism, critical race feminism, antico-lonialism, **postcolonial feminism**, Black feminism, queer theory, and queer feminism. Rather than introduce each theory separately, we draw from the commonalities within them. These theories aim to include voices that are not always heard, recognizing that agency is shaped by and also shapes larger relations of power and social control. While critical feminists and anti-oppressive theorists agree on the importance of identifying individual voices, they differ in how they analyze the relationship between agency and structural relations. Some theories give primacy to patriarchy, others capitalism, others settler colonialism, others sexual and gendered binaries; however, they all agree about the intersection of race, gender, sexuality, class, agency, and voice (Snowden 2011; Gerassi 2015; Moosa-Mitha 2015).

Many critical theorists and feminists aim to challenge the injustices facing sex trade workers without prohibiting sex work. This type of perspective often entails a redistribution of power and wealth, a decriminalization of consensual sexual activity that includes the sex trade, and an empowered workplace. From these critical perspectives, a study of the sex trade must involve the wider economic, social, and political contexts of sex worker's lives, including the ideology of individualism and neoliberal philosophies, as well as in-depth understandings of real people's experiences (Brooks and Schissel 2015). An understanding of the increasing social, sexual, and cultural inequalities related to income, education, health, and welfare is therefore necessary to contextualize prostitution.

Other critical authors expand this analysis to include inequalities related to race, the history of settler colonialism (Bird and Kaye, this volume), and sexual and gender binaries (Laing, Pilcher, and Smith 2015). This work includes, for example, consideration of problems that stem from a lack of power by individuals being sexually exploited by johns and pimps and continued systemic racism on the part of police. An example of this is shown through Tutty and Nixon's (2003: 77) research through the words of a young Indigenous woman:

> [police] pick on you — if you're on the stroll they [police] look at you like you're lower than them. They're above the law. They can do whatever they want. One cops come up to you say, "I'm gonna stick you in jail for seventy-two hours just because I can!"

Similar to others, Nixon and Tutty's research demonstrates how sex trade workers show both agency and lack of agency in negotiating the overdetermining social forces that have come to shape their lives through the sex trade. The women often act with intent in the face of victimization and poverty, but they must choose other conditions that have arisen from their experiences, which are structured by external realities shaped by history and life circumstances. Tutty and Nixon (2003: 74) quote another young woman who was controlled but trying to escape:

> The pimp I was with at the time was very controlling. It [accessing services] would have been dreadful for me ... there was always someone watching me and I don't know what would happen if I had talked to someone. They were always just across the street from me.

In arguing for the intersectionality of oppressions, these theories contend that we cannot single out, for example, class or racial oppression, but rather that all forms of oppression are interrelated (hooks 1990; Hill Collins 1998; Moosa-Mitha 2015). Any attempt to comprehend the nature of the sex trade must also include global inequalities, poverty, sexual and gender binaries, racial and cultural oppressions, and understandings of settler colonialism. Finally, an analysis of the sex trade must involve discussions of state activities, such as criminal and civil law, and how these uphold or alleviate the oppression of individuals working in the sex trade.

By seeking to understand real experiences from the voices of real participants, a series of innovative qualitative listening tools has emerged. As noted, many anti-oppressive and critical feminist theories emphasize the importance of drawing on the voices and stories of those in the sex trade as a way of understanding their lived experiences and disrupting oppressive social, economic, and political structures (Moosa-Mitha 2015). This means that hearing from the diversity of sex workers, including those who are both more and less privileged, is crucial (Dominelli 2002; Moosa-Mitha 2015).

While qualitative interviews and focus group discussions have become prevalent in bringing forward the voices of participants in anti-oppressive and feminist research, visual (e.g., photovoice) and other arts-based approaches (e.g., drama, drawing, rap, hip-hop) have also been recently popularized. In anti-oppressive postcolonial research, for example, authors such as Linda Goulet et al. (2011: 36) argue that theatre with Indigenous youth is both decolonizing and empowering:

> Theatrical processes [are used] both to tell the youth participants' stories and to represent them in images. Their stories describe how Indigenous youth feel constrained by forces of social control within, and external to, their communities and perceive themselves to lack agency to effect space in which Indigenous youth can free their minds and their bodies.

These creative methodologies make it possible for participants to shift from an understanding of their specific lives toward a critical social analysis and to identify possible steps for social and political change. By engaging in this process, those who have experienced marginalization are helping to create counter-hegemonic knowledge by speaking to both the oppressive social forces in their lives and their ideas for social change.

Desyllas (2014), for example, used the arts-based method of photovoice with women in the sex trade. The participants took pictures related to their visions, strengths, experiences, and voices toward engaging community, education, and social/policy change. These reflected intersectionality, experiences of stigma and of resistance, as well as agency. As Desyllas (2013: 496) states,

> participants who were the same age, engaged in the same type of sex work and identified in the same way racially, sexually and economically had completely different experiences of working in the sex industry and may or may not have experienced violence or drug use. The women's intersecting identities informed their unique experiences and served to challenge unidimensional representations of sex workers.

The participants in Desylla's study talked about feeling empowered through the use of taking pictures to describe their involvement in sex work. For example, one said that "it was amazing. I really liked how much it forced me to think about these things in relation to being a sex worker ... especially now that I am redefining my goals" (2013: 494). Arts-based methods such as these have likewise been said to empower participants in resisting the internalization of negative societal messaging about their work.

Outside of research, the use of art as a form of resistance is seen in work from artists such as Rebecca Bellmore's installation, *blood on the snow* (2002). In the year that Pickton was charged with murdering sex trade workers, Bellmore used a blanket of snow and a blood-stained chair to demonstrate the silencing of so many women:

> I was seeking to make a visual silence, imagining the snow that fell and gently covered the massacre at Wounded Knee. I made this sculpture the year [that] serial killer Robert Pickton was finally charged with murdering so many women. For me, it asks if it is finally possible to remove the blanket of snow and release the deafening silence. (Mendel Art Gallery Display, Saskatoon, 2014)

Winnipeg artist Jamie Black developed a public art display called the REDress project to draw further attention to the missing and murdered Indigenous women, showing the utility of art in making political statements. Having the 131 red dresses blowing in the wind aims to remind passersby of the missing women:

> Anti-oppressive and feminist perspectives create an intellectual and emotional space for a diversity of women's voices to be heard. Creating the space for sex trade workers' voices enables insight into the social construction of identity and wider social experiences.

> You can walk right by them and feel as though someone's there and then look and see no one is there. It's a real visceral reminder of the fact that there are so many women no longer here to tell their stories. I hope this project allows spaces for families and community members to tell the stories that need to be told about these women who can no longer speak for themselves. (Kretzel 2014)

Tasha Hubbard, an award-winning Cree filmmaker and professor, said the project is a way to invite people to look at the root problems, including racism and poverty, that continue to impact Indigenous Peoples and communities.

Anti-oppressive and feminist perspectives create an intellectual and emotional space for a diversity of women's voices to be heard. Creating the space for sex trade workers' voices enables insight into the social construction of identity and wider social experiences. This research also helps to highlight the diversity of sex trade workers, including differences within the trade as well as at various intersections of race, class, sexuality, and gender.

Conclusion

The social control and regulation of the sex trade has differed depending on historical time and place. Sex workers have been and continue to be labelled as either deviant or normal, morally acceptable or morally unacceptable, and sex workers have been celebrated and/or punished depending on the context. Yet much work has been done to show that sex work cannot be reduced to these simple dichotomous narratives.

While criminalization continues to be the dominant policy around the world regarding sex work, its regulation is highly contested in Canada. Bill C-36 put forward legislation that decriminalized the sex trade in Canada while criminalizing the behaviour of johns and pimps. The intent of the bill is similar to that in Nordic countries: to eventually eradicate the sex trade while protecting the rights of adult sex trade workers.

This "third way" model has met with mixed reviews: on the one hand, some view it as having good intentions to protect sex trade workers; on the other, it is critiqued for labelling sex workers as victims and all clients as perpetrators, for overlooking diversity within the industry, and for denying the movement toward decriminalizing the buying of sex and destigmatizing johns. Framed with this debate in mind, this chapter focused on the characteristics of those involved, issues of violence, racism, homophobia, socioeconomics, sexuality, and theories that help to explain people's involvement in the sex trade.

Important considerations within this discussion about the sex trade include the overrepresentation of Black and Indigenous youth and adults in the industry and its link to a history of colonialism and the vulnerability of racialized peoples; the underrepresentation of males in research on the sex trade; and the engagement of lesbian, gay, bisexual, transgender, queer-identified, and nonbinary individuals in the sex trade, as well as how transphobia and homophobia shape the lives of LGBTQ+ sex workers. Discussions of LGBTQ+ people also serve to disrupt the moral framing of their engagement in the sex trade and expand definitions of gender and sexuality as more fluid.

As we have seen throughout the chapter, it is important to consider many factors: the experiences of sex workers; those whose lives are characterized by marginalization, poverty, homelessness; where social services are insufficient; and those who celebrate their profession as erotic labour and argue that sex trade workers are entitled to liberties and human rights. The sex trade is experienced and framed as both a site of empowerment and pleasure and/or as a site of oppression and violence. As noted, those involved in sex work are often victims of multiple forms of violence, including sexual and physical abuse, and have a deeply troubling risk to be victims of homicide. Sexual oppression and violence are not the only stories. While research on women, men, and LGBTQ+ people shows that many of those in the sex trade are entering at a younger age and have experienced painful backgrounds, there is another narrative of people engaged in sex work with multiple and diverse histories who experience sex work as a choice and where they are in charge of their own sexuality and bodies.

Sex work needs to be addressed from a position that combines the lived experiences of those involved in the sex trade with an understanding of the intersectionality of sexual, social, racial, and economic inequalities. By combining the insights, real-life situations, and resistance of people working within the sex trade with the stories of sex trade workers in both privileged and oppressed situations, individual and collective responses can be developed to improve the safety and lives of sex workers.

Discussion Questions

1. Discuss how Indigenous people's involvement in the sex trade has been viewed as trafficking. Why is it important to consider Indigenous people's involvement in sex work within the context of colonization?
2. How do theories about the sex trade contribute to the debate on regulation and decriminalization?
3. Upon consideration of the landmark *Canada v. Bedford* case, develop your own position on the decriminalization of the sex trade.
4. While many sex worker activists in Canada have advocated for annulling laws that criminalize sex work, others propose moving toward the Nordic model of regulation. This position is called the "third way." Define this model and discuss its rationale in both Sweden and in Canada.

Recommended Resources

1. West, Donald. 2012 [1993]. *Male Prostitution*. Routledge.
2. Van der Meulen, E., E.M. Durisin, and V. Love (eds.). 2013. *Selling Sex: Experience, Advocacy and Research on Sex Work in Canada*. Vancouver: UBC Press.
3. Canter, David, Maria Ioannou, and Donna Youngs (eds.). 2012. *Safer Sex in the City: The Experience and Management of Street Prostitution*. London: Ashgate.
4. Equality Now. <equalitynow.org/>.
5. Red Light/Green Light (film on preventing sexual exploitation) <redlightgreenlightfilm.com>.

Glossary

bawdy house: a place occupied by one or more people for the purposes of prostitution.
Bill C-36: decriminalizes the sex trade but criminalizes johns and pimps or anyone exploiting sex workers.
decriminalization: the removal of laws against forms of sex work.
human trafficking: the recruitment, transportation, transfer, and harbouring of people for the purpose of exploitation by using threat, force or

other coercion, fraud, deception, or abuse of power.

john: a client of sexual services.

legalization: system of criminal regulation and government control of prostitution.

postcolonial feminism: realizes the intersectionality of oppressions — that class/race/gender/sexuality are interrelated and any attempt to understand the sex trade must include racial and cultural oppressions and understandings of settler colonialism.

pro-sex feminism: highlights prostitution as a form of erotic labour and argues that individuals in the sex industry are entitled to human rights and liberties in the same way as other workers.

sexual exploitation: terminology used to refer to children that are being exploited through the sex trade by perpetrators and pimps.

References

Allman, Dan and Ted Myers. 1998. "Male Sex Work and HIV/AIDS in Canada." In Peter Aggleton (ed.), *Men Who Sell Sex: International Perspectives on Male Prostitution and HIV/AIDS.* London: Routledge.

Armstrong, L. 2016. "From Law Enforcement to Protection? Interactions between Sex Workers and Police in a Decriminalized Street-Based Sex Industry." *British Journal of Criminology* 57, 3.

Barnett, Laura, and Lyne Casavant. 2014. *Prostitution: A Review of Legislation in Selected Countries.* July 21. Ottawa: Library of Parliament (Background Papers). <lop.parl.ca/sites/PublicWebsite/default/en_CA/ResearchPublications/2011115E>.

Barry, K. 1988. "Female Sexual Slavery: The Problems, Policies and Cause for Feminist Action." In E. Boneparth and E. Stoper (eds.), *Women, Power and Policy: Towards the Year 2000.* Oxford: Pergamon Press.

Baumann, Rebekah M., Sarah Hamilton-Wright, Dana Lee Riley, Karen Brown et al. 2018. "Experiences of Violence and Head Injury Among Women and Transgender Women Sex Workers." *Sexuality Research and Social Policy* 1–11.

Benjamin, Harry, and R.E.L. Masters. 1964. *Prostitution and Morality: A Definitive Report on the Prostitute in Contemporary Society and an Analysis of the Causes and Effects of the Suppression of Prostitution.* London: Souvenir Press.

Bittle, Steven. 2002. "Youth Involvement in Prostitution: A literature Review and Annotated Bibliography Department of Justice Canada." Department of Justice Canada: Research and Statistics Division. <publications.gc.ca/collections/Collection/J3-2-2002-13E.pdf>.

Brents, B.G., and K. Hausbeck. 2005. "Violence and Legalized Brothel Prostitution in Nevada: Examining Safety, Risk, and Prostitution Policy." *Journal of Interpersonal Violence* 20, 3.

____. 2001. "State Sanctioned Sex: Negotiating Informal and Formal Regulatory Practices in Nevada Brothels." *Sociological Perspectives* 44, 3.

Brock, Deborah. 2000. "Victim, Nuisance, Fallen Woman, Outlaw, Worker? Making the Identity 'Prostitute' in Canadian Criminal Law." In Dorothy E. Chunn and Dany Lacombe (eds.), *Law as a Gendering Practice*. Toronto: Oxford University Press.

Brooks, Carolyn, and Bernard Schissel. 2015. "Crime, Criminology and Justice." In Carolyn Brooks and Bernard Schissel (eds.), *Marginality and Condemnation: A Critical Introduction to Criminology*, 3rd edition. Halifax: Fernwood Publishing.

Canada (Attorney General) v. Bedford. 2013. Supreme Court judgment SCC 72, [2013] 3 S.C.R. 1101. <scc-csc.lexum.com/scc-csc/scc-csc/en/item/13389/index.do>.

Canter, David, Maria Ioannou, and Donna Youngs (eds.). 2012. *Safer Sex in the City: The Experience and Management of Street Prostitution*. London: Ashgate.

Chapkis, Wendy. 1997. *Live Sex Acts: Women Performing Erotic Labour*. New York: Routledge.

Chesler, Phyllis. 1973. *Women and Madness*. New York: Doubleday.

Cobbina, Jennifer E., and Sharon S. Oselin. 2011. "It's Not Only for the Money: An Analysis of Adolescent Versus Adult Entry into Street Prostitution." *Sociological Inquiry* 81, 3.

Cool, Julie. 2004. *Prostitution in Canada: An Overview*. Ottawa: Library of Parliament.

Davis, K. 1937. "The Sociology of Prostitution." *American Sociological Review* 2, 5.

Deibert, David. 2018. "Publisher Exploring New Edition of 'Halfbreed' after Excised Rape Passage Discovered." *Saskatoon StarPhoenix*, June 1. <thestarphoenix.com/news/local-news/publisher-exploring-new-edition-of-halfbreed-after-excised-rape-passage-discovered>.

Deinema, Michael, and Manuel B. Aalbers. 2015. "A Global Red-light City? Prostitution in *Amsterdam: History, Culture and Geography in a World City*. Amsterdam: Amsterdam University Press.

Dennis, Jeffery P. 2008. "Women Are Victims, Men Make Choices: The Invisibility of Men and Boys in the Global Sex Trade." *Gender Issues* 25, 1.

Desyllas, Moshoula Capous. 2013. "Using Photovoice with Sex Workers: The Power of Art, Agency and Resistance." *Qualitative Social Work* 13, 4.

Dominelli, Lena. 2002. *Feminist Social Work Theory and Practice*. Basingstoke: Palgrave.

Dudash, Tawnya. 1997. "Peepshow Feminism." In Jill Nagle (ed.). *Whores and Other Feminists*. New York: Routledge.

Dworkin, Andrea. 1981. *Pornography: Men Possessing Women* London: Women's Press.

Ellison, Graham, and Ronald Weitzer. 2016. "The Dynamics of Male and Female Street Prostitution in Manchester, England." *Men and Masculinities* 20, 2. <journals.sagepub.com/doi/abs/10.1177/1097184X15625318?journalCode=jmma>.

Farley, Melissa, Jacqueline Lynne, and Ann J. Cotton. 2005. "Prostitution in Vancouver: Violence and the Colonization of First Nations Women." *Transcultural Psychiatry* 42, 2.

Ferris, Shawna. 2008. "Working from the Violent Centre: Survival Sex Work and Urban Aboriginality in Maria Campbell's *Halfbreed*." *ESC: English Studies in Canada* 34, 4. <muse.jhu.edu/article/379846>.

Fletcher, Tor. 2013. "Trans Sex Workers: Negotiating Sex, Gender and Non-Normative Desire." In Emily van der Meulen, Elya M. Durisin, and Victoria Love (eds.), *Selling Sex: Experience, Advocacy, and Research on Sex Work in Canada*. Vancouver: UBC Press.

Gerassi, Lara. 2015. "From Exploitation to Industry: Definitions, Risks, and Consequences of Domestic Sexual Exploitation and Sex Work Among Women and Girls." *Journal of Human Behavior in the Social Environment* 25: 6. <doi:

10.1080/10911359.2014.991055>.

Gibson, Mary. 1999. *Prostitution and the State in Italy, 1860–1915*. Ohio: Ohio State University Press.

Glueck, Sheldon, and Eleanor Glueck. 1934. *Five Hundred Delinquent Women*. New York: Alfred A. Knopf.

Golder, Seana, and T.K. Logan. 2007. "Correlates and Predictors of Women's Sex Trading Over Time among a Sample of Out-of-Treatment Drug Abusers." *HIV and Behavior* 11, 4.

Goulet, Linda, Warren Linds, Jo-Ann Episkenew, and Karen Schmidt. 2011. "Creating a Space for Decolonization: Health through Theatre with Indigenous Youth." *Native Studies Review* 20, 1. <spectrum.library.concordia.ca/975032/1/Creating_a_space_for_decolonization_NSR20(1).pdf>.

Hill Collins, Patricia. 1998. *Black Feminist Thought: Knowledge, Consciousness and the Politics of Empowerment*, 2nd edition. New York: Routledge.

Hodgson, James F. 1997. *Games Pimps Play: Pimps, Players and Wives-in-Law: A Quantitative Analysis of Street Prostitution*. Toronto: Canadian Scholars' Press.

Hoigaard, Cecilie, and Liv Finstad. 1992. *Backstreets: Prostitution, Money and Love*. Cambridge: Polity Press.

hooks, bell. 1990. *Yearning: Race, Gender and Cultural Politics*. Boston: South End Press.

Hugill, David. 2010. *Missing Women, Missing News: Covering Crisis in Vancouver's Downtown Eastside*. Halifax: Fernwood Publishing.

Jiwani, Yasmin, and Mary Lynn Young. 2006. "Missing and Murdered Women: Reproducing Marginality in News Discourse." *Canadian Journal of Communication* 31, 4.

Kelly, Lisa M., and Katrina E. Pacey. 2011. "Why Anti-John Laws Don't Work." *Toronto Star*, October 19. <thestar.com/opinion/editorialopinion/2011/10/19/why_antijohn_laws_dont_work.html>.

Kissil, Karni and Maureen Davey. 2010. "The Prostitution Debate in Feminism: Current Trends, Policy and Clinical Issues Facing an Invisible Population." *Journal of Feminist Family Therapy* 22.

Kretzel, Lasia. 2014. "REDress Project Brings Attention to Missing, Murdered Aboriginal Women." *paNOW*, September 18. <panow.com/article/473344/redress-project-brings-attention-missing-murdered-aboriginal-women>.

Krusi, Andrea, Jill Chettiar, Amelia Ridgway, Janice Abbott et al. 2012. "Negotiating Safety and Sexual Risk Reduction with Clients in Unsanctioned Safer Indoor Sex Work Environments: A Qualitative Study." *American Journal of Public Health*, 102, 6.

Krusi, Andrea, Katrina E. Pacey, Lorna Bird, Jill Chettiar et al. 2014. "Criminalisation of Clients: Reproducing Vulnerabilities for Violence and Poor Health Among Street-Based Sex Workers in Canada — A Qualitative Study." *BMJ Open* 4, 6.

Laing, Mary, Katy Pilcher, and Nicola Smith (eds.). 2015. *Queer Sex Work*. London: Routledge.

Landsberg, Adina, Kate Shannon, Andrea Krusi, Kora DeBeck et al. 2017. "Criminalizing Sex Work Clients and Rushed Negotiations Among Sex Workers Who Use Drugs in a Canadian Setting." *Journal of Urban Health* 94, 4.

Lawphil Project. 2012. "Republic Act No. 10158: An Act Decriminalizing Vagrancy, Amending for this Purpose Article 202 of Act No, 3815, as Amended, Otherwise

Known as the Revised Penal Code." March 27. Manila: Arellano Law Foundation. <prostitution.procon.org/sourcefiles/PhilippinesRevisedPenalCode.pdf>.

Li, Xiaobing Li, and Qiang Fang (eds.). 2013. *Modern Chinese Legal Reform: New Perspectives.* Kentucky: University Press of Kentucky.

Logie, Carmen H., LLana James, Wangari Tharao, and Mona R. Loutfy. 2012. "'We Don't Exist:' A Qualitative Study of Marginalization Experienced by HIV-Positive Lesbian, Bisexual, Queer and Transgender Women in Toronto, Canada." *Journal of the International HIV Society* 15, 2.

Lombroso, Casare, and Guglielmo Ferrero. 1895. *The Female Offender.* D. Appleton.

Lutnick A., and D. Cohan. 2009. "Criminalization, Legalization or Decriminalization of Sex Work: What Female Sex Workers Say in San Francisco, USA." *Reproductive Health Matters* 17, 34.

MacKinnon, Catharine, and Andrea Dworkin (eds.). 1997. *In Harm's Way: The Pornography Civil Rights Hearings.* Cambridge: Harvard University Press.

Maggie's Toronto Sex Workers Action Project. 2014. "Condemnation Grows as More Sex Workers' Groups Speak Out Against Police Harassment, Urge Parliament to Go a Different Route." January 29. <maggiestoronto.ca/press-releases?news_id=116>.

Matthews, Roger. 2014. "Female Prostitution and Victimization: A Realist Analysis." *International Review of Victimology* 21, 1.

Meyers, Diana Tietjens. 2013. "Feminism and Sex Trafficking: Rethinking Some Aspects of Autonomy and Paternalism." *Ethical Theory and Moral Practice* 17, 3.

Millett, Kate. 1969. *Sexual Politics.* London: Granada Publishing.

Ministry of Justice. 2003. "Prostitution Reform Act of 2003." Parliamentary Counsel Office (New Zealand Legislation) (4), June 27. <legislation.govt.nz/act/public/2003/0028/latest/DLM197815.html>.

Moosa-Mitha, Mehmoona. 2015. "Situating Anti-Oppressive Theories within Critical and Difference-Centered perspectives." In Susan Strega and Leslie Brown (eds.), *Research as Resistance: Critical, Indigenous and Anti-Oppressive Approaches.* Toronto: Canadian Scholars' Press.

Murphy, Timothy F. 2014. "Are Gay and Lesbian People Fading into the History of Bioethics?" *Hasting Center Report* 44, s4.

Nagle, Jill. (ed.). 1997. *Whores and Other Feminists.* New York: Routledge.

National Post. 2010. "'I'm a Legend': Picton Interview Transcript Released." August 6. <nationalpost.com/news/canada/pickton-interview-transcripts-released>.

New York Post. 2014. "Germany Experiencing Brothel Boom, But Is Prostitution Safer?" June 10. <nypost.com/2014/06/10/germany-experiencing-brothel-boom-but-is-prostitution-safer/>.

O'Doherty, Tamara. 2011a. "Victimization in Off-Street Sex Industry Work." *Violence Against Women* 17, 7 (July).

___. 2011b. "Criminalization and Off-Street Sex Work in Canada." *Canadian Journal of Criminology and Criminal Justice/La Revue Canadienne de Criminologie et de Justice Nale* 53, 2 (April).

Perrin, Benjamin. 2014. "Oldest Profession or Oldest Oppression? Addressing Prostitution After the Supreme Court of Canada Decision in *Canada v. Bedford.*" *Social Science Research Network,* January 14. <macdonaldlaurier.ca/files/pdf/MLIPerrinPaper01-14-final-Web-Ready.pdf>.

Phoenix, Joanna. 2000. "Prostitute Identities." *British Journal of Criminology* 40, 1. <academic.oup.com/bjc/article-abstract/40/1/37/398950?redirectedFrom=fulltext>.

___. 1999a. *Making Sense of Prostitution*. London: Palgrave MacMillan.

___. 1999b. "Ways of Talking About Prostitutes and Prostitution." In *Making Sense of Prostitution*. London: Palgrave MacMillan.

Pivot. 2014. "Vancouver Sex Workers Release "Know Your Rights" Card" [press release]. <pivotlegal.org/sex_workers_rights_card>.

ProCon.org. 2018. "Countries and Their Prostitution Policies." <prostitution.procon.org/countries-and-their-prostitution-policies/>.

Raymond, Janice G. 2018. "Gatekeeping Decriminalization of Prostitution: The Ubiquitous Influence of the New Zealand Prostitutes' Collective." *Dignity: A Journal on Sexual Exploitation and Violence*, 3, 2 (April). <digitalcommons.uri.edu/cgi/viewcontent.cgi?article=1116&context=dignity>.

Razack, Sherene H. 2002. "Gendered Racial Violence and Spatialized Justice: The Murder of Pamela George." In Sherene H. Razack (ed.), *Race, Space and the Law: Unmapping a White Settler Society*. Toronto: Between the Lines.

Reeve, Kesia. 2013. "The Morality of the 'Immoral': The Case of Homeless, Drug-Using Street Prostitutes." *Deviant Behavior* 34, 10.

Rubin, Gayle. 1984. "Thinking Sex: Note for a Radical Theory of the Politics of Sexuality." In Carol Vance (ed.), *Pleasure and Danger: Exploring Female Sexuality*. Boston: Routledge and Kegan Paul.

Sanders, Teela, Maggie O'Neill, and Jane Pitcher. 2009. *Prostitution: Sex Work, Policy and Politics*. London: Sage Publications.

Save the Children Canada. 2000. <savethechildren.ca/>.

Schrage, Laurie. 1994. *Moral Dilemmas of Feminism: Prostitution, Adultery, and Abortion*. London: Routledge.

___. 1989. "Should Feminists Oppose Prostitution?" *Ethics* 99, 2.

Scott, Gavin. 2018. "'The New Era of Canadian Sex Work' Looks at How Sex Workers Might Be Worse Off Under Legislation Intended to Protect Them." <sbs.com.au/guide/article/2018/02/27/how-one-law-changed-everything-about-prostitution-canada>.

Shannon, Kate, and Joanne Csete. 2010. "Violence, Condom Negotiation, and HIV/STI Risk Among Sex Workers." *Jama* 304, 5.

Shdaimah, Cory S., and Shelly A. Wiechelt. 2012. "Crime and Compassion: Women in Prostitution at the Intersection of Criminality and Victimization." *International Review of Victimology* 19, 1.

Sikka, Anette. 2009. *Trafficking of Aboriginal Women and Girls in Canada*. Ottawa: Institute on Governance.

Snowden, Carisa R. 2011. *Choices Women Make: Agency in Domestic Violence, Assisted Reproduction, and Sex Work*. Minneapolis: University of Minnesota Press.

State of Nevada. 1995a. "Nevada Revised Statute: Engaging in Prostitution or Solicitation for Prostitution: Criminal Penalties; Civil Penalty; Discharge and Dismissal." 201.354 (5), 201.354 (5)(a).

___. 1995b. "Nevada Revised Statute. Restriction on Location of Houses of Ill Fame; Penalty." 201.380 (1).

Strega, Susan, Caitlin Janzen, Jeannie Morgan, Leslie Brown et al. 2014. "Never Innocent

Victims: Street Sex Workers in Canadian Print Media." *Violence Against Women* 20, 1.

Tutty, Leslie Maureen, and Kendra Nixon. 2003. "'Selling Sex? It's Really Like Selling Your Soul': Vulnerability to and the Experience of Exploitation through Child Prostitution." In K. Gorkoff and J. Runner (eds.), *Being Heard: The Experiences of Young Women in Prostitution*. Manitoba: Fernwood Publishing.

Valandra. 2007. "Reclaiming Their Lives and Breaking Free: An Afrocentric Approach to Recovery from Prostitution." *Affilia* 22. <prostitutionresearch.com/pdfs/Breaking_Free_Valandra.pdf>.

Van der Meulen, Emily. 2012. "When Sex Is Work: Organizing for Labour Rights and Protections." *Labour/Le Travail*, 69. <lltjournal.ca/index.php/llt/article/view/5680>.

Van der Meulen, Emily, Elya M. Durisin, and Victoria Love (eds.). 2013. *Selling Sex: Experience, Advocacy, and Research on Sex Work in Canada*. Vancouver: UBC Press.

Vanwesenbeeck, I. 2017. "Sex Work Criminalization Is Barking Up the Wrong Tree." *Archives of Sexual Behaviour* 46, 6.

Weitzer, Ronald. 2005a. "Rehashing Tired Claims About Prostitution: A Response to Farley and Raphael and Shapiro." *Violence Against Women* 11, 7 (July).

____. 2005b. "New Directions in Research on Prostitution." *Crime, Law and Social Change* 43, 4 (June).

West, Donald J. 2012 [1993]. *Male Prostitution*. New York: Haworth Press.

Wonders, N.A., and R. Michalowski. 2001. "Bodies, Borders, and Sex Tourism in a Globalized World: A Tale of Two Cities — Amsterdam and Havana." *Social Problems* 48, 4.

Xiaobing Li and Qiang Fang (eds.). 2013. *Modern Chinese Legal Reform: New Perspectives*. Lexington: University Press of Kentucky.

12

Social Control, Settler Colonialism, and Representations of Violence against Indigenous Women

Danielle Bird and Julie Kaye

After reading this chapter, you will be able to do the following:

1. Examine colonial gendered violence and representations of Indigenous women in Canada.
2. Theorize social control of Indigenous women's bodies in the context of targeted violence and anti-violence campaigns.
3. Understand the interconnected relationship between land and settler colonialism and how multiple, interlocking systems of oppression — colonialism, racism, patriarchy, and capitalism — manifest in and through violent victimization and criminalization.
4. Develop familiarity with key theories and scholars working at the intersection of criminology, social control, Indigenous studies, women's and gender studies, and law.
5. Establish an understanding of social control and ongoing representations of Indigenous women in settler colonial contexts.

Violence against Indigenous women has been the subject of numerous reports, articles and studies conducted by various academics and governmental and non-governmental agencies for decades (Razack 2002; Government of Canada 2008; NWAC 2009, 2010; Pearce 2013; FAFIA and NWAC 2015; Lavell-Harvard and Brant 2016). For years, Indigenous women tried to raise awareness about the crisis of violence they were facing. In 1992,

---

Box 12-1: The Politics of Recognition in the Context of Settler Colonialism

by Cerah Dubé

Through the politics of recognition, the state seeks to mask its continued use of colonial violence against Indigenous Peoples by publicly championing its commitment to reconciliation with and recognition of them (Coulthard 2014). For example, public state recognition of harmful historical colonial processes and legislation like the Indian residential school system, the reserve and pass systems, and the Sixties Scoop often results in government-issued apologies, statements, and inquiries. Supreme Court cases have resulted in the recognition of Indigenous Rights enshrined within Canada's *Charter of Rights and Freedoms*. Officials issue treaty land and territory acknowledgments. While such recognition seems to be a step in the right direction, it is undermined by a hidden and ulterior motive of the state: to limit Indigenous Rights and sovereignty beneath the colonial state structure.

As Glen Coulthard (2014: 41) states, "colonial powers will only recognize the collective rights and identities of Indigenous peoples insofar as this recognition does not throw into question the background legal, political, and economic framework of the colonial relationship itself." The colonial relationship is one of oppression and violent subjugation wherein the power and benefits lay with the colonizer (Simpson 2014a). Therefore, while recognition is seemingly granted by the state to Indigenous Peoples, only select forms of recognition — those that work in tandem with state goals and agendas — are permissible. True and meaningful transformations of Indigenous Rights, sovereignty, and self-determination threaten the presumed legitimacy of the colonial state and require decolonized spaces and knowledge that exist entirely outside the state instead of being limited within colonial confines and structures. The politics of recognition allow for surface-level acknowledgements of the products and wrongdoings of colonialism while simultaneously leaving the structural and institutional roots of colonialism unchecked and unchallenged.

---

the first memorial march was held in Vancouver's Downtown Eastside in response to the murder of a Coast Salish woman. But little support followed until Amnesty International and the Native Women's Association of Canada (NWAC) shone an international spotlight on the issue in their 2004 *Stolen Sisters* report. The report officially noted over five hundred cases of missing and murdered Indigenous women and girls (MMIWG) and detailed the heighted threat of extreme violence and brutality that Indigenous women and girls face in Canada. As the documentation grew, so did calls for a state response. Increasingly, the voices of Indigenous women calling for change were over-shadowed by calls for the state to respond to the crisis of MMIWG and violence against Indigenous women. By troubling the shift to state-centred responses, this chapter explores how violence against Indigenous women in Canada forms a particularly disturbing practice of social control. Such mechanisms of control become apparent when we examine anti-violence campaigns and the Canadian state's response to the disproportionate violence, victimization, and criminalization against Indigenous women in settler colonial Canada. Drawing on theories of social control, we also critically analyze representations of violence against Indigenous women, particularly efforts to uncover the "truth" of such violence within a carceral settler state (see Box 12-1).

Forms of racialized, sexualized, gendered, and colonial violence have been subject to mass inquiry. In particular, a growing body of literature bridges a critique of the past and present social conditions that reproduce racial, gendered, and economic inequities for Indigenous Peoples through state-sponsored modes of social control to reveal what Patricia Hill Collins (2009: 231) describes as a "matrix of domination." Widespread public awareness campaigns and commemorative art installations — such as the REDress art installation at the Canadian Museum for Human Rights, the Walking With Our Sisters commemorative installation and ceremonies, Shades of Our Sisters memorials, and other performances and works by Indigenous artists such as Rebecca Belmore, Lori Blondeau, Angela Sterritt, Christi Belcourt — have brought long overdue attention to the experiences of Indigenous women facing targeted and systemic violence in Canada. Still, ongoing conditions of violence, such as aggressive over-policing and high rates of criminalization and victimization both inside and outside of Indigenous communities, remain unchanged, with severe and lethal implications for Indigenous women in various parts of the world. These revelations have ignited outrage and contributed to a movement where many individuals, including survivors of violence, families of MMIWG, Indigenous leaders, and interest groups, have lobbied the Canadian government for a response, accountability, and, more recently, for systemic change.

However, the numbers of missing and murdered Indigenous women continue to rise. The Native Women's Association of Canada (2009: 92) says that "520 cases of missing and murdered Aboriginal women and girls had been entered into the NWAC database"; of these, 126 were reported missing, 347 died as a result of homicide or negligence, forty-three were unconfirmed, and four were suspicious in nature. A few years later, Pearce (2013) documented that 824 of 3,329 missing women in Canada were Indigenous (greater than 24 percent), despite the fact that Indigenous women make up only 4 percent of the female population in Canada (Statistics Canada 2016). More recently, the Royal Canadian Mounted Police released its 2013–14 operational review, which reported that nearly 1,200 Indigenous women were killed between 1980 and 2012, and in 100 percent of the solved homicide cases, Indigenous women knew the offender. The report stated that in 62 percent of homicide cases, the perpetrators were "current and former spouses and family members" (RCMP 2015: n.p). Pamela Palmater (2016: 257) reminds us that while family and spousal violence contributes to the reality of MMIWG, state agents working within policing, prisons, and child welfare have also contributed to increasing levels of violence. Thus, even though awareness and recognition of MMIWG and the disproportionate violence Indigenous women face in Canada has grown, the culture that produces such violence has remained relatively unaltered. As Sarah Hunt (2014: n.p.) laments: "800 names. 600 names. Thousands of names of missing and murdered women.... Yet, as the numbers climb higher with each new death, will they ever be enough to compel the changes that will transform this culture of violence?"

In this context, another generation of Indigenous youth struggle to survive the daily material conditions of inequality while also resisting ongoing systems of oppression. The continuation of targeted violence alongside heightened awareness of the issue raises a number of questions about social control in Canada: (1) How are state benevolence and portrayals of Canadian innocence employed as a mechanism to control Indigenous women's bodies and Indigenous Peoples' lands? (2) How does recognition of Indigenous women's suffering play a role in the continuation of settler colonial mechanisms of social control? (3) In what ways do "truth-seeking" mechanisms, such as commissions of inquiry and inquests, also function as technologies of social control?

From Canada's Refusal to Acknowledge MMIWG to Emerging Forms of Recognition

Early efforts to draw attention to the ongoing crisis of MMIWG aimed to draw national attention and action. Such efforts sought recognition from the Canadian state about the ongoing and disproportionate violence faced by Indigenous women in Canada. As the former president of the Native Women's Association of Canada (NWAC) (see Box 12-2), Bev Jacobs (Amnesty International 2014), argues:

> I want them to care about what's happening. I want them to care about the families that have been traumatized. I want them to care about why this is happening. I want them to care that this is a systemic problem and that's we're all responsible.

When such efforts fell on deaf ears, international activists and local organizations sought to compel government action. In 2004, the Native Women's Association of Canada and Amnesty International collaborated to document five hundred cases of MMIWG in the *Stolen Sisters* report. The report highlights multiple sites of oppression through which violence against Indigenous women manifests, including government policies such as the *Indian Act*, which has been a significant tool of social control in state-sponsored acts of genocide, involving the imprisonment of children in residential schools, high rates of child welfare apprehension, police inaction when Indigenous women and girls go missing, and ongoing public indifference based on racist assumptions and stereotypes about Indigenous Peoples and their communities.

Stolen Sisters demonstrated that Indigenous women and girls in Canada are specifically targeted in acts of extreme violence and brutality that manifest in ongoing forms of settler colonial gender violence often based on colonial stereotypes and assumptions about who they are and what they represent (see Box 12-3). The report served as a plea to *recognize* the significant human rights violations taking place against Indigenous women in Canada, implicating "overt cultural prejudice and implicit or systemic biases in the policies

---

Box 12-2: What Is NWAC?

by Cerah Dubé

Founded in 1974, the Native Women's Association of Canada is a national, non-governmental, Indigenous-led organization that advocates for First Nations, Métis, and Inuit women, girls, and LGBTQ2S+ people across Canada. They participate in policy and legislative analysis, publish research reports, and bring attention to issues and crises faced by Indigenous women. NWAC's focus areas include health and wellness, violence prevention and safety, employment access, safe and secure housing, and child care, and the association is rooted in cultural and spiritual beliefs, laws, language and traditions. Central to their advocacy, vision, and goals are preserving Indigenous culture and enhancing the well-being of Indigenous women, girls, families, and communities, as well as bolstering processes of sovereignty and self-determination (NWAC n.d.).

and actions of government" (Amnesty International Canada 2004: 3). *Stolen Sisters* revealed incidences where police and justice systems failed to provide protection and in many cases exacerbated the violence, resulting in Indigenous communities facing over-policing and under-protection on a daily basis. One of the cases documented in the report concerns the death of Helen Betty Osborne, a 19-year-old Cree student from northern Manitoba. Osborne had planned to become a teacher, but she was abducted by four white men in 1971 in The Pas, Manitoba, where she was sexually assaulted and murdered. The Manitoba Justice Inquiry into her death indicates:

> Her attackers seemed to be operating on the assumption that Aboriginal women were promiscuous and open to enticement through alcohol or violence. It is evident that the men who abducted Osborne believed that young Aboriginal women were objects with no human value beyond sexual gratification. (Cited in Amnesty International 2004: 17)

In addition to the evident racism in the perpetrators' violence, the Manitoba inquiry also found that the investigation into her death was sloppy, discriminatory, and highlighted how the police had long been aware of white men sexually preying on Indigenous women but did not feel the practice warranted any particular vigilance on their part. The report also details the murder of Pamela George and the subsequent trial of two white men before a white judge and an all-white jury. As a clear means of stigmatization, the trial paid little attention to the life of Pamela George before she became a sex worker, despite the fact that the perpetrators did not attack her while she was working in the sex trade. Nonetheless, Justice Malone instructed the jurors to bear in mind that Pamela was "indeed a prostitute" when they considered whether or not she had consented to sexual activity. In doing so, the judge demonstrated overt abuse of women's sexual history to bias the court in favour of the perpetrators, who were simultaneously portrayed as young men with "bright futures." The portrayal of the men could not be more starkly juxtaposed against the stigmatizing devaluation of Pamela George's humanity, her right to consent, and bodily autonomy.

Similarly, the *Sisters in Spirit* findings reveal that the "intergenerational impact and resulting vulnerabilities of colonization and state policies — such as residential schools, the '60s Scoop, and the child welfare system — are underlying factors in the outcomes of violence experienced by Aboriginal women and girls" (NWAC 2010: i). The report suggests that despite ongoing

Box 12-3: Sexist and Racist Colonial Stereotypes

by Cerah Dubé

An example of these stereotypes is that of Indigenous women as "squaws," a notion that is premised on assumptions and beliefs rooted in gendered, colonial racism. "Squaw" has long dominated colonial discourses and remains deeply ingrained in continued manifestations of colonial gender violence perpetrated against Indigenous women. This stereotype sees an Indigenous woman as "not only a woman but an Indian woman," depicting her as immoral, lustful, dirty, and, ultimately, disposable (LaRoque 1994: 74; Eberts 2014). The degrading stereotype of "squaw" reinforces the notion that violence against Indigenous women is somehow less severe than other forms of violence in society. When Indigenous women are cast in such a dehumanizing light, it normalizes violence against them and their bodies and perpetuates such violence as deserved and allowable.

efforts to highlight these issues, "Aboriginal women continue to be the most at-risk group in Canada for issues related to violence, and continue to experience complex issues linked to intergenerational impacts of colonization ... residential schools and the child welfare system" (NWAC 2010: ii).

In addition to NWAC and Amnesty International, provincial governments have initiated studies related to MMIWG. British Columbia's former attorney general, Wally Oppal (2012: 28), was commissioned to lead a "fact-finding" inquiry into incidences of missing and murdered women in that province. Findings from this inquiry cite decades of strained relationships between Indigenous Peoples and police, stating that "discrimination, systemic and institutional bias, and political and public indifference" all contributed to the disproportionate numbers of missing and murdered women within Vancouver's Downtown Eastside.

Myriad reports reveal that racism, sexism, colonialism, stigma, and discrimination are contributing to incidents of violence against Indigenous women. Yet, despite growing government and public *recognition* of these contributing factors, Canada has failed to implement numerous recommendations put forward by Indigenous women or the Inter-American Commission on Human Rights (IACHR) and the Convention on the Elimination of All Forms of Discrimination Against Women (CEDAW) (on the **politics of recognition**, see Simpson 2014a; Coulthard 2014). Still, various interest groups continued to lobby the federal government for a national inquiry to not only bring attention to the crisis of MMIWG at a national federal level, but also to address how the roots of this crisis are embedded in a gendered colonial legacy and to begin remedying such issues. In lieu of a national inquiry, Stephen Harper's Conservative government responded to this pressure by releasing a report titled *Invisible Women: A Call to Action* in 2014. A portion of the report reads:

> Such forms of social control have resulted in the ongoing regulation of Indigenous women's bodies and lives. Within this context, Indigenous women and girls are targeted in extreme acts of violence not only because they are women, but because they are women who are Indigenous.

> The need [for family members] to keep the memory of their loved ones alive speaks of the great tragedy at the heart of the story on missing and murdered Aboriginal women — the silence in which this tragedy happens. It is the tragedy of not being heard when they call out for help, not being heard when they reported someone missing. That silence is part of the ongoing trend of mainstream society saying to Aboriginal people that they don't count. (Government of Canada 2014: 3)

While speaking directly to the truth underlying the crisis of mmiwg, the Canadian government's report did little to acknowledge that the heteronormative and patriarchal colonial processes, practices, and stereotypes responsible for violence against Indigenous women continue to permeate all aspects of Canadian society. These include more obvious settler colonial modes of social control, such as the gendered and racialized policies legislated within the *Indian Act* and other practices such as the coerced sterilization of Indigenous women by health professionals in Canada (Collier 2017). Such forms of social control have resulted in the ongoing regulation of Indigenous women's bodies and lives. Within this context, Indigenous women and girls are targeted in extreme acts of violence not only because they are women, but because they are women who are Indigenous (Palmater 2016: 258). Combined with state-building projects of land dispossession within settler colonial contexts, gender and race are mechanisms of social control designed to further regulate, surveil, and domesticate Indigenous nations. As Simpson (2014b: 156) states:

> Indian women "disappear" because they have been deemed killable, able to be raped without repercussion, expendable. Their bodies have been *historically* rendered less valuable because of what they are taken to represent: land, reproduction, Indigenous kinship and governance, an alternative to heteronormative and Victorian rules of descent. Theirs are bodies that carry a symbolic load because they

have been conflated with land and are thus contaminating to white, settler social order.

Following the death of 15-year-old Tina Fontaine, the Harper government urged Canadians to understand her death, and the deaths of other MMIWG, not as a sociological phenomenon but as an individual crime problem (Boutilier 2014). However, as Kaye and Béland (2014: 1) clarify, "crime is an inherently sociological phenomenon and the heightened threat of violence faced by Aboriginal women more than warrants a sociologically informed response. Unfortunately, the prime minister seems intent to stick to a reactionary approach of crime resolution." In doing so, the government continued to downplay the demonstrable, systemic inequality and disproportionate violent victimization faced by Indigenous women in the context of settler colonialism.

This rhetoric was part of the Harper Conservatives' tough-on-crime agenda, which aimed to strengthen the reach of the criminal justice system through the use of mandatory minimum sentencing, harsher and lengthier penalties, increased police powers and the provision of additional funding for police investigative resources (Mallea 2010). But the tough-on-crime approach did not challenge the racism, misogyny, and patriarchy that permeates every aspect of the Canadian criminal justice system and shapes the responses of the police, judges, lawyers, prison staff, and parole officers who are deployed in violent incidents. Similarly, the government's plans to increase police powers seemed to ignore multiple government reports and academic research that cite decades of strained relationships between Indigenous Peoples and the police (see Oppal 2012; Human Rights Watch 2013; Stark 2016; Sapers 2016).

According to Dian Million (2013: 39), early feminist efforts to criminalize gendered violence actually contributed to the criminalization and incarceration of the victims of crime rather than the perpetrators, because although victims are made more visible, the processes of racism, misogyny, and patriarchy embedded within the fabric of settler colonial societies remain unchallenged and unaltered. As such, "US and Canadian societies become more hypervigilant around sexual crime but not less misogynistic. They also become more invasive and controlling." Such processes work in tandem with state influence to construct Indigenous women who are victimized by crime as criminals themselves. For example, in 2015, Angela Cardinal was called to a court room in Edmonton, Alberta, to testify at a preliminary hearing for a man who was charged for violently attacking and sexually assaulting her. During the proceedings, Cardinal was held for five nights in a jail cell and was led into the court room, by court staff, with her hands cuffed and legs

---

Box 12-4: Criminalizing Victimized Persons:
Media Representations of Indigenous Women

by Cerah Dubé

Media narratives play a powerful role in constructing public knowledge and opinions. This is especially significant in the social and public construction of the MMIWG crisis in Canada. How the media portrays MMIWG through both its imagery and discourse often results in skewed, troubling, and dehumanizing accounts of their lives and personalities. Media representations of MMIWG tend to focus on aspects such as involvement with the drug and sex trades, substance abuse issues, and homelessness (Hugill 2014). A woman's involvement in street-level sex work is frequently picked apart by media outlets, stigmatized through the use of words like "prostitute" and "hooker," language that depicts them as "dirty," "dangerous," and "deviant" women who are "consumed by addiction" and constantly at risk (Hugill 2014: 132–35). David Hugill (2014) notes that the images of MMIWG produced in print media often appear similar to criminal mugshots. The use of such images reinforces the negative narrative put forward by media that is then further construed in public perceptions of the women.

This narrative lends itself toward the construction of MMIWG as criminals themselves instead of as victims of crimes perpetrated against them. Instead of allowing for the understanding of missing and murdered women as having suffered trauma and violence, they are projected as being "morally corrupt" and "criminally culpable" and thus somehow deserving of their fate of going missing or being murdered (Hugill 2014).

---

shackled (Johnson 2017). Instead of offering her the protection and justice that victims and survivors of brutal violence deserve, officials in the criminal justice system instead treated Cardinal as a criminal, thereby reproducing the fallacy that Indigenous women are not deserving of protection (see Box 12-4).

Nevertheless, many tough-on-crime supporters continued to position federal and provincial government stances as a progressive move toward ending violence against Indigenous women and girls, even when this stance contradicted survivor testimonies and re-silenced the women at the centre of the Canadian government's *Invisible Women* report, reinforcing the message that Indigenous women and girls are, indeed, not being heard. Compounding the problem, the Canadian government refused to acknowledge that strengthening the criminal justice system and expanding police powers are direct forms of social control in settler colonial contexts. These processes of increased surveillance and regulation blame Indigenous women and girls for their own victimization and punish them for not adhering to white, heteronormative notions of femininity, even in death (Jiwani and Young 2006).

The connections between sex, race, gender, colonialism, and settler colonialism reveal mechanisms of social control in ongoing representations of Indigenous women in Canadian anti-violence campaigns as well as in Canada's response to growing awareness of such violence and discrimination.

Settler Colonial State-Building, Benevolence, and Representations of Indigenous Women

Settler colonialism is an ongoing pursuit within Canadian state-building practices and the continued process of settling Canada's socio-legal and political systems through ongoing structured dispossession (Morgensen 2011; Veracini 2011; Tuck and Yang 2012). Such dispossession relies on racialized, gendered, economic, and political domination that seeks to eliminate Indigenous Peoples from the land (Coulthard 2014).

According to Arvin, Tuck, and Morrill (2013: 12), settler colonialism is

> a persistent social and political formation in which newcomers/colonizers/settlers come to a place, claim it as their own, and do whatever it takes to disappear the Indigenous peoples that are there. Within settler colonialism, it is exploitation of land that yields supreme value. In order for settlers to usurp the land and extract its value, Indigenous peoples must be destroyed, removed, and made into ghosts.

Representations of missing and murdered Indigenous women have been used historically to justify Indigenous dispossession while also reinforcing contemporary settler colonial mechanisms of social control over Indigenous lands and lives through "**white possessive logics**" (Moreton-Robinson 2015).

Scholars taking their lead from Indigenous feminists understand that violence against Indigenous women is a continuation of colonial policies and processes of elimination (Dean 2015; Kaye 2017); their theorizing challenges assumptions of Canada's benevolence, neutrality, and democracy, and they bring attention to the connections between colonial notions of the land as "empty" (*terra nullius*) and the genocidal intent of ongoing settler policies and targeted efforts to erase Indigenous Peoples, particularly Indigenous women (i.e., *humanitus nullius*) (Thobani 2012). As Kahnawà:ke Mohawk scholar Audra Simpson (2014b) explains:

> In spite of the innocence of the story that Canada likes to tell about itself: that it is a place of immigrant and settler founding; that in this, it is a place that somehow escapes the ugliness of history. That it is a

place that reconciles, that apologizes ... Canada is just quite simply a settler society. A settler society [whose] multicultural, liberal, and democratic structure and performance of governance seeks an ongoing settling of land. This settling is not, of course, innocent either. It is dispossession: the taking of our land from us. And, it is ongoing. It is killing our women in order to do so; and [it] has historically done this to do so.

The story of Canadian "innocence" underpins the structure of settler colonialism and cements a certain version of truth, power, and knowledge that maintains social control. Drawing upon the work of Foucault, social constructionists recognize that "knowledge is not just a reflection of reality. Truth is a discursive construction and different regimes of knowledge determine what is true and false" (Jorgensen and Phillips 2002:13). This colonial narrative offers Canadians a one-sided version of "truth" that aligns with and supports Canada's ongoing control and regulation of self-determining Indigenous nations.

Contested "Truths"

The concepts of "truth telling" and "reconciliation" have become familiar terms within Canada's socio-political consciousness and are a cornerstone of the National Inquiry into Missing and Murdered Indigenous Women's and Girls. Two of the most influential catalysts for this discursive shift were the creation of the Truth and Reconciliation Commission (TRC) of Canada in 2008 and the resulting ninety-four calls to action in 2015.

Truth-telling commissions are not unique to Canada. Such commissions have been used to uncover state atrocities in various parts of the world, including South Africa, Peru, Uruguay, and Liberia. In Canada, the TRC was established with the mandate to document and uncover the "truth" behind the country's history of the "aggressive project of assimilation" of the Indian residential school system (IRS) (TRC 2015). Even though the Canadian government formally apologized in 2008 for its role in the creation and operations in the residential school system, their contrition came only after hundreds of IRS Survivors came forward with stories of abuse and demanded that the Canadian government take responsibility for the intergenerational devastation associated with the forced incarceration of Indigenous children in the IRS system (Government of Canada 2008; Manuel and Derrickson 2017; James 2012).

Canada's decision to establish the TRC emerged only after IRS Survivors and their families filed a class-action law suit against the Canadian state and won. Consequently, the commission was tasked with witnessing and collecting thousands of IRS Survivors' stories and experiences related to state-sponsored acts of genocide. One of the underlying public assumptions related to such commissions is that educating members of Canadian society of historical and contemporary wrongs inflicted upon Indigenous Peoples, and uncovering "truth," will disrupt and transform the social, economic, political, and cultural structures and processes from which violence and oppression emanates. However, as James (2012: 2) notes, this process raises "general doubts about possible limitations of victim-centred approaches in contexts where the perpetrators and beneficiaries of the injustices continue to be socially dominant."

In this context, some have argued that awareness raising should not take place alongside the further exploitation of those participating in such inquiries. This requires trauma-informed processes that create spaces for healing while addressing systemic forms of violence. Further, it has been argued that Indigenous women should not have to be responsible for educating non-Indigenous women about the trauma that colonization has caused in their lives — an expectation that is exhausting and retraumatizing for them. Rather, the responsibility to learn about and become aware of such systemic violence falls on non-Indigenous Canadians to research and seek out themselves.

In a context in which Indigenous women are both disproportionately criminalized and under-protected by police, there is a colonial dimension to the process by which non-Indigenous Canadians are becoming aware of the systemic violence that Indigenous communities have known and spoken about for decades. The reality remains that almost a century of government initiatives, reports, and recommendations have done little to disrupt the ways in which social, political, legal, and economic oppression is produced and reproduced within settler colonial states such as Canada. Challenges to systemic forms of violence, including contesting the white, heteronormative, colonial, and patriarchal systems of domination on which the colonial relationship is predicated threatens settler colonialism (Coulthard 2014). In turn, the state's refusal to participate in anything but symbolic recognition is indicative of its unwillingness to make space for meaningful and transformative change. As such, these types of commissions have, thus far, only served to offer symbolic reversals of settler colonial power relations (see section on Inquiries and "Fact" Collection as Technologies of Settler Colonial Social Control).

While such reports and apologies acknowledge the historical harms inflicted on Indigenous Peoples and communities, the focus often reverts back to century-old attempts to fix the "Indian problem" via statements of reconciliation and calls for Indigenous communities and individuals to "heal themselves" — seldom, if ever, acknowledging that structures in society that produce extreme violence remain intact to this day. For example, over a decade prior to the release of the TRC report in 2015, the Royal Canadian Mounted Police commissioner offered an apology for the role that they played in the residential school system. It reads:

> While such reports and apologies acknowledge the historical harms inflicted on Indigenous Peoples and communities, the focus often reverts back to century-old attempts to fix the "Indian problem" via statements of reconciliation and calls for Indigenous communities and individuals to "heal themselves" — seldom, if ever, acknowledging that structures in society that produce extreme violence remain intact to this day.

> Many aboriginal people have found the courage to step outside of that legacy of this terrible chapter in Canadian history to share their stories.... To those of you who suffered tragedies at residential schools, we are very sorry for your experience.... Canadians can never forget what happened and they never should. The RCMP is optimistic that we can all work together to learn from this residential school system experience and ensure that it never happens again. The RCMP is committed to working with aboriginal people to continue the healing process. Your communities deserve better choices and better chances. Knowing the past, we must all turn to the future and build a brighter future for all our children. We, I, as Commissioner of the RCMP, am truly sorry for what role we played in the residential school system and the abuse that took place in that system. (Royal Canadian Mounted Police 2004)

Despite the seemingly sympathetic rhetoric from government and police, this statement moves from apology to a commitment to "working with Aboriginal people to heal." Regan (2010: 59) argues that "when non-Native Canadians talk about reconciliation ... the tendency is to speak solely of the need for Native people to heal themselves and reconcile with us, so that the country can put this history behind it and move forward." In other words, the RCMP statement simply apologized for their role in residential schools, while never acknowledging that the system in which it operates continue to function in similar ways.

In 2009, one year after the Canadian government's apology for the role in residential schools, then-prime minister Stephen Harper declared to an international audience at the G20 summit that "Canada has no history of colonialism" (O'Keefe 2009). These types of statements are not uncommon, and in fact frame Indigenous dispossession and subjugation as "liberation" evolving from the labour and sacrifices of "hard working pioneers" (Moreton-Robinson 2015: 6). It conceals ongoing settler colonial regulation of Indigenous lives and lands by reinforcing archaic discourses of social evolution where notions of social, technological, and material progress are associated with white supremacy and the fallacy that "the West provided the best model of living" (McCallum 2014).

Despite the Canadian government's recent push toward reconciliation, this national narrative continues to offer a type of surface-level recognition that, while acknowledging historical Indigenous trauma as a result of the IRS system, ignores contemporary state policies and practices of Indigenous child apprehension, incarceration, and violence against Indigenous women and girls (TRC 2015). Tanana Athabascan scholar Dian Million (2013: 178) intersects **Indigenous feminism** with a Foucauldian analysis of "biopolitics" and argues that such a "therapeutic ethos has often lent itself to a reconciliation that does not change the colonial structures but adapts the colonized to the colonial systems as they change." This means that the continued state recognition of Indigenous Peoples' trauma is falsely portrayed as a natural outcome of colonial *legacies* rather than an ongoing function of settler colonial policies.

The second factor that reinforces the narrative of Canadian benevolence is the portrayal of Indigenous women as "at risk" of facing violence (Clark 2016). Depictions of Indigenous women as "at risk" parallel often-cited representations of a "colonized other," which have been firmly critiqued in the post- and anticolonial literature. As Moreton-Robinson (2015: xii) argues, such representations "portray Indigenous peoples as a deficit model of humanity ... overrepresented as always lacking, dysfunctional, alcoholic, violent, needy, and lazy." For example, as Kaye (2017) details, Canadian anti-trafficking discourses portray Indigenous women simultaneously as "at risk" and as a "risky other," justifying rescue-driven models of intervention alongside **carceral systems** of criminalization and control. The rhetoric of state benevolence, however, has always been juxtaposed in colonial Canada against the "uncivilized" and infantilized positioning of Indigenous Peoples, particularly in the criminal justice system (Erikson 2011).

Along these lines, initial representations of MMIWG emphasized violence against Indigenous women as a *legacy* of colonization. As Kaye (2017: 5) details, "violence against Indigenous women informs many claims for recognition in Canada that, in turn, reinforce the power of the settler colonial state, reify the state as saviour, and undermine alternatives to state mechanisms of justice." Razack (2002: 10) argues that contemporary forms of colonial empire are "a structure of a feeling, a deeply held belief in the need to and the right to dominate others *for their own good*, others who are expected to be grateful." Rather than addressing the root causes of targeted violence, protecting Indigenous women *for their own good* generally reinforces settler colonial strategies of social control and increases forms and technologies of surveillance, which includes the over-policing of Indigenous and underprivileged communities and results in the hypervisibility and over-criminalization of Indigenous women living in these communities. Such was the treatment of Angela Cardinal who — in the absence of suitable housing — suffered from consistent sleep deprivation and lack of food; yet, far from receiving support and compassion, she was treated with criminal distain and forced to testify in shackles against the man who violently attacked and sexually assaulted her.

Through ongoing characterizations of Indigenous women as "at risk," "in need," or "somehow lacking," colonial representations produce and compel the obligations of supposed state benevolence in the form of intervention, rescue, and aid. In such representations, Indigenous women are naturalized as being in need and dysfunctional, while state intervenors are warranted increased powers of intervention and control. However, while such representations remain dominant, truth telling also necessitates ongoing disruptions in settler colonial logics of elimination that produce the conditions whereby Indigenous women and girls — such as Tina Fontaine and Cindy Gladue — are murdered with impunity (Hunt 2014; Macdonald 2015; Kaye 2017). The conditions of continuous displacement through structured dispossession fail to draw attention in anti-violence interventions, which too often emphasize heightened forms of policing, monitoring, and control. Anti-violence intervention must reckon with state-based violence and legal policies that naturalize ongoing forms of victimization and criminalization of Indigenous women.

Inquiries and "Fact" Collection as Technologies of Settler Colonial Social Control

In the context of truth and reconciliation, "Indigenous trauma" is an ever-expanding target of public inquiry in which the discourse of healing and forgiveness dominate while Indigenous dispossession and state-sponsored acts of genocide are ignored (James 2012: 17). Commissioned research projects

and government initiatives provide "solutions" to Indigenous Peoples' disparities in Canada. In particular, three major projects demonstrate the extent to
which researchers, government, and other interest groups have tried to educate
and bring awareness to the disparities that exist between Indigenous and
non-Indigenous peoples.

Hawthorne Recommendations

In 1966–67, anthropologist Harry B. Hawthorne submitted a two-vol-
ume report to the Department of Indian Affairs entitled *A Survey of the
Contemporary Indians of Canada: Economic, Political, Educational Needs and
Policies*. The report, according to Hawthorne (1967: 5), was intended to
nationally examine the "contemporary situation of the Indians of Canada
with a view to understanding the difficulties they faced in overcoming some
pressing problems and their many ramifications." The study aimed to catalogue the effects of Canada's aggressive assimilationist policies, found within
the *Indian Act*, and to "understand" the scope of the "Indian" problem and
"improve the outcomes" of Canada's policies toward Indigenous Peoples. In
the report, Hawthorne and his colleagues concluded that Indigenous Peoples
were treated as "citizens minus" (Hawthorne 1967: 6). Indigenous Peoples
were the most socially, politically, and economically disadvantaged population
within the country, due to decades of failed government policies, including
the residential school system. Recommendations emerging from the report
included calls for the Canadian government to stop all assimilationist policies
and recognize "that Indians can and should retain the special privileges of
their status while enjoying full participation as provincial and federal citizens"
(Hawthorne 1967: 7).

Royal Commission on Aboriginal Peoples (RCAP)

Thirty years after the Hawthorne report, the Royal Commission on Aboriginal
Peoples (1996) released a four-thousand-page document and 440 recommendations in an effort to repair the "relationship" and bridge the socioeconomic
disparities that exist between Indigenous and non-Indigenous Peoples in
Canada after a tense standoff between the people of Kanehsatà:ke, the Sûreté
du Québec, and the Canadian Army, infamously referred to as the Oka Crisis
(see the National Film Board's *270 Years of Resistance*). The report identified
colonialism as a major contributing factor to the disparities that exist between
Indigenous and non-Indigenous peoples across the country, highlighting the
need for national healing and government reparations.

Truth and Reconciliation Commission (TRC) of Canada

Nearly two decades after the RCAP, the TRC (2015) was established as a residential school "truth-seeking" initiative aimed at acknowledging the injustices of the past and "reconciling for the future." It was to explore Canada's legacy of residential school policies and their intergenerational effects on Indigenous Peoples in another effort to repair and bridge the relationships between Indigenous Peoples and their non-Indigenous counterparts through education and understanding.

Reports, articles, and documents that date prior to the nineteenth century emphasize Indigenous Peoples' "dysfunction" and "their" need to heal, but this continued focus on responsibilized forms of "healing" obscures the ways in which the state remains complicit in the silencing and marginalization of Indigenous Peoples. Alongside such reports, the Supreme Court of Canada has identified ongoing systemic discrimination against Indigenous people within the legal system. However, at this point, the Canadian courts and the government of Canada have not provided any transformative and meaningful remedies to address such inequalities (LSC 2015). Reports into the issue of missing and murdered Indigenous women and girls further reveal this disconnect.

The Legal Strategy Coalition (LSC) on Violence Against Indigenous Women examined over two decades of reports and recommendations regarding violence against Indigenous women. The review of fifty-eight reports containing over seven hundred recommendations found that only a few of the recommendations had been fully implemented (Feinstein and Pearce 2015). The Inter-American Commission on Human Rights further documented the legal obligation of Canada, in accordance with international law, to enact preventative measures that address the ongoing systemic and structural inequalities facing Indigenous women in the country. Yet, as the LSC's submission to the United Nations Special Rapporteur on violence against women states, "while there is a general consensus about the root causes of violence against Indigenous women, there has been a complete failure to plan or implement the necessary responses to address the crisis" (LSC 2015: 2). Thus, in spite of growing recognition, a plethora of recommendations on prevention and causes, as well as international legal obligations, many academics, researchers, and government agencies have simply continued to

> Reports, articles, and documents that date prior to the nineteenth century emphasize Indigenous Peoples' "dysfunction" and "their" need to heal, but this continued focus on responsibilized forms of "healing" obscures the ways in which the state remains complicit in the silencing and marginalization of Indigenous Peoples.

push for yet another government-funded "fact-finding" initiative to uncover the "truth" underlying incidences of missing and murdered women in settler colonial Canada.

MMIWG National Commission of Inquiry

Discourses about violence against Indigenous women, including the establishment of the National Inquiry into Missing and Murdered Indigenous Women and Girls (MMIWG), are imbued with a mandate to air the "truth." The inquiry claims that a "truth-telling" approach will "educate the public, to facilitate healing of traumatized communities, to restore public confidence in institutions that have been seriously damaged in the eyes of Canadians, and to make recommendations for action and policy reform aimed at effecting real changes to make Indigenous women and girls safe, sacred, honoured and empowered" (MMIWG-FFADA 2016). However, such an undertaking closely resembles previous government attempts to rectify injustices of the past and promote healing by drawing on personal narratives of Indigenous suffering, trauma, and dysfunction.

After decades of Indigenous advocacy and continued efforts to make the lives of Indigenous women and girls matter to the Canadian government, the Liberal Party of Canada announced the launch of a national inquiry into MMIWG in 2016. The launch was met with widespread support from provinces and territories, each establishing orders in council. However, concerns regarding the implementation became immediately evident. The NWAC, Feminist Alliance for International Action (FAFIA) Canada, and Amnesty International expressed concern that the terms of reference were not explicitly guided by a human rights framework. Although later publications by the national inquiry refer to human rights, such references did not offer a human rights framework (LSC 2015). The CEDAW (2015) further recommended a rights-based approach in order to ensure the mandate addresses the role of policing and public complaints commissions. Even though the inquiry was required to examine the systemic causes of violence against Indigenous women, the mandate made no particular reference to critique the police or criminal justice system, even though police and criminal justice systems worsen violence faced by Indigenous women (see Box 12-5).

Throughout the pre-inquiry process, the families and advocates of missing and murdered Indigenous women raised the importance of scrutinizing policing and the criminal justice system. Some thought the omission from the terms of reference of investigating police was a diplomatic choice that would allow the commission to establish a broad mandate; others, however, raised concern that police might avoid scrutiny from that mandate. In the end, scrutiny of policing in MMIWG cases remained unclear in the implementation of the national inquiry, and since the final inquiry report was published, families have continued to be troubled. For example, some MMIWG families voiced alarm after being contacted by policing agencies in response to referrals submitted by the national inquiry without communication with the families. Senior CBC correspondent Neil Macdonald (2016) responded to public debate about the role of the commission in investigating the police, highlighting that the epidemic of MMIWG occurs in a context where police have been part of the violence toward Indigenous people and where Indigenous women have been disproportionately criminalized.

CEDAW (2015) clearly identified the importance of independent reviews of individual cases, particularly for those involving allegations of police bias or inadequacies. However, rather than establishing an independent review or monitoring of families and survivors with concerns about policing, their cases have been referred back to the very authorities responsible for discriminatory treatment in victims' services in their provinces or territories.

Past inquiries have identified the importance of continuous dialogue with affected communities in formulating the inquiry process. In particular, following the Missing Women Inquiry of British Columbia and the *Forsaken* report (see Oppal 2012), the British Columbia Civil Liberties Association noted the importance of consultation with marginalized communities as well as with organizations that support them at every stage. In spite of such lessons learned, the national inquiry demonstrated poor transparency and communications with communities and families of MMIWG from the outset.

By May 2017, civil society organizations, some of the families and survivors of MMIWG, Two-Spirit community members, and concerned individuals had written an open letter to Chief Commissioner Marion Buller to express their growing concern and crisis of confidence in the direction of the inquiry. The letter specifically flagged the restricted role and the limited information they were able to obtain from the national inquiry:

> We are deeply concerned with the continued lack of communication that is causing anxiety, frustration, confusion, and disappointment in this long-awaited process. We request that you, as the leader of this Inquiry, substantially rework your approach in order to regain trust and ensure that families are no longer feeling re-traumatized in this process. (Culbert 2017: 2)

The process of truth-gathering methods adopted by this inquiry forms a colonial mechanism of raising awareness among non-Indigenous Canadians about systemic injustice, but it does so at the expense of people living the various forms of systemic inequality by failing to address the ongoing nature of the violence and retraumatizing families and communities in the process of recording the violence they continue to face.

A number of senior-level resignations further pointed toward instability within the inquiry's efforts, including the exiting of Commissioner Marilyn Poitras in July of 2017 as well as the director of communications, two executive directors, the lead commission counsel, the director of research, and others. Upon resigning, Poitras revealed the following:

> The model that we're using has legal counsel driving it with an old traditional commission model of setting up hearings. The traditional colonial style says, "You go in, you have a hearing, people come and tell you their problems and you figure it out." ... My main concern is that this commission is going down a tried road. We've been studied, we've been researched, we've gone and looked at Indians and half-breeds and Inuit people for a long time to see what's the problem.... You tell us your sad story and we'll figure out what to do with you. And we're headed down that same path. And if it worked, we would all be so fixed and healthy by now. It doesn't work. (Walsh 2015: 9)

Poitras' comments point out that a "truth-gathering" exercise reproduces colonial systems of domination. Within such processes, "Native peoples become marked as national wounds requiring healing rather than as nations requiring decolonization" (Million 2013, as discussed in Kaye 2017:114). The process of truth-gathering methods adopted by this inquiry forms a colonial mechanism of raising awareness among non-Indigenous Canadians about systemic injustice, but it does so at the expense of people living the various forms of systemic inequality by failing to address the ongoing nature of the violence and retraumatizing families and communities in the process of recording the violence they continue to face.

Within the "truth gathering" methods of family and survivor hearings, many families and survivors confirmed well-known findings that police and criminal justice systems require scrutiny. Such "truths" were shared at risk of the safety, well-being, and security of the families, some of whom later identified that their cases were directly harmed by the sharing of their truths on the national stage. Similar to many reports and inquiries of the past, this national

> **Box 12-5: What Is a National Commission of Inquiry?**
>
> National commissions of inquiry are federally established investigations into issues of national importance. Federal inquiries are established under terms set out in the *Inquiries Act*, which gives the federal Cabinet power and discretion to establish an inquiry at any time. Cabinet also has the discretion to determine the inquiry's subject and scope. The Act is broad and provides flexibility and creativity in designing the inquiry process and methods. This is intended to ensure that an inquiry is a meaningful and sensitive process. However, it also requires that early and thorough research and consultation inform the inquiry's design to facilitate and support a fair, responsive, and effective process.
>
> See the FAQs Sheet on National Inquiries prepared by the Legal Strategy Coalition on Violence Against Indigenous Women (2016).

inquiry acknowledged injustices of the past and recognized the connections between historical and contemporary oppression, but it did little to disrupt the ways in which truth and power are produced and reproduced within the context of settler colonialism. In turn, systemic and material violence against Indigenous women continues at alarming rates.

Refusal and Resistance to Social Control

In a context of settler colonialism, national commissions of inquiry remain inevitably tied to the national, racial, and gendered priorities of the state. Although the *Inquiries Act* provides ample room for creativity and flexibly in the design and implementation of national inquiries, to date, inquiry processes in Canada have maintained a "truth-gathering" methodology that renders the *subjects* of inquiry passive participants in the process rather than engaging them as members of the community. While inquiries continue to examine incidences of missing and murdered women, such reports rarely speak of Indigenous women's resistance and stories of survival within the context of violent oppression. While some might argue that resistance falls outside of the scope of such reports, inquires, and commissions, the grand narrative that emerges is that Indigenous women are vulnerable, are victims, and are highly susceptible to violence, and, even worse, the public, government, police, and their own communities do not care. Significantly, this grand narrative ignores the primary sources of harm to Indigenous women, such as ongoing acts of genocide, as well as settler colonial violence and racism that are upheld at every stage of the criminal justice system and are evident in investigations of mmiwg. This is problematic because survivors of violence and their families, friends, and related interest groups have fought for decades to recentre Indigenous women's

In a settler colonial context, discourses of therapy and healing are used to **responsibilize** Indigenous women and girls, where the onus is on them to heal themselves while white, heteronormative, patriarchal systems of domination that produce such violence remain fully intact and unchallenged.

lives and legacies in relationships of resistance, in a concerted effort to decolonize through processes of reclamation. Families and communities have fought to keep the memories of their loved ones alive, arguing that each was more than a statistic (see Box 12-6).

The dominant narrative of Indigenous women and girls' vulnerability and victimhood raises critical questions regarding how distorted versions of "truth" produce and reproduce systems of domination through interlocking discursive representations of Indigenous women generally and missing, murdered, and disappeared Indigenous women specifically. Such a limited perspective reproduces settler colonial mechanisms of social control through public displays of highly traumatic personal narratives that often reinforce archaic and stereotypical understandings of Indigenous suffering and victimhood (see Box 12-7). For example, historical examinations have consistently revealed how Canadian state agencies such as the Department of Indian Affairs utilized surveillance, punishment, and discipline to regulate Indigenous women and girls when they failed to conform to the white, heteronormative, and patriarchal standards imposed by colonists (Sangster 1999; Lawrence 2003). In a settler colonial context, discourses of therapy and healing are used to **responsibilize** Indigenous women and girls, where the onus is on them to heal themselves while white, heteronormative, patriarchal systems of domination that produce such violence remain fully intact and unchallenged.

As such, scholars and advocates have resisted simplistic images of "victims" and instead raise the question: How can resistance be applied to recentre the complexities of Indigenous women's identities within the context of violent oppression? In *The History of Sexuality*, Foucault (1990: 95) says, "where there is power, there is resistance," meaning that power is not always repressive or inescapable, but rather that power is created and re-created through social relations, though internal and external struggle, and it is reified through

---

Box 12-6: Shades of Our Sisters

An exhibit and online experience co-created by the families of MMIWG that shares the memory of their loved ones and what the loss of their life means. Shades of our Sisters takes audiences through "grief, laughter and love of these families; challenging Canadians to realize the injustice of this national tragedy."

Box 12-7: ReMatriate

The ReMatriate Collective provides an ongoing online campaign to combat stereotypes and appropriation by portraying Indigenous women through empowered lenses of self-determination. The platform features images of Indigenous women portraying situations in which they feel empowered, as they finish the sentence, "We are...." Responses are varied, such as "We are strong women," "We are the resistance," and "We are working on the future of decolonial ceremonies."

discourse. In the context of settler colonialism, Indigenous women's resistance exists alongside and within state building technologies of social control. Anticolonial and decolonial theories are useful for highlighting such resistance because it allows Indigenous women and girls to transcend the boundaries of vulnerability and victimhood and cast a "gaze upon race and racialization process[es]" that intersect with settler colonial systems of power, domination and mechanisms of social control (Dei and Asgharzadeh 2001: 300). Such a positioning pushes back against simplistic images that set Indigenous women as individual "problems" that require healing and therapy, instead re-centring systems of domination — including patriarchy, racism, settler colonialism, and misogyny — as overarching societal problems needing to be eradicated. Such a stance requires active resistance through ongoing refusals.

Refusal, according to Simpson (2014b: 11) "[is] a political and ethical stance that stands in stark contrast to the desire to have one's distinctiveness as a culture, as a people, recognized. Refusal comes with the requirement of having one's *political* sovereignty acknowledged and upheld, and raises the question of legitimacy for those who are usually in the position of recognizing." In the context of settler colonial social control and representations of violence against Indigenous women, the act of "refusal" turns the gaze away from Indigenous women themselves and instead focuses on disrupting and challenging the ongoing legitimacy of white supremacy, patriarchy, heteronormativity, and misogyny within settler colonial Canada by asking: "What is wrong with Canada that it continues to allow colonial gender violence against Indigenous women to occur?" A refusal to engage in settler colonial narratives that pathologize Indigenous women and further blames them for their own victimization. Such rhetoric has only been used to further Canada's nation-building project at the continued expense of Indigenous women's bodies, lives, and livelihoods.

As Sarah Hunt (2013: 1) states:

Transforming our dehumanization must move beyond just poster campaigns and court cases, because their ability to enact change only goes so far. I believe it is only through building stronger relationships with one another, across the generations and across differences in education, ability, sexuality and other social locations, that we can break down the stigma and shame resulting from generations of colonial violence. As we reinstate the roles of women and two-spirit people in systems of Indigenous governance and law, ending gendered violence can be understood as integral to self-determination.

This is a substantive shift in questioning, and it requires that intersectional relationships of resistance are in place to begin stripping away the structures and colonial logics that reproduce systems of power, domination, and a pervasive culture of violence.

Discussion Questions

1. What are the implications of thinking about violence against Indigenous women as a *legacy* of colonialism compared to an *ongoing* form of colonial gendered violence?
2. How does an understanding of the politics of recognition inform representations of Indigenous women in a settler colonial context?
3. What are the transformative possibilities of a culture rooted in violent dispossession and continuing through settler colonial forms of oppression?

Recommended Resources

Chimamanda Ngozi Adichie, TED Global 2009, "The Danger of a Single Story."

Christine Welsh, "Finding Dawn," National Film Board.

Tasha Hubbard and Marilyn Poitras, "7 Minutes" short video.

LEAF. Legal Strategy Coalition on Violence Against Indigenous Women (LSC): <leaf.ca/legal/legal-strategy-coalition-on-violence-against-indigenous-women-lsc/>

Shades of Our Sisters: <shadesofoursisters.com/>.

Alanis Obomsawin, *Kanehsatake: 270 Years of Resistance*. National Film Board.

Glossary

carceral systems: institutions, such as prisons and jails, and systems of justice characterized by intense surveillance, punitive power, discipline, and imprisonment.

Indigenous feminism: a critical paradigm that examines and interrogates the intersections between sex, race, gender, Indigeneity, and nation. The focus of its analysis is on the dynamics that negatively affect Indigenous women.

politics of recognition: how individual and collective identities are shaped through the process of state acknowledgment; the recognition of identities is constructed as a gateway to social, political, and institutional acceptance.

responsibilization: a process strongly associated with neoliberal politics that pressures individuals to take personal responsibility for the choices they make and the outcomes of their own lives. This is in contrast to a model under a social welfare state, in which the state provides public goods and a social safety net and is made responsible for collective outcomes (Wakefield and Fleming 2009).

settler colonialism: an ongoing social, political, and economic societal structure that occurs when newcomers/colonizers/settlers come to a place that is inhabited by Indigenous nations and claim the land as their own. For newcomers/settlers/colonizers to pursue ownership over the land, Indigenous Peoples must disappear. According to Maille et al. (2013), "Within settler colonialism, exploitation of land yields supreme value. In order for settlers to usurp the land and extract its value, Indigenous peoples must be destroyed, removed, and made into ghosts." Note: settler colonialism cannot be isolated from other social processes of racism, sexism, patriarchy, misogyny, and gendered violence.

white possessive logics: a type of rationalization supported by white patriarchal notions of property and possession which reasserts the nation-state's ownership, control, and domination of Indigenous lands (see Aileen Moreton-Robinson 2015).

References

Amnesty International. 2004. "Stolen Sisters: A Human Rights Response to Discrimination and Violence Against Indigenous Women in Canada." October. <amnesty.ca/sites/amnesty/files/amr200032004enstolensisters.pdf>.
Amnesty International. 2014. "Human Rights Now: 'I Want Canadians to Care' — a

Conversation with Bev Jacobs." <amnesty.ca/blog/%E2%80%9Ci-want-canadians-to-care%E2%80%9D-a-conversation-with-bev-jacobs>.

Arvin, Maile, Eve Tuck, and Angie Morrill. 2013. "Decolonizing Feminism: Challenging Connections between Settler Colonialism and Heteropatriarchy." *Feminist Formations* 25, 1.

Boutilier, Alex. 2014. "Native Teen's Slaying a 'Crime,' Not a 'Sociological Phenomenon,' Stephen Harper Says," *Toronto Star*, August 21. <thestar.com/news/canada/2014/08/21/native_teens_slaying_a_crime_not_a_sociological_phenomenon_stephen_harper_says.html>.

Clark, Natalie. 2016. "Shock and Awe: Trauma as the New Colonial Frontier." *Humanities* 5, 1.

Collier, Roger. 2017. "Reports of Coerced Sterilization of Indigenous Women in Canada Mirrors Shameful Past." *Canadian Medical Association Journal* 189, 33.

CEDAW (Committee on the Elimination of Discrimination against Women). 2015. *Report of the Inquiry Concerning Canada of the Committee on the Elimination of Discrimination against Women under Article 8 of the Optional Protocol to the Convention on the Elimination of All Forms of Discrimination against Women*. CEDAW.

Coulthard, Glen. 2014. *Red Skin, White Masks: Rejecting the Colonial Politics of Recognition*. Minneapolis: University of Minnesota Press.

Culbert, Lori. 2017. "Indigenous Families, Without Answers for so Many Years, Frustrated by Slow Start at Federal Inquiry." *The Province*. <theprovince.com/news/local-news/indigenous-families-without-answers-for-so-many-years-frustrated-by-slow-start-at-federal-inquiry>.

Dean, Amber. 2015. *Remembering Vancouver's Disappeared Women: Settler Colonialism and the Difficulty of Inheritance*. Toronto: University of Toronto Press.

Dei, George Sefa, and Alireza Asgharzadeh. 2001. "The Power of Social Theory: The Anti-Colonial Discursive Framework." *Journal of Educational Thought* 35, 3.

Eberts, Mary. 2014. "Victoria's Secret: How to Make a Population of Prey." In Joyce Green (ed.), *Indivisible: Indigenous Human Rights*. Winnipeg: Fernwood Publishing.

Erickson, Lesley. 2011. *Westward Bound: Sex, Violence, the Law, and the Making of a Settler Society*. Vancouver: UBC Press.

FAFIA (Canadian Feminist Alliance for International Action) and NWAC (Native Women's Association of Canada). 2015. "Murders and Disappearances of Aboriginal Women and Girls Report to the Human Rights Committee."

Feinstein, Pippa, and Megan Pearce. 2015. *Violence against Indigenous Women and Girls in Canada: Review of Reports and Recommendations — Executive Summary*. February 26.

Foucault, Michel. 1990. *The History of Sexuality: An Introduction*. New York: Random House.

Government of Canada. 2014. "Invisible Women: A Call to Action, A Report on Missing and Murdered Indigenous Women in Canada." Report of the Special Committee on Violence Against Indigenous Women." <publications.gc.ca/collections/collection_2014/parl/xc2-411/XC2-411-2-1-1-eng.pdf>.

____. 2008. Prime Minister Harper Offers Full Apology on Behalf of Canadians for the Indian Residential Schools System. June 11. <canada.ca/en/news/archive/2008/06/prime-minister-harper-offers-full-apology-behalf-canadians-indian-residential-schools-system.html>.

Hawthorne, Harry. 1967. "A Survey of the Contemporary Indians of Canada Economic, Political, Educational Needs and Policies: Part 2." Indian and Northern Affairs Canada.

Hill Collins, Patricia. 2009. *Black Feminist Thought: Knowledge, Consciousness, and the Politics of Empowerment*. New York: Routledge Publishing.

Hugill, David. 2014. "Dazed, Dangerous, and Dissolute: Media Representations of Street-Level Sex Workers in Vancouver's Downtown Eastside." In G. Balfour and E. Comack (eds.), *Criminalizing Women: Gender and (In)justice in Neo-Liberal Times*, 2nd edition. Winnipeg: Fernwood Publishing.

Human Rights Watch. 2013. "Those Who Take Us Away: Abusive Policing and Failures in Protection of Indigenous Women and Girls in Northern British Columbia, Canada." <hrw.org/report/2013/02/13/those-who-take-us-away/abusive-policing-and-failures-protection-indigenous-women>.

Hunt, Sarah. 2014. "Mourning Carries Us Like a Current," *Voices Rising*. February 14. <nationsrising.org/mourning-carries-us-like-a-current/>

____. 2013. "More than a Poster Campaign: Redefining Colonial Violence." *Decolonization: Indigeneity, Education & Society*, February 14. <decolonization.wordpress.com/2013/02/14/more-than-a-poster-campaign-redefining-colonial-violence/>.

James, Matt. 2012. "A Carnival of Truth? Knowledge, Ignorance and the Canadian Truth and Reconciliation Commission." *International Journal of Transitional Justice* 6.

Jiwani, Yasmin, and Mary Lynn Young. 2006. "Missing and Murdered Women: Reproducing Marginality in News Discourse." *Canadian Journal of Communication* 31, 4.

Johnson, Janice. 2017. "'I'm the Victim and I'm in Shackles:' Edmonton Women Jailed While Testifying Against Her Attacker." CBC News, June. <cbc.ca/news/canada/edmonton/sex-assault-victim-jailed-judge-edmonton-1.4140533>.

Jorgensen, Marianne, and Louise Phillips. 2002. *Discourse as Analysis and Theory*, London: Sage Publications.

Kaye, Julie. 2017. *Responding to Human Trafficking: Dispossession, Colonial Violence, and Resistance Among Indigenous and Racialized Women*. University of Toronto Press.

Kaye, Julie, and Daniel Béland. 2014. "Stephen Harper's Dangerous Refusal to 'Commit Sociology.'" *Toronto Star*, August 22. <thestar.com/opinion/commentary/2014/08/22/stephen_harpers_dangerous_refusal_to_commit_sociology.html>.

LaRocque, Emma. 1994. *Violence in Aboriginal Communities*. Ottawa: National Clearinghouse on Family Violence.

Lavell-Harvard, D. Memee, and Jennifer Brant. 2016. *Forever Loved: Exposing the Hidden Crisis of Missing and Murdered Indigenous Women and Girls in Canada*. Bradford: Demeter Press.

Lawrence, Bonita. 2003. "Gender, Race, and the Regulation of Native Identity in Canada and the United States: An Overview." *Hypatia* 18, 2.

LSC (Legal Strategy Coalition). 2015. "Frequently Asked Questions Resource on Public Inquiries." <leaf.ca/wp-content/uploads/2016/01/LEAF-Legal-Strategy-Coalition-FAQs-re-MMIW-inquiry.pdf>.

Macdonald, Neil. 2016. "Analysis: Justice for Families Requires MMIW Inquiry Investigate Role of Police." CBC News. <cbc.ca/news/politics/murdered-missing-inquiry-macdonald-1.3743744>.

____. 2015. "Welcome to Winnipeg: Where Canada's Racism Problem Is at Its Worst."

Maclean's 128, 4.

Mallea, Paula. 2010. "The Fear Factor Stephen Harper's 'Tough on Crime' Agenda." Canadian Center for Policy Alternatives. <policyalternatives.ca/sites/default/files/uploads/publications/National%20Office/2010/11/Tough%20on%20Crime.pdf>.

Manuel, Arthur, and Ronald Derrickson. 2017. *The Reconciliation Manifesto: Recovering the Land and Rebuilding the Economy*. Toronto: James Lorimer & Company.

McCallum, Mary Jane Logan. 2014. *Indigenous Women, Work and History 1940–1980*. Winnipeg: University of Manitoba Press.

Micner, Tamara. 2017. "'All of a Sudden It Matters': Facing Up to Canada's 1,200 Missing Women." *Prospect*. <prospectmagazine.co.uk/politics/all-of-a-sudden-it-matters-facing-up-to-canadas-1200-missing-women>.

Million, Dian. 2013. *Therapeutic Nations: Healing in an Age of Indigenous Human Rights*. Tucson: University of Arizona Press.

MMIWG-FFADA. 2016. Home page. <mmiwg-ffada.ca/>.

Moreton-Robinson, Aileen. 2015. *The White Possessive: Property, Power, and Indigenous Sovereignty*. Minneapolis: University of Minnesota Press.

Morgensen, Scott Lauria. 2011. "The Biopolitics of Settler Colonialism: Right Here, Right Now." *Settler Colonial Studies* 1, 1.

National Inquiry into Missing and Murdered Indigenous Women and Girls. 2016. "Frequently Asked Questions." <pipsc.ca/news-issues/announcements/final-report-national-inquiry-missing-and-murdered-indigenous-women-and?gclid=EAIaIQobChMI7dvTgruG6QIVysDACh38FwMuEAAYASAAEgJEk_D_BwE>.

NWAC (Native Women's Association of Canada). 2010. "What Their Stories Tell Us: Research Findings from the Sisters in Spirit Initiative." <nwac.ca/wp-content/uploads/2015/07/2010-What-Their-Stories-Tell-Us-Research-Findings-SIS-Initiative.pdf>.

_____. 2009. "Voices of Our Sisters in Spirit: A Report to Families and Communities." 2nd edition, March. <nwac.ca/wp-content/uploads/2015/05/NWAC_Voices-of-Our-Sisters-In-Spirit_2nd-Edition_March-2009.pdf>.

_____. n.d. "About." <nwac.ca/about/>.

O'Keefe, Derrick. 2009. "Harper in Denial at G20: Canada Has 'No History of Colonialism." *Rabble*, September 28. <rabble.ca/blogs/bloggers/derrick/2009/09/harper-denial-g20-canada-has-no-history-colonialism>.

Oppal, Wally. 2012. *Forsaken: The Report of the Missing Women Commission of Inquiry*. British Columbia. <missingwomeninquiry.ca/wp-content/uploads/2010/10/Forsaken-ES-web-RGB.pdf>.

Palmater, Pamela. 2016. "Shining Light on the Dark Places: Addressing Police Racism and Sexualized Violence against Indigenous Women and Girls in the National Inquiry." *Canadian Journal of Women & the Law* 28, 2.

Pearce, Maryanne. 2013. "An Awkward Silence: Missing and Murdered Vulnerable Women and the Canadian Justice System." Faculty of Law, University of Ottawa.

_____. 2002. "Gendered Racial Violence and Spatialized Justice: The Murder of Pamela George." *Race, Space, and the Law*. Toronto: Between the Lines.

Regan, Paulette. 2010. *Unsettling the Settler Within : Indian Residential Schools, Truth Telling, and Reconciliation in Canada*. Vancouver: UBC Press.

Royal Canadian Mounted Police. 2015. "Missing and Murdered Aboriginal Women:

2015 Update to the National Operational Overview." <rcmp-grc.gc.ca/en/missing-and-murdered-aboriginal-women-2015-update-national-operational-overview>.

___. 2004. "RCMP Commissioner, Statement of Apology." <rcmp-grc.gc.ca/aboriginal-autochtone/apo-reg-eng.htm>.

Royal Commission on Aboriginal Peoples. 1996. *The Report of the Royal Commission on Aboriginal Peoples, Vol. 1: Looking Forward, Looking Back.* Ottawa: Government of Canada.

Sangster, Joan. 1999. "Criminalizing the Colonized: Ontario Native Women Confront the Criminal Justice System, 1920–1960." *Canadian Historical Review* 80, 1.

Sapers, Howard. 2016. *Annual Report of the Office of the Correctional Investigator 2015–16.* Ottawa: Office of the Correctional Investigator. <oci-bec.gc.ca/cnt/rpt/annrpt/annrpt20152016-eng.aspx#s7>.

Simpson, Audra. 2014a. "RACE 2014 Keynote 1: 'The Chief's Two Bodies: Theresa Spence and the Gender of Settler Sovereignty.'" Unsettling Conversations, RACE Network's 14th Annual Critical Race and Anticolonial Studies Conference. New York: Vimeo, LLC. <vimeo.com/110948627>.

___. 2014b. *Mohawk Interruptus: Political Life Across the Borders of Settler States.* Durham: Duke University Press.

Stark, Heidi. 2016. "Criminal Empire: The Making of the Savage in a Lawless Land." *Theory & Event* 19, 4.

Statistics Canada. 2016. "First Nations, Métis and Inuit Women." <www150.statcan.gc.ca/n1/pub/89-503-x/2015001/article/14313-eng.htm>.

Thobani, Sunera. 2012. *Exalted Subjects: Studies in the Making of Race and Nation in Canada.* Toronto: Toronto University Press.

TRC (Truth and Reconciliation Commission of Canada). 2015. *Honouring the Truth, Reconciling for the Future: Summary of the Final Report of the Truth and Reconciliation Commission of Canada.* <trc.ca/assets/pdf/Honouring_the_Truth_Reconciling_for_the_Future_July_23_2015.pdf>.

___. n.d. "Our Mandate." <trc.ca/about-us/our-mandate.html>.

Tuck, Eve, and K.W. Yang. 2012. Decolonization Is Not a Metaphor. *Decolonization: Indigeneity, Education & Society* 1, 1.

Veracini, Lorenzo. 2011. "Introducing Settler Colonial Studies." *Settler Colonial Studies* 1, 1.

Wakefield, A., and J. Fleming. 2009. "Responsibilization." *The SAGE Dictionary of Policing.* London: SAGE Publications.

Walsh, Jenna. 2015. "The National Inquiry into the Missing and Murdered Indigenous Women of Canada: A Probe in Peril." *Indigenous Law Bulletin* 8, 30. <classic.austlii.edu.au/au/journals/IndigLawB/2017/27.pdf>.

SECTION FOUR

Surveillance and Resistance to Social Control

The proliferation of internet technologies and the advent of social media have had a profound influence as agents of social change. Many of our social interactions, public or private, have migrated to web-mediated spaces, and many of us depend on consumer technologies for an ever-increasing range of tasks. Of course, these web spaces and tools are not impervious to misuse or intrusion. Research in the field of surveillance studies commonly considers how emergent technologies and information databanks leave us susceptible to increased supervision and personal risk. While authorities have long monitored populations perceived as posing danger, these researchers draw attention to how surveillance capacities have matured over the past twenty (rather tumultuous) years, especially those following September 11, 2001. More often than not, the capacities of the surveillance and data-sharing networks put in place to shield against terrorism have become public courtesy of leaked documents and a succession of scandals surrounding their use against the public at large.

The development of new communication and information-sharing technologies have also offered new capacities for collective resistance. Web-mediated interactions have afforded new capacities for social activism by allowing for the widespread accessibility (and formation) of information resources. Whereas Western populations once had little choice but to draw from traditional sources for "authoritative information" — including the institutions of mass media, politics, medicine, law, and criminal justice — web-based communicative technologies now provide a range of alternative information sources and, by extension, a range of alternative perspectives through which to perceive, and critically engage with, the world. The chapters compiled in this final section assess the ways in which technological innovations assist those who would accumulate our personal information and infringe upon our rights to privacy, but also those who wish to call critical attention to social issues and mobilize protest. The writings to follow demonstrate how technological innovations contribute new questions and perspectives to the ever-evolving field of deviance and social control studies, as well as the emergent ways in which our contemporary social landscape allows new tactics with which to seek out and confront those forms of power that undermine movements toward social justice.

James Popham's "Social and Panoptic Regulation through Digital Technologies" discusses the concept of panopticism — the ability for authorities to surveil our conduct in an expanding range of contexts — and provides case studies to highlight the endangerment of personal privacy. His chapter dissects the myriad ways in which digitized interactions extract our personal information and probes the curious apathy that members of the public express regarding the use of their private data. The chapter incorporates the conceptual tools of Michel Foucault to demonstrate connections between our digital habits and classificatory schemas, governmentality, and disciplinary power. The applicability and significance of these concepts is demonstrated through Popham's consideration of cases ranging from the Boston Marathon bombing to the 2016 presidential election. While the chapter highlights the dangers of digital panopticism, it also demonstrates the ways in which web communication and information distribution also inform strategies of dissent and resistance. To this end, Popham considers the genesis and mobilization of the #MeToo movement as a demonstration of the democratizing repercussions of web-mediated communicative spaces. The chapter concludes in revisiting (and admonishing) the prevalence of the perspective that those with "nothing to hide" should support these trends, and requests that readers critically consider their own positions on the matter.

Chapter 14, Scott Thompson's "National Security, Surveillance, and Colonial Understandings of Indigenous Sovereignty," considers how surveillance technologies are used in service of continuing processes of colonization and highlights their use in undermining Indigenous sovereignty. Thompson points to Canada's economic interests in charting how "civilized" practice came to centre the exploitation of natural resources and how this settler ideology justifies continuing paternalistic relations with "unproductive" Indigenous populations. Characterizing surveillance as a convergence of technological means and the rationalities that justify the imperative to surveil, the chapter demonstrates the past and present-day discourses that continue to naturalize settler authority despite Indigenous self-governance rights. For example, Canada's residential school system is described as a panoptic instrument that sought to indoctrinate Indigenous youth with the moralism of productivity and condition their acquiescence to Western capitalism. Looking to contemporary relations between Nations, Thompson highlights how the disjuncture between Indigenous rights and the self-purported jurisdiction of the Canadian state have informed mobilizations against environmental degradation — and the corresponding deployment of authorities tasked with restoring order and protecting industrial progress. Finally, the chapter contrasts contemporary federal policies (like those of Crown-Indigenous Relations and Northern Affairs Canada) with the aims of the Indian agents of past eras, noting the troubling parallels. For Thompson, these surveillance practices and the ideas that justify them undermine reconciliation.

Chapter 15, Kristen Thomasen's "Beyond Airspace Safety: A Feminist Perspective on Drone Privacy Regulation" uses a feminist lens to critically consider how the expansion of drone technologies endanger the privacy rights of women. Advocating for policy that is sensitive to the unique threats that commercially available drone technologies pose for women, Thomasen introduces the concept of gendered privacy to discuss how such surveillance reinforces patriarchy in promoting gender-specified conduct associated with mainstream gender norms of modesty and deference. The chapter draws attention to long-standing cultural tropes that conceptualize the privacy interests of women from a masculine vantage that places the onus to conform with modest (restrained) gender conduct upon women themselves. As feminized conduct expectations of old resurface in legal discourse that suggests women take responsibility to ensure their own privacy, strategies that could better prevent the nefarious use of drones are neglected. Thomasen also considers the gendered implications associated with law enforcement's expanding use of drone technologies and the prospect that the objective of protecting women will be used to justify federal expansion of drone use to surveil the public. Her chapter considers paths toward forging drone policy that protects the privacy rights of individuals without undermining public safety or perpetuating antiquated gender expectations.

The theme of disconcerting surveillance capacities continues with Jeff Monaghan and Kevin Walby's "Under the Gaze: Policing Social Movements That Resist Extractive Capitalism." Monaghan and Walby demonstrate how the expanding surveillance capacities of the Canadian state, though enacted to defend the public against terrorist threats, are used to surveil groups that threaten corporate interests. The chapter discusses research on policing philosophies and tactics in Canada, highlighting how law enforcement has increasingly been dispatched against social mobilizations — most prominently, Indigenous rights and environmental protection groups — that conflict with industrial interests. Notably, the chapter also demonstrates how, as with mass media and claims makers, federal agencies can be found to produce and promote narratives that overemphasize the threats (if any) posed by the movements they deem problematic. Monaghan and Walby use a series of case studies to demonstrate the expanding avenues through which security agencies collect data and distribute information on the perception of threats, and they discuss how these practices endanger the principles of democracy. Take note of how Monaghan and Walby characterize federal security agency responses to the establishment of the Idle No More movement, as well as the forms of discourse that became embedded through the 2015 passage of Canada's controversial *Anti-Terrorism Act* (Bill C-51).

The final chapter of this collection, "Tweets of Dissent: Observations on Social Movements in the Digital Age," discusses how the onset of network society has affected the constitution and tactics of contemporary social movements. It draws from the neo-Marxian theories of Antonio Gramsci and social movement scholarship derived from the civil rights era to contrast the organization of past social mobilizations with those of the present day. Recounting the genesis of movements like Occupy Wall Street, Idle No More, and Black Lives Matter, it demonstrates the revolutionary potential of using internet platforms and social media to popularize dissent. However, the hardships encountered by these groups is also mined to demonstrate the concurrent emergence of organizational drawbacks focused on identifying leadership and ensuring ideological solidarity among a diverse (and dispersed) membership. The chapter demonstrates how these movements inspired the counter-mobilization of oppositional groups advocating for the retention of "traditional values," contributing to an ideological Western climate described as one entangled in a "culture war."

Looking Forward

Over twenty years, technological progress and the diffusion of new methods of constructing and disseminating information has granted societies the capacities, once unthinkable, that now constitute mundane features of our everyday lives. These changes have inspired research into how institutions regulate the general public — and they have also incited new cultural practices to control the conduct of those classified as deviant. As the chapters of this final section demonstrate, technological progress and the onset of the network society have mobilized the public to challenge the authority and resist the normative expectations imposed by these processes. These patterns are unlikely to slow down, and we'll face new tactics of regulation and control — but also new possibilities for collective resistance and mobilizations toward social change.

13

Social and Panoptic Regulation through Digital Technologies

James F. Popham

After reading this chapter, you will be able to do the following:

1. Develop a critical understanding of Bentham's proposed panopticon and its implications.
2. Relate the panopticon to more abstract forms of surveillance as per Foucault.
3. Apply panoptic principles to social media and participatory media technologies.
4. Explain "sousveillance" and counter-power measures online.

On September 14, 2015, Mike Miller, a freelance videographer in Toronto, stopped to record an interaction between several Toronto Police Service (TPS) officers and two young Black men (Gillis 2017). An edited version of his video, which was still available online when this chapter was written, begins with a shot of an officer speaking to one of the youths, whose hands are against a police cruiser. A second police cruiser pulls into frame and two police officers exit. The initial arresting officer can be heard asking his colleagues to "turn the camera on that guy," gesturing with his thumb in the direction of Miller. The two officers, later identified as constables Shawn Gill and Brian Smith (Winsa and Rankin 2015), then approach Miller and begin to converse with him about his filming. At times the officers take a threatening stance toward Miller, glaring menacingly at the camera and crowding him, while at others they laugh and crack jokes. Throughout the video, constables Gill and Smith try to block Miller's ability to record the arrests occurring in the background.

Miller's recording came at a time of heightened scrutiny about police interactions with Black and Brown people in North America, driven by thousands of instances of US law enforcement officers killing unarmed Black men while on duty (Richardson 2017). This included the high-profile cases of Walter Scott, Michael Brown, and Eric Garner, whose deaths were captured in video or audio formats and shared through social media (Yang 2016). In Canada, Toronto-based freelance journalist Desmond Cole called out the TPS on their controversial "**carding**" tactic. Cole explained that officers will routinely stop individuals they deem to be suspicious and ask them for their identification while also recording personal details. All of this is done without a warrant or cause for arrest, and analyses have demonstrated that this tactic is disproportionately used against people of colour (Cole 2015). Miller, a person of colour himself, is a long-time activist on this matter and had been previously instructed by the deputy chief of the TPS to record any examples of carding that he encountered. This was his purpose for recording a police interaction on that September day (Winsa and Rankin 2015; Gillis 2017).

> Miller's recording viscerally reproduced what Cole and countless other visible minorities had experienced at the hands of police forces throughout Canada: a sense of fear and powerlessness in the face of unsympathetic authority.

In late October 2015, Miller's story and accompanying video was publicized by the *Toronto Star* and widely shared on social media platforms. To date, his recording has been viewed more than 300,000 times and his experiences have been discussed in dozens of television and news stories. Despite being non-violent, Miller's recording viscerally reproduced what Cole and countless other visible minorities had experienced at the hands of police forces throughout Canada: a sense of fear and powerlessness in the face of unsympathetic authority (Cole 2015; Wortley and Owusu-Bempah 2011). Miller's experiences, confirmed through video evidence, directly led to an investigation and charges against the two constables through the Office of the Independent Police Review Director (Gillis 2017). More importantly, open and public dialogue about the officer's actions reverberated with the message of the **Black Lives Matter** movement in the United States, instigating widespread discussions on social media platforms such as Facebook, Twitter, and Reddit (Sheptycki 2016).

As you have likely experienced, the internet has come to dominate our interpersonal relationships in the modern world. It has afforded us the power to access vast repositories of information in a few keystrokes or keep in contact with friends living on other continents. Many of these advancements

As a result, each relaying point in this vast global network has the potential to record and observe who accessed it and what they accessed.

hinge on **informational exchange**, which is a foundational concept in the technical architecture of the internet and the services that make use of it (Comer 2007). Whether reading the latest gossip about a popular celebrity or sharing highly classified documents between federal agencies, the internet is fundamentally about facilitating knowledge sharing. A second principle of the internet is that we must surrender identifying information in order to access other forms of information. At the surface level you might consider this as a login to a specific network or service, but it goes much deeper. For instance, the network technologies that power informational exchange require you to provide a delivery address for this information, be it your home computer, laptop, or mobile phone (Comer 2007). As a result, each relaying point in this vast global network has the potential to record and observe who accessed it and what they accessed. This leads into the third point, which is that true anonymity is rarely achieved on the internet. Rather, the radically transparent nature of these systems establishes a constant trail of breadcrumbs that can often be traced back to the originator — the internet user (Wall 2007).

These same ideas have pervaded the fabric of populist services that now make up the majority of global internet usage. In other words, the architectural underpinnings of the internet, including principles of exchange, identification, and transparency, have informed the structure of web-based services and the social interactions that come along with them (Lyon 2018). Consider social media platforms, which encourage and often require that users surrender control over their personal information in order to gain access to other connected individuals. In a functional sense, social media operates on the idea that we, the users, are willing to exchange a portion of our private and personal information in order to gain access to others' information. When we go on Facebook, Snapchat, or Instagram, we surrender certain expectations of privacy in exchange for a window into the lives of others. Many of these websites insist that you provide your genuine identity to fully access the service. In fact, Facebook and Twitter have devoted significant resources toward **de-anonymizing** users so as to ensure that, at the very least, a modicum of personal identifying information is available through their platforms (Hogan 2012; Cho, Kim, and Acquisti 2012). While these actions in and of themselves have recently warranted greater levels of scrutiny from governments and researchers alike (Elish and Boyd 2018), what is important to this chapter is that most internet users are apathetic about their digital privacy and willing to exchange it for the instant gratification afforded by new media sources (Acquisti, Brandimarte, and Loewenstein 2015; Tapscott 2009).

Despite these now widely known risks — or perhaps because of them — the internet has also come to play an integral role in mobilizing the public (Bonilla and Rosa 2015; Haunss 2014; Mann and Ferenbok 2013). As with Miller's case, discussed previously, it empowers traditionally excluded populations to turn the public's gaze toward their experiences and engage in dialogue with sympathizers (Kidd and McIntosh 2016). Moreover, it provides a powerful tool for organizing social movements, such as Black Lives Matter, the Jasmine Revolution, Occupy Wall Street, Idle No More, or #MeToo (Castells 2015; Wotherspoon and Hansen 2013; Manikonda et al. 2018). This capacity to mobilize emerges from our ability to communicate our sentiments in a one-to-many format, something that philosopher Manuel Castells (2009: 58) describes as "**mass self-communication**." In essence, Castells' (2009) argument is that internet technologies allow members of the public, en masse, to broadcast their opinions with one another in ways that were never previously possible. We can share our uncensored opinions and reach individuals who would historically have been unreachable, while also receiving information from new sources. For instance, you might have witnessed examples of celebrities directly connecting with their fans through social media in ways that were not possible before.

These technologies empower socially disparate groups of individuals to coalesce on shared ideologies, both confirming and legitimizing counter-power ideals. Castells (2009: 8) calls these "resistance identities," which in many cases leverage the transparency afforded by the panoptic nature of the internet to locate one another, engaging in a form of "voluntary surveillance" (Adams 2013). Rather than attempting to hide from those who might wish to monitor them, these groups proudly share their identities in a bid to build momentum and strengthen their cause. Still other groups will make use of this transparency to engage in counter-panoptic "**sousveillance**" (Mann, Nolan, and Wellman 2002: 332) of authority, using internet technologies to undermine traditional media gatekeepers and broadcast images of injustice (Richardson 2017). As Castells (2015: 9) asserts, networked communication paired with sousveillance were critical to the social revolutions that occurred in North Africa and the Middle East through 2012, led by tech-savvy "actors of social change." While the internet-led "weaponisation of visibility" (Trottier 2017) has affected significant social change through the twenty-first century, it can nonetheless be turned upon itself to reaffirm asymmetric balances of power (Hull 2015). That is to say, the undercurrent in most social media platforms is to collect and retain information that can ultimately be employed against the users. Even Castells (2015) had to concede that, in some cases, the internet-informed revolutions led to further subjection of participants. For example, the populist military regime that currently controls the Egyptian government has begun openly spying on its citizens through social media and other internet technologies, despite the fact that it owes its power to the Facebook-inspired 2011 revolution (Herrera 2015).

Since the internet provides a new and powerful mechanism for social control that takes advantage of the information we share online in order to identify and categorize us, we thus turn to panopticism for greater clarity. This chapter provides an introductory framework for critically assessing the relationship between surveillance and modern communication technologies. The next section of this chapter provides a discussion of "panopticism," first defined by philosopher Jeremy Bentham and then adapted by French theorist Michel Foucault. In general terms, panopticism refers to the use of mass or universal surveillance to classify and organize the public for the purposes of social control (Lyon 2018). After further defining the term and providing a contextual background, the chapter then analyzes several case studies that demonstrate the relevance of panopticism to the underlying motivations and residual impacts of pressing issues in our digital society. The chapter concludes with a conversation about why privacy matters. As a whole, it should provide you with greater context about the mechanisms of surveillance embedded in our commonplace digital activities as well as the harms and benefits that come from these social developments. If it gives you pause when you write your next tweet, all the better!

Panopticism

> It's not enough to just connect people. We have to make sure that those connections are positive. It's not enough to just give people a voice. We need to make sure that people aren't using it to harm other people or to spread misinformation. And it's not enough to just give people control over their information. We need to make sure that the developers they share it with protect their information, too. (Facebook, Social Media Privacy, and the Use and Abuse of Data 2018: 1)

These words, read aloud by Facebook founder and CEO Mark Zuckerberg, came near the beginning of his testimony to the United States Senate Committee on Commerce, Science, and Transportation. At issue was the fact that Facebook, the world's largest social media platform, had given research firm Cambridge Analytica millions of users' personal data. The data had been collected from users who participated in an online personality survey (Roose and Kang 2018). While this type of exchange has come to be a commonplace occurrence within the constellation of internet services and is generally met with apathy, a series of revelations by whistleblowers within the research firm suggested that much of this data had been shared without permission. Cambridge Analytica had exploited a loophole in Facebook's privacy policy that allowed for the collection of information about a users' "friends"[1] along with their own personal information. In so doing, the research firm surreptitiously collected data about an estimated eighty-seven million people that was then used to develop psychographic profiles that can be used to classify individuals along a number of different vectors, such as political affiliation (Confessore 2018).

These actions align with many of the concerns raised by Michel Foucault while writing about "panopticism" in the mid-1970s. While his writing occurred nearly two decades before the internet became widely available to the public, it nonetheless relates important observations about how power might be exercised through the use of surveillance. The word itself dates back further and is ideologically grounded in the notion that people will change their behaviours if they sense they are being watched by a person who holds power over them. Panopticism was first popularized by Jeremy Bentham, an eighteenth-century philosopher and social reformist who argued that the contemporary legal system in Great Britain was fraught with injustice and generally failed to redress harms or rehabilitate those who committed them (Semple 1993). He therefore spent much of his career championing change to this system, publishing a series of harsh critiques of the government and its processes related to justice using an assumed name or anonymous credentials.

As his career progressed, Bentham began to focus his energy on designing an improved penitentiary in response to the dungeon-like conditions of existing prisons and the overcrowded gaols (jails) that primarily served as temporary holding facilities for prisoners while they awaited justice (Semple 1993). Bentham framed this holding period as a lost opportunity; as a utilitarian, he argued that the punishment for crimes would better serve the public if they sought to *improve* the individuals who were subject to them. This

Bentham's design was based on a rationale of fear: he argues that prisoners, under constant threat of *potential* scrutiny, would do what they could to avoid additional suffering and punishment.

rationale, and his expressed belief in the morality of hard work, set him on the course to design what came to be known as the **panopticon,** a prison designed to ensure that those confined within would adhere to the rigours of constructive punishment under the observant watch of their captors (Bentham 1830; Semple 1993).

Bentham's panopticon was a radial building that resembled the structure of a wheel. At its centre, where the hub of the wheel normally is, Bentham (1830) described a lodge or circular tower that housed the guards (he called them "inspectors"); at the periphery, or the rim, he called for multiple storeys of open-faced cells that housed the prisoners. In between the lodge and the cells would be an open area, which would allow the guards to look into any of the cells that they wanted to without obstruction. Bentham expected the guard's observation to make up the metaphysical spokes of the wheel, and that it would be one-sided: he explained that the windows of the rotunda should have shades that prevented the inmates from looking in (Bentham 1996) (see Figure 13-1). Bentham's design was based on a rationale of fear: he argues that prisoners, under constant threat of *potential* scrutiny, would do what they could to avoid additional suffering and punishment. In his reformist view, this meant following a rigorous schedule of labour, temperance, and instruction, and the prisoner's adherence to these requirements would be subject to unremitting inspection (Bentham 1830).

Bentham saw great potential in his penitentiary model, both for those who were incapacitated by it and for society at large. As a utilitarian, Bentham ardently called for policy that pursued the greatest good for the largest number of people possible while also minimizing its detrimental effects (intentional and unintentional) (Bentham 1996; Miller and Miller 1987). By extension, he argued that the threat of constant inspection in his panoptic model would afford greater utility to its prisoners, instilling productive values and a sense of allegiance to the greater good of societies. Moreover, he wrote that this process would empower the inspectors to categorize and ostracize persistent offenders from the general population, describing an early form of actuarial risk assessment (Silver and Miller 2002; Bentham 1830). Bentham also argues that the philosophy of panoptic transparency and the resultant sorting can be transferred to the public, creating a mechanism for general classification. In so doing, it would eliminate uncertainty about the underlying circumstance

Figure 13-1: Bentham's Architectural Plans for the Panopticon

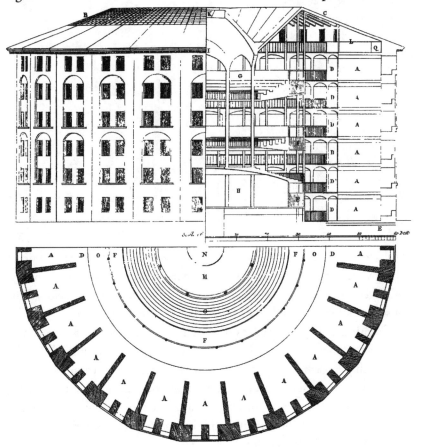

Source: Jeremy Bentham creator QS:P170,Q60887 <commons.wikimedia.org/wiki/File:Panopticon. jpg>, "Panopticon", marked as public domain.

of individual deviance while simultaneously establishing categories of people that could be used for various means of social control (Miller and Miller 1987; Curtis 2002).

Bentham's suggestion that the panoptic philosophy be extended to the public for the purposes of categorization raises an important observation on social control. In fact, he goes so far as to recommend that everyone should be tattooed with some sort of identification marking, as contemporary sailors did with anchors and names on their forearms (Miller and Miller 1987). Doing so would simplify the categorization process, as individuals could be immediately recognized for their name, occupation, or other characteristics. An interesting analogy lies in J.K. Rowling's *Harry Potter* series of novels. One

Box 13-1: The Sorting Hat

Oh, you may not think I'm pretty,
But don't judge on what you see,
I'll eat myself if you can find
A smarter hat than me.
You can keep your bowlers black,
Your top hats sleek and tall,
For I'm the Hogwarts Sorting Hat
And I can cap them all.
There's nothing hidden in your head
The Sorting Hat can't see,
So try me on and I will tell you
Where you ought to be...

Rowling, J. 1998. *Harry Potter and the Philosopher's Stone*: 80–81.

of the series' most pivotal moments comes early on, when all the new students at Hogwarts School of Witchcraft and Wizardry endure a "sorting ceremony" that determines to which of the school's four houses they will belong. The houses are a kind of residence for the young wizards and witches, but also carry significant social bearing as they are in a constant state of competition with one another for academic, sport, and social recognition. Additionally, membership in each house signifies a set of characteristics common to each of the residents, such as bravery, wit, or kindness. Once sorted, the students remain in their assigned house throughout their education at Hogwarts, associating with their housemates and developing rivalries with competing houses (Rowling 1998; see Box 13-1).

As you might imagine, the ability to "sort" people provides a powerful tool for maintaining social order, generally to the benefit of those who are responsible for defining and assigning the categories. These labels can affect who people socialize with, how authorities deal with them, or what opportunities they might receive in life. Moreover, they simplify observation as they eliminate the need to develop background knowledge about the categorized people. Recalling *Harry Potter*, the faculty and staff at Hogwarts do not need to investigate the students' personalities to decide their allegiances; rather, they can monitor and reward or punish actions reminiscent of their house's characteristics. In this perspective, panoptic observation is oriented toward adherence to labels rather than assessing behaviours. Bentham (1830) viewed the power of observation and categorization as an antidote to social ills, providing a mechanism by which the contagions and their carriers could be quarantined from society. More importantly, Bentham (1830) argued that a universal application of this ideology would reconstitute society itself, driving all members of society to improve their own utility

Bentham viewed the power of observation and categorization as an antidote to social ills, providing a mechanism by which the contagions and their carriers could be quarantined from society.

while simultaneously watching and reporting others in order drive them to do the same (Miller and Miller 1987).

This perspective was of particular concern to French philosopher Michel Foucault. Foucault's (1995) text *Discipline and Punish* makes a series of arguments about the effects of observation on the general public and our behaviours. Several important points of Foucault's writing influence our discussion of the internet and society. First is his observation that panoptic inspection has become a normalized part of society through broad engagement in "complete and austere institutions" (Foucault 1995: 231). Essentially, Foucault's (1995) argument is that principles of judgment, such as those championed by Bentham (1830), have come to dominate our day-to-day lives through the institutions that shape them. He uses the experiences of prisoners across the centuries as an illustrative point, demonstrating how each day's activities were controlled, observed, and judged from start to finish, establishing an "unceasing discipline" (Foucault 1995: 237). Rather than inflicting immediate and painful punishment, modern penal systems employ measurements of order to modulate, or scale, the level of harm that prisoners experience. Foucault (1995) argues that these same mechanisms have pervaded beyond the prison to affect the public's lives as well — that we ourselves are subject to complete institutions.

A simple example of the pervasive institutionalization and observation in society would be your experiences with education. Beginning with the earliest years of schooling, most students in North America bring home modular indicators of their educational attainment — we commonly call them "report cards." Reports might come as letter grades or percentage scores, or might simply be pass/fail, but their underlying purpose is the same: they provide a mechanism by which a student can be inspected and classified by the authorities in their life. These observations have serious consequences for social control as they can affect one's social surroundings, punishments, or even opportunities for success. Thinking about your own report cards, what would have happened had you received failing grades? How would your parents have reacted? Your peers? Your institution? Researchers have demonstrated the

Those who define these categories and make the decisions about who belongs in each have great power over the public — they have the ability to cast entire groups of people as outsiders or as sick.

direct consequences of categorization on individuals in an educational setting. In the early 1960s, Harvard psychologist Robert Rosenthal partnered with Lenore Jacobson, a school principal in San Francisco, to explore what happened when teachers were told that certain children in their classroom were likely to experience "unusual intellectual gains during the academic year" (Rosenthal and Jacobson 1966: 116). This determination was based on an intelligence test that was administered to each child attending the school. Eight months later, a follow-up IQ test was administrated to the same school, and many of the students who had been identified to the teachers did in fact experience significant gains in their IQ. The catch to this study was that the flagged students had been randomly selected and that no such indicator for academic potential actually existed. Rosenthal and Jacobson (1966) surmised that their teachers' expectations, being raised by the empirically demonstrated potential, resulted in greater classroom attention and ultimately higher levels of academic achievement. In line with Foucault's (1995) concerns, this experiment demonstrates how social control might manifest through instructional mechanisms of classification. Whereas those students who had been labelled as promising students received additional attention, those who were not similarly labelled did not.

The second point of consideration from Foucault centres on the way the public interacts with these labels. As discussed above, Bentham (1830) suggests that those whose actions or perspectives do not align with public interests might be labelled as contagious. He reasoned that this categorization could lead to better administration of treatments for "social ills," eventually producing a "cure" and inoculating the public. Foucault (1995) argued this point further, suggesting that the designation of deviance as a malaise serves to differentiate and exclude individuals who do not conform to the standards of "good behaviour" set by the observers, and by extension he argues that we seek to avoid being designated as "sick" at all costs. Unlike correctional institutions, which have prescribed tasks that act as measurement of one's malaise (Goffman 2007), categorization of the public is much more haphazard and is influenced by uncontrollable socially constructed factors such as race or economic status as well as arbitrary factors such as timing, location, or associations. Those who define these categories and make the decisions about who belongs in each have great power over the public — they have the ability to cast entire groups of people as outsiders or as sick. Foucault (1995: 192) explains:

> It is the examination which, by combining hierarchical surveillance and normalizing judgement, assures the great disciplinary functions of distributions and classification.... With it are ritualized those disciplines that may be characterized in a word by saying that they are a modality of power for which individual difference is relevant.

Foucault (1995) warned that "distribution and classification" of the public based on inspection pushes us into a state of normalized individuality — what he terms *individuation* — where our relations with one another are driven by a "me-first" attitude. In essence, he argues that our fear of being identified as one of the "sick" members of society leads us to avoid associating with those who might carry the contagion. This inevitably leads to an us-versus-them dichotomy, where people judge others based on whether or not we feel that their categorization will adversely affect our own social standing.

Police culture provides a relatively straightforward example of individuation. During any given shift, police officers run the risk of violent interactions with the public, leading to heightened concern over self-preservation and expectations of danger in all encounters (Barker 1998). This, in turn, leads to a risk-aversive internal culture that "idealizes a hard-nosed, aggressive approach to policing which accords priority to law enforcement and crime fighting" (Paoline, Myers, and Worden 2000: 576) as a way to pre-emptively mitigate harmful encounters with a risky public. Moreover, studies demonstrate that police officers will develop and internalize a sorting mechanism based on personal characteristics that will then dictate the way they interact with suspects (Waddington, Stenson, and Don 2004). While these biases are a product of individual experience, they are influenced by and in turn influence a more or less homogenous policing culture (Chan 1996). Here, individuation materializes as a function of the ad hoc distribution and classification systems that the police apply to their encounters: while there is some variation in the way officers interact with the public, they nonetheless gravitate toward aggression directed against all those who are not members of the fraternal order (Paoline, Myers, and Worden 2000; Ho Shon 2005).

The combined effects of normalized inspection and individuation lead to a third point raised by Foucault (1991: 103), which he termed "governmentality." Broadly defined, governmentality refers to the ways that people self-censure their behaviours in alignment with the opaque interests and intentions of

> We govern our lives to avoid the deleterious effects of being categorized as ungovernable.

the state. In essence, he argues that we govern our lives to avoid the deleterious effects of being categorized as ungovernable. This is the penultimate outcome of normalized discipline and categorization, as it leads the public to automatically and unconsciously act at the behest of authorities without prompt (Dean 2017). Burchell (1991) argues this is a sort of political arithmetic that we are conditioned to internalize and act upon from a very young age, and that these calculations are geared toward accumulating power by establishing our utility within society.

The most important point to draw from this discussion is that Foucault's (1991) sense of governmentality implies that the government, or state, only exists because the public, as a whole, willfully recreates it through their actions. Thus, our routinized judgment and sorting of others continuously recreates the state (Dean 2017). You might think about the way you prepare for a final exam as an example of governmentality. Believe it or not, your professor *wants* you to do well on your coursework but cannot be there to coach you through your preparations. Your study activities are therefore a reflection of what you think the professor expects of you, and you will shape your behaviours in an attempt to meet these expectations. More importantly, Foucault (1991) explains that we also apply these same principles to those around us — in other words, we take on responsibilities that were traditionally those of the state, such as surveillance for deviant activities. Thus, in a roundabout way, governmentality is about the way in which we willingly, and sometimes with great fervour, take on maintenance of the social order.

Case Studies

At this point, you might be wondering what this admittedly dense theoretical discussion has to do with the opening discussion about the internet and the information that we share online; however, if you take a moment to think about it, you might begin to see the connection. Specifically, if you consider the panopticon to take shape as an idea or philosophy as per Foucault's (1995) insistence, you should be able to see how the physical tendrils of observation first proposed by Bentham (1830) can be replaced with the digital lines of communication we rely on today. Near-universal access to the internet in most Westernized nations has drawn enormous swathes of the public into these unprecedented social settings that reflect the technological notions of informational exchange (ITU 2016). This gestalt switch undermines long-standing notions of privacy and instead instills an expectation — and acceptance — of observation. In eschewing privacy barriers, the digital public has developed an expectation of transparency from all corners, creating a culture of surveillance and instilling new expectations of informational accessibility (Lyon 2018). At the same time, these little bits and pieces of our shared lives form enormous repositories of data about us, going beyond personal demographics to include political leanings, relationships, or sexual orientation (Elish and Boyd 2018). This information creates powerful analytic tools that can then be used to predict individual behaviours and detect the communities to which we belong (Papadopoulos et al. 2012). In other words, our infatuation with surveilling ourselves (and others) ensures this machine keeps growing and, as a result, has opened radically exhaustive mechanisms for categorization and surveillance.

> In eschewing privacy barriers, the digital public has developed an expectation of transparency from all corners, creating a culture of surveillance and instilling new expectations of informational accessibility.

This section is devoted to unpacking three examples of how digital surveillance has come to affect us. The first two case studies exemplify negative implications, illustrating how algorithmically determined characteristics were used as a sorting mechanism during the forty-fifth presidential election and then connecting governmentality with the digital "witch hunt" for the Boston Marathon bombers. The third case study draws attention to the counter-power potential of the internet by demonstrating sousveillance through the #MeToo movement.

Facebook, Cambridge Analytica, Categorization, and the Forty-Fifth US Presidential Election

If you have ever had a job interview, you will know that a successful outcome is as much about impression management as it is demonstrating your skills (Von Baeyer, Sherk, and Zanna 1981). These same concerns are experienced by politicians during election periods. The public, acting as interviewers of sorts, have a number of expectations about political candidates, right down to the colour of their clothes. But, much like interviewers, the public can be a fickle bunch whose priorities remain opaque. Some voters might be swayed by far more substantial political issues such as government debt or social service spending, others might be affected by a candidate's visual branding, and most lie somewhere in between (Smith 2001). As a result, many political campaigns employ experimental impression tactics to attract the most voters possible, often going beyond the traditional whistle stops and yard signs to which the public has become accustomed (Issenberg 2016). Starting in the mid-2000s, this experimentation began to incorporate internet-driven technologies focused on motivating candidate and party supporters to get out and vote on election days (Baldwin-Philippi 2016). This approach to experimentation played an important role in the 2008 election of Barack Obama as the forty-fourth president of the United States. His campaign managers made extensive use of big data analytics and modern technologies to constantly shape and reshape Obama's campaign, down to the language and look of the "contact us" button on his election website (Issenberg 2016). More often than not, these decisions were informed by the campaign's ability to partition voters into separate categories based on age, gender, race, or other social measures, and then analyze each group's opinions on certain matters or issues.

The impact of these tactics resonated with political circles throughout the world and kick-started a digital modernization movement in electoral campaign practices, with particular attention paid to voter categorization. While demographic-oriented campaigning was a long-standing tradition by the time of Obama's campaign (Baldwin-Philippi 2016), the phenomenal power of big data analytics to categorize individuals at a granular level gave rise to a new science of computational politics (Tufekci 2014). In essence, computational techniques informed by academic research can make use of available datasets about the public to create **psychographics** — models that blend motivational psychology and personality inventories — to predict human behaviours with great accuracy (Wells 1975; Kosinski, Stillwell, and Graepel 2013). Tufekci (2014: 30) explains:

> the advent of big datasets that contain imprints of actual behavior and social network information — social interactions, conversations, friendship networks, history of reading and commenting on a variety of platforms — along with advances in computational techniques means that political campaigns (and indeed, advertisers, corporations and others with the access to these databases as well as technical resources) can model individual voter preferences and attributes at a high level of precision, and crucially, often without asking the voter a single direct question. Strikingly, the results of such models may match the quality of the answers that were only extractable via direct questions, and far exceed the scope of information that could be gathered about a voter via traditional methods.

For the 2008 and 2012 Obama campaigns, this meant circumventing traditional tacit campaign knowledge and using panoptic data profiles of politically inactive but potential supporters. Informed by these profiles, the campaign

> Research has demonstrated that big data analysis can be used to anticipate a broad range of human conditions, from asthma attacks to pregnancy to purchasing intentions, *before the affected individuals know.*

deployed a series of social media–driven advertisements that zeroed in on motivating these would-be supporters; it functioned with great effect (Tufekci 2014; Issenberg 2016).

Obama's successful campaigns worked as a proof-of-concept for psychographics in elections but also catalyzed more divisive iterations of the technology. As discussed previously, social media and internet communication technologies have ushered in a culture of participatory surveillance that has normalized transparency. The readily available nature of our personal data, paired with rapid computational and human sciences advancements, have empowered psychographic research to develop powerful predictive behavioural models. To demonstrate, Kosinski, Stillwell, and Graepel (2013) created a profiling algorithm that used an individual's Facebook "likes" to make determinations about their personal characteristics. When compared against user profiles, the authors concluded that "a wide variety of people's personal attributes, ranging from sexual orientation to intelligence, can be automatically and accurately inferred using their Facebook Likes" (Kosinski, Stillwell, and Graepel 2013: 5805). Moreover, research has demonstrated that big data analysis can be used to anticipate a broad range of human conditions, from asthma attacks to pregnancy to purchasing intentions, *before the affected individuals know* (Crawford and Shultz 2014; O'Neil 2016).

By extension, these advancements also imply that psychographic profiling can be used to direct behaviours as well, leveraging differences between self-perception and "others" to polarize opinions (Lerman and Hogg 2014). Indeed, this is something that Tufekci (2014: para. 41) warned about, writing that:

> Campaigns, though, until now had to target the whole population, or at least a substantial segment, all at once, with the same message. In contrast, by modeling individual psychologies through computational methods applied to big data, a political campaign hoping to garner votes of a conservative candidate can plausibly (and relatively easily) identify voters that were more likely react to fear by voting conservative and target them individually through "fear–mongering" tactics

designed for their personal weaknesses and vulnerabilities while bypassing individuals on whom fear–mongering would not have the desired effect, perhaps even the opposite of the desired one, all the while communicating with them in a manner invisible to broader publics, say via Facebook ads.

This differentiation manifested in the 2016 US presidential election campaign. Whereas the Obama campaigns used psychographics to encourage voter turnout, the Trump campaign used analytics for divisive purposes (Persily 2017). Specifically, Trump's electoral organization partnered with Cambridge Analytica and, using the aforementioned ill-gotten dataset, hired a team of data scientists whose task was to profile "persuadable voters." The psychographics developed by the Cambridge Analytica team profiled an estimated twenty million potential supporters, mostly drawn from economically marginalized but racially dominant social groups within the United States (primarily representing working-class white Americans) (González 2017). Empowered with the tools to differentiate these potential supporters, the Trump campaign then deployed a "weaponized propaganda machine" (Dean 2017: 93) that emotionally manipulated its targets to understand the election as an "us-versus-them" decision.

Trump and the Republican Party's successful use of divisive rhetoric had the immediate effect of polarizing the population along political lines and transforming political allegiances into rivalry. As Connolly (2017: 29) explains, these divides imbued voters with an all-or-nothing mentality that connected social issues with opposing candidate Hillary Clinton and the Democratic Party:

> One cluster of demeaning associations in a Trump speech draws together the dangers of assertive femininity, minority standing, alien religions, disability, foreignness, weakness, responsiveness, vulnerability and dissolution until each item on the line vibrates with perceived threats posed by the others.… Later, when followers hear the expression of any of these items by Trump critics they will be inclined to associate its bearer with every other item on the list.

This strategy proved to be effective, as was demonstrated by the results of the 2016 election. Despite losing the popular vote by a significant proportion, Donald Trump received a majority of the Electoral College votes to win the presidency. Retrospective analysis of his victory indicates a strategic focus on "white-identity politics" (Lipsitz 2006: 60) in undecided jurisdictions mobilized Republican voters and dissuaded democrats from attending the polls (Lang and Damore 2016). The Trump campaign's partnership with Cambridge Analytica exploited pre-existing schisms in the social makeup of the United States to effectively divide its populace.

You should be able to connect this micro-targeting strategy with Foucault's arguments about panoptic surveillance, particularly his discussion of distribution and classification. An oft-repeated tone of the 2016 electoral was the juxtaposition of Trump as an anti-government working man against Clinton's membership in the so-called political elite (Grossmann and Thaler 2018). This counter-hegemonic framing helped to popularly diagnose the Democratic Party, its candidate, and its supporters with a corruptive malady. In so doing, Trump, representing the Republican Party, was able to mobilize his supporters by challenging them to prove that they too were not sick or degenerate (Connolly 2017). These actions proved doubly fruitful, as they also served to demobilize Trump's opposition (Lang and Damore 2016). Trump's divisive campaign strategy employed what Foucault (1995: 198) called a ritual of exclusion:

> A meticulous tactical partitioning in which individual differentiations [are] the constricting effects of a power that multiplied, articulated and subdivided itself; the great confinement on the one hand; the correct training on the other.

Governmentality and Reddit's Pursuit of the Boston Marathon Bombers

On April 15, 2013, two bombs exploded near the finish line of the annual Boston Marathon. They had been timed to detonate approximately four hours and ten minutes after the start of the third wave of the marathon, which roughly aligned with the average finish time for most runners (Britt 2018). Three people were killed by the bombs and an estimated 264 others were hospitalized; one campus police officer was also killed in the resulting manhunt for the bombers. Subsequent investigations would determine that two brothers, Dzhokhar and Tamerian Tsarnaev, were responsible for the bombing (Nhan, Huey, and Broll 2017). Unfortunately, the attacks had an immediate effect on social media before this conclusion could be met. By 2013, smartphones were ubiquitous and most were equipped with high-resolution cameras. Moreover, Facebook and Twitter included video functions in their platforms, streamlining the deployment of this imagery. Video and photography of the detonations and their immediate after-effect began to circulate within moments, spurring public commentary from all corners of the globe (Nhan, Huey, and Broll 2017).

Acknowledging the panoptic power of mobile computing technology, the US Federal Bureau of Investigations (FBI) asked that anyone with video or photography that might aid in the investigation submit it to the agency. Moreover, the FBI openly called for support from the public in identifying people of interest. **Crowdsourcing** — asking the public to voluntarily contribute knowledge, resources, or time — has long been an effective tool in criminal investigations. One example might be the use of wanted posters or milk carton images to aid in locating wanted individuals or missing children. Grid searches are another example, where volunteers work with police to search a geographic area using assigned locations.

While these activities continue, the internet has added a new dimension to crowdsourced investigations. Parsing the volume of data available online is a resource-intensive proposition that police and governmental agencies simply cannot afford to do; however, pools of unskilled civilian investigators can often be mobilized to aid these processes, particularly with high-profile cases. In September 2006, billionaire Steve Fossett failed to return from a pleasure flight in one of his personal airplanes. He had not filed a flight plan, but his general trajectory was known to authorities. Fossett was believed to have crashed or made an emergency landing somewhere in the mountains that border California and Nevada. Investigators identified a 52,000 square kilometre patch of mountains and dense brush where he was likely to have landed and began traditional search activities to no avail. At this point, with encouragement from Fossett's friend Richard Branson, Google and several satellite photographing firms made high-resolution images of the entire search area available to the public, which was then tasked with visually scanning the images for any sign of a wreckage. An estimated fifty thousand people from all corners of the world contributed to this search (Behrend et al. 2011).

More recent examples of crowdsourcing using similar tactics include investigations of the 2011 Vancouver riots, the search for Malaysia Airlines Flight 370 in 2014, and the OpenStreetMap Ebola mapping project for the Democratic Republic of the Congo (2014–18) (Schneider and Trottier 2012; Walsh et al. 2014; Tambo, Ugwu, and Ngogang 2014). While these speak to the capacity of panoptic surveillance to promote state-public participation, they also have a darker side. In the Fossett case, Civil Air Patrol, the agency responsible for the search, expressed frustration with the volume of misleading information that the crowdsourcing activity produced (Friess 2007), brought on

> The Reddit community's untethered and haphazard analysis of surveillance ultimately led to popular framing of several untrue rumours as "fact."

by public vigour to locate the missing aviator. To this end, Gary Marx (2013: 58), a sociologist at the Massachusetts Institute of Technology (MIT), argues that downloading investigative responsibilities to the public runs the risk of developing into a state of digital vigilantism:

> Contemporary means extend the passive requests of the old "Wanted!" posters for fugitives — many requests are more open ended and vague, describing events that might happen, seeking input on suspicious circumstances and people. As such, they invite an unsettling categorical suspicion, whether across entire populations or within subgroups defined by ethnicity nationality, religion, or dress.

He adds that realization of this advancement instills a world of presumptive surveillance, where the participating public realizes that they are being watched, just as they are watching others. David Lyon (2018: 116) adds that this "participatory turn" blurs the divide between state and public surveillance.

This returns our discussion to the aftermath of the Boston Marathon bombing. Shortly after asking the public to assist in the investigation, the FBI released several photographs and video of the two brothers, whose identities were unknown (at the time). Armed with this information, the public immediately took to their newsfeeds and social media networks in search of the perpetrators (Tapia, LaLone, and Kim 2014). The imagery generated by the public as well as that provided by the FBI did *not* come with any sort of expert interpretation at first, leaving the public to collectively speculate on its veracity, significance, and relevance (Nhan, Huey, and Broll 2017). This process reached a frenzied pace on the discussion forums of Reddit. Here, participants posted their theories about the attacks and commented on others. Notably, these discussions were neither requested nor supported by the FBI or related law enforcement agencies; rather, they emerged organically from conversations between users and often hinged on misinformation or rumour (Starbird et al. 2014).

The Reddit community's untethered and haphazard analysis of surveillance ultimately led to popular framing of several untrue rumours as "fact." The most harmful of these rumours came when Reddit turned its attention to missing MIT student Sunil Tripathi, who bore a passing resemblance to Dzhokhar Tsarnaev, the younger of the two bombers (Nhan, Huey, and Broll 2017; Tapia et al. 2014). Tripathi had gone missing from his student accommodation one day after the bombings, having earlier taken a leave from his studies due to mental health concerns. In a bid to find him, his family had circulated several photographs on social media. In one such photograph of Tripathi in profile view, several blemishes were visible on his right cheek. Vigilant Redditors argued that these marks were also present in a grainy surveillance photo of Tsarnaev and concluded that Tripathi was one of the perpetrators (Nhan, Huey, and Broll 2017; Starbird et al. 2014). Having been identified — or, in popular internet parlance, "doxxed" — Tripathi's family began to receive vitriolic messages, including death threats. While the FBI deployed investigators to participate in online communications to curb such misleading information, the damage had been done: Tripathi was named as a suspect by several news media firms, further aggravating his family's experiences. Sadly, Sunil Tripathi's remains were found several days later. He had taken his life, likely before his name had been associated with the bombings, leaving his family to simultaneously grieve his passing while also attempting to clear his name (Nhan, Huey, and Broll 2017).

The Reddit administrative team (2013) was forced to act in the aftermath of these accusations, issuing an apology to Tripathi's family and to the general public for the website's role in contributing toward Tripathi's defamation. Additionally, the team spoke to the corruptive potential of decentralized, crowd-sourced investigations:

> A few years ago, reddit enacted a policy to not allow personal information on the site. This was because "let's find out who this is" events frequently result in witch hunts, often incorrectly identifying innocent suspects and disrupting or ruining their lives. We hoped that the crowdsourced search for new information would not spark exactly this type of witch hunt. We were wrong. The search for the bombers bore less resemblance to the types of vindictive internet witch hunts our no-personal-information rule was originally written for, but the outcome was no different. (para. 4)

Framed this way, you might perceive the social media–driven quest to identify the Boston Marathon bomber(s) as a function of governmentality. First, as an unrequested and undirected investigation, the public's ardent search for the perpetrators' identities demonstrated an internalized sense of responsibility for the maintenance of order. While many commenters stated that they had performed these inquiries out of a sense of injustice for the bombers' victims, they nonetheless grounded their activities as correcting a wrongdoing rather than redress for the victims (Pantumsinchai 2018). Second, the public naming of Tripathi individuated him as a perpetrator and thereby created a measure of governability. Tripathi's social media presence was thoroughly analyzed and used to inform this category (Tapia, LaLone, and Kim 2014). Cumulatively, these activities reified what Foucault called the "composite reality" (1991: 103) of the state by creating a public narrative of justice and using Tripathi's identity to symbolize its antithesis. The public took on this responsibility without prompt and, in so doing, further entrenched a socially derived sense of what *ought* to be. Here, the panoptic gaze afforded by the internet provided a vital tool in retrenching this sense of order.

Sousveillance and the System: The #MeToo Movement

One of the most striking impacts from the rise of social media has been the speed at which new ideas and sentiments can spread among user networks. You might know these ideas by the more commonly used term **memes**, a concept borrowed from philosopher Richard Dawkins (2006). He wanted to create a "noun that conveys the idea of a unit of cultural transmission, or a unit of imitation" (Dawkins 2006: 192) that would aid in understanding the evolution of human culture. Dawkins' new noun proved to be a fitting term for what would happen to the internet twenty-five years later, as it succinctly describes the constant turnover of imagery and messaging that spread through internet-driven social networks. Memes might come as images, videos, comments, or sometimes as hashtags.

In many cases, memes will turn up as flash-in-the-pan points of levity that temporarily hold the collective public attention and then fizzle out just as quickly. You might remember the Harlem Shake or Tide Pod challenges that rapidly spread through the internet before fading away. But sometimes memic cultural transfer can produce lasting impact. For instance, in late 2013, people began to film themselves in the ice bucket challenge, pouring cold water (often with ice in it) over their heads. The videos began with the would-be victim challenging other friends before drenching themselves. Many of these videos were produced with the goal of raising funds for the ALS[2] Association (2018), which reports that the videos raised US$115 million in the summer of 2014. In other cases, memes have been used to spread social commentary and draw attention to social issues. For instance, in 2014 the Rob Bliss marketing firm

> The wide spread of modern social networks paired with the ease of transmitting messages has equipped the digital generation with the ability to effectively illustrate the depth of social concerns.

partnered with Hollaback!, an anti-harassment organization, to share a video on YouTube that featured a young woman silently walking the streets of New York City. Her experiences were captured on film by a hidden camera, which recorded more than one hundred instances of verbal harassment and countless winks, whistles, or other attempts to catch her attention. At one point in the video, an unnamed man pursues her for more than five minutes despite clear body language from the woman that his advances were unwelcome. The video has since been viewed more than forty-six million times, sparking significant public debate over the day-to-day harassment that many women all over the world encounter (Bailey 2017). It also instigated conversations along racial lines as the video primarily showed people of colour harassing a white-identified woman despite the director's admission that white men had also made harassing comments but these had been edited out (Rentschler 2015; Meyerson 2014).

These socially oriented forms of cultural transfer are symbolic of the democratizing potential of social media, particularly for marginalized groups affected by intersectionality, such as women or people of colour (Yuce, Agarwal, and Wigand 2013; Davary 2017). Recalling Castells' (2009) discussions, the wide spread of modern social networks paired with the ease of transmitting messages has equipped the digital generation with the ability to effectively illustrate the depth of social concerns. The so-called hashtag activism movements that have sprung up over the past decade are illustrative of this point by making use of technology to demonstrate the breadth of a concern or issue. When posting to their news feeds, individuals can pair a hash ("#") with a relevant term to demarcate their comment in alignment with trending subjects. This technology converts the term into a hyperlink which, when clicked on, will link users with others who have also used the hashtag, giving a sense of the number of people who have expressed sentiments about it. Hashtag activism has helped to inform numerous resistance activities, such as the #IdleNoMore protests led by Indigenous Peoples in Canada or the #BlackLivesMatter movement that mobilized protest against police violence toward people of colour in the United States and eventually globally (Coates 2015; Davary 2017).

The #MeToo is a recent example of an impactful hashtag movement. Beginning in the fall of 2017, women around the world began taking to Twitter and other social media services posting the words "me too." The movement started when Hollywood actress Alyssa Milano tweeted out a comment that a friend had made to her reading "if all the women who have been sexually harassed or assaulted wrote 'Me Too' as a status, we might give people a sense of the magnitude of the problem" (@Alyssa_Milano 2017). Her tweet had been inspired by the work of activist Tarana Burke and occurred in the wake of a revelatory *New York Times* article in which actor Ashley Judd disclosed that Hollywood producer Harvey Weinstein had sexually harassed her during what she thought would be a business meeting. Several other women quoted in the story stated that Weinstein had done the same thing to them, using his power in the industry as a bargaining chip for sexual favours. The #MeToo hashtag was used more than twelve million times within the first twenty-four hours of Milano's posting (Mendes, Ringrose, and Keller 2018).

This use of Twitter and hashtag activism to open dialogue and to network against sexism, misogyny, and rape culture was not a unique occurrence, nor was the immediate popularity of the hashtag (for a discussion, see Horeck's [2014] analysis of feminist hashtags). Where the #MeToo movement differs is in the nature of participation asked by victims. Specifically, #MeToo activism rests in the hashtag itself, which provides an ad hoc census of individuals, primarily women, who had endured sexual victimization during their lifetime. This action creates a sort of counter-surveillance that leverages the capacity of panoptic transparency to illustrate overwhelming numbers (Peyrefitte and Sanders-McDonagh 2018). While it started with dialogue about gendered power relations, the rapid growth of the #MeToo movement quickly empowered countless women to share their experiences, regardless of their relationship with the aggressor, to a receptive public. Moreover, the groundswell of support for the hashtag elicited a "call-out culture" (Mendes, Ringrose, and Keller 2018: 236) where victims are empowered to publicly challenge their abusers. As Mendes, Ringrose, and Keller (2018: 244) conclude,

> these platforms are also making women's and girls' voices and participation visible in ways that can generate the type of ripple effect we have witnessed in the aftermath of #MeToo, where many powerful (mainly white) men are being held accountable for historic instances of abuse and harassment.

While it is important to note that a number of voices remain marginalized and unheard within this campaign (see Zarkov and Davis 2018; Peyrefitte and Sanders-McDonagh 2018), its transformational impacts cannot be ignored.

Herein lies a different perspective on the impacts of panoptic surveillance.

As discussed previously, theorists have begun to argue that the reins of observational mechanisms can be wrested from authorities by publicly "watching the watchers." Whereas Foucault was concerned that the normalization of surveillance would indoctrinate (and perhaps has indoctrinated) the public into accepting and acting upon whims of a distant and abstract state, the counter-power strategy of sousveillance, or "watching from below" (Mann and Ferenbok 2013: 19), offers a democratizing perspective on the inculcation of the culture of surveillance. The #MeToo movement — and multiple other protest actions that have occurred through or been empowered by social media (e.g., Castells 2015; Richardson 2017) — demonstrate options to undermine the observational power vested in authorities and turn the gaze inward. The enormity of internet-based communication technologies and the ability of countless users to share their opinions in a one-to-many manner have created a new forum, or space, in which the public can inversely *apply* judgment as a product of *being* observed. By eschewing these boundaries, we can work together to vociferously share new measures of righteousness and justice as well as seek new means for redress that were not previously possible. To this end, surveillance theorist David Lyon (2018: 195) argues that there is hope to counter the nefarious omnipresence of surveillance in modern life by asserting digital rights, adding

> the emergence of the culture of surveillance, of watching as a way of life, is both something that may be readily observed, but also, by definition, something to which constructive contributions are being made. They will be truly constructive if the emerging surveillance imaginaries and practices connect with the large canvas of the common good, human flourishing and the care of the other. This, of course, is easy to say, but it is a risky path to take. Actually to put human flourishing first or to care properly for the other is to put yourself out there, make yourself vulnerable, to make a sacrifice and let go.

Conclusion

The information presented here was intended to provide you with an introduction to the panoptic lens and its implications as we enter an increasingly digitized era of social interaction. As we have explored, the changes to our behaviours due to internet communications, paired with the underlying structure of these technologies, have created an environment that has the potential to further the concerns that Michel Foucault raised about **panopticism** and governmentality. Foucault provides a far more nuanced and reasoned philosophy on surveillance, which has inspired countless essays, articles, and textbooks. But at this point, you should be able to critically assess the way you share information, the way you use others' information, and the way others (including corporate, state, and authoritative interests) make use of your and others' data en masse to influence our actions. At the very least, this chapter hopefully introduced you to critical ways of thinking *about* these potentials, even if it does not direct you to act.

At this juncture, it is worth addressing a frequent counterargument to these concerns. There is a tendency among the public, both before and after the inculcation of digital surveillance technologies, to argue that "I have nothing to hide" (Solove 2007). Indeed, this argument might be bolstered by recent legislation throughout jurisdictions in North America and Europe that concretely defend one's right to digital privacy through acts such as the *Personal Information Protection and Electronic Documents Act (PIPEDA)* in Canada or the European Union's *General Data Protection Regulation*. However, even as legislation, these policies are reactive in nature, meaning that they can only regulate behaviours that are known or can be anticipated (Hull 2015). More importantly, they rely on an assumption of a culture of forbearance, or operating within the spirit of the law, among the institutions that they affect (Levitsky and Zibalatt 2018; Solove 2007). In other words, rules that govern our privacy are only effective if the government and private agencies that access our data are willing to adhere to the public's understanding of what the term means. Considering its nebulous definition among the public (Lyon 2018; Hull 2015), dictating clear-cut privacy regulations becomes an exceedingly difficult task. This leads to the ubiquitous privacy policies to which we implicitly agree to access virtually every social media platform currently available. As Hull (2015) argues, these policies actually contribute to the Foucauldian principles discussed previously by making us subject to each entity's definition of privacy, generally dictated by groups whose interest is to profit from and control your data rather than protect it.

Despite these concerns, we must not undermine the progressive potential of mass self-communication and the sousveillant employment of internet technologies. Indeed, as this chapter has discussed, the new era of surveillance can also be framed as one of empowerment, where mass self-communication has informed new forms of counter-power activities (Castells 2009, 2015). The fact that we can now share images, audio, video, and sentiments with people across the globe is telling of what might yet come and what *has* come.

Rapper Childish Gambino's music video for his song "This is America" was viewed more than two hundred million times in the month after its release, raising significant public debate about the experiences of Black Americans in the twenty-first century (Berman 2018). I depart with a cautionary sense of optimism for the internet and society. We certainly have a long way to go if we are to subvert the panoptic mechanisms described in this chapter, but the revolutionary actions borne by the internet paired with heightened public dissatisfaction about the way privacy has been handled leads me to believe that there is potential.

Discussion Questions

1. What are your thoughts on Bentham's proposals for panopticism? Do you think that total surveillance can be justified?
2. How well do you think Foucault's writing applies to the current state of the internet? What gaps are there in his understanding that new theorists might address?
3. What do you take into consideration when you participate in social media? What factors might influence your participation online?
4. How do you think the internet can be used to elicit social change in the future?

Recommended Resources

Lyon, D. 2018. *The Culture of Surveillance*. Cambridge: Polity Press
Twitter. 2018. "Twitter Privacy Policy." <twitter.com/en/privacy>.
Popham, J.F. 2018. "Microdeviation: Observations on the Significance of Lesser Harms in Shaping the Nature of Cyberspace." *Deviant Behavior* 39, 2.
Cadwalladr, C., and E. Graham-Harrison. 2018. "Revealed: 50 Million Facebook Profiles Harvested for Cambridge Analytica in Major Data Breach." *Guardian*, March 17. <theguardian.com/news/2018/mar/17/cambridge-analytica-facebook-influence-us-election>.

Glossary

Black Lives Matter: a social movement dedicated to communicating the generational trauma endured by Black communities at the hands of authorities, as well as the impacts of systemic racism on their daily lives.
carding: a contested policing practice that entails randomly stopping indi-

viduals and requesting to see their personal identification information. Studies have demonstrated that police disproportionately employ this tactic against visible minorities.

crowdsourcing: harnessing the enormous resources of networked individuals to reach a common goal.

de-anonymizing: attempting to reverse-engineer user data in order to identify them, or their traits, for digital commercial practices.

informational exchange: the underlying principle of the internet and related technologies, which entails relaying information between different points.

mass self-communication: defined by Manuel Castells (2009), this refers to the ability of internet users to engage in one-to-many communications while still maintaining a level of presumed anonymity.

meme: a momentary and often humorous description of an emotion or experience, which will sometimes be widely circulated online for the purpose of shaping public narratives.

panopticism (panopticon): a term defined by Jeremy Bentham (1830) and revisited by Michel Foucault (1995). Refers to total observation of an individual, in physical and metaphysical realms.

psychographics: profiles of personal characteristics or traits based on observed information about an individual, such as their Facebook "likes."

sousveillance: originally defined by Mann, Nolan, and Wellman (2002), this term refers to digital counter-power movements that use panoptic surveillance to observe and protest powerful agents.

Notes

1   The term "friends" has come to be synonymous with something more than our traditional notion of friendship — our Facebook "friends" might not overlap with our spheres of true friendship.

2   Amyotrophic lateral sclerosis is better known as Lou Gehrig's disease.

References

@Alyssa_Milano. 2017. "If you've been sexually harassed or assaulted write 'me too' as a reply to this tweet." [Twitter post], October 15. <twitter.com/Alyssa_Milano/status/919659438700670976>.

Acquisti, A., L. Brandimarte, and G. Loewenstein. 2015. "Privacy and Human Behavior in the Age of Information." *Science* 347, 6221.

Adams, S. 2013. "Post-Panoptic Surveillance through Healthcare Rating Sites: Who's Watching Whom?" *Information, Communication & Society* 16, 2.

ALS Association. 2018. "ALS Ice Bucket Challenge Commitment." *ALS Association*. <alsa.

org/fight-als/ice-bucket-challenge-spending.html>.

Bailey, B. 2017. "Greetings and Compliments or Street Harassment? Competing Evaluations of Street Remarks in a Recorded Collection." *Discourse & Society* 28, 4.

Baldwin-Philippi, J. 2016. "The Cult (ure) of Analytics in 2014." In J.A. Hendricks and D. Schill (eds.), *Communication and Midterm Elections*. New York: Palgrave Macmillan.

Barker, J.C. 1998. *Danger, Duty, and Disillusion: The Worldview of Los Angeles Police Officers*. Long Grove: Waveland Press.

Behrend, T.S., D.J. Sharek, A.W. Meade, and E.N. Wiebe. 2011. "The Viability of Crowdsourcing for Survey Research." *Behavior Research Methods* 43, 3.

Bentham, J. 1996. *The Collected Works of Jeremy Bentham: An Introduction to the Principles of Morals and Legislation*. Oxford: Clarendon Press.

____. 1830. *The Rationale of Punishment*. London: Robert Heward.

Berman, J. 2018. "'This Is America': 8 Things to Read about Childish Gambino's New Music Video." *New York Times*, May 8. <nytimes.com/2018/05/08/arts/music/childish-gambino-this-is-america-roundup.html>.

Bonilla, Y., and J. Rosa. 2015. "#Ferguson: Digital Protest, Hashtag Ethnography, and the Racial Politics of Social Media in the United States." *American Ethnologist* 42, 1.

Britt, R. 2018. "Boston Marathon 2018: Results Analytics, Multi-Year Statistics, Avg Finish Times, Tips, More." *RunTri*. <runtri.com/2007/05/boston-marathon-2008-what-to-expect.html>.

Burchell, G. 1991. "Peculiar Interests: Civil Society and Governing 'The System of Natural Liberty.'" In G. Burchell, C. Gordon, and P. Miller (eds.), *The Foucault Effect: Studies in Governmentality with Two Lectures and an Interview with Michel Foucault*. Chicago: University of Chicago Press.

Cadwalladr, C., and E. Graham-Harrison. 2018. "Revealed: 50 Million Facebook Profiles Harvested for Cambridge Analytica in Major Data Breach." *Guardian*, March 17. <theguardian.com/news/2018/mar/17/cambridge-analytica-facebook-influence-us-election>.

Castells, M. 2015. *Networks of Outrage and Hope: Social Movements in the Internet Age*, 2nd edition. Cambridge: Polity.

____. 2009. *Communication Power*. Oxford: Oxford University Press.

Chan, J. 1996. "Changing Police Culture." *British Journal of Criminology* 36, 1.

Cho, D., S. Kim, and A. Acquisti. 2012. "Empirical Analysis of Online Anonymity and User Behaviors: The Impact of Real Name Policy." *2012 45th Hawaii International Conference on System Science* (HICSS) (January).

Coates, K. 2015. *# IdleNoMore: And the Remaking of Canada*. Regina: University of Regina Press.

Cole, D. 2015. "The Skin I'm In: I've Been Interrogated by Police More Than 50 Times — All Because I'm Black." *Toronto Life*, April 21. <torontolife.com/city/life/skin-im-ive-interrogated-police-50-times-im-black/>.

Comer, D. 2007. *The Internet Book: Everything You Need to Know About Computer Networking and How the Internet Works*, 4th ed. Upper Saddle River: Pearson Prentice Hall.

Confessore, N. 2018. "Cambridge Analytica and Facebook: The Scandal and the Fallout So Far." *New York Times*, April 4. <nytimes.com/2018/04/04/us/politics/cambridge-analytica-scandal-fallout.html>.

Connolly, W.E. 2017. "Trump, the Working Class, and Fascist Rhetoric." *Theory & Event* 20, 1.

Crawford, K., and J. Schultz. 2014. "Big Data and Due Process: Toward a Framework to Redress Predictive Privacy Harms." *Boston College Law Review* 55, 1.

Curtis, B. 2002. "Surveying the Social: Techniques, Practices, Power." *Histoire sociale/ Social History* 35, 69.

Davary, B. 2017. # Black Lives Matter." *Ethnic Studies Review* 37, 1.

Dawkins, R. 2006. *The Selfish Gene*, 30th anniversary ed. Oxford: Oxford University Press.

Dean, J. 2017. "Not Him, Us (and We Aren't Populists)." *Theory & Event* 20, 1.

Elish, M.C., and D. Boyd. 2018. "Situating Methods in the Magic of Big Data and AI." *Communication Monographs* 85, 1.

"Facebook, Social Media Privacy, and the Use and Abuse of Data." 2018. Hearings before the Committee on Commerce, Science, and Transportation, Senate, 115th Cong. (Testimony of Mark Zuckerberg). <judiciary.senate.gov/imo/media/doc/04-10-18%20Zuckerberg%20Testimony.pdf>.

Foucault, M. 1995. *Discipline and Punish: The Birth of the Prison* (Alan Sheridan, trans.). New York: Vintage Books.

___. 1991. "Governmentality." In G. Burchell, C. Gordon, and P. Miller (eds.), *The Foucault Effect: Studies in Governmentality with Two Lectures and an Interview with Michel Foucault*. Chicago: University of Chicago Press.

Friess, S. 2007. "Online Fossett Searchers Ask, Was It Worth It?" *Wired*, November 6. <wired.com/2007/11/online-fossett-searchers-ask-was-it-worth-it/>.

Gillis, W. 2017. Misconduct charges stayed against Toronto cops who blocked citizen filming arrest. *Toronto Star*, January 12. <thestar.com/news/gta/2017/01/12/misconduct-charges-stayed-against-toronto-cops-who-blocked-citizen-filming-arrest.html>.

Goffman, E. 2007. *Asylums: Essays on the Social Situation of Mental Patients and Other Inmates*. New York: Routledge.

González, R.J. 2017. "Hacking the Citizenry? Personality Profiling, 'Big Data' and the Election of Donald Trump." *Anthropology Today* 33, 3.

Grossmann, M., and D. Thaler. 2018. "Mass–Elite Divides in Aversion to Social Change and Support for Donald Trump." *American Politics Research* 46, 5.

Haunss, S. 2014. "Privacy Activism after Snowden: Advocacy Networks or Protest?" *Cultures of Privacy*. <researchgate.net/profile/Sebastian_Haunss/publication/292630367_Privacy_Activism_after_Snowden_Advocacy_Networks_or_Protest/links/56b088ac08ae8e37214f79b3.pdf>.

Herrera, L. 2015. "Citizenship under Surveillance: Dealing with the Digital Age." *International Journal of Middle East Studies* 47, 2.

Hogan, B. 2012. "Pseudonyms and the Rise of the Real-Name Web." In J. Hartley, J. Burgess, and A. Bruns (eds.), *A Companion to New Media Dynamics*. Chichester: Blackwell Publishing.

Horeck, T. 2014. "#AskThicke: 'Blurred Lines,' Rape Culture, and the Feminist Hashtag Takeover." *Feminist Media Studies* 14, 6.

Ho Shon, P.C. 2005. "'I'd Grab the sob by His Hair and Yank Him Out the Window': The Fraternal Order of Warnings and Threats in Police–Citizen Encounters." *Discourse & Society* 16, 6.

Hull, G. 2015. "Successful Failure: What Foucault Can Teach Us About Privacy Self-Management in a World of Facebook and Big Data." *Ethics and Information Technology* 17, 2.

Issenberg, S. 2016. *The Victory Lab: The Secret Science of Winning Campaigns.* New York: Broadway Books.

ITU. 2016. *Measuring the Information Society Report 2016.* Geneva: International Telecommunication Union.

Kidd, D., and K. McIntosh. 2016. "Social Media and Social Movements." *Sociology Compass* 10, 9.

Kosinski, M., D. Stillwell, and T. Graepel. 2013. "Private Traits and Attributes Are Predictable from Digital Records of Human Behavior." *Proceedings of the National Academy of Sciences* 110, 15.

Lang, R.E. and D.F. Damore. 2016. "The End of the Democratic Blue Wall?" 1–17. <digitalscholarship.unlv.edu/brookings_pubs/45/>.

Lerman, K., and T. Hogg. 2014. "Leveraging Position Bias to Improve Peer Recommendation." *PLOS One* 9, 6.

Levitsky, S., and D. Ziblatt. 2018. *How Democracies Die.* New York: Crown.

Lipsitz, G. 2006. *The Possessive Investment in Whiteness: How White People Profit from Identity Politics.* New York: Temple University Press.

Lyon, D. 2018. *The Culture of Surveillance.* Cambridge: Polity.

Manikonda, L., G. Beigi, H. Liu, and S. Kambhampati. 2018. "Twitter for Sparking a Movement, Reddit for Sharing the Moment: #Metoo Through the Lens of Social Media." *arXiv preprint arXiv:*1803.08022.

Mann, S., and J. Ferenbok. 2013. "New Media and the Power Politics of Sousveillance in a Surveillance-Dominated World." *Surveillance & Society* 11, 1/2.

Mann, S., J. Nolan, and B. Wellman. 2002. "Sousveillance: Inventing and Using Wearable Computing Devices for Data Collection in Surveillance Environments." *Surveillance & Society* 1, 3.

Marx, G.T. 2013. "The Public as Partner? Technology Can Make Us Auxiliaries as Well as Vigilantes." *IEEE Security & Privacy* 11, 5.

Mendes, K., J. Ringrose, and J. Keller. 2018. "# MeToo and the Promise and Pitfalls of Challenging Rape Culture Through Digital Feminist Activism." *European Journal of Women's Studies* 25, 2.

Meyerson, C. 2014. "A Hollaback Response Video: Women of Color on Street Harassment." Jezebel, November 6. <jezebel.com/a-hollaback-response-video-women-of-color-on-street-ha-1655494647>.

Miller, J.A., and R. Miller. 1987. "Jeremy Bentham's Panoptic Device." *MIT Press* 41.

Nhan, J., L. Huey, and R. Broll. 2017. "Digilantism: An Analysis of Crowdsourcing and the Boston Marathon Bombings." *British Journal of Criminology* 57, 2.

O'Neil, C. 2016. *Weapons of Math Destruction: How Big Data Increases Inequality and Threatens Democracy.* New York: Broadway Books.

Pantumsinchai, P. 2018. "Armchair Detectives and the Social Construction of Falsehoods: An Actor–Network Approach." *Information, Communication & Society* 21, 5.

Paoline III, E.A., S.M. Myers, and R.E. Worden. 2000. "Police Culture, Individualism, and Community Policing: Evidence from Two Police Departments." *Justice Quarterly* 17, 3.

Papadopoulos, S., Y. Kompatsiaris, A. Vakali, and P. Spyridonos. 2012. "Community

Detection in Social Media." *Data Mining and Knowledge Discovery* 24, 3.

Persily, N. 2017. "Can Democracy Survive the Internet?" *Journal of Democracy* 28, 2.

Peyrefitte, M., and E. Sanders-McDonagh. 2018. "Space, Power and Sexuality: Transgressive and Transformative Possibilities at the Interstices of Spatial Boundaries." *Journal of Feminist Geography* 25, 3.

Popham, J.F. 2018. "Microdeviation: Observations on the Significance of Lesser Harms in Shaping the Nature of Cyberspace." *Deviant Behavior* 39, 2.

Reddit. 2013. "Reflections on the Recent Boston Crisis" (Blog Post). *upvoted*, April 22. <redditblog.com/2013/04/22/reflections-on-the-recent-boston-crisis/>.

Rentschler, C.A. 2015. "Technologies of Bystanding: Learning to See Like a Bystander." In S. Pearl (ed.), *Images, Ethics, Technology*. New York: Routledge.

Richardson, A.V. 2017. "Bearing Witness While Black: Theorizing African American Mobile Journalism after Ferguson." *Digital Journalism* 5, 6.

Roose, K., and C. Kang. 2018. "Mark Zuckerberg Testifies on Facebook Before Skeptical Lawmakers." *New York Times*, April 10: A1.

Rosenthal, R., and L. Jacobson. 1966. "Teachers' Expectancies: Determinants of Pupils' IQ Gains." *Psychological Reports* 19, 1.

Rowling, J.K. 1998. *Harry Potter and the Sorcerer's Stone*. New York: Arthur A. Levine Books.

Schneider, C.J., and D. Trottier. 2012. "The 2011 Vancouver Riot and the Role of Facebook in Crowd-Sourced Policing." *BC Studies* 175.

Semple, J. 1993. *Bentham's Prison: A Study of the Panopticon Penitentiary: A Study of the Panopticon Penitentiary*. Oxford: Clarendon Press.

Sheptycki, J. 2016. "'In There Like a Dirty Shirt': Reflections on Fieldwork in the Police Organization." In G.A. Antonopoulos (ed.), *Illegal Entrepreneurship, Organized Crime and Social Control*. Basel: Springer.

Silver, E., and L.L. Miller. 2002. "A Cautionary Note on the Use of Actuarial Risk Assessment Tools for Social Control." *Crime & Delinquency* 48, 1.

Smith, G. 2001. "The 2001 General Election: Factors Influencing the Brand Image of Political Parties and Their Leaders." *Journal of Marketing Management* 17, 9–10.

Solove, D.J. 2007. "I've Got Nothing to Hide and Other Misunderstandings of Privacy." *San Diego Law Review* 44, 4.

Starbird, K., J. Maddock, M. Orand, P. Achterman, and R.M. Mason. 2014. "Rumors, False Flags, and Digital Vigilantes: Misinformation on Twitter after the 2013 Boston Marathon Bombing." iConference 2014 Proceedings.

Tambo, E., E.C. Ugwu, and J.Y. Ngogang. 2014. "Need of Surveillance Response Systems to Combat Ebola Outbreaks and Other Emerging Infectious Diseases in African Countries." *Infectious Diseases of Poverty* 3, 1.

Tapia, A.H., N.J. LaLone, and H.W. Kim. 2014. "Run Amok: Group Crowd Participation in Identifying the Bomb and Bomber from the Boston Marathon Bombing." Presented at International ISCRAM Conference, University Park, Pennsylvania, May.

Tapscott, D. 2009. *Grown Up Digital: How the Net Generation Is Changing Your World*. New York: McGraw-Hill.

Trottier, D. 2017. "Digital Vigilantism as Weaponisation of Visibility." *Philosophy & Technology* 30, 1.

Tufekci, Z. 2014 "Engineering the Public: Big Data, Surveillance and Computational

Politics." *First Monday* 19, 7.

Twitter. 2018. "Twitter Privacy Policy." <twitter.com/en/privacy>.

Von Baeyer, C.L., D.L. Sherk, and M.P. Zanna. 1981. "Impression Management in the Job Interview: When the Female Applicant Meets the Male (Chauvinist) Interviewer." *Personality and Social Psychology Bulletin* 7, 1.

Waddington, P.A., K. Stenson, and D. Don. 2004. "In Proportion: Race, and Police Stop and Search." *British Journal of Criminology* 44, 6.

Wall, D. 2007. *Cybercrime: The transformation of Crime in the Information Age,* Vol. 4. Cambridge: Polity.

Walsh, B., C. Maiers, G. Nally, J. Boggs, and Praxis Program Team. 2014. "Crowdsourcing Individual Interpretations: Between Microtasking and Macrotasking." *Literary and Linguistic Computing* 29, 3.

Wells, W.D. 1975. "Psychographics: A Critical Review." *Journal of Marketing Research* 12, 2.

Winsa, P., and J. Rankin. 2015. "Video Captures Aggressive Tactics Used by TAVIS Officers." *Toronto Star*, October 27. <thestar.com/news/insight/2015/10/27/video-captures-aggressive-tactics-used-by-tavis-officers.html>.

Wortley, S., and A. Owusu-Bempah. 2011. "The Usual Suspects: Police Stop and Search Practices in Canada." *Policing and Society* 21, 4.

Wotherspoon, T., and J. Hansen. 2013. "The 'Idle No More' Movement: Paradoxes of First Nations Inclusion in the Canadian context." *Social Inclusion* 1, 1.

Yang, G. 2016. "Narrative Agency in Hashtag Activism: The Case of #BlackLivesMatter." *Media and Communication* 4, 4.

Yuce, S., N. Agarwal, and R. Wigand. 2013. "Mapping Cyber-Collective Action Among Female Muslim Bloggers for the *Women to Drive* Movement." In A. Greenberg, W. Kennedy and N. Bos, *Social Computing, Behavioral-Cultural Modeling and Prediction.* Paper presented at Sixth International Conference, SBP, Washington, DC. April 2. New York: Springer.

Zarkov, D., and K. Davis. 2018. "Ambiguities and Dilemmas around #MeToo: #ForHowLong and #Whereto?" *European Journal of Women's Studies* 25, 1.

14

National Security, Surveillance, and Colonial Understandings of Indigenous Sovereignty

Scott Thompson

After reading this chapter, you will be able to do the following:

1. Understand surveillance through Foucault's theory of governmentality and its two key components of "governing rationalities" and "technologies."

2. Understand how the legal category of "Indian" has been used by the Canadian government to govern First Nations, Inuit, and Métis peoples.

3. Understand how "productivity" is a social construction used to justify the governance of First Nations, Inuit, and Métis peoples by the Canadian government.

4. Understand the colonial concepts of social order within society, social Darwinism, the white man's burden, social efficiency, and productivity.

5. Understand how the government of Canada classification of "critical infrastructure" limits First Nations, Inuit, and Métis sovereignty.

Despite attempts to mend relationships between First Nations, Inuit, Métis, and settler peoples in Canada and concrete action items to advance reconciliation (see Truth and Reconciliation Commission of Canada 2015b), the legacy of colonial policy remains within the Canadian government's

Indigenous sovereignty, title to land, and self-determination existed long before their contact with European colonial traders and settlers and are independent of any European law or legal system.

legislation, institutions, and ways of thinking. In *Tsilhqot'in Nation v. British Columbia* (2014), the Supreme Court of Canada established that the sovereignty of First Nations and Inuit peoples predates the *Royal Proclamation* (1763) and the *British North America Act* (1876). Indigenous sovereignty, title to land, and self-determination existed long before their contact with European colonial traders and settlers and are independent of any European law or legal system.

In this sense, the sovereignty of peoples legally defined as "**Indians**" is not bound by British/Canadian settler laws, policy, and practices. In practice, however, this is not the case. Recent legislation regarding national security (Bill C-51), as well as the responses of national security agencies in Canada to teach-ins, hunger strikes, and protests associated with both Idle No More and the 2007 Day of Action — a day of protest organized for June 29, 2007, to call attention to the differential life chances, lived experiences, and cancellation of government funding promises for First Nations, Inuit, and Métis communities (Fontaine 2007) — indicate that Canadian government

Question (study guide).

Box 14-1: The Use of "Indian" as a Classification of Government

by Celine Beaulieu

The term "Indian" is now not commonly heard due to public recognition of its derogatory nature. But Indigenous Peoples are specifically recognized through the historical legal categorization of "Indian" as determined by European settler governments — first under British and later under Canadian law. For this chapter, the term "Indian" is used in reference to the classification of people under the *Indian Act* (1876). The federal policy uses the classification of "Indian" to combine the distinct multiplicities of independent First Nations, Inuit, and Métis peoples in Canada into a singular collective population. This categorization of Indigenous nations aligns with the governments' specific views of what Indigenous identity entails, and works as an external categorization that is imposed upon Indigenous nations. However, this term excludes specific individuals who cannot be recognized as a result of the restrictions imposed historically through the government of Canada's narrow registration process (e.g., unknown or unstated parentage; RSC, 1985, c. I-5, s. 5). Overall, it is important to recognize that the categorization of "Indian" in this chapter aligns with the specific definition constructed by the Canadian federal government, and then imposed upon the many distinct Indigenous nations as a means of shaping their behaviour.

institutions still hold the colonial view of Indigenous sovereignty as limited (see Box 14-1). This chapter addresses how and why the state places defined limits on what Indigenous sovereignty can be, how these limitations are tied to national security surveillance systems, and what legacy of colonial rationalities remains within these processes. It explains how the colonial imposition of state-defined limits on Indigenous sovereignty is reproduced within colonial surveillance practices and how this way of thinking still impacts Indigenous sovereignty.

> Productivity justifies colonial expansion, governance, and settlement and serves to measure the success of the "civilization" and assimilation of Indigenous Peoples. From Confederation to the current day, productivity has played a central role in Canadian policy regarding people legally classified as "Indians" and has placed hard boundaries around Indigenous sovereignty and self-governance.

More specifically, this chapter focuses on the role of the concept of "productivity" as a key driver within the British/Canadian rationality of colonialism. Justified by "order" and "racial superiority," "misused" lands and the labour power of Indigenous Peoples were and are converted to fit Eurocentric, capitalist systems of production and economies. Productivity justifies colonial expansion, governance, and settlement and serves to measure the success of the "civilization" and assimilation of Indigenous Peoples. From Confederation to the current day, productivity has played a central role in Canadian policy regarding people legally classified as "Indians" and has placed hard boundaries

---

Box 14-2: First Nations Sovereignty

by Connor Morrison and Scott Thompson

Although the idea of thinking of Indigenous Peoples as "Nations" might seem new to some, the First Nations have always been sovereign bodies. In pre-colonial times, Indigenous Peoples were self-governing, each nation living in accordance with their own sets of norms, values, traditions, and practices. When King George III issued the *Royal Proclamation* of 1763, a set of settlement guidelines was enacted that recognized Aboriginal Rights of title and land ownership, specifically that "the several Nations or Tribes of Indians with whom We are connected." Furthermore, agreements between the British Crown and First Nations also recognized their sovereignty since, by definition, a treaty under international law can only be agreed upon between two legally equal sovereign nations (an agreement not between sovereign nations being a contract instead). Finally, sovereignty and the claim to territory was upheld by the Supreme Court of Canada in *Tsilhqot'in Nation v. British Columbia* (2014) as the court found that these rights of nationhood predated colonial contact. Aboriginal sovereignty and title to land existed long before colonization.

Surveillance always works against the sovereignty of those under it. Although surveillance is often thought of as a tool of undercover agents or the result of some new high-tech gadget, what is often lost is that surveillance requires a very clear understanding, or belief, that outlines the way that things *ought to be* or how people *ought to behave*.

around Indigenous sovereignty and self-governance.

Drawing on current surveillance practices and historical expansions of productivity within British/Canadian colonial practice, this chapter demonstrates how the concept of productivity is embedded within Canadian understandings of national security and continues to police the boundaries of, and develop knowledge about, what is considered "acceptable" regarding First Nations, Inuit, and Métis sovereignty in Canada. It argues that Indigenous sovereignty in Canada remains limited by knowledge production practices within national security agencies, and this apparatus has worked to assert a colonial relationship whereby First Nations, Inuit, and Métis sovereignty could not impose on British and, later, the Canadian government's, understandings of productivity (see Box 14-2).

Surveillance and Sovereignty

Surveillance always works against the sovereignty of those under it. Although surveillance is often thought of as a tool of undercover agents or the result of some new high-tech gadget, what is often lost is that surveillance requires a very clear understanding, or belief, that outlines the way that things *ought to be* or how people *ought to behave*.

Without this framework, agents or high-tech gadgets would have nothing to identify, collect information on, and work to control. That is, surveillance needs an understanding of who people *are* and what they *should* be doing so it can identify wrongdoers and intervene in their behaviour. For this reason, sovereignty — or the right and ability to exert authority over oneself, or of a group of people over themselves — is necessarily limited, or categorically opposed by, the beliefs, values, and rules of those conducting surveillance. Foucault's concept of governmentality can explain this role of surveillance in colonial policy and practice.

In his writing and lectures at the Collège de France in Paris, Foucault identifies governance as "the conduct of conduct" or, more simply, as activities "aiming to shape, guide or effect the conduct of some person or persons" (Gordon 1991: 2; also see Foucault 2010). Here, governance, or how individuals' lives and their actions are shaped, is understood as having two key parts. The first is "**governing rationalities**," meaning the organizing sets of ideas, or beliefs, that explain what people or objects are to be governed, why they should be governed, what nature and obligations are to be attributed

> Rationalities form the beliefs, values, categories, and roles that set out a very specific understanding of "who is who," "who does what," and "what exactly is the way that things *ought to be*."

to the governed, and finally, how the act of governance is to be carried out (Rose, O'Malley and Valverde 2006: 86). In short, governing rationalities exist as "a way or system of thinking about the nature of the practice of government" that make specific forms of management possible for its practitioners as well as "those upon whom it was practiced" (Gordon 1991: 3). Rationalities form the beliefs, values, categories, and roles that set out a very specific understanding of "who is who," "who does what," and "what exactly is the way that things *ought to be*."

In the case of the British (and, later, the Canadian) state and the surveillance of First Nations, Inuit, and Métis peoples, rationalities were applied based on specific understandings of colonialism, which included categories of race, subjecthood, and religion. These notions established how "Indians" were to live, be "civilized," and develop into productive capitalist subjects.

The second aspect of governance is "technologies." Foucault takes up a broad definition of technology, drawing from the Greek root of *techne*, which refers to the techniques, skills, methods, processes, and policies used in the accomplishment of objectives (Foucault 1978 cited in Behrent 2013). **Technologies of governance** are those that work to bring the ideas, or rationalities (mentioned previously), into being; they work to shape human interaction and human life to make them fit the goals, beliefs, values, and ways of seeing the world of the surveillance system.

Understanding both of these components of surveillance is crucial for charting how government programs sought to use colonial surveillance to impact First Nations, Inuit, and Métis peoples. The following sections take up this understanding of surveillance as consisting of both rationalities — ideas, beliefs, values, about how things *ought to be* — and technologies — the tools, strategies, policies, and practices used in the accomplishment of objectives — that chart how specific surveillance practices worked, and are still working, to

> **Technologies of governance** are those that work to bring the ideas, or rationalities (mentioned previously), into being; they work to shape human interaction and human life to make them fit the goals, beliefs, values, and ways of seeing the world of the surveillance system.

> **Box 14-3: The Historical Process of Surrendering Reserve Land**
> **— An *Indian Act* Technology of Governance**
>
> *by Celine Beaulieu*
>
> Through the *Indian Act*, specific technologies were used by the Department of Indian Affairs to control their actions and to delegitimize First Nations' sovereignty. This was demonstrated historically through the process of surrendering land on First Nations' reserves. Since the federal government, through its own social and legal constructs, deems reserve land as federal property, the adequate procedure to surrendering reserve land is mediated through a process of regulations outlined by the Department of Indian Affairs through the *Indian Act*. As outlined by Harold McGill, the process entailed submitting a proposal for surrendering land by an officer of the Department, to be approved by the superintendent. If approved, the council would hold a meeting witnessed and the votes authorized by the officer of the Department (RG 10, Volume 8287, File 674/7-3-13-103RC). This process demonstrates the restrictions imposed upon First Nations and their inability to exercise their own methods of land distribution under the *Indian Act* (Beaulieu forthcoming).

bring "Indian" productivity into line with a colonial understanding of *how things ought to be* (see Box 14-3).

The Rationality of British/Canadian Colonialism and Productivity

The link between Canadian colonial practice and capitalist pursuit of productive land and labour use can be traced to British colonial rationalities of order/prosperity and racial domination. In the colonial period, which roughly spanned 1607–1763, expansionist colonial rationalities drew heavily from required Church of England sermons and teachings. From 1547, British law required the teaching of particular religious sermons or homilies that asserted values and beliefs supportive of the strict social hierarchy and structure of British society (Aughterson 1998). These state-mandated church teachings included the Homily on Order titled *An Exhortation Concerning Good Order and Obedience to Rulers and Magistrates* ([1562] 1854), which asserted a relationship between God and humanity through which human adherence to God's plan for creation would ensure productivity within the society and prosperity for all. This included not only piety in worshipping God, but also adherence to a strict social hierarchy and order in British society. As noted in the Homily on Order ([1562] 1854):

ALMIGHTY God hath created and appointed all things, in heaven, earth, and waters, in a most excellent and perfect order.... In earth he hath assigned and appointed kings and princes, with other governors under them, in good and necessary order.... Every degree of people, in their vocation, calling, and office, hath appointed to them their duty and order. Some are in high degree, some in low; some kings and princes, some inferiors and subjects; priests and laymen, masters and servants, fathers and children, husbands and wives, rich and poor; and every one have need of other. So that in all things is to be lauded and praised the goodly order of God: without the which no house, no city, no commonwealth can continue and endure; for, where there is no right order, there reigneth all abuse, carnal liberty, enormity, sin, and Babylonical confusion. (Cited in Aughterson 1998: 93)

In this sense, God had a plan to ensure the greatest productivity of land and labour. God had decided where every person should be born and what station and calling they should fulfill. Those in lower stations were to give deference and obedience to those above them, while those in higher stations were to provide guidance and protection (see Box 14-4).

This ordering was applied to British colonization of territories and peoples. According to the teachings, God, in his infallibility, places every person — from the English monarch to an Indigenous woman in the Americas — in their proper place, and each of them was to know their position and play their part within the strict social hierarchy of God's order. This order ensures productivity and prosperity, and to violate it would be to break the order of God's plan and risk the prosperity of all. This was coupled with "social Darwinism," the expansion of early understandings of evolutionary theory and their incorporation into colonial justifications for domination. Social Darwinism established productivity and the capacity for the widening of state influence to new territories and over new peoples as measures of racial success and superiority.

Under the social Darwinism of the time, it was argued that biological concepts of natural selection and "survival of the fittest" should be applied to racial and societal groups as well. It wrongly asserted that some cultures were more evolved than others, and thus more capable of using land and labour power in a more productive manner (Hofstadter 1992 [1944]).

> Social Darwinism established productivity and the capacity for the widening of state influence to new territories and over new peoples as measures of racial success and superiority.

Box 14-4: Rationalities of *Terra Nullius* and the "Doctrine of Discovery"

by Celine Beaulieu

Terra nullius and the Doctrine of Discovery are two additional examples of rationalities (a specific set of thoughts or beliefs) used by European nations during the era of colonial expansion. These foundational ideas and the beliefs originating from these principles continue to influence the Canadian State's present practices, perceptions, and ideas of Indigenous People (Truth and Reconciliation Commission of Canada 2015b: Call 47). The Doctrine, issued by Pope Alexander VI in 1493, viewed colonial expansion as a commendable endeavour by Spanish explorers that would result in the "civilization" and "Christianization" of Indigenous Peoples in America (see Miller et al. 2010). Pope Alexander's edict authorized Spain to explore, "discover," and claim "unoccupied" land in the Americas. Therefore, the Doctrine of Discovery gradually became incorporated into international law, so that other European nations would also be allowed to claim unoccupied territory without disrespecting the authority of the pope. It was within this transition that the principle of *terra nullius* was introduced. Interpreted as "no man's land," terra nullius was used to decree a territory unoccupied, and therefore allowed for European nations to assert their sovereignty over these regions. *Terra nullius* failed to acknowledge the legitimacy of Indigenous Nations' sovereignty over specific territories, thus determining that it was unnecessary for European nations to fight Indigenous Nations in order to occupy their land (Beaulieu forthcoming). Overall, it is important to identify how these rationalities continue to influence present perceptions and limitations to practices of Indigenous sovereignty within Canada. The TRC's forty-ninth call to action asks all religious denominations to repudiate *terra nullius* and the Doctrine of Discovery; in calls 58 to 61, religious denominations are guided to remediate any previous actions that have enforced these concepts (Truth and Reconciliation Commission of Canada 2015b: Calls 47, 58–61).

In addition to God's order, social Darwinism depicted some cultures and racial groups as "savage," representing earlier, less evolved developmental stages. The more "advanced" and "evolved" European cultures were simply living out God's natural order in their colonial expansion and subjugation of First Nations, Inuit, and other peoples of the world. Colonialism was about competing societal productive forces and determining which was "more fit" to best control land and labour resources. As noted by Dherme (1908), a British author writing about colonialism,

> the most important result of colonization is to increase world productivity. It is at the same time a great social force for progress. The earth

belongs to humanity. It belongs to those who know best how to develop it, increase its wealth and in the process augment it, beatify it and elevate humanity.

> Productivity existed as both a justification for British colonial expansion and a measure of the subjugation/"civilization" of Indigenous Peoples.

Colonization is the propagation of the highest form of civilization yet conceived and realized, the perpetuation of the most talented race, the progressive organization of humanity. (Cited in Conklin 1997: 56)

Productivity existed as both a justification for British colonial expansion and a measure of the subjugation/"civilization" of Indigenous Peoples. Productivity was understood as: (1) the capacity to produce surplus value as measured by European economic standards; and (2) the transformation of "misused" labour and land — that is, land or labour not working to ensure the type of production of surplus goods for capitalist economic exchange, which was seen as both the expression of God's will and the biological evolutionary imperative of the natural world. In this way, colonial rule, domination, and settlement were not seen as self-serving or exploitative, but instead as humanitarian acts of bringing the "right way" to live, work, and use the land to the backward, "savage" people of the world. It was the "White Man's Burden," as Kipling (1929) termed it, to take the non-European cultures and peoples of the world under British rule and teach them the "evolved" ways of Western production, agricultural processing, and a wage-based organization of labour power. Although it is argued that Kipling noted this in jest, it was a central component of British colonial rationality (Murphy 2010). As noted at the time, colonialism

> must go on.... It has been the prime condition and mode of progress in the past, therefore it is desirable it should go on. It must go on, it ought to go on.... This genuine and confident conviction about "social efficiency" must be taken as the chief moral support of Imperialism. Human progress requires the maintenance of the race struggle, in which the weakest races shall go under, while the "socially efficient" races survive and flourish: we are the "socially efficient" race. (Hobson 2005 [1938]: 155)

Within colonial rationalities, productivity was the measure through which the sovereignty of a people was tested. For the British, their capacity to expand their cultural influence into the new territories of the Americas and elsewhere, and to assert capitalist application of land and labour power, meant that

> Any disruption of the "proper" use of land and labour power would represent a threat to the order and prosperity of all within the society.

when British authority has been forcibly fastened upon large populations of alien race and colour, with habits of life and thought which do not blend with ours.... We are obliged in practice to make a choice between good order and justice administered autocratically in accordance with British standards, on the one hand, and delicate, costly, doubtful, and disorderly experiments in self-government on British lines upon the other, and we have practically everywhere decided to adopt the former alternative. (Hobson 2005 [1938]: 118, 122)

Productivity, however, also presented a boundary for the sovereignty of both individuals and groups — because productivity required adherence to God's proper ordering of society, and the productivity and prosperity of all was dependant on this order. Importantly, Indigenous sovereignty existed to the extent that productivity — in the form of expanding capitalist production — of land and labour power were not adversely impacted. Conversely, any disruption of the "proper" use of land and labour power would represent a threat to the order and prosperity of all within the society.

In the mid-1800s, the Bagot Commission formally incorporated productivity into its unilaterally developed and imposed goals for First Nations, Inuit, and Métis peoples, defined as "Indians" in Canada. In particular, the commission worked for the centralization of control policy, establishing a formalized organization of Indian land-use rights under colonial supervision and control, including the licensing of timber and the issuance of deeds on Indian lands (Report on the Indians of Canada 1847: Appendix EEE). Furthermore, it asserted the need for "Indians" to be educated in the proper use of land and labour resources and to be taught techniques of European agricultural methods and land management, along with concepts of individual ownership and Christianity. With the later consolidation of these goals and other legislation around Indian management, the *Indian Act* of 1876 was defined as

> rest[ing] on the principle, that the aborigines are to be kept in a condition of tutelage and treated as wards or children of the State ... the true interests of the aborigines and of the State alike require that every effort should be made to aid the Red man in lifting himself out of his condition of tutelage and dependence, and that

is clearly our wisdom and our duty, through education and every other means, to prepare him for a higher civilization by encouraging him to assume the privileges and responsibilities of full citizenship. (Department of the Interior 1876)

> The above genocidal functions of the *Indian Act* (1876) were to "continue until there is not a single Indian in Canada that has not been absorbed into the body politic and there is no Indian question and no Indian Department."

Later, Duncan Campbell Scott, then superintendent-general of the Department of Indian Affairs (the government department managing those defined as "Indians" in Canada), established that the above genocidal functions of the *Indian Act* (1876) were to "continue until there is not a single Indian in Canada that has not been absorbed into the body politic and there is no Indian question and no Indian Department" (cited in Titley 1983: 50).

In its practical application, the *Indian Act's* role of oversight, subjugation, and education took the form of several detailed surveillance systems that targeted First Nations, Inuit, and Métis sovereignty and culture. The following sections demonstrate how British/Canadian understandings of order and productivity were, and remain, key aspects of the rationality of colonialism that shaped, and continues to shape, Canadian institutions — working to assert limitations on Indigenous sovereignty in relation to the "productivity" related to critical infrastructure in Canada.

Early "Indian" Surveillance and Productivity in Canada

With Canada's Confederation in 1867, the management of "Indian" peoples and treaty relations fully came under the central administration of government officials in Ottawa. With this shift came a clear and coordinated push to practice the rationality of colonialism, specifically in its relation to the goals set out in the Bagot Commission concerning education, proper development (in relation to land and labour productivity), and cultural extermination. To do this, the Department of Indian Affairs turned to highly invasive surveillance practices that targeted the lives and resources of people classified as "Indians" under the law. The rationality of British colonialism was *brought into being* through the use of several surveillance technologies — the most notable being those administrated

> To do this, the Department of Indian Affairs turned to highly invasive surveillance practices that targeted the lives and resources of people classified as "Indians" under the law.

Indian agents played the key colonial role of surveillance, oversight, management, and discipline, designed to ensure the proper development of Indians into good, productive British subjects.

by Indian agents, who were tasked with applying and enforcing government policy related to First Nations, Inuit, and Métis populations. Having developed out of the less formal trader/agent social positions that were a staple of French colonial practice in the mid-1700s, the specific duties of Indian agents were established in post-Confederation Canada under the *Indian Act* (Dickason 2002; Milloy 1983). In practice, the role of the Indian agent was the assimilation and education of "Indian" peoples, as described by the Bagot Commission. While the agency was managed from a head office in Ottawa, individual agents lived and acted locally, performing an extensive number of tasks that included overseeing reserve land use and its leasing or sale, distributing treaty gifts and rations, administering elections or appointing leadership positions, administrating relief and on-reserve health care, and managing fishing and hunting practices; they even acted as both judge and jury in legal cases involving "Indians" (Dickason 2002; Barron 1988; Carter 1985; Brownlie 1994; Schreiber 2008).[1]

Legislation in Canada also established "Indians" as wards of the state in a specific legal classification that designated them "not a person" and as having a status similar to that of legal children. This placed legal and financial authority of "Indians'" in the hands of the local Indian agent. As such, those classified as Indians under the law were unable to legally hold a bank account, sell or rent land on the reserve, or even to buy or sell their own goods. Indian agents played the key colonial role of surveillance, oversight, management, and discipline, designed to ensure the proper development of Indians into good, productive British subjects. They applied various technologies to First Nations, Inuit, and Métis peoples, the most notorious and documented being the residential school system.

Although several treaties make specific reference to education and the availability of Western knowledge, the system that was developed instead drew on discourses of assimilation and colonization; it used nearly constant surveillance to assert "proper" Indian development onto Indigenous children to turn them into good British subjects as defined by the Baggot Commission. Although this "schooling" was originally voluntary, amendments to the *Indian Act* in 1894 made attendance for "Indian children," later specified as ages 7 to 18, legally mandatory. Parents of absent children faced punitive measures (Nuu-chah-nulth Tribal Council 1996; Grant 1996).

Schools were designed to separate children from the influence of their parents by housing them in dormitories over the school year, and students were disciplined, often physically, if they continued any aspect of their own culture, including speaking in their familial language. Children's hair was cut to match British gendered norms, and education included a focus

> Children's hair was cut to match British gendered norms, and education included a focus on Christian and capitalist moral and social structure, with an emphasis on European agricultural practice (see Dickason 2002; Truth and Reconciliation Commission of Canada 2015a). These "schools" made the social interactions of children visible to school staff, opening them to behavioural correction and were specifically designed to exterminate culture, languages, and values.

on Christian and capitalist moral and social structure, with an emphasis on European agricultural practice (see Dickason 2002; Truth and Reconciliation Commission of Canada 2015a). These "schools" made the social interactions of children visible to school staff, opening them to behavioural correction and were specifically designed to exterminate culture, languages, and values.

As noted by a designer of this program in the late 1800s,

> if you wish to educate these children you must separate them from their parents during the time that they are being educated. If you leave them in the family they may know how to read and write, but they still remain savages, whereas by separating them in the way proposed, they acquire the habits and tastes — it is to be hoped only the good tastes — of civilized people. (Langevin 1883: 1376)

In this way — children were constantly under surveillance as government policy and school rules pressed for the extermination of First Nations, Inuit, and Métis cultures and the adoption of the behaviour of productive, capitalist British subjects. The measure of "proper" use of land and resources was even incorporated into the stationary that students used within the residential schools, as pencils, erasers, and rulers carried the Government of Canada statement "MISUSE IS ABUSE" (see Image 14-1).

The harms to culture, self, identity, and dignity experienced by the

> The permit system not only made obtaining permission and permits necessary for First Nations, Inuit, and Métis peoples living under this system, but it also rendered visible, actionable, and auditable the productive work of "Indians." Permits were directed at educating "Indians" in the proper manner of using labour and resources, working to "civilize" them as good capitalist British subjects while placing a particular focus on agricultural production.

Image 14-1: Pencil Issued at a Northern Ontario Residential School

Pencil issued at a northern Ontario residential school predominately states that "MISUSE IS ABUSE," referring to the importance for "Indian peoples" to avoid "misusing" resources (Indian Record 1962)

children who attended these institutions cannot be understated, and though not all experiences of abuse can be generalized, cases of physical, sexual, psychological, and emotional abuse as well as horrible living conditions that failed to meet the children's most basic needs are well documented with respect to this state-church managed "educational" system (Truth and Reconciliation Commission of Canada 2015a). An internal government audit of the residential school system found that as many as 35 percent to 60 percent of the children who attended these facilities died of malnutrition, mistreatment, disease, or exposure (Bryce 1909; also see Annett 2001).

Coupled with the residential schools, other surveillance technologies were designed to extinguish sovereignty and ensure the proper development of Indian productive practices. In response to the level of Indian agent oversight and organization of labour and land use on reserves, the Department of Indian Affairs initiated a detailed "permit system" that regulated and formalized capitalist productive practices within these spaces. Permits varied in size over the period of time they were in use, though each identified the regional agency, reserve, individual to whom it applied, as well as the specific action "permitted" by the Indian agent (see Image 14-2).

These documents also bore the signature of the agent who authorized the behaviour. The permit system not only made obtaining permission and permits necessary for First Nations, Inuit, and Métis peoples living under this system, but it also rendered visible, actionable, and auditable the productive work of "Indians." Permits were directed at educating "Indians" in the proper manner of using labour and resources, working to "civilize" them as good capitalist British subjects while placing a particular focus on agricultural production.

The permit system was supplemented with a "pass system" designed to document, monitor, restrict, and track the movement of "Indians" when they travelled off of reserve land (see Image 14-3).

Permits were required for planning or harvesting crops, for any sale or purchase of goods or services, for any building structures, or any business transactions. Under this system, "Indians" could choose how

Image 14-2: Indian Agent Permit Form (1937)

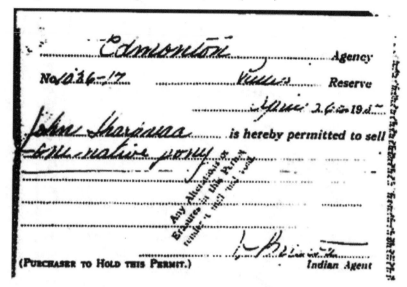

Permits were issued by Indian agents for a variety of reasons. The above permit form gives permission for John Tharpnaa of the Paul Reserve in Alberta to sell a pony to someone off reserve.

Source: Indian Agent. 1937. "Permit — To Sell Native Pony," H2c 156B Control of Indian Reserves by Indian Agents, Catalogue #H89.55.13, Royal Alberta Museum.

to use their labour and resources as long as they fit colonial understandings of proper development and land use. As noted by a person who lived under this system in Alberta, "you needed a permit for everything, you needed a permit to take a shit" (Anon 1988). Although this statement is somewhat hyperbolic, the degree of intrusion, formalization, and discipline enabled by this technology of surveillance is clear. In the western provinces, the permit system was supplemented with a "pass system" designed to document, monitor, restrict, and track the movement of "Indians" when they travelled off of reserve land (see Image 14-3).

Formally put in place between 1882 and 1941 (with evidence indicating its use into the 1960s or later), the pass system required all "Indians" moving off reserve to obtain authorization from Indian agents — even though these restrictions were known by government officials to be in violation of treaty rights (Williams 2016; Carter 1985).

In the early 1900s, a pilot program took the surveillance of the permit and pass systems even further. Known as "model villages," these trial reserve spaces

Image 14-3 Pass System from the Department of Indian Affairs (1896)

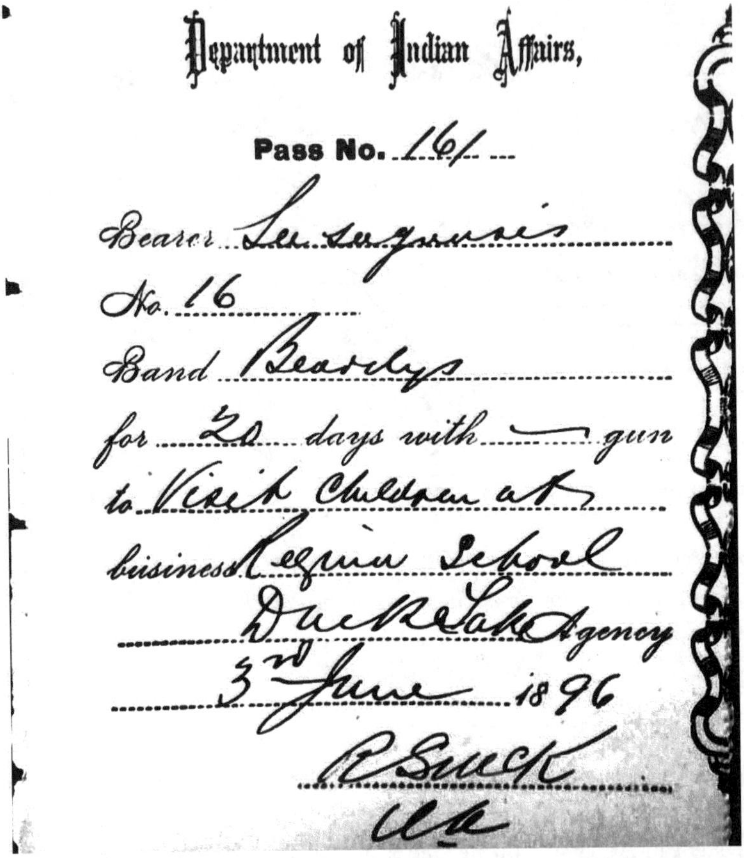

Pass Number 161 Duck Lake Agency, June 3, 1896, Provincial Archives of Saskatchewan, Department of Indian and Northern Affairs, S-E19, file 35a

opened up not only the design and organization of "Indian" labour power and resources but also pushed the surveillance of Indian agents into all areas of social life. Within these model villages, government officials decided who should live where on the reserve, what crops or animals should be raised by what person, how finances should be managed, and they even went so far as to determine who should marry whom and who should be allowed to have and raise children. This level of surveillance and management was thought to effectively foster the development of whiteness, Britishness, and capitalist economic production within these spaces (Dickason 2002; Titley 1983; *Globe and Mail* 1990).

The impact of these surveillance technologies was significant in governing the lives of First Nations, Inuit, and Métis peoples, identified as "Indians" under Canadian law. As the sovereignty, or capacity for self-determination, of the various peoples was bounded by colonial rationalities related to "proper" use of labour and natural resources, this left sovereignty to only exist where it did not come into conflict with the proper development of "Indians" and reserve resources.

Current "Indian" Surveillance Practice and "Proper" Development

Though much has changed from the technologies used in the 1900s, the colonial vision of proper development continues to find expression within current government practices surrounding the use of resources both on lands controlled by the Canadian federal government and those reserve lands upon which Supreme Court and international rulings have recognized the sovereignty of First Nations, Inuit, and Métis peoples (Supreme Court of Canada, *Tsilhqot'in Nation v. British Columbia*, 2014).

The Government of Canada has identified essential elements of the economy in relation to energy and utilities, transportation, manufacturing, government, food, information and communication technology, water, health, finances, and safety (Public Safety Canada 2009). These ten sectors have been determined by the federal government as being "essential to the health, safety, security or economic well-being of Canadians and the effective functioning of government"; however, by defining specific corporate and state assets as "critical infrastructure," this classification also asserts a specific developmental trajectory envisioned by the state in relation to identified "processes, systems, facilities, technologies, networks, assets and services" deemed "essential" (Public Safety Canada 2009: 2). For example, the definition of oil pipelines as critical infrastructure that is essential to the well-being of Canadians lends state support to their current use, and works to validate their socio-environmental impact; however, it also places opposition to pipelines, or actions taken to assert the need for the development of alternatives, in direct conflict with the state and its national security apparatus. This notion of critical infrastructure continues the rationale of order-productivity-prosperity from British/settler culture, where understandings of "proper development" have been updated but remain to be considered as absolutely vital to the prosperity of all people within the society. This means that actions taken against such critical infrastructure and its continuing development put at risk "increases to productivity"

This notion of critical infrastructure continues the rationale of order-productivity-prosperity from British/settler culture, where understandings of "proper development" have been updated but remain to be considered as absolutely vital to the prosperity of all people within the society. This means that actions taken against such critical infrastructure and its continuing development put at risk "increases to productivity" and the "progressive organization of humanity" of the colonial rationalities of social Darwinism and, for that reason, need to be stopped.

and the "progressive organization of humanity" of the colonial rationalities of social Darwinism and, for that reason, need to be stopped. To do this, new surveillance capacities have been developed by the government to tie data collection within government departments directly to national security initiatives as well as private institutions, with the goal of protecting and supporting critical infrastructure (see Dafnos 2013; Dafnos, Thompson, and French 2016; Monaghan and Walby 2012).

The current legislation designed to protect critical infrastructure and its "proper" development falls under the *Emergency Management Act* (2009). Established in 2009, it reasserts the importance of critical infrastructure to the proper functioning of Canadian society. Furthermore, the act conceptualizes the need for an "all-hazards approach" to exist across government departments — that is, each government department must identify and manage their own "risk environment" in relation to critical infrastructure while also communicating their own collected information to other departments as well as receiving information in exchange. The purpose is to develop **situational awareness**, an understanding of the special and temporal makeup of a given environment, and to identify and predict potential risks to pre-emptively mitigate or avoid them. Here, the management and oversight of each department's administrative subject is tied to understandings of essential productive practices and their continued proper development. Although this might seem benign when applied to risks such as forest fires or flooding, it becomes more problematic when applied to people or social groups (Dafnos 2013; Dafnos, Thompson, and French 2016; Hier and Walby 2014; Monaghan and Walby 2012). Since 2007, the *Emergency Management Act* has organized work within Aboriginal Affairs and Northern Development Canada (AANDC) to apply the logic of situational awareness and critical infrastructure to those defined as "Indians." National security and policing agencies have also directed their attention toward First Nations, Inuit, and Métis peoples in cases where actions of Indigenous sovereignty come into conflict with state understandings of "proper" development embedded within their definition of critical infrastructure.

AANDC Surveillance and Colonialism

The "all-hazards approach" and focus on critical infrastructure positioned the Department of Indian Affairs (later Aboriginal Affairs and Northern Development Canada [AANDC] to surveil the First Nations, Inuit, and Métis communities with which they worked. Being only one part of a network sharing knowledge about threats to critical infrastructure across government departments, this surveillance took up the rationales of order-productivity and (re)asserted this relationship within the work of AANDC staff. The all-hazards approach is thus highly problematic, because it perpetuates colonial relationships of surveillance and management of First Nations, Inuit, and Métis peoples. Specifically, it demands conformity to the Canadian state's vision of "proper" land use and development while also working in direct opposition to acts of Indigenous sovereignty around issues of resource extraction, pipelines, waste disposal, flooding, habitat destruction, and other activities conducted as part of the functioning of critical infrastructure.

In 2007, AANDC released its Emergency and Issues Management Directorate (EIMD) as a means of organizing its surveillance work (see Dafnos 2013; Dafnos, Thompson, and French 2016). The policy itself was a direct response to the call made by Phil Fontaine, national chief of the Assembly of First Nations, to create a day marking the expression of First Nations, Inuit, and Métis sovereignty (Fontaine 2007). Known as the National Day of Action, various nations and communities planned actions on June 29, 2007. AANDC/INAC EIMD later identified that "the outcomes of these events have a direct impact on First Nations, and by extension, on the Department" and that the "civil unrest" of protests could "become an emergency by definition," making the surveillance of such events crucial to AANDC's adherence to the all-hazards model (INAC 2010: 18; AANDC 2011: 3). Additionally, AANDC staff were embedded within Canada's Integrated Terrorism Assessment Centre (ITAC), and before and during the Day of Action, they acted as area experts and provided details on communities and demonstration preparations (see Dafnos 2013; Dafnos, Thompson and French 2016). The Day of Action, which included over fifty demonstrations and five blockades, was peaceful. Since 2007, AANDC has continued working with ITAC and has contributed to the production of several reports on "Aboriginal protest," noting the

The "all-hazards approach" and focus on critical infrastructure positioned the Department of Indian Affairs (later Aboriginal Affairs and Northern Development Canada [AANDC] to surveil the First Nations, Inuit, and Métis communities with which they worked.

need for continual surveillance "where there is a threat of politically motivated violence or where protests threaten the functioning of critical infrastructure" (ITAC 2007 cited in Dafnos 2012).

Since 2007, AANDC EIMD policy has also worked to surveil First Nations, Inuit, and Métis communities from AANDC regional offices across the country, synthesizing the data and combining them with information from law enforcement, other departments, and private-sector critical infrastructure partners. Reports are regularly disseminated by AANDC and identify Indigenous community "risks" and "'issues." These reports are circulated back to the department's own staff and then shared with other key governmental departments and agencies, including Transport Canada, the Department of Justice, the Privy Council Office, the Canadian Security Intelligence Service (CSIS), the Royal Canadian Mounted Police (RCMP), and provincial police services. Additionally, the information is transmitted to Public Safety Canada's Government Operations Centre, which is designed to facilitate situational awareness regarding critical infrastructure threats and to develop national, whole-of-government responses.

The impact of this surveillance has been significant. Community members, groups, and warrior societies have been identified and classified as "domestic-issue-based extremism" in Canadian national security reports on terrorist activities (see, for example, ITAC 2007). Furthermore, the expansive scope required by AANDC's need to predict and mediate even potential threats to critical infrastructure has led to extensive monitoring of even Charter-protected actions: events such as teach-ins and peaceful protests have been identified and reported as part of the department's surveillance work (Dafnos 2013; Dafnos, Thompson and French 2016). Additionally, partnerships in national security initiatives have placed external pressures on AANDC to gather further information on Indigenous communities — including a call from the Government Operations Centre in 2014 to compile "a comprehensive listing of all known demonstrations which will occur either in your geographical area or that may touch your mandate" (Pugliese 2014). Movements such as Idle No More face immediate negative identification and are viewed and reported on by AANDC as potential threats to Canadian society.

Conclusion

Part of the process of reconciliation and building an anticolonial relationship requires us to address the continuing impact of government institutional practices — in this case, the state's definition of critical infrastructure and

its link to Canada's national security framework. Although settlers
are learning about the abuses of
past "Indian"-focused government
programs, it is equally important
to look to the administration of
these programs and bring to light
the beliefs and values within them
to fully understand the aspects that made them so destructive.

> Although settlers are learning about the abuses of past "Indian"-focused government programs, it is equally important to look to the administration of these programs and bring to light the beliefs and values within them to fully understand the aspects that made them so destructive.

In this case, surveillance practices on Indigenous Peoples who resist resource extraction have persisted. The focus on productivity and "proper" development establishes a highly restricted understanding of what is "acceptable" Indigenous sovereignty.

In light of the historical and current surveillance practices presented in this chapter, it is difficult to contest First Nations, Inuit, and Métis claims that colonial domination continues. AANDC policy has limited the definition of Indigenous self-determination to one of two options: either Indigenous Peoples must accept the "proper" development and the socio-environmental consequences of Canadian state-defined critical infrastructure programs or, alternately, the national security apparatus of the Canadian state is activated, labelling acts of sovereignty as criminalized "domestic-issue-based extremism." In this way, the limiting of Indigenous sovereignty by means of developmental expectations regarding land and labour use, as established by the Canadian government, remains highly problematic and is an ongoing impediment to reconciliation.

Discussion Questions

1. In the context of surveillance, we often hear, "You have nothing to fear if you have nothing to hide." Does this statement address concerns about how surveillance applies to specific governing rationalities?

2. Do First Nations, Inuit, and Métis peoples have a right to stop the development of major industrial projects such as pipelines or hydroelectric dams?

3. Does First Nations, Inuit, and Métis sovereignty exist if it must act in accordance with Government of Canada definitions of "productivity" and "critical infrastructure?"

4. Do rationales of productivity, development, and settler cultural superiority still exist in Canada?

5. How do we address state surveillance of First Nations, Inuit, and Métis peoples to move forward with reconciliation?

Recommended Resources

CBC News. 2019. "Reports of RCMP Snipers Dispatched to Wet'suwet'en Blockade 'Concerning,' Says Indigenous Services Minister."

Dafnos, Tia. 2019. "Pacification by Pipeline." *Canadian Dimension* 53, 1.

Williams, Alex. 2016. *The Pass System: A Documentary Film* [film]. Tamarack Productions. <thepasssystem.ca>.

Mann, Michael. 1992. *The Last of the Mohicans* [film]. Southbank: Distributed by ViaVision Entertainment.

Dick, Philip K. 2018. *Adjustment Team: Short Story*. New York: Harper-Collins Publishers.

Glossary

critical infrastructure: ten sectors of the economy — energy and utilities, transportation, manufacturing, government, food, information and communication technology, water, health, finances, and safety — that the Government of Canada has identified as essential to government functioning and the health and security of Canadians (Public Safety Canada 2009).

governing rationalities: the organizing sets of ideas, or beliefs, that work to explain what people or objects are to be governed, why they should be governed, what nature and obligations are to be attributed to the governed, and how the act of governance is itself to be carried out.

Indian: an imposed socio-legal category used by the Government of Canada to shape the behaviour and development of First Nations, Inuit, and Métis peoples and communities who fall under the legislation of the *Indian Act*.

situational awareness: an understanding of the special and temporal makeup of a given environment and the capability to identify and predict potential risks to pre-emptively mitigate or avoid them.

technologies of governance: technologies that work to bring the ideas, or rationalities, into being; they work to shape human interaction and human life to make them fit the goals, beliefs, values, and ways of seeing the world of the surveillance system.

Notes

1. The duties and legal authority of Indian agents greatly expanded in scope from 1876 until "Indian" laws and policy were significantly reorganized in 1951. After 1951, the majority of Indian agents were retired, though agents remained active in isolated reserves until 1969 (Brownlie 1994).
2. The official name of the department charged with the management of "Indian" peoples has changed numerous times. At the time this chapter was written, the role is being shared by Crown-Indigenous Relations and Northern Affairs Canada (CIRNAC) and Indigenous Services Canada (ISC).

References

AANDC (Aboriginal Affairs and Northern Development Canada). 2011. Aboriginal Affairs and Northern Development Canada, National Emergency Management Plan. Ottawa: Public Works and Government Services Canada.

Annett, Kevin. 2001. "Hidden from History: The Canadian Holocaust: A Summary of an Ongoing Independent Inquiry into Canadian Native 'Residential Schools' and Their Legacy." Vancouver: Truth Commission into Genocide in Canada.

Anon. 1988. Audio Recording ND H2c 156B Control of Indian Reserves by Indian Agents. Royal Alberta Museum, Edmonton.

Aughterson, Kate. 1998. The English Renaissance: An Anthology of Sources and Documents. London: Routledge.

Barron, Laurie. 1988. "The Indian Pass System in the Canadian West, 1882–1935." Prairie Forum 13, 1.

Beaulieu, Celine. forthcoming. "Is Religious Choice an Elementary Liberty? The Mediation of Religious Freedoms within First Nations Reserves." Undergraduate thesis, University of Saskatchewan, Saskatoon.

Behrent, Michael C. 2013. "Foucault and Technology." History and Technology, An International Journal 29, 1.

Brownlie, Robin. 1994. "Man on the Spot: John Daly, Indian Agent in Parry Sound, 1922–1939." Journal of the Canadian Historical Association 5, 1.

Bryce, Peter. 1909. "Letter to the Superintendent-General of Indian Affairs, November 5th 1909." Department of Indian Affairs, RG 10, DIA Archives, doc. #AW 1-353988. Ottawa: Library and Archives Canada.

Carter, Sarah. 1985. "Controlling Indian Movement: The Pass System." NeWest Review (May).

Conklin, A. 1997. A Mission to Civilize. Stanford: Stanford University Press.

Dafnos, Tia. 2013. "Pacification and Indigenous Struggles in Canada." Socialist Studies 9, 2.

____. 2012. "Beyond the Blue Line: Researching the Policing of Aboriginal Activism Using Access to Information." In Mike Larsen and Kevin Walby (eds.), Brokering Access: Power, Politics, and Freedom of Information Process in Canada. Vancouver: UBC Press.

Dafnos, Tia, Scott Thompson, and Martin French. 2016. "Surveillance and the Colonial Dream: Canada's Surveillance of Indigenous Protest." In Kevin Walby, Randy K. Lippert, Ian Warren and Darren Palmer (eds.), National Security, Surveillance, and Emergencies: Canadian and Australian Sovereignty Compared. London: Palgrave-MacMillan.

Department of the Interior. 1876. "Annual Report for the year ended June 1876." Parliament, Sessional Papers, no. 11, 1877.

Dickason, Olive Patricia. 2002. *Canada's First Nations: A History of Founding Peoples from Earliest Times*. Don Mills: Oxford University Press.

Fontaine, Phil. 2007. "First Nations Call on All Canadians to Stand with Us on June 29th, 2007." <tdrc.net/uploads/file/afnstatement2007.pdf>.

Foucault, Michel. 2010. *The Government of Self and Others: Lectures at the Collège de France 1982–1983*. New York : Palgrave Macmillan.

Globe and Mail. 1990. "Indian Students Forced into Marriage, Farm Life." December 10.

Gordon, Colin. 1991. "Governmental Rationality: An Introduction." In G Burchell, C. Gordon, and P. Miller (eds.), *The Foucault Effect: Studies in Governmentality*. Chicago: University of Chicago Press.

Grant, A. 1996. *No End to Grief: Indian Residential Schools in Canada*. Winnipeg: Pemmican.

Hier, S., and K. Walby. 2014. "Policy Mutations, Compliance, Myths, and Redeployable Special Event Public Camera Surveillance in Canada." *Sociology* 48, 1.

Hobson, J. 2005 [1938]. *Imperialism: A Study*. New York: Cossimo.

Hofstadter, Richard. 1992 [1944]. *Social Darwinism in American Thought*. Boston: Beacon Press.

INAC (Indian and Northern Affairs Canada). 2010. *Final Report — Evaluation of the Emergency Management Assistance Program*. <aadnc-aandc.gc.ca/DAM/DAM-INTER-HQ/STAGING/texte-text/ema_1100100011393_eng.pdf>.

Indian Record. 1962. "Letter to the Editor: A Tribe Without Freedom." XXV 5 (September-October).

ITAC (Integrated Threat Assessment Centre). 2007. "ITAC Threat Assessment Aboriginal Protests Summer 2007." ATI Request to CSIS, no. 117-2008-123.

Kipling, Rudyard. 1929. "The White Man's Burden: The United States & The Philippine Islands, 1899." *Rudyard Kipling's Verse: Definitive Edition*. Garden City: Doubleday.

Langevin, Hector-Lewis. 1883. "Indian Industrial Schools." Canada, House of Commons Debates, May 22.

Milloy, J. 1983. "The Early Indian Acts: Developmental Strategy and Constitutional Change." In L. Getty and A. Lussier (eds.), *As Long as the Sun Shines and the Water Flows: A Reader in Canadian Native Studies*. Vancouver: UBC Press.

Miller, Robert J., Jacinta Ruru, Larissa Behrendt, and Tracey Lindberg. 2010. *Discovering Indigenous Lands: The Doctrine of Discovery in the English Colonies*. New York: Oxford University Press.

Monaghan, J., and K. Walby. 2012. "Making up 'Terror Identities': Security Intelligence and Canada's Integrated Threat Assessment Centre." *Policing & Society* 22, 2.

Murphy, Gretchen. 2010. *Shadowing the White Man's Burden: US Imperialism and the Problem of the Color Line*. New York: NYU Press.

Nuu-chah-nulth Tribal Council. 1996. *Indian Residential Schools: The Nuu-Chah-Nulth Experience Report of the Nuu-Chah-Nulth Tribal Council Indian Residential School Study, 1992–1994*. Port Alberni: Nuu-chah-nulth Tribal Council.

Public Safety Canada. 2009. *National Strategy for Critical Infrastructure*. Ottawa: Government of Canada.

Pugliese, D. 2014. "Government Orders Federal Departments to Keep Tabs on All

Demonstrations Across Country." *Globe and Mail*, June 4. <ottawacitizen.com/news/politics/government-orders-federal-departments-to-keep-tabs-on-all-demonstrations-across-country>.

Report of the Indians of Canada. 1847. Journals of the Legislative Assembly, 8 Vic. 1844–45, Appendix EEE; "Report on the Affairs of the Indians in Canada; submitted to the Honorable the Legislative assembly for their information." Province of Canada. Journals of the Legislative Assembly, 11 Victoria A. 1847. Sessional Papers. Appendix T.

Rose, Nikolas, Pat O'Malley, and Mariana Valverde. 2006. "Governmentality." *Annual Review of Law and Social Science* 2, 1.

Schreiber, Dorothee. 2008. "'A Liberal and Paternal Spirit': Indian Agents and Native Fisheries in Canada." *Ethnohistory* 55, 1.

Supreme Court of Canada. 2014. *Tsilhqot'in Nation v. British Columbia*. 2014. 2 S.C.R. 256. Docket: 34986. *Supreme Court of Canada: Ottawa*. <scc-csc.lexum.com/scc-csc/scc-csc/en/item/14246/index.do>.

Titley, Brian. 1983. "W.M. Graham: Indian Agent Extraordinaire." *Prairie Forum* 1.

Truth and Reconciliation Commission of Canada. 2015a. *The Survivors Speak: A Report of the Truth and Reconciliation Commission of Canada*. Winnipeg: Truth and Reconciliation Commission of Canada.

____. 2015b. *Truth and Reconciliation Commission of Canada: Calls to Action*. Winnipeg: Truth and Reconciliation Commission of Canada.

Williams, Alex. 2016. *The Pass System: A Documentary Film* [film]. Tamarack Productions.

15

Beyond Airspace Safety

A Feminist Perspective on Drone Privacy Regulation

Kristen M.J. Thomasen

> **After reading this chapter, you will be able to do the following:**
> 1. Identify and explain the gendered nature of UAV/drone regulation.
> 2. Describe different theoretical perspectives on privacy and the historical influences of paternalistic notions of modesty.
> 3. Connect privacy and gendered regulations with current and future technological mechanisms of surveillance.

In 2015, William H. Meredith of Kentucky was arrested with charges of first-degree endangerment and criminal mischief. He had used his personal shotgun to shoot down a drone operated by one of his neighbours. Meredith felt that the drone was violating his family's privacy and cited concerns that a predator may have been photographing his 16-year-old daughter who was sunbathing in the yard (Bilton 2016). The charges against Meredith were later dropped in the Bullitt County District Court, with Judge Rebecca Ward stating that "he had a right to shoot at this drone, and I'm going to dismiss this charge" (Volokh 2015).

No technology emerges in a social or legal vacuum (Mason and Magnet 2012; Leenes and Lucivero 2014). Rather, the ways in which we use technologies are often governed by norms, laws, and regulations that significantly influence the ways in which these technologies benefit or disadvantage different individuals and communities (Mason and Magnet 2012). Growing public and private use of **drones** as surveillance tools has begun to impact the privacy of different communities, including women's privacy, which has garnered sensational attention in media and popular discussions. News headlines frequently splash stories about drones spying on sunbathing or naked women and girls, or drones being used to stalk women through public spaces, or drones delivering abortion pills to women who might otherwise lack access (Sheldon 2018).

> Drone regulators, such as Transport Canada, cannot continue to treat the technology as though it is value-neutral; rather, it argues that future policy *must* address the fact that surveillance technologies affect different members of society in dissimilar ways.

Yet despite this popular attention, and the immense literature that has emerged analyzing the privacy implications of drone technology (e.g., Calo 2011; Froomkin and Colangelo 2015; Bracken-Roche et al. 2014; Kaminski 2013; Villasenor 2013; Rule 2015), the ways in which the drone might enhance or undermine women's privacy in particular have not yet been the subject of significant academic analysis. This chapter therefore contributes a critical discussion about the impact of this technology, and its regulation, on women and their privacy. It argues that drone regulators, such as Transport Canada, cannot continue to treat the technology as though it is value-neutral; rather, it argues that future policy *must* address the fact that surveillance technologies affect different members of society in dissimilar ways. A gendered perspective can provide a critical lens through which to identify some of the difficult privacy challenges — not only for women — that are raised by drones at a time when the laws guiding the permissible uses and designs of the technology continue to influence the trajectory of innovation. Going forward, the social context in which drone technology is emerging must inform both drone-specific regulations and the ways in which we approach privacy generally. This chapter provides a starting point for a further discussion on how this can be done within the Canadian context and elsewhere.

First, a brief note on terminology. "Drone" refers to remotely piloted aerial vehicles that range in scale and function from military weapons to children's toys. This chapter is concerned with the devices that are commercially available to individuals, companies, and domestic law enforcement (i.e., non-military devices). These drones are typically small, often weighing no more than several kilograms. They may be equipped with a variety of additional sensors, like high-resolution cameras, that are either already installed at the point of sale or added to the device by the operator. Drones of this size and function can also be manufactured at home (see Figure 15-1).

With this technological focus in mind, this chapter first explains why these domestic-use drones raise gendered privacy concerns and then why a gendered analysis is relevant when thinking about their regulation and privacy

Figure 15-1: Typical Consumer Unmanned Arial Vehicle (UAV) or "Drone"

Alejandro Pena, Air Force <commons.wikimedia.org/wiki/File:Autumn_Drone_(cropped).jpg>, "Autumn Drone"

implications. This includes examining the implications of heteronormative expectations for modesty on legal protections for women's privacy, as these concepts fail to provide effective protections against the kinds of intrusions that primarily affect women. Notably, while this chapter draws on law and theory relating to women's privacy experiences, these and other weaknesses in regulations and norms can also differentially affect the privacy interests of nonbinary persons in public spaces. The second section of the chapter considers how gendered notions of modesty have undermined women's privacy in public space — a space where women already face gender-based intrusions upon their privacy, which may be further exacerbated by drone technology. The current approach of Canadian and US aviation authorities and their regulations — which focus primarily on physical safety concerns associated with drone use, sometimes to the exclusion of privacy issues — incorrectly treats the technology as though it is value-neutral. The chapter concludes by arguing that drone technology in particular (though not exclusively) requires a more nuanced approach to regulation that considers social context and the differential impacts of the technology on individuals and groups.

The current regulatory approach focuses on the artifact (the physical drone), while overlooking the broader cultural and social practices associated with drone technology, as well as the social context into which it is introduced (Wajcman 2007). This narrow focus obscures the ways in which drone technology can reproduce, enhance, alter, or ameliorate existing social inequalities through, among other things, its impact on privacy (Layne et al. 2010). Such perspective is relevant to the current and ongoing debates about drone regulation, particularly in light of the sometimes granular ways in which the drone's gendered impact has already come under scrutiny in popular discussions (e.g., Perritt and Plawinski 2015; Clarke and Moses 2014; Rao, Gopi, and Maione 2016).

The "Sunbathing Teenager" and Drone Privacy Regulation

North American news stories about drones spying on naked, topless, or sunbathing women and girls make regular headlines, as do stories of drones peering into women's homes, apartments, backyards, or over swimming pools (see Box 15-1). These themes also appear in some of the academic writing on drone privacy (McNeal 2014; Rule 2015). Similar stories about drones spying on men — particularly in a state of undress — are relatively rare.

Box 15-1: "I Feel Completely Violated"

In August of 2015, a woman from Vancouver, British Columbia, took to Reddit to describe her victimization at the hands of an anonymous drone operator. Kathryn Redford had been sunbathing topless on a private balcony when she noticed a drone hovering overhead, writing:

> This is embarrassing for me to tell but it shouldn't be, and I guess that's why I'm posting. I was sunbathing topless on my private balcony ... I was lying on the ground — the only view of me would be from the portion of sky that allows for a nice sliver of sun. This is where the drone hovered. The drone was a yellow colour and came from behind the building, hovered for about 10–20 seconds with a small flashing light (camera? video?) then went behind the building, came back a few seconds later and hovered again for about 30 seconds before taking off. I covered myself with my book, feeling completely vulnerable and completely violated. The first thing I did was call the non [emergency] police line. As someone who LOVES the potential for drones I can't help but feel huge disappointment. The few people using them to invade privacy are the people who will be responsible for over-the-top restrictions on drones in public areas.

According to Redford, the police told her that this was becoming a common occurrence in the city but that there was little they could do without her being able to identify the pilot.

Source: <reddit.com/r/vancouver/comments/3gs694/drones_hovering_outside_windowsbalconies_in/>

Law professor Margot Kaminski (2016: para. 5) labels this theme in popular discussions about drone-based privacy violations the "sunbather narrative." She asks, "With all we know about the complexities of information privacy [which is deeply engaged by drone technology], why is the female sunbather the story that keeps capturing attention?" In an attempt to explain the narrative's popularity, Kaminski (2016) refers to the old English legend of **Lady Godiva**, whose husband, Count Leofric, claimed he would lower oppressive taxes on the residents of Coventry, England, if she rode naked through the streets on horseback. As the tale goes, she did exactly that. Out of respect for their heroine's modesty, the city folk averted their eyes with the exception of one man — the **peeping Tom** — who was promptly punished for his offence of undermining the noble woman's honour (Donoghue 2003). The legend of Lady Godiva connects with the contemporary issues surrounding drone regulation:

> The sunbather disrupted by drones is a Lady Godiva story, of sorts, without the tax policy. A young woman expresses liberation by wearing a bikini in her backyard or on the beach. Everyone generally follows social norms and refrains from staring for too long, or taking photos or video. But the hovering drone breaks that agreement and must be punished, just like Tom. Often it's dad who does the punishing, but sometimes it's just a Good Samaritan. Law isn't very helpful. (Kaminski 2016: para. 8)

Kaminski (2016) argues that the sunbather trope is a distraction that "provides a woefully incomplete account of the kinds of privacy concerns that drones raise" (para. 9), ignoring, for instance, the significant impact that drones might have on informational privacy; the implications of facial recognition for anonymity; risks stemming from the use of drones to eavesdrop on electronic communications; and so on. She expresses concern about the possibility that legislators will focus on protecting the modesty of sunbathing teenagers while ignoring the potentially far more widespread and problematic impacts that drones can have on informational privacy.

While Kaminski (2016) is right that lawmakers would be foolish (and sexist) to focus drone regulations around outdated norms of women's modesty, this gendered narrative also reveals that this technology is particularly adept at taking advantage of weaknesses in privacy protections. The early origins of legal privacy doctrine *did* in fact focus on women's modesty as a central facet of women's privacy (and privacy generally). But the modesty theory understands and protects only a limited notion of privacy. What does this mean for women's privacy in the context of growing drone use?

Accordingly, in order to have protection, women must become invisible, which might be accomplished if they "exhibit speech, dress, and behaviour calculated to deflect attention from their bodies, views, or desires."

The Modesty Theory of Privacy

The **modesty theory of privacy** that underlies the "sunbather" narrative is grounded in a traditional expectation of a woman's confinement and seclusion within the home (Allen 1988). Specifically, it holds that when *she* is confined or secluded in such a way, *she* ought not be interfered with or gazed upon by others — particularly uninvited men (including where that gaze is mediated by a drone). This understanding of a woman's "privacy" only narrowly protects her from intrusions in circumstances where she is concealed, secluded, and behaving virtuously. Accordingly, in order to have protection, women must become invisible, which might be accomplished if they "exhibit speech, dress, and behaviour calculated to deflect attention from their bodies, views, or desires" (Allen and Mack 1991: 444). This does little to actually protect a woman's experience of privacy, as heteronormative expectations of the sub-servient housewife and mother conflict with the notion of an invasion-free home life. Nor would this theory protect a woman perceived by traditional norms to be immodest — one who ventures into public, engages in sexual activity outside of marriage, or enters the workforce. The modesty theory of privacy bestowed heavily class-, race-, and sexuality-limited protections against visibility and interference by others, reliant upon on a woman's self-enforced concealment and seclusion in the marital or family home, and her meeting antiquated standards of virtue (Allen and Mack 1991).

Allen and Mack's (1991) critique of the modesty theory of privacy illus-trates how the sunbather narrative recreates patriarchal notions of ownership over the female body: as Kaminski (2016) notes, the drone that flies over a woman in her backyard or in her home, invading her privacy and undermining her modesty (and most importantly, undermining the patriarch's control over who can see her) is deserving of punishment. The same has not been the case where a drone is used in a similarly invasive way in a public space — again echoing this understanding of privacy as based on concealment, seclusion, and invisibility. While a modesty-based analysis of a woman's right to privacy seems antiquated now, the next section examines how this notion shaped the early development of privacy jurisprudence, which effectively lingers today.

Modesty within Privacy Jurisprudence

Anita Allen and Erin Mack (1991) highlight the roles that traditional norms of female modesty and virtue played in the early development of American privacy tort (laws that define legal liabilities for actions that cause harm or loss to a claimant), which affected Canadian tort law as well. These norms of modesty laid the groundwork for courts' modern understanding of the scope and limits of privacy protection. For instance, Allen and Mack (1991: 442) identify the "outmoded normative assumptions about female modesty and seclusion" at the core of the tort's early development through their examination of early privacy tort cases and the foundational paper on "The Right to Privacy" by Samuel Warren and Louis Brandeis (1890; see Box 15-2).

Warren and Brandeis (1890) rely on cases in which parents and husbands could claim financial losses against male seducers of their daughters and wives or where the shame and dishonour caused by a daughter's seduction was judicially remedied. Intrusions upon a woman's modesty were framed as an offence to her husband or father and deserving of compensation (rather than as an offence to her control over her own body or environment, solitude, dignity, or anonymity). These are among the early cases that set the scope and boundaries of the "right to be let alone" in Warren and Brandeis' (1890) famous paper — which ultimately underscored the development of the American privacy tort. Allen and Mack (1991) observe that "women appear in Warren and Brandeis' article as seduced wives and daughters" (459), while the implications of a "private home" and "family life" for women, and in particular women's privacy, go completely overlooked.

Allen and Mack (1991) also refer to numerous tort cases where the courts went remarkably far to compensate a female plaintiff for a privacy loss, on the reasoning that any intrusion that amounted to a loss of her modesty should be sufficient reason to take legal action. The basis on which male judges rationalized such large remedies was a "paternalistic, patriarchal concern for feminine modesty and virtuous seclusion" (Allen and Mack 1991: 464) rather than concern for a woman's equal right to be left alone or her right to benefit from the values that privacy protection can afford. Were that to be the case, then the many intrusions upon a woman within the marital or family home would also be protected.

Women's modesty and concealment from the gaze of strangers within the home has also factored into the development of constitutional privacy protections. For instance, Jeannie Gersen (2008) examines the central role of women's modesty in US Fourth Amendment precedents. In *Kyllo v. United*

Box 15-2: The Right to Privacy

The turn of the twentieth century brought new and often instantaneous technologies like photography, newsprint, and the gramophone to the forefront of society. While these innovations marked enormous steps forward in the conveyance of information, they also gave rise to important questions about personal privacy. For instance, photography now offered a means to accurately reproduce an individual's personal characteristics in an identifiable manner (for instance, think about the advent of so-called mug shots used by police forces beginning around this time). By extension, this meant that a photograph could be used to track an individual — for instance, an image of a city street might show someone entering a store, loitering, being truant. Samuel Warren and Louis Brandeis, two Harvard-educated lawyers, took on this question in their article on "The Right to Privacy" in 1890. One of their important discussions frames privacy as being akin to a possession, to which they note:

> The right of one who has remained a private individual, to prevent his public portraiture, presents the simplest case for such extension; the right to protect one's self from pen portraiture, from a discussion by the press of one's private affairs, would be a more important and far-reaching one. If casual and unimportant statements in a letter, if handiwork, however inartistic and valueless, if possessions of all sorts are protected not only against reproduction, but against description and enumeration, how much more should the acts and sayings of a man in his social and domestic relations be guarded from ruthless publicity. If you may not reproduce a woman's face photographically without her consent, how much less should be tolerated the reproduction of her face, her form, and her actions, by graphic descriptions colored to suit a gross and depraved imagination. (213–14)

States, 533 US 27 (2001), which involved the use of a forward-looking infrared device (see Figure 15-2) by police to examine the amount of heat emanating from a home, Justice Scalia centres his concerns about the invasiveness of this technique on the potential visibility of the "lady of the house taking her bath and sauna" (10). Gersen (2008: 488) elaborates that this focus on the lady in her sauna (which appears nowhere in the facts of the case), "evokes the privacy interest of the man [of the house] entitled to see the lady of the house naked and his interest in shielding her body from prying eyes. Privacy is figured as a woman, an object of the male gaze." She explains that the hypothetical "lady in the bath" evokes concerns about prying eyes lusting after a man's wife and the threat to the woman's virtue by the suggestion of sexual infidelity in the eyes of the voyeur. Anxiety about an intrusion into the man's home "can be expressed as anxiety about female sexual virtue. A meaning of a man's home as his castle that emerges here is the need to shield his

> This decision held that the students had no reasonable expectation of privacy for the parts of their bodies that were visible to everyone.

wife's body from other men's desire" (Gersen 2008: 491).

While such explicitly gendered rhetoric has not appeared in Canadian constitutional privacy cases, the judicial protection of privacy on the basis of concealment within the sanctity and privacy of the home — developed through reference to US case law, including that cited previously — certainly does (see Molnar and Parsons 2016). For instance, a recent Ontario Court of Appeal (ONCA) decision reflected the idea that only modestly secluded people deserve protection. This case, *R v. Jarvis* 2017 ONCA 778, involved a high school teacher who photographed and filmed young women students in his high school covertly using a pen camera. The focus of the footage was on the women's cleavage. Jarvis was charged with voyeurism, an offence with three elements, including that the accused surreptitiously (non-consensually) observed or made a recording of a complainant, in a context in which the complainant has a reasonable expectation of privacy, and that the observation was sexual in nature (Slane 2010).

The majority of the Ontario Court of Appeal, meaning two of the three judges hearing the case, held that the Crown failed to prove that the second element of voyeurism (a reasonable expectation of privacy) was present in this offence. This decision held that the students had no reasonable expectation of privacy for the parts of their bodies that were visible to everyone. To illustrate, the ONCA contrasted this expectation with the hypothetical example of "upskirt photos," where an accused uses a camera affixed to a shoe or other low vantage point to covertly take pictures under women's skirts (Plaxton 2018). Women in these cases can expect privacy vis-à-vis the parts of their bodies that are concealed, by virtue of this concealment. Rather than premise the *Jarvis* complainants' expectation of privacy around the social circumstances in which the filming occurred, or the right of young women not to be filmed by men in a position of power over them (regardless of whether this is done openly or secretly), or the young women's right to control information about themselves, the majority in *Jarvis* relied on concealment as necessary to any expectation of privacy against sexual observation (Plaxton 2018).

Notably, this decision was overturned by the Supreme Court of Canada in *R v. Jarvis*, 2019 SCC 10. The majority of the Supreme Court, in this case six of the nine judges, rejected the idea that privacy is an all-or-nothing concept and that once you venture into public you lose all expectation of

Figure 15-2: An Example of Forward-Looking Infrared Imagery

FLIR *imagery from a US Navy helicopter: Alleged drug traffickers are being arrested by Colombian naval forces. This technology records infrared radiation, typically emitted from a heat source. The brighter white colours indicate greater heat emission. This technology is often used by military and police helicopters to locate individuals who might be overlooked by more traditional technologies.*
Official Navy Page from United States of America US Navy photo/U.S. Navy <commons.wikimedia. org/wiki/File:Flickr_-_Official_U.S._Navy_Imagery_-_Alleged_drug_traffickers_are_arrested_by_ Colombian_naval_forces..jpg>.

privacy. The majority held that depending on the circumstances, people can expect some privacy in public, including that students can expect not to be recorded by a teacher in the manner at issue in this case. So the ONCA decision no longer stands as the law in Canada, but it does serve as a reminder that the early modesty theory of privacy can still emerge in judicial reasoning, even in recent cases.

The reciprocal effect of modesty as the standard for assessing privacy underpins a legal groundwork that fails to adequately offer protections against common invasions of privacy experienced predominantly by women, such as street harassment. In other words, privacy laws were not designed by or for women; the role of women within the development of privacy jurisprudence has been as wives, daughters, and lovers of the (cisgender, heterosexual, home-owning, white) men whose interests shaped the development of the doctrine. The lasting impact of the modesty theory of privacy may in fact reconcile the different legal outcomes in a number of popular drone privacy stories. On the one hand, aggressive measures taken to disarm a drone flying over private property and purportedly exposing women (particularly young women) to the gaze of a male stranger — to the extreme of shooting down the drone over a residential area — have been deemed socially if not legally acceptable (Kaminski 2016). Yet on the other hand, no legal protection has been offered to women encountering intrusions in public spaces. For example, a woman who aggressively responded to a drone operator who had been viewing her remotely led to her being charged and ultimately convicted of criminal assault (Landau 2014). In another case, the privacy concerns of a sex worker did not figure into her experiences of being filmed by a vigilante while she was with a john — even when the vigilante posted his video online. Meanwhile, she was sentenced to a year in prison based on the drone footage (Farivar 2015).

The next section of this chapter explores how the gaps in legal protections of privacy outside the realm of seclusion and modesty (particularly in public spaces) have an inequitable impact upon and among women, and how several features of drones make the technology particularly adept at taking advantage of some of these legal gaps.

Drones and Gendered Privacy Invasions

As noted, one central implication of the traditional modesty theory of women's privacy is that in public spaces, individuals enjoy considerably less, or no, privacy. Feminist privacy scholarship has explained the implications of this for women — particularly with respect to harassment on public streets, a form of privacy invasion that overwhelmingly targets women yet is underprotected in law. This section first describes how the features of the drone make the technology especially adept at intruding on the privacy of individuals in public spaces. It then draws from feminist privacy literature to demonstrate how women's experiences of privacy in public are underprotected in ways that drone technology is apt to exploit. This section provides the basis for the final section of this chapter, which argues that drone regulation requires broader consideration of the social implications of the technology, including the ways in which it might differentially impact some individuals and groups.

Privacy-Invasive Drone Features

Drones have several features that combine to create unique privacy challenges compared to other, more static surveillance technologies (the following two paragraphs come from Thomasen 2017). For instance, two of the most significant physical features of the drone that challenge privacy are also two of its most fundamental features — the fact that drones fly, and that they do so without a human on board. The aerial nature of drone technology permits an operator to access potentially unexpected vantage points of the ground below, compared to ground-based or stationary tools of observation like CCTV cameras or cellphone video. Additionally, the unmanned nature of the technology means that drones tend be smaller than manned aircraft and can be operated in areas that are too dangerous or difficult for a manned craft to access. This unmanned aerial nature also makes the technology well suited for longer-term monitoring and tracking, to the extent that fuel sources permit (see Rao, Gopi, and Maione 2016). Furthermore, since drones can be purchased at relatively low costs (depending on the sophistication of the device) and are widely accessible on the consumer market, they can be put to wide-scale use by a variety of operators. These features and capabilities, among others, can combine to cause a "panoptic" chilling effect on individuals on the ground below (Calo 2011; Waghorn 2016; Završnik 2016; for discussion of panoptic surveillance see Popham, this volume). Drone technology affords its operators access to enormous amounts of information from the ground below using unprecedented, invasive means.

While the normalization of drone technologies may eventually undercut the **panoptic chill** they create, another legally important feature of drones stems from the machine's separation from its operator, raising further challenges related to privacy and accountability. An individual may feel that a drone has invaded her privacy, but if she cannot identify the operator — because the pilot was located at a distance — then she may not know whom to pursue, or through which legal mechanism (Froomkin and Colangelo 2015). Furthermore, an individual might not know what information a drone is collecting or for what purpose, which makes it difficult to know which legal remedy, if any, is available. This uncertainty may also serve to compound the panoptic implications. The drone's detachment from the pilot therefore disempowers the observed, as she has no immediate way to gain more information about the drone's operation or operator (Završnik 2016).

Drones and Women's Experience of Privacy in Public Space

In her book *Uneasy Access*, Anita Allen (1988) demonstrated ways in which women experience too much of the *wrong* kinds of privacy, and too little of the *right* kinds of privacy. The first section of this chapter touched on some of the wrong kinds of women's privacy stemming from gender-biased standards of modesty that emerge from paternalistic notions of seclusion within the home and invisibility from strangers. The wrong privacy has also included the ways in which privacy doctrine has historically shielded domestic abusers from legal accountability by protecting the "sanctity of the home" at the expense of women seeking state assistance or protection from their domestic abusers (MacKinnon 1987; Schneider 1991). Meanwhile, women continue to lack the right kinds of privacy: decisional autonomy, particularly over marriage, reproduction, and sex, as well as the ability to seek replenishing solitude outside the confines of the home. The carry-over of these mores into jurisprudence has meant a lack privacy protection in public, which translates into the disruptions caused by sexual harassment and other intrusions in public spaces and the workplace.

Allen (1988: 123) defines "privacy in public" as the "inaccessibility of persons, their mental states, and information about them to the senses and surveillance devices of others." She further explains that "seclusion, achieved through physical distancing, and anonymity, achieved through limited attention paid, are the forms of inaccessibility that significantly constitute privacy in public" (Allen 1988: 124). Through different cases, the Supreme Court of Canada has similarly recognized that there can be some expectation of privacy in public — either through an expectation that encounters with others in public will be fleeting/limited in temporal scope (*R v. Wise*, [1992] 1 SCR 527); will be anonymous (*R v. Spencer* [2014] 2 SCR 212); and/or that observations and personally identifying information collected in public will not be widely shared (*Aubry v. Éditions Vice-Versa Inc*, [1998] 1 SCR 591) — however, access to and the importance of this realm of privacy have been, and continue to be, gendered.

The public realm, as Allen (1988) describes, can be a place of private tasks where women can alleviate or escape the stresses of home or employment. However, intrusions into one's solitude or **right to be left alone** through malicious acts like street harassment can "break the flow of thought and distract a woman's attention, utterly without purpose, from her own concerns" (Allen 1988: 128). Private tasks and repose are replaced with experiences of leering, insulting, prying, and offensive touching, and imposing the silencing, intimidation, and objectification of women when they enter public space. These intrusions often leave women with little legal or normative recourse (Allen 1988). Viewed individually, these privacy invasions can seem *de minimis* (a legal term that translates to "about minimal things" and refers to harms that are not significant enough to merit a legal remedy) and perhaps receive little or no legal protection in part for this reason. Yet when their frequency and cumulative effect is considered, the impact of these invasions on women's access to privacy is significant.

Women can also face non-consensual filming and photography of their bodies and activities, sometimes accompanied by the sharing of these images online, which not only interrupt one's enjoyment of public space but also disempowers them by undermining their control over their personal information.

Canadian and US statistics illustrate just how widespread these intrusions, in the form of street harassment, are. By some measures, women's experiences with catcalling and similar intrusions extend nearly universally (Macmillan, Nierobisz, and Welsh 2000; Wesselmann and Kelly 2010). Moreover, public harassment is often experienced differently among different groups of women. For example, in the United States, Black women not only experience quantitatively more street harassment, but it is qualitatively different and often rooted in histories of slavery and sexism (Davis 1993; Thompson 1993). Furthermore, verbal or physical harassment can escalate into even more intrusive, dangerous, or violent forms of public harassment, including stalking and rape, which are also experienced differently at intersecting axes of marginalization (Macmillan, Nierobisz, and Welsh 2000; Farmer and Jordan 2017). Women can also face non-consensual filming and photography of their bodies and activities, sometimes accompanied by the sharing of these images online, which not only interrupt one's enjoyment of public space but also disempowers them by undermining their control over their personal information (Blanke 2018). By interfering with a woman's safety, security, repose, solitude, her anonymity, and even her control over images of herself, street harassment, stalking, and other sexual violence in public constitute invasions of a woman's privacy in public space, with very little opportunity for legal recourse.

These existing conditions of inequality will impact and be impacted by the development and adoption of new technologies like the drone (Monahan 2009), and with its ever-growing adoption in new social contexts, street harassment and stalking, as well as their accompanying normative, social, and legal problems, are exacerbated. How might the technology impact that social context — and how might (or should) social context impact the development and regulation of the technology? On one hand, the combination of several key attributes of drone technology — in particular, the "silent observer" and remote nature of the technology — could actually discourage people from using it for street harassment, as it minimizes the personal interaction that harassers seek from their victims (Thompson 1993). On the other hand, these features can also make the drone more appealing for use in escalated forms of harassment like stalking, where the stalker can remain anonymous — not to mention more capable of accessing unexpected or invasive vantage points. Additionally, the dislocation of the drone from its operator deepens the power imbalance between the harasser and the person whose privacy is invaded. Where there is already little legal or social recourse for privacy invasion by a person, the drone adds a further informational and accountability barrier — a person might not know who is operating the drone, why, or how to prevent it.

Furthermore, the nature of the drone as an anonymous observer objectifies the person being observed by reducing them to images and ignoring any objections they might have to being photographed or recorded (Koskela 2000; Harraway 1988; Adey 2016). In this case, rather than reducing its potential for harassment, the drone's unique combination of features might simply change the nature and experience of harassment. Perhaps, then, it is unsurprising that stories are already proliferating about drones being used to sexually harass, stalk, and objectify women in public (Grove 2015; Kaminski 2016). Here, concern about women's public harassment and privacy can be distinguished from the **"sunbather narrative"** focus on women's modesty, as the focus shifts away from modesty to the invasion of a woman's personal privacy and her right to dignity, repose, solitude, and anonymity — rights that are also central to men's privacy in public space.

None of the prior discussion is intended to suggest that drones may not be used the same way against men; however, the gendered social context and deeper history of sexual violence, stalking, and objectification, particularly in public, cannot be overlooked. While drone technology, and the surveillance payloads that can be attached to it, will engage the privacy interests of men as well as women and nonbinary persons in public spaces, the intersections of gender with race, colonialism, sexuality, class, disability, and age continue to affect the ways in which one's expectations and assertions of personal privacy outside the home are protected by law and social norms (Allen 2000).

Privacy Consequences of Drones as a Tool to "Protect Women" in Public Space

As I will outline, drone technologies have also been adapted in ways that focus on protecting women from gender-based violence in public space. Two such examples include the use of drones as personal streetlamps, which can be summoned through a cellphone application to follow an individual around projecting bright lights while recording their movements during times that they feel unsafe (Directline.com 2018). A second suggestion is to use drones to monitor public spaces perceived as high risk for crime — including using small surveillance drones equipped with night vision and thermal imaging cameras to attempt to reduce rates of rape (Steele 2014). These proposed uses, among other proposals by both state and private actors, could very well have beneficial outcomes for women. Yet such proposals must be critically analyzed first, particularly where the justification for this drone usage is the purported "protection of women."

As professors Corinne Mason and Shoshana Magnet (2012: 114–15) observe,

> it is a difficult task to critique surveillance technologies aimed at ensuring women's safety against abusers. When made visible as anti-violence tools, technologies of surveillance appear to be uncontroversial to a range of actors ... [but] by overlooking the complex ways that surveillance practices and technologies are entrenched within the prison industrial complex, one might miss key challenges that surveillance technologies pose to anti-violence strategies. Whether it is smartphones, iPhone applications, Google maps, or home surveillance, feminist surveillance studies scholars must investigate the ways that existing inequalities may be exacerbated by their use.

Future conversations about drone privacy and drone regulation must be attentive to the ways in which the protection of one marginalized group could be co-opted to justify, for example, increasing public surveillance or surveillance of particular people and places, leading to greater social control (Dubrofsky and Magnet 2015). This aligns with similar concerns posed in other chapters about the use of big data analytics, which can arbitrarily direct police attention to specific neighbourhoods or communities through a tautological amplification of nuisance data (O'Neil 2016; discussed in Chapter 4, this text). For instance, the construction of the "woman as a victim" in need of protection can lead to her own forced surveillance. Wesely and Gaardener (2004) highlight the difficult trade-off women can experience between wanting to feel safe when outdoors and their discomfort with the increased surveillance that brings.

There are likewise many examples where the fear of victimization of white women has justified racial discrimination, criminalization, and surveillance

Assessing the increased state use of drones through a feminist lens requires considering the ways in which drones — potentially utilized with the goal of protecting of women — may actually increase the surveillance of women in public, particularly marginalized women.

of marginalized groups, including other women (Backhouse 1999). Further, such narratives can justify state refusal to surveil or criminalize those who abuse members (including women) of these marginalized groups, such as the Canadian government's refusal to investigate the murders of Indigenous women and girls while simultaneously supporting state surveillance of Indigenous women (see Bird and Kaye, this text; also, Bailey 2015; Smith 2015; Crosby and Monaghan 2018).

While drones do not cause or necessitate this outcome, the technology is well suited to facilitate and expand state surveillance, particularly when coupled with the seemingly beneficial promise of improving women's security. This is supported by, among other things, the drone's relatively low cost (both to acquire and to operate, compared to police foot or helicopter patrol), capacity to enter otherwise difficult-to-access areas, and software that requires less skill and training to operate (Rao, Gopi, and Maione 2016). In other words, the drone overcomes many of the resource barriers that would ordinarily limit such surveillance. Accordingly, assessing the increased state use of drones through a feminist lens requires considering the ways in which drones — potentially utilized with the goal of protecting of women — may actually increase the surveillance of women in public, particularly marginalized women (Bailey 2015).

Hille Koskela's (2002) analysis of the effectiveness of CCTV cameras used to protect women reveals a number of added concerns, including that these soundless cameras failed to protect women from verbal assaults and that the cameras transformed into a form of voyeurism for the predominantly male security personnel. It stands to reason that similar critiques can be levelled at drone technology, which is likely unable to intervene an assault, yet might objectify the victims of these crimes.

Finally, we must critically assess the assumption that video or other evidence collected by a drone would assist a complainant in the event of violence in public. For example, courts are inconsistent in their use of digital evidence in criminal prosecutions of sexual violence. In her examination of several recent Canadian cases, Alexa Dodge (2018) explains how even digital evidence that seems to confirm a complainant's testimony could be used against her in ways bolstered by rape myths. In the case *R v. JR* (2016 ABQB 414), an accused was depicted in surveillance footage grabbing the complainant's breasts and buttock. The judge at first instance concluded that the complainant was unclear or ambiguous in the video about whether she was consenting to the touching; in fact, the video was interpreted as contradicting her verbal testimony. While this decision was later overturned, it nevertheless underscores Dodge's (2018) observation that digital evidence is never truly objective, particularly when interpreted by another individual (e.g., a judge) under different circumstances. The justification of increasing public surveillance to protect women should therefore be subjected to further critique on the basis that the purported evidence obtained from drones might not even serve the purpose of protecting women, particularly when scrutinized in the context of pervasive cultural rape myths.

Summary

The goal of this section has been to highlight some of the ways in which drones can intrude upon women's privacy. These are just some examples of the gendered implications of this emerging technology and each will require deeper analysis as drone technology becomes more widely adopted. A further observation that can be drawn from this discussion is that the experience and personal consequences of privacy invasions and surveillance in public space have been known to members of subordinated groups, including women, for a long time (Bailey 2015). While the drone might be viewed as a "**privacy catalyst**" (Calo 2011) — a tool with the potential to draw greater social attention to the value and precarity of privacy protections — its real advantage is that the technology may cause members of empowered groups, who (possibly by virtue of a privileged status) have not been subject to significant privacy invasions and surveillance, to become increasingly aware of the personal and social consequences of such monitoring (Bailey 2015). Critically, though, any response prompted by an increased recognition of the importance of privacy must comprehend the differential experiences of privacy, including vis-à-vis drones, for that response to be meaningful. Drawing on this examination, the final section of this chapter considers whether and how these differential implications can be addressed through the current North American approach to drone regulation.

Reflecting on the "Safety-First" Focus of Canadian and US Drone Regulation

Having considered some ways in which drone technology might differentially affect women's privacy, particularly in ways that might not be addressed under privacy laws of general application, this section assesses the regulatory outcomes of Canadian and US drone-specific regulation. First, this section identifies the general themes and priorities in the regulation of drones, as well as how regulations purport to apply to the technology itself and the social contexts into which it is adopted. The goal here is not to set out a detailed summary of all drone laws in Canada and the United States, many of which are in a state of frequent flux, but rather to draw out some generalizations that will be helpful for the subsequent analysis in light of issues raised in the preceding section. This section then explains why the value-neutral approach to drone regulation taken by these regulators will not sufficiently address the ways in which this technology can negatively impact individuals beyond their personal physical safety. Finally, the section argues that such social impacts of the technology need to be better addressed not only in technology-neutral privacy laws, but also through the rules that regulate drone design and permissible uses.

The North American Approach to Drone Regulation

In both Canada and the United States, regulators treat drone technology like it is here to stay. While in both countries there are some significant regulatory limits on widespread drone use, the federal governments of both states take the position that drone technology will bring economic benefits to society as a whole and that it is worth having and encouraging for further adoption (Chong and Sweeney 2017; United States 2015). Accordingly, we are not operating within a regulatory space where the object of regulation is perceived to need preventative prohibition (at least, not anymore). This is significant in the sense that, while regulators might strive to address and minimize risks associated with the technology, there is ultimately an expectation and a pressure to increasingly permit non-risky uses.

Drone regulation also focuses on safety. In both Canada and the United States, the primary regulators of drone technology are federal safety agencies — Transport Canada and the Federal Aviation Administration, respectively. The specific rules promulgated by these agencies unsurprisingly focus on safety, particularly with respect to other airspace users, as well as people, animals, and property on the ground. In both countries, drone regulations vary according to where and how the drone will be used (riskier opera-

In Canada, privacy concerns raised by drones received relatively little attention from drone regulators until recently.

tions over dense populations are more strictly regulated than operations in open spaces), and according to the size of the drone (smaller drones are subject to less regulation than larger drones). In both countries, recreational users (those who fly drones for personal reasons, not for commercial or research purposes) were largely unregulated until recently. On the other hand, commercial drone operators (who use their drone for a business purpose) have traditionally been highly regulated (Canada 2018). The extent of regulation has not been predicated on the purpose of the operation (beyond the commercial versus recreational distinction), nor on the types of surveillance or other payloads attached to the drone. Both countries also restrict drones from certain airspace, including near military installations, prisons, and national parks. While these safety rules have some beneficial consequences for personal privacy — particularly limits on the use of drones in populated areas — privacy is not the central philosophy of drone regulation (see Box 15-3). Accordingly, as the safety of drone technology improves, some of these laws that currently consequentially protect privacy will likely change.

In Canada, privacy concerns raised by drones received relatively little attention from drone regulators until recently (Canada 2018: para. 3). In spring 2019, Transport Canada provided some non-binding but helpful privacy guidelines for drone operators (Canada 2019). Regulators in the United States have also set out non-binding guidance for operators (United States 2015). These privacy practices seem generally designed to ensure the economic success and social integration of the technology for commercial and non-commercial operators. While these privacy ideals are positive starting points, they have provided no actual legal recourse for individuals negatively affected by drone use. Indeed, accountability and recourse for privacy concerns have not been the primary focus for either of the national regulators.

Implications of the Safety-Based Approach to Drone Regulation

None of the drone laws in Canada or the United States are explicitly gendered — there are no laws restricting or mandating gender-driven access to or use of drone technology. However, as Langdon Winner (1986) famously observed, "artifacts" like the drone have politics, and regulatory frameworks that fail to consider these politics may permit the perpetuation of inequalities

BOX 15-3: Rules for Recreational Drones in Canada

With the increasing popularization of drones as a hobbyist and recreational activity, the Canadian government has begun to develop and communicate guidelines for their operation. However, these guidelines tend to focus on the "safe" operation of these technologies while omitting issues relating to privacy. For instance, the following abstract is taken directly from Transport Canada's website on flying drones safely and legally:

> To fly a recreational drone (or model aircraft), you must follow the safety rules in the Interim Order Respecting the Use of Model Aircraft ... Following the safety rules helps you keep people, aircraft, and property safe. If you fly where you are not allowed or you break the rules below, you could be fined up to $3,000.

Fly your drone:

+ Below 90 m above the ground
+ At least 30 m away from vehicles, vessels, and the public (if your drone weighs over 250 g and up to 1 kg)
+ At least 76 m away from vehicles, vessels, and the public (if your drone weighs over 1kg and up to 35 kg)
+ At least 5.6 km away from aerodromes (any airport, seaplane base, or area where aircraft take off and land)
+ At least 1.9 km away from heliports or aerodromes used by helicopters only
+ Outside of controlled or restricted airspace
+ At least 9 km away from a natural hazard or disaster area
+ Away from areas where its use could interfere with police or first responders
+ During the day and not in clouds
+ Within your sight at all times
+ Within 500 m of yourself
+ Only if clearly marked with your name, address, and telephone number

through such technologies (Wajcman 2007; Johnson 2010). In other words, even though the laws regulating drones appear to be gender-neutral, these regulations can in fact obscure the differential impacts of the technology.

In the case of drones, the primary regulatory focus on safety presumes that this technology presents the same types of risks (physical injury and property damage) of the same level of importance to everyone. This approach fails to account for the other "politics" of the device — such as lending an operator a degree of anonymity, or perpetuating an informational and power imbalance between the operator and the object of observation, or enhancing the feeling of objectification to an individual being observed by a drone. It is quite feasible that for some, physical safety from a drone is not the first priority or concern for regulation. For instance, prevention of easier forms of harassment, intimidation, or voyeurism permitted by the technology — and the subsequent publication of information emanating from such encounters — might be a higher or equivalent priority, at least at the point of encountering the device. Prevention of state-sanctioned pervasive surveillance in public spaces (including those that would be hard to access on foot or expensive to access by manned aircraft) might be the predominant concern for others.

Furthermore, the regulatory approach does not explicitly distinguish between the different social contexts in which drones might be operated. While regulations can apply differently in populated versus unpopulated areas, these regulations are not designed with social context in mind and do not distinguish between different social contexts arising in populated/unpopulated areas. They are also subject to change and become more permissive as the technology becomes safer. Additionally, drone regulations do not consider the impact of different payloads in different contexts or on different individuals. Regulations instead focus on regulating the artifact (the "drone" as an unmanned vehicle that takes to the airspace) rather than on how it integrates into society. Accordingly, the social politics reflected by the technology remain unaddressed. Of course, as discussed earlier, Transport Canada has begun to turn its attention toward privacy. This is a positive step for addressing some of the social concerns that drones raise — however, to date, this has generated little actual legal or normative protection or recourse, particularly for the kinds of privacy invasions that disproportionately affect women.

Preliminary Responses to Regulatory Challenges

Recognizing that the primary responsibility for drone regulation in both Canada and the United States falls to safety agencies, this section sets out some possible next steps toward addressing some of the differential impacts of drones within the current framework. However, without a broader rethinking of privacy law, particularly in public space (Wilson 1990), as well as the systems for drone regulation, these recommendations are limited in their scope and impact. The ultimate solution would be the dismantling of the systems of oppression that lead to these differential privacy experiences and to other inequities and injustices (hooks 2000). This section simply sets out some preliminary ideas for how regulators might start to rebalance the attributes of drone technology through regulation to address a broader range of concerns beyond airspace safety.

First, regulators can place greater emphasis on developing mechanisms for accountability. Namely, they must develop requirements that rebalance the informational and power asymmetries between the operator of the drone and the individual encountering the drone, which would subsequently provide an avenue for redress and future prevention. This may admittedly be a difficult task due to technological and resourcing complexities. For example, while drones could be required to bear the equivalent of a licence plate, which can aid with identifying the operator, how can regulators ensure that it is visible from a distance or while the drone is in movement? Emitting information from the drone to, for instance, a cellphone application could be useful, but this presumes that individuals experiencing negative encounters also own and carry a phone. Similarly, listing all drone flights on a website would be useful, except to those without regular access to the internet. Providing a mechanism or reporting outlet for drone encounters, or even a dedicated investigator or mediator, can also further this endeavour — although such an option would either be resource-heavy or potentially ineffective.

Michael Froomkin and Zak Colangelo (2015) have suggested mechanisms to address the information imbalance between the drone operator and an individual encountering a drone as a means for reducing uncertainty about the device. For instance, a drone could be equipped with coloured lights or other markers to inform individuals about the drone's capabilities (e.g., whether or not it is filming). This may also help to address the power imbalance between the operator and the observed by giving the observed greater awareness relating to the encounter — though this still must be accompanied by a recourse mechanism to address the privacy harm (Froomkin and Colangelo 2015). While none of these suggestions definitively tackles the issue of gendered privacy invasions, at least these combined factors could begin to address some of the attributes of drones that risk worsening the state of public privacy for women and others in public space.

Regulators can simultaneously focus on increasing public participation in all stages of the regulatory process by developing mechanisms for intervention at both the design phase and in the contexts of sale and use (Faulkner 2001). Transport Canada, for instance, provided opportunities for public input when the agency recently revised its drone regulations. Another mechanism for this can be to adopt a critical feminist technology assessment, extending existing technology assessment procedures by "first, giving voice to the full range of interested groups in technological design and, second, starting from a critical debate about what and whose needs are to be met, rather than from existing technologies" (Faulkner 2001: 91). In other words, focus on democratizing the technology from the outside in.

As a final observation, regulators can also adopt policies and targets

In other words, focus on democratizing the technology from the outside in.

to enable women to increase their technical competence and access to drone technology. There are already numerous endeavours targeted at increasing women's involvement in the industry, as well a number of women in prominent positions within the drone sector (McCue 2015). Nevertheless, men still heavily dominate the industry, as with many other technology-driven fields (Dutta and Omolayole 2016). Greater diversity of voices both within and external to these sectors can help to democratize the technology in a meaningful way. However, encouraging women into the industry cannot be the sole or primary solution to addressing the issues raised in this chapter. First, it places an expectation on women to accept the system as is and learn to adapt to and within it, which is itself a system that some women may perceive as socially harmful. Second, while becoming increasingly affordable, drone technology is still a luxury to many, who may not have the financial or time resources to dedicate to entering into an industry, particularly out of a "gender obligation" (Bray 2007). Encouraging more women to become involved with the technology from a technical or policy perspective will be a positive development but cannot be the sole solution to addressing the differential impacts of the technology.

Conclusion

This chapter considered some of the gendered ways in which drone technology might engage privacy law and norms, demonstrating how traditional "norms" of women's privacy and modesty persist in popular and legal discussions of drone technology. The persistence of this narrative undermines the ability of women to assert their privacy in public spaces, including gendered invasions of their privacy that have been exacerbated by the attributes of drone technology. Moreover, the purported concern about women's safety in public could simultaneously lead to greater surveillance by drone technology — both of and among women — to the detriment of privacy in public spaces. In light of these concerns, it becomes apparent that the current approaches to regulating drones in Canada and the United States treat the technology as value-neutral rather than as a system embedded with particular politics. Regulatory agencies should place greater emphasis on addressing some of the politics of the drone — for instance, by eliminating the power imbalance caused by the drone's dislocation from its operator, by bringing more voices into policy and regulatory discussions at the development, sale, and use phases, and increasing women's involvement in the industry and in using the technology. Ultimately, though, the most rewarding solution to many of these concerns will come from broader social and legal change.

Discussion Questions

1. Other than drones, what technologies do you think have a gendered effect? What can be done to address these effects?
2. How do you define "privacy in public"?
3. What solutions can you think of for identifying drones, their owners, and their purposes?
4. How might drone-based surveillance disproportionately affect marginalized, colonized, or racialized groups within Canada?

Recommended Resources

Koskela, H. (2000). "'The Gaze without Eyes': Video-surveillance and the Changing Nature of Urban Space." *Progress in Human Geography*, 24, 2.

Transport Canada's Instructions for Flying a Drone Safely and Legally. <https://www.tc.gc.ca/en/services/aviation/drone-safety/flying-drone-safely-legally.html>.

Will the Proliferation of Domestic Drone Use in Canada Raise New Concerns for Privacy? Report prepared by the Research Group of the Office of the Privacy Commissioner of Canada. <https://www.priv.gc.ca/en/opc-actions-and-decisions/research/explore-privacy-research/2013/drones_201303/>.

Glossary

drones: a colloquial term commonly used to described *unmanned aerial vehicles* (UAV).

Lady Godiva: the noble woman who agreed to traverse through a village in the nude, in order that her husband would reduce taxes for the villagers.

modesty theory of privacy: legal and moral standards that assume privacy for women entails protecting them from sexualized observation.

panoptic chill: an assumption that knowledge of the presence (or possibility thereof) of automated surveillance technologies will lead people to alter or curb their behaviours in public.

peeping Tom: a common term in the English lexicon that extended from the Lady Godiva story. The peeping Tom was the one person in the village who gazed at the nude lady and was subsequently punished for this transgression.

privacy catalyst: defined by Calo (2011), these are tools or artifacts that can have the effect of drawing attention to or shaping public discussion about privacy and related rules, laws, and morals — in this case, drones are an example.

right to be left alone: a historic argument for privacy, stated by Warren and Brandeis and premised on protection of the private realm.

sunbather narrative: defined by Kaminski (2016), used to describe the press's sensationalism of drone-based invasions of privacy that target young women, often in a state of undress.

Note

This chapter is adapted from an article written for the *Canadian Journal of Law and Technology* (2018) 16, 2: 307–38. My sincerest thanks go to Sinziana Gutiu, Madeleine Elish, and the participants at the We Robot 2017 conference; Bita Amani, Kathleen Lahey and the participants of the Feminist Legal Studies Queen's (FLSQ) speaker series; James Popham, Tanya Andrusieczko, and previous anonymous reviewers for their immensely insightful comments and feedback. I am also grateful to Joanna Pawlowski and Cherlene Cheung for their fantastic research assistance, and to my doctoral supervisor, Dr. Ian Kerr, for his abounding support and encouragement.

References

Adey, P. 2016. "Making the Drone Strange: The Politics, Aesthetics and Surrealism of Levitation." *Geographica Helvetica* 71, 4.

Allen, A.L. 2000. "Gender and Privacy in Cyberspace." *Stanford Law Review* 52.

____. 1988. *Uneasy Access: Privacy for Women in a Free Society*. Lanham: Rowman & Littlefield.

Allen, A.L., and E. Mack. 1991. "How Privacy Got Its Gender." *Northern Illinois University Law Review* 10, 1990–1.

Aubry v. Éditions Vice-Versa Inc. 1 SCR 591, 1998.

Backhouse, C. 1999. *Colour-Coded: A Legal History of Racism in Canada, 1900–1950*. Toronto: University of Toronto Press.

Bailey, J. 2015. "Gendering Big Brother: What Should a Feminist Do." *Journal of Law & Equality* 12.

Bilton, N. 2016. "When Your Neighbor's Drone Pays an Unwelcome Visit." *New York Times*, January 28, D5.

Blanke, J.M. 2018. "Privacy and Outrage." *Journal of Law, Technology & the Internet* 9, 1.

Bracken-Roche, D. Lyon, M.J. Mansour, A. Molnar et al. 2014. *Surveillance Drones: Privacy Implications of the Spread of Unmanned Aerial Vehicles (UAVs) in Canada*. A Report to the Office of the Privacy Commissioner of Canada, under the 2013-2014 Contributions Program. <sscqueens.org/sites/sscqueens.org/files/Surveillance_Drones_Report. pdf>.

Bray, F. 2007. "Gender and Technology." *Annual Review of Anthropology* 36.

Calo, R. 2011. "The Drone as Privacy Catalyst." *Stanford Law Review Online* 64.

Canada. 2019. "Privacy Guidelines for Drone Users." Transport Canada. <tc.gc.ca/en/services/aviation/drone-safety/privacy-guidelines-drone-users.html>.

___. 2018. "Flying Your Drone Safely and Legally." Transport Canada. <tc.gc.ca/en/services/aviation/drone-safety/flying-drone-safely-legally.html>.

Chong, J., and N. Sweeney. 2017. *Civilian Drone Use in Canada*. Ottawa: Library of Parliament [publication no. 2017-23-E].

Clarke, R., and L. Moses. 2014. "The Regulation of Civilian Drones' Impacts on Public Safety." *Computer Law & Security Review* 30.

Crosby, A., and J. Monaghan. 2018. *Policing Indigenous Movements: Dissent and the Security State*. Halifax: Fernwood Publishing.

Davis, D. 1993. "The Harm That Has No Name: Street Harassment, Embodiment, and African American Women." UCLA *Women's Law Journal* 4, 2.

Directline.com. 2018. "Fleetlights Search and Rescue: A Direct Line Initiative." <directline.com/fleetlights>.

Dodge, A. 2018. "The Digital Witness: The Role of Digital Evidence in Criminal Justice Responses to Sexual Violence." *Feminist Theory* 19, 3.

Donoghue, D. 2003. *Lady Godiva: A Literary History of the Legend*. London: Blackwell.

Dubrofsky, R., and S. Magnet. 2015. "Introduction." In R. Dubrofsky and S. Magnet (eds.), *Feminist Surveillance Studies*. Durham: Duke University Press.

Dutta, S., and O. Omolayole. 2016. "Are There Differences Between Men and Women in Information Technology Innovation Adoption Behaviors: A Theoretical Study." *Journal of Business Diversity* 16, 1.

Farivar, C. 2015. "Alleged John, Prostitute Busted by Drone, Face Criminal Charges. Beware the Sousveillance State: Anyone Can Find You in Public." *Ars Technica*, December 4. <arstechnica.com/tech-policy/2015/12/john-and-alleged-prostitute-busted-by-drone-face-criminal-charges/>.

Farmer, O., and S. Smock Jordan. 2017. "Experiences of Women Coping with Catcalling Experiences in New York City: A Pilot Study." *Journal of Feminist Family Therapy* 29, 4.

Faulkner, W. 2001. "The Technology Question in Feminism: A View from Feminist Technology Studies." *Women's Studies International Forum* 24, 1.

Froomkin, A.M., and P.Z. Colangelo. 2015. "Self-Defense Against Robots and Drones." *Connecticut Law Review* 48, 1.

Gersen, J.S. 2008. "Is Privacy a Woman?" *Georgetown Law Journal* 97.

Grove, N.S. 2015. "The Cartographic Ambiguities of HarassMap: Crowdmapping Security and Sexual Violence in Egypt." *Security Dialogue* 46, 4.

Haraway, D. 1988. "Situated Knowledges: The Science Question in Feminism and the Privilege of Partial Perspective." *Feminist Studies* 14, 3.

hooks, b. 2000. *Feminism Is for Everybody: Passionate Politics*. London: Pluto Press.

Johnson, D. 2010. "Sorting Out the Question of Feminist Technology." In L. Layne, S. Vostral, and K. Boyer (eds.), *Feminist Technology*. Chicago: University of Illinois Press.

Kaminski, M. 2016. "Enough with the 'Sunbathing Teenager' Gambit." *Slate*, May 17. <slate.com/articles/technology/future_tense/2016/05/drone_privacy_is_about_much_more_than_sunbathing_teenage_daughters.html>.

___. 2013. "Drone Federalism: Civilian Drones and the Things They Carry." *California*

Law Review Circuit 4.

Koskela, H. 2002. "Video Surveillance, Gender, and the Safety of Public Urban Space: 'Peeping Tom' Goes High Tech?" *Urban Geography* 23, 3.

____. 2000. "'The Gaze Without Eyes': Video-Surveillance and the Changing Nature of Urban Space." *Progress in Human Geography* 24, 2.

Kyllo v. United States, 533 US 27, 2001.

Landau, J. 2014. "See It: Connecticut Woman Who Assaulted Teen for Flying Drone at Beach Requests Probation." *New York Daily News*, August 23. <nydailynews.com/news/crime/conn-woman-attacked-teen-drone-seeks-probation-article-1.1836545>.

Layne, L., S. Vostral, and K. Boyer. 2010. *Feminist Technology*. Chicago: University of Illinois Press.

Leenes, R., and F. Lucivero. 2014. "Laws on Robots, Laws by Robots, Laws in Robots: Regulating Robot Behaviour by Design." *Law, Innovation and Technology* 6, 2.

MacKinnon, C.A. 1987. *Feminism Unmodified: Discourses on Life and Law*. Harvard: Harvard University Press.

Macmillan, R., A. Nierobisz, and S. Welsh. 2000. "Experiencing the Streets: Harassment and Perceptions of Safety among Women." *Journal of Research in Crime and Delinquency* 37, 3.

Mason, C., and S. Magnet. 2012. "Surveillance Studies and Violence Against Women." *Surveillance & Society* 10, 2.

McCue, M. 2015. "Meet the Women Shaping the Future of the Drone Business." *Fortune*, July 1. <fortune.com/2015/07/01/women-drone-industry/>.

McNeal, G. 2014. "Drones and Aerial Surveillance: Considerations for Legislature." Pepperdine University Legal Studies Research Paper No. 2015/3.

Molnar, A., and C. Parsons. "Unmanned Aerial Vehicles (UAVs) and Law Enforcement in Australia and Canada: Governance through 'Privacy' in an Era of Counter-Law?" In R. Lippert, K. Walby, I. Warren, and D. Palmer (eds.), *National Security, Surveillance and Terror*. London: Palgrave Macmillan.

Monahan, T. 2009. "Dreams of Control at a Distance: Gender, Surveillance, and Social Control." *Cultural Studies? Critical Methodologies* 9, 2.

O'Neil, C. 2016. *Weapons of Math Destruction: How Big Data Increases Inequality and Threatens Democracy*. New York: Broadway Books.

Perritt, H., and Al Plawinski. 2015. "One Centimeter Over My Back Yard: Where Does Federal Pre-Emption of State Drone Regulation Start?" *North Carolina Journal of Law & Technology* 17, 2.

Plaxton, M. 2018. "Privacy, Voyeurism, and Statutory Interpretation." *Criminal Law Quarterly*.

Rao, B., A. Gopi, and R. Maione. 2016. "The Societal Impact of Commercial Drones." *Technology in Society* 45.

Rule, T. 2015. "Airspace in an Age of Drones." *Boston University Law Review* 95.

R v. Jarvis 2017 ONCA 778, 2017.

R v. Jarvis 2019 SCC 10.

R v. JR ABQB 414, 2016.

R v. Spencer, 2 SCR 212, 2014.

R v. Wise, 1 SCR 527, 1992.

Schneider, M. 1991. "The Violence of Privacy." *Connecticut Law Review* 23.

Sheldon, S. 2018. "Empowerment and Privacy? Home Use of Abortion Pills in the Republic of Ireland." *Signs: Journal of Women in Culture and Society* 43, 4.

Slane, A. 2010. "From Scanning to Sexting: The Scope of Protection of Dignity-Based Privacy in Canadian Child Pornography Law." *Osgoode Hall Law Journal* 48.

Smith, A. 2015. "Not-Seeing: State Surveillance, Settler Colonialism, and Gender Violence." In R. Dubrofsky and S. Magnet (eds.), *Feminist Surveillance Studies*. Durham: Duke University Press.

Steele, A. 2014. "Will Drones Keep India's Women Safe from Rape?" *Christian Science Monitor*, December 11. <csmonitor.com/World/Global-News/2014/1211/Will-drones-keep-India-s-women-safe-from-rape>.

Thomasen, K. 2017. "Flying Between the Lines: Drone Laws and the (Re)Production of Public Spaces." In E. Hilgendorf and U. Seidel (eds.), *Robotics, Automatics, and the Law: Legal Issues Arising from the* AUTONOMICS *for Industry 4.0 Technology Programme of the German Federal Ministry for Economic Affairs and Energy*. Berlin: Nomos.

Thompson, D.M. 1993. "The Woman in the Street: Reclaiming the Public Space from Sexual Harassment." *Yale Journal of Law & Feminism* 6.

United States. 2015. "Voluntary Best Practices for UAS Privacy, Transparency, and Accountability." Washington, DC: National Telecommunications and Information Administration. <ntia.doc.gov/files/ntia/publications/voluntary_best_practices_for_uas_privacy_transparency_and_accountability_0.pdf>.

Villasenor, J. 2013. "Observations from Above: Unmanned Aircraft Systems and Privacy." *Harvard Journal of Law & Public Policy* 36.

Volokh, E. 2015. "Man vs. Drone, vs. the Law." *Washington Post*, August 20. <washingtonpost.com/news/volokh-conspiracy/wp/2015/08/20/man-vs-drone-vs-the-law/>.

Waghorn, N.J. 2016. "Watching the Watchmen: Resisting Drones and the 'Protester Panopticon.'" *Geographica Helvetica* 71, 2.

Wajcman, J. 2007. "From Women and Technology to Gendered Technoscience." *Information, Community and Society* 10, 3.

Warren, S.D., and L.D. Brandeis. 1890. "The Right to Privacy." *Harvard Law Review* 4, 5.

Wesely, J.K., and E. Gaarder. 2004. "The Gendered 'Nature' of the Urban Outdoors: Women Negotiating Fear of Violence." *Gender & Society* 18, 5.

Wesselmann, E.D., and J.R. Kelly. 2010. "Cat-Calls and Culpability: Investigating the Frequency and Functions of Stranger Harassment." *Sex Roles* 63, 7–8.

Wilson, B. 1990. "Will Women Judges Really Make a Difference." *Osgoode Hall Law Journal* 28, 3.

Winner, L. 1989. *The Whale and the Reactor: A Search for Limits in an Age of High Technology*. Chicago: University of Chicago Press.

Završnik, A. 2016. "Introduction: Situating Drones in Surveillance Societies." In A. Završnik (ed.), *Drones and Unmanned Aerial Systems*. Switzerland: Springer International Publishing.

16

Under the Gaze

Policing Social Movements
That Resist Extractive Capitalism

Jeffrey Monaghan and Kevin Walby

After reading this chapter, you will be able to do the following:

1. Briefly describe the policing of social movements in Canada.
2. Explain foundational security studies concepts.
3. Explain key trends that have intensified practices of security governance.
4. Outline a critique of how the "war on terror" has impacted security and policing practices in Canada.
5. Understand the role of critical infrastructure protection in the policing of social movements.

Social movements are forms of contentious politics that challenge and disrupt the status quo (Tarrow 1998). Police and security agencies have long held antagonistic views toward social movements, predominantly movements of the political left. Some of these antagonisms are rooted in the conservative orientation of police culture (Reiner 1992). Another source is the function that policing plays in protecting and advancing the interests of corporations in Western societies (Williams 2015). In Canada, policing has a long history of suppressing Indigenous, labour, queer, environmental, and student movements (Kinsman, Buse, and Steedman 2000). Recently, policing and **surveillance** practices in Canada have been significantly shaped by extractivism, which refers to a model of economic growth that prioritizes the extraction of resources to sell on international markets (Veltmeyer and Petras

2014). Given the centrality of resource extraction to the Canadian political economy, the targets of this policing and surveillance are likely to be people who organize against pipelines, the tarsands, fracking, mining and drilling operations, and similar projects that seek to expand resource commodification in a time of climate emergency.

Practices of policing and security organized by governmental authorities are being entrenched across more and more aspects of social life. Prompted by immense increases in spending on security and policing, surveillance practices have become more prolific, more opaque, less identifiable, less subject to juridical or democratic control, and more antagonistic toward perceived threats to security, including social movement groups raising awareness about and resisting **extractive capitalism** in Canada. During this expansion of security governance, surveillance as a social control practice has incorporated tendencies that both centralize and decentralize its instrumentations. While the "centres" of security, such as security intelligence agencies, have become more powerful, so have the many decentred appendages that recirculate through assemblages of policing. Nowhere is this more evident than in relation to "national security" policing, including the surveillance of social movements.

In this chapter, we outline how contemporary policing practices that target social movements are animated by a convergence of "**war on terror**" security governance and Canada's increasing dependence on extractive capitalism. We consider three aspects of these security governance practices in Canada. First, we detail the recent transformations of national security policing and mission creep, including how "national security" policing has shifted to focus on Indigenous and anti-extraction movements. Second, we examine how national security entities conduct surveillance, with a specific emphasis on pre-emption as a trend in contemporary surveillance. Third, we explore how the integration of corporate interests into the national security policing assemblage has resulted in an increasingly powerful influence over the policing of extraction opponents. We review cases of policing and surveillance in relation to protests that challenge extractive capitalism across the country. Providing an overview of how national security has been an umbrella for policing and corporate entities to suppress Indigenous and environmental movements, we underline that social conditions allowing the diffusion of security into everyday life present an anti-democratic social force that must be contested.

"War on Terror" Security Governance

Practices of policing and security governance have been shaped and influenced by the "war on terror." While the characteristics of security governance predated 9/11, the political and social climate that followed 9/11 accelerated and intensified many of the elements of policing that we detail in this chapter. It is worth thinking of the governmental responses to 9/11 as a *security enactment*, or ways in which a broadened spectrum of social relations and groups have been reframed and governed through their problematizations as "security" (Huysmans 2011, 2014). Resulting efforts to "govern through security" (Valverde 2001: 83) have had profound implications on domestic policing and the policing of social movements. We suggest that three core elements have steered the amplified character of security governance in the "war on terror."

1. Mission Creep

Often used in military and policing literature, "**mission creep**" refers to agencies that engage in an enlarged field of activities — that is, beyond their original mandate. Unlike the police diversification concept, which describes how policing agencies have expanded their mandates through community policing and other doctrines, mission creep is not a formal expansion of responsibilities. Rather, mission creep entails taking on extra responsibilities in the course of fulfilling an original set of duties. In the domain of policing and security, mission creep also means "surveillance creep" (Nelkin and Andrews 1999: 689), which refers to the use of surveillance technologies and techniques for purposes other than originally intended.

One example of mission creep is in policing social movements in the "war on terror." Due to the significant resources allocated to the "war on terror" and counterterrorism, social movements have been recast through the filters of national security policing. While Muslims in Canada remain by far the most scrutinized population by counterterrorism practices (Nagra 2017), the extremely few instances of Muslim-related terrorism or threats have resulted in other groups being targeted by counterterrorism resources. Insofar as the mandates of the "war on terror" were originally framed around Al-Qaeda or other organizations

> Unlike the police diversification concept, which describes how policing agencies have expanded their mandates through community policing and other doctrines, mission creep is not a formal expansion of responsibilities. Rather, mission creep entails taking on extra responsibilities in the course of fulfilling an original set of duties.

Security intelligence agencies use terminology such as "eco-terrorism," yet policing agencies use elastic or looser language that can fit a variety of social movements under the category of national security. The use of "extremism" and "extremists" is an example of elastic security discourses, and agencies use iterations of "environmental extremists" or "Aboriginal extremists" as a mechanism to direct national security resources toward localized policing conflicts.

that engage in politically motivated violence against civilian populations, "mission creep" has meant that a far broader array of groups or actors have been labelled and scrutinized as potential terrorists, ranging from security for and policing of anti-pipeline movements to the anti-Olympics movement (Boykoff 2011; Monaghan and Walby 2012a, 2012b).

With a broadened mission, national security policing has targeted a comprehensive scope of activities. Legal repression is one technique (Ellefsen 2016), and in this chapter we reflect on legal developments that target environmental movement participants. It is not only public security and policing agencies undertaking these surveillance and suppression practices; private security and intelligence have also played a role in tracking animal rights and environmental movements across Canada (Walby and Monaghan 2011), as well as in England, Wales (Button and John 2002), and elsewhere (Birss 2017).

In addition to the legal repression of movements, the "war on terror" has produced discursive ways of labelling and categorizing social movements. As such, activists have been increasingly framed as national security threats. Security intelligence agencies use terminology such as "eco-terrorism," yet policing agencies use elastic or looser language that can fit a variety of social movements under the category of national security (Dominique-Legault 2016). The use of "extremism" and "extremists" is an example of elastic security discourses, and agencies use iterations of "environmental extremists" or "Aboriginal extremists" as a mechanism to direct national security resources toward localized policing conflicts. Take the following comments from a declassified intelligence report by the RCMP's National Security Criminal Investigations division from January 2014. In the document, RCMP analysts describe a wide range of Indigenous, civil society, and environmental groups by warning of "a growing, highly-organized and well-financed, anti-Canadian petroleum movement, that consists of peaceful activists, militants and violent extremists" who are engaging "in criminal activity to promote their anti-petroleum ideology" (RCMP 2016-1140: 87). To demonstrate the level of organization and financing of this "anti-Canadian petroleum movement," the

RCMP analysts canvassed a number of internet sources — from Sun Media to right-wing bloggers — suggesting that the movement is growing in size because of support from US foundations. Regardless of the actual funding, size, dynamics, tactics, or other complexities of social movements, RCMP documents such as these reconstruct multi-faceted dynamics by enacting a singular category: the "anti-Canadian petroleum movement." While no such "thing" actually exists, the category serves a purpose in reducing opposition to pipelines into a frame of criminality deserving of scrutiny.

As an enterprise of criminal "kind making," the RCMP report reproduces selective and inaccurate artifacts to construct activists as national security threats. As Luscombe and Lutfy (2016) argue, the potency of threat construction is a result of its simple, binary framing. These categories of threat reflect assumptions and stereotypes that are presented as objective facts about criminality. Bonelli and Ragazzi (2014: 483) use the concept of "conjectural reasoning" to demonstrate how threat construction is based on the selection and politicization of scattered and sometimes dubious "facts." Detailing the operations of French security agencies, they write: "[intelligence reports] show — sometimes to the point of caricature — how scattered elements are assembled to create a coherent narrative of threat." In the RCMP report, the narrative of threat is straightforward in its depiction of environmentalists as national security problems — the simplicity is ostentatious. Nowhere outside of the RCMP security establishment is there an "anti-petroleum movement." This movement and its supposed "anti-petroleum ideology" are themselves constructs of the security establishment, and perhaps the right-wing blogs relied upon as evidence in RCMP intelligence reports.

Consider another example of simplistic reasoning found in these reports:

> Natural resource exploration and development projects — notably on disputed land — have historically been a contentious issue within aboriginal extremist groups, and are often the catalyst for aboriginal/ industry/law enforcement confrontation. (RCMP 2016-1140: 77)

The report goes on to detail the 2013 land conflict at Elsipogtog, New Brunswick, as a major site of extremist activity. The land conflict at Elsipogtog was a complex and protracted affair, steeped in long-standing conflicts arising from colonial land theft, broken treaties, corporate control over politicians, rural racism, and economic marginalization of the Indigenous (as well as rural settler) communities (Howe 2015). When the province approved shale gas exploration on unceded land, tensions boiled over into a series of blockades that were punctuated by extremely high levels of police provoca-tions, unrelenting surveillance, and eventually an unnecessary but highly punitive and violent police raid (Howe 2015). The complexity of the situation has been regularly ignored by policing agencies, who have used the conflict at Elsipogtog to demonize Indigenous movements. The Canadian Security Intelligence Service (csis) also makes regular mention of the Elsipogtog conflict in claiming national security threats related to domestic protests (see Box 16-1). In one example from a "secret" intelligence assessment from December 2016 on protests related to the Trans Mountain pipeline, csis describes the conflict without any mention of land claims or the high levels of violence toward Indigenous communities. The assessment concludes with a quote from rcmp Assistant Commissioner Brown, who warned that the police raid found "ieds" (improvised explosive devices) that "were akin to a Boston Marathon-type of bombing" (csis 2017-123: 4). Though members of the Mi'kmaq Warrior Society contend that the alleged explosives were planted by agent provocateurs, the report eschews attempts by the Warriors to negotiate a peaceful solution (which included appeals for mediation by the Canadian military) and portrays the conflict as not only criminal but tied to an invocation of the high-profile terrorist attack against civilians during the Boston Marathon. This is an example of national security threat construction,

---

Box 16-1: Elsipogtog First Nation

In October 2013, Indigenous leaders from Elsipogtog First Nation issued an eviction notice to Texas-based swn Resources Inc., ordering the corporation — who was being supported by many within the New Brunswick bureaucratic, political, and policing communities — to stop seismic testing for shale gas development on Mi'kmaq territories. Elsipogtog's chief, Arren Sock, read aloud a band council resolution reclaiming First Nations stewardship over all unoccupied Crown land. The resolution proclaims:

> we are capable of managing our lands better than other governments or corporations ... [that] we have lost all confidence in governments for the safekeeping of our lands held in trust by the British Crown ... [and that] ... we have been compelled to act and save our water, land and animals from ruin. (see Howe 2015: 134)

Though protecting their lands and treaty rights, the Mi'kmaq were systematically undermined by the New Brunswick government, the rcmp, and private companies. Instead of respecting Indigenous laws and the treaty entitlements of the Mi'kmaq, the rcmp engaged in a number of dirty tricks that resulted in the criminalization and the demonization of the land defenders (see Howe 2015).

whereby the RCMP took the images and meaning conjured by the terror attack in Boston and applied them in a blanket manner to a land dispute so as to signify Indigenous land defenders as terrorists.

> Threat entrepreneurs create security intelligence categories that are encoded with damaging stereotypes, allegations, and insinuations, and these categories are subsequently deployed in actual policing work.

The intelligence workers who write these reports are what Sorenson (2016: 42) refers to as "terrorism entrepreneurs" or what we have called threat entrepreneurs (Monaghan and Walby 2017). Threat entrepreneurs create security intelligence categories that are encoded with damaging stereotypes, allegations, and insinuations, and these categories are subsequently deployed in actual policing work. Such categories also mirror the stereotypical claims of conservative politicians. For example, as Joe Oliver, the former natural resources minister, wrote in an open letter in support of the Northern Gateway pipeline, "there are environmental and other radical groups that would seek to block this opportunity" (in Stewart and Tanner 2015: 77). The coupling of "environmental" and "radical" is meant to discredit social movement groups and justify police surveillance. As these categories are applied ever more widely, the surveillance apparatus expands. Then, as a result of this mission creep, the imaginary threat of terrorism is fed into localized policing situations.

2. Pre-Emption and Surveillance

The "war on terror" has dramatically accelerated surveillance practices in contemporary society. Surveillance has been defined as "systematic focus on personal information in order to influence, manage, entitle, or control those whose information is collected" (Bennett et al. 2014: 6). Though the rise of surveillance practices is intimately tied to the development of the modern state, the types of "watching" that occur and the collection of information from these surveillance practices has intensified, widened, and deepened.

The transformation of police work over the past three decades demonstrates the intensifying character of surveillance. Emerging from 1990s discourses, "intelligence-led" policing was a conceptual framework that influenced the development of "a managerial model of evidence-based resource allocation through prioritization ... that places an emphasis on information sharing and collaborative, strategic solutions to crime problems" (Ratcliffe 2008: 85). These efforts have privileged the priority of "manag[ing] information about threats and risks in order to strategically manage the policing mission" (Sheptycki

> Playing a central role in police operations, intelligence-led policing has shifted much of the daily practice of policing away from reactive functions of crime control toward a proactive focus on "risk, surveillance, and security."

2005). As Ratcliffe, Strang, and Taylor (2014: 1) explain, an intelligence-led framework integrates "the 'old knowledge' of policing, such as criminal informants and information gleaned from suspect interviews, with the 'new knowledge' of policing, crime analysis and the surveillance of national databases" such as those managed by csis.

Playing a central role in police operations, intelligence-led policing has shifted much of the daily practice of policing away from reactive functions of crime control toward a proactive focus on "risk, surveillance, and security" (Ericson and Haggerty 1997: 18). While the transformations within what Ericson and Haggerty called "policing the risk society" display a dramatic reorientation toward calculating and managing future risk, the "war on terror" has added an additional emphasis on pre-emptive actions. One of the impacts of 9/11, argues Zedner (2007: 264), has been the "significantly increased … pressure on governments to think and act pre-emptively. The trajectory toward anticipatory endeavour, risk assessment and intelligence gathering is accelerating." The enactment of security has impacted a broad spectrum of governance, not only in policing. De Goede, Simon, and Hoijtink (2014: 412) suggest that "institutions and sectors across the security landscape have embraced the drive to incorporate uncertain futures and pre-emptive protocols into their everyday bureaucratic practice."

Security governance has dispersed this call for anticipatory action throughout multiple agencies and institutions of governance. In Canada, security governance is centred in the major policing and security institutions such as csis, but it also incorporates many lesser institutions, like municipal police, into a security and policing assemblage (Brodeur 2010). We discuss these organizational developments shortly but stress here that the operational logic of the security assemblage is pre-emptive: it uses surveillance, databanking, and intelligence sharing to prepare — and act against — future threats. The police goal through pervasive surveillance of Idle No More activists and Northern Gateway pipeline protestors is to get ahead of contentious politics. Not only is this contrary to typical criminal procedure predicated on gathering of evidence for prosecution (McCulloch and Pickering 2009), it is explicitly aimed at monitoring and disrupting specific political practices, making such surveillance equivalent to political policing. This trend toward pre-emption extends into a new institutionalized form of security intelligence: **fusion centres.**

3. Fusion Centres and Anti-Terror Laws

Under the Bush and Obama administrations in the United States, "fusion centers" were created as intelligence-sharing hubs in the "war on terror." Regan, Monahan, and Craven (2015: 742) explain that fusion centres have a "mandate to share data across government agencies as well as across the public and private sectors" (see also Monahan 2010). Operating under the umbrella of the Department of Homeland Security, seventy-seven officially designated fusion centres existed as of 2013 at state and regional levels (Regan, Monahan, and Craven 2015). The "fusion" aspect of these centres refers to the integration of multiple agencies across the security spectrum into one physical space. Involving sometimes dozens of regional and federal policing and security agencies, these hubs also incorporate private security companies as well as military and customs agencies (Taylor and Russell 2012). The appeal of the fusion centre model was a vision of integration — where multiple agencies could collaborate, share databanks and intelligence resources, and coordinate responses to terrorist threats.

While fusion centres have become established in the United States, the model, as well as the overarching logic of integration and data sharing, has developed slowly in Canada. Notably, Canadian officials have not developed a fusion-centre approach with the publicity and fanfare that occurred in the United States. Instead, fusion centres emerged as makeshift responses to protest "flashpoints" and the need to develop information-sharing practices (King and Waddington 2005). With major events such as the Winter Olympics and G20 Summit in 2010, the CSIS and RCMP created massive, although temporary, "integrated security units" and specialized "joint intelligence groups" that explicitly borrowed from the integrated, intelligence-led doctrines of the US fusion centres (Monaghan and Walby 2012a, 2012b). As an outgrowth of these efforts to pre-emptively police major protests, forms of intelligence-sharing models were integrated at multiple levels of the security apparatus, the most significant being the Government Operations Centre (GOC).

Housed within Public Safety Canada (PSC), the GOC — according to its website — functions in the following manner:

> It provides 24/7 monitoring and reporting, national-level situational awareness, warning products and integrated risk assessments, as

well as national-level planning and whole-of-government response management. During periods of heightened response, the GOC is augmented by staff from other government departments/agencies (OGD) and non-governmental organizations (NGO) who physically work in the GOC and connect to it virtually. (PSC 2017)

Following the fusion centre model, the GOC incorporates an array of actors into its intelligence collection, analysis, and dissemination network. Much like fusion centres in the United States (Regan, Monahan, and Craven 2015), the GOC actively engages in information sharing and surveillance of social movements. Access to information data revealed that the GOC catalogued over eight hundred public demonstrations from 2006 to 2014; these included protests against a Canadian mining company in Brazil, a Montreal march and vigil for missing and murdered Indigenous women, a protest by lobster fishers in New Brunswick, and a rally in Ottawa by the Public Service Alliance of Canada (Boutilier 2014). Integrating agencies including PSC, police, security agencies such as CSIS, the military, CIRNAC, as well as private agencies, the scope of surveillance and intelligence sharing is pervasive. A significant amount of GOC surveillance targeted environmentalists and Indigenous protests.

A prominent example of the GOC's targeting of social movements is illustrated by the policing of Idle No More in 2012–13. Given the scope of Indigenous mobilization at the outset of the movement — upward of one thousand actions across the country — the response involved potentially unprecedented resources dedicated toward a campaign of mass surveillance (Crosby and Monaghan 2016). The campaign was centred in entities such as the GOC, which used the fusion centre approach and acted as a hub for intelligence sharing across all levels of the security apparatus. At one secretive, high-level Assistant Deputy Minister's National Security Operations Committee (ADM NSOPS) meeting held on January 15, 2013, Idle No More was the first item of discussion under the agenda heading "Domestic Extremism and Government Model for Decision Making" (CSIS 2016-93: 6). In handwritten notes from a meeting with the CSIS-run Integrated Terrorism Assessment Centre (ITAC), officials detailed their strategy for **pre-emptive policing** responses; they would create a more permanent "central fusion centre for Native problems" (CSIS 2016-93: 1). While the status of this "fusion centre" is currently unknown, the responsibility for coordinating intelligence and policing information during Idle No More fell to Craig Oldham, director of the GOC, who was also charged with relaying information to the prime minister's national security advisor.

Within these points of contestation and protest, the function of policing and security agencies as protectors of the status quo becomes increasingly clear. Idle No More was perhaps the most surveilled social movement in Canadian history — with policing and security agencies aiming to monitor every event, action, and participant and store this information in a variety of databases (Crosby and Monaghan 2016, 2018). Much of the surveillance

Idle No More was perhaps the most surveilled social movement in Canadian history — with policing and security agencies aiming to monitor every event, action, and participant and store this information in a variety of databases (Crosby and Monaghan 2016, 2018). Much of the surveillance and cataloguing had nothing to do with criminal activity, yet the movement itself presented a weighty challenge to extractive capitalism as well as settler colonialism: it challenged the status quo and was therefore subjected to extensive policing and surveillance practices.

and cataloguing had nothing to do with criminal activity, yet the movement itself presented a weighty challenge to extractive capitalism as well as settler colonialism: it challenged the status quo and was therefore subjected to extensive policing and surveillance practices. These surveillance practices that target social movements often exist in extra-legal spaces, where they remain opaque and avoid scrutiny. That was certainly the case with Idle No More. Beginning with demonstrations in the mid-2000s, police and security agencies have sought to officialize the fusion centre practices to become normal aspects of policing work. To do so, the government proposed a new information-sharing law within the contentious new *Anti-Terrorism Act* of 2015 known as Bill C-51.

The *Anti-Terrorism Act* was itself subject to unpresented protests against the "war on terror" and in support of civil liberties. Bill C-51 created the *Security of Canada Information Disclosure Act* (SCIDA),[1] which formalized the capacities for a diverse number of agencies to engage in widespread intelligence sharing under the rationale of national security. Specifically, SCIDA provides all federal government institutions with a new, explicit authority to disclose information related to an "activity that undermines the security of Canada" to designated federal institutions with national security responsibilities (SCIDA 2015: c. 20, s. 2). In a move that significantly enhances information-sharing practices among federal agencies, SCIDA lists seventeen institutions that have national security responsibilities and can share information about "activities that undermine the security of Canada." These institutions include health, revenue, finance, and security and policing agencies. According to SCIDA, an activity undermines the security of Canada "if it undermines the sovereignty, security or territorial integrity of Canada or the lives or the security of the people of Canada" (SCIDA 2015: c. 20, s. 2, S.2). Indigenous movements fit squarely within this ambit because of their focus on sovereignty and territorial integrity. However, the vagueness of the provisions allows for broad interpretations of "security" — interpretations that policing agencies have already been exploiting in the "war on terror" to direct counterterrorism resources against social movements.

Analyzing some deficiencies with SCIDA, Roach and Forcese (2015: 154) detail the expansive scope of this definition — including contrasts to current legal definitions of "national security" — and warn that "it risks sweeping virtually everything under the security label." SCIDA contains one exception on information sharing specifically addressing activities pertaining to "advocacy, protest, dissent and artistic expression" (SCIDA 2018: c. 20, s. 2, S.2 (i)). This exception has been widely cited by the Liberal government as a responsible limit on policing powers, including in the Green Paper released as part of the national security consultation (Canada 2016). More or less similar to the 2001 *Anti-Terrorism Act*, which declares protests and dissent immune from surveillance powers, these exceptions have proven to have no bearing on policing practices for an obvious reason: they are explicit intelligence practices and are never challenged in court. Much of the intelligence collected remains in the catalogues and databanks managed by security and policing agencies, often unbeknownst even to those who are charged with crimes. Surveillance data on these activists are not relied upon as evidence in trials but remain

---

Box 16-2: Project SITKA and Pre-emptive Surveillance

Project SITKA was a year-long quasi-criminal investigation run by the RCMP from 2014 to 2015, uncovered by researcher Andrew Crosby using access to information requests. During the investigation, RCMP used existing police databases to collect an extensive array of information on prominent Indigenous rights activists. Spanning protests and campaigns from 2010 to 2014, the RCMP gathered data on and evaluated 313 targeted individuals, who were profiled and categorized according to their "background, motivation and rhetoric." Using a risk profile, each person was rated for "anticipated threats" and potential future criminality. In total, eighty-nine were classified as high risk. None of the individuals under investigation were notified, nor are there any clear mechanisms for contesting the accuracy of the data or contesting the dubious legality of the data cataloguing and profiling practices.

For more on Project SITKA, see Crosby and Monaghan 2018 and Barrera 2016.

in police databanks as intelligence and, because these practices are not challenged in courts, they remain secretive (see Box 16-2).

Justin Trudeau's Liberal government introduced new national security legislation that dramatically

> In addition to normalizing "extremism" discourse, the "fusion centre" approach to information sharing is likely to become further entrenched due to the influence and power of security agencies in expanding their own mandates and fields of practice.

increased security powers under the guise of adding accountability and failed to substantively address overly broad authorizations for intelligence gathering and sharing. In parallel to a lack of political will at curtailing security powers, media reporting has been prone to inflate issues of insecurity. Research on news messaging in the time period around Bill C-51 is illustrative of the problematic media coverage, wherein the *National Post* and *Globe and Mail* published favourable articles on Bill C-51 and emphasized notions of threat, terrorism, extremism, and a decline in public safety (Foley 2018). This type of media rhetoric strengthens support for policing and surveillance of social movement participants and environmental and anti-pipeline activists as if they pose a terrorist threat to Canadians. In addition to normalizing "extremism" discourse, the "fusion centre" approach to information sharing is likely to become further entrenched due to the influence and power of security agencies in expanding their own mandates and fields of practice. As we outline in the following section, these trends in security governance will only continue through the programs and sectors that fall under the rubric of critical infrastructure protection.

Critical Infrastructure Protection

We have detailed how three trends have shaped security and policing in Canada, specifically security and policing that target social movements. Here we discuss an example of the convergence of national security mission creep, pre-emptive surveillance, and information-sharing practices in the proliferating domain of **critical infrastructure protection** (CIP). CIP is not only illustrative of trends in security governance; it also provides a useful demonstration of how protest policing is shaped by the current socio-political climate of extractive capitalism.

Critical infrastructure protection is an elastic notion that can refer to state protection of technologies, networks, assets, utilities, and more (also see Boyle and Dafnos 2019; Boyle and Speed 2018). CIP has been a growing component of the reorganization of security governance since 9/11 (Monaghan and Walby

> Protest is conflated with crime and terrorism through repeated reference to radicalization and extremism, which is a major cue in "war on terror" discourse.

2017). While CIP has its roots in the Cold War, the post-9/11 milieu shifted the focus from industrial sabotage to a more diverse and dynamic range of threats. Now the category includes spaces such as railways, pipelines, and nuclear factories (Monaghan and Walby 2017). Critical infrastructure includes a wide array of sites as well as natural disasters and "human induced" emergencies (Canada 2009a, 2009b), with protests falling under the latter category. As Dafnos, Thompson and French (2017) argue, CIP motivates policing and surveillance of social movements and, specifically, of Indigenous movements for land reclamation. For Dafnos and colleagues (2017), the notion of CIP is a cover for more political, targeted surveillance of Indigenous groups carried out by entities such as the ITAC and the RCMP's Aboriginal Joint Intelligence Group and Critical Infrastructure Intelligence Team (CIIT). These entities collect information about social movement groups and share it with intelligence hubs or fusion centres.

The surveillance comprises a vast network of information gatherers and analysts. The RCMP CIIT encourages what it calls suspicious incident reporting among a variety of public- and private-sector stakeholders. These stakeholders also receive information and tips from the RCMP CIIT. One focus of these intelligence groups has been the anti-Keystone pipeline protests. RCMP officer Timothy O'Neil, with the CIIT, reflected on a security briefing for a protest in Ottawa in November 2011 that "environmental activists' actions may inadvertently result in personal injury/death, damage to a facility's infrastructure, and harm to the natural environment" (RCMP 2012-2817: 1). It is bizarrely ironic that this threat entrepreneur would claim social movement groups might "harm the natural environment" given that the goal of the movement is to protect it; moreover, Young (2015) found, through freedom of information requests, that pipelines in Alberta have been responsible for an average of an oil spill a day in that province for the past four decades.

These briefings are shared with the RCMP's "security partners," including local policing and the private security arms of extractive corporations, prompting them to profile and stereotype purported threats. Appearing under a heading of "Environmental Extremism," the document continues: "these radicalized individuals have the expressed intent and demonstrated capability to engage in criminal activity" (RCMP 2012-2817: 5). These excerpts begin to demonstrate the ways in which social movement participants and activists are framed as threats. The RCMP views persons protesting against pipelines as a dangerous element: a danger to themselves, to others, and even to the environment. Protest is conflated with crime and terrorism through repeated reference to radicalization and extremism, which is a major cue in "war on terror" discourse.

> The exclusion of the names of energy company representatives illustrates the treatment accorded to these private partners in extractivism: while activists have their identities searched, catalogued, and released to the public, energy company personnel are protected.

Perhaps the most advanced illustration of these surveillance networks is the semi-annual Energy and Utility Sector Stakeholder briefings organized by CSIS and Natural Resources Canada (NRCan). Representatives of the energy sector and members of Canada's intelligence and law-enforcement community attend these briefings, conducted at CSIS headquarters in Ottawa. Energy sector representatives all possess at least Level II (secret) security clearance, allowing them to view classified intelligence. The purpose is to "provide intelligence to select energy representatives so they are able to implement the required security precautions to protect their assets." The briefings also "provide a forum for the private sector to brief the Canadian intelligence and law-enforcement community on issues we would not normally be privy to" (RCMP A008499: 2). The principal moderator and organizer of the briefings was threat entrepreneur Tim O'Neil. Briefings can involve up to one hundred participants, and typical of the fusion centre approach, an invitee list from May 2011 meetings lists Government of Canada participants including the RCMP, CSIS, the Department of National Defense, Transport Canada, the Communications Security Establishment, the National Energy Board, Industry Canada, NRCan, Public Safety, and Atomic Energy of Canada Limited, among others. Law enforcement representatives from other provinces (New Brunswick, Alberta, Quebec) were also in attendance. Some fifty names are redacted, likely representing industry and private security personnel. The exclusion of the names of energy company representatives illustrates the treatment accorded to these private partners in extractivism: while activists have their identities searched, catalogued, and released to the public, energy company personnel are protected.

Participants at the Energy and Utility Sector Stakeholder meetings are treated to briefings led by government experts on topics from cybersecurity to economic and corporate espionage, to the global risk environment (NRCan 2013). Many of the presentations focus on social movements. Following

Greenpeace protests targeting nuclear facilities in the Great Lakes region, energy companies were treated to a briefing called "security challenges presented by radicalized individuals/groups to Canada's energy sector — the Great Lakes examples." Following the conflict near Elsipogtog First Nation, a working group held a meeting under the theme "North American Resource Development at Risk" that featured a number of sessions on potential disruptions presented by social movement actors; these meetings concluded with sessions on suspicious incident reports, as well as a panel on the "legal challenges of infrastructure protection: collecting evidence for prosecutions in Canada" (NRCan 2013: 13–17). Meetings in May 2011 included an "overview and assessment of Aboriginal Issues of Interest: Summer 2011" and a session called "G8/G20 debriefs," while May 2010 meetings included a session on "Eco-extremism under G20 updates."

These Energy and Utility Sector Stakeholder briefings also feature roundtable discussions on energy sector security with government and industry participants. The meetings entrench the relations and mutual shared values between national security representatives and their security colleagues from the energy sector, and the energy sector has likewise contributed to the cordiality of the meetings. Agendas for the meetings in May 2013 (NRCan 2013: 1) included advertisements for receptions co-hosted by Bruce Power and Brookfield, while breakfast, lunch, and coffee were sponsored by the Northern Gateway pipeline applicant, Enbridge.

An email from O'Neil to participants in March 2012 explains that the meetings allow for two-way intelligence flows. Addressing Scott Stauffer, from the Canadian Natural Resources Ltd. Horizon Oil Sands project, O'Neil writes: "Scott, the Oil Sands will continue to be a target for many more years so an assessment from an owner operators perspective would be appreciated … we would welcome your input from your involvement with the Oil Sands Intelligence Working Group" (RCMP A008499: 1). O'Neil concludes, "The purpose of the panel would be to provide a briefing to the Government of Canada so that it is aware of your initiatives, and secondly and of more value to 'your security peers,' discuss your security procedures, lessons learned, etc." (2). CIP is thus a means of integrating and deputizing corporations into the national security policing assemblage as "security peers." The surveillance network allows the RCMP and CSIS to convey how security agencies are defining contemporary and emerging threats and, correspondingly, allows private companies to keep the Canadian security establishment apprised of their initiatives. As Pasternak and Dafnos (2018) note, these forms of policing and surveillance protect circuits of capital and elite class interests. CIP encourages surveillance of social movement participants and is an example of surveillance creep, as the Canadian state's security intelligence apparatus more closely tracks the daily lives of individuals who oppose extractive resources projects or even the politics of extractive capitalism more broadly.

Conclusion

Trends in security governance have significantly impacted the surveillance and policing of social movements in Canada. Social movements have become increasingly scrutinized due to the reorganization of resources and practices around trends in national security, mission creep, pre-emptive surveillance and information sharing practices, all of which have intensified through a consensus among political and corporate leaders to pursue extractivism. In addition to the negative impacts that surveillance and over-policing have on the ability of individuals and groups to engage in public protest — a condition referred to as the "chilling effect" (Cunningham and Noakes 2008; Starr et al. 2008) — these intelligence-driven practices of the "war on terror" present conditions that foster opportunities for police to criminalize and disrupt social movements.

Social movement scholars have noted a shift in policing strategies from the 1990s doctrines of "negotiation and accommodation" to the current model of "strategic incapacitation" (Gillham, Edwards, and Noakes 2013; Gillham 2011; Wood 2014). **Strategic incapacitation** involves heightened levels of surveillance and intelligence gathering, along with pre-emptive policing techniques. Yet strategic incapacitation also involves abandoning the tenets of "objectivity" and "neutrality" that were aspects of the negotiated management model. Instead, the new approach conceptualizes police-protester relations as antagonistic. To control protests, strategic incapacitation models involve surveillance and pre-emptive attacks on protesters who are deemed "high risk." These arrest and disruption strategies often target core organizers and involve high levels of police violence and criminalization (King 2017; Vitale 2005). In the Canadian context, strategic incapacitation strategies have coincided with the rise of CIP and the integration of the petro-state into the policing assemblage. The Canadian case is yet another example of how CIP-inspired "counter-terrorism is re-shaping policing and security arrangements" in Western countries (Palmer and Whelan 2006: 461). The result is that movements challenging extractive capitalism face antagonistic policing strategies and the increased likelihood of criminalization, as police and security agencies create categories that conflate activism with terrorism. We have used the notion of "threat entrepreneurs" to theorize the key role in these networks of security personnel, who direct these surveillance practices.

The integration of extractive corporations into the policing assemblage, and the deep ties between Canada's corporate elite and what Carroll (2017: 225) calls Canada's carbon-capital elite, have systematically targeted opponents of extractive capitalism. This group reflects what Carroll calls "an entrenched oligarchy" that wields incredible power in Canadian politics and economics, and we have demonstrated here the existence of equally entrenched policing and security apparatuses dedicated to neutralizing perceived threats on behalf of this corporate elite. The terminology and techniques used by these policing and security agencies extend to controlling social movement participants who organize against extractive petro-economies and the deleterious environmental effects of tarsands and pipeline development. Intelligence fusion centres have been created in response, and labels and categories such as extremism applied to activists and Indigenous groups exercising their rights and freedoms. As Harbisher (2015) notes, there is a need to resist discourses and categories of extremism and radicalization applied to social movements (and more generally, as well). There is also a need to problematize, investigate, and resist the policing, security, and surveillance practices that are buttressed by the discourses and categories of threat entrepreneurs.

Discussion Questions

1. What do Nelkin and Andrews mean by "surveillance creep"?
2. Who are the key agencies involved in the policing efforts associated with the "war on terror"?
3. What does the policing of social movements have to do with anti-terror laws?
4. What is the role of critical infrastructure protection in the policing of social movements?
5. What is the effect of this policing and surveillance on Indigenous communities?
6. What does Carroll mean by Canada's "carbon-capital elite"?
7. What is the relationship between political economy and policing?

Recommended Resources

Surveillance and Society, journal <ojs.library.queensu.ca/index.php/surveillance-and-society/about>.

Monahan, Torin, and David Murakami Wood (eds.). 2017. *Surveillance Studies: A Reader.* London: Oxford University Press.

Bowles, Paul, and Henry Veltmeyer (eds.). 2014. *The Answer Is Still No: Voices of Pipeline Resistance.* Halifax: Fernwood Publishing.

Howe, Miles. 2015. *Debriefing Elsipogtog: The Anatomy of a Struggle.* Halifax: Fernwood Publishing.

Kinsman, Gary, and Patrizia Gentile. 2010. *The Canadian War on Queers: National Security as Sexual Regulation.* Vancouver: UBC Press.

CBC News. "'Just the Beginning': Anti-Pipeline Protesters Vow 'Rise of Resistance.'" October 30. <cbc.ca/news/canada/british-columbia/just-the-beginning-anti-pipeline-protesters-vow-rise-of-resistance-1.4378845>.

Livesey, Bruce. 2017. "Spies in Our Midst: RCMP and CSIS Snoop on Green Activists." *National Observer*, May 5. <nationalobserver.com/2017/05/05/news/spies-our-midst-rcmp-and-csis-snoop-green-activists>.

Glossary

critical infrastructure protection: a government discourse that outlines a multi-agency, networked approach to defending public and private infrastructure from supposed risks and hazards, which has been used in a blanket manner to characterize anti-pipeline activists and organizers as threats to state operations and the national interest.

extractive capitalism: a mode of political economy that focuses on resource extraction and foreign-market sales as key principles for economic accumulation.

fusion centres: intelligence-sharing agencies that "fuse" the surveillance capacities, databanks, and resources into collaborative assemblages.

mission creep: an enlargement of an agency or organizations activities beyond an original mandate, often animated by bureaucratic objectives.

pre-emptive policing: a trend toward policing future activities using techniques of risk assessment, anticipatory reasoning, and intelligence and surveillance practices that result in actions that aim to stop supposed threats before they happen.

strategic incapacitation: a term developed to explain a shift in contemporary protest policing strategies toward more extensive surveillance, selective incapacitation and disruption, pre-emptive actions, heightened attention to communication strategies, high deference to spatial regulation and control, as well as excessive — yet strategically deployed —

punishment and brutality.

surveillance: the systematic collection of personal information to influence, manage, enable, or control those whose information is collected.

war on terror: an assemblage of exceptionalist discourses and practices organized around the object of terrorism and deployed as an extension of military and security practices targeting groups or activities self-referentially identified as terroristic.

Note

1. Originally named the *Security of Canadian Information Act* (scisa) when included in Bill C-51 (2015), the act was renamed the *Security of Canada Information Disclosure Act* (scida) in 2018.

References

Barrera, Jorge. 2016. "rcmp Intelligence Centre Compiled List of 89 Indigenous Rights Activists Considered 'Threats.'" *aptn National News*, November 8. <aptnnews. ca/2016/11/08/rcmp-intelligence-centre-compiled-list-of-89-indigenous-rights-activists-considered-threats/>.

Bennett, Colin J., Kevin D. Haggerty, David Lyon, and Valerie Steeves (eds.). 2014. *Transparent Lives: Surveillance in Canada*. Edmonton: Athabasca University Press.

Birss, M. 2017. "Criminalizing Environmental Activism." *nacla Report on the Americas* 49, 3.

Bonelli, Laurent, and Francesco Ragazzi. 2014. "Low-Tech Security: Files, Notes, and Memos as Technologies of Anticipation." *Security Dialogue* 45, 5.

Boutilier, Alex. 2014. "Ottawa Admits to Tracking Hundreds of Protests." *Toronto Star.* <thestar.com/news/canada/2014/09/18/ottawa_admits_to_tracking_hundreds_of_protests.html>.

Boykoff, Jules. 2011. "The Anti-Olympics." *New Left Review* 67.

Boyle, P., and T. Dafnos. 2019. "Infrastructures of Pacification: Vital Points, Critical Infrastructure, and Police Power in Canada." *Canadian Journal of Law & Society/La Revue Canadienne Droit et Société* 34, 1.

Boyle, P., and S. Speed. 2018. "From Protection to Coordinated Preparedness: A Genealogy of Critical Infrastructure in Canada." *Security Dialogue* 49, 3.

Brodeur, J.P. 2010. *The Policing Web*. Oxford: University of Oxford Press.

Button, Mark, and Tim John. 2002. "'Plural Policing' in Action: A Review of the Policing of Environmental Protests in England and Wales." *Policing and Society* 12, 2.

Canada. 2016. *Our Security, Our Rights: National Security Green Paper*. Ottawa: Public Safety Canada.

____. 2009a. *National Strategy for Critical Infrastructure*. Ottawa: Government of Canada.

____. 2009b. *Action Plan for Critical Infrastructure*. Ottawa: Government of Canada.

Carroll, William. 2017. "Canada's Carbon-Capital Elite: A Tangled Web of Corporate Power." *Canadian Journal of Sociology* 43, 2.

Crosby, Andrew and Jeffrey Monaghan. 2018. *Policing Indigenous Movements: Dissent and the Security State*. Halifax: Fernwood Publishing.

____. 2016. "Settler Colonialism and the Policing of Idle No More." *Social Justice* 43, 2.

CSIS (Canadian Security Intelligence Service). 2017-123. Access to Information Act request. Ottawa: CSIS.

____. 2016-93. Access to Information Act request. Ottawa: CSIS.

Cunningham, David, and John Noakes. 2008. "'What if She's from the FBI?' The Effects of Covert Forms of Social Control on Social Movements." In M. Deflem and J.T. Ulmer (eds.), *Surveillance and Governance: Crime Control and Beyond*. New York: Emerald Group Publishing Limited.

Dafnos, T., S. Thompson, and M. French. 2017. "Surveillance and the Colonial Dream: Canada's Surveillance of Indigenous Protest." In R.K. Lippert, K. Walby, and I. Warren (eds.), *National Security, Surveillance, and Terror: Canadian and Australian in Comparative Perspective*. Basingstoke: Palgrave.

de Goede, Marieke, Stephanie Simon, and Marijn Hoijtink. 2014. "Performing Preemption." *Security Dialogue* 45, 5.

Dominique-Legault, Pascal. 2016. "Des savoirs policiers sur les 'mouvements marginaux.' Les constructions du projet GAMMA du SPVM." *Criminologie* 49, 2.

Ellefsen, Rune. 2016. "Judicial Opportunities and the Death of SHAC: Legal Repression Along a Cycle of Contention." *Social Movement Studies* 15, 5.

Ericson, Richard, and Kevin Haggerty. 1997. *Policing the Risk Society*. Toronto: University of Toronto Press.

Foley, R. 2018. "(Mis)Representing Terrorist Threats: Media Framing of Bill C-51." *Media, War and Conflict* 11, 2.

Gillham, Patrick. 2011. "Securitizing America: Strategic Incapacitation and the Policing of Protest Since the 11 September 2001 Terrorist Attacks." *Sociology Compass* 5, 7.

Gillham, Patrick, Bob Edwards, and John Noakes. 2013. "Strategic Incapacitation and the Policing of Occupy Wall Street Protests in New York City, 2011." *Policing and Society* 23, 1.

Harbisher, Ben. 2015. "Unthinking Extremism: Radicalizing Narratives that Legitimise Surveillance." *Surveillance & Society* 13, 3/4.

Howe, Miles. 2015. *Debriefing Elsipogtog: The Anatomy of a Struggle*. Halifax: Fernwood Publishing.

Huysmans, Jef. 2014. *Security Unbound*. London: Routledge.

____. 2011. "What's in an Act? On Security Speech Acts and Little Security Nothings." *Security Dialogue* 42, 4–5.

King, Mike. 2017. *When Riot Cops Are Not Enough: The Policing and Repression of Occupy Oakland*. London: Rutgers University Press.

King, Mike, and David Waddington. 2005. "Flashpoints Revisited: A Critical Application to the Policing of Anti-Globalization Protest." *Policing & Society* 15, 3.

Kinsman, Gary, Dieter Buse, and Mercedes Steedman (eds.). 2000. *Whose National Security? Canadian State Surveillance and the Creation of Enemies*. Toronto: Between the Lines Press.

Luscombe, Alex, and Michael-Anthony Lutfy. 2016. "Peeking Behind the Curtain: Accessing the Backstage of Security Intelligence Threat Assembly." In J. Brownlee and K. Walby (eds.), *Access to Information and Social Justice: Critical Research Strategies for Journalists, Activists and Scholars*. Winnipeg: Arbeiter Ring Publishing.

McCulloch, Jude, and Sharon Pickering. 2009. "Pre-Crime and Counter-Terrorism:

Imagining Future Crime in the 'War on Terror.'" *British Journal of Criminology* 49, 5.

Monaghan, Jeffrey, and Kevin Walby. 2017. "Surveillance of Environmental Movements in Canada: Critical Infrastructure Protection and the Petro-Security Apparatus." *Contemporary Justice Review* 20, 1.

____. 2012a. "Making Up 'Terror Identities': Security Intelligence, Canada's Integrated Threat Assessment Centre, and Social Movement Suppression." *Policing and Society* 22, 2.

____. 2012b. "'…They Attacked the City': Security Intelligence, the Sociology of Protest Policing, and the Anarchist Threat at the 2010 Toronto G20 Summit." *Current Sociology* 60, 5.

Monahan, Torin. 2010. "The Future of Security? Surveillance Operations at Homeland Security Fusion Centers." *Social Justice* 37, 2–3.

Nagra, Baljit. 2017. *Securitized Citizens: Canadian Muslims' Experiences of Race Relations and Identity Formation Post-9/11*. Toronto: University of Toronto Press.

Nelkin, Dorothy, and Lori Andrews. 1999. "DNA Identification and Surveillance Creep." *Sociology of Health & Illness* 21, 5.

NRCan (Natural Resources Canada). 2013. 7040-13-094. Access to Information Act request.

Palmer, Darren, and Chad Whelan. 2006. "Counter-Terrorism Across the Policing Continuum." *Police Practice and Research* 7, 5.

Pasternak, Shiri, and Tia Dafnos. 2018. "How Does a Settler State Secure the Circuitry of +Capital?" *Environment and Planning D: Society and Space* 36, 4.

PSC (Public Safety Canada). 2017. "Government Operations Centre." <publicsafety.gc.ca/cnt/mrgnc-mngmnt/rspndng-mrgnc-vnts/gvrnmnt-prtns-cntr-en.aspx>.

Ratcliffe, Jerry. 2008. *Intelligence-Led Policing*. Portland: Willan.

Ratcliffe, Jerry, S. Strang, and B. Taylor. 2014. "Assessing the Success Factors of Organized Crime Groups: Intelligence Challenges for Strategic Thinking." *Policing: An International Journal of Police Strategies & Management* 37, 1.

RCMP (Royal Canadian Mounted Police). A008499. Access to information Act request.

____. 2016-1140. Access to Information Act request. Ottawa: RCMP.

____. 2012-2817. Access to Information Act request. Ottawa: RCMP.

Regan, Priscilla, Torin Monahan, and Krista Craven. 2015. "Constructing the Suspicious: Data Production, Circulation, and Interpretation by DHS Fusion Centers." *Administration & Society* 47, 6.

Reiner, Robert. 1992. *The Politics of Police*, 2nd edition. Toronto: University of Toronto Press.

Roach, Kent, and Craig Forcese. 2015. *False Security: The Radicalization of Canadian Anti-Terrorism*. Toronto: Irwin Law.

SCIDA (Security of Canada Information Disclosure Act). 2015. Ottawa: Canada.

Sheptycki, James. 2005. "Transnational Policing." *Canadian Review of Policing Research*, 2. <crpr.icaap.org/index.php/crpr/article/viewArticle/31/48>.

Sorenson, J. 2016. *Constructing Ecoterrorism: Capitalism, Speciesism, and Animal Rights*. Winnipeg: Fernwood Publishing.

Starr, Amory, Luis A. Fernandez, Randall Amster, Lesley J. Wood, and Manuel J. Caro. 2008. "The Impacts of State Surveillance on Political Assembly and Association: A Socio-Legal Analysis." *Qualitative Sociology* 31, 3.

Stewart, K., and K. Tanner. 2015. "Using Access to Information to Separate Oil and State in Canada." In J. Brownlee and K. Walby (eds.), *Access to Information and Social Justice: Critical Research Strategies for Journalists, Activists and Scholars*. Winnipeg: Arbeiter Ring Publishing.

Tarrow, Sydney. 1998. *Power in Movement: Social Movements and Contentious Politics*, 2nd edition. Cambridge: Cambridge University Press.

Taylor, Robert, and Amanda Russell. 2012. "The Failure of Police 'Fusion' Centers and the Concept of a National Intelligence Sharing Plan." *Police Practice and Research* 13, 2.

Valverde, Mariana. 2001. "Governing Security, Governing Through Security." In R. Daniels, P. Macklem, and K. Roach (eds.), *The Security of Freedom: Essays on Canada's Antiterrorism Bill*. Toronto: University of Toronto Press.

Veltmeyer, Henry, and James Petras. 2014. *The New Extractivism: A Post-Neoliberal Development Model or Imperialism of the Twenty-First Century?* London: Zed Books.

Vitale, Alex. 2005. "From Negotiated Management to Command and Control: How the New York Police Department Polices Protests." *Policing & Society* 15, 3.

Walby, Kevin, and Jeff Monaghan. 2011. "Private Eyes and Public Order: Policing and Surveillance in the Suppression of Animal Rights Activists in Canada." *Social Movement Studies* 10, 1.

Williams, Kristian. 2015. *Our Enemies in Blue: Police and Power in America*. Oakland: AK Press.

Wood, Lesley. 2014. *Crisis and Control: The Militarization of Protest Policing*. Chicago: Pluto Press.

Young, L. 2015. "The Power of Numbers: Holding Governments Accountable with Their Own Data." In J. Brownlee and K. Walby (eds.), *Access to Information and Social Justice: Critical Research Strategies for Journalists, Activists and Scholars*. Winnipeg: Arbeiter Ring Publishing.

Zedner, Lucia. 2007. "Pre-Crime and Post-Criminology?" *Theoretical Criminology* 11, 2.

17

Tweets of Dissent

Observations on Social Movements in the Digital Age

Mitch D. Daschuk

After reading this chapter, you will be able to do the following:

1. Differentiate between types of social movements.
2. Identify the characteristics of social movements.
3. Describe the stages in the life cycle of social movements.
4. Define the concept of the network society.
5. Explain the benefits and limitations that contemporary social movements experience due to new forms of communicative technologies.

Developed by the United States government as a computer-based communication network, the internet has profoundly affected the way that people access information and interact with each other. Dating back to the 1960s and gradually made publicly accessible throughout the 1990s, the World Wide Web stoked the hopes and fears of social scientists. Though some focused on the prospect that global communication capacities would usher in a truly global community born of universalized information and communicative action, others cautioned for an appreciation of the panoptic capacities of web technologies. With the better part of twenty years of web mediation to reflect on, both lines of thought have enjoyed a measure of validation given the influence and issues now attributed to social media. Exemplified by Facebook (est. 2004) and Twitter (est. 2006), social media afforded web users the ability to congregate and exchange information through digital platforms. Freed of the traditional constraints posed by time and space, news could be instantaneously shared across international boundaries, and information could be distributed by social actors as opposed to corporatized mainstream media. The onset of network society (van Dijk 1999; Castells 1996) forecast the democratization of knowledge and the dissolution of social barriers both at home and abroad.

When historians reflect on the early decades of the new millennium, social media sites will be cited as key players in events ranging from the occupation of Wall Street to the election of Donald Trump. Those tasked with describing the social movements of the early digital era will also need to unpack ambiguities surrounding the distinctions between social movements and hashtags (if any) as well as whether the authority to speak on behalf of a movement resides in the statements of their founders or those who took to the streets in their name. Our current era appears likely to be affiliated most closely with the onset of "culture wars" and the deepening of ideological divisions as opposed to progress and egalitarianism.

This chapter presents an overview of sociological perspectives regarding social movements and collective expressions of dissent. It highlights how the emergence of web-communicative technologies ameliorate some of the obstacles long associated with collective mobilization and identifies drawbacks associated with the constitution of modern social movements. Contrasting pre-digital perspectives with tendencies observed in recent mobilizations, it highlights the genesis and difficulties encountered by movements such as Occupy Wall Street, Idle No More, and Black Lives Matter, and identifies variables limiting their impact on contemporary society. Most prominently, the chapter highlights the absence of authoritative leadership and the presence of ideological ambiguity as variables contributing to a lack of clarity in these movements; however, these are not characteristic of the corresponding resurgence of radical and extremist groups. By the end of the chapter, readers will be introduced to canonical submissions from social movement studies and asked to critically consider how they might assist in understanding the limitations associated with the mobilizations of the digital era.

Organization and Mobilization

Neo-Marxist Antonio Gramsci (2008) theorized how to accomplish social change by understanding hegemony and the significance of **intellectuals** in inspiring "practical action." Gramsci uses the term **hegemony** to denote the process through which the leadership of those with social power is maintained through social consensus affirming their authority. This social consensus, in turn, is ensured due to the popularity of politically and culturally significant intellectuals who embody the ideologies of the powerholders. These intellectuals represent the ideologies embedded within our social institutions, and we become conditioned to identify with and pattern ourselves after them. Potential intellectuals include political figures, teachers, medical professionals, military leaders, police, academics, and those with alternative claims to distinction. By Gramsci's account, figures ranging from Prime Minister Justin Trudeau to former hockey analyst Don Cherry could be approached as intellectuals; they both promote Canadian nationalism, and the latter advocates that our law enforcement and military figures be extended the unconditional support of the Canadian public. Their wishes that we emulate these figures draws our collective attention away from our shared exploitation and the inequities rooted in our systems.

Gramsci also suggests that any mass mobilization for social change demand that the marginalized consecrate their *own* intellectuals. These leaders would advocate for the recognition of shared interests among the marginalized and organize their collective efforts toward practical actions — or forms of **praxis** — attuned to their cause. In many respects, the groups and leaders associated with the emergence of the 1950s civil rights era, and the subsequent mobilization of gender equality and queer rights movements in the 1960s, appeared to validate Gramsci's points on the significance of leadership. Whether personified in individuals such as Martin Luther King Jr. and Gloria Steinem or advocacy groups such as the Gay Liberation Front, charismatic representation and the clear articulation of collective aims were credited for mobilizing a variety of iconic movements. The social movement research of the era was inspired greatly by observations collected in bearing witness to their rise and decline, as well as a burgeoning perspective, within the social sciences, that the role of the researcher ought to advance lessons through which the movements of the future might optimize their potential to make change.

Classic Perspectives on the Constitution of Social Movements

Social movements are public mobilizations signifying widespread interest in changes to social attitudes or institutional practices. While they vary in methods of expression (they can take the form of mass protests, political parties, criminal activities, and trending hashtags) and formation (in immediate response to an event or gradually over weeks, months, or decades), all social movements share the central aim of drawing mass attention to the presence of a problem and demanding a solution. In many respects, modern social thought has drawn great influence from the social movements of the twentieth century. While the mainstream social sciences of the postwar period worked in service of a bureaucratic rationality that affiliated social stability with the maintenance of traditional social relations, the prospect that social observation should coincide with mobilization drew inspiration from the civil rights, feminist, and queer activists of the 1960s. They threatened claims to scientific objectivity in openly advocating for systemic social change and identified the components of successful mobilization, including the development of information distribution networks, centralization of leadership, entrenchment of clearly understood and agreed-upon goals, and organization of opportunities to express dissent to the public at large. The next section focuses on social movement research pertaining to prevalent types of movements, characteristics vital to their success, and the stages of their life cycle.

A Loose Typology of Social Movements

Vago (1999) identifies four generalized categories of movements based on the directionality of their goals and the social impact they covet: reformative, reactionary, expressive, and revolutionary. **Reformative social movements** include groups that advocate for changes to specific attitudes, institutional practices, or forms of authority. Reformative movements typically attempt to instigate change through commonplace or conventional methods such as political affiliation, engaging directly in the political process, or seeking out and supporting political representatives whose values and intentions parallel

> While the mainstream social sciences of the postwar period worked in service of a bureaucratic rationality that affiliated social stability with the maintenance of traditional social relations, the prospect that social observation should coincide with mobilization drew inspiration from the civil rights, feminist, and queer activists of the 1960s. They threatened claims to scientific objectivity in openly advocating for systemic social change and identified the components of successful mobilization.

their own. This would include the groups that organized to advocate for the decriminalization of marijuana prior to Canada's shift in policy, such as the Marijuana Party of Canada (which campaigned for legal changes to cannabis) and those who have partaken publicly in the tradition of 4:20. **Reactionary social movements**, on the other hand, include groups that protest, or try to prevent, the onset of social, political, or institutional changes. Often advocating for the retention of "traditional values," reactionary social movements sometimes pursue mainstream institutional processes to influence laws or promote certain social attitudes. Anti-abortion groups, for example, have employed a range of tactics to advocate against laws decriminalizing abortion, including rallying on behalf of politicians who share their sentiments and picketing outside of reproductive health care clinics (while harassing people who are accessing services).

Expressive social movements advocate for cultural change and the empowerment of groups that are marginalized based on demographic variables such as ethnicity, gender identity, religious affiliation, and sexual orientation. They often mobilize in opposition to certain policies or events but take on additional significance as sources of representations that shift public attitudes or garner public attention. One example of an expressive movement is the one that formed to protest the Diagnostics and Statistical Manual's classification of non-heterosexual desire as mental pathology. While this collection of queer community leaders and allied academics sought to achieve a specific goal, they also tried to alter public attitudes that equated homosexuality with illness. While the specific goal of amending the *Diagnostic and Statistical Manual* was realized in 1974 (Conrad and Angell 2004), expressive queer rights and pride-based movements achieved gradual success over the following decades.

Finally, **revolutionary social movements** stem from the mobilization of groups that harbour a great deal of discontent with the organization of society and advocate for drastic reorganization at the political, social, or institutional level. Revolutionary movements argue against the prospect that social change can be achieved through conventional institutional means, instead advocating for a broad consensus that society be organized in accordance with alternative principles. The Front de libération du Québec (FLQ) is a historically significant example of a revolutionary movement. Perhaps best described as a militant sovereignty group, the FLQ advocated for Quebec's independence from Canada and engaged in acts of terrorism, including kidnapping and murder, while attempting to overthrow Quebec's provincial government (Pinkoski 2012); the federal government responded by declaring the War Measures Act in 1970.

Characteristics of Social Movements

Based on observations derived from the social movements of the postwar era, Gerlach and Hine (1970) suggest that, despite differences in their broader aims, all social movements pursue the concurrent goals of attracting membership, identifying common goals, and deciding upon their preferred forms of mobilization. Five characteristics are required of successful social movements: the development of an organizational structure, establishing systems of recruitment, the formation of a shared ideology, the presence of committed members, and identifying a shared opponent.

The **development of an organizational structure** entails establishing positions of authority. Should a movement seek to broaden its membership and attract public attention, it must develop an internal leadership structure to identify who holds authority over decisions on messaging and tactics. While not necessary for any given "leader" to be formally anointed, a system must exist for strategizing, coordinating, and resolving internal disputes. Difficulties would arise in the absence of representatives to articulate the specific goals of the movement to outsiders and lobby for the support of figures in positions of power.

Lobbying is also central to **recruiting new members**. Variables related to the formation of the movement and the resources available to it will influence different tactics. Many movements request that participants use their interpersonal social networks to attract new adherents (even if only to the extent of light social media marketing, such as creating Facebook groups) and use media distribution channels, be they grassroots or mainstream, to provide some insight into the goals of the group.

Third, Gerlach and Hine note that movements require the **formation of a shared ideology** to ensure that all who participate recognize and abide by the central values and beliefs of the movement. Notably, this point suggests that social movements do not merely emerge around the recognition of a common cause or social situation that "must be dealt with": a movement's distinct ideology will inform the movement's strategies and solutions for social change.

The identification and collective recognition of a common ideological core coincides closely with a requirement for the **commitment of membership**. Members of a group must act in accordance with the values of the movement through their personal conduct and interactions with others. If members of a social movement endorse a common group ideology yet contradict it in their conduct, the overarching credibility of the group might be questioned. For example, a revolutionary social movement that endorsed a mainstream political candidate in the lead-up to an election would be perceived as work-ing in collusion with (as opposed to challenging) the mainstream political system, a move that would undermine the group's credibility. Because social movements that fail to "practice what they preach" risk losing credibility, they must surveil and regulate the conduct of their membership to protect the legitimacy of the movement.

Finally, Gerlach and Hine suggest that a social movement must **identify a shared opponent** against whom its membership can rally. Groups forming around the identification of a common ideology typically undergo a process — be it discursive or representational — whereby groups united around alternative or diametrically oppositional ideologies are characterized as oppo-nents who must be defeated. Should a movement fail to explicitly identify an opposition, its members might no longer perceive a common "enemy" and have little motivation to continue participating.

Five Stages in the Life Cycle of Social Movements

In addition to Gerlatch and Hine's characteristics of social movements, research conducted by Armand Mauss (1975) identifies five stages of social movements. First, Mauss suggests that movements initially pass through a stage of **incipiency**, during which the foundational members collectively perceive of a problem and work toward devising strategies for its remedy. In incipiency, the progenitors of a social movement begin to formulate a shared ideology and identify tangible goals through which to attract additional mem-bers and mobilize against the perceived problem at hand. Following incipiency, the second stage in the life cycle of social movements is **coalescence.** Given a measure of success in attracting additional members, this stage requires that movements necessarily begin to establish hierarchies of leadership and take on an explicit organizational structure. As coalescence requires members occupy specific positions associated with clearly demarcated responsibilities, this stage in the life cycle coincides with the entrenchment of a bureaucratic organization to deduce the most effective and efficient forms of mobiliza-tion. Given the successful entrenchment of a leadership hierarchy and the continued populism of a movement, the third stage is **institutionalization**. Institutionalization occurs as a movement achieves public accreditation as a viable ideological force and a legitimate representative within the broader sphere of social policy and governance. While progressing to this stage con-stitutes a degree of success in terms of better drawing public attention to the presence of a problem, it also necessitates that the movement itself enter a fourth stage of **fragmentation.** In some cases, fragmentation is instigated in the wake of group success, as members come to view the movement as having achieved its goals. Success can also instigate fragmentation as factions within the movement alienate adherents by identifying new goals and refining the ideological tenets at its core. Whether these ideological shifts stem from pressures to remain relevant despite their victories or the emergence of conflict among members, fragmentation occurs when external achievements or internal disruptions undermine the movement's ability to retain consensus. Finally, Mauss associates the emergence of these fractures with a stage of inevitable **demise.** Movements might enter this stage based on success in achieving their central goals, the emergence of splinter groups born of ideological divisiveness among members, or institutionalization such that mainstream social institutions in and of themselves usurp the authority once held by participants.

While Mauss characterizes fragmentation and demise as inevitable stages in the life cycle of a movement, the culture of activism that remained in the wake of the civil rights movements of the 1960s associated their inability to effect more drastic forms of change with the formation of relationships with dominant social institutions. This relates to sentiments, popular within activist subcultures, that Heath and Potter (2004) characterize as a **theory of co-optation.** This theory posits that the failure of previous movements rests primarily in their willingness to bureaucratize and assimilate into the mainstream institutional landscape, and that co-operation with the system risks undermining the credibility of the movement and allowing the personal wishes of leadership to transcend the original goals of the group. Activist cultures expressed particular misgivings with mainstream media institutions and approached the corporate press as **information gatekeepers** wielding the power to select what constituted news and frame information in service to their ideological and corporate interests. These perspectives inspired the sanctification of do-it-yourself ideologies that championed underground networks through which to organize and distribute alternative media, including fanzines and niche media such as the anti-consumerist publication *Adbusters* and other activist publishers such as AK Press (Irzik 2010).

Resistance and the Network Society

The emergence of web-communicative technologies provided new means to distribute information illustrating the problems that movements identify (and outlining their proposed remedies), attract new participants, orchestrate forms of mobilization — such as the planning of rallies, marches, or product boycotts

No longer bound to traditional forms of producing and distributing physical texts, alternative media's transition to easily accessible web-mediated formats has granted them access to broader audiences, increased their authority within countercultural circles, and improved their capacity to challenge the ideological frames used in mainstream media.

— and mobilize new participants that are unfettered by traditional constraints of time, space, accessibility, and gatekeeping. While the mainstream media still sway public opinions and attitudes, web users now have access to a broad range of information sources and digital meeting centres that allow for social movements to partake in the incipiency stage free of the aforementioned traditional constraints. This transition has been particularly significant for alternative forms of media that do not stem from the corporatized realm of the mainstream press. No longer bound to traditional forms of producing and distributing physical texts, alternative media's transition to easily accessible web-mediated formats has granted them access to broader audiences, increased their authority within countercultural circles, and improved their capacity to challenge the ideological frames used in mainstream media (Skinner 2015; Funke and Wolfson 2014; Osman 2014; McCurdy 2012). Forms of recruitment and consciousness-raising once resigned to root in material spaces have found significant empowerment in the transition to digitized spaces, where information can be accessed through search engines and hyperlinks. Cyber-activism refers to the unique methods of advancing dissenting agendas online, from online petitions, Twitter hashtags, and Facebook groups (Carty and Onyett 2007; Earl 2006; Meikle 2002) to more disruptive methods of protest such as **hacktivism**, which is defined by Gunkel (2005: 595) as "the creative use of computer technology for the purposes of facilitating online protests, performing civil disobedience in cyberspace and disrupting the flow of information by deliberately intervening in the networks of global capital." Noteworthy acts of hacktivism include the establishment of "Wikileaks" — a "multi-national media organization and associated library" (Wikileaks 2015: para. 1) that distributes confidential government information to public spaces — including Edward Snowden's release of classified National Security Agency documents pertaining to the covert (and illegal) surveillance of American citizens following 9/11 (NBC News 2014).

One group that has taken extreme measures to demonstrate the capacities for hacktivism is Anonymous, an international hacktivist community established in 2003 around the loosely defined goals of promoting free speech, protecting the free movement of web-based information, and challenging the authority of mainstream political, corporate, and religious institutions (Infosec Institute 2011). While the identities and number of participants have never been disclosed, the group has achieved international recognition based around their appropriated image of Guy Fawkes (executed for attempting to destroy England's House of Lords in 1605 and celebrated by the influential graphic novel *V for Vendetta*). Anonymous has claimed responsibility for illegally infiltrating, and then disabling or altering, the web domains of targets including the US Department of Homeland Security, the Westboro Baptist Church, the Recording Industry Association of America, the Motion Picture Association of America, and the Trump Foundation. Further, members of Anonymous have also demonstrated an interest in engaging in forms of web-based vigilantism. Following reports that the four young men who sexually assaulted and influenced the suicide of Nova Scotia teenager Rehtaeh Parsons were not likely to be charged due to a lack of evidence, Anonymous announced that their "independent investigation" had produced evidence of the identity of her assailants that would be revealed to the public should police fail to reopen the criminal case. Shortly thereafter, and despite claims that law enforcement would only co-operate with the hacktivist group under the condition that they reveal their true identities, police reopened the case, pressed charges, and won convictions (*Herald News* 2015; McGuire 2013).

Three Case Studies in Digital Mobilization

Though emergent web technologies have clearly had positive implications for those wishing to circulate classified information or join clandestine hacktivist groups, their influence in social movements is more difficult to measure. While web-based capacities for information distribution, consciousness raising, and strategizing are well represented in the cultural profile of movements such as Occupy Wall Street, Idle No More, and Black Lives Matter, each of these groups have encountered difficulties around the absence of clear representatives and ambiguities regarding the values they advocate. Each movement should prompt us to ask whether seeking growth through socially mediated means — including Facebook groups and Twitter hashtags — undermines the likelihood that movements can consecrate intellectuals capable of authoritatively speaking on their behalf and, by extension, a group solidarity born of specific and consensually recognized goals. The following section provides three case studies to demonstrate how the unique hardships encountered by Occupy Wall Street, Idle No More, and Black Lives Matter reflect the difficulties of establishing consensus through the communicative practices of the digital age.

Occupy Wall Street

Occupy Wall Street arose in response to the 2008 collapse of the American economy. For years prior, American banks extended excessive homeowner loans to clients with limited means of repaying them, and "sold" this home-owner debt to third parties to turn a profit. The sheer number and frequency of home foreclosures instigated a domino effect as the perilous financial state of the average consumer obliterated the profit margins of major corporations, which in turn threatened the collapse of the entire North American economy. To prevent the onset of another Great Depression, the United States govern-ment dipped into taxpayer reserves to provide billions of dollars in "bail-out packages" to automotive, insurance, and banking companies. While this stimu-lus prevented the bankruptcy of a rash of corporate entities, the state did not advance comparable assistance to people who had been made unemployed or homeless by the crisis. Noting that these bail-out initiatives protected the wealthy while neglecting the working class, the Canadian anti-consumerist magazine *Adbusters* (Caste 2011) proposed that disgruntled Americans col-lectively protest the bailing out of the already-rich. At first, the plan was to hold a day of dissent on September 17, 2011; instead, protestors inhabited New York's financial district until November 15, 2011. Media images sug-gest thousands took part at any given stage during the movement, though no conclusive numbers are available. Further, the events in New York would also instigate "Occupy" movement demonstrations in cities across the United States and internationally, including Canada (Poisson 2011). Though instigated by the housing market crash, many of the slogans focused on class stratification and the inequitable global distribution of wealth. The newfound technological capacities of the contemporary protestor were also granted demonstration in broadcasts "from the ground," as alternative media and organized activist groups asserted new capacities through which to counter mainstream media representations of the occupation (Campbell 2017).

While contemporary communication technologies allotted Occupy dem-onstrators new avenues through which to access and distribute information untainted by the gatekeepers of corporate media, Occupy encountered indomitable barriers stemming from the absence of centralized leadership and the lack of ideological consensus. While Occupy Wall Street reached out to a disgruntled mass within the American citizenry, less attention was focused on ensuring that participants shared a uniform understanding of the ideologies and explicit goals that informed the movement. Part of this stemmed from the movement's fear of co-optation, as reflected in the insistence that the occupation refuse any explicit hierarchy of leadership (CNN 2011). Recalling Gerlach and Hine's note on the importance of facilitating an organizational structure and developing a shared ideology, the difficulty Occupy experienced in accomplishing either contributed significantly to its dissolution. As the occupation continued through fall 2011, mainstream media critiqued the absence of an overarching manifesto or consensually identified list of goals (Gibson 2013). When Occupy participants caved to the insistence that a manifesto be compiled, the resulting document identified multiple and diverse aims reflecting the wishes of numerous subfactions within the group (*Washington Times* 2011). The occupation dissipated shortly thereafter without having instigated substantive systemic changes. This suggests that, while social movements garner a great deal of publicity through social media and can attract participants very quickly, these variables of speed and mass interfere with the traditionally recognized stages of incipiency and coalescence. Occupy Wall Street attracted a phenomenal amount of mainstream attention but did not substantively engage in the consecration of specific values and goals or develop an internal leadership structure to guide the conduct of the group.

Idle No More

Founded in Saskatoon, Canada, in late 2012, Idle No More has developed an international profile based on its advocacy for the improved recognition of Indigenous sovereignty (Crosby and Monaghan 2016; Gray and Gordo 2014). Idle No More was a response to Canada's passage of Bill C-45, which revoked regulations put in place to protect the environment; the movement website (2018: para. 1) states that the goal is "peaceful revolution" based around "[pressuring] Government and industry to protect the environment [and] building allies in order to reframe the nation to nation relationship" between Indigenous Nations and the Canadian state. Shortly after its founding, Idle No More attracted international media attention by using social media to organize a successful national day of protest responding to Bill C-45 (Raynauld, Richez, and Morris 2017; Wood 2015), and it has been celebrated for providing Indigenous populations a platform through which to advocate for the recognition of their sovereignty and increase public awareness of Indigenous issues (CBC News 2013a). The movement's mobilization also coincides with a pronounced level of public interest surrounding the 2015 release of findings from the Truth and Reconciliation Commission (Idle No More 2015).

In the months following its rise in profile, however, Idle No More experienced internal tensions centring primarily on questions of leadership and intent. Tanya Kappo, one of the early organizers of Idle No More, publicly requested greater differentiation between the grassroots nature of Idle No More and actions of Indigenous chiefs and figures in positions of political authority: "From day one we wanted [Idle No More] to be something that was led by everyday people, a horizontal movement.... If this was ever really going to take off, it had to come from the ground up, not the other way around" (*National Post* 2013). This coincides with Idle No More's public statement respectfully disaffiliating the group from the highly publicized hunger strike initiated by Attawapiskat's chief, Theresa Spence, in protest of environmental deregulations and the perilous status of many on-reserve communities:

> The Chiefs have called for action and anyone who chooses can join with them, however this is not part of the Idle No More movement as the vision of this grassroots movement does not coincide with the visions of the Leadership.... While we appreciate the individual support we have received from chiefs and councilors, we have been given a clear mandate to work outside of the systems of government and that is what we will continue to do. (*National Post* 2013)

Idle No More's wish to distinguish Spence's protest from Idle No More emanated from concerns about reflecting the grassroots. Reports around the first anniversary of Idle No More's founding suggested further tensions between early organizers and activists who founded splinter groups such as the Indigenous Nationhood Movement (CBC News 2013b). Similar to Occupy Wall Street, Idle No More encountered hardships that can be attributed to issues related to leadership and ideological consensus. In contrast, however, the ambiguity surrounding Idle No More's leadership resided in the simultaneous presence of competing actors who erroneously claimed affiliation as well as originators who authoritatively denounced the development of a centralized group authority. The hardships that Idle No More encountered in establishing consensus demonstrate how social media allows the instantaneous dissemination of information and calls to action; however, success in this regard ensures that group slogans and iconographies effectively become property of the public domain. An absence of verified spokespersons appears to allow for the creative liberties of social media to reshape public perceptions and invite ideological fracture.

Black Lives Matter

Black Lives Matter started as a web-based group to call attention to racialized systemic discrimination. It was founded by three women who sought to formalize guiding principles to inform grassroots activism against systemic injustice and the high rates of police brutality committed against Black people (Russell-Brown 2017). Inspired by the 2013 acquittal of George Zimmerman, who had been charged with the shooting death of unarmed 17-year-old Trayvon Martin, the women popularized the use of the Twitter hashtag #BlackLivesMatter to signify discontent with the verdict (Campbell 2017). #BlackLivesMatter gathered momentum as it resurfaced in response to a string of high-profile cases of police killing African-Americans (Cox 2017). These cases include the police shootings of 18-year-old Michael Brown in Ferguson, Missouri, and 12-year-old Tamir Rice in Cleveland in 2014; the choking death of Eric Garner in New York in 2014; and the suspicious death of Freddie Gray in Baltimore in 2015 (BBC 2015).

When the decision not to press charges against the officer responsible for Brown's death incited riots in Ferguson, representatives of #BlackLivesMatter entered media discussions of the race-related issues and incidents that influenced Brown's killing and the ensuing standoff between protestors and law enforcement personnel. Black Lives Matter subsequently established chapters throughout North America and made headlines by pledging to select regional leadership in accordance with anti-patriarchal principles to empower female, queer, and trans participants (Black Lives Matter 2018a). As a movement, Black Lives Matter is best described as a network of regionally dispersed groups that, independent of centralized organization and in response to specific incidents and issues, are autonomously organized and primarily involved with regional matters and local events. As a hashtag, #BlackLivesMatter has recently become closely affiliated with the protests inspired by NFL quarterback Colin Kaepernick, who signified discontent with the American judicial system by kneeling throughout the American national anthem.

Nonetheless, the principles motivating Black Lives Matter remain poorly understood (Desmond-Harris 2016). The prevalent misconceptions that

Black Lives Matter promotes "anti-white" interests, for example, found reflection in the popularization of the hashtag #AllLivesMatter, a digitally mediated demonstration of popular disapproval that achieved trending status in the wake of high-profile demonstrations. Other responses suggest that the group is believed to advocate for racialized violence, including movements to designate Black Lives Matter a domestic terrorist group (Fox News 2017) and the onset of White Lives Matter rallies (Allison 2017). Most prominently, the group has been affiliated with anti-patriotism — an erroneous interpretation inspired in no small measure by media coverage and US president Donald Trump's statements regarding the "anthem controversy." When NFL players, led by Kaepernick, took a knee during the American anthem to protest police brutality against African-Americans, Trump characterized those who refused to stand for the anthem as anti-patriots who did not appreciate their privileged position in American society (Global News 2017).

Issues surrounding the centralization of leadership of Black Lives Matter partially stem from the prevalence of competing misinformation resources. Examples include popular Facebook pages that were developed by Russian operatives seeking to sow Western cultural discord (Black Lives Matter 2018b, Frenkel and Qiu 2018), misrepresentative media narratives (with the Fox and Breitbart News Networks serving as prime examples), and white nationalist factions seeking recruits. Though these risks could potentially be mitigated by electing intellectuals with organizational titles to represent the group in the national press, centralized leadership (formally known as the Black Lives Matter Global Network) has not elected to do so. Further, statements released in 2017 pertaining to alleged ideological fracture conceded a conscious effort to remain vague on points of possible contention in the interest of accumulating strength in numbers:

> The Movement for Black Lives is a space where groups working toward black liberation can come together, combine our collective powers and dream big. Our organizations are of varying sizes and take different approaches. Individually, we are a spectrum of gender identity, sexuality, region, age, class and political belief. We are not always in full agreement, we have competing ideas and we will undoubtedly upset each other in the process of making difficult decisions. We are here because we believe that our victories in service of black people are bigger and better when we win together.
>
> Our work is not about ego or celebrity assigned by an often irresponsible press corps. We know that our movement is made up of

countless people, whose dedication is tireless, and whose names most will never know. It is made up of the quiet leadership of those who agree to keep coming back to the work, to each other and to our people. (Mic 2017: paras. 3, 6)

> The case studies of the Occupy Wall Street, Idle No More, and Black Lives Matter movements demonstrate the benefits associated with the onset of new technological capacities.

In part, the quest for "quiet leadership" signals an attempt to retain credibility as a grassroots network (as opposed to an authority structure). Arguably, the absence of designated spokespersons with a high media profile allots the group's detractors greater power in shaping how Black Lives Matter is popularly characterized through misinformation and social media.

Conclusion: The Ambiguities of Digital Activism

The case studies of the Occupy Wall Street, Idle No More, and Black Lives Matter movements demonstrate the benefits associated with the onset of new technological capacities. All three highlight how social media platforms can be used to very quickly mobilize considerable numbers of demonstrators and, in doing so, succeed in attracting public attention to a particular cause. All three organized demonstrations of collective dissent attracted massive press coverage, impressed upon the public consciousness, and, undoubtedly, inspired future waves of advocation for change. Nevertheless, they also demonstrate the presence of new challenges: all three experienced a measure of fragmentation that can be attributed to the presence of differing opinions on the values and goals of the group.

Through the lens of Gerlach and Hine (1970), this lack of consensus can be attributed, at different turns, to issues related to structure, shared ideology, and membership commitment. Occupy Wall Street had numbers and slogans, but no organizational structure through which to promote solidarity among a variety of ideological camps. Despite the principles posted to their websites, Idle No More and Black Lives Matter's induction into

> All three organized demonstrations of collective dissent attracted massive press coverage, impressed upon the public consciousness, and, undoubtedly, inspired future waves of advocation for change. Nevertheless, they also demonstrate the presence of new challenges: all three experienced a measure of fragmentation that can be attributed to the presence of differing opinions on the values and goals of the group.

public discourse by way of social media allowed for the concurrent flow of misinformation and misrepresentation. While ensuring strength in numbers (measured in protestors or hashtags retweeted) does well with respect to spreading awareness of the issue and movement, these gains are undercut should members disagree on the mission and methods of the group. These variations in perspective might also be responsible for a decreased level of commitment among members, who could understandably hesitate in the absence of clear leadership and goals.

Much of this ambiguity could be remedied by identifying authoritative spokespersons to take the role of the intellectuals whom Gramsci described as crucial to mobilizations of praxis. The fact that all three groups elected not to anoint figures of group authority in an apparent bid to retain authenticity suggests the influence of fears surrounding co-optation. Maintaining a grass-roots character aligns with the prevalent activist logic that authority structures undermine the legitimacy of such groups. The alternative method of resisting these stages is associated with the equally problematic absence of consensus.

The imperative of overcoming issues of ambiguity and group fracture resides in the fact that white supremacist mobilizations have not appeared to encounter similar issues. Beyond attracting recruits by stoking anxieties inspired by #BlackLivesMatter and other movements for progressive social change, white nationalist sentiments are increasingly being advocated through high-profile figures such as Richard Spencer and Steve Bannon under the euphemistic banner of the "alt right" movement (GQ 2017). The organization of such groups is most salient in the 2017 "Unite the Right" rallies, conducted in Charlottesville, Virginia. Organized over social media in part by Ku Klux Klan affiliates, early rallies devolved into tiki-torchlit white pride parades replete with Nazi imagery and semi-automatic weapons (Heim et al. 2017). When white nationalists ran down anti-fascist counter-protestor Heather Heyer, "Unite the Right" representatives, including Richard Spencer and David Duke, justified the rally as a response to the left-wing terrorist threat of groups such as Black Lives Matter (CNN 2017).

At the time of this writing, however, cause for hope has emerged in the organization and mobilization of survivors of the February 2018 Parkland school shooting in Florida (CNN 2018). Shortly following this deadliest school shooting in American history, surviving students took to Twitter to criticize a response, among politicians, focused around sharing "thoughts and prayers" as opposed to revisiting gun control legislation. Under representation by designated spokespeople, including Emma Gonzalez and David Hogg, Parkland students successfully organized a nationwide walkout, among high school students, to demonstrate collective support for gun control initiatives (*Globe and Mail* 2018). Given the traction that clear organization and representation have granted the cause of the Parkland survivors, it will be worthwhile to note whether subsequent movements for progress and change follow the model they continue to establish.

Discussion Questions

1. What is the significance of intellectuals for the initiation of praxis?
2. What are the five characteristics associated with all successful social movements?
3. What are the stages in the life cycle of social movements?
4. How did the Occupy Wall Street, Idle No More, and Black Lives Matter movements attempt to prevent their co-optation?
5. What variables are associated with the limitations of the Occupy Wall Street, Idle No More, and Black Lives Matter movements?

Recommended Resources

Idle No More <idlenomore.ca/>.
This Is What Democracy Looks Like (Friedberg and Rowley 2002).
The Sixties: The Years That Shaped a Generation (PBS 1995).

Glossary

coalescence: second stage in the life cycle of social movements; involves the development of authority structures and deployment of consciousness-raising strategies.

demise: final stage in the life cycle of social movements; occurs when movements dissolve in the wake of success or the collective recognition of failure.

expressive social movements: social movements that advocate for cultural change and the empowerment of groups that are marginalized based on demographic variables such as ethnicity, gender identity, religious affiliation, and sexual orientation.

fragmentation: fourth stage in the life cycle of social movements; occurs as success or failure splinters a group into competing factions.

hacktivism: forms of activism, such as hacking and making confidential documents publicly available, associated with the use of web-mediated technology.

hegemony: the process of maintaining the authority to lead society through corresponding methods of applying force and manufacturing consent.

incipiency: first stage in the life cycle of social movements; involves the initial recognition of issues and formation of collective strategies through which to draw attention to them.

information gatekeepers: perspective that mainstream media formerly took on the task of selecting what forms of information would be distributed throughout the wider public.

institutionalization: third stage in the life cycle of social movements; involves the process whereby the movement becomes absorbed into institutional society and the mainstream political system.

intellectuals: authority figures who embody and promote class ideologies. Intellectuals of empowered classes contribute to public consensus for the status quo, while intellectuals of disempowered classes advocate for mobilization against the status quo.

praxis: forms of practical action toward achieving collective aims centred on the reorganization of society.

reactionary social movements: social movements that mobilize in response to the onset of social change.

reformative social movements: social movements that mobilize to change problematic aspects of society.

revolutionary social movements: movements advocating for the drastic reorganization of society.

theory of co-optation: perspective among activist cultures that any degree of co-operation with mainstream social institutions corrupts the authenticity of a movement.

References

Allison, Natalie. 2017. "4 Extremist Groups That Will Be Part of Weekend's White Lives Matter Rallies." *USA Today*, October 25. <usatoday.com/story/news/nation-now/2017/10/25/groups-behind-white-lives-matter/798600001/>.

bbc News. 2015. "Freddie Gray Death: Protesters Highlight Other Police Deaths." April 28. <bbc.com/news/world-us-canada-30341927>.

Black Lives Matter. 2018a. "Herstory." <blacklivesmatter.com/about/herstory/>.

___. 2018b. "Statement from Black Lives Matter Global Network on Fraudulent Social Media Accounts." April 10. <blacklivesmatter.com/pressroom/statement-from-black-lives-matter-global-network-on-fraudulent-social-media-accounts/>.

Campbell, Perri. 2017. "Occupy, Black Lives Matter and Suspended Mediation: Young People's Battles for Recognition in/between Digital and Non-Digital Spaces." *young* 26, 2.

Carty, Victoria, and Jake Onyett. 2007. "Protest, Cyber Activism and New Social Movements: The Re-Emergence of the Peace Movement Post 9/11." *Social Movement Studies* 5, 3.

Caste, Martin. 2011. "Exploring Occupy Wall Street's 'Adbuster' Origins." NPR, October 20. <npr.org/2011/10/20/141526467/exploring-occupy-wall-streets-adbuster-origins>.

Castelles, Manuel. 1996. *The Rise of the Network Society*. Hoboken: Wiley.

CBC News. 2013a. "Idle No More Prepares for Day of Action." October 7. <cbc.ca/news/canada/idle-no-more-prepares-for-day-of-action-1.1913429>.

____. 2013b. "Idle No More Anniversary Sees Divisions Emerging." November 10. <cbc.ca/news/canada/idle-no-more-anniversary-sees-divisions-emerging-1.2420524>.

City News. 2015. "Anonymous Vigilantism Filling Gap in Justice System, Says Beneficiary." August 3. <toronto.citynews.ca/2015/08/03/anonymous-vigilantism-fills-hole-in-traditional-justice-system-says-beneficiary/>.

CNN. 2018. "Parkland Survivors Rip Politicians' 'Pathetic' Responses." February 19. <cnn.com/2018/02/19/politics/parkland-survivors-cnntv/index.html>.

____. 2017. "Trump's Mixed Messaging Sparks Concerns of 'Emboldened' White Supremacists." August 8. <cnn.com/2017/08/19/politics/trump-remarks-alt-right/index.html>.

____. 2011. "Occupy Wall Street Is Going Nowhere Without Leadership." October 27. <cnn.com/2011/10/27/opinion/linsky-occupy-wall-street-leadership/index.html>.

Conrad, Peter, and Allison Angell. 2004. "Homosexuality and Remedicalization." *Society* 41.

Cox, Jonathan. 2017. "The Source of a Movement: Making the Case for Social Media as an Informational Source Using Black Lives Matter." *Ethnic and Racial Studies* 40, 11.

Crosby, Andrew, and Jeffrey Monaghan. 2016. "Settler Colonialism and the Policing of Idle No More." *Social Justice* 43, 2.

Desmond-Harris, Jenée. 2016. "Everyone Should Stop It with the Black Lives Matter-Inspired Slogans." *Vox*, September 14. <vox.com/2016/9/14/12904894/black-lives-matter-slogans-racism>.

Earl, Jennifer. 2006. "Pursuing Social Change Online: The Use of Four Protest Tactics on the Internet." *Social Science Computer Review* 24, 3.

Fox News. 2017. "FBI Cites Black Extremists as New Domestic Terrorist Threat." October 10. <foxnews.com/us/2017/10/10/fbi-cites-black-extremists-as-new-domestic-terrorist-threat.html>.

Frenkel, Shira, and Linda Qiu. 2018. "Fact Check: What Mark Zuckerberg Said about Facebook, Privacy and Russia." *New York Times*, April 10. <nytimes.com/2018/04/10/technology/zuckerberg-elections-russia-data-privacy.html>.

Friedberg, Jill, and Rick Rowley. 2002. *This Is What Democracy Looks Like* [film]. MVD Entertainment Group. <kanopy.com/product/what-democracy-looks>.

Funke, Peter, and Todd Wolfson. 2014. "Class In-Formation: The Intersection of Old and New Media in Contemporary Urban Social Movements." *Social Movement Studies* 13, 3.

Gerlach, Luther, and Virginia Hine. 1970. *People, Power, Change: Movements of Social Transformation*. Indianapolis: Bobbs-Merrill.

Gibson, Morgan. 2013. "The Anarchism of the Occupy Movement." *Australian Journal of Political Science* 48, 3.

Global News. 2017. "Take a Knee Protest: Why Athletes Are Refusing to Stand for US National Anthem." September 25. <globalnews.ca/news/3767075/take-a-knee-why-athletes-refusing-to-stand-anthem/>.

Globe and Mail. 2018. "US Students Walk Out of Classes in Call for Gun Control on Columbine Anniversary." April 20. <theglobeandmail.com/world/article-us-students-set-for-walkout-to-call-for-gun-reform-on-columbine/>.

Gramsci, Antonio. 2008. Selections from the Prison Notebooks. New York: International Publishers.

Gray, Chris Hables, and Angel J. Gordo. 2014. "Social Media in Conflict: Comparing Military and Social-Movement Technocultures." Cultural Politics 10, 3.

GQ. 2017. "The New Uniform of White Supremacy." August 17. <gq.com/story/uniform-of-white-supremacy>

Gunkel, David. 2005. "Editorial: Introduction to Hacking and Hacktivism." New Media and Society 7, 5.

Heath, Joseph, and Andrew Potter. 2004. The Rebel Sell: Why the Culture Can't Be Jammed. New York: Harper.

Heim, Joe, Ellie Silverman, T. Rees Shapiro, and Emma Brown . 2017. "One Dead as Car Strikes Crowds amid Protests of White Nationalists Gathering in Charlottesville; Two Police Die in Helicopter Crash." Washington Post, August 12. <washingtonpost.com/local/fights-in-advance-of-saturday-protest-in-charlottesville/2017/08/12/155fb636-7f13-11e7-83c7-5bd5460f0d7e_story.html?noredirect=on&utm_term=.b7ccfae395ff >.

Herald News. 2015. "Anonymous Vigilantism Filling Gap in Justice System: Glen Canning." August 3. <thechronicleherald.ca/canada/1303046-anonymous-vigilantism-filling-gap-in-justice-system-glen-canning>.

Idle No More. n.d. Home page. <idlenomore.ca/>.

___. 2015. "The 94 TRC Calls to Action." June 4. <idlenomore.ca/the_94_trc_calls_to_action>.

Infosec Institute. 2011. "A History of Anonymous." October 24. <resources.infosecinstitute.com/a-history-of-anonymous/#gref>.

Irzik, Emrah. 2010. "A Proposal for Grounded Cultural Activism: Communication Strategies, Adbusters and Social Change." Thamyris/Intersecting 21.

Mauss, Armand. 1975. Social Problems as Social Movements. Philadelphia: J.B. Lippincourt.

McCurdy, Patrick. 2012. "Social Movements, Protests and Mainstream Media." Sociology Compass 6, 3.

McGuire, Patrick. 2013. "Inside Anonymous's Operation to Out Rehtaeh Parsons' Rapists." Vice News, April 15. <vice.com/sv/article/nn4py8/inside-anonymouss-operation-to-out-rehtaeh-parsonss-rapists>.

Meikle, Graham, 2002. Future Active: Media Activism and the Internet. New York: Routledge.

Mic.com. 2017. "The Movement for Black Lives Responds to Recent Claims of a Fractured Coalition." June 23. <mic.com/articles/180730/the-movement-for-black-lives-responds-to-recent-claims-of-a-fractured-coalition#.xav7qBItw>.

National Post. 2013. "Idle No More Founders Distance Themselves from Chiefs." January 1. <nationalpost.com/news/politics/idle-no-more-founders-distance-themselves-from-chiefs>.

NBC News. 2014. "Who Is Edward Snowden, the Man Who Spilled the

NSA's Secrets?" May 26. <nbcnews.com/feature/edward-snowden-interview/who-edward-snowden-man-who-spilled-nsas-secrets-n114861>.

Osman, Wazhmah. 2014. "On Media, Social Movements and Uprisings: Lessons from Afghanistan, Its Neighbors, and Beyond." *Journal of Women in Culture and Society* 39, 4.

Picket, Kerry. 2011. "Picket: Occupy Wall Street Protestors Post Manifesto of Demands." *Washington Times*, October 3. <washingtontimes.com/blog/watercooler/2011/oct/3/picket-occupy-wall-street-protesters-post-manifest/>.

Pinkoski, Kevin Lee. 2012. "The Historiography of the Front de Liberation du Quebec: Frameworks, Identity and Future Study." *Constellations* 3, 2.

Poisson, Jayme. 2011. "Occupy Toronto: Copycat Protest or the Start of a True People's Revolution?" *Toronto Star*, October 14. <thestar.com/news/gta/2011/10/14/occupy_toronto_copycat_protest_or_the_start_of_a_true_peoples_revolution.html>.

Raynauld, Vincent, Emmanuelle Richez, and Katie Boudreau Morris. 2017. "Canada Is #IdleNoMore: Exploring Dynamics of Indigenous Political and Civic Protest in the Twitterverse." *Communication & Society* 21, 4.

Russell-Brown, Katheryn. 2017. "Critical Black Protectionism, Black Lives Matter, and Social Media: Building a Bridge to Social Justice." *Howard Law Journal* 60, 2.

Skinner, David. 2015. "Alternative and Community Media in Canada: Policy and Prospects." In Chris Atten (ed.), *The Routledge Companion to Alternative and Community Media*. New York: Routledge.

The Sixties: The Years That Shaped a Generation. 1995. PBS Films. <youtube.com/watch?v=jTspDh6C3yY>.

Vago, Steven. 1999. *Social Change*, 5th ed. Toronto: Pearson.

Van Dijk, Jan. 1999. *The Network Society: Social Aspects of New Media*. Thousand Oaks: Sage.

Wikileaks. 2015. "What Is Wikileaks." <wikileaks.org/What-is-Wikileaks.html>.

Wood, Lesley J. 2015. "Idle No More, Facebook and Diffusion." *Social Movement Studies* 14, 5.

Index